500 best
comfort
food
recipes

Johanna Burkhard

Robert
ROSE

500 Best Comfort Food Recipes
Text copyright © 2010 Johanna Burkhard
Photographs copyright © 2010 Robert Rose Inc.
Cover and text design copyright © 2010 Robert Rose Inc.

For complete cataloguing information, see page 560.

Disclaimer
The recipes in this book have been carefully tested by our kitchen and our tasters. To the best of our knowledge, they are safe and nutritious for ordinary use and users. For those people with food or other allergies, or who have special food requirements or health issues, please read the suggested contents of each recipe carefully and determine whether or not they may create a problem for you. All recipes are used at the risk of the consumer.

We cannot be responsible for any hazards, loss or damage that may occur as a result of any recipe use.

For those with special needs, allergies, requirements or health problems, in the event of any doubt, please contact your medical adviser prior to the use of any recipe.

Design and Production: Daniella Zanchetta/PageWave Graphics Inc.
Editors: Sue Sumeraj and Jennifer MacKenzie
Proofreader: Sheila Wawanash
Indexer: Gillian Watts
Photography: Mark T. Shapiro
Food Styling: Kate Bush
Prop Styling: Charlene Erricson
Photo of Creamy Tuna Pasta Bake: Colin Erricson
Food Styling for Creamy Tuna Pasta Bake: Kathryn Robertson

The publisher and author wish to express their appreciation to the following supplier of dishes, linens and accessories used in the interior food photography:

The Kitchen and Glass Place
840 Yonge Street, Toronto, Ontario, Canada M4W 2H1
Tel: (416) 927-9925

Cover image: Old-Fashioned Beef Stew (page 196)

We acknowledge the financial support of the Government of Canada through the Book Publishing Industry Development Program (BPIDP) for our publishing activities.

Published by Robert Rose Inc.
120 Eglinton Avenue East, Suite 800, Toronto, Ontario, Canada M4P 1E2
Tel: (416) 322-6552 Fax: (416) 322-6936

Printed and bound in Canada

1 2 3 4 5 6 7 8 9 CPL 18 17 16 15 14 13 12 11 10

Contents

Acknowledgments

A COOKBOOK IS NEVER a solo effort, and I would like to sincerely thank the Robert Rose creative team of publisher Bob Dees and sales and marketing manager Marian Jarkovich for their ingenuity and marketing skills; editor Sue Sumeraj, a superb organizer and a delight to work with; Jennifer MacKenzie, recipe tester, for her expert advice; Daniella Zanchetta at PageWave Graphics for the beautiful book design and layout.

This book is dedicated to my children, Nicole and Patrick, who are now adults and have become wonderful cooks. I marvel at the pleasure and pride they take in preparing wholesome foods — it's a tribute to the many happy and loving memories spent in our family kitchen and the meals we shared around the table.

Also warm thanks to my partner, Ron, whose kindheartedness and infectious humor make every day an adventure, and to my family and friends, who have been so supportive in my career.

Introduction

I REMEMBER COMING HOME from school to the fragrant aroma of a pot roast in the oven or a smoky ham and pea soup simmering away on the back burner. Everyone has a cupboardful of food memories that evoke a sense of family and home. We call them our comfort foods.

For some, the words "comfort food" might evoke a special occasion spent with family, such as gathering for Thanksgiving with a roast turkey and pumpkin pie or celebrating a birthday with chocolate layer cake and ice cream. Others may recall warm childhood memories of being soothed by mom's chicken soup when home from school with a cold. Comfort food can be as simple as a treasured family recipe — perhaps a favorite potato salad served at a family reunion. For me, comfort food means anything that evokes a sense of nurturing, with a good measure of love and care stirred into the pot.

Whatever the association, comfort foods all have two things in common: they make us feel good and they taste great. My goal in writing *500 Best Comfort Food Recipes* is to help recreate the "feel good" times and draw people back to the kitchen to soul-satisfying recipes that everyone enjoys: pot roast, macaroni and cheese, date squares. These traditional dishes are so much a part of our food heritage and culture, yet the recipes are rarely found grouped together in one book.

This book includes not only classic dishes that have never lost their appeal, such as Old-Fashioned Beef Stew (page 196), Thyme-Roasted Chicken with Garlic Gravy (page 264) and Cinnamon Apple Crumble Pie (page 512), but also new comfort foods that have become a staple in contemporary kitchens, including Wild Mushroom Risotto (page 375), Bistro Lentils with Smoked Sausage (page 388) and Tiramisu (page 543).

Most of the recipes in the book follow today's guidelines for healthy eating, calling for fresh ingredients and moderate use of fat. Many of the recipes are vegetarian, to appeal to those who opt not to eat meat, including Black Bean and Corn Soup (page 171), Spicy Noodles with Vegetables and Peanut Sauce (page 350) and Middle Eastern Couscous with Chickpeas (page 392). They're sure to become favorite comfort foods for the entire family, vegetarian or not.

When my children were growing up, their idea of comfort food included many of the old favorites, but they were also influenced by fast-food tastes, so I've included recipes that will appeal to the younger set, such as Taco Pitas (page 60), Turkey Fajitas (page 63), burgers (pages 310–312) and pizzas (pages 54–55). This homemade "fast food" is far more nutritious than the fat- and calorie-laden fare served in fast-food restaurants. Ideally, these recipes will entice kids to help with the preparation and, for teens, learn how to cook these easy dishes themselves.

Another reason I like to serve comfort foods is that they are reliable. How many times have you labored over a stove to make a wonderful meal only to hear your family issue groans of disappointment? With comfort foods, everyone is rewarded, including the cook. *500 Best Comfort Food Recipes* is geared toward cooks who want recipes that are easy, dependable and reassuringly familiar. Many of these dishes are personal favorites that have become standards in my house.

Cooking today is as much about the demands on our time as it is about what we want to serve for dinner. We're all trying to balance jobs with a busy family life, and very often dinner plays second fiddle to juggling work, homework and a host of activities. Yet suppers need to be appetizing and nutritious. With our hectic schedules, it's almost impossible to make a meal from scratch every night. That's why many of the recipes in this book provide for next-day encores that can be reheated in the microwave. Others can be prepared ahead, so that when you do have a spare hour, you can assemble a meal and stash it in the freezer. In about the same time it takes to order a pizza and have it delivered, you can have a delicious meal on the table.

Of course, the frantic pace can sometimes take over our lives, and once in a while, we need to take the time to make a leisurely meal — to tuck a pot of Molasses Baked Beans (page 384) in the oven and just sit back and enjoy the restorative effect of the soothing aroma. Spending time in the kitchen has other benefits, too. Cooking and eating with our children provides us with a nurturing environment in which we can spend time together and communicate with each other. It also gives us an opportunity to teach our children how sound eating habits can make a lifelong difference to their health. Try to set aside time with your family — perhaps two or three nights a week — and plan a dinner of your favorite comfort food dishes. It doesn't have to be fancy; even just a good bowl of homemade soup is all it takes to make a meal a special event.

Nowadays, thanks to convenience products and the proliferation of fast-food outlets, we are spending less and less time in the kitchen. Even making a basic meatloaf is an event. Baking banana bread is a lost art. *500 Best Comfort Food Recipes* is intended to be only cookbook you'll ever need: it covers all the basics and includes the most popular, sought-after comfort food recipes. The directions are easy to follow, and the recipes call for ingredients that are readily available in supermarkets. I even provide practical information, such as recipe shortcuts and serving suggestions, to help you get dinner on the table. In addition, this introduction includes a list of the basic equipment needed for a well-stocked kitchen, as well as helpful tips on preparing recipes, shopping effectively, saving time in the kitchen and streamlining your kitchen.

There's no greater pleasure than the hours spent around the table, sharing a meal with family and friends, whether it's something as simple as a bowl of Harvest Vegetable Barley Soup (page 175) with a warm slice of Honey Oatmeal Bread (page 434) or an elaborate family get-together featuring Sunday Roast Beef with Wine Gravy (page 237). I hope this book inspires you to get back in the kitchen and create some special memories around your table — and perhaps establish some new food traditions of your own.

Basic Equipment

We all have a few useless kitchen tools stashed away in our cupboards, bought in the hopes that they would turn us into cooking pros. Before you are tempted to buy yet another kitchen gadget, make sure you have the basics in your kitchen. Though cookware can be expensive, it pays to buy the very best quality you can afford, for a lifetime of great cooking and baking.

Skillets, Pots and Pans

- 8- or 10- inch (20 or 25 cm) nonstick skillet (for frying eggs, making pancakes and small-batch cooking)
- 12-inch (30 cm) heavy nonstick skillet (for pan-frying and sautéing)
- 1-quart (1 L) saucepan (for boiling eggs, making sauces and reheating single servings)
- 3-quart (3 L) saucepan (for cooking vegetables, rice, grains and small-batch stews)
- 5-quart (5 L) heavy-bottomed stainless steel or enameled cast-iron Dutch oven (for cooking stews and chilis and braising meats)
- 8-quart (8 L) stockpot (for cooking pasta, big-batch soups and stocks)
- Large, shallow, dark roasting pan (for roasting turkey, ham and chicken)

Cutting and Chopping Equipment

- Chef's knife (the size of the blade will depend on how the knife feels in your hand — it should fit like a glove; test the grip and weight before buying)
- Paring knives
- Serrated bread knife
- Sturdy kitchen shears
- Honing steel

Cutting Boards

- Large wooden board (for vegetables)
- Large plastic board (for raw meats and poultry)
- Wooden pastry board (if you are an avid baker)

Baking Pans

Please note this important distinction: a baking pan is a metal pan, while a baking dish is glass. For the best results, use the equipment specified in the recipe.

- 8-inch (20 cm) square baking pan
- 9-inch (23 cm) square baking pan
- 13- by 9-inch (33 by 23 cm) baking pan
- Two 9-inch (23 cm) round cake pans
- 9-inch (23 cm) springform pan (for heavier cakes, such as coffee cakes and cheesecakes)
- 10-inch (25 cm) tart pan with removable bottom
- Two 9- by 5-inch (23 by 13 cm) loaf pans (for loaf cakes and yeast breads)
- 12-cup muffin pan
- Two heavy baking sheets (I prefer rimmed baking sheets, as they can also be used to roast vegetables)
- Wire cooling rack (for cooling cakes, cookies and breads)

Glassware and Casserole Dishes

Every kitchen should have an assortment of ovenproof glassware for baking, roasting and microwaving and for use as storage containers for the refrigerator and freezer. The basics include:

- Two 9-inch (23 cm) glass pie plates
- 8-inch (20 cm) square baking dish
- 13- by 9-inch (33 by 23 cm) baking dish (for lasagna, baking and roasting)

- 8-cup (2 L) casserole dish with lid
- 12-cup (3 L) casserole dish with lid

Bowls

You'll need an assortment of stainless steel and glass mixing bowls in various sizes. You can never have too many of these stashed away in your cupboard, especially for marathon baking and batch-cooking sprees.

Electrical Equipment

The top kitchen appliances include:

- Microwave oven
- Food processor
- Blender
- Electric hand mixer or hand blender (for whipping cream and egg whites)
- Stand mixer (a definite asset for serious bakers)

Utensils

Here is a checklist of other kitchen essentials:

- Heavy rolling pin
- Wooden spoons in several sizes
- Soup ladle
- Slotted metal spoon
- Rubber and metal spatulas
- Wire whisk
- Tongs
- Pastry brush
- Microplane or other rasp grater
- Box grater
- Fine metal sieve
- Colander
- Metal or plastic measuring cups for dry ingredients
- Glass measuring cups for liquids
- Measuring spoons
- Bulb baster
- Juice squeezer
- Vegetable peeler
- Can opener
- Corkscrew/bottle opener
- Oven mitts/potholders
- Black pepper mill

Easy Steps for Preparing a Recipe

1. Read the entire recipe carefully before you start.

2. Assemble all the ingredients on the counter.

3. Set out necessary cooking equipment, such as saucepans, skillets and wooden spoons. Preheat the oven and prepare cooking utensils — for example, grease a casserole dish or line a baking sheet with foil. This prevents you from hunting through a drawer in the middle of a recipe to find a piece of equipment or waiting for the oven to preheat once the dish is ready to go.

4. Chop onions, garlic and vegetables before you start cooking and place on a plate, tray or sheet of waxed paper within easy reach. Measure herbs, spices and seasonings; place in small custard cups or on plates.

5. Clean up as you go. Not only does this save time, but you'll find it's far more efficient to work in an uncluttered kitchen.

How to Make the Most of Your Shopping Trip

1. Before you go, get organized. How many times have you wandered the aisles of a supermarket randomly picking up familiar foods? This is a recipe for costly impulse purchases. Getting organized before you go shopping will make your life easier in the kitchen and save you money.

2. Make a list. Decide what meals you are going to make. Scan your pantry and refrigerator and jot down missing staples. Add to the list any other items called for in the recipes. Organize your shopping list according to the supermarket layout, grouping food items such as fresh meats, dairy, produce and canned goods together, so you won't have to backtrack.

3. Go shopping at the right time. You're likely to purchase more than you intend if you shop when you're hungry. Also, try not to shop when you're tired or not in the mood — shopping is a weekly necessity, so make it as pleasant and enjoyable as possible.

4. Take advantage of time-saving products. Pasta-ready tomato sauces, precut vegetables and shredded cheeses cost more but are worth the price when it comes to saving time in the kitchen.

5. Try warehouse and bulk shopping. Buying in bulk can save you both time and money. However, the cost savings can evaporate if the products aren't used at peak freshness. Plan carefully when purchasing in bulk, so you don't overbuy.

6. Make shopping a family event. Food selection is an important life skill that goes hand in hand with cooking. Children need to learn how to make wise food choices.

Time-Saving Kitchen Strategies

1. Wash lettuce as soon as you get home from the supermarket. Fill a sink with cold water, swish the leaves around and scoop them into a salad spinner to dry. Wrap lettuce in a clean, dry kitchen towel and place in a plastic bag or store right in the salad spinner in the refrigerator.

2. Peel a week's worth of onions and store them in a plastic bag in the refrigerator. Not only will you save time prepping onions for recipes, but the cold temperature will help minimize tears when you chop the onions.

3. Keep handy bags of chopped onions, bell peppers and hot peppers in the freezer to add to soups, casseroles and stews. They can be frozen for up to 2 months.

4. Separate a head of garlic into cloves and remove the skins. Place in an airtight container in the refrigerator; use within a week.

5. Peel ginger and store in a glass jar filled with sherry in the refrigerator. Use the ginger-flavored sherry in recipes.

6. To get a head start on another meal, cook extra rice, pasta and potatoes. Pack in airtight containers and store in the refrigerator for up to 3 days.

7. Double a recipe, where indicated, and freeze for another meal. Use masking tape and a permanent marker to label and date all freezer foods. Take stock of the foods often, so items will be used at peak quality.

8. Batch-cook on weekends, so you can rely on the refrigerator or freezer for make-ahead meals.

9. Don't let forgotten leftovers become costly throwaways. Place leftovers in an airtight container, label and date. Store

on a designated shelf in the refrigerator so everyone in the family knows where to find them.

10. Take advantage of your microwave to steam vegetables for stir-fries, melt butter and chocolate and make quick sauces.

Ways to Streamline Your Kitchen

1. Knick-knacks and non-essential appliances clutter a kitchen counter. Keep only essential cooking equipment, such as a food processor and a coffee maker, handy on your counter. Keep less frequently used items in the cupboard, within easy reach.

2. Get a jug or container for wooden spoons, tongs and spatulas and keep it on the counter next to the stove.

3. Organize your kitchen drawers to keep similar utensils and kitchen tools together — for example, paring knives with vegetable peelers.

4. Store frequently used saucepans, mixing bowls and baking equipment within easy reach at the front of the cupboard; store any equipment not used on a regular basis at the back of the cupboard.

5. Organize your pantry so you can find items easily and quickly see what's missing when making a grocery list. Group canned and packaged goods, such as pastas, on the same shelf. Arrange bottled vinegars and oils together, along with condiments such as ketchup and sauces such as soy sauce.

6. Place your cutting board next to the sink, so you can wash and chop produce easily. Have a bowl nearby to dispose of vegetable waste for composting.

7. Make sure everyone in the family is familiar with the kitchen set-up so that when it's their turn to clean up or put groceries away, everything will be put in the right place.

Breakfast and Brunch

Scrambled Eggs and Ham Burritos

Makes 4 burritos

Forget forks and knives when serving this tasty pick-up sandwich that has all the appeal of a traditional breakfast of ham and scrambled eggs.

Tip

Medium salsa gives a burst of heat. For a tamer breakfast, use mild salsa.

- Preheat oven to 350°F (180°C)
- Baking sheet

4	9-inch (23 cm) flour tortillas	4
1 cup	shredded Cheddar cheese	250 mL
6	eggs	6
1 tbsp	milk	15 mL
¼ tsp	salt	1 mL
	Freshly ground black pepper	
2 tsp	butter	10 mL
½ cup	diced smoked ham	125 mL
2	green onions, sliced	2
½ cup	mild or medium salsa, drained	125 mL

1. Place tortillas on baking sheet; sprinkle with cheese. Place in oven for 5 minutes or until cheese melts.

2. Meanwhile, in a bowl, beat together eggs, milk, salt and pepper to taste. In a large nonstick skillet, melt butter over medium heat; cook ham and green onions, stirring, for 1 minute or until onion is softened. Add eggs; cook, stirring often, for about 2 minutes or until eggs are just set.

3. Spoon egg mixture along bottom third of tortillas; top each with a heaping tbsp (15 mL) of salsa. Fold 1 inch (2.5 cm) of right and left sides of tortilla over filling, starting from the bottom, and roll up tortillas around filling. Serve immediately.

Egg Tomato Muffin Melt

In my house, eggs Benedict is most often reserved for a special occasion weekend breakfast or brunch, so I rely on these yummy eggs instead, and not just for breakfast. They make a great supper dish when you're looking for something fast and easy.

- Preheat broiler
- Baking sheet

	Butter	
4	thin slices smoked ham	4
1	large tomato, cut into 4 thick slices	1
	Salt and freshly ground black pepper	
4	eggs	4
2	English muffins, split	2
4	thin slices aged Cheddar cheese	4

1. In a large nonstick skillet, melt 2 tsp (10 mL) butter over medium heat and cook ham slices for 1 minute per side or until lightly browned. Transfer to a plate and keep warm. Add tomato slices to skillet and cook for about 30 seconds per side or until softened. Season to taste with salt and pepper.

2. Meanwhile, poach, pan-fry or scramble eggs as desired. Toast English muffins; spread with butter if desired. Arrange cut side up on baking sheet.

3. Layer each muffin half with 1 ham slice, 1 tomato slice and 1 egg. Top with sliced cheese. Broil for 1 to 2 minutes or until cheese is melted. Serve immediately.

Eggs Benedict with Blender Hollandaise

Makes 4 servings

This classic dish, made with English muffins topped with Canadian bacon and poached eggs drizzled with buttery hollandaise, was created at New York's famed Delmonico's in the 1920s for Mr. and Mrs. LeGrand Benedict, who complained there was nothing new on the lunch menu.

Variations

Instead of hollandaise, layer thinly sliced Cheddar cheese over poached eggs and place under preheated broiler for 2 minutes or until cheese is melted.

Substitute thickly sliced smoked ham for the Canadian bacon.

Eggs Benedict Florentine

Steam 8 oz (250 g) baby spinach leaves until wilted; drain well. Layer over English muffins and top with poached eggs and hollandaise sauce.

- Preheat oven to 250°F (120°C)
- Rimmed baking sheet

1 tsp	vinegar	5 mL
1 tsp	salt	5 mL
1 tbsp	butter	15 mL
8	slices Canadian bacon	8
4	English muffins, split	4
8	eggs	8
	Blender Hollandaise (see recipe, opposite)	

1. In a large deep skillet, bring about 2 inches (5 cm) of water, vinegar and salt to a simmer over high heat. Reduce heat to medium-low and keep water simmering until ready to poach eggs.

2. In a large nonstick skillet, melt butter over medium-high heat. Cook bacon for 1 to 2 minutes per side or until lightly browned.

3. Toast English muffins. Arrange on baking sheet and top each half with a slice of bacon. Place in preheated oven to keep warm.

4. Break each egg into a small dish or measuring cup and slip into simmering water. (By all means use a poaching ring if you have one.) Cook until whites and yolks are set to desired doneness, about 4 to 5 minutes for medium-set yolks. Remove eggs using a slotted spoon and place on a double paper towel-lined plate to blot moisture.

5. Place 2 English muffin halves on serving plates and top each with a poached egg. Spoon warm hollandaise sauce over eggs and serve immediately.

Tips

To help keep hollandaise sauce hot, half-fill the blender container with hot water to warm it; drain well just before using.

Hollandaise sauce can be made up to 4 hours ahead; cover and refrigerate. To reheat, place in the top of a double boiler or in a stainless-steel bowl set over a saucepan of simmering water; whisk constantly until warm.

Blender Hollandaise

Makes ⅔ cup (150 mL)

4	egg yolks, at room temperature	4
1 tbsp	fresh lemon juice	15 mL
¼ tsp	salt	1 mL
Pinch	cayenne pepper	Pinch
½ cup	butter, cut into pieces	125 mL

1. In a blender, combine egg yolks, lemon juice, salt and cayenne. Blend on high for a few seconds until frothy.

2. Place butter in a 2-cup (500 mL) glass measure and microwave on High for 1 to 1½ minutes or until melted and bubbly. Turn blender on high and add hot butter to egg yolk mixture in a thin steady stream until thickened. Serve immediately.

Creamed Eggs with Smoked Ham

8	eggs	8
¼ cup	milk	60 mL
¼ tsp	salt	1 mL
¼ tsp	freshly ground black pepper	1 mL
1 tbsp	butter	15 mL
½ cup	smoked ham, cut into thin strips	125 mL
3	green onions, sliced	3
¼ cup	light cream cheese, cut into cubes	60 mL
2 tbsp	chopped fresh parsley	30 mL

1. In a bowl, beat eggs, milk, salt and pepper; set aside.

2. In a large nonstick skillet, melt butter over medium heat. Cook ham and green onions, stirring, for 2 to 3 minutes or until onions are softened. Stir in cream cheese until melted and smooth.

3. Add egg mixture and cook, stirring often, for about 4 minutes or until eggs are almost set but still moist. Sprinkle with parsley and serve.

Western Omelet

1 tbsp	butter	15 mL
2	green onions, sliced	2
½	small green bell pepper, diced	½
½ cup	diced smoked ham	125 mL
4	eggs	4
1 tbsp	milk or water	15 mL
¼ tsp	salt	1 mL
	Freshly ground black pepper	

1. In a large nonstick skillet, heat butter over medium heat. Add green onions, pepper and ham; cook, stirring often, for 5 minutes or until pepper is softened.

2. Meanwhile, in a bowl, whisk eggs with milk, salt and pepper; pour into skillet.

3. Cook over medium heat, stirring gently with wooden spatula, for about 30 seconds or until eggs just start to set. Continue to cook, without stirring, until firm, about 3 minutes. Fold in half and carefully slide onto a serving plate. Serve immediately.

Cheese and Mushroom Oven Omelet

Versatile mushrooms star in this terrific dish that's perfect to serve for brunch or a light supper.

Tips

Use a variety of white and exotic mushrooms such as shiitake, portobello and oyster.

Herbed soft goat cheese can replace the cream cheese, if desired.

- Preheat oven to 350°F (180°C)
- Well-buttered 9- or 10-inch (23 or 25 cm) pie plate, sprinkled with 1 tbsp (15 mL) fine dry bread crumbs

4	eggs, separated	4
2 tbsp	milk	30 mL
	Salt and freshly ground black pepper	
1 tbsp	butter	15 mL
3 cups	sliced assorted mushrooms	750 mL
3	green onions, sliced	3
¼ cup	light or herb cream cheese	60 mL
⅓ cup	shredded Cheddar cheese	75 mL
2 oz	smoked ham, cut into thin strips, or 3 slices bacon, cooked crisp and crumbled	60 g

1. In a small bowl, beat egg yolks with milk; season with salt and pepper. In a bowl, using an electric mixer, beat egg whites until stiff peaks form. Slowly beat in yolk mixture on low speed until blended into egg whites. Pour into prepared pie plate. Bake for 15 minutes or until just set in the center.

2. Meanwhile, in a large nonstick skillet, melt butter over medium-high heat. Cook mushrooms and green onions, stirring, for 5 minutes or until tender and liquid is evaporated. Remove from heat; stir in cream cheese until smooth.

3. Spoon evenly over omelet; sprinkle with cheese and ham. Bake for 8 minutes more or until cheese is melted.

Baked Layered Tuscan Omelet

Having a special weekend brunch and don't know what to serve? Here's an impressive egg dish that is sure to please. Accompany with baked ham, if you wish, and a selection of scones, muffins or rolls and fresh fruit.

Tips

Hate shedding tears when chopping onions? To minimize the weeping problem, use a razor-sharp knife to prevent loss of juices and cover the cut onions with a paper towel as you chop them to prevent the vapors from rising to your eyes.

To seed tomatoes, cut in half crosswise and gently squeeze out seeds.

- Preheat oven to 350°F (180°C)
- 9-inch (23 cm) springform pan, greased
- Rimmed baking sheet

1 tbsp	olive oil	15 mL
1	onion, chopped	1
1	red bell pepper, chopped	1
1	small zucchini, halved lengthwise, then sliced crosswise	1
2 cups	sliced mushrooms	500 mL
1½ cups	seeded and chopped tomatoes	375 mL
3 tbsp	tomato paste	45 mL
3 tbsp	chopped fresh basil	45 mL
	Salt and freshly ground black pepper	
12	eggs	12
8 tsp	butter, divided	40 mL
1½ cups	shredded fontina or provolone cheese	375 mL

1. In a large nonstick skillet, heat oil over medium heat. Cook onion, red pepper, zucchini and mushrooms, stirring, for 5 minutes or until softened. Add tomatoes and tomato paste; cook, stirring often, for 8 to 10 minutes or until vegetables are tender and sauce is thickened. Stir in basil and season with salt and pepper to taste. Transfer to a bowl and set aside. (Can be made a day ahead; cover and refrigerate.)

2. In a bowl, beat 3 eggs with 1 tsp (5 mL) water and season with salt and pepper. In a 10-inch (25 cm) nonstick skillet, melt 2 tsp (10 mL) butter over medium heat. Pour in egg mixture and cook for 2 to 3 minutes, gently lifting edge to allow uncooked egg to flow underneath, until top is almost set. Carefully turn omelet over and cook for 1 minute or until completely set and golden. Transfer to a plate. Repeat, making 3 more omelets, separating each omelet with parchment or waxed paper.

Variation

Instead of the vegetable filling suggested in the recipe, layer the omelet with Ratatouille Salsa (page 83) and substitute Monterey Jack cheese for the fontina.

3. To assemble, place 1 omelet in prepared springform pan. Sprinkle with $\frac{1}{3}$ cup (75 mL) of the cheese. Spread one-quarter of the vegetable mixture over omelet. Repeat, assembling three more layers. Top with remaining vegetable mixture, then cheese.

4. Place pan on baking sheet and bake for 35 to 40 minutes or until cheese is melted and a knife inserted in the center is hot to the touch. Remove sides of pan and carefully slide omelet off springform base onto a large serving plate. Cut into wedges and serve.

Basic Omelet

In a bowl, whisk 3 eggs with 1 tbsp (15 mL) water and a pinch of salt and pepper. In an 8-inch (20 cm) nonstick skillet, heat 2 tsp (10 mL) butter over medium-high heat. Pour in egg mixture and cook, using a spatula to push egg to center and lifting edge to allow uncooked egg to flow underneath, for 1 to 2 minutes or until top is almost set. Sprinkle your favorite fillings, such as shredded cheese, diced ham, tomato or red pepper, or sautéed mushroom, over half the omelet. Fold the other half over the filling and slide out of the pan onto a plate. Makes 1 serving.

Breakfast Hash Brown and Sausage Bake

Make-ahead dishes are always appreciated for a special breakfast or brunch. I doubled this recipe and also prepared a vegetarian version to serve at a post-wedding brunch. The dishes were baked just before the guests arrived, and the food stayed nicely warm on the buffet table. Leftovers the next day were just as delicious!

Tip

This recipe can be doubled and baked in a 13- by 9-inch (33 by 23 cm) baking dish for 45 to 50 minutes.

Variation

For a vegetarian version, omit sausage and add 1 diced red bell pepper along with hash browns and onion in skillet.

- Preheat oven to 350°F (180°C)
- 8-inch (20 cm) square baking dish, well greased

8 oz	lean pork or chicken sausages, casings removed	250 g
1 tbsp	vegetable oil	15 mL
3 cups	frozen diced hash brown potatoes	750 mL
1	onion, chopped	1
½ tsp	dried crumbled sage	2 mL
¼ tsp	dried thyme leaves	1 mL
1 cup	shredded Cheddar cheese	250 mL
4	eggs	4
1 cup	milk	250 mL
2 tbsp	freshly grated Parmesan cheese	30 mL
1	green onion, finely sliced	1
	Freshly ground black pepper	

1. In a large nonstick skillet over medium-high heat, cook sausage, breaking up meat with back of a wooden spoon, for 5 minutes or until no longer pink. Transfer to a plate lined with paper towel to absorb any fat. Let cool. Chop sausage meat, using a knife or pulsing in a food processor.

2. Return skillet to medium-high heat and add oil. Cook potatoes, onion, sage and thyme, stirring often, for 10 minutes or until potatoes are nicely browned. Arrange potato mixture in prepared dish. Top with sausage and Cheddar cheese.

3. In a bowl, beat together eggs, milk, Parmesan cheese and green onion. Season with pepper. Pour over cheese layer. (Can be prepared ahead. Cover and refrigerate for up to 1 day.)

4. Bake in preheated oven for 35 to 40 minutes (10 minutes longer if refrigerated) or until top is golden and a knife inserted in the center comes out clean. Transfer to a wire rack and let stand for 10 minutes before serving.

Tomato and Asiago Cheese Strata

- Preheat oven to 350°F (180°C)
- 8-inch (20 cm) square baking dish, well greased

2 tbsp	olive oil	30 mL
1 cup	chopped Spanish onion	250 mL
2	cloves garlic, finely chopped	2
2 cups	chopped seeded plum tomatoes (about 5 to 6)	500 mL
½ tsp	salt	2 mL
¼ tsp	freshly ground black pepper	1 mL
2 tbsp	chopped fresh basil	30 mL
6 cups	cubed stale Italian or French bread (see Tip, left)	1.5 L
1½ cups	shredded Asiago or fontina cheese	375 mL
4	eggs	4
1 cup	vegetable or chicken stock	250 mL

1. In a large nonstick skillet, heat oil over medium-high heat. Cook onion and garlic, stirring, for 2 minutes. Stir in tomatoes, salt and pepper; cook, stirring often, for 5 minutes or until tomatoes are sauce-like. Stir in basil.

2. Layer half of the bread cubes in prepared baking dish. Top with half of the tomato mixture and sprinkle with half of the cheese. Layer with remaining bread and tomato mixture.

3. In a bowl, beat eggs with stock; pour over bread mixture. Sprinkle with remaining cheese. Let stand for 10 minutes for bread to absorb egg mixture. (Can be made a day ahead; cover and refrigerate.)

4. Bake in preheated oven for 35 to 40 minutes (5 to 10 minutes longer if refrigerated), until top is golden and center is set when tested with a knife. Serve warm or at room temperature.

Leek, Bacon and Gruyère Strata

Makes 8 servings

This appealing egg dish makes a wonderful breakfast or brunch, or serve it along with a salad for a light supper.

Tips

To clean leeks: Trim dark green tops. Cut down center almost to root end and chop. Rinse in a sink full of cold water to remove sand; scoop up leeks and place in colander to drain or use a salad spinner.

Recipe can be halved and baked in an 8-inch (2 L) baking dish for 30 to 40 minutes.

• 13- by 9-inch (33 by 23 cm) baking dish, greased

2 tbsp	butter	30 mL
2	leeks, white and light green part only, chopped (see Tip, left)	2
2	cloves garlic, finely chopped	2
1	large red bell pepper, diced	1
10 cups	cubed day-old Italian bread (¾-inch/2 cm cubes)	2.5 L
12	slices bacon, cooked crisp and crumbled	12
2 cups	shredded Gruyère or Cheddar cheese	500 mL
8	eggs	8
2 cups	milk	500 mL
½ tsp	salt	2 mL
¼ tsp	freshly ground black pepper	1 mL
¼ tsp	freshly grated nutmeg	1 mL

1. In a large nonstick skillet, melt butter over medium heat. Cook leeks, garlic and red pepper, stirring, for 5 minutes or until softened.

2. Layer half of the bread cubes in baking dish. Top with half each of the leek mixture, bacon and cheese. Repeat layers.

3. In a bowl, beat eggs, milk, salt, pepper and nutmeg. Pour evenly over bread mixture. Press down with a spatula to help bread absorb egg mixture. Cover and refrigerate for at least 2 hours or overnight.

4. Preheat oven to 350°F (180°C).

5. Uncover and bake for 40 to 50 minutes or until center is set and top is puffed. Let stand for 10 minutes before serving.

Variation

Ham, Leek and Gruyère Strata

Substitute 1 cup (250 mL) diced smoked ham for the bacon.

How to Cook Bacon in the Microwave

The amount of time needed to cook bacon in the microwave depends not only on the power of your microwave oven, but also on the thickness of the bacon and its salt, sugar and moisture content. Always check at the earlier time to make sure it doesn't overcook, then continue cooking in 30-second increments until crisp.

Line a large plate with a double layer of paper towels and place the bacon in a single layer on the paper; top with a paper towel to prevent splatters, Cook bacon on High.

Suggested times

2 slices: $1\frac{1}{2}$ to $2\frac{1}{2}$ minutes
4 slices: 3 to 5 minutes
6 slices: 5 to 7 minutes

Cooking Bacon for a Crowd

Line bottom of a shallow 11- by 7-inch (2 L) baking dish with a double thickness of paper towels. Arrange 4 or 5 slices per layer, separated by a double sheet of paper towels; top with paper towel. Microwave on High, allowing for 3 to 4 minutes per layer, or until bacon is crisp. For best results, do no more than three layers at a time. Watch carefully to ensure bacon doesn't overcook.

Ham and Potato Frittata

Makes 6 servings

Nothing beats a delicious egg dish like this frittata for a special occasion breakfast or brunch, or for an easy supper dish. A frittata is an Italian version of an omelet. Unlike its finicky cousin, which needs careful flipping and turning, a frittata doesn't require any major cooking skills other than stirring — so it's almost impossible to ruin this dish.

Tip

Bake or microwave 2 large potatoes the day before and refrigerate so cubes keep their shape during cooking.

Variation

Bacon and Potato Frittata

Instead of ham, add 6 bacon slices, cooked until crisp and crumbled, to egg mixture.

• Preheat oven to 375°F (190°C)

2 tbsp	butter	30 mL
1	small onion, finely chopped	1
2 cups	peeled cooked potatoes, cut into ½-inch (1 cm) cubes	500 mL
1	small red bell pepper, finely diced (optional)	1
¾ cup	diced smoked ham (about 4 oz/125 g)	175 mL
8	eggs	8
2 tbsp	milk	30 mL
2 tbsp	finely chopped fresh parsley	30 mL
	Salt and freshly ground black pepper	
1 cup	shredded Cheddar, Edam or Havarti cheese	250 mL

1. In a large nonstick skillet, melt butter over medium-high heat. Add onion, potatoes, red pepper and ham; cook, stirring often, for 5 minutes or until vegetables are tender. Reduce heat to medium-low.

2. Meanwhile, in a large bowl, beat together eggs, milk and parsley; season with salt and pepper. Pour over potato mixture in skillet; cook, stirring gently, for about 1 minute, or until eggs start to set. (The eggs will appear semi-scrambled.) Stir in cheese.

3. If skillet handle is not ovenproof, wrap in double layer of foil to shield it from oven heat. Place skillet in preheated oven for 15 to 20 minutes or until eggs are just set in center. Let cool for 5 minutes. Turn out onto large serving plate and cut into wedges.

Crustless Zucchini Quiche

You can always count on eggs for an economical meal. This oven-baked crustless quiche is perfect for brunch or an easy supper, served with juicy sliced tomatoes and good bread.

Tips

Wrap zucchini in a clean, dry kitchen towel to remove excess moisture.

To make fresh bread crumbs, process 1 slice white sandwich bread in a food processor until finely crumbed.

- Preheat oven to 325°F (160°C)
- 10-inch (25 cm) pie plate or quiche dish, greased

1 tbsp	butter	15 mL
3 cups	grated zucchini (unpeeled), squeezed dry	750 mL
4	green onions, sliced	4
1	red bell pepper, diced	1
6	eggs	6
¾ cup	shredded Cheddar or fontina cheese	175 mL
½ cup	soft fresh bread crumbs	125 mL
¼ tsp	salt	1 mL
¼ tsp	freshly ground black pepper	1 mL

1. In a large nonstick skillet, melt butter over medium-high heat. Add zucchini, green onions and red pepper; cook, stirring often, for 5 minutes or until softened. Let cool slightly.

2. In a large bowl, beat eggs; stir in zucchini mixture, cheese, bread crumbs, salt and pepper. Pour into pie plate. Bake for 35 to 40 minutes or until set in center.

Mushroom Spinach Quiche

Makes 6 servings

Mushrooms paired with spinach or broccoli is a favorite filling for quiche. Serve for brunch, lunch or dinner with a salad.

Tips

To wash or not wash mushrooms? You can wipe them with a damp cloth, if you wish. However, I feel it's important to wash all produce that comes into my kitchen. I quickly rinse mushrooms under cold water and immediately wrap in a clean, dry kitchen towel or paper towels to absorb excess moisture.

The taste of freshly grated nutmeg is so much better than the pre-ground variety. Whole nutmeg can be found in the spice section of your supermarket or bulk food store. Use a rasp grater (such as a Microplane) to grate nutmeg.

- 9-inch (23 cm) pie plate or quiche dish
- Pie weights or dried beans

	Pastry for a single-crust 9-inch (23 cm) pie (see recipe, page 508)	
8 cups	lightly packed fresh baby spinach (6 oz/175 g)	2 L
1 tbsp	butter	15 mL
1	small onion, finely chopped	1
1½ cups	chopped assorted mushrooms, such as cremini, shiitake and white button	375 mL
¼ tsp	dried thyme leaves	1 mL
¾ cup	shredded Jarlsberg or Cheddar cheese	175 mL
3	eggs	3
1 cup	milk or light (5%) cream	250 mL
¼ tsp	salt	1 mL
¼ tsp	freshly ground black pepper	1 mL
	Freshly grated nutmeg	

1. On a lightly floured surface, roll out pastry to a 12-inch (30 cm) round. Fit into pie plate and trim edge, leaving a generous ½-inch (1 cm) overhang. Turn pastry edge under and crimp edge. Prick pastry bottom in several places with a fork. Refrigerate for 30 minutes.

2. Preheat oven to 425°F (220°C) and arrange oven rack in bottom third of oven.

3. Line pastry with a sheet of parchment paper or foil and fill with pie weights. Bake in lower third of oven for 10 minutes. Remove pie weights and bake for 5 minutes more or until edges are golden. Place on rack to cool. Reduce oven temperature to 375°F (190°C).

4. Rinse spinach and shake off excess water. Heat a large nonstick skillet over medium-high heat. Cook spinach, stirring often, until just wilted. (Or place in covered casserole dish and microwave on High for 1½ to 2 minutes.) Squeeze out excess moisture and chop. (There should be ½ cup/125 mL.) Set aside.

Instead of spinach, substitute 1½ cups (375 mL) small broccoli florets. Blanch broccoli in boiling water for 1 minute or until crisp and bright green. (Or place in a covered glass dish with 2 tbsp (30 mL) water and microwave on High for 1 to 1½ minutes until crisp and bright green.) Plunge into cold water to chill, then drain. Add to pie shell along with mushrooms.

5. In same nonstick skillet, melt butter over medium-high heat. Add onion, mushrooms and thyme and cook, stirring, for 3 to 4 minutes or until mushrooms are softened. Let cool slightly.

6. Sprinkle pastry with cheese, then with mushroom mixture and spinach. In a bowl, whisk together eggs, milk, salt, pepper and nutmeg to taste. Pour evenly into pie crust.

7. Bake for about 35 minutes or until knife inserted in the center comes out clean. Transfer to a rack and let stand for 10 minutes before serving.

Quiche Lorraine

This ever-popular egg pie with bacon bits is an instant problem solver when you're wondering what to make for a do-ahead brunch or special lunch.

Tip

Instead of bacon slices that require cooking, use ½ cup (125 mL) real bacon bits.

Variation

Smoked Salmon Asparagus Quiche

Replace bacon with 4 oz (125 g) thinly sliced smoked salmon or Black Forest ham, cut into strips, and add 1 cup (250 mL) chopped uncooked asparagus. Reduce cheese to ¾ cup (175 mL).

- 9-inch (23 cm) pie plate or quiche dish
- Pie weights or dried beans

	Pastry for a single-crust 9-inch (23 cm) pie (see recipe, page 508)	
8	slices bacon, cooked crisp and crumbled	8
1 cup	shredded Swiss, Gruyère or Gouda cheese	250 mL
3	green onions, thinly sliced	3
4	eggs	4
1¼ cups	half-and-half (10%) cream	300 mL
¼ tsp	salt	1 mL
¼ tsp	freshly ground pepper	1 mL
	Freshly grated nutmeg	

1. On a lightly floured surface, roll out pastry into a 12-inch (30 cm) round. Fit into pie plate and trim edge, leaving a generous ½-inch (1 cm) overhang. Turn pastry edge under and crimp edge. Prick pastry bottom in several places with a fork. Refrigerate for 30 minutes.

2. Preheat oven to 425°F (220°C) and arrange oven rack in bottom third of oven.

3. Line pastry with a sheet of parchment paper or foil and fill with dried beans or pie weights. Bake in preheated oven for 10 minutes. Remove pie weights and bake for 5 minutes more or until edges are golden. Transfer to a rack to cool. Reduce oven temperature to 375°F (190°C).

4. Sprinkle bacon, cheese and green onions evenly over crust. In a bowl, beat eggs; add cream, salt, pepper and nutmeg to taste. Pour over bacon mixture. Bake in oven for 35 to 40 minutes or until a knife inserted in centre comes out clean. Let stand for 10 minutes before serving.

Oatmeal with Apples and Cranberries

Oatmeal is such a wonderful, healthy breakfast. The addition of apples and dried cranberries makes it even more appealing and nourishing. By eating breakfast, even a simple bowl of cereal, we tend to burn more calories during the day. Choose large-flake (old-fashioned) rolled oats over quick-cooking oats. They help moderate blood sugar levels better, so you won't feel hungry by mid-morning.

Tips

Instead of cranberries, add chopped dried apricots, figs, prunes, mangos or raisins.

To make cinnamon sugar, combine 1/4 cup (60 mL) granulated sugar with 1 tbsp (15 mL) ground cinnamon.

1 1/3 cups	water or apple juice	325 mL
Pinch	salt (optional)	Pinch
2/3 cup	large-flake (old-fashioned) rolled oats	150 mL
1	apple, peeled and chopped	1
1/4 cup	dried cranberries	60 mL
	Milk	
	Cinnamon sugar, honey or maple syrup to taste	

Stovetop Method

1. In a medium saucepan, bring water to a boil over high heat. Season with salt (if using). Stir in oats, apple and cranberries and return to a boil, stirring constantly. Reduce heat to low, partially cover and let simmer, stirring occasionally, for 5 to 7 minutes or until oats are tender.

2. Thin with milk to desired consistency. Sweeten with cinnamon sugar to taste.

Microwave Method

1. In a large 8-cup (2 L) glass measure or casserole dish, combine water, salt, oats, apple and cranberries. Microwave, uncovered, on High for 4 to 6 minutes, stirring twice, until mixture comes to a full rolling boil and thickens. (Watch carefully to prevent mixture from boiling over.)

2. Thin with milk to desired consistency. Sweeten with cinnamon sugar to taste.

French Toast with Cinnamon Sugar

This cinnamon-flavored French toast is delicious with bacon or sausages, fresh fruit and yogurt. The cinnamon sugar adds a nice sweetness to the French toast, but you may also want to serve maple or fruit-based syrup with it.

Tip

Use stale, slightly thicker cut bread rather than soft, sliced sandwich bread when you make French toast. You'll find the toast will not be as soggy and will nicely puff up.

- Preheat oven to 200°F (100°C)
- Baking sheet

6	eggs	6
1½ cups	milk	375 mL
1 tbsp	granulated sugar	15 mL
2 tsp	vanilla	10 mL
4 tsp	butter (approx.), divided	20 mL
12	thick-cut slices day-old egg (challah), raisin or whole-grain bread	12

Cinnamon Sugar

¼ cup	granulated sugar	60 mL
1 tbsp	ground cinnamon	15 mL

1. In a large shallow dish, whisk together eggs, milk, sugar and vanilla.

2. In a large nonstick skillet, melt 2 tsp (10 mL) of the butter over medium heat. Dip bread into egg mixture, turning once, until well soaked. Cook in batches for about 3 minutes per side or until crisp and golden brown. Transfer to baking sheet and keep warm in preheated oven while preparing remaining slices. Add more butter to skillet and adjust heat between batches as necessary.

3. *Cinnamon Sugar:* In a shallow bowl or pie plate, combine sugar and cinnamon.

4. Cut warm toast in half on the diagonal and dip both sides in cinnamon sugar, coating generously. Arrange on serving plates and serve immediately.

Overnight Oven French Toast

Makes 4 servings

Expecting company and want to get a head start on the cooking? Here's a great breakfast dish that can be assembled a day ahead or frozen. When ready to serve, arrange the toasts on greased baking sheets and pop in the oven while you make the coffee and fry the bacon.

Tips

Freeze unbaked slices in a single layer on a baking sheet lined with plastic wrap; when frozen, transfer to plastic storage bags and freeze. No need to defrost before baking; bake as directed in recipe, increasing baking time by about 5 minutes.

Buy French bread that is 4 inches (10 cm) in diameter or increase slices to 10 if slightly smaller.

Variation
Fruit Kabobs
Add colorful fruit kabobs to dress up the breakfast plate. Thread assorted fresh fruit chunks, such as apple, banana, strawberries, kiwi, pear and pineapple, onto 4-inch (10 cm) wooden skewers. (Trim or cut skewers in half, if necessary, to get the right length.)

- Preheat oven to 425°F (220°C)
- 13- by 9-inch (33 by 23 cm) baking dish
- Baking sheet, well greased or lined with parchment paper

4	eggs	4
1 cup	milk	250 mL
1 tbsp	granulated sugar	15 mL
1 tsp	vanilla	5 mL
12	slices day-old French bread, cut ¾ inch (2 cm) thick	12
3 tbsp	melted butter	45 mL

1. In a bowl, whisk together eggs, milk, sugar and vanilla. Arrange bread slices in a single layer in baking dish. Pour egg mixture over. Turn slices over and let stand until egg mixture is absorbed. Cover and refrigerate until ready to bake. (Recipe can be prepared up to this point the night before.)

2. Arrange toasts in a single layer on prepared sheet and brush tops with half of melted butter.

3. Bake in preheated oven for 10 minutes. Turn slices over; brush tops with remaining melted butter. Bake for 8 minutes longer or until puffed and golden.

Stuffed French Toast with Ricotta and Blueberries

Makes 6 servings

Bored with ordinary French toast? Try this version stuffed with creamy ricotta and blueberries. Serve with maple syrup or dipped in cinnamon sugar (see recipe, page 30).

Tips

If you don't have a rasp grater, such as a Microplane, to grate lemon zest, use a zester to remove the zest in thin shreds, then finely chop with a knife.

When lemons are bargain-priced, stock up for the future. Grate the zest and squeeze the juice; place in separate containers and freeze.

- Preheat oven to 200°F (100°C)
- Baking sheet

4	eggs	4
1 cup	milk	250 mL
3 tbsp	granulated sugar, divided	45 mL
1½ tsp	vanilla	7 mL
1 cup	ricotta cheese	250 mL
1 tsp	grated lemon zest	5 mL
1½ cups	fresh or frozen blueberries, thawed and drained	375 mL
12	slices day-old egg bread (challah), raisin bread or whole-grain bread	12
6 tsp	butter, divided (approx.)	30 mL

1. In a large, shallow dish, whisk together eggs, milk, 1 tbsp (15 mL) of the sugar and vanilla.

2. In a bowl, combine ricotta, remaining sugar and lemon zest. Spread a generous tablespoonful of ricotta mixture over each bread slice, leaving a ½-inch (1 cm) border. Layer half the bread slices with blueberries. Cover with remaining bread slices and gently press down.

3. In a large nonstick skillet or griddle, melt 2 tsp (10 mL) of the butter over medium heat. In batches, dip both sides of sandwiches in egg mixture until well soaked. Cook in batches for about 3 minutes per side or until golden brown. Transfer to a baking sheet and keep warm in preheated oven while preparing remaining slices. Add more butter to skillet and adjust heat between batches as necessary.

Buttermilk Pancakes with Spiced Maple Apples

If I had to name one dish that used to bring my kids out from under their down comforters on a lazy weekend morning, this would be it. For a different twist, try these irresistible pancakes topped with spiced pear slices, too.

Tips

To keep pancakes warm, place on rack in warm oven.

Extra pancakes can be wrapped and frozen, then popped in the toaster for a quick breakfast.

To get a head start on a weekend breakfast, I measure out the dry ingredients for several batches of pancakes in advance, place in plastic bags and store in the cupboard. Beat in the liquid ingredients and the batter is ready for the griddle.

- Preheat oven to 200°F (100°C)
- Baking sheet with rack

Spiced Maple Apples

2 tbsp	butter	30 mL
4	apples or pears, peeled, cored and sliced	4
1/3 cup	maple syrup	75 mL
1/2 tsp	ground cinnamon	2 mL
1/2 tsp	ground ginger	2 mL
1/4 tsp	freshly grated nutmeg	1 mL

Pancakes

1¾ cups	all-purpose flour	425 mL
1 tbsp	granulated sugar	15 mL
2 tsp	baking powder	10 mL
1/2 tsp	baking soda	2 mL
1/2 tsp	salt	2 mL
2	eggs	2
2 cups	buttermilk	500 mL
2 tbsp	melted butter	30 mL

1. *Spiced Maple Apples:* In a large nonstick skillet, melt butter over medium-high heat. Add apples, maple syrup, cinnamon, ginger and nutmeg; cook, stirring often, for 5 minutes or until apples are just tender. Keep warm.

2. *Pancakes:* In a bowl, combine flour, sugar, baking powder, baking soda and salt. In another bowl, beat eggs; add buttermilk and melted butter. Whisk into flour mixture to make a smooth thick batter.

3. On an oiled griddle or in a large nonstick skillet over medium heat, drop 1/4 cupfuls (60 mL) of batter and spread to a 4-inch (10 cm) circle. Cook for about 1 1/2 minutes or until bubbles appear on top; turn over and cook until browned on other side. Transfer to rack on baking sheet and keep warm in preheated oven while preparing remaining pancakes. Serve with spiced maple apples over top.

Apple Puff Pancake

You can have this impressive oven pancake assembled and in the oven in very short order. Then set the table, make the coffee and call everyone for breakfast. Serve with a drizzle of maple syrup and vanilla yogurt.

Tip

The brown sugar you use in recipes is totally your preference. Brown sugar comes in both light and dark brown. Dark brown sugar is noticeably darker in color and has a stronger molasses taste.

• Preheat oven to 400°F (200°C)
• Two 8- or 9-inch (20 or 23 cm) cake pans or 9-inch (23 cm) glass pie plates

1 cup	all-purpose flour	250 mL
1 cup	milk	250 mL
4	eggs	4
2 tbsp	granulated sugar	30 mL
¼ tsp	salt	1 mL
4 tbsp	butter, divided	60 mL
3	apples, peeled and thinly sliced (about 4 cups/1 L)	3
¼ cup	packed brown sugar	60 mL
1½ tsp	ground cinnamon	7 mL
	Confectioner's (icing) sugar	

1. In a blender or food processor, blend flour, milk, eggs, sugar and salt to make a smooth batter. Let stand while cooking apples.

2. In a large nonstick skillet, melt 2 tbsp (30 mL) butter over medium heat. Add apple slices, brown sugar and cinnamon. Cook, stirring often, for 5 minutes or until apples are softened.

3. Add 1 tbsp (15 mL) butter to each baking pan and place in preheated oven until melted. Swirl to coat bottom and sides. Pour batter into pans, dividing evenly, and top each with an even layer of warm apple mixture.

4. Bake for 20 to 25 minutes or until puffed and golden. Sprinkle with confectioner's sugar and serve.

Crêpes

**Makes about
14 crêpes**

This is an all-purpose crêpe recipe, ideal for blintzes (page 36), Brown Sugar Pears (page 539) or savory fillings, such as Seafood Supreme (page 229).

Tip

To make ahead, place crêpes, separated with waxed paper, in a plastic storage bag or rigid container (such as a large cookie tin). Refrigerate for up to 3 days or freeze for up to 1 month.

- 8-inch (20 cm) nonstick skillet

4	eggs	4
1 cup	milk	250 mL
1/2 cup	water	125 mL
1 1/4 cups	all-purpose flour	300 mL
1/4 tsp	salt	1 mL
2 tbsp	butter, melted	30 mL

1. In a blender or food processor, blend eggs, milk and water. Add flour and salt; blend on low speed until smooth, scraping down sides with a spatula. Let batter stand for 30 minutes.

2. Heat skillet over medium-high heat and brush lightly with some of the melted butter. Pour in a scant 1/4 cup (60 mL) batter, swirling pan quickly to spread evenly. Cook for about 1 minute or until edges curl and underside of crêpe is lightly browned. Transfer to a plate, browned side up.

3. Repeat with remaining batter, brushing skillet lightly with melted butter before adding batter to pan and adjusting heat as necessary. Stack crêpes on plate, separating each with waxed paper. Let cool.

Cheese Blintzes with Lemon Blueberry Sauce

Makes 14 blintzes

These popular crêpe bundles with a lemony cheese filling are perfect for a special brunch or dessert.

Tips

If you don't have a rasp grater, such as a Microplane, to grate lemon zest, use a zester to remove the zest in thin shreds, then finely chop with a knife.

When lemons are bargain-priced, stock up for the future. Grate the zest and squeeze the juice; place in separate containers and freeze.

To get more juice out of a lemon, roll on countertop or microwave on High for 20 seconds before squeezing.

- Preheat oven to 200°F (100°C)
- Baking sheet

1 lb	pressed cottage cheese, crumbled	500 g
4 oz	light cream cheese, cubed	125 g
1/3 cup	granulated sugar	75 mL
1	egg	1
2 tsp	grated lemon zest	10 mL
1 tbsp	fresh lemon juice	15 mL
14	crêpes (see recipe, page 35)	14
2 tbsp	butter (approx.)	30 mL
	Sour cream	
	Lemon Blueberry Sauce (see recipe, page 505) or warm preserves	

1. In a food processor, blend cottage cheese, cream cheese, sugar, egg, lemon zest and lemon juice until smooth. Transfer to a bowl.

2. Place each crêpe, browned side up, on work surface. Place a generous 2 tbsp (30 mL) of filling in center and spread to a 3- by 2-inch (7.5 by 6 cm) rectangle. Turn up bottom edge to cover filling and flatten slightly. Fold in sides and then fold top of crêpe over to create a rectangular package. Flip over again and place on large plate. Repeat with remaining crêpes and filling. (Can be made up to 1 day ahead. Cover well and refrigerate.)

3. In a large nonstick skillet, heat 2 tsp (10 mL) butter over medium heat. Add 4 blintzes to skillet and cook for 1 to 2 minutes per side, turning once, until golden brown. Place blintzes on baking sheet and keep warm in preheated oven. Repeat with remaining blintzes, adding butter as needed for each batch. Serve hot with sour cream and Lemon Blueberry Sauce.

Sandwiches and Light Suppers

Egg Salad on a Kaiser

This versatile egg salad is great on a Kaiser or tucked into pita pockets with shredded lettuce or sprouts and tomato wedges.

Tip

To hard-cook eggs: Place eggs in saucepan; add cold water to cover eggs by 1 inch (2.5 cm). Place over medium-high heat; bring to a gentle rolling boil. Boil for 2 minutes; cover and remove from heat. Let stand for 10 minutes. Drain and chill eggs in cold water.

Variation

Egg Salad Tortilla Spirals

Spread egg salad on two 9-inch (23 cm) flour tortillas, leaving a 1-inch (2.5 cm) border. Layer with lettuce. Fold bottom over filling, then sides; roll up tightly. Wrap in plastic wrap and refrigerate overnight. To make easy-pick-up sandwiches for kids' lunches, cut into 1-inch (2.5 cm) pieces.

2 tbsp	cream cheese, softened	30 mL
2 tbsp	plain yogurt	30 mL
1 tsp	Dijon mustard	5 mL
1/4 tsp	salt	1 mL
1/4 tsp	freshly ground black pepper	1 mL
3	hard-cooked eggs, finely chopped (see Tip, left)	3
1	small green onion, finely chopped	1
2	whole wheat Kaiser rolls, split	2
	Leaf or romaine lettuce	
6	thin slices tomato	6

1. In a bowl, combine cream cheese, yogurt, mustard, salt and pepper. Stir in eggs and green onion. (Make ahead, cover and refrigerate for up to 2 days.)

2. Spread egg salad over top halves of rolls. Arrange lettuce and tomato slices on bottom halves; sandwich together.

Dilled Salmon and Egg Salad on Pumpernickel

Makes 4 sandwiches

I like to add inexpensive eggs to help stretch more costly canned sockeye salmon or solid white tuna when making sandwiches.

Tip

To prevent cucumber from turning soggy, assemble sandwiches the same day they are served.

Variation

Dilled Salmon

Instead of eggs and salmon, use 2 cans (7½ oz/213 g) sockeye salmon.

3	hard-cooked eggs, finely chopped (see Tip, page 38)	3
1	can (7½ oz/213 g) sockeye salmon, drained and flaked	1
¼ cup	light mayonnaise	60 mL
1	large green onion, finely chopped	1
2 tbsp	chopped fresh dill or parsley	30 mL
1 tsp	grated lemon zest	5 mL
¼ tsp	salt	1 mL
¼ tsp	freshly ground black pepper	1 mL
8	slices pumpernickel bread	8
½	seedless cucumber, thinly sliced	½

1. In a bowl, combine eggs, salmon, mayonnaise, green onion, dill, lemon zest, salt and pepper. (Made ahead, cover and refrigerate for up to 2 days.)

2. Divide salad among pumpernickel slices, spreading evenly. Layer with cucumber slices. Serve open-faced or sandwich together. Cut in half.

Curried Chicken Salad Sandwiches

Chicken salad sandwich has never been the same in my house since I added some pizzazz to the old standby with apples and a hint of curry.

Tip

Simmer 1 large boneless skinless chicken breast (about 8 oz/250 g), halved lengthwise, in lightly salted water or chicken stock for 10 minutes; remove from heat. Let cool in stock for 15 minutes.

Variation

Mango Chicken Salad Sandwiches

Replace apple with diced fresh mango. Add ¼ cup (60 mL) chopped fresh cilantro.

⅓ cup	light mayonnaise	75 mL
2 tbsp	mango chutney	30 mL
1 tsp	mild curry paste, or to taste	5 mL
1½ cups	finely diced cooked chicken	375 mL
½ cup	finely diced unpeeled apple	125 mL
3 tbsp	golden raisins or dried cranberries	45 mL
2 tbsp	finely chopped green onions	30 mL
	Salt	
4	slices thick-cut whole-grain bread	4
	Red leaf or Boston lettuce	
	Additional mayonnaise	

1. In a bowl, blend mayonnaise with chutney and curry paste. Stir in chicken, apple, raisins and green onions; season with salt to taste.

2. Spread bread slices with additional mayonnaise. Spread 2 bread slices generously with chicken mixture; top with lettuce and remaining bread. Cut in half.

Smoked Salmon and Watercress Tea Sandwiches

**Makes
16 sandwich pieces**

The contrast of the dark pumpernickel bread and rosy salmon filling makes for colorful tea sandwiches.

Variation
Instead of watercress, use cucumber slices and fresh dill sprigs.

5 oz	smoked salmon, coarsely chopped	150 g
4 oz	light cream cheese, softened	125 g
2 tsp	fresh lemon juice	10 mL
1 tsp	Worcestershire sauce	5 mL
	Hot pepper sauce	
8	thin slices pumpernickel or whole-grain bread	8
2 tbsp	butter (approx.), softened	30 mL
1	bunch watercress, large stems removed	1

1. In a food processor, combine salmon, cream cheese, lemon juice, Worcestershire sauce and hot pepper sauce to taste. Process until smooth. (If preparing ahead, transfer to a bowl, cover and refrigerate.)

2. Spread bread lightly with butter. Spread salmon mixture thinly on bread slices. Arrange watercress sprigs on half of the slices. Top with remaining bread slices, pressing together lightly.

3. Trim off crusts and cut sandwiches into quarters (either squares or triangles). Arrange on a serving platter and garnish with watercress.

Tea Sandwiches

What could be more inviting than tea sandwiches for a bridal or baby shower, garden party or afternoon tea? Plan on serving a variety of sandwich shapes, including triangles, squares, rectangles and pinwheels, with assorted fillings. These bite-size morsels are always popular, so expect to make 4 to 6 tea sandwiches per person, depending on whether you plan to serve other appetizer-style finger foods or salads.

Types of Bread

Tea sandwiches are typically made using thinly sliced square loaves of white and/or whole wheat bread. You can place an order for these specialty loaves at your favorite bakery. Be adventurous and try whole-grain, nut, rye and pumpernickel breads too. Just make sure to use top-quality breads. Large flavored tortillas, such as spinach and sun-dried tomato, also make creative tea sandwiches.

Fillings

When it comes to flavorful fillings, the possibilities are endless. Go traditional with egg salad, cucumber or ham and pickle, or try updated fillings of goat cheese with basil pesto or prosciutto with roasted red pepper spread.

Assembling Sandwiches

Freeze bread slices until firm to make it easier to spread the butter and fillings. To prevent sandwiches from getting soggy, always spread a thin layer of softened butter on the bread first, spreading it right to the edges. To ensure neat edges, use a serrated knife to cut off the crusts only *after* sandwiches are filled. The exception is pinwheel sandwiches (see page 43.)

Squares, Triangles, Fingers and Cut-Out Sandwiches

Use a sandwich loaf cut into 16 thin slices (and don't use the end pieces). Spread each slice with softened butter (you'll need about $^{1}/_{3}$ cup/75 mL butter in total). Spread filling (about $1^{1}/_{2}$ cups/375 mL) evenly over 8 of the slices. Top with remaining slices, pressing together lightly. Trim off crusts and cut each sandwich into quarters (either squares or triangles) or into 3 fingers. You can also use cookie cutters to cut sandwiches into decorative shapes, but there is more waste.

Ribbon Sandwiches

Spread 2 slices of white bread and 1 slice of whole wheat bread with softened butter. Spread filling on the whole wheat bread and 1 slice of the white bread. Place whole wheat slice, filling side up, on top of white slice, then top with the other white slice. Press together lightly. Trim off crusts and cut into 3 fingers.

Pinwheel Sandwiches

Use a square loaf cut horizontally into 5 long slices. Use a serrated knife to trim off the crusts, then lightly roll slices with a rolling pin to flatten slightly. Spread slices with softened butter, then filling. Place 1 asparagus spear, thin strips of roasted red pepper (patted dry) or 2 baby gherkins along a short end of each slice, then roll up tightly. Wrap in plastic wrap and refrigerate for at least 1 hour. Trim ends and cut each roll into 6 slices.

Tortilla Spirals

Spread filling evenly over large tortillas (no need to use butter). Roll up tightly. Wrap in plastic wrap and refrigerate for at least 1 hour. Trim ends and cut on the diagonal into thick slices.

Make Ahead

Place assembled uncut sandwiches on a tray covered with a damp kitchen towel. Wrap tightly with plastic wrap to prevent drying out. (If you have made rolls, wrap each roll in plastic wrap.) Most sandwiches can be refrigerated for up to 1 day. Sandwiches made with cucumber, watercress, fresh herbs or other salad greens should be assembled no more than 4 hours ahead to prevent wilting.

Cucumber Tea Sandwiches

Here is an updated version of the classic tea sandwich, spread with butter flavored with basil and orange zest.

Tips

To make orange twists, cut an orange into thin round slices. Make a cut to the center of each round and twist each cut end in opposite directions.

Assemble sandwiches no more than 4 hours before serving so the cucumber remains crisp.

⅓ cup	butter, softened	75 mL
1 tbsp	finely chopped fresh basil	15 mL
1 tsp	grated orange zest	5
¼ tsp	freshly ground black pepper	1 mL
8	thin slices white or whole-grain bread	8
½	seedless cucumber, thinly sliced	½
	Orange twists (optional; see Tip, left)	

1. In a bowl, blend butter with basil, orange zest and pepper. Spread thinly on bread slices. Layer half of the bread slices with cucumber. Top with remaining bread slices, pressing together lightly.

2. Trim off crusts and cut sandwiches into quarters (either squares or triangles). Arrange on a serving platter and garnish with orange twists, if desired.

Tuna Tea Sandwiches

**Makes
32 sandwich pieces**

Looking for inspiration
when making a tuna
sandwich? For a
Mediterranean spin, try
this tasty version with
red pepper, feta and
black olives.

Tips

Buy roasted red peppers
either in a jar or from the
supermarket deli counter.
Blot dry before dicing to
remove excess moisture.

If making sandwiches
the day before, do not
trim crusts. Wrap several
sandwiches together in
plastic wrap and place in
airtight storage containers.
Refrigerate.

2	cans (each 6 oz/170 g) solid white tuna, drained	2
1/2 cup	crumbled feta cheese	125 mL
1/3 cup	light mayonnaise	75 mL
1/4 cup	finely chopped green onions	60 mL
1/4 cup	finely diced roasted red peppers	60 mL
2 tbsp	finely chopped black olives, such as kalamata	30 mL
	Freshly ground black pepper	
16	thin slices white or whole wheat sandwich bread	16
1/3 cup	butter, softened	75 mL

1. In a small bowl, flake tuna with a fork and combine with feta. Blend in mayonnaise, green onions, red peppers and olives. Season with pepper.

2. Spread bread lightly with butter. Spread about 1/4 cup (60 mL) tuna mixture evenly over half of the bread slices and top with remaining bread slices, pressing together lightly.

3. Trim off crusts and cut sandwiches into quarters (either squares or triangles).

Grilled Italian Sandwiches

Makes 2 sandwiches

The classic grilled cheese sandwich takes on a Mediterranean spin with basil pesto and Italian cheese. Great for lunch, or serve as an appetizer!

4	thick slices crusty Italian bread	4
3 tbsp	store-bought or homemade Basil Pesto (see recipe, page 334)	45 mL
4	slices provolone, fontina or mozzarella cheese	4
6	thin tomato slices	6
	Salt and freshly ground black pepper	
2 tbsp	olive oil	30 mL

1. Lightly spread bread slices with pesto. Layer 2 bread slices with 1 slice of cheese. Layer with tomato slices; season with salt and pepper to taste. Top with remaining cheese and bread slices. Brush top bread slices lightly with olive oil.

2. Place oiled-side down in a large nonstick skillet over medium heat; brush sandwich tops with remaining olive oil. Grill for 2 to 3 minutes per side or until nicely toasted and cheese is melted. Cut into quarters and serve.

Grilled Ham and Cheese Sandwiches

Makes 2 sandwiches

There's nothing better for lunch than a golden grilled sandwich oozing with melted cheese. This version includes ham — however, you can omit it and the mustard if you wish.

2 tbsp	light mayonnaise	30 mL
2 tsp	Dijon mustard	10 mL
4	thick slices home-style white or whole-grain bread	4
4	thin slices smoked ham	4
2 oz	aged Cheddar cheese, sliced	60 g
4 tsp	soft butter	20 mL

1. In a small bowl, combine mayonnaise and mustard; spread over bread slices. Cover each with a slice of ham. Top 2 of the slices with Cheddar cheese and top with remaining bread slices so that cheese is sandwiched between the ham. Spread top bread slices each with 1 tsp (5 mL) butter.

2. In a large nonstick skillet over medium heat, place sandwiches buttered-side down in pan and spread top of bread slices with remaining butter. Grill for 2 to 3 minutes per side or until nicely golden and cheese is melted. Cut into halves and serve immediately.

Classic Bruschetta with Tomato and Parmesan

Makes 2 servings

Bruschetta is an Italian open-faced sandwich. It can be served unadorned, with garlic and olive oil, or with a myriad of popular toppings such as juicy ripe tomatoes, fresh basil and Parmesan. When summer tomatoes and fresh basil beckon, make bruschettas for a simple light lunch or as an appetizer for a barbecue.

Tip

To serve as an appetizer, use 8 thick slices French bread instead of Italian bread.

Variation

Greek Bruschetta with Feta-Tomato Topping

Spread toasted bread slices with Greek White Bean Spread and top with feta-tomato topping (see Pita Crisps with Feta and Tomatoes, page 87.)

● Preheat broiler

2	large ripe tomatoes, seeded and diced	2
2 tbsp	coarsely chopped fresh basil	30 mL
1	small clove garlic, minced	1
2 tbsp	olive oil, divided	30 mL
1 tsp	balsamic vinegar	5 mL
	Salt and freshly ground black pepper	
4	thick slices crusty Italian bread	4
	Shaved Parmesan cheese	

1. In a small bowl, combine tomatoes, basil, 1 tbsp (15 mL) oil and balsamic vinegar; season with salt and pepper to taste. Gently toss and let stand for up to 1 hour.

2. Toast bread in a grill pan over medium heat or under broiler for about 2 minutes per side or until golden brown. Brush bread tops lightly with remaining oil. Arrange on a serving plate.

3. Spoon tomato mixture over warm toast and top with shavings of Parmesan cheese. Serve immediately.

Herb Garlic Bread

Who doesn't love this fragrant accompaniment to a steaming bowl of pasta or tossed salad greens?

Tip

Store Parmesan wedges wrapped in plastic wrap, then in foil, in the refrigerator; it keeps well for weeks.

● Preheat oven to 350°F (180°C)

½ cup	butter, softened	125 mL
2	cloves garlic, minced	2
⅓ cup	freshly grated Parmesan cheese	75 mL
2 tbsp	finely chopped fresh parsley	30 mL
¼ tsp	dried basil leaves	1 mL
¼ tsp	dried oregano leaves	1 mL
2 tsp	fresh lemon juice	10 mL
1	large loaf French or Italian bread, cut into ¾-inch (2 cm) thick slices	1

1. In a bowl, cream together butter, garlic, Parmesan, parsley, basil, oregano and lemon juice.

2. Spread butter mixture on one side of bread slices; reassemble into loaf shape and wrap loaf tightly in foil.

3. Bake in preheated oven for 20 minutes or until heated through.

Tuna Cheddar Melt

Makes 2 sandwiches

When I'm too busy to cook dinner, I often rely on this simple satisfying sandwich instead of ordering takeout.

● Preheat broiler
● Baking sheet

1	can (6 oz/170 g) tuna, drained and flaked	1
¼ cup	light mayonnaise	60 mL
¼ cup	finely chopped celery	60 mL
1	green onion, finely chopped	1
1 tsp	fresh lemon juice	5 mL
4	slices whole-grain bread	4
8	thin tomato slices	8
	Salt and freshly ground black pepper	
4	slices Cheddar cheese	4

1. In a bowl, combine tuna, mayonnaise, celery, green onion and lemon juice.

2. Spread bread slices with tuna mixture. Layer with tomato slices; season with salt and pepper. Top with Cheddar cheese slices.

3. Arrange on baking sheet; place under broiler for about 3 minutes or until cheese is melted. Serve immediately.

Mushroom Cheese Dreams

These tasty melts are undeniable proof that there's more to lunch or a quick dinner than an ordinary sandwich or pizza.

Variation

Pizza Cheese Dreams

Cook vegetable topping as directed, reducing mushrooms to 1 cup (250 mL) and adding 1 small green bell pepper, cut into strips. Instead of herbed cream cheese, spread English muffins generously with your favorite pizza sauce. Layer with mushroom mixture and bacon. Top with mozzarella cheese instead of Gouda. Broil as directed.

- Preheat broiler
- Baking sheet

2 tsp	butter	10 mL
2 cups	thinly sliced mushrooms	500 mL
2	green onions, sliced	2
½ tsp	dried fines herbes	2 mL
	Salt and freshly ground black pepper	
Dash	Worcestershire sauce	Dash
2	English muffins, split	2
¼ cup	herbed cream cheese	60 mL
4	slices bacon, cooked until crisp, halved	4
4	thin slices Gouda, fontina or Gruyère cheese	4

1. In a medium nonstick skillet, melt butter over medium heat. Cook mushrooms, green onions and fines herbes, stirring often, for 3 minutes or until mushrooms are softened. Season with salt, pepper and Worcestershire sauce.

2. Toast English muffins and place cut side up on baking sheet. Spread each with cream cheese and layer with 2 half slices bacon. Top with mushroom mixture and a cheese slice.

3. Place baking sheet under preheated broiler for 1 to 2 minutes or until cheese melts. Serve immediately.

Panini with Prosciutto and Provolone

Makes 4 servings

Like all good things Italian, these wonderful pressed sandwiches can be made with a variety of fillings. Here's one of my favorite combinations.

Tip

If you don't have a panini grill, you can cook these sandwiches in a nonstick or cast-iron skillet or on a stovetop grill or outdoor grill. As they cook, press down with a spatula. Cook for 3 to 4 minutes per side. If you're using a grill, rotate the sandwiches halfway through cooking each side to create crossed grill marks.

- Preheat panini grill to medium
- Preheat oven to 200°F (100°C)
- Baking sheet

4	panini, ciabatta or crusty buns, split in half lengthwise	4
	Dijon, whole-seed or honey mustard (optional)	
8	thin slices provolone or fontina cheese	8
8	slices prosciutto or smoked ham	8
8	oil-packed sun-dried tomato halves, blotted dry and cut into thin strips	8
1½ cups	lightly packed fresh baby spinach	375 mL

1. Place buns on work surface, cut side up. Thinly spread with mustard, if using. Layer each half with a slice of cheese and prosciutto. Layer bottom halves with sun-dried tomatoes and spinach. Cover with top halves and press lightly to pack.

2. Place 2 sandwiches in grill, close the top plate and cook for 2 minutes. Rotate sandwiches to create crossed grill marks and cook for 1 to 2 minutes or until cheese is melted and buns are golden brown and crusty.

3. Place cooked panini on baking sheet and keep warm in preheated oven while grilling the remaining sandwiches. Cut sandwiches in half and serve.

Tip

How to Grill Vegetables:
Trim ends off eggplant and zucchini. Cut into 1/4-inch (0.5 cm) thick slices. Core, seed and cut peppers into lengthwise quarters. Cut onions crosswise into thick slices and skewer with wooden toothpicks in several places to prevent rings from separating. Brush vegetables with olive oil and season with salt and pepper. Place on greased outdoor grill or in batches on a stovetop grill over medium heat. Grill, turning vegetables occasionally, until tender, about 10 minutes.

Creating Great Panini

The possibilities are limitless when it comes to panini. Mix and match your favorite bread and fillings to create your own specialty, then follow the basic method on page 50 to assemble and cook your sandwiches. Here are some suggestions to get you started:

Bread

Panini buns, ciabatta rolls or loaves, focaccia, sliced home-style white or whole-grain bread, pita bread

Fillings

- Sliced cheese such as mozzarella, provolone, Gouda, Cheddar, Gruyère (any good melting cheese), plain or herbed soft goat cheese, herbed cream cheese

- Deli meats such as smoked or baked ham, salami, pepperoni or prosciutto; roasted meats such as roast beef, chicken or turkey; canned tuna; bean spreads such as hummus

- Grilled vegetables such as zucchini, eggplant, bell peppers or onion (see Tip, left)

- Sliced tomatoes, fresh herbs and salad greens such as baby spinach, arugula or lettuce

- Condiments such as mayonnaise, pesto, mustard, salsa, pizza sauce, pickles, olives or capers

Hot Roast Beef Heroes

Makes 4 sandwiches

These huge sandwiches are stuffed to overflowing with lots of great things. Grill extra flank or round steak or use store-bought sliced roast beef in this family favorite.

Tip

To soften cream cheese: Place cream cheese in glass bowl and microwave on Medium (50%) for 45 to 60 seconds.

- Preheat broiler
- Baking sheet

4	large crusty rolls	4
1/4 cup	cream cheese, softened	60 mL
2 tbsp	plain yogurt or sour cream	30 mL
2 tbsp	Dijon mustard	30 mL
2	tomatoes, thinly sliced	2
1 tbsp	olive oil	15 mL
1/2	large green bell pepper, cut into thin strips	1/2
1	small onion, thinly sliced	1
1	large clove garlic, finely chopped	1
1 cup	sliced mushrooms	250 mL
1/2 tsp	dried oregano leaves	2 mL
1 cup	thin strips cooked flank or round steak	250 mL
	Salt and freshly ground black pepper	

1. Split rolls along one side and open like a book. (Do not cut all the way through.) Place on baking sheet and broil cut side until toasted.

2. In a bowl, combine cream cheese, yogurt and mustard; spread over cut sides of rolls. Line bottom halves with tomato slices.

3. In a large nonstick skillet, heat oil over medium-high heat; cook green pepper, onion, garlic, mushrooms and oregano, stirring occasionally, for 5 minutes. Add beef; cook, stirring, 1 minute more or until hot. Season with salt and pepper to taste. Spoon into rolls and serve immediately.

Beefy Pizza Subs

Why order out when it's so easy to prepare these pizza-style sandwiches at home? Make them with leftover grilled steak or store-bought deli roast beef for a fast dinner.

Tip

Prepare sandwich filling ahead, cover and refrigerate. Layer rolls with cheese; spoon in beef filling. Wrap in paper towels and microwave on Medium-High (70%) for 2½ to 3 minutes for 2 rolls, or 1½ minutes for 1 roll, or until heated through.

- Preheat broiler
- Baking sheet

1 tbsp	olive oil	15 mL
2 cups	sliced mushrooms	500 mL
1	green bell pepper, cut into thin strips	1
1	onion, cut into thin wedges	1
1	large clove garlic, finely chopped	1
1 tsp	dried basil or oregano leaves	5 mL
¼ tsp	hot pepper flakes	1 mL
1½ cups	thinly sliced cooked flank steak or 6 oz (175 g) deli roast beef, cut into strips	375 mL
¾ cup	pizza sauce or tomato pasta sauce	175 mL
	Salt and freshly ground black pepper	
4	crusty rolls	4
6 oz	thinly sliced mild provolone or mozzarella cheese	175 g

1. In a large nonstick skillet, heat oil over medium-high heat. Add mushrooms, green pepper, onion, garlic, basil and hot pepper flakes; cook, stirring, for 5 minutes or until softened. Stir in beef and pizza sauce; cook until heated through. Remove from heat; season with salt and pepper to taste.

2. Cut rolls along one side and open like a book; layer with cheese slices. Place on baking sheet under preheated broiler for 1 minute or until cheese melts. Watch carefully. Spoon beef mixture into rolls and serve immediately.

Deep-Dish Chicago-Style Pizza

Deep-dish pizza, made famous by Pizzeria Uno in Chicago, is a treat to make in your home kitchen.

Tips

Pizza may be baked and frozen. Reduce cooking time by 5 minutes. Let pizza cool completely; wrap well and freeze. Defrost completely before reheating in a preheated 400°F (200°C) oven for 15 to 20 minutes or until crust is golden brown.

Store Parmesan wedges wrapped in plastic wrap, then in foil, in the refrigerator; it keeps well for weeks.

- Preheat oven to 450°F (230°C)
- Two 9-inch (23 cm) round baking pans or springform pans, sprinkled lightly with cornmeal
- Large baking sheet, inverted and placed on bottom rack of oven

	Pizza Dough (see recipe, page 432)	
1 tbsp	olive oil	15 mL
1	green bell pepper, diced	1
1	onion, chopped	1
12 oz	mild or hot Italian sausage, casing removed, crumbled	375 g
1	can (28 oz/796 mL) Italian plum tomatoes, drained, crushed	1
2	cloves garlic, finely chopped	2
1 tsp	dried basil leaves	5 mL
1 tsp	dried oregano leaves	5 mL
1/4 tsp	salt	1 mL
1/4 tsp	freshly ground black pepper	1 mL
12 oz	mozzarella cheese, thinly sliced, divided	375 g
1/4 cup	freshly grated Parmesan cheese	60 mL

1. Divide pizza dough in two and shape each into a ball. On a lightly floured work surface, stretch or roll dough into 12-inch (30 cm) rounds. Press into bottom and 1 inch (2.5 cm) up the sides of prepared pans. Set aside for 15 minutes to let dough rise.

2. Meanwhile, in a medium skillet, heat oil over medium heat; cook green pepper and onion, stirring, for 2 minutes or until slightly softened. Transfer to a bowl.

3. Add sausage meat to skillet; cook, breaking up with back of a spoon, for 5 minutes or until no longer pink. Drain on paper towels. Chop, if necessary, into small pieces.

4. In a bowl, combine tomatoes, garlic, basil, oregano, salt and pepper. Layer half of the mozzarella cheese over each dough; spread with half of the tomato sauce, onion mixture and sausage. Sprinkle tops with Parmesan cheese.

5. Place pans on inverted baking sheet in preheated oven; bake pizzas for 20 to 25 minutes, until crust is golden. Place on racks for 5 minutes. Cut into wedges and serve.

All-Dressed Pizza

Makes 4 servings

"Let's order pizza!" The next time you hear this request from your kids, assemble the ingredients here and get them cooking. Why order out when making pizza at home using store-bought bread bases and sauces is such a breeze? It's more economical, too.

Tips

This recipe is the perfect solution to deal with the odd bits of vegetables, cheese and deli left in my fridge by week's end. Vary the toppings according to what you have on hand, including sliced pepperoni, chopped ham or broccoli.

Four 7-inch (18 cm) pitas or 6 split English muffins can also be used. If necessary, arrange on two baking sheets; rotate halfway during baking so breads bake evenly. Reduce baking time to 10 minutes.

- Preheat oven to 400°F (200°C)
- Baking sheet

1 tbsp	vegetable or olive oil	15 mL
1	small onion, thinly sliced	1
1	clove garlic, finely chopped	1
1 cup	sliced mushrooms	250 mL
1	small green or red bell pepper, cut into thin strips	1
1/2 tsp	dried basil leaves	2 mL
1/2 tsp	dried oregano leaves	2 mL
1	12-inch (30 cm) prebaked pizza base or 9-by 12-inch (23 by 30 cm) focaccia	1
1/2 cup	pizza sauce (approx.)	125 mL
2 cups	shredded cheese, such as mozzarella, fontina or provolone	500 mL

1. In a large nonstick skillet, heat oil over medium-high heat. Add onion, garlic, mushrooms, pepper, basil and oregano; cook, stirring, for 4 minutes or until softened.

2. Arrange pizza shell on baking sheet; spread with pizza sauce. Top with vegetables and shredded cheese.

3. Bake in preheated oven for 20 to 25 minutes or until cheese is melted and crust is golden.

Focaccia with Roasted Peppers and Brie

Use this recipe as a guideline and be adventurous. Grill vegetables, such as assorted colored peppers, eggplant and zucchini, or rely on supermarket delis that stock a great selection of antipasti. Sliced salami and other cheeses, such as Asiago and provolone, are other tasty options to layer in this hearty sandwich. See page 51 for other suggestions.

Variations

A French baguette or 4 panini buns can be substituted for the focaccia.

Instead of pesto, use black olive tapenade.

½ cup	light mayonnaise	125 mL
¼ cup	store-bought or homemade Basil Pesto (see recipe, page 334)	60 mL
1	focaccia loaf, square or round (about 8 inches/20 cm)	1
2 cups	lightly packed salad greens, such as mesclun or arugula	500 mL
8 oz	Brie or goat cheese, sliced	250 g
1 cup	roasted red peppers (see Tips, page 80), drained, cut into strips	250 mL

1. In a bowl, combine mayonnaise and pesto. Cut focaccia lengthwise in half. Spread both halves with mayonnaise mixture.

2. Arrange greens on bottom half; layer Brie and red pepper strips over greens. Top with remaining half. Cut into quarters, wrap and refrigerate. Best served the day sandwich is made to prevent greens from wilting.

Greek Chicken Pitas

When I'm in the mood
for something easy for
dinner, this is what I make.
It beats sandwiches or
burgers from fast-food
restaurants hands down.

Tip

The combination of lemon
juice, garlic and oregano
is the classic marinade for
souvlaki. Use as a quick
marinade, adding 1 tbsp
(15 mL) olive oil, and
pour over chicken breasts
or pork loin chops. Let
marinate for 15 minutes
at room temperature or
refrigerate for up to 1 day
ahead. Place on greased
grill and barbecue.

1 lb	boneless skinless chicken breasts, cut into very thin strips	500 g
1 tbsp	fresh lemon juice	15 mL
1	large clove garlic, finely chopped	1
¾ tsp	dried oregano leaves	3 mL
¼ tsp	salt	1 mL
¼ tsp	freshly ground black pepper	1 mL
2 tsp	olive oil	10 mL
1	small red onion, halved lengthwise, thinly sliced	1
1	red or green bell pepper, cut into thin 2-inch (5 cm) strips	1
4	7-inch (18 cm) pitas, halved to form pockets	4
¾ cup	store-bought or homemade Tzatziki Sauce (see recipe, page 136)	175 mL
4 cups	shredded romaine lettuce	1 L
2	tomatoes, cut into wedges	2

1. In a bowl, combine chicken, lemon juice, garlic, oregano, salt and pepper; marinate at room temperature for 10 minutes.

2. In a large nonstick skillet, heat oil over medium-high heat; cook chicken, stirring, for 5 minutes or until no longer pink. Add onion and pepper; cook, stirring, for 2 minutes or until vegetables are softened.

3. Wrap pitas in paper towels; microwave on Medium (50%) for 1½ minutes or until warm. Spoon chicken mixture into pita halves; top with a generous spoonful of tzatziki sauce, shredded lettuce and tomato wedges.

Falafel Burgers
with Parsley Tahini Sauce

Makes 4 servings

Falafels are as popular a fast food in the Middle East as hot dogs are in North America. In this recipe, the spiced chickpea mixture is shaped into patties instead of traditional balls and pan-fried instead of deep-fried. These burgers are so tasty they may just entice meat eaters to try more vegetarian dishes.

Tip

When I crave fast food, I reach for falafel burgers that I've cooked ahead, wrapped individually in plastic wrap and stored in my freezer. Microwave on a plate lined with paper towels at Medium-High (70%) for 1 to 1½ minutes or until warmed through. Patties can be frozen for up to 1 month.

2 tbsp	olive oil (approx.), divided	30 mL
1	small onion, minced	1
2	cloves garlic, minced	2
2 tsp	ground cumin	10 mL
1 tsp	ground coriander	5 mL
½ tsp	paprika	2 mL
¼ tsp	salt	1 mL
Pinch	cayenne pepper	Pinch
1	can (19 oz/540 mL) chickpeas, drained and rinsed	1
1	egg	1
2 tbsp	all-purpose flour	30 mL
2 tbsp	chopped fresh parsley	30 mL
½ cup	panko bread crumbs or fine dry bread crumbs	125 mL
2	7-inch (18 cm) whole wheat pitas, halved to form pockets	2
	Parsley Tahini Sauce (see recipe, opposite)	
1	large tomato, cut into wedges	1
	Shredded romaine lettuce	

1. In a small nonstick skillet, heat 2 tsp (10 mL) oil over medium-high heat. Cook onion, garlic, cumin, coriander, paprika, salt and cayenne, stirring often, for 3 minutes or until softened. Remove from heat.

2. In a food processor, combine chickpeas, egg and flour. Pulse to form a coarse mixture that holds together, scraping down sides as necessary. Add onion mixture and parsley. Pulse just until blended. Transfer to a bowl and form into 4 patties, each about 4 inches (10 cm) in diameter.

3. Place bread crumbs in a shallow bowl. Coat patties in crumb mixture, pressing lightly so crumbs stick. Discard any excess crumbs.

Tahini is a smooth, thick paste made from ground sesame seeds and commonly used in Middle Eastern cooking. Look for it in the imported food section of well-stocked supermarkets.

Tip

Use yogurt with 2% to 4% milk fat; nonfat yogurt has too thin a consistency for this recipe.

4. In a large nonstick skillet, heat remaining oil over medium-high heat. Cook patties, in batches, for 3 to 4 minutes per side or until golden brown, adding more oil as needed between batches. Transfer to a plate. (Patties are slightly soft when you remove them from the skillet but become firmer as they cool).

5. Cut warm burgers in half and serve in pita pockets, topped with Parsley Tahini Sauce, tomato wedges and romaine.

Parsley Tahini Sauce

Makes 1 cup (250 mL)

¾ cup	plain yogurt	175 mL
¼ cup	tahini	60 mL
1 tbsp	fresh lemon juice, or to taste	15 mL
1	large clove garlic, minced	1
½ cup	finely chopped fresh parsley	125 mL

1. In a bowl, whisk together yogurt, tahini, lemon juice and garlic until smooth. Stir in parsley. Store in an airtight container in the refrigerator for up to 2 weeks.

Taco Pitas

Ever since I devised these yummy tacos, I walk right on by the prepackaged taco mixes and shells in supermarkets. Once the meat is browned, it takes no time to add the beans and seasonings to make the tasty filling.

Tip

To heat pitas: Wrap pitas in foil and place in a 350°F (180°C) oven for 15 to 20 minutes. Or wrap 4 at a time in paper towels and microwave on High for 1 to 1½ minutes.

Variation
Sloppy Joe Pitas

Increase beef to 1 lb (500 g). Omit beans and add 1 can (7½ oz/ 213 mL) tomato sauce; cook 3 minutes more or until sauce is slightly thickened.

8 oz	lean ground beef	250 g
1	small onion, finely chopped	1
1	large clove garlic, finely chopped	1
2 tsp	chili powder	10 mL
2 tsp	all-purpose flour	10 mL
½ tsp	dried oregano leaves	2 mL
½ tsp	ground cumin	2 mL
Pinch	cayenne pepper	Pinch
½ cup	beef stock	125 mL
1	can (19 oz/540 mL) pinto, black or red kidney beans, drained and rinsed	1
4	7-inch (18 cm) pitas, halved to form pockets, warmed	4
	Salsa, shredded lettuce, tomato wedges, bell pepper strips, shredded mozzarella or Cheddar cheese	

1. In a large nonstick skillet over medium-high heat, cook beef, breaking up with the back of a wooden spoon, for 4 minutes or until no longer pink.

2. Reduce heat to medium. Add onion, garlic, chili powder, flour, oregano, cumin and cayenne pepper. Cook, stirring often, for 5 minutes or until onions are softened.

3. Pour in stock; cook, stirring, until slightly thickened. Stir in beans; cook 2 minutes more or until heated through.

4. Spoon ¼ cup (60 mL) of the mixture into pita pockets; top with salsa, lettuce, tomato, peppers and cheese.

Chicken Caesar Wraps

Makes 6 wraps

I've taken the classic chicken Caesar salad and transformed it into a popular wrap, for a great-tasting, portable lunch or dinner sandwich.

Tip

Instead of cooking chicken breasts, use 2 cups (500 mL) diced leftover cooked chicken or turkey.

2	boneless skinless chicken breasts (each 6 oz/175 g)	2
2 tsp	olive oil	10 mL
1	small clove garlic, minced	1
½ cup	light mayonnaise	125 mL
1 tbsp	fresh lemon juice	15 mL
1 tsp	Dijon mustard	5 mL
6	slices bacon, cooked crisp and crumbled	6
¼ cup	oil-packed sun-dried tomatoes, chopped (optional)	60 mL
2 tbsp	freshly grated Parmesan cheese	30 mL
	Freshly ground black pepper	
6	9-inch (23 cm) flour tortillas	6
6 cups	shredded romaine lettuce	1.5 L

1. Slice chicken breasts horizontally into two thin pieces each. In a nonstick skillet, heat oil over medium-high heat. Cook chicken for 3 minutes per side or until no longer pink inside. Transfer to a cutting board and cut into thin strips.

2. In a bowl, combine garlic, mayonnaise, lemon juice and mustard. Add bacon, sun-dried tomatoes, if using, and Parmesan cheese. Season to taste with pepper.

3. Thinly spread mayonnaise mixture over each tortilla, leaving a 1-inch (2.5 cm) border. On bottom half of each tortilla, layer with some of the chicken strips and 1 cup (250 mL) romaine. Fold 1 inch (2.5 cm) of the right and left sides of tortilla over filling; starting from bottom, roll tortillas around filling. Serve immediately.

It's a BLT Wrap!

I've taken the classic BLT and fashioned it into a wrap, adding fresh basil to the mayonnaise for a thoroughly modern twist.

Variation
Club Wrap
Cut 2 grilled or cooked chicken breasts into thin strips. Spread tortillas with basil mayonnaise; layer with tomato, lettuce, chicken and bacon. Roll tortillas as directed.

8	slices bacon, cut into quarters	8
1/3 cup	light mayonnaise	75 mL
2 tbsp	chopped fresh basil or 1/2 tsp (2 mL) dried	30 mL
4	9-inch (23 cm) flour tortillas	4
2	large tomatoes	2
4 cups	shredded romaine lettuce	1 L

1. Place bacon on a large plate lined with a double layer of paper towels; loosely cover with another layer of paper towels. Microwave at High for 5 minutes or until cooked and almost crisp. Let cool.

2. In a bowl, combine mayonnaise and basil. Spread over tortillas, leaving a 1-inch (2.5 cm) border around edge. Cut tomatoes in half crosswise and gently squeeze out seeds; slice thinly. Layer tortillas with tomato slices, lettuce and bacon. Fold 1 inch (2.5 cm) of the right and left sides of tortilla over filling. Starting from the bottom, roll up tortillas around filling. Serve immediately or cover in plastic wrap and store in the refrigerator for up to 1 day.

Turkey Fajitas

Makes 6 fajitas

I love this recipe because it's a quick and easy main dish, yet it calls for only a few ingredients. It's ideal to serve for an impromptu dinner. I set out bowls of the cheese, sour cream and salsa, and let everyone help themselves.

Tips

Turkey can also be barbecued. Marinate as directed and brush with 1 tbsp (15 mL) oil; grill over medium heat for 3 minutes per side or until no longer pink.

To warm tortillas: Wrap tortillas in foil and place in a 350°F (180°C) oven for 15 to 20 minutes. Or grill tortillas over medium heat for 30 to 60 seconds per side.

1 lb	boneless turkey breast or boneless skinless chicken breasts, cut into thin slices	500 g
1 tbsp	fresh lime juice	15 mL
1	clove garlic, finely chopped	1
1 tsp	dried oregano leaves	5 mL
½ tsp	ground cumin	2 mL
½ tsp	ground coriander	2 mL
½ tsp	salt	2 mL
Pinch	cayenne pepper	Pinch
2 tbsp	olive oil	30 mL
1	red onion, thinly sliced	1
1	small red bell pepper, cut into thin 2-inch (5 cm) strips	1
1	small green bell pepper, cut into thin 2-inch (5 cm) strips	1
6	9-inch (23 cm) flour tortillas, warmed (see Tips, left)	6
	Salsa, sour cream, shredded lettuce and shredded Cheddar cheese for garnishes	

1. In a bowl, toss turkey with lime juice, garlic, oregano, cumin, coriander, salt and cayenne pepper. Marinate for 15 minutes at room temperature, or longer in the refrigerator.

2. In a large nonstick skillet, heat 1 tbsp (15 mL) oil over high heat; cook turkey for 2 to 3 minutes per side or until lightly browned and no longer pink in center. Transfer to plate; keep warm.

3. Add remaining oil to skillet; cook onion and peppers, stirring, for 3 minutes or until tender-crisp. Remove from heat. Cut turkey into thin diagonal strips; toss with onion-pepper mixture. Spoon turkey mixture down center of each tortilla; add a small spoonful of salsa and sour cream, if desired, and sprinkle with shredded lettuce and cheese. Roll up.

Amazing Chicken Enchiladas

Makes 6 enchiladas

Instead of turning chicken leftovers into cold sandwiches, whip up this fast-fix dinner with loads of family appeal.

Tip

You can assemble this dish a day ahead of baking; just top with salsa and cheese prior to popping in the oven.

Variation

Cooked turkey or 1½ cups (375 mL) small cooked shrimp can be used instead of chicken.

- Preheat oven to 350°F (180°C)
- 13- by 9-inch (33 by 23 cm) baking dish, greased

4 oz	cream cheese	125 g
½ cup	plain yogurt or sour cream	125 mL
2 cups	cooked chicken, cut into thin strips	500 mL
3	green onions, sliced	3
2	tomatoes, seeded and diced	2
¼ cup	chopped fresh cilantro or parsley	60 mL
6	9-inch (23 cm) flour tortillas	6
1½ cups	mild or medium salsa	375 mL
1 cup	shredded Cheddar or Monterey Jack cheese	250 mL

1. Place cream cheese in a large bowl; microwave on Medium (50%) for 1 minute to soften. Stir well. Stir in yogurt, chicken, green onions, tomatoes and cilantro.

2. Spread about ½ cup (125 mL) of the chicken mixture down center of each tortilla and roll up. Arrange tortillas in a single layer, seam side down, in prepared baking dish. Spread each tortilla with salsa and sprinkle with cheese. Bake for 30 to 35 minutes or until heated through. Sprinkle with extra chopped cilantro, if desired.

Microwave Method

1. Do not sprinkle with the cheese. Cover dish with waxed paper; microwave on Medium-High (70%) for 7 to 9 minutes or until heated through. Sprinkle with cheese; microwave on High for 1 minute or until cheese melts.

Dilled Salmon and Egg Salad on Pumpernickel (page 39)

Smoked Salmon Mousse (page 85)

Vegetable Minestrone with
Sun-Dried Tomato Pesto (page 167)

Caesar Salad (page 117)

Cheese-Smothered Onion Soup (page 177)

Creamy Tomato Soup (page 181)

Creamy Tuna Pasta Bake (page 368)

Cheese and Salsa Quesadillas

Makes 4 quesadillas

Here's my modern rendition of grilled cheese: thin flour tortillas replace sliced bread, mozzarella substitutes for processed cheese and chunky salsa stands in for the ketchup. And the beans? They're optional, but make a wholesome addition.

Tips

I often serve these warm cheesy wedges with soup for an easy dinner. They're also great as a snack that both kids and grownups applaud.

Use mild salsa to appease those with timid taste buds, but add a dash of hot pepper sauce to the filling for those who like a burst of heat.

½ cup	salsa, plus additional for serving	125 mL
4	9-inch (23 cm) flour tortillas	4
1 cup	canned black or pinto beans, drained and rinsed	250 mL
1 cup	shredded mozzarella, Monterey Jack or Cheddar cheese	250 mL

1. Spread 2 tbsp (30 mL) salsa on half of each tortilla. Sprinkle with ¼ cup (60 mL) each of the beans and the cheese. Fold tortillas over and press down lightly.

2. In a large nonstick skillet over medium heat, cook tortillas, 2 at a time, pressing down lightly with the back of a metal spatula, for about 2 minutes per side, until lightly toasted and cheese is melted. (Or place directly on barbecue grill over medium heat until lightly toasted on both sides.)

3. Cut into wedges and serve warm with additional salsa, if desired.

Roasted Vegetable and Goat Cheese Quesadillas

Quesadillas sound complicated, but they are really just grilled sandwiches made with flour tortillas. The sky's the limit when it comes to fillings. This version, using roasted vegetables and goat cheese, is easy and delicious.

Tips

Don't be intimidated by the fennel. It's simple to handle; just trim the top and cut in half lengthwise. Remove and discard the tough core.

Wraps can be assembled ahead. Cover in plastic wrap and refrigerate. Just pop them on the grill or in a nonstick skillet until toasted and cheese melts. Keep an eye on them — they cook quickly.

- Preheat oven to 400°F (200°C)
- Rimmed baking sheet, greased

1	small red onion, finely chopped	1
1	large red bell pepper, diced	1
½	fennel bulb, cored and diced	½
1 tbsp	olive oil, plus extra for grilling	15 mL
½ tsp	salt	2 mL
½ tsp	freshly ground black pepper	2 mL
¼ cup	chopped kalamata olives	60 mL
1 tbsp	balsamic vinegar	15 mL
2 tbsp	chopped fresh basil	30 mL
6	7-inch (18 cm) flour tortillas	6
6 oz	creamy goat cheese or cream cheese, softened	175 g
	Olive oil for brushing	

1. Spread onion, red pepper and fennel on baking sheet. Drizzle with oil; season with salt and pepper. Roast in preheated oven for 20 minutes, stirring occasionally, until vegetables are tender-crisp. Transfer to a bowl. Stir in olives and vinegar. Cover and refrigerate. (Can be made up to 3 days ahead.) Stir in basil.

2. Spread each tortilla with 2 tbsp (30 mL) of the goat cheese. Sprinkle each half with ¼ cup (50 mL) of the vegetable mixture; fold over filling, pressing down lightly. (Can be assembled ahead, wrapped in plastic wrap and refrigerated for up to 4 hours.)

3. Brush quesadillas lightly with oil. Place on greased grill over medium heat or cook in batches in a large nonstick skillet over medium heat for 1 to 2 minutes on each side or until toasted. Cut into wedges and serve warm.

Black Bean Vegetable Burritos

Mexican dishes are a big hit with teens — and their parents. It makes a nourishing snack or supper. For a meat version, add strips of ham, cooked turkey or chicken.

Tip

Make a batch of burritos, wrap each in a paper towel, then in plastic wrap. Keep handy in the fridge, ready to microwave for school lunches or after-school snacks. Remove plastic wrap before microwaving.

1 tbsp	vegetable oil	15 mL
3	green onions, sliced	3
1	large clove garlic, finely chopped	1
1 cup	diced zucchini	250 mL
1	red or green bell pepper, diced	1
1 tsp	dried oregano leaves	5 mL
1 tsp	ground cumin	5 mL
1	can (19 oz/540 mL) black beans or kidney beans, drained and rinsed	1
8	9-inch (23 cm) flour tortillas, preferably whole wheat	8
1 cup	shredded Monterey Jack or Cheddar cheese	250 mL
1 cup	mild or medium salsa	250 mL
½ cup	sour cream	125 mL

1. In a large nonstick skillet, heat oil over medium heat. Add green onions, garlic, zucchini, bell pepper, oregano and cumin; cook, stirring, for 5 minutes or until vegetables are tender-crisp. Stir in beans; cook 1 to 2 minutes or until heated through.

2. Spoon ¼ cup (60 mL) of the bean mixture on the bottom half of each tortilla. Top each with 2 tbsp (30 mL) shredded cheese, 2 tbsp (30 mL) salsa and 1 tbsp (15 mL) sour cream. Fold 1 inch (2.5 cm) of the right and left sides of tortillas over filling; starting from bottom, roll tortillas around filling. Wrap each burrito in a paper towel. Place 4 at a time on a plate; microwave on Medium-High (70%) for 3 to 4 minutes or until heated through. To heat a single burrito, microwave on Medium-High (70%) for 1 minute.

Swiss Cheese Fondue

Fondue is perfect for an informal get-together and takes very little time to make. It's especially inviting on a cold blustery day, after being outdoors, to dip chunks of bread into a pot of melted cheese.

Tips

An earthenware fondue pot is traditionally used to make a cheese fondue because it maintains an even, gentle heat to melt the cheese. Metal fondue pots are designed for meat and seafood using hot oil or broths.

If you don't have a ceramic fondue pot, use a heavy-bottomed saucepan instead and take care not to melt the cheese at too high a temperature. When serving the fondue and cheese starts to firm when dipping in bread cubes, place over low heat, stirring, until melted.

• Earthenware fondue pot or heavy-bottomed saucepan

8 oz	Emmenthal cheese, coarsely grated (2 cups/500 mL)	250 g
8 oz	Gruyère cheese, coarsely grated (2 cups/500 mL)	250 g
4 tsp	cornstarch	20 mL
1	large clove garlic, halved lengthwise	1
1¼ cups	dry white wine, such as Riesling or Sauvignon Blanc	300 mL
1 tbsp	kirsch or lemon juice	15 mL
	Freshly ground nutmeg and black pepper	
1	French baguette, cut into bite-size cubes	1
1	apple, cored and sliced (optional)	1
1	pear, cored and sliced (optional)	1

1. In a bowl, combine cheeses and toss with cornstarch.

2. Rub inside of a fondue pot with cut sides of garlic. Add wine and garlic to pot. Bring to a boil over medium heat. Remove and discard garlic.

3. Reduce heat to low and gradually add cheese to pot, a handful at a time, stirring constantly in a zigzag pattern (not a circular motion) to prevent cheese from balling up, until cheese is just melted and creamy (do not let boil). Add kirsch and season with nutmeg and pepper to taste.

4. To serve, place the fondue pot over medium-low heat of a fondue burner, adjusting heat as necessary to keep the mixture at a low simmer, stirring often. Serve with bread along with apple and pear slices, if using, for dipping. (If fondue thickens as you dip in bread pieces, stir in a small amount of white wine.)

Appetizers

continued...

Hot Appetizers (continued)

Creamy Spinach Dip

Makes 3 cups (750 mL)

Here's a dip that's so much tastier than the ones made with salty soup mixes. Serve with vegetable dippers such as carrot, pepper, cucumber, celery, broccoli, fennel and cauliflower. I use any leftovers as a dressing for pasta or potato salads, or as a spread for sandwiches.

Tip

To make a bread bowl for serving: Using a serrated knife, slice 2 inches (5 cm) off top of small (1 lb/500 g) unsliced round whole wheat or sourdough bread. Hollow out loaf, reserving contents, leaving a shell about 1 inch (2.5 cm) thick. Spoon dip into bread bowl. Cut reserved bread into strips or cubes and serve along with vegetable dippers.

1	package (10 oz/300 g) fresh or frozen spinach	1
1 cup	crumbled feta cheese (about 4 oz/125 g)	250 mL
⅓ cup	chopped green onions	75 mL
¼ cup	chopped fresh dill	60 mL
1	clove garlic, minced	1
1 tsp	grated lemon zest (see Tips, left)	5 mL
1½ cups	sour cream (regular or light)	375 mL
½ cup	light mayonnaise	125 mL
	Hot pepper sauce	

1. Remove tough stem ends from fresh spinach; wash in cold water. Place spinach with moisture clinging to leaves in a large saucepan. Cook over high heat, stirring, until just wilted. (If using frozen spinach, see Tips, page 74.) Place spinach in a colander to drain. Squeeze out moisture by hand; wrap in a clean, dry towel and squeeze out excess moisture.

2. In a food processor, combine spinach, feta, green onions, dill, garlic and lemon zest. Process until very finely chopped.

3. Add sour cream and mayonnaise; process, using on-off turns, just until combined. Transfer to a serving bowl and add hot pepper sauce to taste. Cover and refrigerate until ready to serve. Serve in a bread bowl (see Tips, left), if desired, and accompany with vegetable dippers.

Warm Salsa Dip

**Makes 3 cups
(750 mL)**

This dip will draw raves from a gang of starving teens or a crowd around the TV set when the ball game is in progress. In our house, we usually can't agree if we want the dip hot or mild. The solution? I use mild salsa as the base and, once the dip is made, divide it into two bowls. I leave one mild and add plenty of hot sauce or minced pickled jalapeños to spice up the other. Give the dip a quick reheat in the microwave if it cools — assuming it lasts that long, of course!

1	can (19 oz/540 mL) white kidney beans, drained and rinsed	1
1 cup	mild or hot salsa	250 mL
2	cloves garlic, minced	2
1 tsp	ground cumin	5 mL
1 tsp	dried oregano leaves	5 mL
4 oz	cream cheese, cubed and softened	125 g
1 cup	shredded mozzarella cheese or Monterey Jack or white Cheddar cheese	250 mL
	Tortilla chips or pita crisps (see page 87)	

1. In a bowl, mash beans with a fork until quite smooth.

2. In a medium saucepan, combine beans, salsa, garlic, cumin and oregano. Place over medium heat, stirring often, until piping hot.

3. Stir in cream cheese; stir until dip is smooth. Add mozzarella; stir until melted. Serve warm with tortilla or pita crisps.

Microwave Method

1. Combine all the ingredients in microwave-safe bowl. Microwave at Medium-High (70%), stirring twice, for 5 to 7 minutes, or until heated through and cheese is melted. Serve warm with tortilla or pita crisps.

5-Minute Crab Dip

With a can of crabmeat in the pantry and cream cheese in the fridge, you're all set to make a quick dip in 5 minutes flat. You can make it in the microwave or just as easily on the stovetop over medium heat.

Tip

Serve with Melba toast rounds or crisp vegetable dippers.

Variation

5-Minute Clam Dip

Substitute 1 can (5 oz/ 142 g) drained clams for the crab. Stir in 1 minced garlic clove, if desired.

8 oz	cream cheese	250 g
1	can (6 oz/170 mL) crabmeat, drained, liquid reserved	1
¼ cup	finely chopped green onions	60 mL
2 tsp	fresh lemon juice	10 mL
½ tsp	Worcestershire sauce	2 mL
¼ tsp	paprika	1 mL
	Hot pepper sauce	

1. Place cream cheese in a medium-size microwave-safe bowl; microwave on Medium (50%) for 2 minutes or until softened. Stir until smooth.

2. Stir in crab, green onions, 2 tbsp (30 mL) reserved crab liquid, lemon juice, Worcestershire sauce, paprika and hot pepper sauce to taste. Microwave on Medium-High (70%) for 2 minutes or until piping hot. Serve warm.

Warm Spinach and Cheese Dip

When you've got the gang coming over, serve this warm dip and watch it disappear. I like to accompany it with white or blue corn tortilla chips.

Tips

If you want a hot version, use 2 fresh or pickled jalapeño peppers. Or for a mild version, use 1 can (4 oz/113 g) green chiles, drained and chopped.

To defrost spinach:
Remove frozen spinach from packaging and place in a 4-cup (1 L) casserole dish. Cover and microwave on High, stirring once, for 6 to 8 minutes or until defrosted and hot. Place in a sieve and press out excess moisture.

1	package (10 oz/300 g) fresh or frozen chopped spinach	1
8 oz	cream cheese, softened	250 g
1 cup	mild or medium salsa	250 mL
2	green onions, finely chopped	2
1	clove garlic, minced	1
1/2 tsp	dried oregano leaves	2 mL
1/2 tsp	ground cumin	2 mL
1/2 cup	shredded Monterey Jack or Cheddar cheese	125 mL
1/2 cup	milk (approx.)	125 mL
	Salt	
	Hot pepper sauce	

1. Remove tough stem ends from fresh spinach; wash in cold water. Place spinach with moisture clinging to leaves in a large saucepan. Cook over high heat, stirring, until just wilted. (If using frozen spinach, see Tips, left.) Place spinach in a colander to drain. Squeeze out moisture by hand; wrap in a clean, dry towel and squeeze out excess moisture.

2. In a medium saucepan, combine spinach, cream cheese, salsa, green onions, garlic, oregano and cumin. Cook over medium heat, stirring, for 2 to 3 minutes or until smooth and piping hot.

3. Stir in cheese and milk; cook for 2 minutes or until cheese melts. Add more milk to thin dip, if desired. Season with salt and hot pepper sauce to taste. Spoon into serving dish.

Microwave Method

1. In an 8-cup (2 L) casserole dish, combine spinach, cream cheese, salsa, onions, garlic, oregano and cumin; cover and microwave on Medium (50%) for 4 minutes, stirring once. Add cheese and milk; cover and microwave on Medium-High (70%), stirring once, for 2 to 3 minutes, or until cheese is melted. Season with salt and hot pepper sauce to taste.

Do-Ahead Herb Dip

Makes 2 cups
(500 mL)

This creamy dip relies on lower-fat dairy products and zesty herbs, so it clocks in with a lot less fat and calories than you might imagine. Make it at least a day ahead to let flavors develop. Serve with fresh veggies.

Tips

Other fresh herbs, including basil, can be added according to what you have in the fridge or growing in your garden.

This dip also makes a great dressing for pasta and potato salads. Store in an airtight container in the fridge for up to 1 week.

1 cup	ricotta or creamed cottage cheese	250 mL
½ cup	plain yogurt or sour cream	125 mL
½ cup	light mayonnaise	125 mL
⅓ cup	finely chopped fresh parsley	75 mL
2 tbsp	finely chopped fresh chives or minced green onions	30 mL
2 tbsp	chopped fresh dill	30 mL
2 tsp	honey Dijon mustard	10 mL
1 tsp	red wine vinegar or lemon juice	5 mL
	Salt	
	Hot pepper sauce	

1. In a food processor, purée ricotta, yogurt and mayonnaise until very smooth and creamy.

2. Transfer to a bowl; stir in parsley, chives, dill, mustard and vinegar. Season with salt and hot pepper sauce to taste. Cover and refrigerate.

Curry Lemon Dip

**Makes 1 cup
(250 mL)**

Whisk these few
ingredients together for a
simple dip to serve with
crunchy vegetables, such as
cauliflower florets, English
cucumber spears, sugar
snap peas, baby carrots
and bell pepper strips.

Variation

Pesto Dip

Instead of curry powder,
use 2 tbsp (30 mL) basil
or sun-dried tomato
pesto, or to taste, and
omit cilantro.

¾ cup	light or regular sour cream	175 mL
¼ cup	light mayonnaise	60 mL
½ to 1 tsp	curry powder, or to taste	2 to 5 mL
1 tsp	grated lemon zest	5 mL
2 tbsp	chopped fresh cilantro or chives	30 mL
	Salt and freshly ground black pepper	

1. In a bowl, combine sour cream, mayonnaise, curry
powder, lemon zest and cilantro. Season with salt and
pepper to taste. Cover and refrigerate until ready to
serve or for up to 2 days.

Chilled Asparagus with Curry Lemon Dip

Try this tasty dip with chilled cooked asparagus
for an easy appetizer when entertaining. Snap
off wooden ends of asparagus. Fill a wide skillet
with water and bring to a boil. Add asparagus and
return to boil. Reduce heat, cover and simmer
for 2 to 4 minutes or until bright green and still
slightly crisp. Plunge into ice water to chill. Drain
and wrap in damp paper towels and refrigerate
until ready to serve.

Always Popular Layered Bean Dip

Makes 8 servings

Variations of the popular bean dip always make the party circuit. Here's my updated version. It has an oregano-bean base, a creamy jalapeño cheese layer and a vibrant fresh topping of tomatoes, olives and cilantro.

Tip

Fresh cilantro, also called coriander and Chinese parsley, lasts only a few days in the fridge before it deteriorates and turns tasteless. Wash cilantro well, spin dry and wrap in paper towels; store in plastic bag in the fridge. Leave the roots on — they keep the leaves fresh.

● 8-inch (20 cm) shallow round serving dish or pie plate

1	can (19 oz/540 mL) red kidney beans or black beans, drained and rinsed	1
1	clove garlic, minced	1
1 tsp	dried oregano leaves	5 mL
1/2 tsp	ground cumin	2 mL
1 tbsp	water	15 mL
1 cup	shredded Monterey Jack or Cheddar cheese	250 mL
3/4 cup	sour cream	175 mL
1 tbsp	minced seeded fresh or pickled jalapeño peppers	15 mL
2	tomatoes, seeded and finely diced	2
1	Hass avocado, peeled and diced (optional)	1
2	green onions, sliced	2
1/3 cup	sliced black olives	75 mL
1/3 cup	chopped fresh cilantro or parsley	75 mL

1. In a food processor, combine beans, garlic, oregano, cumin and water; process until smooth. Spread in serving dish.

2. In a bowl, combine cheese, sour cream and jalapeño peppers. Spread over bean layer. (Can be assembled earlier in day; cover and refrigerate.)

3. Just before serving, sprinkle with tomatoes, avocado (if using), green onions, olives and cilantro. Serve with tortilla chips or pita crisps (see page 87).

Italian White Bean Spread

I like to serve this tasty easy-to-make spread with warm squares of focaccia or crostini.

Tip

Dip can be made up to 3 days ahead.

Variation

Greek White Bean Spread: Instead of fresh basil, increase chopped parsley to 2 tbsp (30 mL) and add ½ tsp (2 mL) dried oregano leaves to the onions when cooking.

2 tbsp	olive oil	30 mL
1	small onion, finely chopped	1
2	large cloves garlic, finely chopped	2
1 tbsp	red wine vinegar	15 mL
1	can (19 oz/540 mL) white kidney beans, drained and rinsed	1
2 tbsp	finely chopped oil-packed sun-dried tomatoes	30 mL
1 tbsp	chopped fresh parsley	15 mL
1 tbsp	chopped fresh basil leaves	15 mL
	Freshly ground black pepper	

1. In a small skillet, heat oil over medium heat. Cook onion and garlic; stirring occasionally, for 3 minutes or until softened (do not brown). Add vinegar and remove from heat. In a food processor, purée kidney beans and onion mixture until smooth.

2. Transfer to a bowl. Stir in sun-dried tomatoes, parsley and basil; season with pepper to taste. Cover and refrigerate.

Hummus

You can buy hummus,
the classic spread from
the Middle East, in
supermarkets, but I find
it so easy to make in my
home kitchen. Serve it as
a dip with pita wedges or
use as a sandwich spread.

Tip

Thin hummus, if desired,
by stirring in additional
water.

1	can (19 oz/540 mL) chickpeas, rinsed and drained	1
¼ cup	tahini	60 mL
2 to 3	cloves garlic, chopped	2 to 3
¼ cup	olive oil	60 mL
¼ cup	fresh lemon juice	60 mL
2 tbsp	water	30 mL
2 tbsp	finely chopped fresh parsley	30 mL
	Salt and freshly ground black pepper	

1. In a food processor or blender, purée chickpeas, tahini, garlic, olive oil, lemon juice and water until smooth.

2. Transfer to a bowl; stir in parsley and season with salt and pepper to taste.

Hummus Pita Bites

2	thin soft 7-inch (18 cm) pitas, split	2
1 cup	hummus	250 mL
½	small seedless cucumber	½
½	small red bell pepper, cut into thin strips	½

1. Spread the rough sides of each pita generously with hummus, leaving a small border.

2. Cut cucumber into 5-inch (12 cm) long strips, each ¼ inch (0.5 cm) thick. Place a few cucumber and red pepper strips along edge of pita halves and roll into a tight bundle. Wrap each in plastic wrap and refrigerate up until serving time.

3. To serve, trim ends and slice into 1-inch (2.5 cm) pieces. Place cut side up on a serving plate.

Red Pepper Cheese Spread

Most deli counters feature roasted red peppers, or you can buy them in jars. Or roast a fresh red pepper (see Tips, below). This spread is fabulous served with crostini (toasted baguette slices) or pita crisps.

Tips

I used 1 bottled roasted red pepper that measured 1/3 cup (75 mL).

To roast your own pepper: Arrange 1 whole pepper on rimmed baking sheet and place under preheated broiler, 4 inches (10 cm) from source of heat, turning often, until skin is charred. Place in a bowl and cover with plastic wrap to allow pepper to steam (this helps loosen the skin). When cool, peel and seed; cut into strips. Drain on paper towels.

1 cup	ricotta cheese	250 mL
5 oz	feta cheese, crumbled	150 g
1/3 cup	roasted red bell pepper (see Tips, left)	75 mL
1/4 cup	chopped fresh parsley	60 mL
2 tbsp	chopped fresh basil	30 mL
2 tbsp	chopped fresh chives	30 mL
1/2 tsp	freshly ground black pepper	2 mL

1. In a food processor, purée ricotta, feta cheese and red pepper until very smooth.

2. Transfer to a bowl; stir in parsley, basil, chives and pepper. Cover and refrigerate for up to 5 days.

Rosy Shrimp Spread

Makes 1¼ cups (300 mL)

You can whip up this reliable recipe in only a few minutes using ingredients you keep on hand in the pantry and in the fridge. It's equally good with crackers or vegetable dippers. You'll turn to it, as I have, time and time again.

Tips

Microwave cold cream cheese at Medium (50%) for 1 minute to soften.

Spread can be prepared up to 2 days ahead, covered and refrigerated.

4 oz	cream cheese, softened	125 g
¼ cup	sour cream or plain yogurt	60 mL
2 tbsp	prepared chili sauce	30 mL
1 tsp	prepared horseradish	5 mL
	Hot pepper sauce	
1	can (4 oz/113 g) small shrimp, drained and rinsed	1
1 tbsp	minced green onion tops or chopped fresh chives	15 mL

1. In a bowl, beat cream cheese until smooth. Stir in sour cream, chili sauce, horseradish and hot pepper sauce to taste.

2. Fold in shrimp and green onions. Transfer to serving dish; cover and refrigerate until serving time.

Sicilian Caponata

This sweet-sour relish, typical of Sicilian cooking, is excellent as a topping for crostini (see Tips, page 91), or pair it with soft goat cheese. It's also great as a relish spread on crusty baguettes layered with one of Italy's prized cheeses, such as Taleggio, Gorgonzola or Asiago.

Tip

Place in an airtight container and refrigerate for up to 1 week or freeze for up to 1 month.

1	eggplant (1 lb/500 g)	1
1 tbsp	coarse salt	15 mL
2 tbsp	olive oil	30 mL
1	red onion, halved lengthwise, thinly sliced	1
2	stalks celery, diced	2
¼ cup	tomato paste	60 mL
¼ cup	balsamic or red wine vinegar	60 mL
2 tbsp	granulated sugar	30 mL
¼ cup	water	60 mL
⅓ cup	sliced black or green olives	75 mL
1 tbsp	capers, rinsed (optional)	15 mL
2 tbsp	pine nuts	30 mL
	Freshly ground black pepper	

1. Peel eggplant and cut into ½-inch (1 cm) cubes. Place in a colander and sprinkle with salt. Place a plate over eggplant, then top with several cans to extract bitter eggplant juices. Let stand for 30 minutes. Rinse and pat dry with a clean kitchen towel.

2. In a large saucepan, heat 1 tbsp (15 mL) of the oil over medium heat; cook eggplant, stirring, for 5 minutes or until softened. Transfer to a bowl.

3. Add remaining oil to pan; cook onion and celery, stirring, for 5 minutes or until softened. Add tomato paste, balsamic vinegar, sugar and water; cook, stirring, for 2 minutes.

4. Return eggplant to pan along with olives and capers, if using. Reduce heat to medium-low and simmer, partially covered, stirring occasionally, for 15 minutes, until eggplant is tender. (Add additional water, if needed, to prevent mixture from sticking.) Stir in pine nuts and season with pepper to taste.

Ratatouille Salsa

Supermarket shelves are lined with great-tasting salsas. Take your favorite salsa, throw in a few roasted vegetables and voila! — you've got yourself a snazzy spread. This versatile sauce makes a wonderful condiment for sandwiches with cold cuts or cheese, or as a pizza topping.

Tips

Dice vegetables into ¼-inch (0.5 cm) pieces.

Prepare ratatouille salsa ahead. It keeps well in an airtight container in the refrigerator for 3 days or 1 month in the freezer.

- Preheat oven to 425°F (220°C)
- Rimmed baking sheet, greased

1½ cups	diced eggplant	375 mL
1½ cups	diced zucchini	375 mL
1	red bell pepper, diced	1
1 tsp	dried basil leaves	5 mL
1 tbsp	olive oil	15 mL
1½ cups	medium salsa	375 mL
¼ cup	chopped fresh parsley	60 mL
1	clove garlic, minced	1
	Tortilla chips	

1. Spread eggplant, zucchini and red pepper on prepared baking sheet. Sprinkle with basil; drizzle with oil. Roast in preheated oven, stirring occasionally, for about 20 minutes or until vegetables are tender and lightly colored.

2. Transfer to a bowl; stir in salsa, parsley and garlic. Cover and refrigerate. Serve with tortilla chips.

Ratatouille Nachos

Makes 24 appetizers

Here's a more appealing version of nachos and cheese — and it's lower in fat.

- Preheat broiler
- Baking sheet

24	round nacho tortilla chips	24
1 cup	Ratatouille Salsa (see recipe, above)	250 mL
1 cup	shredded mild Asiago or provolone cheese	250 mL

1. Arrange nachos in a single layer on baking sheet. Top each with about 2 tsp (10 mL) salsa; sprinkle with cheese. Place under preheated broiler for 2 minutes or until cheese melts. Watch carefully; serve warm.

Guacamole

Makes 6 servings

There are many versions of this popular Mexican appetizer. Here I've enhanced the mashed avocados with green onions, tomato and jalapeño pepper.

2	Hass avocados, peeled	2
1	tomato, seeded and diced	1
⅓ cup	coarsely chopped fresh cilantro	75 mL
2	green onions, sliced	2
1 to 2 tbsp	minced seeded jalapeño peppers	15 to 30 mL
1 tbsp	fresh lime juice	15 mL
	Salt	
	Tortilla chips	

1. In a bowl, mash avocados with a fork. Stir in tomato, cilantro, green onions, jalapeño pepper and lime juice. Season with salt to taste.

2. Place in a serving dish and accompany with tortilla chips.

Smoked Trout Pâté

Makes 1¼ cups (300 mL)

This tasty pâté is so easy to make. With just a whirl of the food processor, it's ready. Serve with toast points for an elegant presentation.

Tip

When buying a whole smoked trout, buy one that is 12 oz (375 g) in weight.

Variation

Salmon that has been hot smoked or any other smoked fish, such as whitefish or cod, can be used instead of the trout.

8 oz	boneless skinless smoked rainbow trout (see Tip, left), flaked	250 g
¼ cup	sour cream	60 mL
¼ cup	cream cheese	60 mL
1 tsp	grated lemon zest	5 mL
1 tbsp	fresh lemon juice	15 mL
2 tbsp	chopped fresh chives or minced green onion tops	30 mL
	Salt (optional)	
	Hot pepper sauce	

1. In a food processor, process trout until finely chopped. Add sour cream, cream cheese and lemon zest and juice; process until smooth.

2. Transfer to a bowl; add chives and season with salt, if needed, and hot pepper sauce to taste. Serve immediately or make ahead, cover and refrigerate for up to 3 days. Serve with crackers or toast points.

Smoked Salmon Mousse

This is one of my most-requested recipes. It delivers a wonderful smoked salmon flavor, but uses relatively little of that costly ingredient. My secret? I work magic with canned salmon, which keeps the cost reasonable so I can serve this appetizer more often.

Tips

I prefer to use canned sockeye salmon (instead of the pink variety) for its superior color and flavor.

The mousse can be prepared up to 4 days ahead for easy entertaining.

To get more juice out of a lemon, roll on countertop or microwave on High for 20 seconds before squeezing.

Spoon mousse into three 1-cup (250 mL) bowls and have handy in the fridge to serve over the holidays.

1	can (7½ oz/213 g) sockeye salmon (see Tips, left)	1
1	package (¼ oz/7 g) unflavored gelatin	1
½ tsp	grated lemon zest	2 mL
1 tbsp	fresh lemon juice (see Tips, left)	15 mL
¼ tsp	salt	1 mL
1½ cups	sour cream	375 mL
4 oz	smoked salmon, finely chopped	125 g
2 tbsp	minced green onions	30 mL
2 tbsp	finely chopped fresh dill	30 mL
	Hot pepper sauce	
	Dill sprigs and lemon zest for garnish	
	Melba toasts or pumpernickel rounds	

1. Drain salmon and place juice in small measuring cup. Add enough water to make ¼ cup (60 mL). Sprinkle in gelatin. Let stand for 1 to 2 minutes to soften. Microwave on Medium (50%) for 45 to 60 seconds or until dissolved.

2. Remove any skin from salmon and discard. Place in a food processor with gelatin mixture, lemon zest and juice and salt. Process until smooth.

3. Transfer mixture to a bowl. Stir in sour cream, smoked salmon, green onions and dill. Season with hot pepper sauce to taste.

4. Spoon mixture into serving bowls (see Tips, left). Cover loosely with plastic wrap (it should not touch surface of the mousse); refrigerate until set, for 4 hours or overnight. Garnish top with dill sprigs and lemon zest; serve with Melba toast or pumpernickel rounds.

Party Pâté

Here's a modern spin to an old standby, chicken liver spread. Even if you're not a big fan of liver, you'll be instantly won over when you try this lightly sweetened pâté with currants and port. Serve with crostini.

Tips

Make the pâté up to 3 days ahead. Cover surface with plastic wrap and refrigerate. Or pack into containers and freeze for up to 1 month.

The taste of freshly grated nutmeg is so much better than the pre-ground variety. Whole nutmeg can be found in the spice section of your supermarket or bulk food store. Use a rasp grater (such as a Microplane) to grate nutmeg.

3 tbsp	dried currants	45 mL
3 tbsp	ruby port	45 mL
1 lb	chicken livers	500 g
½ cup	water	125 mL
2 tbsp	butter	30 mL
1	onion, finely chopped	1
1 cup	peeled chopped apples	250 mL
¾ tsp	salt	3 mL
½ tsp	dried sage leaves	2 mL
½ tsp	freshly ground black pepper	2 mL
¼ tsp	freshly grated nutmeg (see Tips, left)	1 mL
⅓ cup	butter, cut into small cubes	75 mL
	Crostini (see Tips, page 91)	

1. In a small glass dish, combine currants and port; microwave on High for 1 minute, until plump. Set aside.

2. Trim chicken livers and cut into quarters. Place in a large nonstick skillet with water. Bring to a boil over medium heat; cook, stirring often, for 5 minutes or until no longer pink. Drain in sieve; transfer liver to food processor.

3. Rinse and dry skillet; add 2 tbsp (30 mL) butter and melt over medium heat. Add onion, apples, salt, sage, pepper and nutmeg; cook, stirring often, for 5 minutes or until softened.

4. Add onion-apple mixture to liver in bowl of food processor; purée until very smooth. Let cool slightly. Add butter cubes to liver mixture and purée until creamy. Add reserved currants and port; pulse, using on-off turns, until just combined.

5. Spoon into a serving bowl. Cover surface with plastic wrap and refrigerate until firm, about 4 hours or overnight. Serve with crostini.

Pita Crisps
with Feta and Tomatoes

These wholesome nibblers
are so easy to make and are
always a crowd pleaser.

Tips

Assemble these nibblers
just before serving as the
crisps tend to soften.

You can also set out a crock
of the bean spread, along
with a bowl of the tomato
topping. Place pita crisps
in a bread basket and let
guests help themselves.

Variation

Instead of Greek
White Bean Spread,
use homemade or
store-bought hummus
or the Lebanese
eggplant spread known
as baba ghanouj.

3	ripe tomatoes, seeded and diced	3
1 cup	finely cubed or crumbled feta cheese	250 mL
1/3 cup	kalamata olives, pitted and diced	75 mL
2	green onions, thinly sliced	2
1/4 cup	finely chopped fresh parsley	60 mL
	Freshly ground black pepper	
	Greek White Bean Spread (see Variation, page 78)	
48	pita crisps (see below) or crostini (see Tips, page 91)	48

1. In a bowl, combine tomatoes, feta cheese, olives, green onions and parsley. Season generously with pepper. Cover and refrigerate until ready to serve.

2. To serve, spread bean spread on crisps and top with tomato topping. Arrange on platters and serve.

Pita Crisps

A lower-fat alternative to tortilla chips are pita crisps. Separate three 7-inch (18 cm) thin pitas into rounds and cut each into 8 wedges. Place in a single layer on baking sheets; bake at 350°F (180°C) for 8 to 10 minutes or until crisp and lightly toasted. Let cool. Store in an airtight container. The pita crisps can be made 1 day ahead or layered in a rigid container and frozen for up to 2 weeks.

Antipasto Nibblers

**Makes
24 appetizers**

Here's another last-minute idea for tasty bites to serve when friends drop over. These small nibblers are a throwback to the cocktail/lounge scene of the 1960s, when appetizers often meant cold cuts wrapped around a pickle. I like them because they can be assembled in a few minutes and are a colorful addition to a tray of warm appetizers.

Tip

This recipe can be varied according to what you have on hand. Thin slices of salami or ham folded in half, cocktail onions and marinated artichoke pieces make for other easy combinations.

24	stuffed green olives or kalamata olives	24
8 oz	fontina cheese, cut into 3/4-inch (2 cm) cubes	250 g
1	small red bell pepper, cut into 1-inch (2.5 cm) squares	1
1	small green bell pepper, cut into 1-inch (2.5 cm) squares	1
1 tbsp	olive oil	15 mL
1 tbsp	balsamic vinegar	15 mL
	Freshly ground black pepper	
2 tbsp	chopped fresh basil leaves or parsley	30 mL

1. Thread 1 olive, 1 cheese cube, then 1 pepper square on cocktail toothpicks. Arrange in attractive shallow serving dish. Cover and refrigerate until serving time.

2. In a small bowl, whisk together oil and balsamic vinegar; pour over kabobs. Season generously with pepper, sprinkle with basil and serve.

Cheddar Pepper Rounds

Makes about 48 rounds

This recipe may seem to call for a lot of peppercorns, but it's not all that peppery. It just has a lively zip.

Tip

To crack peppercorns: Place in a heavy plastic bag and, on a wooden board, crush using a rolling pin.

Variation

Cheddar Walnut Rounds
Substitute ⅓ cup (75 mL) finely chopped walnuts for cracked peppercorns.

8 oz	aged Cheddar cheese, shredded	250 g
4 oz	cream cheese, cubed	125 g
2 tbsp	brandy or sherry	30 mL
¼ cup	finely chopped fresh parsley	60 mL
1 tbsp	cracked black peppercorns (see Tip, left)	15 mL

1. In a food processor, combine Cheddar cheese, cream cheese and brandy. Process until mixture is very smooth. Transfer to a bowl; refrigerate for 3 hours or until firm.

2. Divide mixture into two pieces; wrap each in plastic wrap. Roll on a flat surface and shape into a smooth log measuring about 6 by 1½ inches (15 by 4 cm).

3. Place parsley and cracked peppercorns on a plate. Unwrap cheese logs and roll in parsley-peppercorn mixture until evenly coated. Wrap again in plastic wrap and refrigerate until firm.

4. To serve, cut each log into ¼-inch (0.5 cm) slices and place on small toasted bread rounds, Melba toasts or crackers.

Irresistible Smoked Salmon Bites

Makes 24 appetizers

Everyone loves smoked salmon and these popular appetizers are always the first to go at a party.

Tip

These appetizers can be made earlier in the day or even the day ahead — just cover and refrigerate. Garnish shortly before serving.

4 oz	cream cheese	125 g
1 tbsp	finely chopped fresh dill	15 mL
2 tsp	honey Dijon mustard	10 mL
2 tsp	whole-seed mustard	10 mL
2 tsp	fresh lemon juice	10 mL
6	slices dark rye or pumpernickel bread, crusts trimmed	6
6 oz	sliced smoked salmon	175 g
	Capers and dill sprigs	

1. Place cream cheese in a bowl; microwave on Medium for 1 minute to soften. Stir well. Blend in dill, mustards and lemon juice.

2. Generously spread mustard mixture over bread slices; layer with smoked salmon. Cut each slice into 4 triangles or squares, or 6 rectangles. Garnish with capers and dill. Cover with plastic wrap and refrigerate.

Fresh Spring Rolls with Shrimp

Great for entertaining, these fresh-tasting, low-calorie spring rolls are so simple to assemble and roll.

Tips

Fish sauce, also called *nam pla*, is a salty brown seasoning that is the backbone of Thai cooking. Look for it in the Asian foods section of large supermarkets or Asian markets.

Make rolls up to 4 hours before serving. Cover and refrigerate.

¼ cup	fish sauce	60 mL
2 tbsp	fresh lime juice	30 mL
2 tsp	packed brown sugar	10 mL
1 tsp	Asian chili sauce, or to taste	5 mL
1	green onion, sliced	1
24	small cooked shrimp, peeled, tails removed	24
6	Vietnamese rice paper sheets (8 inches/20 cm)	6
6	small Boston lettuce leaves	6
1	piece (3 inches/7.5 cm) seedless cucumber, cut into thin strips	1
½	red bell pepper, cut into thin strips	½
12	fresh cilantro stems with leaves	12

1. In a bowl, combine fish sauce, lime juice, brown sugar, chili sauce and green onion. Place shrimp in bowl and toss with 2 tbsp (30 mL) of the fish sauce mixture. Set rest of mixture aside to use in the rolls and as a dipping sauce.

2. Pour hot water into a large bowl. Using tongs, dip 1 rice paper sheet in water for 5 seconds. Remove and place on damp kitchen towel. Let stand for 30 seconds or until soft and pliable; if still stiff, sprinkle with more water.

3. Place lettuce leaf across top half of rice paper sheet. Arrange 4 shrimp on lettuce. Top with some of the cucumber and red pepper strips. Drizzle with ½ tsp (2 mL) of the fish sauce mixture. Top with 2 cilantro stems with leaves. Fold sides of rice paper sheet over ends of filling. Starting at filled side, roll into cylinder. Cut in half on the diagonal and arrange on serving plate. Repeat with the remaining sheets and ingredients and assemble rest of rolls in the same way. Serve with reserved dipping sauce.

Creamy Mushroom Walnut Toasts

Want a great start to a meal? Begin here. I always have containers of this delicious mushroom spread in my freezer ready to defrost in the microwave when friends or family drop by. The same applies for the bread, which I slice, pack into plastic bags and freeze.

Tips

Mushroom-walnut filling can be frozen for up to 1 month.

Spread toasts with mushroom mixture just before baking to prevent them from turning soggy.

Crostini

Cut 1 thin baguette into 1/3-inch (8 mm) thick slices. Arrange on baking sheet; brush lightly with 2 tbsp (25 mL) olive oil or melted butter. Bake in 375°F (190°C) oven for 5 minutes or until edges are lightly toasted.

- Preheat oven to 375°F (190°C)
- Baking sheet

1 lb	mushrooms (an assortment of white, oyster and portobello), coarsely chopped (see Tip, page 182)	500 g
2 tbsp	butter	30 mL
1/3 cup	finely chopped green onions	75 mL
2	cloves garlic, minced	2
1/2 tsp	dried thyme leaves	2 mL
4 oz	cream cheese or goat cheese, cut into pieces	125 g
1/3 cup	freshly grated Parmesan cheese (plus extra for topping)	75 mL
1/3 cup	finely chopped walnuts	75 mL
2 tbsp	finely chopped fresh parsley	30 mL
	Salt and freshly ground black pepper	
40	crostini (see Tips, left)	40

1. In a food processor, finely chop mushrooms in batches using on-off turns.

2. In a large skillet, heat butter over medium-high heat. Add mushrooms, green onions, garlic and thyme; cook for 5 to 7 minutes or until mushrooms are softened. Cook 1 to 2 minutes more, if necessary, until all moisture has evaporated. (Mixture should be dry and almost crumbly.) Remove from heat.

3. Add cream cheese, stirring until smooth. Add Parmesan cheese, walnuts and parsley. Season with salt and pepper to taste. Transfer to a bowl; cover and let cool.

4. Spread crostini with a generous teaspoonful (5 to 7 mL) of mushroom mixture. Arrange on baking sheet. Sprinkle tops with additional Parmesan cheese. Bake in preheated oven for 8 to 10 minutes or until edges are toasted.

Cheddar Jalapeño Toasts

Get a head start on your party preparations with these tasty appetizers designed to be stored in the freezer. When friends arrive, just pop them into a hot oven.

Tips

To freeze, spread bread slices with cheese mixture; arrange in a single layer on baking sheets and freeze. Transfer to a rigid container, separating layers with waxed paper; freeze for up to 1 month. No need to defrost before baking.

To avoid skin irritation, wear rubber gloves when handling jalapeño peppers.

- Preheat oven to 375°F (190°C)
- Baking sheets

8 oz	aged Cheddar cheese, shredded	250 g
4 oz	cream cheese, cubed	125 g
2 tbsp	finely diced red bell pepper	30 mL
2 tbsp	minced seeded jalapeño peppers or 1 tbsp (15 mL) minced pickled jalapeño peppers	30 mL
2 tbsp	finely chopped fresh parsley	30 mL
36	baguette slices, cut ⅓-inch (8 mm) thick	36

1. In a food processor, purée Cheddar and cream cheese until very smooth. Transfer to a bowl; stir in red pepper, jalapeño peppers and parsley.

2. Spread bread slices with a generous teaspoonful (5 mL) of cheese mixture; arrange on baking sheets.

3. Bake in preheated oven for 10 to 12 minutes (up to 15 minutes, if frozen), until tops are puffed and edges toasted. Serve warm.

Parmesan Crostini with Caramelized Onion Jam

**Makes
32 appetizers**

Nutty-sweet Parmigiano Reggiano is the preferred Parmesan cheese to use in this simple cheese spread. Buy a wedge and grate it yourself at home as needed in recipes so the cheese doesn't lose it's wonderful rich flavor or aroma. Or buy a wedge from a cheese shop and ask that they grate it for you. Store the freshly grated Parmesan in a container in the freezer. The Caramelized Onion Jam works wonders as a topping for Parmesan crostini and also for crostini spread with herbed goat cheese.

Tip

Make this recipe ahead. Prepare Parmesan crostini as directed in Steps 1 and 2. Place on baking sheets, cover with plastic wrap and freeze. Transfer to a covered container separating layers with waxed paper. Freeze for up to 1 month. No need to defrost before baking.

- Preheat oven to 375°F (190°C)
- Rimmed baking sheets

1 cup	freshly grated Parmesan cheese	250 mL
1/4 cup	cream cheese, softened	60 mL
1 tsp	chopped fresh rosemary (optional)	5 mL
1/2 tsp	freshly ground black pepper	2 mL
32	crostini (see Tips, page 91)	32
	Caramelized Onion Jam (see recipe, below)	

1. In a bowl, blend Parmesan with cream cheese, rosemary, if using, and pepper. (Can be covered and refrigerated for up to 5 days or frozen for up to 2 weeks.)

2. Spread each crostini with a scant 1 tsp (5 mL) of the Parmesan mixture. Arrange on baking sheets. Bake in preheated oven for 10 to 12 minutes or until golden. Top warm toasts with a spoonful of the Caramelized Onion Jam and serve.

Caramelized Onion Jam

Makes 2 cups (500 mL)

1/4 cup	olive oil	60 mL
6 cups	thinly sliced red onions	1.5 L
1/3 cup	red wine vinegar	75 mL
1	bottle (12 oz/341 mL) beer	1
1/2 cup	packed brown sugar	125 mL
1 tbsp	chopped fresh thyme or rosemary	15 mL
1/2 tsp	salt	2 mL
1/2 tsp	freshly ground black pepper	2 mL

1. In a Dutch oven or large saucepan, heat oil over medium-high heat. Cook onions, stirring often, for 15 to 20 minutes or until lightly colored.

2. Add vinegar and cook, stirring, until almost evaporated. Stir in beer, brown sugar, thyme, salt and pepper. Bring to a boil; reduce heat and boil gently, stirring occasionally, for 15 to 20 minutes or until most of the liquid is reduced and is syrupy.

3. Let cool. Transfer to an airtight container and refrigerate for up to 1 month.

Sun-Dried Tomato and Goat Cheese Puffs

Makes about 40 appetizers

These puffs are known as gougères, savory French cheese pastries made with the same choux pastry used to make dessert cream puffs and éclairs. This combination of goat cheese, sun-dried tomatoes and fresh basil makes melt-in-your mouth appetizers.

Tip

The cheese puffs can be baked earlier in the day and reheated just before serving. Or place baked puffs in rigid airtight containers, layered between parchment or waxed paper, and freeze for up to 2 weeks. To reheat, place frozen puffs on a baking sheet and bake in 350°F (180°C) oven for 6 to 8 minutes or until heated through.

Variation

Bacon and Cheddar Cheese Puffs

Replace goat cheese with 1 cup (250 mL) shredded aged Cheddar cheese and add 8 slices bacon, cooked crisp and crumbled. Omit salt and sun-dried tomatoes. Use chives instead of basil.

- Preheat oven to 375°F (190°C), with racks in top third and bottom third of oven
- Baking sheets, lined with parchment paper

½ cup	butter, cut into pieces	125 mL
¼ tsp	salt	1 mL
¼ tsp	freshly ground black pepper	1 mL
Pinch	cayenne pepper	Pinch
1¼ cups	all-purpose flour	300 mL
4	eggs, chilled	4
6 oz	soft goat cheese, crumbled	175 g
⅓ cup	finely chopped drained oil-packed sun-dried tomatoes (blotted dry)	75 mL
2 tbsp	finely chopped fresh basil	30 mL
1	egg yolk	1

1. In a medium saucepan, combine 1 cup (250 mL) water, butter, salt, pepper and cayenne. Place over high heat until butter melts and mixture comes to a full boil.

2. Reduce heat to medium and remove pan from heat. Using a wooden spoon, stir in flour all at once. Return pan to heat and stir vigorously for 1 minute or until dough leaves sides of pan. Remove from heat and let dough cool slightly, about 3 minutes.

3. Using an electric mixer, or by hand using a wooden spoon, beat in whole eggs, one at a time, until batter is glossy. Beat in goat cheese until incorporated. Fold in sun-dried tomatoes and basil.

4. Drop rounded spoonfuls of batter (the size of large cherry tomatoes) onto prepared baking sheets, 1½ inches (4 cm) apart. In a small bowl, beat egg yolk with 1 tsp (5 mL) water. Brush pastries with egg yolk mixture and smooth any uneven edges.

5. Bake in preheated oven for 25 to 30 minutes, rotating baking sheets halfway through baking, until gougères are puffed and golden. Serve warm or at room temperature.

Pancetta Pepper Bites

Making hot hors d'oeuvres to serve to guests at a large party can be time-consuming. That's why I like to have these do-ahead savory pastries on hand in the freezer to pop into the oven shortly before guests arrive.

Tip

Pancetta is Italian cured bacon that is not smoked; use prosciutto or double-smoked instead, if desired. For a vegetarian version, omit the pancetta; increase olive oil to 2 tbsp (30 mL).

Variation

For a Greek variation, replace sage with 2 tbsp (30 mL) chopped fresh oregano or 2 tsp (10 mL) dried oregano leaves. Add 1/4 cup (60 mL) finely chopped kalamata olives to pepper mixture. Sprinkle baked pastries with crumbled feta cheese instead of herb cream cheese.

- Preheat oven to 375°F (190°C)
- Baking sheets, lined with parchment paper

1 tbsp	olive oil	15 mL
3 oz	pancetta, finely chopped	90 g
1/3 cup	minced shallots	75 mL
4	cloves garlic, minced	4
1	red bell pepper, finely diced	1
1	yellow bell pepper, finely diced	1
2 tbsp	chopped fresh sage leaves	30 mL
1/2 tsp	salt	2 mL
1/2 tsp	freshly ground black pepper	2 mL
2 tbsp	chopped fresh parsley	30 mL
1	package (14 to 16 oz/400 to 450 g) frozen puff pastry, thawed (see Tip, page 96)	1
8 oz	herb and garlic cream cheese, such as Boursin, or soft goat cheese	250 g

1. In a large nonstick skillet, heat oil over medium-high heat; cook pancetta, shallots and garlic, stirring, for 2 minutes. Add red pepper, yellow pepper, sage, salt and pepper; cook, stirring, for 3 minutes or until peppers are softened. Transfer to a bowl; stir in parsley. Let cool completely. (Can be covered and refrigerated for up to 1 day.)

2. Divide puff pastry in half. On a lightly floured surface, roll out each half into a 12- by 10-inch (30 by 25 cm) rectangle. Place on baking sheets; freeze for 15 minutes for easier handling. Trim pastry edges to even; cut each rectangle into thirty 2-inch (5 cm) squares. Place on prepared baking sheets; prick each square in several places with a fork.

3. Spread each square with a generous teaspoonful (5 mL) of the pepper mixture. (Can be covered and refrigerated for up to 4 hours. Or freeze on baking sheets and transfer frozen pastries to containers, separating layers with parchment or waxed paper. Freeze for up to 1 month. No need to defrost before baking.)

4. Bake in preheated oven for 15 to 18 minutes or until golden. Top each with about 1/2 tsp (2 mL) of cream cheese. Return to oven for 2 to 3 minutes, until cheese is melted. Serve warm or at room temperature.

Samosas with Cilantro Yogurt Sauce

Makes 30 turnovers

These flaky nibblers are always the first to go at a party. Although a bit time-consuming to make, they are well worth the effort because they can be made ahead and frozen. Serve with Cilantro Yogurt Sauce or your favorite chutney.

Tips

Store-bought curry pastes vary in flavor and strength depending on the brand. Some pastes are labeled as mild but have more heat than expected. Add a smaller amount of curry paste to the recipe to test the strength and add more to get the depth of curry flavor you prefer.

Frozen butter puff pastry is preferred, but any brand of frozen puff pastry in a 14- to 16-oz (400 to 450 g) package will work well in this recipe.

- Preheat oven to 375°F (190°C)
- Baking sheets, lined with parchment paper

1 lb	lean ground lamb or beef	500 g
1	potato, peeled and grated	1
1	onion, finely chopped	1
2	cloves garlic, finely chopped	2
1 tbsp	minced gingerroot	15 mL
2 tsp	mild or medium curry paste or powder	10 mL
½ tsp	ground cumin	2 mL
½ tsp	salt	2 mL
Pinch	cayenne pepper	Pinch
¼ cup	chopped fresh cilantro	60 mL
1	package (14 to 16 oz/400 to 450 g) frozen puff pastry, thawed	1
1	egg yolk	1
	Cilantro Yogurt Sauce (optional)	

1. In a large nonstick skillet, cook lamb over medium-high heat, breaking up with the back of a spoon, for 5 minutes or until no longer pink. Drain any fat in skillet.

2. Add potato, onion, garlic, ginger, curry paste, cumin, salt and cayenne. Cook, stirring, for 5 minutes or until potato and onion are softened. Stir in cilantro. Let filling cool.

3. On lightly floured surface, thinly roll half of the pastry into a 15- by 9-inch (38 by 23 cm) rectangle. Cut pastry into fifteen 3-inch (7.5 cm) squares. Place a generous tablespoon (15 mL) of the filling in center of each. Fold into a triangle; pinch edges to seal. Repeat with remaining pastry and filling.

4. Arrange pastries on prepared baking sheets in a single layer. Freeze for 20 minutes or until pastry is firm. Using a sharp knife, trim ragged edges of pastry. Using a fork, prick tops of pastries. (Pastries can be frozen at this point; do not defrost before baking.)

Tip

Fresh cilantro, also called coriander and Chinese parsley, lasts only a few days in the fridge before it deteriorates and turns tasteless. Wash cilantro well, spin dry and wrap in paper towels; store in plastic bag in the fridge. Leave the roots on — they keep the leaves fresh.

5. In a bowl, beat egg yolk with 1 tsp (5 mL) water. Brush pastries lightly with egg mixture. Bake in preheated oven for 18 to 20 minutes or until puffed and golden. Serve warm or at room temperature accompanied with Cilantro Yogurt Sauce, if desired.

Cilantro Yogurt Sauce

Makes 1 cup (250 mL)

¾ cup	plain yogurt	175 mL
1 cup	lightly packed fresh cilantro with tender stems	250 mL
1 tbsp	fresh lemon juice	15 mL
1 tbsp	coarsely chopped gingerroot	15 mL
½ tsp	salt	2 mL
Pinch	cayenne pepper	Pinch

1. In a food processor, combine yogurt, cilantro, lemon juice, ginger, salt and cayenne. Process until smooth. Refrigerate until ready to serve. Can be made up to 2 days ahead.

Artichoke Phyllo Triangles

Phyllo pastry makes great crisp wrappers for a variety of savory fillings. The pastry is used extensively in Mediterranean cooking and fits in perfectly with the modern notion of comfort foods because it delivers taste, style and convenience, too. I make batches of these Greek-inspired appetizers ahead and then freeze them. The only thing left to do is pop them in the oven and serve.

Tips

To freeze, place unbaked triangles on baking sheets; freeze until firm. Place in waxed paper–lined containers; freeze for up to 2 months. No need to defrost before baking.

The artichoke filling also freezes well. Pack into containers and freeze for 1 month.

Variation

Spread artichoke filling on crostini (see Tips, page 91). Sprinkle with additional Parmesan cheese. Bake in preheated oven for 8 minutes or until heated through.

- Preheat oven to 375°F (190°C)
- Baking sheet, lightly greased

1 tbsp	olive oil	15 mL
1	can (14 oz/398 mL) artichoke hearts or bottoms, drained well, finely chopped	1
4	green onions, finely chopped	4
2	cloves garlic, minced	2
1 tsp	dried oregano leaves	5 mL
1/4 cup	finely chopped oil-packed sun-dried tomatoes	60 mL
1/4 cup	finely chopped kalamata olives	60 mL
1 cup	shredded Gruyère or Asiago cheese	250 mL
1/4 cup	freshly grated Parmesan cheese (plus extra for topping)	60 mL
	Freshly ground black pepper	
6	sheets phyllo pastry	6
1/3 cup	olive oil or melted butter (approx.)	75 mL

1. In a large nonstick skillet, heat oil over medium-high heat. Add artichokes, green onions, garlic and oregano; cook, stirring, for 3 minutes or until softened. Stir in sun-dried tomatoes and olives. Remove from heat; transfer to a bowl and let cool slightly.

2. Stir in Gruyère and Parmesan cheeses; season with pepper. (Recipe can be prepared up to this point, then kept covered and refrigerated, up to 3 days.)

3. Place 1 phyllo sheet on work surface. (To prevent remaining sheets from drying out, keep them covered with waxed paper, then a damp kitchen towel.) Brush pastry lightly with oil or melted butter. Cut crosswise into 8 strips, each 2 inches (5 cm) wide.

4. Place 1 tsp (5 mL) filling at bottom-left corner of each strip; fold right corner over filling to meet the left side to form a triangle. Continue wrapping pastry around filling, maintaining a triangular shape.

5. Place on prepared baking sheet. Brush top lightly with olive oil. Continue making triangles with remaining phyllo and filling in the same way. Bake in preheated oven for 14 to 16 minutes or until golden.

Easy Artichoke Cheese Melts

**Makes
24 appetizers**

Everyone likes to have a breezy appetizer in their repertoire. This is one of mine. It takes no time to prepare and tastes great.

Tip

Make this spread up to 3 days ahead, cover and refrigerate. Assemble appetizers just before serving or toasts will soften.

- Preheat oven to 375°F (190°C)
- Baking sheet

1	jar (6 oz/170 mL) marinated artichokes, well drained and finely chopped	1
½ cup	shredded Monterey Jack, Gouda or Cheddar cheese	125 mL
¼ cup	freshly grated Parmesan cheese	60 mL
¼ cup	light mayonnaise	60 mL
24	crostini (see Tips, page 91)	24
¼ cup	finely diced red bell pepper	60 mL
8	kalamata olives, cut into thin slivers	8

1. In a bowl, combine artichokes, Monterey Jack, Parmesan and mayonnaise. Spread over toasts; top with red pepper and olive slivers.

2. Arrange on baking sheet; bake in preheated oven for 10 to 12 minutes or until tops are bubbly and edges are golden. Serve warm.

Spanakopita

Spinach and feta pie, a classic Greek comfort food, can be served warm or at room temperature as an appetizer or part of a buffet.

• Preheat oven to 375°F (190°C)
• 13- by 9-inch (33 by 23 cm) baking pan, greased

2	packages (each 10 oz/300 g) fresh spinach	2
6 tbsp	olive oil (approx.), divided	90 mL
1 cup	sliced green onions	250 mL
2	eggs	2
1½ cups	finely crumbled feta cheese (about 6 oz/175 g)	375 mL
¼ cup	chopped fresh dill	60 mL
	Freshly ground black pepper	
11	sheets phyllo pastry	11

1. Rinse spinach in cold water; remove tough ends. Place in Dutch oven or large saucepan with just the water clinging to leaves; cook over medium-high heat, stirring, until just wilted. Drain well and squeeze dry; finely chop.

2. In a large nonstick skillet, heat 1 tbsp (15 mL) oil over medium-high heat; cook spinach and green onions, stirring, for 4 minutes or until spinach is just tender. Let cool.

3. In a bowl, beat eggs; add spinach mixture, feta and dill and season with pepper.

4. Place 1 sheet of phyllo on work surface. (To prevent remaining phyllo sheets from drying out, keep covered with waxed paper, then a damp kitchen towel.) Brush pastry lightly with oil. Fit into baking pan with ends hanging over sides. Layer 5 more phyllo sheets in pan, brushing each with oil before adding the next. Evenly spread with spinach filling and fold ends over filling. Layer remaining 5 phyllo sheets on top, brushing each lightly with oil before adding the next. Carefully fold pastry edges under bottom pastry.

5. Using a sharp knife, cut the top phyllo layers into squares or diamond patterns. Brush top with oil. Bake in preheated oven for 35 to 40 minutes or until golden. Let cool for 10 minutes before cutting into serving-size pieces.

Nippy Parmesan Cheese Straws

I make double batches
of these wonderfully
cheese-laden sticks,
especially at holiday
time. They are perfect as
appetizers and great to
serve along with soup.
To obtain the richest flavor,
buy a wedge of authentic
Parmigiano Reggiano and
have it finely grated for
you at the cheese shop.

Tips

Frozen butter puff pastry
is preferred, but any brand
of frozen puff pastry in a
14- to 16-oz (400 to 450 g)
package will work well in
this recipe.

Baked straws can be stored
in covered container for
up to 5 days. Or freeze
unbaked straws for up to
2 months in an airtight
container lined with waxed
paper. No need to defrost
before baking.

- Preheat oven to 375°F (190°C)
- Baking sheet(s), lined with parchment paper

1 cup	freshly grated Parmesan cheese	250 mL
½ tsp	paprika	2 mL
¼ tsp	cayenne pepper	1 mL
1	package (14 to 16 oz/400 to 450 g) frozen puff pastry, thawed	1

1. In a bowl, combine Parmesan, paprika and cayenne pepper.

2. Sprinkle work surface with 2 tbsp (30 mL) of the Parmesan mixture to cover an area approximately the same size as 1 pastry sheet. Top with pastry sheet; sprinkle with another 2 tbsp (30 mL) of the Parmesan mixture.

3. Roll out half the pastry to make a 10-inch (25 cm) square. Sprinkle half the sqaure with 2 tbsp (30 mL) of the Parmesan mixture; fold dough over in half. Sprinkle with 2 tbsp (30 mL) more Parmesan mixture. Roll out to make a thin 12- by 10-inch (30 by 25 cm) rectangle. Cut dough in half to make two 12- by 5-inch (30 by 12.5 cm) rectangles.

4. With a sharp knife and using a ruler as a guide, cut pastry into strips measuring 5 by ¾ inches (13 by 2 cm); twist each strip three or four times to make a spiral. Arrange on prepared baking sheets, pressing the ends onto the sheets to hold them in place.

5. Repeat Steps 2 through 4 with remaining pastry and Parmesan mixture.

6. Freeze for 15 minutes or until pastry is firm. Bake in preheated oven for 14 to 16 minutes or until puffed and golden. Transfer to a rack to cool.

Baked Brie with Cranberry-Pear Chutney

Makes 4 servings

This makes a very simple but delicious appetizer. If you are expecting a large crowd, buy a larger wheel of Brie and top with generous layer of chutney and chopped walnuts. Bake a few minutes longer or until sides are soft to the touch.

Tips

Make extra batches of the chutney and pack the hot mixture into sterilized 1-cup (250 mL) preserving jars and fit with two-piece lids. Process in boiling water bath for 10 minutes to ensure a vacuum seal.

A jar of this chutney tied with a colorful swatch of fabric and a pretty ribbon makes a wonderful hostess gift.

It also makes a fabulous condiment to serve with Roast Turkey (see recipe, page 278), or try it with Tourtière (see recipe, page 307).

- Preheat oven to 350°F (180°C)
- Baking sheet, lined with parchment paper

1	round of Brie cheese (7 oz/200 g)	1
¼ cup	Cranberry-Pear Chutney (see recipe, below)	60 mL
2 tbsp	finely chopped walnuts	30 mL
	Baguette slices	

1. Arrange Brie on prepared baking sheet. Spread top with chutney; sprinkle with walnuts.

2. Bake in preheated oven for 5 to 7 minutes or until sides of Brie are soft to the touch. Using a metal spatula, transfer to a serving plate; surround with bread slices. Serve warm.

Cranberry-Pear Chutney

Makes about 3 cups (750 mL)

3 cups	fresh or frozen cranberries	750 mL
1½ cups	peeled, finely diced pears, such as Anjou	375 mL
1	small onion, finely chopped	1
1 cup	packed brown sugar	250 mL
½ cup	orange juice	125 mL
½ cup	cider vinegar	125 mL
½ cup	golden raisins	125 mL
1 tbsp	grated orange zest	15 mL
1 tsp	ground ginger	5 mL

1. In a large saucepan, combine cranberries, pears, onion, brown sugar, orange juice, vinegar, raisins, orange zest and ginger. Bring to a boil over medium heat.

2. Simmer, uncovered, stirring occasionally, for 15 to 20 minutes or until mixture has thickened and fruit is tender.

Spinach-Stuffed Mushroom Caps

These very impressive appetizers are the perfect pop-in-the-mouth treat and are ideal for a buffet table or cocktail party. You can opt to leave out the bacon for a vegetarian version or add the cooked bacon to just half of the filling and offer both options.

Tip

Stuffed mushroom caps can be prepared up to 2 hours ahead of serving and refrigerated.

• Preheat oven to 375°F (190°C)
• Rimmed baking sheet, lined with parchment paper or foil

1	package (10 oz/300 g) fresh spinach	1
36	mushrooms (1½ inches/4 cm in diameter)	36
4 tsp	olive oil	20 mL
4 oz	finely chopped double-smoked bacon or pancetta	125 g
4	green onions, thinly sliced	4
2	cloves garlic, finely chopped	2
4 oz	herbed cream cheese	125 g
2 tbsp	freshly grated Parmesan cheese (approx.)	30 mL

1. Rinse spinach in cold water; remove large stems. Place in Dutch oven with just the water clinging to leaves; cook over medium-high heat, stirring, until just wilted. Drain well and squeeze dry; finely chop.

2. Remove mushrooms stems and finely chop. Set aside. Place mushroom caps, hollow side down, on prepared baking sheet. Brush with oil. Bake in preheated oven for 7 to 9 minutes or until softened. Let cool; drain off liquid. Place, hollow side up, on baking sheet.

3. In a large nonstick skillet, cook bacon over medium heat, stirring often, for 5 minutes or until crisp. Drain off fat, if necessary. Add reserved mushroom stems, green onions and garlic; cook, stirring, for 3 minutes or until softened. Add spinach and cook, stirring, for 3 minutes. Stir in cream cheese.

4. Spoon a heaping teaspoonful (5 mL) of the mixture into each mushroom cap, mounding slightly. Sprinkle tops with Parmesan.

5. Bake in preheated oven for 10 to 12 minutes or until top is lightly browned. Serve warm.

Grilled Thai Shrimp

Shrimp and red cocktail sauce is overdone on the party circuit. Here's a very easy and flavorful way to serve shrimp that always has lots of crowd appeal.

Tip

Fish sauce, also called *nam pla*, is a salty brown seasoning that is the backbone of Thai cooking. Look for it in the Asian foods section of large supermarkets or in Asian markets.

1	large clove garlic, minced	1
2 tbsp	chopped fresh cilantro	30 mL
1 tbsp	packed brown sugar	15 mL
2 tbsp	fresh lime juice	30 mL
2 tbsp	Thai fish sauce or soy sauce	30 mL
1 tbsp	vegetable oil	15 mL
1/2 to 1 tsp	Asian chili sauce, or to taste	2 to 5 mL
1 lb	large raw shrimp, peeled, with tails left on (about 30)	500 g
	Coarsely chopped fresh cilantro and lime wedges	

1. In a large bowl, combine garlic, cilantro, brown sugar, lime juice, fish sauce, oil and chili sauce. Add shrimp and toss. Cover and refrigerate, stirring occasionally, for at least 1 hour or up to 4 hours.

2. Preheat a barbecue grill, stovetop grill pan or large nonstick skillet over medium-high heat. Grill or cook shrimp, turning once, for 2 to 3 minutes or until shrimp are pink and opaque. Transfer to a serving bowl or platter. Garnish with cilantro and lime wedges. Serve warm or at room temperature along with toothpicks for guests to serve themselves.

Coconut Sesame Shrimp

These crunchy shrimp with an Asian spin thanks to the sesame oil are irresistible and always a party favorite. I particularly like the fact that I can fry the shrimp ahead and reheat quickly in the oven once guests arrive. Serve with Peanut Dipping Sauce (see recipe, page 109) or your favorite sweet-and-sour dipping sauce.

Tip

Make this recipe ahead. Fry shrimp as directed. Let cool. Cover loosely with plastic wrap and refrigerate for up to 4 hours; place on a rack on baking sheet and reheat in a 350°F (180°C) oven for 5 minutes or until heated through.

● Baking sheet with rack

30	large raw shrimp, peeled and deveined, with tails on	30
2	eggs	2
3 tbsp	all-purpose flour	45 mL
1 tbsp	toasted sesame oil	15 mL
½ tsp	salt	2 mL
½ tsp	Asian chili sauce, or to taste	2 mL
¾ cup	unsweetened shredded coconut	175 mL
3 tbsp	sesame seeds	45 mL
	Vegetable oil for deep-frying	

1. Butterfly shrimp by cutting lengthwise along outside curve almost but not completely through. Pat shrimp dry with paper towels.

2. In a bowl, lightly beat eggs; stir in flour, sesame oil, salt and chili sauce. In another bowl, combine coconut and sesame seeds.

3. Holding shrimp by the tail, dip into egg mixture, then dip into coconut mixture, turning to coat all over. Set on a rack on a baking sheet. Discard any excess egg and coconut mixtures.

4. Pour oil into a deep-fryer or deep heavy-bottomed large saucepan to come at least 2 inches (5 cm) up side. Heat to 375°F (190°C) or until 1-inch (2.5 cm) cube of white bread turns golden brown in 30 seconds.

5. Deep-fry shrimp, in batches, turning once, for about 1 minute or until golden. Using a slotted spoon, transfer to paper towels to drain. Arrange warm shrimp on serving plate and accompany with your favorite dipping sauce.

Cajun Crab Cakes with Herb Dipping Sauce

Always a popular hit when
entertaining, watch these
tasty crab cakes disappear!

Tips

To prevent soggy crab
cakes, make sure to
squeeze crabmeat of
excess moisture.

To make ahead, prepare
crab cakes as directed
in recipe. Let cool, place
on greased baking sheet,
cover and refrigerate. To
reheat, place in preheated
400°F (200°C) oven for
8 to 10 minutes.

● Baking sheet, lined with waxed paper

Herb Dipping Sauce

½ cup	light mayonnaise	125 mL
½ cup	sour cream	125 mL
2 tsp	whole-seed mustard	10 mL
2 tsp	fresh lemon juice	10 mL
2 tbsp	finely chopped fresh flat-leaf (Italian) parsley	30 mL
2 tbsp	finely chopped fresh chives	30 mL
	Hot pepper sauce	

Crab Cakes

1	egg	1
¼ cup	light mayonnaise	60 mL
1 tbsp	Dijon mustard	15 mL
2 tsp	Cajun spice	10 mL
1 tsp	Worcestershire sauce	5 mL
1 lb	crabmeat, squeezed dry	500 g
3	green onions, finely chopped	3
½ cup	minced red bell pepper	125 mL
½ cup	minced celery	125 mL
1½ cups	soft fresh bread crumbs	375 mL
1 cup	finely crushed flavored baked tortilla or corn chips	250 mL
¼ cup	olive oil (approx.)	60 mL

1. *Herb Dipping Sauce:* In a bowl, combine mayonnaise, sour cream, mustard, lemon juice, parsley and chives. Season with hot pepper sauce to taste. Set aside.

2. *Crab Cakes:* In a bowl, beat egg; add mayonnaise, mustard, Cajun spice and Worcestershire sauce. Stir in crabmeat, green onions, red pepper and celery. Stir in bread crumbs. Shape heaping tablespoons into 2-inch (5 cm) patties.

3. Place crushed tortilla chips in shallow bowl and coat patties on both sides with crumbs. Place on prepared baking sheet.

4. In a large nonstick skillet, heat half of the oil over medium-high heat. Fry crab cakes in batches, adding more oil if needed, for 2 minutes per side or until golden. Accompany with Herb Dipping Sauce.

Honey Garlic Chicken Wings

Makes 8 servings as an appetizer or 4 as a main course

These spicy wings are always a party hit. They're deliciously messy, so be sure to have plenty of napkins on hand.

Tip

You can also partially cook the wings in the oven for the first 20 minutes and complete the cooking on the barbecue over medium heat.

- Preheat oven to 375°F (190°C)
- Rimmed baking sheet, lined with foil, with rack brushed with oil or nonstick cooking spray

3 lbs	chicken wings, separated and tips removed	1.5 kg
1/3 cup	soy sauce	75 mL
1/4 cup	liquid honey	60 mL
2 tbsp	hoisin sauce	30 mL
2 tbsp	rice vinegar	30 mL
2	large cloves garlic, finely chopped	2
2 tsp	hot pepper sauce, or to taste	10 mL

1. Place chicken wings in a large, heavy plastic bag and set in a large bowl. In a small bowl, combine soy sauce, honey, hoisin sauce, vinegar, garlic and hot pepper sauce. Pour over wings, close tightly and seal. Let marinate in fridge for several hours or overnight.

2. On prepared baking sheet, arrange wings in a single layer on rack set on prepared baking sheet; roast in preheated oven for 30 minutes. Pour off pan juices and turn wings over.

3. Meanwhile, place marinade in a small saucepan. Bring to a boil over medium heat; cook 3 to 5 minutes or until slightly thickened. Baste wings liberally with marinade.

4. Roast for 25 to 30 minutes or until wings are tender and nicely glazed.

Spicy Barbecue Chicken Wings

Makes 8 to 10 servings

Whether you're watching the big game on TV or hosting a laid-back summer barbecue, there is nothing better than wings for a hungry crowd at a casual get-together.

Tips

The sauce makes about 2 cups (500 mL). Transfer what you need for basting to a separate bowl, then place remaining barbecue sauce in an airtight container and refrigerate for up to 1 month. Use to baste other grill favorites, such as ribs and burgers.

For barbecued wings, first roast wings basted with sauce for 30 minutes, as in Step 3. Place wings on greased grill over medium heat. Grill, turning wings and basting with sauce occasionally, for about 20 minutes or until nicely glazed and tender. Watch carefully, as the sauce burns easily.

- Preheat oven to 375°F (190°C)
- Rimmed baking sheet, lined with foil, with rack brushed with oil or nonstick cooking spray

1½ cups	ketchup	375 mL
¼ cup	packed brown sugar	60 mL
¼ cup	balsamic vinegar	60 mL
2 tbsp	Worcestershire sauce	30 mL
2	large cloves garlic, finely chopped	2
1½ tsp	chili powder	7 mL
1 tsp	ground cumin	5 mL
1 tsp	dry mustard	5 mL
1 tbsp	Asian chili sauce, or to taste	15 mL
4 lbs	chicken wings, separated and tips removed	2 kg

1. In a bowl, combine ketchup, brown sugar, vinegar, Worcestershire sauce, garlic, chili powder, cumin, mustard and chili sauce to taste.

2. Pat wings dry with paper towels. Place in a large bowl and toss with ½ cup (125 mL) of the sauce. Arrange wings in a single layer on rack set on prepared baking sheet. Baste both sides of wings liberally with sauce.

3. Roast in preheated oven for 30 minutes. Pour off pan juices. Baste both sides of wings liberally with sauce.

4. Roast for 25 to 30 minutes or until wings are tender and nicely glazed.

Chicken Satays with Peanut Dipping Sauce

• Twenty-four 6-inch (15 cm) wooden skewers, soaked

Satays

3	boneless skinless chicken breasts (about 1 lb/500 g)	3
1/4 cup	soy sauce	60 mL
1 tbsp	vegetable oil	15 mL
1 tbsp	minced gingerroot	15 mL
1 tsp	granulated sugar	5 mL
2	cloves garlic, minced	2

Peanut Dipping Sauce

1/3 cup	peanut butter	75 mL
3 tbsp	fresh lime juice	45 mL
2 tbsp	soy sauce	30 mL
1 tbsp	packed brown sugar	15 mL
2 tsp	minced gingerroot	10 mL
1 tsp	Asian chili sauce, or to taste	5 mL
1	clove garlic, minced	1
2 tbsp	chopped fresh cilantro	30 mL

1. *Satays:* Place chicken on a plate and cover with plastic wrap. Freeze for 1 to 2 hours or until firm to the touch but not solidly frozen. Cut each breast against the grain into 8 long thin strips, each about 1/4 inch (0.5 cm) thick. Thread chicken onto skewers accordion-style. Arrange in a shallow baking dish.

2. In a bowl, combine soy sauce, oil, ginger, sugar and garlic. Pour over chicken. Cover and refrigerate; marinate for 1 hour or overnight, turning chicken occasionally.

3. *Peanut Dipping Sauce:* In a bowl, whisk together peanut butter, lime juice, soy sauce, brown sugar, ginger, chili sauce and garlic until smooth. (Can be covered and refrigerated up to 1 day.) Stir in cilantro.

4. Preheat greased barbecue grill to medium. Remove chicken from marinade, discarding marinade, and place on grill; grill for 3 minutes on each side or until cooked through. Serve warm with dipping sauce.

Appetizer Chicken Meatballs

Delicious meatballs made with chicken are a tasty alternative to the beef that has always been a meatball mainstay. Buy extra chicken and make several batches to store in your freezer for quick appetizers or to add to soups, chilis and stroganoffs for fast mid-week meals.

Tip

Cooked meatballs can be made up to 1 day ahead and kept covered in the refrigerator or frozen for up to 1 month. To freeze, place meatballs in a single layer on trays; when frozen, transfer to airtight containers. To defrost quickly, place meatballs in a casserole dish and microwave on High for 4 to 5 minutes until just warmed through, stirring once.

- Preheat oven to 375°F (190°C)
- Rimmed baking sheets, lined with parchment paper

1 tbsp	vegetable oil	15 mL
2	cloves garlic, minced	2
1	onion, finely chopped	1
1 tbsp	dried fines herbes	15 mL
½ tsp	salt	2 mL
½ tsp	freshly ground black pepper	2 mL
2	eggs	2
2 lbs	lean ground chicken or turkey	1 kg
½ cup	fine dry bread crumbs	125 mL
½ cup	freshly grated Parmesan cheese	125 mL

1. In a medium nonstick skillet, heat oil over medium heat. Add garlic, onion, fines herbes, salt and pepper. Cook, stirring often, for 5 minutes or until softened. Let cool slightly.

2. In a bowl, whisk eggs with a fork. Add onion mixture, chicken, bread crumbs and Parmesan; mix gently until evenly combined.

3. Using wet hands, form chicken mixture into 1-inch (2.5 cm) meatballs. Place 1½ inches (4 cm) apart on prepared baking sheets.

4. Bake in preheated oven for 15 to 20 minutes or until meatballs are lightly browned and no longer pink inside.

Chicken Meatballs with Plum Mustard Sauce

Makes 36 meatballs

Batch-cook tasty chicken meatballs ahead and have them handy in your freezer to toss with this easy sauce for a last-minute appetizer.

Tips

Store-bought frozen cooked chicken and beef meatballs, available in the frozen foods section of supermarkets, can also be used as a convenient substitute for homemade meatballs. Look for ones lower in fat and sodium as a healthy food choice.

If you prefer to sauce the meatballs with a bit of heat, add 1 tsp (5 mL) Asian chili sauce, or to taste, with the plum sauce.

Variation
Substitute Appetizer Beef Meatballs (page 112).

¾ cup	plum sauce	175 mL
2 tbsp	soy sauce	30 mL
1 tbsp	minced gingerroot	15 mL
1 tbsp	Dijon mustard	15 mL
36	frozen Appetizer Chicken Meatballs (see recipe, page 110)	36
1	green onion, sliced	1

1. In a medium saucepan, combine 2 tbsp (30 mL) water, plum sauce, soy sauce, ginger and mustard. Add meatballs and stir to coat with sauce.

2. Cover and simmer over medium heat, stirring often, for 15 minutes or until piping hot and meatballs are heated through. Transfer to a warmed serving dish and sprinkle with green onions.

Appetizer Beef Meatballs

Makes about 72 meatballs

Who doesn't love meatballs as an appetizer? Serve them in any one of the tasty sauces provided. As fast as you fill the serving bowls, watch them disappear.

Tip

Cooked meatballs can be made up to 1 day ahead and kept covered in the refrigerator, or frozen for up to 1 month. To freeze, place meatballs in a single layer on baking sheets; when frozen, transfer to airtight containers. To defrost quickly, place meatballs in a casserole dish and microwave on High for 4 to 5 minutes until just warmed through, stirring once.

- Preheat oven to 400°F (200°C)
- Rimmed baking sheet, greased

1 tbsp	vegetable oil	15 mL
1	onion, finely chopped	1
2	cloves garlic, minced	2
¾ tsp	salt	3 mL
½ tsp	dried thyme leaves	2 mL
½ tsp	freshly ground black pepper	2 mL
½ cup	beef stock	125 mL
2 tsp	Worcestershire sauce	10 mL
2 lbs	lean ground beef	1 kg
1 cup	soft fresh bread crumbs	250 mL
2 tbsp	finely chopped fresh parsley	30 mL
1	egg, lightly beaten	1

1. In a medium nonstick skillet, heat oil over medium heat. Add onion, garlic, salt, thyme and pepper; cook, stirring often, for 5 minutes or until softened. Stir in beef stock and Worcestershire sauce; let cool slightly.

2. In a bowl, combine onion mixture, ground beef, bread crumbs, parsley and egg; mix thoroughly.

3. Form beef mixture into 1-inch (2.5 cm) balls; arrange on prepared baking sheet spacing 1½ inches (4 cm) apart. Bake in preheated oven for 18 to 20 minutes or until nicely browned. Transfer to a paper towel–lined plate to drain.

Party Meatballs
with Sweet-and-Sour Sauce

This versatile dipping sauce
is also good with chicken
or pork kebabs, or with
chicken wings. For a spicy
version, add hot pepper
sauce to taste.

Tip

The brown sugar you use
in recipes is totally your
preference. Brown sugar
comes in both light and
dark brown. Dark brown
sugar is noticeably darker
in color and has a stronger
molasses taste.

½ cup	orange juice	125 mL
¼ cup	soy sauce	60 mL
¼ cup	ketchup	60 mL
¼ cup	packed brown sugar	60 mL
2 tbsp	balsamic vinegar	30 mL
1	clove garlic, minced	1
1½ tsp	cornstarch	7 mL
36	Appetizer Beef Meatballs (see recipe, page 112)	36

1. In a medium saucepan, stir together orange juice, soy sauce, ketchup, brown sugar, vinegar, garlic and cornstarch until smooth. Bring to a boil over medium heat, stirring constantly, until sauce is thick and smooth.

2. Stir in cooked meatballs; cover and simmer for 5 minutes or until heated through.

Party Meatballs with Spicy Chili Sauce

For sauce with a fiery kick, add more Asian chili sauce or use your favorite hot pepper sauce to taste.

Tip

A pound (500 g) of store-bought frozen cooked chicken and beef meatballs, available in the frozen foods section of supermarkets, can be used as a convenient substitute for homemade meatballs. Look for ones lower in fat and sodium as a healthy food choice.

¾ cup	chili sauce	175 mL
½ cup	grape jelly	125 mL
1 to 2 tsp	Asian chili sauce	5 to 10 mL
36	frozen Appetizer Beef Meatballs (see recipe, page 112) or Appetizer Chicken Meatballs (see recipe, page 110)	36

1. In a medium saucepan, combine chili sauce, grape jelly and Asian chili sauce to taste. Place over medium heat and cook until jelly melts. Add meatballs and stir to coat with sauce.

2. Cover and simmer over medium heat, stirring often, for 15 minutes or until meatballs are heated through. Transfer to a warmed serving dish.

Salads

continued...

Main Course Salads

Caesar Salad

The king of tossed salads was named after a Tijuana restaurateur by the name of Caesar Cardini. Here, mayonnaise gives this classic salad an even creamier texture than the original.

Tips

Raw or coddled eggs are considered taboo in salads because they may contain salmonella bacteria. Mayonnaise is used instead.

Make sure salad greens are washed and dried thoroughly, preferably in a salad spinner, for best results. Homemade croutons make a definite flavor difference, but 3 cups (750 mL) store-bought croutons work in a pinch.

1/3 cup	olive oil	75 mL
2 tbsp	light mayonnaise	30 mL
2 tbsp	fresh lemon juice	30 mL
2 tbsp	water	30 mL
1 tsp	Dijon mustard	5 mL
2	cloves garlic, minced	2
3	anchovy fillets, chopped, or 1 tbsp (15 mL) anchovy paste	3
1/4 tsp	freshly ground black pepper	1 mL
1	large head romaine lettuce, torn into bite-size pieces (about 12 cups/3 L)	1
6	slices bacon, cooked crisp and crumbled (optional)	6
	Garlic croutons (see recipe, below)	
1/3 cup	freshly grated Parmesan cheese	75 mL
	Salt	

1. In a food processor, combine oil, mayonnaise, lemon juice, water, mustard, garlic, anchovy fillets and pepper; process until smooth and creamy.

2. Arrange lettuce in salad bowl; pour dressing over and toss lightly. Add croutons; sprinkle with crumbled bacon, if using, and Parmesan cheese. Toss again. Taste and season with salt and pepper, if needed. Serve immediately.

Garlic Croutons

- Preheat oven to 375°F (190°C)
- Rimmed baking sheet

4 cups	cubed crusty bread (1/2-inch/1 cm cubes)	1 L
2 tbsp	olive oil	30 mL
1	clove garlic, minced	1
2 tbsp	freshly grated Parmesan cheese	30 mL

1. Place bread cubes in a bowl. Combine oil and garlic; drizzle over bread cubes and toss. Sprinkle with Parmesan and toss again. Arrange on baking sheet in single layer. Toast in preheated oven, stirring once, for about 10 minutes or until golden.

Classic Greek Salad

Greek's signature salad sings when you use the ripest tomatoes and really good olive oil, along with imported Greek feta and oregano.

Tip

As in all salads, I use the finest extra virgin olive oils for best flavor. Experiment with oils from different countries. Greece, for example, is a major olive-producing country, and you can find a selection of oils in fine food shops and in some supermarkets that stock various good oils. (See page 149 for more information about olive oil.)

2	ripe tomatoes, halved lengthwise, cut into wedges	2
1	small Vidalia or red onion, halved, cut into wedges	1
½	English cucumber, quartered lengthwise, cut into thick slices	½
1	red bell pepper, cut into cubes	1
1	yellow or green bell pepper, cut into cubes	1
¼ cup	olive oil (see Tip, left)	60 mL
2 tbsp	fresh lemon juice	30 mL
1 tsp	dried oregano leaves	5 mL
¼ tsp	salt	1 mL
	Freshly ground black pepper	
2 tbsp	chopped fresh flat-leaf (Italian) parsley	30 mL
4 oz	feta cheese, cubed	125 g
12	kalamata olives	12

1. In a salad bowl, combine tomatoes, onion, cucumber and peppers.

2. In a separate bowl, whisk together oil, lemon juice, oregano, salt and pepper. Pour dressing over vegetables and gently toss. Sprinkle with parsley and garnish with feta and olives. Serve immediately.

Gazpacho Salad

2 pints	cherry tomatoes, halved or quartered, if large	1 L
1	red bell pepper, diced	1
1	yellow bell pepper, diced	1
1	green bell pepper, diced	1
1	sweet onion, such as Vidalia, coarsely chopped	1
½	seedless cucumber, quartered lengthwise, thickly sliced	½
⅓ cup	olive oil	75 mL
¼ cup	sherry or red wine vinegar	60 mL
	Salt and freshly ground black pepper	
⅓ cup	coarsely chopped fresh cilantro or parsley	75 mL

Makes 6 to 8 servings

Savor the vibrant, fresh flavors of Spain's cold summer soup in a salad instead.

Tip

The vegetables can be prepared earlier in the day and refrigerated. Toss them with the vinaigrette just before serving to prevent them from getting waterlogged.

1. In a large serving bowl, combine tomatoes, peppers, onion and cucumber.

2. In a small bowl, whisk together oil, vinegar and salt and pepper to taste.

3. Just before serving, pour vinaigrette over vegetables and toss. Sprinkle with cilantro. Serve immediately.

Napa Cabbage Salad with Sesame Ginger Dressing

The appealing combination of ginger and sesame makes for a refreshing, light salad.

Tip

To toast sesame seeds: Heat a nonstick skillet over medium heat. Add seeds and toast, stirring often, for 2 to 3 minutes or until nicely colored.

Variation

To make this a main course salad, add thin strips of grilled steak (such as Easy Asian Flank Steak, page 240) or roasted chicken.

4 oz	snow peas, ends trimmed, cut in half on the diagonal	125 g
4 cups	shredded Napa cabbage, lightly packed	1 L
1	red bell pepper, cut into thin 2-inch (5 cm) long strips	1
3	green onions, thinly sliced on the diagonal	3
1 tbsp	toasted sesame seeds	15 mL

Ginger Sesame Dressing

2 tbsp	rice vinegar	30 mL
1 tbsp	vegetable oil	15 mL
1 tbsp	soy sauce	15 mL
2 tsp	finely grated gingerroot	10 mL
1	clove garlic, grated	1
2 tsp	brown sugar	10 mL
1 tsp	toasted sesame oil	5 mL

1. In a small saucepan of boiling water, cook snow peas for 30 seconds, until bright green and crisp. Drain and chill in cold water. Place in a kitchen towel to dry.

2. In a serving bowl, combine snow peas, cabbage, red pepper and green onions.

3. *Dressing:* In a small saucepan, whisk together vinegar, oil, soy sauce, ginger, garlic and brown sugar. Heat over medium-low heat for about 2 minutes or until dressing is warm and fragrant. Stir in sesame oil.

4. Pour warm dressing over salad and toss well. Sprinkle with sesame seeds. Serve immediately (the salad turns limp quickly).

Greens with Grapefruit and Avocado

This is a favorite salad to serve for brunch. Assemble it just before serving to prevent the greens from wilting. Make the dressing ahead and store in a condiment squeeze bottle for easy drizzling over the salad.

Tip

If preparing fennel ahead, thinly slice and place in ice water to prevent discoloration. Drain well and pat dry before adding to salad.

Variation

Use orange juice in the dressing instead of grapefruit juice and 3 oranges on the salad.

2 tbsp	fresh grapefruit juice	30 mL
4 tsp	red wine vinegar	20 mL
4 tsp	honey Dijon mustard	20 mL
1/4 cup	light mayonnaise	60 mL
1/4 cup	olive oil	60 mL
	Salt and freshly ground black pepper	
1	head Boston lettuce	1
1	bunch watercress, tough stems removed	1
1	small fennel bulb, ends trimmed	1
2	grapefruit, peeled and sectioned	2
1	Hass avocado, peeled and sliced	1

1. In a bowl, whisk together grapefruit juice, vinegar and mustard until smooth. Whisk in mayonnaise and oil. Season with salt and pepper. Transfer to a squeeze bottle or jar.

2. Tear lettuce into bite-size pieces and arrange on a large serving platter. Top with an even layer of watercress.

3. Cut fennel lengthwise into quarters; remove core and cut into thin lengthwise strips. Scatter over greens. Drizzle salad with dressing; top with grapefruit sections and avocado. Serve immediately.

Baby Greens with Roasted Pears and Roquefort

Makes 6 servings

Here's a popular salad on restaurant menus that is easy to make at home for a special dinner. Serve it as a starter course or at the end of the meal as a cheese course.

Tips

If desired, replace part of the olive oil with walnut oil in the dressing.

You can use any creamy blue cheese or goat cheese.

- Preheat oven to 400°F (200°C)
- Rimmed baking sheets

Roasted Pears

4	Bartlett or Anjou pears	4
¼ cup	ruby port or pomegranate juice	60 mL
1 tbsp	olive oil	15 mL

Salad

½ cup	coarsely chopped walnuts	125 mL
⅓ cup	olive oil	75 mL
2 tbsp	red wine vinegar	30 mL
1 tbsp	honey Dijon mustard	15 mL
	Salt and freshly ground black pepper	
10 cups	lightly packed mixed baby salad greens	2.5 L
8 oz	Gorgonzola or Roquefort cheese, cut into pieces	250 g

1. *Roasted Pears:* Peel pears, cut into quarters and core. Cut each pear quarter into 3 to 4 thick slices. Place in a bowl and toss with port and olive oil. Arrange in a single layer on baking sheet and roast in preheated oven for 15 to 20 minutes or until slices are just tender. Let cool. (Can be roasted up to 1 day ahead. Place in an airtight container and refrigerate.)

2. *Salad:* Reduce oven temperature to 350°F (180°C). Place walnuts on another baking sheet. Place in oven, stirring once, for 5 to 7 minutes or until lightly toasted. Let cool.

3. In a bowl, whisk together olive oil, vinegar and mustard. Season with salt and pepper to taste.

4. Place greens in a large bowl. Pour dressing over and lightly toss. Arrange on large salad plates. Sprinkle with cheese and walnuts. Arrange pear slices over salad and serve immediately.

Orange Spinach Salad with Almonds

This is one of my favorite salads to serve for a brunch. It's a good match with egg-based dishes thanks to the sweetness of the oranges and the dressing.

Tips

Remove peel and white pith from oranges. Working over medium bowl, cut between membranes to release segments.

To toast almonds: Place nuts on a baking sheet in a 350°F (180°C) oven for 6 to 8 minutes, stirring occasionally, until lightly toasted.

Variation

Strawberry Spinach Salad with Poppy Seed Dressing

In dressing, omit fines herbes and add 1 tbsp (15 mL) poppy seeds. Instead of oranges, use 1½ cups (375 mL) sliced strawberries.

Dressing

¼ cup	olive oil	60 mL
2 tbsp	white wine or rice vinegar	30 mL
1 tbsp	honey Dijon mustard	15 mL
1 tsp	dried fines herbes or tarragon leaves	5 mL
1 tsp	grated orange zest	5 mL
¼ tsp	salt	1 mL
¼ tsp	freshly ground black pepper	1 mL

Salad

8 cups	baby spinach	2 L
3	seedless oranges, peeled and sectioned (see Tips, left)	3
1	large Hass avocado, peeled and diced	1
3	green onions, sliced	3
⅓ cup	slivered almonds, toasted (see Tips, left)	75 mL

1. *Dressing:* In a bowl, whisk together oil, vinegar, honey mustard, fines herbes, orange zest, salt and pepper.

2. *Salad:* In a large bowl, combine spinach, orange sections, avocado and green onions. Pour dressing over salad and lightly toss. Sprinkle with almonds and serve immediately.

Spinach, Mushroom and Carrot Salad

This party salad is not complicated to make, neither is it expensive to prepare. But the flavors make it special enough to serve for company — with tangy lime juice, mustard and cumin balancing the sweetness of raisins and carrots.

Tip

This colorful salad can be made up to 4 hours ahead and refrigerated. Add the dressing and toss just before serving.

Variation

Use 1½ tsp (7 mL) dried fines herbes instead of cumin.

8 cups	lightly packed baby spinach	2 L
1½ cups	sliced mushrooms	375 mL
2 cups	peeled shredded carrots	500 mL
1½ cups	seedless cucumber, halved lengthwise and sliced crosswise	375 mL
1	small red onion, thinly sliced	1
⅓ cup	dark raisins	75 mL

Dressing

¼ cup	olive oil	60 mL
2 tbsp	fresh lime juice	30 mL
1 tbsp	liquid honey	15 mL
2 tsp	Dijon mustard	10 mL
¾ tsp	ground cumin	3 mL
1	clove garlic, minced	1
½ tsp	salt	2 mL
¼ tsp	freshly ground black pepper	1 mL

1. In a serving bowl, layer one-third of the spinach, all the sliced mushrooms, another one-third of the spinach, all the shredded carrots, then remaining spinach. Layer cucumbers, onion and raisins over top. Cover and refrigerate up to 4 hours.

2. *Dressing:* In a bowl, whisk together oil, lime juice, honey, mustard, cumin, garlic, salt and pepper. Just before serving, drizzle over salad and toss gently.

Grilled Portobello Salad with Goat Cheese

Makes 4 servings as a main course or 6 as a side dish

Meaty portobello mushrooms team up deliciously with creamy goat cheese. This elegant dish is perfect with crusty bread for a simple Sunday brunch or a light supper.

Tips

Soak wooden skewers in water for at least 15 minutes to prevent burning.

If desired, replace half the olive oil with walnut oil.

- Preheat greased barbecue grill or stovetop grill pan to medium-high
- Wooden skewers, soaked

1/3 cup	olive oil	75 mL
3 tbsp	balsamic vinegar	45 mL
1 tbsp	honey Dijon mustard	15 mL
1 tbsp	chopped fresh thyme or 1 tsp (5 mL) dried thyme leaves	15 mL
1/2 tsp	salt	2 mL
1/2 tsp	freshly ground black pepper	2 mL
4	large portobello mushrooms (about 1 1/4 lbs/625 g)	4
8 cups	baby romaine lettuce	2 L
8	strips bacon, cooked crisp and crumbled (optional)	8
5 oz	goat cheese, crumbled	150 g
1/2 cup	toasted walnuts, coarsely chopped	125 mL

1. In a bowl, whisk together oil, vinegar, mustard, thyme, salt and pepper.

2. Wash mushrooms and wrap in a kitchen towel to dry. Separate stems from tops and set tops aside. Thread stems onto wooden skewers. Brush stems and mushroom tops with 1/4 cup (60 mL) of the dressing.

3. Place skewers and mushroom tops on grill or in batches in grill pan; cook for 6 to 8 minutes, turning once and brushing with dressing, until softened. Transfer to a cutting board and cut mushroom tops into thick slices.

4. Place lettuce in a large bowl. Pour in enough of the remaining dressing to coat the lettuce; toss to coat. Divide among 4 serving plates and top with mushrooms. Sprinkle with bacon bits (if using), goat cheese and walnuts. Serve immediately.

Bean Salad with Mustard Dill Dressing

Bean salad is another staple we've grown up with over the years. Originally this salad used canned string beans, but fresh beans give it a new lease on taste, as does the addition of fiber-packed chickpeas.

Variation

Instead of chickpeas, use canned mixed beans. This includes a combination of chickpeas, red and white kidney beans and black-eyed peas. It's available in supermarkets.

1 lb	green beans	500 g
1	can (19 oz/540 mL) chickpeas, drained and rinsed	1
⅓ cup	chopped red onions	75 mL

Dressing

2 tbsp	olive oil	30 mL
2 tbsp	red wine vinegar	30 mL
1 tbsp	Dijon mustard	15 mL
1 tbsp	granulated sugar	15 mL
¼ tsp	salt	1 mL
¼ tsp	freshly ground black pepper	1 mL
2 tbsp	finely chopped fresh dill	30 mL

1. Trim ends of beans; cut into 1-inch (2.5 cm) lengths. In a large pot of boiling salted water, cook beans for 3 to 5 minutes (start timing when water returns to a boil) or until tender-crisp. Drain; rinse under cold water to chill. Wrap in a clean, dry towel to absorb moisture.

2. In a serving bowl, combine green beans, chickpeas and onions.

3. *Dressing:* In a small bowl, whisk together oil, vinegar, mustard, sugar, salt and pepper until smooth. Stir in dill.

4. Pour over beans and toss well. Refrigerate until serving time.

Green Bean and Plum Tomato Salad

When preparing this dish ahead, I like to keep the blanched green beans, tomatoes and dressing separate and toss them just before serving to prevent the salad from getting soggy.

Tip

Use the terrific mustardy dressing with other favorite vegetable salad mixtures and crisp greens.

1 lb	young green beans, trimmed	500 g
8	small plum tomatoes (about 1 lb/500 g)	8
2	green onions, sliced	2

Dressing

¼ cup	olive oil	60 mL
4 tsp	red wine vinegar	20 mL
1 tbsp	whole-seed mustard	15 mL
1	clove garlic, minced	1
½ tsp	granulated sugar	2 mL
¼ tsp	salt	1 mL
¼ tsp	freshly ground black pepper	1 mL
¼ cup	chopped fresh parsley	60 mL

1. In a medium saucepan of boiling salted water, cook beans for 3 to 5 minutes or until just tender-crisp. Drain and rinse under cold water to chill; drain well. Wrap in a clean, dry towel to absorb moisture.

2. Cut plum tomatoes in half lengthwise; using a small spoon, scoop out centers. Cut each piece again in half lengthwise; place in a bowl. Just before serving, combine beans, tomatoes and green onions in a serving bowl.

3. *Dressing:* In a small bowl, whisk together oil, vinegar, mustard, garlic, sugar, salt and pepper. Stir in parsley. Pour dressing over salad and toss well.

Grilled Vegetable Salad

Makes 4 servings

This delectable grilled salad can be made with whatever vegetables you have on hand. Other vegetables suggestions include sliced baby eggplant, thickly sliced fennel or thick asparagus spears.

Tips

Soak wooden skewers in cold water for 15 minutes to prevent them from burning when you're grilling the onions.

If desired, add 1 or 2 small Italian eggplants, cut into thin slices, as part of the vegetable assortment for grilling.

● Wooden skewers, soaked

1	Vidalia onion	1
1	red bell pepper	1
1	yellow bell pepper	1
3	small zucchini	3

Dressing

2 tbsp	olive oil	30 mL
1 tbsp	balsamic vinegar	15 mL
1 tbsp	red wine vinegar	15 mL
1 tsp	Dijon mustard	5 mL
1	large clove garlic, minced	1
1 tbsp	finely chopped fresh parsley	15 mL
2 tsp	finely chopped fresh rosemary or thyme leaves	10 mL
½ tsp	salt	2 mL
½ tsp	freshly ground black pepper	2 mL

1. Cut onion into 4 thick slices; insert skewers through slices to prevent them from falling apart when grilling. Cut peppers into quarters; remove ribs and seeds. Cut zucchini crosswise into halves and then cut each piece in half lengthwise. Arrange vegetables on a baking sheet.

2. *Dressing:* In a bowl, combine oil, vinegars, mustard, garlic, parsley, rosemary, salt and pepper. Brush vegetables with vinaigrette and let marinate at room temperature for 30 minutes or for up to 4 hours.

3. Preheat greased barbecue grill to medium-high. Grill vegetables for 10 to 15 minutes, turning occasionally; remove vegetables as they become tender-crisp. Transfer to a serving platter; serve warm or at room temperature.

Blue Cheese Dressing or Dip

You'll never go back to store-bought blue cheese dressing once you try this tasty homemade version. Buttermilk is low in fat, and if you use light sour cream, you'll lighten the calories on your salad while keeping the rich, creamy taste. This dressing also makes a fabulous dip for vegetables or chicken wings.

Tip

Use the dressing the same day you make it. It doesn't maintain its thick creaminess when stored in the refrigerator for more than a day.

4 oz	crumbled blue cheese	125 g
½ cup	regular or light sour cream	125 mL
½ cup	buttermilk	125 mL
1 tbsp	white wine vinegar	15 mL
2 tsp	Dijon mustard	10 mL
2 tbsp	finely chopped fresh chives or parsley	30 mL
	Salt and freshly ground black pepper	

1. In a bowl, mash blue cheese with sour cream until smooth but with a few chunks remaining. Stir in buttermilk, vinegar and mustard. Add chives and season with salt and generously with pepper.

Creamy Avocado Dressing or Dip

Follow the recipe above, but replace the blue cheese with 1 small ripe Hass avocado, peeled and chopped, and use 2 tbsp (30 mL) fresh lime juice instead of vinegar. Purée ingredients, except chives, in a food processor until smooth. Transfer to a bowl. Add chives, 2 tbsp (30 mL) chopped fresh cilantro and 1 jalapeño pepper, seeded and minced, or hot pepper sauce to taste.

This makes a thick dressing, ideal as a topper for a tomato salad or cold poached salmon or as a dip for tortilla chips or vegetables. Place in an airtight container, with the surface of the dip covered with plastic wrap to prevent discoloration, and refrigerate for up to 4 hours. Makes 1⅓ cups (325 mL).

French Salad Dressing

Makes ½ cup (125 mL)

Why buy expensive bottled salad dressings when it's so convenient to have this great-tasting salad dressing on hand?

Variation

Italian Salad Dressing

Use balsamic vinegar instead of red wine vinegar and replace the fines herbes with ½ tsp (2 mL) each dried basil and oregano.

⅓ cup	olive or vegetable oil	75 mL
2 tbsp	red wine vinegar	30 mL
1½ tsp	Dijon mustard	7 mL
1	small clove garlic, minced	1
1 tsp	dried fines herbes	5 mL
Pinch	granulated sugar	Pinch
	Salt and freshly ground black pepper	

1. In a bowl, stir together oil, vinegar, mustard, garlic and fines herbes. Season with sugar, salt and pepper to taste. Store in covered jar in the refrigerator.

Creamy Coleslaw

Makes 6 servings

A family barbecue and picnic calls for a generous bowl of old-fashioned cabbage slaw with a creamy mayonnaise-mustard dressing.

Variation

Waldorf Coleslaw

Substitute 2 chopped large stalks celery for the carrots, and add 2 diced apples and ¾ cup (175 mL) coarsely chopped walnuts.

8 cups	finely shredded green cabbage	2 L
5	green onions, sliced	5
2	carrots, peeled and shredded	2
2 tbsp	chopped fresh parsley	30 mL
½ cup	light mayonnaise	125 mL
2 tbsp	liquid honey	30 mL
2 tbsp	cider vinegar	30 mL
1 tbsp	Dijon mustard	15 mL
½ tsp	celery seeds (optional)	2 mL
½ tsp	salt	2 mL
¼ tsp	freshly ground black pepper	1 mL

1. In a serving bowl, combine cabbage, green onions, carrots and parsley.

2. In another bowl, stir together mayonnaise, honey, vinegar, mustard, celery seeds, if using, salt and pepper. Pour over cabbage mixture; toss to coat well. Refrigerate until ready to serve.

Warm Bacon Cabbage Slaw

You'll find that kids love this stir-fry version of a cabbage salad — and so will you. It's a great way to appreciate this nutritious and economical vegetable.

Tip

Buy a convenient bag of shredded cabbage at your supermarket and this salad is made in no time.

1/4 cup	sour cream or plain yogurt	60 mL
2 tbsp	light mayonnaise	30 mL
2 tbsp	cider vinegar	30 mL
1 tbsp	Dijon mustard	15 mL
1 tbsp	packed brown sugar	15 mL
4	slices bacon, chopped	4
4 cups	shredded green cabbage	1 L
2	stalks celery, sliced	2
3	green onions, sliced	3
	Salt and freshly ground black pepper	

1. In a small bowl, whisk together sour cream, mayonnaise, vinegar, mustard and brown sugar.

2. In large nonstick skillet over medium-high heat, cook bacon, stirring, for 3 minutes or until crisp. Transfer to paper towels to drain. Drain all but 2 tsp (10 mL) fat from skillet. Add cabbage, celery and green onions; cook, stirring, for 2 to 3 minutes or until cabbage is wilted.

3. Remove from heat; stir in sour cream mixture. Sprinkle with bacon; season with salt and pepper to taste. Serve immediately.

Carrot Raisin Salad

If you find it challenging to get your kids to eat vegetables, try this easy-to-prepare carrot salad, sweetened with raisins and with a creamy dressing. It certainly was a hit with my kids when they were growing up.

Tip

This salad holds well and can be made up to 1 day ahead.

3 cups	coarsely shredded carrots (about 5 to 6)	750 mL
1/4 cup	golden raisins or dried cranberries	60 mL
1/4 cup	chopped fresh parsley	60 mL
1/4 cup	light mayonnaise	60 mL
1/4 cup	plain yogurt	60 mL
1 tbsp	cider vinegar	15 mL
2 tsp	honey Dijon mustard	10 mL
2 tsp	grated orange zest	10 mL
	Salt and freshly ground black pepper	

1. In a serving bowl, combine carrots, raisins and parsley.

2. In a bowl, whisk together mayonnaise, yogurt, vinegar and mustard. Add orange zest and season with salt and pepper. Pour over salad and mix well. Serve chilled.

Best-Ever Potato Salad

If anything signals the arrival of summer days and backyard barbecues, it's a trusty potato salad. My version goes beyond tossing potatoes with mayonnaise. In this recipe, warm potatoes are steeped in a tasty marinade before mayonnaise is added. The result? A summertime family favorite.

Variation

You can also add 3 chopped hard-cooked eggs and ¾ cup (175 mL) frozen peas, rinsed under hot water and drained well.

6	new potatoes (about 2 lbs/1 kg)	6
2 tbsp	red wine vinegar	30 mL
1 tbsp	Dijon mustard	15 mL
1	clove garlic, minced	1
4	green onions, sliced	4
2	stalks celery, diced	2
¼ cup	chopped fresh parsley or dill	60 mL
½ cup	light mayonnaise	125 mL
¼ cup	sour cream or plain yogurt	60 mL
½ tsp	salt	2 mL
	Freshly ground black pepper	

1. In a medium saucepan of boiling salted water, cook whole potatoes for 20 to 25 minutes, until just tender. Drain; when cool enough to handle, peel and cut into ½-inch (1 cm) cubes. Place in a serving bowl.

2. In a small bowl, stir together vinegar, mustard and garlic; pour over warm potatoes and toss gently. Let cool to room temperature. Stir in green onions, celery and parsley.

3. In a bowl, combine mayonnaise, sour cream, salt and pepper to taste. Fold into potato mixture until evenly coated. Refrigerate until serving time.

Caesar Potato Salad

Here, I've borrowed ingredients from the popular Caesar salad dressing to give new potatoes a tasty twist.

If you like, cook or microwave 4 bacon strips until crisp, then crumble and sprinkle over salad along with the parsley.

Tips

Refrigerate the salad if making ahead, but let it come to room temperature before serving.

Use potatoes the same size so they cook evenly.

2 lbs	small new potatoes, scrubbed	1 kg
¼ cup	light mayonnaise	60 mL
2 tbsp	olive oil	30 mL
2 tbsp	fresh lemon juice	30 mL
2 tsp	Dijon mustard	10 mL
2 tsp	anchovy paste or 2 minced anchovy fillets	10 mL
1 tsp	Worcestershire sauce	5 mL
1	large clove garlic, minced	1
	Salt and freshly ground black pepper	
	Romaine lettuce	
2 tbsp	chopped fresh parsley	30 mL

1. In a large saucepan of boiling salted water, cook potatoes for 15 minutes or until just tender when pierced. Drain; let cool slightly. Cut into halves or quarters. Place in a bowl.

2. In a small bowl, whisk together mayonnaise, oil, lemon juice, mustard, anchovy paste, Worcestershire sauce and garlic; season with salt and pepper to taste. Pour over warm potatoes; gently toss to coat. Cover and refrigerate up to 4 hours.

3. Arrange in a lettuce-lined serving bowl; sprinkle with parsley.

Deli Egg and Potato Salad

Why settle for takeout at your supermarket deli when you can make this chunky potato and egg salad flecked with dill pickles? Add crusty rolls and sliced cold cuts for a ready-to-go picnic lunch.

Tip

Can be prepared ahead, covered and refrigerated, for up to 2 days.

1½ lbs	small new potatoes	750 g
⅓ cup	light mayonnaise	75 mL
⅓ cup	sour cream	75 mL
1 tbsp	whole-seed mustard	15 mL
½ tsp	salt	2 mL
¼ tsp	freshly ground black pepper	1 mL
4	hard-cooked eggs, chopped (see Tip, page 38)	4
½ cup	diced celery	125 mL
½ cup	diced dill pickle	125 mL
3	green onions, sliced	3
2 tbsp	chopped fresh dill or parsley	30 mL

1. In a saucepan of lightly salted boiling water, cook potatoes for 15 minutes or until tender when pierced. Drain; when cool enough to handle, cut into ½-inch (1 cm) cubes.

2. In a bowl, combine mayonnaise, sour cream, mustard, salt and pepper. Pour over potatoes. Add eggs, celery, pickles, green onions and dill; gently toss to coat. Cover and refrigerate. Remove from refrigerator 30 minutes before serving.

Italian Pasta Salad

Pasta salads are always a hit. They brighten up a buffet, backyard barbecue or your dinner table. Served with Herb Garlic Bread (see recipe, page 48), this salad is a meal in itself.

Tip

Dried basil and oregano can be replaced with 1 tbsp (15 mL) each chopped fresh. (As a general rule, when substituting fresh for dried herbs use three times the amount of fresh for the dried.)

Variation

You can also add 4 oz (125 g) pepperoni, salami or ham, cut into thin 1-inch (2.5 cm) strips.

8 oz	pasta such as fusilli or penne	250 g
4 oz	provolone cheese, cut into small cubes	125 g
1 cup	cherry tomatoes, halved or quartered, if large	250 mL
1/3 cup	diced red onions	75 mL
1/2	large red bell pepper, cut into thin 1 1/2-inch (4 cm) strips	1/2
1/2	large green bell pepper, cut into thin 1 1/2-inch (4 cm) strips	1/2
1/3 cup	kalamata olives (optional)	75 mL
1/3 cup	finely chopped fresh parsley	75 mL

Dressing

1/4 cup	olive oil	60 mL
2 tbsp	red wine vinegar	30 mL
1 tbsp	Dijon mustard	15 mL
1	large clove garlic, minced	1
1 tsp	dried basil leaves	5 mL
1 tsp	dried oregano leaves	5 mL
1/2 tsp	salt	2 mL
1/4 tsp	freshly ground black pepper	1 mL

1. Cook pasta in a large pot of boiling salted water until tender but still firm. Drain; rinse under cold water and drain well.

2. In a large serving bowl, combine pasta, cheese cubes, tomatoes, onions, peppers, olives and parsley.

3. *Dressing:* In a bowl, combine oil, vinegar, mustard, garlic, basil, oregano, salt and pepper.

4. Pour dressing over pasta mixture; toss until well coated. Let stand at room temperature for up to 30 minutes, allowing flavors to blend. Refrigerate if making ahead.

Greek Pasta Salad

Makes 6 servings

Cut preparation time way down by using store-bought tzatziki in this salad. The garlicky Greek sauce made with yogurt and cucumber is not only great for souvlaki, but also makes a delicious salad dressing to use instead of mayonnaise.

Tip

Tzatziki Sauce can be stored in an airtight container in refrigerator for up to 5 days. This recipe makes about 2 cups (500 mL).

8 oz	penne or spiral pasta	250 g
1	small red onion, chopped	1
2	red bell peppers, diced	2
¾ cup	crumbled feta cheese	175 mL
½ cup	kalamata olives	125 mL
¼ cup	chopped fresh parsley	60 mL

Dressing

¾ cup	Tzatziki Sauce (see recipe, below)	175 mL
2 tbsp	olive oil	30 mL
1 tbsp	red wine vinegar	15 mL
1 tsp	dried oregano leaves	5 mL
¼ tsp	freshly ground black pepper	1 mL

1. Cook pasta in a large pot of boiling salted water until tender but firm. Drain; rinse under cold water to chill. Drain well. In a serving bowl, combine pasta, onion, peppers, feta, olives and parsley.

2. *Dressing:* In a bowl, combine Tzatziki Sauce, oil, vinegar, oregano and pepper; toss with pasta mixture to coat. Cover and refrigerate. Remove from fridge 30 minutes before serving.

Tzatziki Sauce

3 cups	plain yogurt	750 mL
1 cup	finely chopped cucumber	250 mL
1 tsp	salt	5 mL
2	cloves garlic, minced	2
2 tsp	fresh lemon juice or red wine vinegar	10 mL

1. Place yogurt in a coffee filter– or double paper towel–lined sieve set over a bowl; cover and let drain in the refrigerator for 4 hours or until reduced to 1½ cups (375 mL).

2. In a bowl, sprinkle cucumber with salt. Let stand 20 minutes. Drain in a sieve; squeeze out excess moisture and pat dry with paper towels. In a bowl, combine yogurt, cucumber, garlic and lemon juice.

Greek Orzo Salad with Grilled Vegetables

Makes 4 servings

To accompany this vibrant salad, place thick Greek-style pita breads on the grill until lightly toasted and heated through.

Tip

The orzo salad can be made up to 4 hours ahead and is best kept at room temperature.

• Preheat greased barbecue grill or stovetop grill pan to medium-high

Dressing

1/3 cup	olive oil	75 mL
2 tbsp	red wine vinegar	30 mL
2 tbsp	balsamic vinegar	30 mL
2 tbsp	chopped fresh oregano or 2 tsp (10 mL) dried oregano leaves	30 mL
3	cloves garlic, finely chopped	3
1/2 tsp	salt	2 mL
1/2 tsp	freshly ground black pepper	2 mL

Salad

1 1/4 cups	orzo pasta	300 mL
1/3 cup	chopped fresh parsley	75 mL
3	zucchini	3
1	red bell pepper	1
1	yellow bell pepper	1
1	large sweet onion, such as Vidalia (about 12 oz/375 g)	1
4 oz	feta cheese, coarsely crumbled	125 g
12	kalamata olives	12

1. *Dressing:* In a bowl, whisk together olive oil, red wine vinegar, balsamic vinegar, oregano, garlic, salt and pepper.

2. *Salad:* In a large pot of lightly salted boiling water, cook orzo until just tender but firm. Drain; rinse under cold water to chill. Drain well. Transfer to a serving bowl; add parsley. Toss 1/3 cup (75 mL) of the dressing with orzo mixture; set aside at room temperature.

3. Cut zucchini into lengthwise quarters. Cut red and yellow peppers into 4 sections each, removing ribs and seeds. Cut onion into 4 thick slices. Brush with remaining dressing. Place on grill or in batches in grill pan; cook for 12 to 16 minutes, turning occasionally and brushing with remaining dressing, until tender-crisp.

4. Transfer vegetables to a cutting board and cut into 1-inch (2.5 cm) pieces. Add to orzo and toss lightly. Just before serving, sprinkle top with feta cheese and olives.

Mexicali Rice and Black Bean Salad

Your turn to bring the salad to the next reunion or neighborhood get-together? Here's a sure-fire winner that can be easily doubled to feed as many folks as the occasion demands. Even better, it can be made a day ahead.

Tip

To cook rice: Rinse ¾ cup (175 mL) basmati rice under cold water; drain. In a medium saucepan, bring 1½ cups (375 mL) water to a boil. Add rice and ½ tsp (2 mL) salt; cover and simmer for 15 minutes or until tender. Spread hot rice on baking sheet to cool.

2 cups	cooked basmati rice (see Tip, left)	500 mL
1	can (19 oz/540 mL) black beans, drained and rinsed	1
1 cup	cooked corn kernels	250 mL
1	red bell pepper, diced	1
4	green onions, sliced	4

Dressing

½ cup	sour cream	125 mL
2 tbsp	olive oil	30 mL
4 tsp	fresh lime or lemon juice	20 mL
1	jalapeño pepper, seeded and minced	1
1 tsp	dried oregano leaves	5 mL
1 tsp	ground cumin	5 mL
½ cup	chopped fresh cilantro or parsley	125 mL

1. In a large serving bowl, combine rice, black beans, corn, red pepper and green onions.

2. *Dressing:* In a bowl, combine sour cream, olive oil, lime juice, jalapeño, oregano and cumin. Pour over rice mixture; toss well. Cover and refrigerate for up to 8 hours. Stir in cilantro just before serving.

Tabbouleh

Makes 8 servings

The Lebanese salad, tabbouleh, made with nutty-tasting bulgur, is a good example of the vibrant comfort foods from the Mediterranean that have become so popular in recent years. This refreshing green salad is often displayed next to traditional favorites, such as potato salad and coleslaw, in the deli section of supermarkets. But you'll find it very inexpensive and easy to make in your home kitchen.

Tips

Bulgur is precooked cracked wheat that has been dried; it needs only to be soaked in water before using.

This salad keeps well for several days. It's better to add the tomatoes as a garnish just before serving to prevent the salad from becoming soggy.

¾ cup	fine bulgur (see Tips, left)	175 mL
2 cups	finely chopped fresh parsley, preferably flat-leaf (Italian)	500 mL
4	green onions, finely chopped	4
¼ cup	finely chopped fresh mint or 2 tbsp (30 mL) dried crumbled (optional)	60 mL
¼ cup	olive oil	60 mL
¼ cup	fresh lemon juice	60 mL
1 tsp	salt	5 mL
½ tsp	paprika	2 mL
¼ tsp	freshly ground black pepper	1 mL
2	tomatoes, seeded and diced	2

1. Place bulgur in a bowl; add cold water to cover. Let stand for 30 minutes. Drain in a fine sieve. Using the back of a spoon, or with your hands, squeeze out as much water as possible.

2. In a serving bowl, combine softened bulgur, parsley, green onions and mint, if using.

3. In a small bowl, stir together oil, lemon juice, salt, paprika and pepper. Pour over bulgur mixture; toss well. Cover and refrigerate until serving time. Just before serving, sprinkle with tomatoes.

Couscous Salad with Orange and Basil

I always keep couscous in my cupboard for quick-fix salads and side dishes. Here's a tasty salad that's an ideal accompaniment to grilled lamb chops or patties.

Tip

To toast almonds: Place nuts on a baking sheet in a 350°F (180°C) oven for 6 to 8 minutes, stirring occasionally, until lightly toasted.

Variation

Couscous Salad with Cumin and Cilantro
Use chopped cilantro instead of basil and add 1 tsp (5 mL) ground cumin to the dressing.

1¼ cups	chicken stock	300 mL
¼ cup	raisins or dried cranberries	60 mL
¼ cup	chopped dried apricots	60 mL
1 cup	regular or whole wheat couscous	250 mL
1	small red bell pepper, finely diced	1
3	green onions, sliced	3
¼ cup	slivered almonds, lightly toasted	60 mL
¼ cup	chopped fresh basil or parsley	60 mL
3 tbsp	olive oil	45 mL
4 tsp	red wine vinegar	20 mL
1 tsp	grated orange zest	5 mL
2 tbsp	fresh orange juice	30 mL
	Salt and freshly ground black pepper	

1. In a small saucepan, combine stock, raisins and apricots. Bring to a boil over high heat. Remove from heat and stir in couscous. Cover and let stand for 5 minutes. Fluff with a fork and let cool to room temperature, uncovered.

2. In a serving bowl, combine couscous, red pepper, green onions, almonds and basil.

3. In a small bowl, combine oil, vinegar, orange zest and orange juice. Season with salt and pepper to taste. Pour over salad and toss to coat well. Serve at room temperature.

Quinoa and Corn Salad with Cumin Lime Dressing

Quinoa, with its mild, nutty taste and high protein content, makes a great alternative to other grains in salads and soups or as a side dish. This great-tasting summer salad with corn, tomatoes and avocados can stand alone as a main dish. Or pair it with grilled chicken.

Tips

When you buy quinoa, it has been rinsed and air-dried to remove the naturally occurring bitter saponins, a resin-like coating. Still, rinse it again before use to remove any powdery residue that may remain.

Look for other interesting and healthful oils, such as avocado, pumpkin seed or almond oil, in specialty food shops and use instead of olive oil.

Instead of pumpkin seeds, try almonds, walnuts or pine nuts.

Cook extra cobs of corn, cut off the kernels and use in soups and salads.

1 cup	quinoa, rinsed well	250 mL
	Salt	
1/4 cup	olive oil	60 mL
1 tsp	grated lime zest	5 mL
2 tbsp	fresh lime juice	30 mL
1 1/2 tsp	ground cumin	7 mL
1/2 tsp	hot pepper sauce, or to taste	2 mL
	Freshly ground black pepper	
3	green onions, thinly sliced	3
2	tomatoes, seeded and diced	2
1/2	seedless cucumber, diced	1/2
2 cups	cooked fresh corn kernels (about 3 cobs)	500 mL
2	Hass avocados, peeled and diced	2
1/2 cup	coarsely chopped fresh cilantro	125 mL
1/3 cup	raw pumpkin seeds (optional)	75 mL

1. In a medium saucepan, bring 2 cups (500 mL) water to a boil over high heat. Add quinoa and 1/2 tsp (2 mL) salt. Cover, reduce heat to medium-low and simmer for 15 minutes or until quinoa is tender and water is absorbed. Uncover and fluff with a fork. Let cool.

2. In a small bowl, combine oil, lime zest and juice, cumin, hot pepper sauce and salt and pepper to taste.

3. In a serving bowl, combine quinoa, green onions, tomatoes, cucumber and corn. Pour in half the dressing and toss to coat. (Can be prepared up to 4 hours ahead; cover and refrigerate.)

4. Shortly before serving, add avocados, cilantro and pumpkin seeds, if using. Drizzle with remaining dressing and toss lightly.

Taco Salad

Makes 4 servings		

For a casual lunch or dinner, rely on this colorful salad with a Mexican flair that is a snap to assemble.

Tips

Hate shedding tears when chopping onions? To minimize the weeping problem, use a razor-sharp knife to prevent loss of juices and cover the cut onions with a paper towel as you chop them to prevent the vapors from rising to your eyes.

Fresh cilantro, also called coriander and Chinese parsley, lasts only a few days in the fridge before it deteriorates and turns tasteless. Wash cilantro well, spin dry and wrap in paper towels; store in plastic bag in the fridge. Leave the roots on — they keep the leaves fresh.

12 oz	lean ground beef	375 g
1	large clove garlic, finely chopped	1
2 tsp	chili powder	10 mL
½ cup	mild or medium salsa	125 mL

Dressing

⅓ cup	olive oil	75 mL
2 tbsp	fresh lime juice or red wine vinegar	30 mL
1 tsp	granulated sugar	5 mL
1 tsp	chili powder	5 mL
½ tsp	dried oregano leaves	2 mL
½ tsp	ground cumin	2 mL
¼ tsp	salt	1 mL
¼ tsp	freshly ground black pepper	1 mL

Salad

8 cups	torn iceberg or romaine lettuce	2 L
1	can (19 oz/540 mL) black beans, drained and rinsed	1
2	tomatoes, diced	2
1	Hass avocado, peeled and diced	1
1	small red onion, chopped	1
1 cup	shredded Cheddar cheese	250 mL
⅓ cup	sliced black olives	75 mL
⅓ cup	chopped fresh cilantro	75 mL
	Tortilla chips	

1. In a large nonstick skillet, over medium-high heat, cook beef, breaking up with a wooden spoon, for 5 minutes or until no longer pink. Drain any fat in skillet.

2. Add garlic and chili powder. Cook, stirring often, for 2 minutes. Stir in salsa and transfer to a bowl.

3. *Dressing:* In a bowl, whisk together oil, lime juice, sugar, chili powder, oregano, cumin, salt and pepper.

4. *Salad:* Place lettuce in a large shallow salad bowl. Pour in half of the dressing and lightly toss. In another bowl, combine beans, tomatoes, avocado and onion. Pour in remaining dressing and toss lightly. Spoon over lettuce and top with beef mixture. Layer with cheese, olives and cilantro. Arrange tortilla chips around edge of bowl and serve immediately.

Cobb Salad

This substantial salad made famous at Hollywood's Brown Derby in the 1930s has remained a favorite over the years.

Tip

To hard-cook eggs: Place eggs in saucepan; add cold water to cover eggs by 1 inch (2.5 cm). Place over medium-high heat; bring to a gentle rolling boil. Boil for 2 minutes; cover and remove from heat. Let stand for 10 minutes. Drain and chill eggs in cold water.

Dressing

1/3 cup	olive oil	75 mL
2 tbsp	red wine vinegar	30 mL
2 tsp	whole-seed mustard	10 mL
1/2 tsp	dried tarragon leaves	2 mL
1/2 tsp	salt	2 mL
1/4 tsp	freshly ground black pepper	1 mL

Salad

8 cups	baby salad greens	2 L
1 1/2 cups	diced cooked chicken	375 mL
2	ripe but firm tomatoes, seeded and diced	2
1	Hass avocado, peeled and cut into slices	1
2	hard-cooked eggs, sliced (see Tip, left)	2
6	slices bacon, cooked crisp and crumbled	6
3/4 cup	crumbled blue cheese	175 mL
2 tbsp	chopped fresh chives	30 mL

1. *Dressing:* In a bowl, whisk together olive oil, vinegar, mustard, tarragon, salt and pepper.

2. *Salad:* Place lettuce in a large, wide, shallow salad or serving bowl. Pour half of the dressing over greens and toss to coat well.

3. Layer with chicken, tomato, avocado, egg, bacon bits and blue cheese. Sprinkle with chives and drizzle with remaining dressing. Serve immediately.

Orange Sesame Beef and Noodle Salad

Lean beef and crunchy vegetables team with Asian seasonings in this tasty, vibrant salad. It is equally delicious made with chicken, pork or extra-firm tofu. Leftovers are great for next day's bagged lunches.

Tips

If you don't have a rasp grater, such as a Microplane, to grate orange zest, use a zester to remove the zest in thin shreds, then finely chop with a knife.

When oranges are bargain-priced, stock up for the future. Grate the zest and squeeze the juice; place in separate containers and freeze.

To get more juice out of an orange, roll on countertop or microwave on High for 20 seconds before squeezing.

Dressing

¼ cup	soy sauce	60 mL
2 tbsp	toasted sesame oil	30 mL
1 tbsp	vegetable oil	15 mL
2 tbsp	rice vinegar	30 mL
1½ tsp	grated orange zest	7 mL
2 tbsp	fresh orange juice	30 mL
1 tbsp	minced gingerroot	15 mL
2	cloves garlic, finely chopped	2
1½ tsp	granulated sugar	7 mL
1 tsp	Asian chili sauce, or to taste	5 mL

Salad

1¼ lb	flank steak or thick-cut sirloin tip steak	625 g
8 oz	linguine or spaghettini pasta	250 g
3 cups	small broccoli florets	750 mL
1	large red bell pepper, cut into thin 2-inch (5 cm) strips	1
4	green onions, sliced	4
⅓ cup	chopped fresh cilantro	75 mL

1. *Dressing:* In a bowl, combine soy sauce, sesame oil, vegetable oil, vinegar, orange zest, orange juice, ginger, garlic, sugar and chili sauce.

2. *Salad:* Place steak in a heavy, sealable plastic bag. Add ⅓ cup (75 mL) dressing, squeeze out air, seal securely and set in a bowl. Refrigerate for at least 4 hours or overnight. Refrigerate remaining dressing separately.

3. In a large saucepan of boiling salted water, cook pasta until almost tender. Add broccoli; cook for 1 minute or until tender-crisp and bright green. Drain pasta and broccoli. Rinse under cold water. Drain well.

4. In a large serving bowl, combine pasta, broccoli, red pepper and green onions. Add remaining dressing and toss to coat. Cover and refrigerate for up to 4 hours. Bring to room temperature before serving.

5. Preheat greased barbecue grill or stovetop grill pan to medium-high. Remove steak from marinade; discard marinade. Place steak on grill or in grill pan; cook for 7 to 8 minutes on each side or until browned on outside and still pink inside. Transfer to a cutting board. Let rest for 10 minutes, then cut on the diagonal into thin slices.

6. Add beef and cilantro to pasta mixture; toss gently.

Terrific Thai Chicken Salad

Many supermarkets stock a wide variety of Asian food products, including fish sauce and chili sauce. Fish sauce, also called *nam pla*, is a salty brown seasoning that is the backbone of Thai cooking.

Variations

Substitute 3 tbsp (45 mL) soy sauce for the fish sauce.

Replace rice vermicelli with the same amount of spaghettini, cooked according to package directions.

1 lb	boneless skinless chicken breasts	500 g
4 oz	rice vermicelli	125 g
½	seedless cucumber, cut into thin 2-inch (5 cm) strips	½
1	large red bell pepper, cut into thin 2-inch (5 cm) strips	1
¼ cup	chopped fresh basil, mint or cilantro	60 mL

Dressing

¼ cup	fish sauce	60 mL
3 tbsp	fresh lime juice	45 mL
2 tbsp	packed brown sugar	30 mL
1 tbsp	minced gingerroot	15 mL
1	large clove garlic, minced	1
1 tsp	Asian chili sauce or hot pepper sauce	5 mL

1. In a large saucepan, bring 2 cups (500 mL) lightly salted water to a boil; reduce heat to medium-low. Add chicken; poach for 10 to 12 minutes or until no longer pink inside. Let cool in poaching liquid. Remove and cut chicken into thin strips. (Reserve poaching liquid to use in soups and stews.)

2. Place vermicelli in a bowl and cover with boiling water. Let soak for 3 minutes to soften. Drain; chill under cold water and drain well.

3. In another bowl, combine chicken, vermicelli, cucumber, red pepper and basil.

4. *Dressing:* In a bowl, combine fish sauce, lime juice, brown sugar, ginger, garlic and chili sauce to taste. Just before serving, pour over chicken mixture; toss well. Garnish with additional basil.

Pesto Chicken Caesar Salad

Fresh basil gives a new
spin to traditional
Caesar salad.

Tips

For best results, dry
romaine leaves thoroughly,
preferably in a salad
spinner, to prevent dilution
of the creamy basil
dressing.

If fresh basil is unavailable,
substitute ½ cup (125 mL)
fresh parsley and 1½ tsp
(7 mL) dried basil.

For homemade Garlic
Croutons, see the recipe
on page 117.

Dressing

½ cup	lightly packed fresh basil leaves	125 mL
⅓ cup	olive oil	75 mL
¼ cup	fresh lemon juice	60 mL
1 tbsp	Worcestershire sauce	15 mL
1 tbsp	Dijon mustard	15 mL
2	cloves garlic, coarsely chopped	2
½ tsp	salt	2 mL
½ tsp	freshly ground black pepper	2 mL

Salad

1 lb	boneless skinless chicken breasts	500 g
3 tbsp	light mayonnaise	45 mL
10 cups	torn romaine lettuce	2.5 L
2 cups	halved cherry tomatoes	500 mL
2 cups	croutons	500 mL
⅓ cup	freshly grated Parmesan cheese	75 mL

1. *Dressing:* In a food processor, combine basil, oil, lemon juice, Worcestershire sauce, mustard, garlic, salt and pepper.

2. *Salad:* Arrange chicken in a single layer in a shallow bowl; coat with ¼ cup (60 mL) of the dressing. Cover and refrigerate for at least 30 minutes or for up to 2 hours. Refrigerate remaining dressing separately.

3. Preheat greased barbecue grill or stovetop grill pan to medium-high. Remove chicken from marinade; discard marinade. Place chicken on grill or in grill pan; cook, turning once, for 12 to 15 minutes or until no longer pink inside. Transfer to cutting board; let cool 5 minutes. Cut into diagonal slices.

3. In a small bowl, whisk remaining dressing with mayonnaise. In a salad bowl, combine romaine and cherry tomatoes. Toss with enough of the dressing to coat. Add croutons and sprinkle with Parmesan cheese. Toss lightly.

4. Divide among four serving plates; top with warm chicken slices and serve immediately.

Grilled Salmon and Romaine Salad

You won't believe how easy it is to make this elegant grilled salmon on a bed of freshly tossed greens. This meal-in-one dish is ideal for a patio supper with friends. The dressing, made quickly in the food processor, does double duty as a marinade for the salmon and a dressing for the salad.

Tip

Instead of grilling, place salmon on a broiler pan 4 inches (10 cm) below preheated broiler for the same cooking time.

- Preheat greased barbecue grill to medium-high
- Wooden skewers, soaked

Dressing

2 cups	lightly packed fresh parsley	500 mL
¼ cup	fresh orange juice	60 mL
2 tbsp	olive oil	30 mL
2 tbsp	red wine vinegar	30 mL
1 tbsp	Dijon mustard	15 mL
½ tsp	salt	2 mL
½ tsp	freshly ground black pepper	2 mL
1	clove garlic, minced	1
1 tsp	grated orange zest	5 mL

Salad

1	center-cut piece salmon fillet (1¼ lbs/625 g)	1
8 cups	torn romaine lettuce	2 L
2 cups	halved cherry tomatoes	500 mL
½	medium seedless cucumber, halved lengthwise and sliced	½

1. *Dressing:* In a food processor, process parsley, orange juice, oil, vinegar, mustard, salt and pepper until parsley is very finely chopped. Transfer to a glass measure. Stir in garlic and orange zest.

2. *Salad:* Remove skin from salmon and slice lengthwise into 4 long strips. Thread salmon lengthwise onto skewers. Place in shallow baking dish to hold salmon in an even layer. Spread with ¼ cup (60 mL) of the dressing. Let marinate at room temperature for 15 minutes, turning occasionally.

3. Place salmon on preheated grill; grill, brushing with dressing, turning once, for about 4 minutes per side or until fish flakes easily.

4. Meanwhile, in a bowl, combine romaine, cherry tomatoes and cucumber. Pour over remaining dressing; toss to lightly coat. Divide salad among serving plates; top with salmon.

All about Olive Oil

Olive oil is the pressed juice from olives, a fruit, and there are dozens of varieties, each with its own distinct flavor and characteristics.

Olive oils add not only great flavor to foods, they also have certain health advantages. Rich in monounsaturated fats, olive oils reduce the level of harmful cholesterol in our blood and at the same time leave the good cholesterol intact.

There are two grades of oil available in our market. Extra virgin olive oil is the best quality, retaining the fresh, natural flavor of the olives and with a maximum acidity level of 1% oleic acid. It's ideal for cooking and salads and for flavoring dishes before serving. Regular olive oil comes from olives that have been refined to produce a colorless and flavorless oil. Virgin olive oil is added to give it some added character. It is used primarily in cooking. "Light" olive oil is not lighter in calories, only in flavor. It's a refined oil and overpriced when compared to other quality oils in the same price bracket. If you want a mild-flavored oil, mix canola oil with some good-quality extra virgin instead.

What to look for in an oil

Olives oils are a lot like wines — there are many to choose from and they vary greatly in price and quality. Sample a variety to decide what appeals most to your taste buds, as well as budget.

- Read the bottle label to help you make an informed choice. Lower-priced brands of oils, although bottled in a particular country, are often a blend from several different countries. The more expensive olive oils, however, often include the name of the producer and region, along with a vintage date on their labels.

- Don't judge an oil by its color. Oils range from buttery yellow to vivid green depending on the olive variety and stage of ripeness at harvest time. Color does, however, give a clue to flavor. Generally, light-colored oils are more subtle than the robust darker oils.

- Olive oil loses it flavor and color over time, so use soon after purchase. Store oils in a cool, dark place, away from direct light. Do not store in the refrigerator. When properly capped, oil will keep for 1 year.

Tuna Niçoise Salad

This Mediterranean dish is more of a main course than a salad. Tuna, potatoes, green beans, tomatoes, eggs, capers, and black olives give this dish a wonderful balance of flavors. It's simple to make and very sophisticated to serve.

Tip

To hard-cook eggs: Place eggs in saucepan; add cold water to cover eggs by 1 inch (2.5 cm). Place over medium-high heat; bring to a gentle rolling boil. Boil for 2 minutes; cover and remove from heat. Let stand for 10 minutes. Drain and chill eggs in cold water.

Dressing

1/3 cup	olive oil	75 mL
2 tbsp	red wine vinegar	30 mL
1 tbsp	balsamic vinegar	15 mL
1 tbsp	Dijon mustard	15 mL
2	cloves garlic, minced	2
1/4 tsp	salt	1 mL
1/4 tsp	freshly ground black pepper	1 mL

Salad

1 lb	small new potatoes, halved or quartered	500 g
8 oz	green beans, ends trimmed, cut into 2-inch (5 cm) pieces	250 g
1	small red onion, thinly sliced	1
1	can (6 oz/170 g) solid white tuna, drained and flaked	1
2	hard-cooked eggs, quartered (see Tip, left)	2
2	ripe tomatoes, cut into wedges	2
12	Niçoise or other black olives	12
2 tbsp	capers, rinsed	30 mL
2 tbsp	chopped fresh parsley or chives	30 mL

1. *Dressing:* In a bowl, whisk together oil, red wine and balsamic vinegars, mustard, garlic, salt and pepper.

2. *Salad:* In a large saucepan of boiling salted water, cook potatoes for 10 minutes or until tender when pierced. Remove with slotted spoon to a bowl. Add 2 tbsp (25 mL) of the dressing and toss to coat.

3. Add green beans to same saucepan and bring to a boil; cook for 3 to 5 minutes or until tender-crisp. Drain and chill under cold water; pat dry with paper towels. Place in another bowl with onion. Add 2 tbsp (30 mL) of the dressing and toss to coat.

4. On a serving platter, arrange potatoes in center and surround with green bean mixture. Arrange tuna on top of potatoes. Surround with eggs, tomato wedges and olives. Sprinkle with capers and parsley; drizzle with remaining dressing. Serve immediately.

Soups

continued...

Vegetable and Cream Soups (continued)

Chicken Stock

It's easy to make homemade stock instead of resorting to commercial stock cubes and powders, which are loaded with salt.

3 lbs	chicken bones (such as neck, backbones and wing tips)	1.5 kg
2	carrots, coarsely chopped	2
2	stalks celery, including leaves, chopped	1
1	large onion, chopped	1
½ tsp	dried thyme leaves	2 mL
1	bay leaf	1
	Salt and freshly ground black pepper	

1. Place chicken bones in a large stockpot. Add water to cover (about 10 cups/2.5 L). Add carrots, celery, onion, thyme and bay leaf. Bring to a boil and skim. Simmer, covered, for 2 hours; strain through a fine sieve. Season with salt and pepper to taste.

Turkey Stock

Make stock the day after roasting a turkey or place bones in a heavy plastic bag and freeze for up to 1 month.

Tip
Refrigerate stock in airtight containers for up to 3 days or freeze for up to 3 months.

	Bones from 1 cooked turkey (about 12- to 14-lb/6 to 7 kg bird), cut into large pieces	
2	carrots, coarsely chopped	2
2	stalks celery, including tops, coarsely chopped	2
1	large onion, chopped	1
¼ cup	coarsely chopped fresh parsley, with stems	60 mL
1 tsp	dried thyme leaves	5 mL
4	whole cloves	4
	Salt and freshly ground black pepper	

1. Place turkey bones in a large stockpot. Add cold water to cover (about 8 cups/2 L). Add carrots, celery, onion, parsley, thyme and cloves. Bring to a boil and skim. Simmer, covered, for 2 hours; strain through a fine sieve. Remove any meat from bones and add to stock. Season with salt and pepper to taste.

Asian Beef Noodle Soup

Loaded with vegetables, this Vietnamese-style soup is low in calories and full of flavor. A brimming bowlful makes a great meal-in-one supper that takes less than 10 minutes to cook.

Tips

Get all the ingredients assembled and prepared before you begin cooking.

To pull apart rice noodles, place bundle of noodles in a paper bag to prevent them from flying all over the kitchen.

Variation

Angel hair pasta can be substituted for the rice noodles.

8 oz	boneless lean tender beef, such as sirloin	250 g
2 tbsp	soy sauce	30 mL
8 cups	beef stock	2 L
2	thin slices gingerroot, smashed with side of knife	2
2 cups	rice vermicelli, broken into 3-inch (7.5 cm) pieces	500 mL
2	carrots, peeled and shredded	2
2 cups	sliced Napa cabbage or bok choy	500 mL
2 cups	mung bean sprouts	500 mL
¼ cup	coarsely chopped fresh cilantro	60 mL
2	green onions, sliced	2
	Toasted sesame oil (optional)	

1. Slice beef into very thin strips. In a bowl, combine beef with soy sauce. Set aside.

2. In a large saucepan over high heat, bring stock and ginger to a boil. Add vermicelli; boil for 2 minutes or until softened. Add beef, carrots and cabbage.

3. Return to a boil; cook for 2 minutes. Add bean sprouts; cook for 1 minute or until heated through. Ladle into soup bowls; garnish with cilantro and chopped green onions. Drizzle with sesame oil, if desired.

Beef Consommé with Roasted Garlic and Winter Vegetables

Makes 6 servings

In the past, consommé was often served as part of a formal dinner. I like this comforting version. It has a flavorful broth accented with roasted garlic and winter vegetables and can serve as a light starter with a special roast beef or chicken dinner.

Tips

To clean leeks: Trim dark green tops. Cut down center almost to root end and chop. Rinse in a sink full of cold water to remove sand; scoop up leeks and place in colander to drain or use a salad spinner.

Use a sherry that is dry or has just a hint of sweetness.

Have all of the ingredients ready; bring consommé to a boil and add vegetables shortly before serving so vegetables don't overcook.

● Preheat oven to 350°F (180°C)

1	large head garlic	1
2 tsp	olive oil	10 mL
1	carrot, peeled	1
1	small leek, white and light green parts only (see Tip, left)	1
1	small turnip, peeled	1
3	cans (each 10 oz/284 mL) condensed beef consommé or broth	3
3 cups	water	750 mL
1/2 cup	dry sherry	125 mL
Pinch	cayenne pepper	Pinch
1 1/2 cups	thinly sliced shiitake mushrooms	375 mL
2 tbsp	chopped fresh parsley	30 mL

1. Using a sharp knife, trim 1/4 inch (0.5 cm) off the larger bulb end of garlic and place cut side down on large piece of heavy-duty foil. Drizzle with oil and wrap in foil to enclose. Place in small ovenproof dish and roast garlic in preheated oven until soft, about 40 minutes. Set aside to cool. Press garlic cloves between fingertips to release from skins and place in a bowl. (Can be prepared up to 2 days ahead and refrigerated.)

2. Cut carrot, leek and turnip into very thin 1 1/2-inch (4 cm) long matchsticks (julienne strips).

3. In a large saucepan, bring garlic, consommé, water, sherry and cayenne to boil over high heat, stirring occasionally. Add carrots, leek, turnip and mushrooms. Reduce heat, cover and simmer for 8 to 10 minutes or until vegetables are just tender. Ladle into warm soup bowls and sprinkle with parsley.

Beef Goulash Soup

Beef slowly stewed in a rich broth flavored with sweet Hungarian paprika makes for a substantial comforting soup that mimics a stew — perfect when you come in from the cold after a day of skiing. Accompany with thick slices of crusty bread.

Tip

Unless you're using expensive tomato paste from a tube, you can freeze leftover tomato paste. Put tablespoons (15 mL) of leftover canned tomato paste on a waxed paper–lined plate or in ice cube trays; freeze until firm. Transfer to a small freezer bag and have handy in the freezer to add to recipes.

1 tbsp	vegetable oil (approx.)	15 mL
1½ lbs	boneless stewing beef, cut into 1-inch (2.5 cm) cubes	750 g
2	onions, halved lengthwise and sliced	2
2	red bell peppers, diced	2
3	cloves garlic, finely chopped	3
½ tsp	salt	2 mL
½ tsp	freshly ground black pepper	2 mL
2 tbsp	sweet Hungarian paprika	30 mL
¼ cup	tomato paste	60 mL
4 cups	beef stock (approx.)	1 L
2	potatoes, peeled and diced	2

1. In a large Dutch oven, heat oil over medium-high heat. Cook beef in batches, adding more oil as necessary, until browned on all sides. Transfer to a plate.

2. Reduce heat to medium; cook onions, bell peppers, garlic, salt and pepper, stirring often, for 10 minutes or until softened and onions are light golden. Stir in paprika and tomato paste; cook, stirring, for 1 minute.

3. Return beef to pot along with stock. Bring to a boil; reduce heat, cover and simmer for 1 hour.

4. Add potatoes; simmer, covered, for 30 minutes or until beef and potatoes are tender. Add additional water or stock, to thin soup, if desired. To serve, ladle into bowls.

Hearty Beef and Barley Soup

Makes 12 servings

I can't think of a better combination than thick slices of warm bread from the oven and steaming bowls of soup when you come in from the cold. This tried-and-true soup has a hearty beefy mushroom taste and lots of old-fashioned appeal.

Tip

If I'm going to the trouble of making homemade soup, I like to make a big pot so there are plenty of leftovers for my freezer. Ladle soup into containers and freeze for up to 3 months.

1 tbsp	vegetable oil	15 mL
1½ lbs	meaty beef shanks (about 2 or 3), trimmed of fat	750 g
1 lb	mushrooms, chopped	500 g
2	large onions, chopped	2
4	cloves garlic, finely chopped	4
2	bay leaves	2
2 tsp	salt	10 mL
1 tsp	dried thyme leaves	5 mL
¼ tsp	freshly ground black pepper	1 mL
12 cups	water	3 L
¾ cup	pearl or pot barley, rinsed	175 mL
4	carrots, peeled and chopped	4
2	large stalks celery including leaves, chopped	2

1. In a Dutch oven or stockpot, heat oil over medium-high heat. Add beef and cook until nicely browned on both sides. Transfer to a plate.

2. Reduce heat to medium. Add mushrooms, onions, garlic, bay leaves, salt, thyme and pepper; cook, stirring often, for 5 minutes or until softened. Return beef to pan. Pour in water and bring to a boil. Reduce heat to medium-low and simmer, covered, stirring occasionally, for 1 hour.

3. Add barley, carrots and celery. Cover and simmer, stirring occasionally, for 1 hour more or until beef is tender.

4. Remove beef with slotted spoon. Discard bones; finely chop the meat and return to soup. Discard bay leaves; adjust seasoning with salt and pepper to taste.

Chicken Noodle Soup

Often called "Jewish penicillin," chicken soup is the perfect antidote to an oncoming cold. But there's more to its restorative powers. Rich and delicious, it can banish the winter blues and make you feel just plain good any day of the year.

Tip

You don't have to slave over the stove to make this soul-satisfying soup. Adding the chicken and the vegetables to the pot at the same time streamlines the process and does away with the chore of making stock first. The results are every bit as pleasing.

3 lbs	whole chicken or chicken pieces, such as legs and breasts	1.5 kg
10 cups	water (approx.)	2.5 L
1	large onion, finely chopped	1
3	carrots, peeled and chopped	3
2	stalks celery including leaves, chopped	2
2 tbsp	chopped fresh parsley	30 mL
$\frac{1}{2}$ tsp	dried thyme leaves	2 mL
2 tsp	salt	10 mL
$\frac{1}{4}$ tsp	freshly ground black pepper	1 mL
1	bay leaf	1
2 cups	medium or broad egg noodles	500 mL
1 cup	finely diced zucchini or small cauliflower florets	250 mL
2 tbsp	chopped fresh dill or parsley	30 mL

1. Rinse chicken; remove as much skin and excess fat as possible. Place in a large stockpot; add water to cover. Bring to a boil over high heat; using a slotted spoon, skim off foam as it rises to the surface.

2. Add onion, carrots, celery, parsley, thyme, salt, pepper and bay leaf. Reduce heat to medium-low; cover and simmer for about $1\frac{1}{4}$ hours or until chicken is tender.

3. Remove chicken with slotted spoon and place in a large bowl; let cool slightly. Pull chicken meat off the bones, discarding skin and bones. Cut meat into bite-size pieces. Reserve 2 cups (500 mL) for soup. (Use remainder for casseroles and sandwiches.)

4. Skim fat from surface of soup; bring to a boil. Add cubed chicken, noodles, zucchini and dill; cook for 10 minutes or until noodles and vegetables are tender. Remove bay leaf. Adjust seasoning with salt and pepper to taste.

Thai Chicken Soup with Sweet Potatoes

Supermarkets today have well-stocked international food sections, so you can recreate many of the comfort food dishes served in popular ethnic restaurants.

Tips

To clean leeks: Trim dark green tops. Cut down center almost to root end and chop. Rinse in a sink full of cold water to remove sand; scoop up leeks and place in colander to drain or use a salad spinner.

Instead of Thai green curry paste, use 2 tsp (10 mL) mild or medium Indian curry paste, or to taste.

2 cups	chicken stock	500 mL
2	boneless skinless chicken breasts	2
1 tbsp	vegetable oil	15 mL
1	leek, white and light green part only, chopped (see Tip, left)	1
1 cup	thinly sliced celery (about 2 stalks)	250 mL
2	cloves garlic, minced	2
1 tsp	Thai green curry paste, or to taste	5 mL
1½ cups	diced peeled sweet potato	375 mL
1	red bell pepper, diced	1
2 tbsp	cornstarch	30 mL
1 cup	coconut milk	250 mL
	Salt	
2 tbsp	chopped fresh cilantro	30 mL
2 tbsp	chopped fresh basil	30 mL
1	green onion, thinly sliced	1

1. In a medium saucepan, bring stock and 2 cups (500 mL) water to a boil. Add chicken, reduce heat and simmer, covered, for 15 minutes or until chicken is no longer pink inside. Remove chicken and reserve broth. Cut chicken on the diagonal into very thin strips and reserve.

2. In a large saucepan, heat oil over medium heat. Cook leek, celery, garlic and curry paste, stirring often, for 5 minutes or until vegetables are softened. Add reserved poaching broth, sweet potatoes and red pepper; bring to a boil. Cover, reduce heat and simmer for 10 minutes or until vegetables are just tender.

3. In a small bowl, blend cornstarch with 2 tbsp (30 mL) water; stir into soup along with coconut milk. Bring to a boil, stirring, until slightly thickened. Add chicken strips; cook for 1 minute or until heated through. Season with salt to taste.

4. In a bowl, combine cilantro, basil and green onion. Ladle soup into warm bowls and sprinkle with herb mixture.

Turkey Vegetable Chowder

Roasting a turkey has added benefits besides using leftovers for next-day sandwiches. Make an easy homemade stock as the base for this simply, satisfying chowder that also calls for leftover cooked turkey.

Variation

For a creamier version, use 1 cup (250 mL) milk and ½ cup (125 mL) half-and-half (10%) cream.

1 tbsp	butter	15 mL
1	onion, chopped	1
2	potatoes, peeled and diced	2
2 cups	frozen mixed vegetables	500 mL
2 cups	turkey or chicken stock	500 mL
½ tsp	salt	2 mL
	Freshly ground black pepper	
2 tbsp	all-purpose flour	30 mL
1½ cups	milk	375 mL
1½ cups	finely diced cooked turkey	375 mL
1 cup	shredded Cheddar cheese	250 mL
2 tbsp	chopped fresh basil or parsley	30 mL

1. In a large saucepan, melt butter over medium heat. Cook onion, stirring, for 3 minutes or until softened.

2. Add potatoes, frozen vegetables, turkey stock, salt and pepper. Bring to a boil; reduce heat, cover and simmer for 15 minutes or until vegetables are tender.

3. In a bowl, blend flour with ¼ cup (60 mL) of the milk to make a smooth paste; add remaining milk. Stir into saucepan; bring to a boil and cook, stirring, until thickened. Add turkey, Cheddar cheese and basil; cook for 2 minutes or until piping hot.

Creole Fish Soup

Makes 4 servings as a main course or 6 as a starter

The trademark ingredients of Creole cooking — onions, green pepper and celery — have been combined in a tomato and cream base to create this luscious fish soup.

Tip

Any kind of fish, such as cod, sole, haddock or bluefish, can be used. If using frozen fish fillets, remove packaging and arrange fish on plate; microwave on High for 3 to 4 minutes or until partially defrosted. Cut fish into small cubes; let stand 15 minutes to complete defrosting.

1 tbsp	olive oil	15 mL
4	green onions, sliced	4
1	large clove garlic, finely chopped	1
2	stalks celery including leaves, chopped	2
1	green bell pepper, diced	1
1 tsp	paprika	5 mL
1/2 tsp	dried thyme leaves	2 mL
Pinch	cayenne pepper	Pinch
2 cups	diced peeled potatoes	500 mL
1	can (19 oz/540 mL) stewed tomatoes, including juice, chopped	1
2 cups	fish or vegetable stock (approx.)	500 mL
1 lb	fresh or frozen fish fillets (see Tip, left)	500 g
1/2 cup	whipping (35%) cream (optional)	125 mL
	Salt and freshly ground black pepper	

1. In a large saucepan, heat oil over medium heat. Add green onions, garlic, celery, green pepper, paprika, thyme and cayenne pepper; cook, stirring, for 3 minutes or until softened. Add potatoes, stewed tomatoes with juice and stock; bring to a boil. Reduce heat, cover and simmer for 15 minutes or until vegetables are tender.

2. Add fish; simmer for 2 minutes or until fish flakes when tested with a fork. Stir in cream, if using. (Add more stock if soup is too thick.) Season with salt and pepper to taste.

Mediterranean Seafood Soup

Here's an inviting soup that's fragrant with garlic and brimming with fresh seafood in a rich wine and tomato broth. It delivers pleasure from the first to the last spoonful.

Tip

For a less expensive version of this recipe, replace shrimp and scallops with an equal quantity of mild fish.

Variation

For a change, add steamed mussels. Place 1 lb (500 g) mussels in a saucepan with 1/4 cup (60 mL) white wine or water. Place over high heat; cover and steam for 3 to 5 minutes or until shells open. Strain liquid and use as part of the fish stock called for in recipe. Discard any mussels that do not open. Add mussels to soup just before serving (leave in the shells, if desired).

2 tbsp	olive oil	30 mL
1	Spanish onion, chopped (about 1 lb/500 g)	1
3	cloves garlic, finely chopped	3
1	red bell pepper, diced	1
1	green bell pepper, diced	1
1	large stalk celery including leaves, chopped	1
1	bay leaf	1
1 tsp	salt	5 mL
1 tsp	paprika	5 mL
1/4 tsp	hot pepper flakes	1 mL
1/4 tsp	saffron threads, crushed	1 mL
1	can (19 oz/540 mL) tomatoes, including juice, chopped	1
4 cups	fish or chicken stock (approx.)	1 L
1 cup	dry white wine or vermouth or stock	250 mL
1 lb	halibut or other mild white fish, cubed	500 g
8 oz	medium raw shrimp, peeled and deveined, with tails left on	250 g
8 oz	scallops, halved if large	250 g
1/3 cup	finely chopped fresh parsley	75 mL

1. In a Dutch oven or large saucepan, heat oil over medium-high heat. Add onion, garlic, peppers, celery, bay leaf, salt, paprika, hot pepper flakes and saffron; cook, stirring often, for 5 minutes or until vegetables are softened.

2. Add tomatoes with juice, stock and wine. Bring to a boil; reduce heat to medium-low and simmer, covered, for 30 minutes. (Recipe can be prepared to this point up to a day ahead, or frozen for up to 3 months; when reheating, bring back to a full boil.)

3. Stir in halibut, shrimp, scallops and parsley; cover and simmer for 3 to 5 minutes or until fish is opaque. Serve immediately in warm soup bowls.

Clam Chowder

Thick and creamy, laden with chunks of potatoes and featuring the smoky flavor of bacon, this restaurant favorite is easy to recreate in your home kitchen.

Variation

Fish Chowder

Omit canned clams. Increase fish stock to 2 cups (500 mL). Add 12 oz (375 g) cubed fish, such as cod, haddock or bluefish, at end of cooking along with bacon bits. Simmer for 5 minutes or until fish flakes. Add more stock, if necessary, to thin soup to desired consistency.

4	slices bacon, chopped	4
1	can (5 oz/142 g) clams, drained, juice reserved	1
1	small onion, finely chopped	1
1	stalk celery, finely diced	1
1	clove garlic, finely chopped	1
1	bay leaf	1
1½ cups	potatoes, peeled, cut into ½-inch (1 cm) cubes	375 mL
1 cup	fish or chicken stock	250 mL
2 cups	milk	500 mL
3 tbsp	all-purpose flour	45 mL
2 tbsp	finely chopped fresh parsley	30 mL
	Salt and freshly ground black pepper	

1. In a large saucepan, cook bacon over medium heat, stirring, for 4 minutes or until crisp. Remove; blot with paper towels and set aside.

2. Add drained clams, onion, celery, garlic and bay leaf; cook, stirring often, for 3 minutes or until vegetables are softened.

3. Stir in reserved clam juice, potatoes and stock; bring to a boil. Reduce heat to medium-low, cover and simmer for 15 minutes or until vegetables are tender.

4. In a bowl, blend flour with ⅓ cup (75 mL) of the milk to make a smooth paste. Stir in remaining milk. Add to saucepan; bring to a boil over medium-high heat, stirring often, until mixture thickens.

5. Stir in bacon bits and parsley; season with salt, if needed, and pepper to taste. Remove bay leaf before serving.

Hearty Mussel Chowder

**Makes 4 servings
as a main course
or 6 as a starter**

Cultivated mussels are the perfect fast food. They come debearded (meaning the thread that holds them to stationary objects has already been removed) and require only a quick rinse under cold water before cooking. Just throw them in a pot, steam for 4 to 5 minutes and they're ready to eat.

Tip

To store mussels: Place mussels in a bowl and cover with damp paper towels. Never keep in a closed plastic bag or the mussels will suffocate. Also never put in a sink full of water or they will drown. For maximum freshness, use within 2 days of purchase.

Variation
Turkey Chowder
Follow recipe as directed. Omit wine; use 2 cups (500 mL) turkey stock instead of mussel broth. Replace mussels with 1½ cups (375 mL) diced cooked turkey or chicken.

2 lbs	cultivated mussels	1 kg
1 cup	white wine or water	250 mL
4	slices bacon, chopped	4
1	large leek, white and light green part only, chopped (see Tips, page 159)	1
2	stalks celery, chopped	2
1½ cups	diced peeled potatoes	375 mL
½ tsp	salt	2 mL
¼ tsp	freshly ground black pepper	1 mL
½ cup	diced red bell pepper	125 mL
2 tbsp	all-purpose flour	30 mL
1½ cups	milk or light (5%) cream	375 mL
2 tbsp	finely chopped fresh parsley	30 mL

1. Place mussels and wine in a large saucepan. Cover and place over high heat; bring to a boil. Steam for 4 minutes or just until shells open. Drain, reserving cooking liquid. Add enough water or stock to make 2 cups (500 mL) liquid. Remove mussel meat from shells and place in a bowl; discard any that do not open.

2. In a large saucepan over medium heat, cook bacon, stirring often, for 4 minutes or until crisp. Remove with slotted spoon; drain on paper towels. Drain all but 2 tsp (10 mL) fat from pan. Add leek and celery; cook, stirring, for 3 minutes or until softened. Add potatoes, reserved mussel broth, salt and pepper. Bring to a boil; reduce heat, cover and simmer for 15 minutes or until potatoes are tender. Stir in red pepper.

3. In a bowl, blend flour with ¼ cup (60 mL) milk to make a smooth paste; add remaining milk. Stir into saucepan; bring to a boil and cook, stirring, until thickened. Add reserved mussels, bacon bits and parsley; cook 2 minutes or until piping hot.

Shrimp Bisque

Makes 4 servings

Bisques are creamy, rich soups often made with seafood that traditionally rely on long-grain rice as the soup's thickener.

Tips

For the fish stock, use all fish stock or 1 cup (250 mL) bottled clam juice and 2 cups (500 mL) chicken or vegetable stock.

I prefer to use a blender here instead of a food processor to make this extra smooth.

2 tbsp	butter, divided	30 mL
12 oz	medium raw shrimp, peeled and deveined, with tails left on	375 g
1	onion, chopped	1
2	stalks celery, chopped	2
1	carrot, peeled and chopped	1
Pinch	cayenne pepper	Pinch
3 cups	fish stock (approx.) (see Tips, left)	750 mL
3 tbsp	long-grain white rice	45 mL
2 tbsp	tomato paste	30 mL
1 cup	half-and-half (10%) cream	250 mL
1/3 cup	medium-dry sherry	75 mL
1 tbsp	chopped fresh tarragon or 1 tsp (5 mL) dried tarragon leaves	15 mL
1 tsp	grated lemon zest	5 mL
	Salt and freshly ground black pepper	

1. In a large saucepan, heat 1 tbsp (15 mL) of the butter over medium heat. Cook shrimp, stirring often, for 2 to 3 minutes or until pink. Remove with a slotted spoon to a bowl. Set aside 4 shrimp with tails for garnish. Remove tails from remaining shrimp. Reserve shrimp, discarding tails.

2. Melt remaining butter in saucepan. Cook onion, celery, carrot and cayenne, stirring often, for 5 minutes or until softened. Stir in fish stock, rice and tomato paste.

3. Bring to a boil; reduce heat to low, cover and simmer until rice and vegetables are tender, about 25 minutes. Remove from heat. Add shrimp.

4. In a blender (see Tips, left), purée in batches until very smooth. Return soup to saucepan. Add cream, sherry, tarragon and lemon zest. Season with salt and pepper to taste. Thin with additional stock, if desired. Heat soup over medium heat until piping hot. (Do not let boil or soup may curdle.) Ladle soup into bowls and garnish with reserved shrimp.

Chunky Minestrone

This nourishing soup is chockfull of vegetables and excels at chasing away the winter chills. It's soothing both to the body and the soul.

Tip

Extras of this soup freeze well for up to 3 months.

Variations

Meatball Minestrone

Add 1 lb (500 g) small meatballs (about 36), either homemade (see page 315) or store-bought, along with chickpeas and parsley. Increase cooking time to 10 minutes or until meatballs are heated through. Add additional stock, if necessary, to thin soup.

Chicken or Turkey Minestrone

Add 2 cups (500 mL) diced cooked chicken or turkey along with chickpeas.

2 tbsp	olive oil	30 mL
2	onions, chopped	2
4	cloves garlic, finely chopped	4
3	carrots, peeled and diced	3
2	stalks celery including leaves, chopped	2
1½ tsp	dried basil leaves	7 mL
1 tsp	dried oregano or marjoram leaves	5 mL
½ tsp	freshly ground black pepper	2 mL
10 cups	chicken or vegetable stock	2.5 L
1	can (19 oz/540 mL) tomatoes, including juice, chopped	1
2 cups	small cauliflower florets	500 mL
1½ cups	green beans, cut into 1-inch (2.5 cm) lengths	375 mL
¾ cup	small-shaped pasta, such as tubetti or shells	175 mL
1	can (19 oz/540 mL) chickpeas or white kidney beans, drained and rinsed	1
⅓ cup	chopped fresh parsley	75 mL
	Freshly grated Parmesan cheese	

1. In a Dutch oven or large stockpot, heat oil over medium heat. Add onions, garlic, carrots, celery, basil, oregano and pepper; cook, stirring, for 5 minutes or until softened.

2. Stir in stock, tomatoes with juice, cauliflower and beans. Bring to a boil; reduce heat to medium-low and simmer, covered, for 20 minutes or until vegetables are tender.

3. Stir in pasta; cover and simmer for 10 minutes, stirring occasionally, until pasta is just tender.

4. Add chickpeas and parsley; cook 5 minutes more or until heated through. Ladle soup into heated bowls and sprinkle with Parmesan.

Vegetable Minestrone with Sun-Dried Tomato Pesto

Makes 8 servings

I always make a double batch of this soup each fall when vegetables are at their prime. I pack it into containers and put in the freezer for easy mid-week meals on chilly days. Any combination of vegetables can be used in this hearty vegetable soup, depending on what's in your fridge. Sun-Dried Tomato Pesto is optional, but it adds a wonderful jolt of flavor and dresses up the soup. You can also use whatever pesto you have on hand.

Tip

Serve with additional Parmesan cheese at the table. Refrigerate soup for up to 5 days or freeze in airtight containers for up to 3 months.

1 tbsp	olive oil	15 mL
2	large onions, chopped	2
3	cloves garlic, finely chopped	3
2	carrots, peeled and chopped	2
2	stalks celery, chopped	2
10 cups	vegetable or chicken stock (approx.)	2.5 L
2 cups	shredded cabbage	500 mL
2 cups	small cauliflower florets	500 mL
1/3 cup	short fine noodles or other small-shaped pasta, such as shells	75 mL
1 cup	frozen peas	250 mL
1	can (19 oz/540 mL) Romano or navy beans, drained and rinsed	1
3/4 cup	Sun-Dried Tomato Pesto (see recipe, page 334)	175 mL
	Freshly grated Parmesan cheese (optional)	

1. In a Dutch oven or large stockpot, heat oil over medium heat. Add onions, garlic, carrots and celery; cook, stirring occasionally, for 10 minutes or until softened.

2. Add stock and cabbage; bring to a boil over high heat. Reduce heat, cover and simmer for 20 minutes or just until vegetables are tender. Stir in cauliflower and pasta; simmer, covered, for 8 minutes or just until pasta is tender. Stir in peas and beans; cook for 2 minutes.

3. Ladle into bowls; swirl a generous tablespoon (15 mL) Sun-Dried Tomato Pesto into each. Sprinkle with Parmesan cheese, if desired. Soup thickens slightly as it cools; add more stock, if necessary.

Vegetable Tortellini Soup

2 tsp	olive oil	10 mL
1	small onion, finely chopped	1
2	cloves garlic, finely chopped	2
½ tsp	dried basil leaves	2 mL
3 cups	chicken stock	750 mL
1	can (19 oz/540 mL) Italian stewed tomatoes	1
2 cups	fresh or frozen cheese- or meat-filled tortellini	500 mL
2 cups	frozen mixed Italian vegetables	500 mL
	Salt and freshly ground black pepper	
	Freshly grated Parmesan cheese	

1. In large saucepan, heat oil over medium heat. Cook onion, garlic and basil, stirring, for 3 minutes or until softened. Add chicken stock and tomatoes; bring to a boil. Add tortellini. Reduce heat, cover and simmer, stirring occasionally, for 5 minutes.

2. Add frozen vegetables. Cover and simmer for 8 minutes more or until pasta and vegetables are just tender. Season with salt and pepper to taste. Ladle into soup bowls; sprinkle generously with Parmesan cheese.

Pasta and Bean Soup

Your fridge can be bare, but chances are you'll have these basic items on hand to make this hearty soup that is the most famous and loved soup in Italy, where it's known as *pasta e fagioli.*

Variations

Bean, Pasta and Swiss Chard Soup
Increase stock to 6 cups (1.5 L). Stir in 4 cups (1 L) shredded fresh Swiss chard or spinach along with pasta.

Other kinds of canned beans or lentils can be used instead of white kidney beans.

1 tbsp	olive oil	15 mL
1	onion, chopped	1
2	cloves garlic, finely chopped	2
1 cup	chopped drained canned plum tomatoes	250 mL
5 cups	chicken or vegetable stock (approx.)	1.25 L
1	can (19 oz/540 mL) white kidney beans, drained and rinsed, divided	1
¾ cup	small pasta shapes, such as ditali or shells	175 mL
2 tbsp	chopped fresh basil or parsley	30 mL
	Salt and freshly ground black pepper	
	Freshly grated Parmesan cheese	

1. In a large saucepan, heat oil over medium heat. Cook onion and garlic, stirring, for 3 minutes or until softened. Add tomatoes and cook, stirring occasionally, for 5 minutes or until sauce-like.

2. Add stock; bring to a boil over high heat. In a bowl, using a fork, mash half of the beans. Stir into stock along with pasta; reduce heat to medium, partially cover and cook, stirring occasionally, for 8 to 10 minutes or until pasta is just tender.

3. Add remaining whole beans and basil; heat until piping hot. Season with salt and pepper to taste. Thin with additional stock, if necessary. Ladle soup into bowls; sprinkle generously with Parmesan cheese.

Spicy Black Bean Gazpacho

A generous bowlful of this nourishing soup makes an ideal lunch or light supper. Just add some pita bread or whole-grain crackers.

Tips

Cold soups taste best when refrigerated overnight, giving the flavors a chance to blend. Always check the seasoning of a cold soup, however. Often you will need to add extra salt, pepper or hot pepper sauce.

If tomatoes aren't fully ripened when you buy them, place in a paper bag on your counter for a day a two. The ethylene gas given off by the tomatoes speeds up the ripening process. Never store tomatoes in the fridge — the cold temperature numbs their sweet flavor. A sunny windowsill may seem like a good place to ripen tomatoes, but a hot sun often bakes rather than ripens them.

1	red bell pepper, coarsely chopped	1
3	green onions, coarsely chopped	3
3	ripe tomatoes, coarsely chopped	3
1	can (19 oz/540 mL) black beans, drained and rinsed	1
2 cups	canned tomato juice (approx.)	500 mL
2 tbsp	balsamic vinegar	30 mL
1 tbsp	red wine vinegar	15 mL
1	large clove garlic, minced	1
	Salt and freshly ground black pepper	
½ tsp	hot pepper sauce, or to taste	2 mL
⅓ cup	chopped fresh cilantro or parsley	75 mL
	Sour cream or plain yogurt	

1. In a food processor, finely chop red pepper and green onions, using on-off turns; transfer to a large bowl. Add tomatoes to food processor; finely chop, using on-off turns. Add to pepper-onion mixture along with black beans and tomato juice. Add balsamic and red wine vinegars and garlic; season with salt, pepper and hot pepper sauce. Cover and refrigerate for 4 hours, or preferably overnight.

2. Add more tomato juice or water to thin soup to desired consistency. Adjust seasoning with vinegars, salt, pepper and hot pepper sauce to taste. Ladle into chilled bowls; sprinkle with cilantro and top with a spoonful of sour cream.

Black Bean and Corn Soup

Makes 6 servings

My idea of a no-fuss dinner is this easy soup served with warm bread. It's especially reassuring to know that when I come home late from work, I can reach in my cupboard and pull out some convenient canned products — and dinner is on the table in no time!

Tip

Soups that call for canned products, such as tomatoes and beans, contain hefty quantities of salt (as do commercial stock bases), so be cautious about adding extra. Instead, rely on your pepper mill for a seasoning boost.

Variation

Supermarkets are full of beans these days. With this recipe, why not try chickpeas, Romano or white kidney beans?

1 tbsp	olive oil	15 mL
1	onion, chopped	1
2	cloves garlic, finely chopped	2
1	green bell pepper, diced	1
1	large stalk celery, diced	1
1 tsp	dried oregano leaves	5 mL
1 tsp	ground cumin	5 mL
1/2 tsp	dried thyme leaves	2 mL
Pinch	cayenne pepper	Pinch
4 cups	chicken or vegetable stock	1 L
1	can (19 oz/540 mL) tomatoes, including juice, chopped	1
1	can (19 oz/540 mL) black beans, drained and rinsed	1
1 cup	corn kernels (fresh, frozen or canned)	250 mL
1 cup	diced smoked sausage, such as kielbasa, or smoked ham (optional)	250 mL
1/4 cup	chopped fresh cilantro or parsley	60 mL

1. In a large saucepan, heat oil over medium-high heat. Add onion, garlic, pepper, celery, oregano, cumin, thyme and cayenne pepper; cook, stirring, for 5 minutes or until softened.

2. Add stock and tomatoes with juice; bring to a boil. Reduce heat to medium-low and simmer, covered, for 20 minutes.

3. Stir in beans, corn and sausage, if using. Cook 5 minutes more or until vegetables are tender. Stir in cilantro; ladle into warm bowls.

Old-Fashioned Pea Soup with Smoked Ham

Makes 8 servings

My family came from the Netherlands to Southern Ontario in the 1950s and we were raised on this warming Dutch soup. When I lived in Quebec for several years, I discovered pea soup was also a key staple in that province's food heritage and I felt right at home.

Tip

For a wonderful rich flavor, I like to add a meaty ham bone to the soup as it simmers. As most hams sold today in supermarkets are boneless, however, the addition of both chopped smoked ham and chicken stock make a good substitute. Do add a ham bone, though, if you have one, and use water instead of stock. Smoked pork hock is another alternative if a ham bone is not available. Remove ham bone at end of cooking; scrape off any meat, chop and add to soup.

2 tbsp	butter	30 mL
1	leek, white and light green parts only, chopped (see Tip, page 183)	1
1	large onion, chopped	1
2	large cloves garlic, finely chopped	2
3	carrots, peeled and chopped	3
1	large stalk celery including leaves, chopped	1
1½ tsp	dried marjoram leaves	7 mL
1	bay leaf	1
¼ tsp	freshly ground black pepper	1 mL
8 cups	chicken stock (approx.)	2 L
2 cups	chopped smoked ham	500 mL
1½ cups	dried yellow or green split peas, rinsed and picked over	375 mL
	Salt	
¼ cup	chopped fresh parsley	60 mL

1. In a Dutch oven or stockpot, melt butter over medium heat. Add leek, onion, garlic, carrots, celery, marjoram, bay leaf and pepper; cook, stirring often, for 8 minutes or until softened.

2. Stir in stock, ham and split peas. Bring to a boil; reduce heat, cover and simmer, stirring occasionally, for about 1½ hours or until split peas are tender.

3. Remove bay leaf. Adjust seasoning with salt and pepper to taste. Stir in parsley. Soup thickens as it cools; thin with additional stock or water to desired consistency.

Curried Split Pea Soup

Makes 8 servings

Here's a homey, satisfying soup that's perfect to serve as the main event on cold, blustery days.

Tip

This recipe makes a large batch of soup; freeze extra for another meal.

Variation

If you have any leftover baked ham, dice into small cubes and add along with the split peas. Another option is to add diced smoked sausage, such as kielbasa, for the last 15 minutes of cooking.

1 tbsp	vegetable oil	15 mL
2	onions, chopped	2
4	cloves garlic, finely chopped	4
1 tbsp	mild curry paste, or to taste	15 mL
1 tsp	ground cumin	5 mL
1 tsp	paprika	5 mL
1/4 tsp	cayenne pepper	1 mL
3	large carrots, peeled and chopped	3
2	large stalks celery including leaves, chopped	2
2 cups	dried yellow or green split peas, rinsed and sorted	500 mL
1/4 cup	tomato paste	60 mL
10 cups	vegetable or chicken stock	2.5 L
1/3 cup	chopped fresh cilantro or parsley	75 mL
	Salt and freshly ground black pepper	
	Plain yogurt (optional)	

1. In a large Dutch oven or stockpot, heat oil over medium heat. Add onions, garlic, curry paste, cumin, paprika and cayenne pepper; cook, stirring, for 3 minutes or until softened.

2. Add carrots, celery, split peas, tomato paste and stock. Bring to a boil; reduce heat, cover and simmer for about 1 to 1 1/2 hours or until peas are tender.

3. Stir in cilantro; season with salt and pepper to taste. Ladle into bowls; top with a dollop of yogurt, if desired. Soup thickens as it cools, so you may want to thin with additional stock before serving.

Suppertime Lentil Soup

Of all dried legumes, lentils are my favorite. They're fast and easy to cook — and healthy too!

Tip

To save time, I chop the mushrooms, onions, carrots and celery in batches in the food processor. If you have any leftover baked ham, chop it and add to the soup along with the stock.

Variation

Lentil-Rice Soup

Use ⅔ cup (150 mL) lentils and ⅓ cup (75 mL) long-grain white or brown rice instead of 1 cup (250 mL) lentils.

8 cups	chicken or vegetable stock	2 L
1 cup	green lentils, rinsed and sorted	250 mL
8 oz	mushrooms, chopped	250 g
3	carrots, peeled and chopped	3
2	stalks celery including leaves, chopped	2
1	large onion, chopped	1
2	cloves garlic, finely chopped	2
1 tsp	dried thyme or marjoram leaves	5 mL
¼ cup	chopped fresh dill or parsley	60 mL
	Salt and freshly ground black pepper	

1. In a large Dutch oven or stockpot, combine stock, lentils, mushrooms, carrots, celery, onion, garlic and thyme.

2. Bring to a boil; reduce heat, cover and simmer 35 to 40 minutes or until lentils are tender. Stir in dill or parsley. Adjust seasoning with salt and pepper to taste.

Harvest Vegetable Barley Soup

Variation

Instead of sweet potatoes, add 1 cup (250 mL) each diced peeled potatoes and diced carrots. Add along with the rutabaga.

2 tbsp	butter	30 mL
1	large onion, chopped	1
3	cloves garlic, finely chopped	3
1½ cups	diced peeled rutabaga	375 mL
½ tsp	dried thyme or marjoram leaves	2 mL
8 cups	chicken or vegetable stock (approx.)	2 L
½ cup	pearl barley, rinsed	125 mL
1½ cups	diced peeled sweet potatoes	375 mL
1½ cups	diced zucchini	375 mL
	Salt and freshly ground black pepper	

1. In a large Dutch oven or stockpot, melt butter over medium heat. Add onion, garlic, rutabaga and thyme; cook, stirring often, for 5 minutes or until vegetables are lightly colored.

2. Stir in stock and barley; bring to a boil. Reduce heat, cover and simmer for 20 minutes. Add sweet potatoes and zucchini; simmer, covered, for 15 minutes or until barley is tender. Season with salt and pepper to taste.

Basil Tomato-Rice Soup

Makes 6 servings

My pantry can be sparse, but I can always count on having these few ingredients on hand to make this last-minute soup to serve with crusty whole-grain bread and cheese.

Tips

Instead of canned tomatoes, use 4 large ripe tomatoes, peeled and chopped.

If you have fresh basil on hand, substitute 2 tbsp (25 mL) of the chopped fresh herb for the dried basil in recipe and add along with parsley.

Variation

To make a creamy tomato-rice soup, add ½ cup (125 mL) whipping (35%) cream along with the parsley.

1 tbsp	olive oil	15 mL
1	large onion, chopped	1
2	stalks celery, chopped	2
2	cloves garlic, finely chopped	2
1 tsp	dried basil leaves	5 mL
1	can (28 oz/796 mL) plum tomatoes, including juice	1
6 cups	chicken or vegetable stock	1.5 L
½ cup	long-grain white rice	125 mL
1 tsp	granulated sugar (approx.)	5 mL
	Salt and freshly ground black pepper	
2 tbsp	chopped fresh parsley	30 mL

1. In a Dutch oven or stockpot, heat oil over medium heat. Add onion, celery, garlic and basil; cook, stirring, for 5 minutes or until softened.

2. In a food processor, purée tomatoes with juice. Add to pot with stock and rice; season with sugar, salt and pepper to taste. Bring to a boil; reduce heat, cover and simmer for 30 to 35 minutes or until rice is tender. Stir in parsley.

Cheese-Smothered Onion Soup

Makes 6 servings

A good melting cheese with a nice nutty flavor, such as Gruyère or raclette, works very well in this savory soup that will warm you up on cold blustery days. The assertive flavor of onions mellows and sweetens when cooked until golden. This classic makes an easy transition from an everyday dish to an entertainment standout.

Tips

Buy French bread 3 to 4 inches (8 to 10 cm) in diameter. Or, if using a thin baguette, use 2 slices of bread in each bowl.

The onion soup base can be made ahead and refrigerated for up to 5 days or frozen for up to 3 months.

• Large shallow baking pan

3 tbsp	butter	45 mL
8 cups	thinly sliced Spanish onions (about 2 to 3)	2 L
1/4 tsp	dried thyme leaves	1 mL
1/4 tsp	freshly ground black pepper	1 mL
2 tbsp	all-purpose flour	30 mL
6 cups	beef stock	1.5 L
1 tbsp	olive oil	15 mL
1	large clove garlic, minced	1
6	slices French bread, about 3/4-inch (2 cm) thick	6
2 cups	shredded Gruyère cheese	500 mL

1. In a Dutch oven or large heavy saucepan, melt butter over medium heat. Add onions, thyme and pepper; cook, stirring often, for 15 minutes or until onions are tender and a rich golden color. Blend in flour; stir in stock. Bring to a boil, stirring, until thickened. Reduce heat to medium-low, cover and simmer for 15 minutes.

2. Meanwhile, position oven rack 6 inches (15 cm) from broiler; preheat broiler.

3. In a small bowl, combine olive oil and garlic; lightly brush oil mixture over both sides of bread. Arrange on baking sheet; place under broiler and toast on both sides.

4. Place toasts in deep ovenproof soup bowls; sprinkle with half the cheese. Arrange bowls in baking pan. Ladle hot soup into bowls. Sprinkle with remaining cheese. Place under broiler for 3 minutes or until cheese melts and is lightly browned. Serve immediately.

Roasted Parsnip Soup with Stilton

Pears add a just a hint of sweetness to this winter soup — a perfect match with the Stilton cheese.

Tip

Hate shedding tears when chopping onions? To minimize the weeping problem, use a razor-sharp knife to prevent loss of juices and cover the cut onions with a paper towel as you chop them to prevent the vapors from rising to your eyes.

- Preheat oven to 375°F (190°C)
- Rimmed baking sheet, greased

1 lb	parsnips, peeled and diced	500 g
3	Bartlett pears, peeled, cored and diced	3
1	large potato, diced	1
1	large onion, coarsely chopped	1
2	cloves garlic, chopped	2
1 tbsp	olive oil	15 mL
	Salt and freshly ground black pepper	
4 cups	chicken or vegetable stock (approx.)	1 L
1 cup	half-and-half (10%) cream	250 mL
¾ cup	crumbled Stilton cheese	175 mL
2 tbsp	chopped fresh chives or parsley	30 mL

1. On baking sheet, arrange parsnips, pears, potato, onion and garlic in a single layer. Drizzle with oil and season with salt and pepper.

2. Roast in preheated oven, stirring occasionally, for 30 minutes or until vegetables are just tender and lightly colored.

3. Transfer to a large saucepan over high heat; add chicken stock. Bring to a boil; reduce heat and simmer for 20 minutes or until vegetables are very tender.

4. In a food processor or blender, purée in batches until very smooth. Add cream; thin with additional stock, if necessary. Return to saucepan and heat just until piping hot. (Do not let boil or soup may curdle.) Season with salt and pepper to taste. Ladle into bowls; sprinkle with Stilton cheese and chives.

Cheddar Broccoli Chowder

If you have a vegetarian in your family, this is a recipe you can count on. It's no fuss to prepare, easy to reheat and makes a complete meal.

Tip

Depending on what I have in the fridge, I make variations on this versatile, tasty soup by using other vegetables, such as carrots and cauliflower.

2 tbsp	butter	30 mL
1	small onion, finely chopped	1
¼ cup	all-purpose flour	60 mL
3 cups	vegetable or chicken stock	750 mL
2 cups	potatoes, peeled and cut into ½-inch (1 cm) cubes	500 mL
1	bay leaf	1
3 cups	finely chopped broccoli florets and peeled stalks	750 mL
1½ cups	milk	375 mL
1½ cups	shredded Cheddar cheese	375 mL
	Freshly ground black pepper	

1. In a large saucepan, melt butter over medium heat. Cook onion, stirring, for 2 minutes or until softened. Blend in flour; stir in stock. Bring to a boil, stirring, until thickened.

2. Add potatoes and bay leaf; reduce heat, cover and simmer, stirring occasionally, for 10 minutes.

3. Add broccoli; simmer, stirring occasionally, for 10 minutes more or until vegetables are tender.

4. Stir in milk and cheese; heat just until cheese melts and soup is piping hot. (Do not boil or soup may curdle.) Remove bay leaf; adjust seasoning with pepper to taste.

Corn and Red Pepper Chowder

Sweet, young corn, combined with tender leeks and bell pepper, make a delicately flavored fall soup. Kernels cut from cooked cobs of corn are ideal for this recipe. You'll need about 3 cobs.

Tip

To cut kernels from the cob easily, stand the ears on end and cut downward using a sharp knife.

1 tbsp	butter	15 mL
2	leeks, white and light green parts only, finely chopped (see Tip, page 183)	2
½ tsp	dried thyme leaves	2 mL
2½ cups	chicken or vegetable stock	625 mL
1½ cups	cooked or frozen corn kernels	375 mL
1	large red bell pepper, diced	1
3 tbsp	all-purpose flour	45 mL
2 cups	milk	500 mL
	Salt and freshly ground black pepper	
2 tbsp	chopped fresh parsley or chives	30 mL

1. In a large saucepan, melt butter over medium heat. Add leeks and thyme; cook, stirring often, for 4 minutes or until softened. Do not brown. Stir in stock and frozen corn, if using. Bring to a boil; reduce heat, cover and simmer for 10 minutes. Add corn and red pepper; cover and simmer for 5 minutes or until vegetables are tender.

2. In a bowl, blend flour with ⅓ cup (75 mL) milk to make a smooth paste; stir in remaining milk. Stir into saucepan; bring to a boil, stirring, until thickened. Season with salt and pepper to taste. Ladle into soup bowls; sprinkle with parsley or chives.

Creamy Tomato Soup

I always look forward to late summer — when baskets of lush ripe tomatoes are the showpiece in outdoor markets — so I can make this silky smooth soup. In winter, vine-ripened greenhouse tomatoes make a good stand-in, particularly if you use a little tomato paste for extra depth. Just add 1 to 2 tbsp (15 to 25 mL) when puréeing soup.

Tip

If tomatoes aren't fully ripened when you buy them, place in a paper bag on your counter for a day a two. The ethylene gas given off by the tomatoes speeds up the ripening process. Never store tomatoes in the fridge — the cold temperature numbs their sweet flavor. A sunny windowsill may seem like a good place to ripen tomatoes, but a hot sun often bakes rather than ripens them.

- Preheat oven to 400°F (200°C)
- Large shallow roasting pan or heavy rimmed baking sheet

1 tbsp	olive oil	15 mL
6	ripe tomatoes, cored and quartered, (about 2 lbs/1 kg)	6
1	leek, white and light green parts only, chopped (see Tip, page 183)	1
1	small onion, coarsely chopped	1
2	carrots, peeled and coarsely chopped	2
1	stalk celery including leaves, chopped	1
2	large cloves garlic, sliced	2
1/2 tsp	salt	2 mL
1/4 tsp	freshly ground black pepper	1 mL
1/4 tsp	freshly grated nutmeg	1 mL
3 cups	chicken or vegetable stock (approx.)	750 mL
1 cup	table (18%) cream	250 mL
2 tbsp	chopped fresh herbs such as parsley, basil or chives	30 mL

1. Drizzle oil over bottom of roasting pan. Add tomatoes, leek, onion, carrots, celery and garlic; season with salt, pepper and nutmeg.

2. Roast, uncovered, in preheated oven, stirring occasionally, for 45 minutes or until vegetables are tender, but not brown.

3. Transfer to a stockpot and add 2 cups (500 mL) of the stock. Bring to a boil, cover and reduce heat. Simmer for 15 minutes or until vegetables are very tender.

4. Purée mixture in batches, preferably in a blender or a food processor, until very smooth. Strain soup through a sieve into large saucepan.

5. Add cream and enough of the remaining stock to thin soup to desired consistency. Adjust seasoning with salt and pepper to taste. Heat until piping hot. (Do not let boil or soup may curdle.) Ladle into warm bowls; sprinkle with fresh herbs.

Cream of Mushroom Soup

Use shiitake mushrooms along with less inexpensive cremini mushrooms to create this intensely flavored soup that makes a great starter for a special dinner.

Tip

To wash or not wash mushrooms? You can wipe them with a damp cloth, if you wish. However, I feel it's important to wash all produce that comes into my kitchen. I quickly rinse mushrooms under cold water and immediately wrap in a clean, dry kitchen towel or paper towels to absorb excess moisture.

2 tbsp	butter	30 mL
1	large onion, finely chopped	1
2	cloves garlic, finely chopped	2
8 oz	assorted mushrooms, such as shiitake and cremini, sliced (see Tip, left)	250 g
1½ tsp	chopped fresh thyme or ½ tsp (2 mL) dried thyme leaves	7 mL
2 tbsp	all-purpose flour	30 mL
4 cups	chicken stock	1 L
½ tsp	salt	2 mL
¼ tsp	freshly ground black pepper	1 mL
1 cup	table (18%) cream	250 mL
¼ cup	medium-dry sherry (optional)	60 mL
2 tbsp	chopped fresh chives or parsley	30 mL

1. In a Dutch oven or large saucepan, heat butter over medium-high heat. Cook onion and garlic, stirring, for 2 minutes, until softened. Stir in mushrooms and thyme; cook, stirring often, for 5 minutes or until mushrooms are tender.

2. Blend in flour; stir in stock, salt and pepper. Bring to a boil over high heat. Reduce heat to medium-low, cover and simmer for 25 minutes. Let cool slightly.

3. In a food processor or blender, purée soup in batches. Return to saucepan. Place over medium heat; stir in cream and sherry, if using. Adjust seasoning with salt and pepper to taste. Heat until piping hot. Ladle into heated bowls and sprinkle with chives.

Creamy Cauliflower Soup with Feta

Feta and dill are a terrific flavor combination in this creamy soup that has become one of my most requested recipes when served to friends and family. Serve it either hot or cold.

Tip

To clean leeks: Trim dark green tops. Cut down center almost to root end and chop. Rinse in a sink full of cold water to remove sand; scoop up leeks and place in colander to drain or use a salad spinner.

1	leek, white and light green parts only, sliced (see Tip, left)	1
5 cups	small cauliflower florets (about 1 small head)	1.25 L
1 cup	diced peeled potato (about 1 medium potato)	250 mL
2 cups	chicken stock (approx.)	500 mL
1 cup	half-and-half (10%) cream or milk	250 mL
2 tbsp	chopped fresh dill or parsley	30 mL
	Salt and freshly ground black pepper	
½ cup	crumbled feta cheese	125 mL
	Dill sprigs as garnish	

1. In a large saucepan, combine leek, cauliflower, potato and stock. Bring to a boil; reduce heat, cover and simmer for 25 minutes or until vegetables are very tender. Let cool slightly.

2. In a food processor or blender, purée in batches until smooth. Return to pan and stir in cream and dill. Season with salt and pepper to taste.

3. Reheat until piping hot. (Do not let boil or soup may curdle.) Thin with additional stock, if necessary. Ladle into bowls and top each with 2 tbsp (30 mL) feta cheese. Garnish bowls with sprigs of dill. Serve immediately.

Carrot Orange Soup

Looking for a great opener for a meal? Here it is. The sweetness of carrots and orange are balanced by the tang of yogurt in this low-calorie soup.

Tip

Normally yogurt will curdle if you add it to a soup or sauce, but blending it with cornstarch as a binder overcomes this problem.

1 tbsp	vegetable oil	15 mL
1	onion, chopped	1
1	large clove garlic, finely chopped	1
2 tsp	mild curry paste, or to taste	10 mL
4 cups	sliced carrots	1 L
4 cups	chicken stock	1 L
1 cup	orange juice	250 mL
1 cup	plain yogurt	250 mL
1 tbsp	cornstarch	15 mL
	Salt and freshly ground black pepper	
2 tbsp	chopped fresh parsley or chives	30 mL
	Grated orange zest	

1. In a large saucepan, heat oil over medium heat. Add onion, garlic and curry paste; cook, stirring, for 2 minutes or until softened. Add carrots, chicken stock and orange juice. Bring to a boil; cover and simmer for 45 minutes or until carrots are very tender. Let cool 10 minutes.

2. In a food processor or blender, purée in batches; return to saucepan. In a bowl, blend yogurt with cornstarch; stir into soup. Cook over medium heat, stirring, for 5 minutes or until slightly thickened. Season with salt and pepper to taste. Ladle into bowls; sprinkle with parsley and orange zest.

Cream of Sweet Pea Soup with Mint

Makes 6 servings

This updated green pea soup is wonderful served hot but is also delicious served cold on a hot summer's day. Either way, add the Minted Pea Swirl for an impressive presentation.

Variations

Instead of Minted Pea Swirl, add ¼ cup (60 mL) lightly packed mint leaves to soup mixture when puréeing.

When serving the soup cold, use buttermilk instead of cream.

1 tbsp	butter	15 mL
1	large onion, chopped	1
2	cloves garlic, finely chopped	2
1½ cups	diced peeled potatoes	375 mL
4 cups	chicken or vegetable stock	1 L
4 cups	frozen green peas	1 L
1 cup	table (18%) cream	250 mL
	Salt and freshly ground black pepper	

Minted Pea Swirl

¾ cup	frozen green peas	175 mL
⅓ cup	fresh mint leaves	75 mL
½ cup	chicken or vegetable stock	125 mL

1. In a large saucepan, melt butter over medium-high heat. Cook onion and garlic, stirring, for 2 minutes or until softened. Add potatoes and stock. Bring to a boil. Reduce heat, cover and simmer for 20 minutes or until potatoes are very tender.

2. Add peas and cook for 5 minutes or until just tender but still bright green. Let cool slightly.

3. In a food processor or blender, purée soup in batches until smooth. Stir in cream. Season with salt and pepper to taste.

4. If serving warm, return soup to saucepan and heat until piping hot. (Do not let boil or soup may curdle.) If serving cold, place in an airtight container and refrigerate for 8 hours or overnight.

5. *Minted Pea Swirl:* In a food processor, purée frozen peas, mint and stock until smooth. Transfer to a bowl and refrigerate.

6. To serve, ladle soup into bowls. Add small spoonfuls of Minted Pea Swirl to the center of each and run a skewer through to create an attractive pattern. Serve immediately.

Ginger Squash Soup

Serve cupfuls of this colorful soup as an elegant starter to a fall menu. I turn to it when fresh-picked squash are plentiful in the market. I often make extra purée and freeze it in containers. It takes no time at all to make the soup if you have the purée on hand in the freezer. The finished soup also freezes well.

Tip

To make squash purée: Cut 1 small butternut or large acorn squash (about 2 lbs/1 kg) into quarters; remove seeds. Place in large casserole dish with ½ cup (125 mL) water. Cover and microwave on High for 15 to 20 minutes or until squash is tender when pierced with a fork. (Cooking time varies with size and type of squash.) Let stand 15 minutes or until cool enough to handle. Scoop out pulp; place in food processor and purée. Makes about 2 cups (500 mL).

1 tbsp	butter	15 mL
1	large onion, chopped	1
2	cloves garlic, finely chopped	2
4 tsp	minced gingerroot	20 mL
2 tbsp	all-purpose flour	30 mL
3 cups	chicken stock	750 mL
2 cups	cooked squash purée (see Tip, left)	500 mL
½ cup	table (18%) cream or whipping (35%) cream	125 mL
1 tsp	grated orange zest	5 mL
	Salt, freshly ground black pepper and freshly grated nutmeg	
2 tbsp	chopped fresh chives or parsley	30 mL

1. In a large saucepan, melt butter over medium heat. Add onion, garlic and ginger; cook, stirring often, for 3 minutes or until onion is softened. Blend in flour; stir in stock and squash. Bring to a boil and cook, stirring, until thickened. Reduce heat to medium-low, cover and simmer for 10 minutes.

2. In a food processor or blender, purée in batches until smooth. Return to saucepan. Add cream and orange zest; season with salt, pepper and nutmeg to taste. Heat until piping hot. Ladle into bowls; sprinkle with chives.

Curried Root Vegetable Soup

Here's a seductive soup with a Caribbean accent to serve for a special dinner. The surprising combination of earthy root vegetables, married with spices like ginger and curry, gives the soup a delicious Island flare. My friends always go home with the recipe.

Tip

The carrots, sweet potato and rutabaga, cut into $\frac{1}{2}$-inch (1 cm) cubes, should total 4 cups (1 L).

Variation
Curried Butternut Squash and Apple Soup
Substitute 5 cups (1.25 L) peeled and cubed butternut squash for the carrots, sweet potato and rutabaga.

2 tbsp	butter	30 mL
1½ cups	diced peeled apples	375 mL
1	onion, chopped	1
2	cloves garlic, finely chopped	2
1 tbsp	minced gingerroot	15 mL
1½ tsp	mild curry paste, or to taste	7 mL
½ tsp	ground cumin	2 mL
½ tsp	ground coriander	2 mL
¼ tsp	dried thyme leaves	1 mL
Pinch	cayenne pepper	Pinch
2	carrots, peeled and cubed	2
1	sweet potato, peeled and cubed	1
1 cup	cubed rutabaga	250 mL
4 cups	chicken or vegetable stock	1 L
1 cup	half-and-half (10%) cream	250 mL
¼ cup	chopped fresh cilantro or parsley	60 mL
	Sour cream or yogurt (optional)	

1. In a large saucepan, heat butter over medium heat. Add apples, onion, garlic, ginger, curry paste, cumin, coriander, thyme and cayenne pepper; cook, stirring, for 5 minutes or until softened.

2. Add carrots, sweet potato, rutabaga and stock. Bring to a boil; reduce heat to medium-low and simmer, covered, for 30 minutes or until vegetables are very tender. Let cool slightly.

3. In a food processor or blender, purée soup in batches until smooth. Return to saucepan; stir in cream and heat until piping hot. (Do not let boil or soup may curdle.) Ladle into bowls; sprinkle with cilantro and add dollop of sour cream or yogurt, if using.

Borscht

If you are a fan of beets, as I am, you will love this simple version of the classic Russian soup. Serve it piping hot or chilled as a refreshing summer soup. Try it using fresh fennel and fennel seeds. Although not essential to creating delicious borscht, fennel complements the sweetness of the beets.

Tip

To prevent beet stains, wear rubber gloves when handling beets and cover your cutting board with a sheet of waxed paper.

1 tbsp	butter	15 mL
1	large onion, chopped	1
1 cup	chopped celery or fennel bulb	250 mL
1	large clove garlic, finely chopped	1
½ tsp	fennel seeds (optional)	2 mL
1½ lbs	fresh beets, peeled and diced	750 g
5 cups	chicken stock	1.25 L
	Salt and freshly ground black pepper	
2 tbsp	chopped fresh dill	30 mL
	Sour cream or plain yogurt	

1. In a large saucepan, melt butter over medium heat. Add onion, celery, garlic and fennel seeds, if using; cook, stirring, for 5 minutes or until softened.

2. Stir in beets and chicken stock. Bring soup to a boil; reduce heat and simmer, partially covered, for 45 minutes or until beets are very tender. Let cool slightly.

3. In a food processor or blender, purée soup in batches until smooth. Season with salt and pepper to taste. Stir in dill. If serving warm, return to saucepan and heat until piping hot. Or refrigerate until chilled.

4. Ladle soup into bowls and top with a dollop of sour cream or yogurt.

Vichyssoise

Makes 6 servings

This classic cold soup made famous on French restaurant menus in the 1960s relies on the simple combo of potatoes, leeks and cream. I like to serve it very chilled with fresh cut garden chives.

Tip

You can make this soup up to 2 days ahead. It also can be served warm. Reheat until piping hot; do not let boil.

Variation

Vichyssoise with Watercress

Watercress adds a vibrant color and nip to classic vichyssoise. Remove tough stems from 1 bunch watercress. Add watercress leaves to soup at end of cooking when potatoes are tender. Simmer for 1 minute, until watercress is limp and bright green in color. Purée soup as directed.

1 tbsp	butter	15 mL
2	leeks, white and light green parts only, chopped (see Tips, page 190)	2
2 cups	diced peeled potatoes	500 mL
1 tsp	dried tarragon leaves or fines herbes	5 mL
2 tbsp	all-purpose flour	30 mL
4 cups	chicken stock	1 L
1 cup	half-and-half (10%) cream	250 mL
	Salt and freshly ground black pepper	
2 tbsp	chopped fresh chives	30 mL

1. In a large saucepan, melt butter over medium heat. Add leeks, potatoes and tarragon; cook, stirring, for 5 minutes or until leeks are softened but not browned.

2. In a bowl, blend flour with $\frac{1}{4}$ cup (60 mL) of the chicken stock until smooth; add to saucepan along with remaining chicken stock. Bring to a boil, stirring, until slightly thickened; reduce heat, cover and simmer, stirring occasionally, for 20 minutes or until potatoes are very tender.

3. In a blender or food processor, purée soup in batches until smooth. Transfer to a bowl. Stir in cream; season with salt and pepper to taste. Refrigerate. To serve, ladle into bowls and sprinkle with chives.

Leek, Potato and Cabbage Soup

With all the glamorous foods out there now, cabbage is often neglected. That's a shame. Cabbage is an excellent partner to soothing potatoes and smoky sausage in this robust soup — which shows just how rich an addition this underrated vegetable can be. Taste it and you'll see.

Tips

To clean leeks: Trim dark green tops. Cut down center almost to root end and chop. Rinse in a sink full of cold water to remove sand; scoop up leeks and place in colander to drain or use a salad spinner.

Store soup in an airtight container in the refrigerator for up to 5 days.

2 tbsp	olive oil	30 mL
2	leeks, white and light green parts only, chopped (see Tips, left)	2
2	cloves garlic, finely chopped	2
¼ tsp	freshly ground black pepper	1 mL
¼ tsp	caraway seeds (optional)	1 mL
3	potatoes, such as Yukon gold, peeled and cut into ½-inch (1 cm) cubes	3
4 cups	finely shredded green cabbage	1 L
6 cups	beef stock	1.5 L
8 oz	kielbasa, or other cooked smoked sausage, cut into ½-inch (1 cm) cubes	250 g
¼ cup	chopped fresh parsley	60 mL

1. In a large saucepan, heat oil over medium heat. Add leeks, garlic, pepper and caraway seeds, if using; cook, stirring, for 4 minutes or until softened.

2. Stir in potatoes, cabbage and stock. Bring to a boil; reduce heat to medium-low and simmer, covered, for 20 minutes or until vegetables are tender.

3. Add sausage and parsley; cook 5 minutes more or until sausage is heated through.

Stews, Pot Roasts and One-Pot Simmers

continued...

Chicken

Fish and Seafood

Italian Sausages Braised with Potatoes (page 213)

Chicken Vegetable
Cobbler (page 220)

Bistro Steak (page 238)

Barbecued Ribs with Zesty Barbecue Sauce (page 262)

Thyme-Roasted Chicken with Garlic Gravy (page 264)

Yummy Parmesan Chicken Fingers (page 271)

Rosemary Beef Ragoût

Stews are very convenient for reheating and freezing, so they can be a real time saver. Keep stew in an airtight container in the refrigerator for up to 3 days. Or double the recipe and freeze half for another meal.

Variation

Substitute 1 fennel bulb for the celery, if desired. Trim top from fennel; cut in half lengthwise and remove core. Cut into strips.

1 lb	stewing beef, cut into 1-inch (2.5 cm) cubes	500 g
2 tbsp	olive oil, divided	30 mL
2	large onions, chopped	2
3	cloves garlic, finely chopped	3
1½ tsp	dried rosemary, crumbled	7 mL
2 tbsp	balsamic or red wine vinegar	30 mL
2 tbsp	all-purpose flour	30 mL
2½ cups	beef stock	625 mL
2 tbsp	tomato paste	30 mL
½ tsp	salt	2 mL
½ tsp	freshly ground black pepper	2 mL
12 oz	peeled baby carrots	375 g
3	stalks celery, thickly cut	3

1. Pat beef dry with paper towels. In a Dutch oven or large saucepan, heat 1 tbsp (15 mL) oil over medium-high heat. Brown beef on all sides; transfer to a plate.

2. Add remaining oil to pan. Reduce heat to medium and cook onions, garlic and rosemary, stirring, for 5 minutes or until softened. Add vinegar; cook until almost evaporated. Blend in flour. Add stock, tomato paste, salt and pepper. Bring to a boil; cook, stirring, until slightly thickened.

3. Return meat and accumulated juices to pan; reduce heat, cover and simmer for 1¼ hours. Add carrots and celery; simmer, covered, for 30 minutes or until beef and vegetables are tender.

Boeuf Bourguignon

Makes 6 servings

This richly flavored French beef stew with red wine and smoky bacon is especially delicious when served with creamy mashed potatoes.

Tips

To brown meat without having to add a lot of oil, pat meat dry with paper towels before cooking. Add a bit of the oil to the pan and heat until hot but not smoking. Add a small amount of the meat at a time until nicely colored; remove. Add a bit more oil to pan if necessary and reheat before adding next batch of meat.

To wash or not wash mushrooms? You can wipe them with a damp cloth, if you wish. However, I feel it's important to wash all produce that comes into my kitchen. I quickly rinse mushrooms under cold water and immediately wrap in a clean, dry kitchen towel or paper towels to absorb excess moisture.

2½ lbs	boneless beef blade or shoulder pot roast, trimmed and cut into 1½-inch (4 cm) cubes	1.25 kg
2 tbsp	vegetable oil (approx.)	30 mL
4	slices thick-cut smoky bacon, chopped	4
1	large onion, chopped	1
4	cloves garlic, finely chopped	4
¼ cup	all-purpose flour	60 mL
2 cups	red wine	500 mL
1½ cups	beef stock	375 mL
2 tsp	chopped fresh thyme or ¾ tsp (3 mL) dried thyme leaves	10 mL
1	bay leaf	1
½ tsp	salt	2 mL
½ tsp	freshly ground black pepper	2 mL
2 cups	peeled baby carrots	500 mL
1	package (10 oz/300 g) pearl onions (about 20)	1
1 tbsp	butter	15 mL
8 oz	cremini mushrooms, quartered	250 g
¼ cup	chopped fresh parsley	60 mL

1. Pat beef dry with paper towels. In a Dutch oven or large saucepan, heat 1 tbsp (15 mL) oil over medium-high heat. Cook beef, in batches, until nicely browned on all sides, adding more oil as needed. Transfer to a plate as meat browns.

2. Reduce heat to medium and cook bacon, stirring, for about 5 minutes or until crisp. Remove bacon and set aside. Pour off all but 1 tbsp (15 mL) fat from pan. Cook chopped onion and garlic, stirring, for 3 minutes or until softened. Sprinkle flour over onion mixture and cook, stirring, for 1 minute.

3. Add wine, stock, thyme, bay leaf, salt and pepper. Scrape up brown bits from bottom of pan and cook, stirring, until sauce comes to a boil and thickens. Return meat and accumulated juices to pan. Bring to boil, reduce heat to medium-low and simmer, covered, for 1½ hours or until beef is almost tender. Add carrots and bacon. Simmer for 15 minutes.

The stew tastes even
better if you make it a
day ahead. Let cool,
cover and refrigerate, and
reheat before serving. It
also freezes well. Place in
an airtight container and
freeze for up to 3 months.

4. Meanwhile, in a saucepan of boiling water, cook pearl
onions for 4 minutes. Place in strainer and chill under
cold water; peel.

5. In a large nonstick skillet, melt butter over medium
heat. Cook pearl onions, stirring often, for 3 minutes or
until nicely colored. Add mushrooms and cook, stirring,
for 5 minutes or until mushrooms are softened. Add
vegetables to beef. Cover and simmer for 15 minutes
or until beef and vegetables are tender. Transfer to a
serving dish and sprinkle with parsley.

Freezing and Reheating Soups and Casseroles

- Label and date containers and casseroles before refrigerating
  or freezing.

- Meat- and chicken-based soups, stews and casseroles can be kept
  safely for up to 3 days in the refrigerator; vegetable-based dishes can
  be kept refrigerated for 5 days.

- To reheat, place in saucepan over medium heat, stirring occasionally,
  until piping hot; or place in covered casserole and bake in 350°F
  (180°C) oven for 30 to 45 minutes or until piping hot; or microwave,
  covered with lid or microwave-safe plastic wrap, on Medium-High
  (70%) for 9 to 15 minutes, stirring occasionally, or until heated
  through to center. For single servings, microwave, covered, on
  Medium-High (70%) for 3 to 5 minutes.

- Stews, soups and casseroles can be frozen for up to 3 months. Defrost
  in refrigerator overnight and reheat as directed above.

Old-Fashioned Beef Stew

What's more comforting than a satisfying stew? You start feeling good the minute you set this one-pot dish to simmer on the stovetop. As the herb-infused aroma wafts through your kitchen, the good feeling grows. The first forkful confirms that this stew is comfort food at its best.

Tip

A word about parsley. Use either the curly leaf variety or the more strongly flavored flat-leaf (Italian) type. Wash well in plenty of water to remove dirt; dry parsley in a salad spinner or wrap in clean towel. The drier the parsley, the longer it lasts in your refrigerator. Wrap in paper towels, then in a plastic bag and refrigerate. To save time, I finely chop a few bunches of parsley, pack into a container and freeze. Though not suitable for fresh salads, the frozen parsley is perfect to add to soups, stews, meatloaves and casseroles.

1½ lbs	stewing beef, cut into 1½-inch (4 cm) cubes	750 g
¼ cup	all-purpose flour	60 mL
1 tsp	salt	5 mL
½ tsp	freshly ground black pepper	2 mL
2 tbsp	vegetable oil (approx.)	30 mL
2	onions, chopped	2
3	cloves garlic, finely chopped	3
1 tsp	dried thyme leaves	5 mL
1 tsp	dried marjoram leaves	5 mL
1	bay leaf	1
1 cup	red wine or additional beef stock	250 mL
3 tbsp	tomato paste	45 mL
3 cups	beef stock (approx.)	750 mL
5	carrots	5
2	stalks celery	2
4 to 5	potatoes (about 1½ lbs/750 g)	4 to 5
12 oz	green beans	375 g
¼ cup	chopped fresh parsley (see Tip, left)	60 mL

1. Pat beef dry with paper towels. Combine flour, salt and pepper in a heavy plastic bag. In batches, add beef to flour mixture and toss to coat. Transfer to a plate. Reserve remaining flour mixture.

2. In a Dutch oven or large saucepan, heat 1 tbsp (15 mL) oil over medium-high heat; brown beef, in batches, adding more oil as needed. Transfer to a plate as meat browns.

3. Reduce heat to medium. Cook onions, garlic, thyme, marjoram and bay leaf, stirring, for 3 minutes or until softened. Blend in remaining flour. Add wine and tomato paste; cook, stirring, to scrape up brown bits. Return beef and any accumulated juices to pan; pour in stock.

4. Bring to a boil, stirring, until slightly thickened. Reduce heat, cover and simmer over medium-low heat, stirring occasionally, for 1 hour.

5. Meanwhile, peel carrots and halve lengthwise. Cut carrots and celery into 1½-inch (4 cm) chunks. Peel potatoes and quarter. Add vegetables to pan. Cover and simmer for 30 minutes.

Tip

Instead of green beans, use 2 cups (500 mL) cubed rutabaga (1-inch/2.5 cm cubes) and add with the carrots.

6. Trim ends of beans and cut into 2-inch (5 cm) lengths. Stir into stew mixture, adding more stock if necessary, until vegetables are just covered. Cover and simmer for 30 minutes or until vegetables are tender. Remove bay leaf and stir in parsley. Adjust seasoning with salt and pepper to taste.

Irish Beef Stew

Makes 6 to 8 servings

Guinness, a dark Irish beer, adds a rich, intense flavor to this simple beef stew that benefits from being made a day ahead.

Tip

Instead of Guinness, substitute another dark beer, such as stout or dark ale. If the beer you use is only available in 12-oz (341 mL) bottles or cans, add an extra ½ cup (125 mL) beef stock to the stew.

3 lbs	lean stewing beef or lamb, cut into 1½-inch (4 cm) cubes	1.5 kg
2 tbsp	vegetable oil (approx.)	30 mL
2	large onions, thinly sliced	2
4	cloves garlic, finely chopped	4
1 tbsp	chopped fresh thyme or 1 tsp (5 mL) dried thyme leaves	15 mL
1	large bay leaf	1
1 tsp	salt	5 mL
½ tsp	freshly ground black pepper	2 mL
2 tbsp	all-purpose flour	30 mL
1	can (16 oz/440 mL) pub draft Guinness	1
½ cup	beef stock	125 mL
¼ cup	chopped fresh parsley	60 mL

1. Pat beef dry with paper towels. In a Dutch oven or large saucepan, heat 1 tbsp (15 mL) oil over medium-high heat. Brown beef, in batches, adding more oil as needed. Transfer to a plate as meat browns.

2. Reduce heat to medium; cook onions, garlic, thyme, bay leaf, salt and pepper, stirring often, for 5 minutes or until softened. Blend in flour. Add beef, including juices, beer and stock to pan.

3. Bring to a boil over high heat; reduce heat, cover and simmer for 1½ hours. Remove lid; simmer for 30 minutes or until beef is very tender. Adjust seasoning with salt and pepper to taste; remove bay leaf. Sprinkle with parsley before serving.

Beef Brisket with Beer and Caramelized Onions

When I was growing up, briskets and pot roasts were a staple in my house. I can remember coming home from school to the tantalizing smell of a roast slowly braising in the oven. This recipe features a richly colored sauce from caramelized onions and a subtle sweet-sour taste from the beer and brown sugar. It's delicious served with creamy mashed potatoes or egg noodles.

● Preheat oven to 325°F (160°C)

1	beef brisket or pot roast, such as cross-rib or rump (about 3 to 4 lbs/1.5 to 2 kg)	1
¼ cup	all-purpose flour	60 mL
2 tbsp	vegetable oil (approx.), divided	30 mL
4	onions, halved lengthwise and thinly sliced (about 1¼ lbs/625 g)	4
2 tbsp	packed brown sugar	30 mL
2	bay leaves	2
1 tsp	salt	5 mL
½ tsp	ground cinnamon	2 mL
½ tsp	ground ginger	2 mL
½ tsp	freshly ground black pepper	2 mL
3	large cloves garlic, finely chopped	3
2 tbsp	balsamic vinegar	30 mL
1	bottle (12 oz/341 mL) beer	1
1	can (7½ oz/213 mL) tomato sauce	1
1½ lbs	carrots (about 8)	750 g
1	small rutabaga (about 1 lb/500 g)	1

1. Pat beef dry with paper towels. On a large plate, roll meat in flour to coat. Shake off excess; reserve remaining flour.

2. In a Dutch oven, heat 1 tbsp (15 mL) oil over medium-high heat. Brown meat on all sides, about 6 minutes. Transfer to a plate.

3. Reduce heat to medium. Add remaining oil to Dutch oven. Cook onions, brown sugar, bay leaves, salt, cinnamon, ginger and pepper, stirring often, for 12 to 15 minutes or until onions are softened and nicely colored. (Add more oil, if needed, to prevent onions from burning.)

4. Add reserved flour and garlic; cook, stirring, for 30 seconds. Add vinegar; cook until evaporated. Pour in beer and tomato sauce; bring to a boil, stirring, until thickened. Return meat and accumulated juices to pan. Cover and roast in preheated oven for 2 hours.

5. Meanwhile, peel carrots and rutabaga; cut into 2- by ½-inch (5 by 1 cm) strips. Add to beef. Cover and cook 1 to 1½ hours or until meat is tender.

6. Remove roast from pan; cut into thin slices. Arrange on serving platter; surround with vegetables. Skim any fat from sauce; remove bay leaves and spoon some sauce over meat and pour the rest into a warmed sauceboat to serve on the side.

Braised Beef Short Ribs

Makes 4 servings

When it comes to favorite recipes, these slowly braised short ribs in a rich herb-orange-flavored sauce served with lots of creamy mashed potatoes are the quintessence of comfort food.

3 lbs	beef short ribs	1.5 kg
2 tbsp	olive oil (approx.)	30 mL
2	onions, chopped	2
3	cloves garlic, finely chopped	3
1 tsp	dried rosemary or thyme leaves, crumbled	5 mL
1 tsp	salt	5 mL
½ tsp	freshly ground black pepper	2 mL
1½ cups	beef stock (approx.)	375 mL
1 cup	canned tomatoes, including juice, chopped	250 mL
2 tbsp	Worcestershire sauce	30 mL
3	strips (3 inches/7.5 cm) orange peel	3

1. Pat short ribs dry with paper towels. In a Dutch oven or large saucepan, heat 1 tbsp (15 mL) oil over medium-high heat; brown short ribs, in batches, adding more oil as needed, until nicely browned on all sides. Transfer to a plate.

2. Reduce heat to medium; cook onions, garlic, rosemary, salt and pepper, stirring often, for 5 minutes or until softened.

3. Add stock, tomatoes with juice, Worcestershire sauce and orange peel. Return beef and accumulated juices to pan; bring to a boil. Cover and reduce heat; simmer for 2 hours, adding additional stock to keep beef covered while braising, until beef is fork-tender.

Saucy Braised Round Steak

This dish creates lots of yummy gravy to spoon over mashed potatoes or sweet potatoes. Serve with broccoli or green beans for a family-pleasing supper.

Tip

This is a great recipe to double and have stashed in the freezer for those nights when you don't want to cook from scratch. Place meat and sauce in an airtight container and freeze for up to 3 months.

1½ lbs	boneless beef round steak	750 g
¼ cup	all-purpose flour	60 mL
2 tbsp	vegetable oil (approx.)	30 mL
1	large onion, chopped	1
2	cloves garlic, finely chopped	2
1 tsp	ground coriander	5 mL
1 tsp	ground cumin	5 mL
½ tsp	freshly ground black pepper	2 mL
1 cup	beef stock	250 mL
3	strips (3 inches/7.5 cm) orange peel	3
⅓ cup	fresh orange juice	75 mL
⅓ cup	ketchup	175 mL
2 tbsp	soy sauce	30 mL
1 tbsp	balsamic vinegar	15 mL

1. Pat beef dry with paper towels. Cut into 6 pieces and pound with a meat mallet to ½-inch (1 cm) thickness. Dredge in flour, shaking off excess. Reserve any remaining flour.

2. In a Dutch oven, heat 1 tbsp (15 mL) oil over medium-high heat. Cook steak, in batches, until nicely browned on all sides, adding more oil as needed between batches. Transfer to a plate.

3. Reduce heat to medium. Cook onion, garlic, coriander, cumin and pepper, stirring, until onion is softened, about 3 minutes. Blend in remaining flour.

4. Add stock, orange peel, orange juice, ketchup, soy sauce and vinegar. Bring to a boil, stirring and scraping up any brown bits from bottom of pan, until thickened.

5. Return steaks and any accumulated juices to pan. Cover and simmer over low heat for 1 hour. Turn steaks and simmer for 1 hour or until tender. Discard orange peel.

Slow Cooker Method

1. Follow Steps 1 and 2 and transfer meat to slow cooker. Follow Steps 3 and 4, reducing beef stock to ½ cup (125 mL). Pour sauce over meat in slow cooker. Cover and cook on Low for 7 to 8 hours or on High for 3½ to 4 hours, until tender, turning meat twice during cooking.

Country Pot Roast

Makes 6 to 8 servings

This homey standby always provides me with welcome leftovers for later in the week or even to have stashed away in the freezer for an easy supper.

Tip

Pot roast always tastes better the next day; let cool, cover and refrigerate. Also freezes well.

● Preheat oven to 350°F (180°C)

1	boneless beef pot roast, such as rump or brisket (about 3 to 4 lbs/ 1.5 to 2 kg)	1
¼ cup	all-purpose flour	60 mL
2 tbsp	olive oil	30 mL
1	large onion, chopped	1
3	cloves garlic, finely chopped	3
1½ tsp	dried oregano leaves	7 mL
1	bay leaf	1
1 tsp	salt	5 mL
½ tsp	freshly ground black pepper	2 mL
¼ cup	red wine vinegar	60 mL
1	can (19 oz/540 mL) stewed tomatoes, including juice	1
½ cup	beef stock	125 mL
2 tbsp	fancy molasses or brown sugar	30 mL

1. Pat roast dry with paper towels. Place flour on a plate and coat beef with flour; reserve remaining flour.

2. In a Dutch oven, heat oil over medium-high heat and brown roast on all sides, about 6 minutes. Transfer to plate.

3. Reduce heat to medium. Cook onion, garlic, oregano, bay leaf, salt and pepper, stirring, for 3 minutes or until lightly colored. Add vinegar; scrape up brown bits from bottom of pan. Blend in remaining flour; add tomatoes with juice, stock and molasses. Bring to a boil; return beef to pan. Cover and place in preheated oven; braise for 2½ to 3 hours or until meat is fork-tender.

4. Cut beef into slices and arrange on a platter. Discard bay leaf and purée sauce in a food processor or blender until smooth. Spoon some of the sauce over meat; transfer rest to a gravy boat. Serve with mashed potatoes.

Veal Ragoût with Sweet Peppers

I like to make this delicious comfort stew ahead and have it tucked away in the freezer ready for company. Adding the peppers at the end of cooking helps keep their shape and lends a slightly smoky taste that lingers in your memory long after the last bite.

Tips

Use a combination of green, red and yellow peppers for maximum color effect.

The recipe can be prepared through Step 3 up to 48 hours ahead, then covered and refrigerated — or freeze for up to 3 months. Before reheating, let defrost in fridge overnight. Bring to a boil; cover and simmer for 20 minutes or until veal is thoroughly heated.

Variation

Beef can be substituted for the veal.

3 lbs	lean stewing veal, cut into 1-inch (2.5 cm) cubes	1.5 kg
2 tbsp	all-purpose flour	30 mL
4 tbsp	olive oil (approx.), divided	60 mL
1	Spanish onion, chopped (about 1 lb/500 g)	1
4	large cloves garlic, finely chopped	4
1 tsp	dried thyme leaves	5 mL
1 tsp	paprika	5 mL
1	bay leaf	1
1 tsp	salt	5 mL
1/2 tsp	freshly ground black pepper	2 mL
1 cup	red wine or beef stock	250 mL
4	tomatoes, chopped	4
4	bell peppers (any color), cubed	4
1/3 cup	chopped fresh parsley	75 mL

1. Pat veal dry with paper towels. In a bowl, toss veal cubes with flour until well coated. In a Dutch oven or large heavy saucepan, heat 1 tbsp (15 mL) oil over medium-high heat. Brown veal, in batches, adding more oil as needed. Transfer to a plate as meat browns.

2. Reduce heat to medium. Add remaining oil. Cook onion, garlic, thyme, paprika, bay leaf, salt and pepper, stirring often, for 5 minutes or until softened.

3. Add wine and bring to a boil. Stir in veal along with accumulated juices; add tomatoes. Bring to a boil; reduce heat to medium-low and simmer, covered, for 1 1/4 to 1 1/2 hours or until veal is tender.

4. Shortly before serving, heat 1 tbsp (15 mL) oil in a large nonstick skillet over high heat; cook pepper cubes, stirring, for 2 to 3 minutes or until lightly colored. Reduce heat to medium-low, cover and simmer for 8 to 10 minutes or until tender-crisp.

5. Add peppers to veal; stir in parsley and simmer for 5 minutes to let the flavors blend. Adjust seasoning with salt and pepper to taste. Remove bay leaf.

Veal Braised with Onions

Richly flavored braised meats like veal are always a welcome choice for a family meal. I make them in advance, since their flavor improves when refrigerated and reheated the next day. Serve this simple dish with noodles or creamy mashed potatoes.

Tip

To brown meat without having to add a lot of oil, pat meat dry with paper towels before cooking. Add a bit of the oil to the pan and heat until hot but not smoking. Add a small amount of the meat at a time until nicely colored; remove. Add a bit more oil to pan if necessary and reheat before adding next batch of meat.

2 lbs	lean stewing veal, cut into ¾-inch (2 cm) cubes	1 kg
2 tbsp	olive oil (approx.), divided	30 mL
2	large onions, chopped	2
2	cloves garlic, finely chopped	2
2 tbsp	all-purpose flour	30 mL
1½ cups	chicken stock	375 mL
½ cup	dry white wine or additional stock	125 mL
2 tbsp	tomato paste	30 mL
1 tsp	salt	5 mL
½ tsp	freshly ground black pepper	2 mL
¼ cup	chopped fresh parsley	60 mL
1 tsp	grated lemon zest	5 mL

1. Pat veal dry with paper towels. In a Dutch oven or large saucepan, heat 1 tbsp (15 mL) oil over high heat. Brown veal, in batches, adding more oil as needed. Transfer to a plate as meat browns.

2. Reduce heat to medium; add remaining oil. Cook onions and garlic, stirring, for 5 minutes or until lightly colored. Blend in flour; stir in stock, wine and tomato paste. Add veal along with accumulated juices; season with salt and pepper. Bring to a boil.

3. Reduce heat, cover and simmer, stirring occasionally, for 50 minutes. Stir in parsley and lemon zest; cook, covered, for 10 minutes or until veal is tender.

Osso Buco

The rich flavors of this classic Italian dish come from the slow braising of the succulent veal shanks. While not essential, the addition of the gremolata adds a fragrant seasoning to fork-tender veal. Serve with rice or polenta.

Tip

Hate shedding tears when chopping onions? To minimize the weeping problem, use a razor-sharp knife to prevent loss of juices and cover the cut onions with a paper towel as you chop them to prevent the vapors from rising to your eyes.

4	thick slices veal shank	4
2 tbsp	all-purpose flour	30 mL
2 tbsp	butter	30 mL
1	onion, chopped	1
2	large cloves garlic, finely chopped	2
2	small carrots, peeled and diced	2
1	stalk celery, finely chopped	1
2 tsp	chopped fresh rosemary or thyme leaves or ¾ tsp (3 mL) dried rosemary or thyme leaves	10 mL
¾ tsp	salt	3 mL
½ tsp	freshly ground black pepper	2 mL
½ cup	white wine	125 mL
¾ cup	chicken stock (approx.)	175 mL
2 tbsp	tomato paste	30 mL

Gremolata (optional)

¼ cup	chopped fresh parsley	60 mL
2 tsp	grated lemon zest	10 mL
1	clove garlic, minced	1

1. Pat veal dry with paper towels. Place flour on a plate; coat veal in the flour, shaking off excess.

2. In a Dutch oven or large saucepan, heat butter over medium-high heat; brown veal on all sides. Transfer to a plate and set aside.

3. Add onion, garlic, carrots, celery, rosemary, salt and pepper to pan; cook, stirring for 3 minutes, until lightly colored. Stir in wine, scrapping up brown bits from bottom of pan; add stock and tomato paste. Return veal to pan; bring to a boil. Reduce heat; cover and simmer, adding more stock if needed, for 1¼ to 1½ hours or until veal is very tender.

4. *Gremolata:* In a small bowl, combine parsley, lemon zest and garlic. Transfer veal to a serving platter; spoon sauce over top. Sprinkle with gremolata and serve.

Braised Lamb Shanks

Lamb shanks are back in fashion and served in the trendiest of restaurants. Served on a mound of creamy mashed potatoes, this is comfort food at its best.

Tip

Lamb shanks vary in size depending on whether they are locally sourced or come from New Zealand or Australia. Estimate each lamb shank to be 12 to 16 ounces (375 to 500 g) per person. Increase the number of shanks if they are on the small side.

● Preheat oven to 325°F (160°C)

2 tbsp	olive oil	30 mL
4	lamb shanks, trimmed	4
2	onions, chopped	2
4	cloves garlic, chopped	4
2	carrots, peeled and chopped	2
1	stalk celery, chopped	1
2	sticks cinnamon	2
1	bay leaf	1
1 tsp	each dried oregano and thyme leaves	5 mL
1 tsp	salt	5 mL
1/4 tsp	hot pepper flakes	1 mL
1	can (19 oz/540 mL) stewed tomatoes	1
1 cup	beef stock (approx.)	250 mL
1 cup	red wine or additional beef stock	250 mL

Topping

3 tbsp	chopped fresh parsley	45 mL
1 tbsp	coarsely grated lemon zest	15 mL
1/2 tsp	freshly ground black pepper	2 mL

1. In a large Dutch oven or saucepan, heat oil over medium-high heat. Cook lamb shanks, in batches, until browned on all sides. Transfer to plate.

2. Reduce heat to medium. Cook onions, garlic, carrots, celery, cinnamon sticks, bay leaf, oregano, thyme, salt and hot pepper flakes, stirring often, for 5 minutes or until vegetables are softened.

3. Add tomatoes, stock and wine; bring to a boil. Return shanks and any accumulated juices to pan. Cover and cook in preheated oven for 2 hours or until lamb is tender and falling off the bone.

4. Transfer meat to a plate. Skim fat; remove and discard cinnamon sticks and bay leaf. In a food processor or blender, purée sauce until smooth, adding more stock if necessary. Return sauce to pan and cook over medium-high heat for 5 minutes or until slightly reduced. Return lamb to pan; place over medium heat until piping hot.

5. *Topping:* Combine parsley, zest and pepper. Arrange lamb on a platter and sprinkle with mixture.

Greek Lamb and Bean Stew

Makes 6 servings

Oregano-scented tomato sauce with a burst of heat from hot pepper flakes is the perfect foil for buttery lima beans and lamb.

Tip

Stew can be cooked ahead and stored in an airtight container in the refrigerator for up to 3 days or frozen for up to 3 months.

2 cups	large dried lima beans	500 mL
2 tbsp	olive oil, divided	30 mL
1 lb	lean boneless lamb, cut into 1-inch (2.5 cm) pieces	500 g
1	Spanish onion (1 lb/500 g), chopped	1
4	cloves garlic, finely chopped	4
1 tbsp	dried oregano leaves	15 mL
1/2 tsp	hot pepper flakes	2 mL
1	can (19 oz/540 mL) tomatoes, including juice, chopped	1
1 tsp	salt	5 mL
1/2 tsp	freshly ground black pepper	2 mL
1	large red bell pepper, chopped	1
1	large green bell pepper, chopped	1
1/2 cup	kalamata olives	125 mL
1/4 cup	chopped fresh parsley	60 mL

1. Sort and rinse beans. In a large saucepan, bring beans and 8 cups (2 L) cold water to a boil; cover and cook for 15 minutes. Drain and return to pot. Add 8 cups (2 L) water: bring to a boil. Reduce heat and simmer, partially covered, for 45 minutes or until tender. Drain.

2. Meanwhile, in a Dutch oven, heat 1 tbsp (15 mL) oil over medium-high heat; cook lamb until browned on all sides. Transfer to a plate.

3. Add remaining oil to pan; reduce heat to medium. Cook onion, garlic, oregano and hot pepper flakes, stirring, for 5 minutes or until softened. Return meat to pan along with any juices. Add tomatoes with juice, salt and pepper; bring to a boil. Reduce heat, cover and simmer for 45 minutes.

4. Preheat oven to 350°F (180°C). Add beans, red and green peppers, olives and about 1/2 cup (125 mL) water to lamb to make a sauce-like consistency. Cover and bake in oven for 40 minutes or until lamb is tender. Stir in parsley.

Spicy Lamb Stew

Sometimes you crave a dish that explodes with spicy flavors. The ginger and hot pepper flakes used here will satisfy that craving — and soothe your soul, too. I like to serve this spice-infused stew with basmati rice.

Tips

To cook basmati rice: Rinse 1½ cups (375 mL) rice in several changes of cold water. Place in bowl; add cold water to cover. Let soak 15 minutes; drain. In a saucepan, bring 2¼ cups (550 mL) water to a boil; add rice and 1 tsp (5 mL) salt. Return to boil, reduce heat to low and simmer, covered, for 10 minutes. Remove and let stand, covered, for 5 minutes. Uncover and fluff with a fork.

Buy a 3-lb (1.5 kg) leg of lamb or shoulder roast to get 1½ lbs (750 g) boneless lamb.

Variation

Beef can be substituted for the lamb; increase cooking time to 1½ hours or until meat is tender.

2 tbsp	vegetable oil (approx.)	30 mL
1½ lbs	lean boneless lamb, cut into 1-inch (2.5 cm) cubes	750 g
1	large onion, chopped	1
2	cloves garlic, finely chopped	2
1 tbsp	minced gingerroot	15 mL
1 tsp	ground cumin	5 mL
1 tsp	ground coriander	5 mL
½ tsp	ground cinnamon	2 mL
½ tsp	salt	2 mL
¼ tsp	hot pepper flakes, or to taste	1 mL
Pinch	ground cloves	Pinch
1 tbsp	all-purpose flour	15 mL
½ cup	plain yogurt	125 mL
1	large tomato, chopped	1
½ cup	lamb or chicken stock	125 mL
¼ cup	chopped fresh cilantro or parsley	60 mL

1. In a large saucepan, heat 1 tbsp (15 mL) oil over medium-high heat; brown lamb, in batches, adding more oil as needed. Transfer to a plate as meat browns.

2. Reduce heat to medium. Cook onion, garlic, ginger, cumin, coriander, cinnamon, salt, hot pepper flakes and cloves, stirring, for 2 minutes or until softened.

3. Sprinkle with flour; stir in yogurt. Cook for 1 minute or until thickened. Add lamb with any accumulated juices, tomato and stock; bring to a boil. Reduce heat and simmer, covered, for 45 minutes or until lamb is tender. Sprinkle with cilantro or parsley before serving.

Lamb Tagine with Chickpeas and Apricots

Tagine is a Moroccan stew accented with rich spices. It is traditionally slow-cooked in a pottery dish with a cone-shaped lid of the same name. Serve with Moroccan-Style Couscous (see recipe, page 393), without the added raisins.

Tip

Buy a 3-lb (1.5 kg) leg of lamb or shoulder roast to get 1½ lbs (750 g) boneless lamb.

2 tbsp	olive oil (approx.)	30 mL
1½ lbs	lean boneless lamb, cut into 1-inch (2.5 cm) cubes	1.5 kg
5	carrots, peeled and thickly sliced	5
1	large onion, chopped	1
3	cloves garlic, finely chopped	3
1 tsp	ground ginger	5 mL
1	ground cumin	5 mL
1 tsp	ground cinnamon	5 mL
1 tsp	ground turmeric	5 mL
½ tsp	salt	2 mL
½ tsp	freshly ground black pepper	2 mL
1	can (14 oz/398 mL) tomatoes, including juice, chopped	1
1 cup	chicken stock (approx.)	250 mL
1	can (19 oz/540 mL) chickpeas, rinsed and drained	1
½ cup	dried apricots or figs, roughly chopped	125 mL
¼ cup	liquid honey	60 mL

1. In a Dutch oven, heat 1 tbsp (15 mL) oil over medium-high heat. Brown lamb, in batches, adding more oil as needed. Transfer to a plate as meat browns.

2. Reduce heat to medium. Add carrots, onion, garlic, ginger, cumin, cinnamon, turmeric, salt and pepper to pan; cook, stirring, for about 5 minutes or until onion is softened.

3. Add tomatoes, stock and lamb, along with any accumulated juices; bring to a boil. Reduce heat to medium-low, cover and simmer for 1½ hours or until lamb is just tender.

4. Add chickpeas, apricots and honey. Add more stock, if necessary. Cover and simmer for 30 minutes or until lamb is very tender.

Slow Cooker Method

1. Follow Step 1 and transfer lamb to slow cooker. Follow Step 2, then stir in tomatoes and stock; bring to a boil. Transfer to slow cooker. Cover and cook on Low for 6 hours or on High for 3 hours, until almost tender. Add chickpeas, apricots and honey. Cover and cook on Low for 1 hour or on High for 30 minutes.

Sweet-and-Sour Pineapple Pork

1	can (8 oz/214 mL) pineapple tidbits	1
¼ cup	soy sauce	60 mL
¼ cup	rice vinegar	60 mL
3 tbsp	packed brown sugar	45 mL
1 tbsp	cornstarch	15 mL
2 tbsp	vegetable oil, divided	30 mL
1 lb	lean boneless pork loin, cut into thin strips	500 g
1	small onion, halved lengthwise, sliced	1
2	cloves garlic, finely chopped	2
1 tbsp	minced gingerroot	15 mL
2	carrots, peeled, thinly sliced on the diagonal	2
1	zucchini, halved lengthwise, thinly sliced	1
1	red bell pepper, cut into thin 2-inch (5 cm) strips	1

1. Drain pineapple, reserving juice; set pineapple aside. Pour juice in a glass measure; add soy sauce, rice vinegar and brown sugar. Blend in cornstarch until smooth.

2. In a large nonstick skillet, heat 1 tbsp (15 mL) of the oil over medium-high heat. Cook pork until browned on all sides. Transfer to a plate.

3. Add remaining oil to pan; cook onion, garlic and ginger, stirring, for 30 seconds or until fragrant. Add carrots, zucchini and red pepper; cook, stirring, for 1 minute.

4. Add soy sauce mixture; bring to a boil, stirring, until thickened. Reduce heat, cover and cook for 1 to 2 minutes or until vegetables are tender-crisp.

5. Return pork to pan, including any accumulated juices and reserved pineapple. Heat, stirring, for 1 minute or until piping hot. Serve immediately.

Pulled Pork

Pile this juicy, tender pork, with its sweet-spicy sauce, into buns when you want an economical way to please a crowd.

Tip

Place leftover pulled pork in sauce in an airtight container and refrigerate for up to 3 days or freeze for up to 3 months.

● Preheat oven to 300°F (150°C)

4 lbs	boneless pork shoulder blade roast	2 kg
1 tbsp	chili powder	15 mL
2 tsp	dry mustard	10 mL
2 tsp	dried oregano leaves	10 mL
2 tsp	ground cumin	10 mL
1 tsp	paprika	5 mL
½ tsp	freshly ground black pepper	2 mL

Sauce

1	large onion, finely chopped	1
4	cloves garlic, finely chopped	4
2 cups	chili sauce or ketchup	500 mL
¼ cup	packed brown sugar	60 mL
¼ cup	cider vinegar	60 mL
2 tbsp	Worcestershire sauce	30 mL
2 tsp	liquid smoke or to taste	10 mL
	Soft buns (white or whole wheat), warmed and split	

1. Remove any netting from pork, if necessary. Trim off excess fat.

2. In a bowl, combine chili powder, mustard, oregano, cumin, paprika and pepper. Coat pork all over with seasoning and place meat in a Dutch oven or large casserole.

3. *Sauce:* In a bowl, combine onion, garlic, chili sauce, brown sugar, vinegar, Worcestershire sauce and liquid smoke. Pour sauce over meat.

4. Cover and braise in preheated oven, turning roast over halfway through cooking, for 4 to 4½ hours or until very tender. Skim any fat from surface of sauce.

5. Transfer pork to a cutting board, tent with foil and let stand for 10 minutes. Using two forks, shred or pull meat into strands, discarding excess fat. Return pork to sauce in Dutch oven and keep warm until serving. Spoon shredded pork with sauce into buns and serve.

Slow Cooker Method

1. Place pork roast coated in seasonings in slow cooker. Pour sauce over. Cover and cook on Low for 9 to 10 hours or on High for 4½ to 5 hours, turning meat once, until meat is very tender. Shred pork and return to slow cooker to keep warm until serving time.

Southwestern Pork Stew

Here's a soothing dish to serve for casual get-togethers. This stew requires no more preparation time than a stir-fry or one-pot dish. Cutting the meat into smaller pieces also shortens the cooking time.

Variation

Lean stewing beef can be substituted for the pork. For a vegetarian dish, replace meat with cubes of firm tofu. Add along with kidney beans.

2 tbsp	olive oil, divided	30 mL
1 lb	lean stewing pork, cut into 3/4-inch (2 cm) cubes	500 g
2	onions, chopped	2
3	cloves garlic, finely chopped	3
4 tsp	chili powder	20 mL
1 1/2 tsp	dried oregano leaves	7 mL
1 tsp	ground cumin	5 mL
3/4 tsp	salt	3 mL
1/2 tsp	hot pepper flakes, or to taste	2 mL
3 tbsp	all-purpose flour	45 mL
2 cups	beef or chicken stock	500 mL
1	can (28 oz/796 mL) tomatoes, including juice, chopped	1
2	bell peppers (assorted colors), cubed	2
2 cups	frozen corn kernels	500 mL
1	can (19 oz/540 mL) kidney beans or black beans, drained and rinsed	1
	Chopped cilantro (optional)	

1. In a Dutch oven or large saucepan, heat 1 tbsp (15 mL) oil over medium-high heat. Cook pork until browned on all sides. Transfer to a plate.

2. Add remaining oil to pan; reduce heat to medium. Cook onions, garlic, chili powder, oregano, cumin, salt and hot pepper flakes, stirring, for 2 minutes or until softened.

3. Blend in flour; stir in stock and tomatoes with juice. Bring to a boil, stirring until thickened. Return pork and accumulated juices to pan; reduce heat, cover and simmer for 1 hour or until meat is tender.

4. Add bell peppers, corn and kidney beans; simmer, covered, for 15 minutes or until vegetables are tender. Garnish with chopped cilantro, if desired.

Choucroute with Smoked Sausages

Makes 4 servings

This rustic French dish from the Alsace region is perfect for those occasions when you want something hearty and causal to serve. Smoked pork chops or ribs can also be used instead of sausages. Don't forget the Dijon mustard.

Tip

Make sure to pierce the skins of whole sausage using a skewer to prevent skins from bursting. Or cut into large chunks and add to dish.

1 tbsp	vegetable oil	15 mL
2	onions, chopped	2
2	cloves garlic, chopped	2
½ tsp	whole black peppercorns	2 mL
8	juniper berries (optional)	8
1	can (28 oz/796 mL) sauerkraut, rinsed and well-drained (3 cups/750 mL)	1
1 cup	chicken stock (approx.)	250 mL
½ cup	dry white wine or additional stock	125 mL
4 oz	piece smoked bacon, cut into 4 pieces	125 g
4	smoked sausages (see Tip, left)	4
4	knackwurst or wieners	4

1. In a large Dutch oven or saucepan, heat oil over medium heat. Cook onions, garlic, peppercorns and juniper berries, if using, stirring, for 5 minutes or until onion is softened.

2. Stir in sauerkraut, stock and wine. Bury bacon in sauerkraut. Reduce heat to medium-low; cover and simmer, stirring occasionally, for 1 hour. Add more stock, if needed, to keep sauerkraut moist.

3. Prick sausages in several places. Bury smoked sausages in sauerkraut. Cover and cook for 30 minutes. Add knackwurst and cook for 15 minutes more or until heated through.

4. To serve, place sauerkraut in center of a large platter and surround with sausages. Accompany with boiled potatoes.

Italian Sausages Braised with Potatoes

Makes 4 servings

This rustic dish is perfect with a glass of red wine on a wind-down Friday night. Do give the fennel a try; when raw, this vegetable has an assertive anise taste. However, when cooked, it's much more mellow and inviting.

Variation

Instead of fennel, use about 3 cups (750 mL) shredded cabbage.

1 lb	mild or hot Italian sausages	500 g
2 tbsp	water (approx.)	30 mL
1 tbsp	olive oil	15 mL
1	large onion, halved lengthwise, sliced	1
1	fennel bulb, trimmed, cored and cut into strips	1
2	cloves garlic, finely chopped	2
1 tsp	dried oregano leaves	5 mL
4	potatoes, peeled and cubed (about 1½ lbs/750 g)	4
1	can (14 oz/398 mL) tomatoes, including juice, chopped	1
½ cup	beef stock	125 mL
½ tsp	salt	2 mL
¼ tsp	freshly ground black pepper	1 mL
2 tbsp	chopped fresh parsley	30 mL

1. With a fork, prick sausages all over. Place in a large nonstick skillet over medium-high heat. Add water and cook, turning often and adding more water as needed (to prevent sausages from sticking), for 10 to 12 minutes or until browned and no longer pink in center. Transfer to a cutting board. Let cool slightly; cut into slices.

2. Drain fat from skillet; add oil, onion, fennel, garlic and oregano. Cook, stirring, for 3 minutes or until softened. Add potatoes, tomatoes with juice, stock, salt and pepper; bring to a boil. Reduce heat, cover and cook for 15 minutes or until potatoes are almost tender.

3. Return sausage to pan; cover and cook for 8 minutes or until potatoes are tender. Sprinkle with parsley.

Chorizo and Black Bean Stew

**Makes 4 to
6 servings**

Handy cans of baked beans have remained a kitchen staple over the years and spell comfort for many. Newcomers, such as versatile black beans, are also moving into that comfort zone as they gain in popularity as a tasty base for easy one-pot meals.

Tip

Use whatever mode of hot seasoning you prefer — chopped fresh jalapeño or chile peppers, or your favorite hot pepper sauce to taste.

1 tbsp	olive oil	15 mL
1 lb	chorizo or hot Italian sausages	500 g
2	onions, chopped	2
3	cloves garlic, finely chopped	3
2	red bell peppers, diced	2
2 tsp	dried oregano leaves	10 mL
2 tsp	ground cumin	10 mL
1/2 tsp	salt	2 mL
1/4 tsp	hot pepper flakes, or to taste (see Tip, left)	1 mL
1	can (28 oz/796 mL) tomatoes, including juice, chopped	1
2 tbsp	balsamic vinegar	30 mL
1 tbsp	packed brown sugar	15 mL
1	can (19 oz/540 mL) black beans, drained and rinsed	1
1/2 cup	coarsely chopped fresh cilantro	125 mL

1. In a Dutch oven or large saucepan, heat oil over medium heat. Prick sausages with a fork in several places and add to pan; cook for 10 minutes or until browned on all sides. Transfer to a plate; let cool slightly and cut into diagonal slices.

2. Add onions, garlic, peppers, oregano, cumin, salt and hot pepper flakes to pan; cook, stirring often, for 7 minutes or until vegetables are softened.

3. Add sausage slices, tomatoes with juice, vinegar and brown sugar; bring to a boil. Reduce heat; cover and simmer, stirring occasionally, for 15 minutes.

4. Stir in beans; cover and simmer for 10 minutes. Stir in cilantro and serve.

Cajun Cassoulet

Makes 6 servings

Here's a streamlined version of the French peasant bean dish. Andouille is highly seasoned smoked pork sausage, but you can substitute smoked garlic sausage, such as kielbasa.

Variation

Serve this tasty cassoulet in baked tortilla shells. Fit six 7-inch (18 cm) flour tortillas into ovenproof deep bowls set on a baking sheet. (Bake in batches if you don't have enough bowls.) Place in preheated 350°F (180°C) oven for 14 to 17 minutes or until crisp. (Can be done ahead.) Reheat shells in warm oven before serving.

2 tbsp	olive oil, divided	30 mL
1 lb	boneless skinless chicken thighs, cut into 1-inch (2.5 cm) cubes	500 g
8 oz	andouille or smoked garlic sausage, cut into thick slices or chunks	250 g
1	large red onion, finely chopped	1
3	cloves garlic, finely chopped	3
1	red bell pepper, cubed	1
1	green bell pepper, cubed	1
3	stalks celery, chopped	3
1 tbsp	Cajun spice	15 mL
½ tsp	dried thyme leaves	2 mL
1 cup	chicken stock (approx.)	250 mL
2 cups	frozen corn	500 mL
1	can (19 oz/540 mL) black beans, drained and rinsed	1
	Salt	
⅓ cup	chopped fresh cilantro or parsley	75 mL

1. In a Dutch oven or large saucepan, heat 1 tbsp (15 mL) oil over medium-high heat; cook chicken until browned on all sides. Transfer to a plate. Add sausage slices; cook until lightly browned. Add to chicken.

2. Reduce heat to medium; add remaining oil to pan. Cook onion, garlic, red and green peppers, celery, Cajun spice and thyme, stirring, for 7 minutes or until vegetables are softened.

3. Stir in stock and bring to a boil. Return chicken and sausage to pan along with corn and beans. Reduce heat to low, cover and simmer for 10 minutes. Add more stock and season with salt to taste, if necessary. Sprinkle with cilantro.

Coq au Vin

A fancy name for a chicken stew, but oh, what a stew! Smoky bacon, herbs, mushrooms and red wine turn humble chicken into a comforting dish that has made French cooking so famous and appreciated.

Variation

Instead of chicken thighs, use a good-sized chicken (about 4 lbs/2 kg) in this recipe, cut into pieces.

6	slices regular or double-smoked bacon, chopped	6
3 lbs	skinless bone-in chicken thighs	1.5 kg
1	large onion, chopped	1
3	carrots, peeled and thickly sliced	3
2	cloves garlic, finely chopped	2
2	stalks celery, thickly sliced	2
1 tsp	dried thyme leaves	5 mL
1	bay leaf	1
½ tsp	salt	2 mL
¼ tsp	freshly ground black pepper	1 mL
2 cups	dry red wine	500 mL
3 tbsp	all-purpose flour	45 mL
1 cup	chicken stock	250 mL
1 tbsp	butter	15 mL
4 cups	mushrooms, quartered	1 L

1. In a Dutch oven, cook bacon over medium heat, stirring, for 5 minutes or until crisp. Transfer to paper towels to drain; set aside. Drain all but 1 tbsp (15 mL) fat from skillet.

2. Add chicken to pan and cook until browned on all sides. Transfer to a plate.

3. Reduce heat to medium. Cook onion, carrots, garlic, celery, thyme, bay leaf, salt and pepper, stirring, for 5 minutes or until vegetables are softened. Add wine. Bring to a boil.

4. In a bowl, blend flour with ¼ cup (60 mL) of the chicken stock until smooth. Add to pan with remaining stock. Bring to a boil, stirring, until slightly thickened. Return chicken to pan. Reduce heat and simmer, partially covered, until chicken is just tender, about 45 minutes.

5. Meanwhile, melt butter in a large nonstick skillet over medium-high heat. Cook mushrooms, stirring, for 5 minutes or until mushrooms are tender. Add to chicken along with reserved bacon; simmer for 5 minutes for flavors to blend.

Chicken Cacciatore

Makes 4 servings

To survive the 6 o'clock
weeknight rush, batch-cook
stews and sauce-based
meals on weekends and
keep in fridge for up to
3 days or freeze for easy
reheating. When you
breeze through the door at
night, you simply have to
decide whether you'll serve
the stew with pasta
or rice — and dinner's
on the table.

Tip

Sun-dried tomatoes
sold dry in packages are
more economical than
those packed in oil. To
reconstitute, place in
a bowl and cover with
boiling water. Or cover with
cold water and microwave
on High for 2 minutes or
until just boiling. Let stand
for 10 minutes or until
softened; drain and chop.

3 tbsp	all-purpose flour	45 mL
½ tsp	salt	2 mL
½ tsp	freshly ground black pepper	2 mL
2 lbs	skinless bone-in chicken thighs	1 kg
2 tbsp	olive oil, divided	30 mL
1	small onion, chopped	1
2	cloves garlic, finely chopped	2
3 cups	sliced mushrooms	750 mL
½ cup	white wine or chicken stock	125 mL
2 cups	canned tomatoes, including juice, chopped	500 mL
⅓ cup	chopped sun-dried tomatoes (see Tip, left)	75 mL
¼ cup	chopped fresh basil leaves or parsley or a mixture of both	60 mL

1. In a heavy plastic bag, shake together flour, salt and pepper. In batches, toss chicken to coat, shaking off excess.

2. In a Dutch oven or large saucepan, heat 1 tbsp (15 mL) oil over medium-high heat. Brown chicken on all sides. Transfer to a plate.

3. Add remaining oil; cook onion, garlic and mushrooms, stirring, for 5 minutes or until softened.

4. Add wine; return chicken and any juices to pan along with tomatoes with juice and sun-dried tomatoes. Bring to a boil; reduce heat, cover and simmer for 35 minutes or until chicken is tender. Stir in basil; season with salt and pepper to taste.

Chicken and Sweet Potato Stew

Economical chicken thighs make a comforting weeknight supper. Here they star in a full-bodied stew with chunks of wholesome sweet potatoes. It's equally good when made with a winter squash, such as butternut, instead.

Tips

Replace sweet potatoes, if desired, with 4 potatoes, peeled and cubed, and 4 sliced carrots.

This recipe can be made ahead. Cover and refrigerate for up to 3 days or freeze for up to 1 month.

3 tbsp	all-purpose flour	45 mL
1 tsp	salt	5 mL
½ tsp	freshly ground black pepper	2 mL
2 lbs	skinless bone-in chicken thighs	1 kg
2 tbsp	vegetable oil, divided	30 mL
1	large onion, chopped	1
2	cloves garlic, finely chopped	2
1½ tsp	mild curry paste, or to taste	7 mL
1 tsp	dried thyme leaves	5 mL
½ tsp	dried marjoram leaves	2 mL
1½ cups	chicken stock	375 mL
3	sweet potatoes (about 2 lbs/1 kg)	3
¼ cup	chopped fresh parsley	60 mL

1. In a heavy plastic bag, shake together flour, salt and pepper. In batches, add chicken; shake to coat.

2. In a Dutch oven or large saucepan, heat 1 tbsp (15 mL) oil over medium-high heat; brown chicken on all sides. Transfer to a plate.

3. Add remaining oil to pan; reduce heat to medium. Cook onion, garlic, curry paste, thyme and marjoram, stirring, for 5 minutes or until softened.

4. Add stock; bring to boil. Return chicken and any juices to pan; cover and simmer for 20 minutes. Peel and quarter sweet potatoes; cut into 2-inch (5 cm) chunks. Add to pan; simmer, covered, for 20 minutes or until tender. Stir in parsley.

Chicken and Vegetable Stew

Even if you don't have a lot of time to spend in the kitchen, you can rustle up a great-tasting stew using boneless chicken thighs and convenient frozen vegetables. This satisfying dish does away with browning the chicken. You'll save time but not lose any flavor. Serve over noodles.

Tip

Use 5 cups (1.25 L) fresh vegetables instead of frozen, if you wish. Cut them into bite-size pieces. For slower-cooking vegetables, such as carrots and celery, add them along with the chicken. For faster-cooking ones, such as broccoli and zucchini, add in the last 10 minutes of cooking.

1 tbsp	butter	15 mL
1	large onion, chopped	1
2	cloves garlic, finely chopped	2
1 tsp	dried Italian herbs or fines herbes	5 mL
1 lb	boneless skinless chicken thighs (about 8), cut into 1-inch (2.5 cm) cubes	500 g
3 tbsp	all-purpose flour	45 mL
2 cups	chicken stock	500 mL
1	package (1 lb/500 g) frozen mixed vegetables	1
	Salt and freshly ground black pepper	

1. In a Dutch oven or large saucepan, melt butter over medium heat. Add onion, garlic and Italian herbs; cook, stirring, for 4 minutes or until lightly colored.

2. In a bowl, toss chicken with flour until well-coated. Add to pan along with any remaining flour; stir in chicken stock. Bring to a boil and cook, stirring, until sauce thickens. Reduce heat, cover and simmer, stirring occasionally, for 20 minutes.

3. Add frozen vegetables; return to a boil. Season with salt and pepper to taste. Reduce heat, cover and simmer for 10 minutes or until chicken and vegetables are tender.

Chicken Vegetable Cobbler

Makes 6 servings

Some dishes never lose their appeal — like this old-fashioned favorite, which is perfect to make on a lazy Sunday afternoon. It requires a little time to prepare, but once the creamy chicken mixture and its golden biscuit crust is bubbling away in the oven, you'll be glad you made the effort. And so will your family.

Tip

I've chosen a biscuit crust to make this a cobbler, but you can cover the savory chicken filling with your favorite pie pastry or frozen puff pastry to make a pot pie. Or you can omit the topping altogether and serve over rice or noodles.

• 12-cup (3 L) deep casserole dish

2 lbs	chicken legs, with thighs, skin and excess fat removed	1 kg
3½ cups	water	875 mL
1 tsp	salt	5 mL
	Freshly ground black pepper	
1	bay leaf	1
2 tbsp	butter	30 mL
2 cups	quartered mushrooms	500 mL
1	onion, chopped	1
1	large clove garlic, finely chopped	1
2 tsp	dried fines herbes or dried basil leaves	10 mL
⅓ cup	all-purpose flour	75 mL
3	carrots, peeled and sliced	3
2	stalks celery, chopped	2
½ cup	whipping (35%) cream or table (18%) cream	125 mL
1 cup	frozen peas	250 mL
¼ cup	chopped fresh parsley	60 mL
	Cheddar Biscuit Crust (see recipe, opposite)	

1. In a large saucepan, combine chicken, water, salt, pepper and bay leaf. Bring to a boil; reduce heat to medium-low, cover and simmer for 1 hour. Let stand until chicken is cool enough to handle. Pull chicken meat from bones; cut into bite-size pieces. Strain stock and skim off any fat; there should be 2½ cups (625 mL) of stock. Add water, if necessary. Discard bay leaf. Set aside.

2. In a large saucepan, melt butter over medium heat; cook mushrooms, onion, garlic and fines herbes, stirring often, for 5 minutes or until softened.

3. Blend flour with small amount of stock until smooth; add rest of stock. Stir into mushroom mixture; bring to a boil, stirring, until thickened and smooth.

Tips
The chicken-vegetable mixture without the crust freezes well for up to 2 months.

Fines herbes, available in the spice section of your grocery store, contains dried parsley, chives, tarragon and chervil. You can also use an Italian herb mix of basil, oregano and marjoram.

4. Add carrots and celery; cover and simmer over low heat, stirring occasionally, for 15 minutes or until vegetables are just tender.

5. Add chicken, cream, peas and parsley; season with additional salt and pepper to taste. Heat through. Spoon hot chicken mixture into casserole dish.

6. Preheat oven to 400°F (200°C). Meanwhile, make Cheddar Biscuit Crust (see recipe, below). Roll out on lightly floured board to make a circle large enough to cover casserole. Arrange on top of hot chicken mixture. (If making chicken mixture ahead, cover and refrigerate; microwave on Medium-High (70%), or reheat in saucepan on stovetop, until piping hot before topping with crust.)

7. Bake in preheated oven for about 25 to 30 minutes or until crust is golden and filling is bubbly.

Cheddar Biscuit Crust

1⅓ cups	all-purpose flour	325 mL
2 tsp	baking powder	10 mL
½ tsp	baking soda	2 mL
¼ tsp	salt	1 mL
½ cup	shredded Cheddar cheese	125 mL
½ cup	buttermilk	125 mL
¼ cup	butter, melted	60 mL

1. In a bowl, combine flour, baking powder, baking soda and salt. Add cheese. Combine buttermilk and butter; stir into flour mixture to make a soft dough.

Company Chicken Mushroom Pot Pie

Makes 6 to
8 servings

Looking for a winning dish to serve for a buffet or potluck? Look no further than this pastry-topped chicken pie with lots of tasty mushrooms.

Tips

Instead of topping the chicken filling with pie pastry, use half a 14- to 16-oz (400 to 450 g) package of frozen puff pastry, thawed. On a lightly floured surface, roll out pastry to fit baking dish. Brush rim of baking dish with water. Cover filling with pastry, pressing down edges. Cut steam vents in top. Bake for 30 to 35 minutes or until pastry is golden.

To wash or not wash mushrooms? You can wipe them with a damp cloth, if you wish. However, I feel it's important to wash all produce that comes into my kitchen. I quickly rinse mushrooms under cold water and immediately wrap in a clean, dry kitchen towel or paper towels to absorb excess moisture.

- Preheat oven to 400°F (200°C)
- 8-cup (2 L) casserole dish

3 tbsp	butter, divided	45 mL
6	boneless skinless chicken breasts (2 lbs/1 kg), cut into ¾-inch (2 cm) cubes	6
12 oz	shiitake or cremini mushrooms, sliced	375 g
¼ cup	finely chopped shallots	60 mL
2	cloves garlic, finely chopped	2
2 tsp	finely chopped fresh thyme or ¾ tsp (3 mL) dried thyme leaves	10 mL
1 tsp	salt	5 mL
¼ tsp	freshly ground black pepper	1 mL
½ cup	dry white wine or additional chicken stock	125 mL
3 tbsp	all-purpose flour	45 mL
½ cup	chicken stock	125 mL
½ cup	whipping (35%) cream	125 mL
2 tbsp	chopped fresh parsley or chives	30 mL
	Pastry for a single-crust 9-inch (23 cm) pie (see recipe, page 508)	
1	egg, lightly beaten	1

1. In a Dutch oven or large saucepan, heat 1 tbsp (15 mL) butter over medium-high heat; brown half the chicken. Transfer to a bowl. Add 1 tbsp (15 mL) butter to pan; brown remaining chicken. Transfer to a bowl.

2. Add remaining butter to pan. Cook mushrooms, shallots, garlic, thyme, salt and pepper, stirring, for 3 minutes or until mushrooms are softened. Add wine; bring to a boil. Cook for 3 minutes or until slightly reduced.

Tip

This recipe can be made ahead. Let chicken mixture cool. Cover and refrigerate for up to 1 day. Reheat filling until piping hot. Place in baking dish; top with pastry.

3. In a bowl, blend flour with $\frac{1}{4}$ cup (60 mL) stock until smooth. Stir in remaining stock. Stir into pan; cook until sauce boils and thickens. Return chicken and any juices to pan. Stir in cream; bring to a boil. Reduce heat, cover and simmer for 5 minutes or until chicken is just tender. Stir in parsley and transfer to baking dish.

4. On a lightly floured surface, roll out pastry slightly larger than size of baking dish and fit over filling. Trim edge, leaving a $\frac{1}{2}$-inch (1 cm) overhang; turn under and seal to edge of dish. Cut slits for steam vents. Lightly brush with egg. Bake in preheated oven for 25 to 30 minutes or until filling is bubbly and pastry is golden.

Mediterranean Chicken

This is a favorite chicken dish that's tasty and easy to make. Just prepare the vegetables to top the chicken breasts and cook the dish in your oven or microwave. Serve with rice or pasta and a green salad.

Tip

Instead of canned tomatoes, use 1 cup (250 mL) peeled, seeded and chopped fresh tomatoes.

- Preheat oven to 350°F (180°C)
- 11- by 7-inch (28 by 18 cm) baking dish

1 tbsp	olive oil	15 mL
1	onion, finely chopped	1
2	cloves garlic, finely chopped	2
1½ tsp	chopped fresh thyme or ½ tsp (2 mL) dried thyme leaves	7 mL
¼ tsp	fennel seeds, crushed (optional)	1 mL
½ tsp	salt	2 mL
¼ tsp	freshly ground black pepper	1 mL
1	yellow or green bell pepper, cut into thin 2-inch (5 cm) long strips	1
1 cup	drained canned whole plum tomatoes, seeded and chopped	250 mL
⅓ cup	small black olives, such as sun-dried	75 mL
2 tbsp	chopped fresh parsley	30 mL
4	boneless skinless chicken breasts (1¼ lbs/625 g)	4

1. In a large nonstick skillet, heat oil over medium heat. Cook onion, garlic, thyme, fennel seeds, salt and pepper, stirring, for 3 minutes or until softened.

2. Stir in bell pepper and tomatoes. Cook, stirring, for 5 minutes or until tomatoes are sauce-like and pepper strips are softened. Add olives and parsley. (To make ahead, place in an airtight container and refrigerate up to 1 day.)

3. Arrange chicken in a single layer in baking dish and spoon sauce over breasts. Bake, uncovered, in preheated oven for about 30 minutes or until chicken is no longer pink in center or an instant-read thermometer registers 165°F (74°C).

Microwave Method

1. Assemble as directed above, cover dish with lid or vented plastic wrap and microwave on Medium-High (70%) for 6 to 9 minutes, rearranging breasts once during cooking, until chicken is no longer pink in the center. Let stand, covered, for 5 minutes before serving.

Easy Curried Fish Stew

Makes 4 servings

Gingerroot adds a sparkling flavor to this low-cal stew. Serve steaming bowls with chunks of crusty whole-grain bread. It's a complete meal!

Tip

Store-bought curry pastes vary in flavor and strength depending on the brand. Some pastes are labeled as mild but have more heat than expected. Add a smaller amount of curry paste to the recipe to test the strength and add more to get the depth of curry flavor you prefer.

Variation

Instead of fish, add 1½ cups (375 mL) small cooked shrimp.

1 tbsp	vegetable oil	15 mL
1	small onion, finely chopped	1
1 tbsp	minced gingerroot	15 mL
2 tsp	mild curry paste, or to taste	10 mL
2 cups	diced peeled potatoes	500 mL
1½ cups	thinly sliced carrots	375 mL
2¼ cups	fish or chicken stock	550 mL
1 tbsp	cornstarch	15 mL
	Salt and freshly ground black pepper	
1½ cups	snow peas, ends trimmed, halved	375 mL
1 lb	fish fillets, cut into chunks	500 g

1. In a large saucepan, heat oil over medium heat. Cook onion, ginger and curry paste, stirring, for 2 minutes or until softened. Add potatoes, carrots and fish stock. Bring to a boil; reduce heat, cover and simmer for 10 to 12 minutes or until vegetables are just tender.

2. In a bowl, blend cornstarch with 2 tbsp (30 mL) water. Add to stew and cook, stirring, until thickened. Season with salt and pepper to taste.

3. Stir in snow peas and fish; cover and cook for 2 to 3 minutes or until snow peas are tender-crisp and fish is opaque. Ladle into bowls and serve.

Bouillabaisse

Makes 6 servings

I like to serve guests this wonderful fish stew from Marseille, France, when there's a diverse array of fresh fish and shellfish in the market. I start the meal with a substantial salad and end with a fruit-based dessert.

Tip

Vary the type of fresh fish and seafood according to what's available in the market. Suggestions include cod, halibut, haddock, monkfish, tilapia, scallops, shrimp, lobster, clams and mussels.

Variation

Instead of a mixture of fish and seafood, use 2 lbs (1 kg) fish, such as cod and halibut.

- Preheat oven to 375°F (190°C)
- Baking sheet

1	French baguette, cut on the diagonal into ½-inch (1 cm) slices	1
2 tbsp	olive oil	30 mL
1 lb	mussels	500 g
1 lb	littleneck clams	500 g
	Bouillabaisse Broth (see recipe, opposite)	
1 lb	firm fish, such as cod, halibut or monkfish, cut into 1-inch (2.5 cm) cubes	500 g
8 oz	medium raw shrimp, peeled and deveined, with tails left on	250 g
8 oz	scallops, halved or quartered, if large	250 g
	Salt and freshly ground black pepper	
¼ cup	chopped fresh parsley	60 mL
	Rouille (see recipe, page 228)	

1. Brush baguette slices with oil. Arrange on baking sheet and lightly toast in preheated oven for 7 minutes or until golden.

2. Scrub mussels and clams under cold water. Remove any beards from mussels. Discard any mussels or clams with cracked shells or that do not close when tapped.

3. In a Dutch oven or large saucepan, bring broth to a boil over medium-high heat. Add mussels and clams. Cover and cook for about 4 minutes or until shells open. Remove from heat. Using a ladle, transfer mussels and clams to a large bowl. Discard any that do not open. Set aside 12 clams and 12 mussels in the shell. Shuck remaining meat from shells.

4. Return broth to a boil over medium-high heat. Add fish, cover and cook until almost opaque, about 2 minutes. Add shrimp and scallops; cook for 2 minutes or just until shrimp turn pink and fish flakes with a fork.

5. Divide fish and seafood among heated wide soup plates. Add 2 mussels and 2 clams with shells to each plate, along with shucked mussels and clams.

6. Place broth over high heat and bring to a boil; season with salt and pepper to taste. Ladle hot broth over fish and shellfish and sprinkle with parsley.

7. Spread 12 baguette toasts generously with rouille and arrange 2 on top of each plate. Serve immediately. Pass any remaining toasts and rouille at the table.

Bouillabaisse Broth

Makes about 6 cups (1.5 L)

2 tbsp	olive oil	30 mL
1	onion, chopped	1
1	leek, white and light green parts only, thinly sliced (see Tip, left)	1
1	fennel bulb, top trimmed and bulb chopped	1
3	cloves garlic, chopped	3
2	bay leaves	2
4	fresh thyme stems or 1/4 tsp (1 mL) dried thyme leaves	4
1/4 tsp	saffron threads, crushed	1 mL
4	large tomatoes, cored and chopped	4
4 cups	fish or chicken stock	1 L
3/4 cup	dry white wine	175 mL
2	strips (3 inches/7.5 cm) orange peel	2
	Salt and freshly ground black pepper	

1. In a Dutch oven, heat oil over medium heat. Cook onion, leek, fennel, garlic, bay leaves, thyme and saffron, stirring, for 8 minutes or until vegetables are softened.

2. Add tomatoes, stock, wine and orange peel; bring to a boil. Reduce heat to medium-low, cover and simmer for 30 minutes or until vegetables are very tender.

3. Strain through a fine sieve, pressing down on vegetables with a wooden spoon to extract as much broth as possible. Discard vegetables. Season broth with salt and pepper to taste. Use immediately or place in an airtight container and refrigerate for up to 2 days or freeze for up to 2 months.

continued…

If you are able to get fish bones from the market, add them along with the tomatoes and use water instead of stock.

Tip

To clean leeks: Trim dark green tops. Cut down center almost to root end and chop. Rinse in a sink full of cold water to remove sand; scoop up leeks and place in colander to drain or use a salad spinner.

This spicy, garlicky mayonnaise is spread on toasted baguette slices to top the seafood and flavorful broth. It can also be used as an appetizer dipping sauce for shrimp.

Tip

Buy roasted red peppers either in a jar or from the supermarket deli counter. Blot dry before dicing to remove excess moisture.

Rouille

½ cup	diced roasted red bell peppers (see Tip, left)	125 mL
⅔ cup	mayonnaise	150 mL
2	cloves garlic, coarsely chopped	2
2 tsp	fresh lemon juice	10 mL
¼ tsp	cayenne pepper, or to taste	1 mL

1. Pat red pepper dry in paper towels to remove as much moisture as possible.

2. In a food processor, purée red pepper, mayonnaise, garlic, lemon juice and cayenne until smooth. Transfer to a bowl. (If preparing ahead, cover and refrigerate for up to 3 days.)

Seafood Supreme

Do you remember the days when elegant luncheons were in fashion? Here's a special dish reminiscent of days gone by when richly flavored seafood sauces were served in puff pastry shells. You could serve this dish the same way, or tuck the seafood sauce into crêpes, serve over rice, or toss with pasta.

Variations

Cooked lobster can replace part of the shellfish.

For a less expensive version, omit scallops and shrimp; increase the amount of sole, haddock or cod to 1½ lbs (750 g).

1 cup	fish or chicken stock (approx.)	250 mL
½ cup	dry white wine or vermouth	125 mL
8 oz	sole or other white fish, cut into 1-inch (2.5 cm) cubes	250 g
8 oz	small scallops	250 g
8 oz	small cooked peeled shrimp	250 g
3 tbsp	butter	45 mL
⅓ cup	finely chopped green onions	75 mL
¾ cup	diced red bell pepper	175 mL
¼ cup	all-purpose flour	60 mL
½ cup	whipping (35%) cream	125 mL
	Salt and ground white pepper	
2 tbsp	chopped fresh dill or parsley	30 mL

1. In a saucepan, bring stock and wine to a boil over medium heat. Add sole cubes; poach 2 minutes (start timing when fish is added to stock). Add scallops; poach 1 to 2 minutes more or until seafood is opaque. Remove using a slotted spoon; place in a bowl along with shrimp and set aside.

2. Strain stock into glass measure; there should be 2 cups (500 mL). Add water, if necessary; reserve.

3. In a saucepan, melt butter over medium heat. Add green onions and red peppers; cook, stirring, for 3 minutes or until softened. Blend in flour; pour in reserved stock mixture. Bring to a boil, stirring, until sauce is very thick and smooth. Stir in cream; bring to a boil.

4. Just before serving, add seafood and heat through. Season with salt and white pepper to taste; stir in dill. Serve immediately.

Steamed Mussels
with Herb Cream Sauce

As today's cultivated
mussels just need a quick
scrub, it takes no time to
turn out this tasty dish
to serve as an appetizer
or as a main course for
dinner. Accompany with
crusty bread to mop up
the delicious sauce.

Variation

**Steamed Mussels in
Curry Cream Sauce**
Add 2 tsp (10 mL) mild
curry paste, or to taste,
with the cream, and use
¼ cup (60 mL) chopped
fresh cilantro instead of
parsley and basil.

2 lbs	mussels	1 kg
1 tbsp	butter	15 mL
¼ cup	finely chopped shallots	60 mL
3	cloves garlic, finely chopped	3
1 cup	dry white wine	250 mL
½ cup	whipping (35%) cream	125 mL
2 tbsp	chopped fresh parsley	30 mL
2 tbsp	chopped fresh basil, chives or tarragon	30 mL

1. Scrub mussels under cold water and remove any beards. Discard any with cracked shells or that do not close when tapped.

2. In a Dutch oven or large saucepan, melt butter over medium heat. Cook shallots and garlic, stirring, for 2 minutes or until softened.

3. Add wine and bring to a boil over medium-high heat. Add mussels, cover and steam for 4 to 5 minutes or until shells open. Using a slotted spoon, transfer mussels to a large bowl. Discard any that do not open.

4. Add cream to pan. Reduce heat and boil gently for 3 to 5 minutes or until sauce is reduced to about 1 cup (250 mL). Remove from heat and stir in parsley and basil.

5. Arrange mussels in large bowls and ladle sauce over top. Serve immediately.

Mussels Marinara

My idea of a perfect simple meal is a bowlful of these plump mussels served with crusty bread to dip into the garlicky tomato broth.

Tip

To remove the mussel's beard (a clump of string-like material that clings to the shell), tug it off with your fingers.

Variation

Linguine Mussels Marinara

Remove mussels from their shells and toss mussels and broth with 8 oz (250 g) cooked string pasta such as linguine.

2 lbs	mussels	1 kg
1 tbsp	olive oil	15 mL
1	small onion, chopped	1
3	cloves garlic, minced	3
½ tsp	salt	2 mL
Pinch	hot pepper flakes	Pinch
4	ripe tomatoes, seeded and chopped	4
½ cup	dry white wine	125 mL
2 tbsp	chopped fresh parsley	30 mL

1. Scrub mussels under cold water; remove any beards. Discard any that do not close when tapped.

2. In a large saucepan, heat oil over medium heat; cook onion, garlic, salt and hot pepper flakes, stirring, for 2 minutes or until softened. Add tomatoes and wine; cover and cook for 10 minutes or until sauce-like.

3. Add mussels; increase heat to medium-high. Cover and steam for 4 to 5 minutes or until shells open. Discard any mussels that do not open.

4. To serve, spoon mussels in their shells along with sauce into serving bowls. Sprinkle with parsley.

Jambalaya

Makes 6 to 8 servings

Jambalaya is the perfect party dish. A one-pot wonder originating from New Orleans, it pleases all palates with its piquant flavors and mix of chicken, sausage and shrimp. Set this dish on the table and watch it disappear.

Tips

Try not to stir the jambalaya or the rice will turn sticky.

If using chicken thighs with the bone in, increase cooking time by 5 to 10 minutes.

Variation

Replace the sausage with 8 oz (250 g) cubed smoked ham.

- Preheat oven to 350°F (180°C)
- 12-cup (3 L) baking dish or ovenproof serving dish

2 tbsp	olive oil (approx.)	30 mL
1½ lbs	boneless skinless chicken thighs (about 12)	750 g
8 oz	andouille, chorizo or other smoked sausage, thinly sliced	250 g
1	large onion, chopped	1
3	cloves garlic, finely chopped	3
2	stalks celery, diced	2
2	bell peppers, any color, diced	2
1 tsp	dried thyme leaves	5 mL
1 tsp	paprika	5 mL
½ tsp	salt	2 mL
¼ tsp	ground allspice	1 mL
¼ tsp	cayenne pepper	1 mL
1½ cups	long-grain white rice	375 mL
1	can (14 oz/398 mL) tomatoes, including juice, chopped	1
1¾ cups	chicken stock	425 mL
8 oz	medium raw shrimp, peeled and deveined, with tails left on	250 g
⅓ cup	chopped fresh parsley	75 mL
3	green onions, finely chopped	3

1. In a Dutch oven, heat 1 tbsp (15 mL) oil over medium-high heat. Brown chicken, in batches, adding more oil as needed. Transfer to a plate.

2. Add sausage, onion, garlic, celery, peppers, thyme, paprika, salt, allspice and cayenne; cook, stirring often, for 5 minutes or until vegetables are softened. Return chicken to dish along with accumulated juices.

3. Stir in rice, tomatoes with juice and stock; bring to a boil. Transfer to baking dish. Cover and bake in preheated oven for 30 minutes or until rice and chicken are just tender.

4. Stir in shrimp, parsley and green onions; cover and bake for 5 to 8 minutes more or until shrimp turn pink.

Shrimp Étouffée

Makes 4 servings

This signature dish of New Orleans relies on a base of garlic, celery and green pepper in a fresh tomato sauce and, of course, hot pepper sauce to spice it up a notch or two. Serve over steamed rice.

Tip

Use only red ripe tomatoes, such as vine-ripened, in this robust shrimp stew. If good fresh tomatoes are unavailable, substitute 1 can (28 oz/796 mL) plum tomatoes, drained and chopped.

1 tbsp	butter	15 mL
1	small onion, chopped	1
4	green onions, chopped	4
1	green bell pepper, diced	1
½ cup	diced celery	125 mL
2	cloves garlic, finely chopped	2
1	bay leaf	1
1 tsp	chopped fresh thyme or ¼ tsp (1 mL) dried thyme leaves	5 mL
¼ tsp	salt	1 mL
	Freshly ground black pepper	
1½ cups	peeled, seeded and chopped fresh tomatoes (see Tip, left)	375 mL
3 tbsp	all-purpose flour	45 mL
1½ cups	fish or vegetable stock	375 mL
1 lb	large raw shrimp, peeled and deveined, with tails left on	500 g
2 tbsp	chopped fresh parsley	30 mL
½ tsp	hot pepper sauce, or to taste	2 mL
2 tbsp	fresh lemon juice	30 mL

1. In a large saucepan, melt butter over medium heat. Cook onion, green onions, green pepper, celery, garlic, bay leaf, thyme, salt and pepper, stirring often, for 5 minutes or until vegetables are softened. Add tomatoes; cook, stirring, for 5 minutes or until sauce-like.

2. Place flour in a small bowl and blend in ⅓ cup (75 mL) of the stock until smooth. Add to pan along with remaining stock. Bring to a boil, stirring, until slightly thickened. Reduce heat, cover and simmer, stirring occasionally, for 15 minutes.

3. Add shrimp, parsley and hot pepper sauce. Simmer for 3 to 4 minutes or until shrimp turn pink. Remove bay leaf; add lemon juice and season with salt and pepper to taste.

Skillet Shrimp and Rice Creole

Makes 4 servings

Makes 4 servings

Attractive and colorful, this classic Southern specialty relies on the flavors of tomato, celery, thyme and bay leaf. It's a spicy one-dish meal that takes only 30 minutes to cook.

Variation

Skillet Sausage and Rice Creole

Substitute 12 oz (375 g) mild or hot Italian sausages for the shrimp. Cut sausages in half lengthwise. Place cut side down in skillet; cook over medium heat, turning occasionally, for 10 minutes or until no longer pink. Cut into thick slices; add to recipe as you would the shrimp.

1 tbsp	vegetable oil	15 mL
1	large onion, chopped	1
2	cloves garlic, finely chopped	2
2	stalks celery, chopped	2
½ tsp	dried thyme leaves	2 mL
1	bay leaf	1
1 cup	long-grain white rice	250 mL
1	red bell pepper, diced	1
1	can (14 oz/398 mL) tomatoes, including juice, chopped	1
1 cup	fish or chicken stock	250 mL
½ tsp	salt	2 mL
Pinch	cayenne pepper	Pinch
2	small zucchini, halved lengthwise and thinly sliced	2
1 lb	large raw shrimp, peeled and deveined, with tails left on	500 g

1. In a large nonstick skillet, heat oil over medium heat. Cook onion, garlic, celery, thyme and bay leaf, stirring, for 5 minutes or until softened.

2. Stir in rice and red pepper; cook for 2 minutes. Add tomatoes with juice, stock, salt and a generous pinch cayenne pepper. Bring to a boil; reduce heat, cover and simmer for 15 minutes. Stir in zucchini; bury shrimp in rice. Cover and cook for 8 minutes or until zucchini are tender and shrimp are pink and firm.

Main Dishes

continued...

Chicken and Turkey (continued)

Fish

Sunday Roast Beef with Wine Gravy

Makes 6 servings

When growing up, Sunday dinner in my home was often a standing rib roast seasoned simply with salt and pepper and served with pan gravy. This recipe moves it up a notch with the addition of a thyme-pepper rub and red wine to enhance the gravy. Serve with another side-dish classic, Yorkshire Pudding (see recipe, page 441).

- Preheat oven to 450°F (230°C)
- Roasting pan

4 lb	standing rib roast	2 kg
1	large clove garlic, cut in small slivers	1
2 tbsp	Dijon mustard	30 mL
1 tbsp	chopped fresh thyme or 1 tsp (5 mL) dried thyme leaves	15 mL
½ tsp	salt	2 mL
1 tsp	coarsely ground black pepper	5 mL

Wine Gravy

½ cup	red wine	125 mL
1½ cups	beef stock	375 mL
1 tbsp	cornstarch	15 mL
2 tbsp	water	30 mL
1 tbsp	Worcestershire sauce	15 mL
	Salt and freshly ground black pepper	

1. Make small slits in roast and insert garlic slivers. Let roast stand for 30 minutes. In a bowl, combine mustard, thyme, salt and pepper. Spread over roast.

2. Place rib side down in shallow roasting pan. Roast in preheated oven for 15 minutes; reduce heat to 350°F (180°C) and continue to roast for 1¼ to 1½ hours or until meat thermometer registers 140°F (60°C) for medium-rare. Transfer to carving board, covered loosely with foil, for 15 minutes.

3. *Wine Gravy:* Skim fat from drippings in pan. Place over medium heat; add wine. Cook, scraping up brown bits from bottom, until reduced by half. Stir in beef stock; strain sauce through a fine sieve into a saucepan. Bring to a boil; cook for 5 minutes or until slightly reduced.

4. In a small bowl, blend cornstarch with water and Worcestershire sauce. Add to pan, stirring constantly, until sauce boils and thickens. Season with salt and pepper to taste. Cut beef into thin slices and accompany with sauce.

Bistro Steak

Makes 4 servings

Dressed up with wine, garlic and herbs, this steak recipe becomes a special dish when you're entertaining friends.

Tips

Serve with Roasted Garlic Potatoes (see recipe, page 399).

Herbes de Provence is a blend of French herbs that often includes thyme, rosemary, basil and sage. If you can't find this blend in your supermarket, substitute a generous pinch of each of these herbs.

4	boneless striploin steaks, each 6 oz (175 g)	4
½ tsp	coarsely ground black pepper	2 mL
2 tsp	olive oil	10 mL
2 tsp	butter	10 mL
	Salt	
¼ cup	finely chopped shallots	60 mL
1	large clove garlic, finely chopped	1
¼ tsp	dried herbes de Provence (see Tip, left)	1 mL
⅓ cup	red wine or additional beef stock	75 mL
½ cup	beef stock	125 mL
1 tbsp	Dijon mustard	15 mL
2 tbsp	chopped fresh parsley	30 mL

1. Pat steaks dry with paper towels. Season with pepper.

2. Heat a large heavy skillet over medium heat until hot; add oil and butter. Increase heat to high; brown steaks about 1 minute on each side. Reduce heat to medium; cook to desired degree of doneness. Transfer to a heated serving platter; season with salt and keep warm.

3. Add shallots, garlic and herbes to skillet; cook, stirring, for 1 minute. Stir in red wine; cook, scraping up any brown bits from bottom of pan, until liquid has almost evaporated.

4. Stir in stock, mustard and parsley; season with salt and pepper to taste. Cook, stirring, until slightly reduced. Spoon sauce over steaks. Serve immediately.

Filet Mignon with Green Peppercorn Sauce

Makes 4 servings

My version of the classic beef dish uses coarsely ground black peppercorns to season the beef before cooking and tangy green peppercorns to flavor the brandy-cream sauce. Serve with creamy mashed potatoes and a vegetable such as green beans or asparagus.

Tip

To lightly crush the green peppercorns, place on a cutting board and crush using the flat side of a large knife.

● Preheat oven to 200°F (100°C)

4	beef tenderloin (filet mignon) steaks (1 inch/2.5 cm thick), each 5 oz (150 g)	4
½ tsp	coarsely ground black pepper	2 mL
2 tsp	butter	10 mL
2 tsp	olive oil	10 mL
¼ cup	finely chopped shallots	60 mL
3 tbsp	cognac or brandy	45 mL
½ cup	undiluted canned condensed beef broth	125 mL
½ cup	whipping (35%) cream	125 mL
1 tbsp	green peppercorns in brine, rinsed, drained and lightly crushed	15 mL
2 tsp	whole-seed mustard	10 mL

1. Pat steaks dry with paper towels and season with pepper. In a large nonstick skillet, heat butter and oil over medium-high heat until foamy. Cook steaks for 2 to 3 minutes per side or until desired doneness. Transfer to a plate and keep warm in preheated oven.

2. Reduce heat to medium. Cook shallots, stirring, for 1 minute. Add cognac and cook until liquid is almost evaporated. Stir in broth, cream, peppercorns and mustard. Bring to a boil and cook, stirring often, until thickened and reduced to about ¾ cup (175 mL).

3. Spoon sauce evenly over steaks and serve.

Easy Asian Flank Steak

Makes 6 servings

Here's my favorite way to prepare beef on the barbecue. Flank steak is economical and easy to marinate ahead, and leftovers make great-tasting sandwiches.

Tips

Flank steak becomes more tender the longer it's marinated. Thick-cut round steak can also be prepared in the same way.

If you love to grill foods, consider using a stovetop grill pan instead of a barbecue. Sold in kitchenware and department shops, these versatile pans give foods an outdoor grill flavor right on your stovetop.

¼ cup	hoisin sauce	60 mL
2 tbsp	soy sauce	30 mL
2 tbsp	fresh lime juice	30 mL
1 tbsp	vegetable oil	15 mL
4	cloves garlic, finely chopped	4
2 tsp	Asian chili sauce or 1 tsp (5 mL) hot pepper flakes	10 mL
1½ lbs	flank steak	750 g

1. In a shallow glass dish, whisk together hoisin sauce, soy sauce, lime juice, oil, garlic and chili sauce; add steak, turning to coat both sides with marinade. Refrigerate, covered, for at least 8 hours or up to 24 hours. Remove meat from refrigerator 15 minutes before cooking.

2. Preheat greased barbecue grill to medium-high (or preheat broiler).

3. Remove steak from marinade, discarding marinade. Grill steak for 7 to 8 minutes per side or until medium-rare. (Alternatively, place steak on a foil-lined baking sheet; broil 4 inches (10 cm) below preheated broiler for 7 to 8 minutes on each side.) Transfer to cutting board and cover loosely with foil; let stand for 5 minutes. Thinly slice at right angles to the grain of meat.

Beef Stroganoff

Makes 4 servings

This ever-popular dish of sautéed beef strips and sour cream originated in Russia and is especially delicious served with noodles or rice.

Variation

Use chicken or pork instead of beef.

1 tbsp	butter (approx.)	15 mL
2 tbsp	vegetable oil (approx.), divided	30 mL
1 lb	lean boneless sirloin steak, trimmed, cut into 2- by ¼-inch (5 by 0.5 cm) strips	500 g
	Salt and freshly ground black pepper	
1	onion, halved lengthwise, thinly sliced	1
1	large clove garlic, finely chopped	1
3 cups	thickly sliced cremini mushrooms	750 mL
2 tbsp	all-purpose flour	30 mL
1¼ cups	beef stock	300 mL
1 tsp	Dijon mustard	5 mL
1 tsp	Worcestershire sauce	5 mL
⅓ cup	sour cream	75 mL
2 tbsp	finely chopped fresh parsley	30 mL

1. In a large nonstick skillet, heat 1½ tsp (7 mL) each butter and oil over medium-high heat until foamy. Cook beef, in two batches, stirring, for 2 minutes or until browned, adding more butter and oil as needed between batches. Transfer to a plate and season with salt and pepper.

2. Add remaining 1 tbsp (15 mL) oil to skillet. Cook onion, garlic and mushrooms, stirring, for 3 minutes or until vegetables are lightly colored.

3. In a bowl, blend flour with ¼ cup (60 mL) stock until smooth. Add to skillet along with remaining stock, mustard and Worcestershire sauce. Bring to a boil and cook, stirring, until sauce is thickened. Reduce heat to medium-low and simmer, covered, for 2 minutes.

4. Stir in beef strips and sour cream. Cook for 1 minute or until heated through. Season with salt and pepper to taste. Sprinkle with parsley and serve immediately.

Chili-Rubbed Grilled Beef with Roasted Garlic Horseradish Cream

Dry rubs made with herbs and spices are a simple and easy way to infuse a lot of flavor into grilled meats. Make extras of this rub and have on hand to use with other grill favorites, such as ribs and chicken.

Variation

The beef is also great to use in a sandwich. Grill the beef the day ahead and serve it cold or grill it just before serving. Cut the beef into thin slices. Spread a cut baguette with Roasted Garlic Horseradish Cream and top with sliced beef. Cut sandwich into thick diagonal slices and serve.

• Preheat greased barbecue grill to high

1 tbsp	chili powder	15 mL
1 tbsp	dried oregano leaves	15 mL
2 tsp	ground cumin	10 mL
2 tsp	ground coriander	10 mL
½ tsp	cayenne pepper, or to taste	2 mL
2 lbs	boneless sirloin steak, cut 1 inch (2.5 cm) thick	1 kg
2 tbsp	olive oil	30 mL
	Salt	
	Roasted Garlic Horseradish Cream (see recipe, opposite)	

1. In a bowl, combine chili powder, oregano, cumin, coriander and cayenne. Pat steak dry with paper towels; coat with seasoning mixture and rub into meat.

2. Brush beef with oil and place on prepared grill. Grill for about 5 minutes per side or until just medium-rare. Remove to a plate; season with salt to taste.

3. To serve, thinly slice beef on the diagonal into thin slices and arrange on a serving plate. Accompany with Roasted Garlic Horseradish Cream.

This is an all-purpose sauce to serve with a variety of beef recipes, whether a classic roast beef or juicy beef burgers layered with tomatoes and lettuce.

Tip

To roast garlic: Trim ¼ inch (0.5 cm) off the larger, stem end of a whole bulb of garlic. Place cut side down on a sheet of foil. Drizzle with 2 tsp (10 mL) olive oil. Wrap and place in small casserole dish. Roast in 350°F (180°C) oven for about 45 minutes or until soft. Squeeze the whole garlic bulb so pulp slips out of skins; add to potatoes when mashing. I often roast several heads at a time and refrigerate the roasted garlic to use during the week.

Roasted Garlic Horseradish Cream

Makes 1¼ cups (300 mL)

2	bulbs garlic, roasted (see Tip, left)	2
½ cup	mayonnaise	125 mL
½ cup	sour cream	125 mL
2 tbsp	finely grated peeled fresh horseradish or drained bottled horseradish	30 mL
1 tsp	Worcestershire sauce	5 mL
	Salt and hot pepper sauce	

1. Squeeze out roasted cloves of garlic into a bowl and mash with a fork. Stir in mayonnaise, sour cream, horseradish, Worcestershire sauce, salt and hot pepper sauce to taste. Use immediately or cover and refrigerate for up to 3 days.

Beef and Broccoli Stir-Fry

1 lb	lean boneless sirloin steak, cut into thin strips	500 g
2 tbsp	hoisin sauce	30 mL
2	cloves garlic, finely chopped	2
1 tbsp	minced gingerroot	15 mL
1 tsp	grated orange zest	5 mL
½ cup	orange juice	125 mL
3 tbsp	soy sauce	45 mL
2 tsp	cornstarch	10 mL
¼ tsp	hot pepper flakes	1 mL
1 tbsp	vegetable oil	15 mL
6 cups	small broccoli florets and peeled chopped stems (about 1 large bunch)	1.5 L
3	green onions, sliced	3

1. In a bowl, toss beef strips with hoisin sauce, garlic and ginger. Let marinate at room temperature for 15 minutes. (Cover and refrigerate if preparing ahead.)

2. In a glass measuring cup, combine orange zest and juice, soy sauce, cornstarch and hot pepper flakes.

3. In a large nonstick skillet, heat oil over high heat; cook beef, stirring, for 2 minutes or until no longer pink. Transfer to a plate.

4. Add broccoli and soy sauce mixture to skillet; reduce heat to medium, cover and cook for 2 to 3 minutes or until broccoli is tender-crisp. Add beef strips with any accumulated juices and green onions; cook, stirring, for 1 minute or until heated through.

Veal Paprikash

We've somehow forgotten this delicious classic preparation — and it's worth considering again. Together, the golden red paprika and tangy sour cream bring out the best in tender veal and meaty mushrooms.

Tip

Fettuccine or broad egg noodles make a delicious companion to this creamy veal in mushroom sauce.

1 lb	grain-fed veal scallops	500 g
2 tbsp	vegetable oil, divided	30 mL
4 cups	quartered mushrooms (about 12 oz/375 g)	1 L
1	large onion, halved lengthwise and thinly sliced	1
2	cloves garlic, finely chopped	2
4 tsp	paprika	20 mL
1/2 tsp	dried marjoram leaves	2 mL
1/2 tsp	salt	2 mL
1/4 tsp	freshly ground black pepper	1 mL
1 tbsp	all-purpose flour	15 mL
3/4 cup	chicken stock	175 mL
1/2 cup	sour cream	125 mL
	Salt and freshly ground black pepper	

1. Pat veal dry with paper towels. In a large nonstick skillet, heat 1 tbsp (15 mL) oil over medium-high heat; stir-fry veal in two batches, each for 3 minutes or until browned but still pink inside. Transfer to a plate along with pan juices; keep warm.

2. Reduce heat to medium. Add remaining oil. Cook mushrooms, onion, garlic, paprika, marjoram, salt and pepper, stirring often, for 7 minutes or until lightly colored.

3. Blend in flour; pour in stock. Cook, stirring, for 2 minutes or until thickened. Stir in sour cream. Return veal and accumulated juices to pan; cook 1 minute more or until heated through. Adjust seasoning with salt and pepper to taste; serve immediately.

Tuscan Roast Veal with Rosemary and White Wine

Makes 6 to
8 servings

You will be delighted by the tantalizing aromas of rosemary and garlic wafting through your kitchen whenever you prepare this delicious roast — ideal for a Sunday or other special occasion.

Tip

Pancetta is unsmoked Italian bacon. It is available at supermarket deli counters.

- Preheat oven to 350°F (180°C)
- Roasting pan

2 oz	pancetta, finely diced, or bacon	60 g
1/4 cup	finely chopped fresh parsley	60 mL
2	cloves garlic, finely chopped	2
1 tsp	grated lemon zest	5 mL
	Salt and freshly ground black pepper	
3 lbs	boneless leg of veal roast, well trimmed, tied	1.5 kg
2 tbsp	olive oil	30 mL
1 tbsp	chopped fresh rosemary or 1 tsp (5 mL) dried rosemary leaves, crumbled	15 mL
1 cup	dry white wine, divided	250 mL
1 cup	chicken or veal stock, divided	250 mL

1. In a bowl, combine pancetta, parsley, garlic and zest; season with salt and pepper.

2. Remove strings from veal roast; trim excess fat. Cover with plastic wrap and pound using a meat mallet to flatten slightly. Spread stuffing down center of meat. Roll the veal around the stuffing and tie securely at six intervals with butcher's string. (Prepare earlier in the day and refrigerate to allow flavors to penetrate veal.)

3. Place veal in pan. Brush with oil; season with rosemary, salt and pepper. Place in preheated oven and roast, uncovered, for 30 minutes. Add 1/2 cup (125 mL) each wine and stock to roasting pan. Tent loosely with foil and continue to roast for 1 1/2 hours more, adding more wine and stock to the pan as necessary, until meat thermometer registers 170°F (80°C).

4. Transfer meat to serving platter and keep warm. Pour remaining wine and stock into roasting pan and place on stovetop over high heat. Bring to a boil, scraping up any brown bits from bottom of pan. Strain into a saucepan and boil until partially reduced. Slice veal into slices and drizzle with some of the pan juices. Serve remainder in a sauceboat.

Veal Scaloppini with Marsala

This easy-to-make saucy veal is one of my all-time favorite dishes to serve when I'm entertaining. Delicious served with noodles and a green vegetable such as asparagus.

Tip

If you prefer a cream sauce, stir in ¼ cup (60 mL) whipping (35%) cream at end of cooking and heat through.

1 lb	thin veal or pork cutlets	500 g
½ tsp	salt	2 mL
¼ tsp	freshly ground black pepper	1 mL
¼ cup	all-purpose flour	60 mL
1 tbsp	butter (approx.)	15 mL
1 tbsp	olive oil (approx.)	15 mL
⅓ cup	minced shallots	75 mL
¾ lb	assorted mushrooms, such as shiitake, oyster and button mushrooms, sliced	375 g
1 tbsp	chopped fresh thyme or 1 tsp (5 mL) dried thyme leaves	15 mL
½ cup	dry Marsala or white wine	125 mL
½ cup	chicken stock	125 mL

1. Blot veal dry with paper towels. Season with salt and pepper; dredge in flour, shaking off excess.

2. In a large nonstick skillet, heat 1½ tsp (7 mL) each butter and oil over high heat; cook veal in batches, adding more butter and oil as needed, for 1 minute per side or until lightly browned. Transfer to a plate.

3. Reduce heat to medium; cook shallots, mushrooms and thyme, stirring, for 5 minutes or until softened. Add Marsala and stock; cook for 2 minutes or until slightly reduced. Return veal to skillet. Cook for 2 to 3 minutes, turning occasionally, until heated through and coated in sauce. Adjust seasoning with salt and pepper to taste.

Herb Wiener Schnitzel

Makes 4 servings

Tender milk-fed veal is preferred over grain-fed in this classic pan-fried recipe with flavorful herbs. Schnitzel is typically served with French fries, but you could also serve with a salad of mixed baby greens.

Tips

Make sure cutlets are thin; if necessary, pound meat thin between sheets of plastic wrap using a meat mallet or rolling pin.

Herbes de Provence is a blend of French herbs that often includes thyme, rosemary, basil and sage. If you can't find this blend in your supermarket, substitute a generous pinch of each of these herbs.

- Preheat oven to 200°F (100°C)
- Baking sheet

1 lb	thin veal or turkey cutlets (8 cutlets)	500 g
½ tsp	salt	2 mL
½ tsp	freshly ground black pepper	2 mL
1 cup	plain dry bread crumbs	250 mL
⅓ cup	lightly packed fresh parsley	75 mL
¾ tsp	dried herbes de Provence (see Tips, left) or thyme leaves	3 mL
⅓ cup	all-purpose flour	75 mL
2	eggs, beaten	2
2 tbsp	butter (approx.)	30 mL
2 tbsp	vegetable oil (approx.)	30 mL
	Lemon wedges	

1. Pat veal dry with paper towels. Season with salt and pepper.

2. In a food processor, process bread crumbs, parsley and herbes de Provence.

3. Place flour, beaten eggs and bread crumb mixture in three separate shallow bowls. Just before cooking, dredge veal in flour, shaking off excess; dip in egg and then coat well in bread crumb mixture. Discard any excess flour, eggs and bread crumb mixture.

4. In a large nonstick skillet, heat 1 tbsp (15 mL) each butter and oil over medium-high heat. Cook veal in batches, adding more butter and oil as needed and wiping skillet clean with paper towels between batches, for 1½ minutes per side or until golden. Transfer to baking sheet; place in warm oven while cooking remaining schnitzel. Serve accompanied with lemon wedges.

Grilled Lamb Chops with Mustard Baste

Makes 4 servings

Lamb chops are wonderful au naturel, but even more wonderful with a mustard glaze and a sweet hint of maple. Here's a quick and tasty way to dress up lamb chops when entertaining.

Tip

Instead of fresh herbs, use 1 tsp (5 mL) dried rosemary or thyme leaves.

Variation

Try this marinade with lamb kabobs, as well as chicken and pork.

2 tbsp	Dijon mustard	30 mL
2 tbsp	maple syrup	30 mL
2 tbsp	balsamic vinegar	30 mL
1 tbsp	chopped fresh rosemary or thyme (see Tip, left)	15 mL
2	cloves garlic, finely chopped	2
1/2 tsp	freshly ground black pepper	2 mL
1 1/2 lbs	lamb loin chops (about 8), 1 inch (2.5 cm) thick, trimmed	750 g
	Salt	

1. In a shallow glass dish big enough to accommodate the lamb chops, combine Dijon mustard, maple syrup, balsamic vinegar, rosemary, garlic and pepper; add chops and turn to coat. Marinate at room temperature for 15 minutes, or cover and refrigerate, turning occasionally, for up to 8 hours. Remove meat from refrigerator 15 minutes before cooking.

2. Preheat greased barbecue grill to medium-high (or preheat broiler).

3. Remove lamb from marinade, discarding marinade. Grill lamb for 5 to 7 minutes on each side for medium-rare or desired doneness. (Alternatively, place on a broiler pan about 4 inches/10 cm below preheated broiler for 5 to 7 minutes on each side for medium-rare or desired doneness.) Season with salt to taste.

Rosemary Roast Lamb with New Potatoes

Makes 8 servings

Lamb is often my first choice when planning a special dinner. It's always a crowd pleaser. I love the heavenly aroma of garlic and rosemary in this recipe — it fills my house and makes an especially warm welcome for friends as they come through the door.

Tips

Take the lamb out of the fridge about 30 minutes before roasting.

Choose potatoes that are the same size so they roast evenly.

- Preheat oven to 350°F (180°C)
- Large shallow roasting pan, greased

8	cloves garlic	8
1	leg of lamb (about 5 to 6 lbs/ 2.5 to 3 kg)	1
	Grated zest and juice of 1 lemon	
2 tbsp	olive oil	30 mL
2 tbsp	chopped fresh rosemary or 2 tsp (10 mL) dried rosemary leaves, crumbled	30 mL
1/2 tsp	salt	2 mL
1/2 tsp	freshly ground black pepper	2 mL
12	whole new potatoes, scrubbed (about 3 lbs/1.5 kg)	12
1 tbsp	all-purpose flour	15 mL
1/2 cup	white wine	125 mL
1 cup	chicken stock	250 mL

1. Cut 6 cloves garlic into 8 to 10 slivers each. Using the tip of a knife, cut shallow slits all over lamb and insert a garlic sliver into each.

2. Finely chop remaining 2 garlic cloves. In a bowl, combine garlic, lemon zest and juice, oil, rosemary, salt and pepper. Place lamb in prepared roasting pan; surround with potatoes. Brush lamb and potatoes generously with lemon-garlic mixture.

3. Roast in preheated oven for about 1 1/2 hours, turning potatoes over halfway through roasting, until an instant-read thermometer registers 135°F (57°C) for medium-rare. (For medium, remove the potatoes and continue to roast lamb for 15 to 20 minutes more or to your liking.)

Tip

If you don't want to open a bottle of white wine, a good substitute is dry white vermouth. Keep a bottle handy in the cupboard for those recipes that call for white wine.

4. Remove lamb to a platter; tent with foil and let rest 10 minutes before carving. Transfer potatoes to a dish; keep warm.

5. Skim fat in pan; place over medium heat. Stir in flour and cook, stirring, until lightly colored. Pour in wine; cook, scraping up any brown bits, until wine is reduced by half. Stir in stock; bring to a boil, stirring, until thickened. Strain through a fine sieve into a warm sauceboat.

6. Carve the lamb. Arrange slices on a serving plate and moisten with some of the sauce; surround with roasted potatoes. Serve with remaining sauce.

Garlic and Herb–Crusted Rack of Lamb

Makes 4 servings

Here's a classic lamb dish, often featured on restaurant menus, that can be easily prepared in your home kitchen for a special dinner. Much of it can be prepared ahead so you need only to place the meat in the oven when guests arrive. Serve it with small oven-roasted potatoes and tender green beans.

Tip

Have the butcher remove chine bone, excess fat and meat between the bones.

- Preheat oven to 425°F (220°C)
- Heavy rimmed baking sheet or shallow roasting pan

2	racks of lamb, each with 7 ribs	2
	Salt and freshly ground black pepper	
2 tbsp	olive oil	30 mL

Garlic and Herb Crust

1½ cups	soft fresh bread crumbs (about 3 slices bread)	375 mL
¾ cup	finely chopped flat-leaf (Italian) parsley	175 mL
2 tsp	chopped fresh rosemary leaves	10 mL
2 tsp	chopped fresh thyme leaves	10 mL
5 to 6	cloves garlic, finely chopped	5 to 6
½ tsp	salt	2 mL
½ tsp	freshly ground black pepper	2 mL
3 tbsp	butter, softened	45 mL
2 tbsp	Dijon mustard	30 mL

1. Season lamb with salt and pepper. In a large nonstick skillet, heat oil over medium-high heat; sear lamb on all sides until lightly browned. Transfer to baking sheet and let cool slightly.

2. *Garlic and Herb Crust:* In a bowl, combine bread crumbs, parsley, rosemary, thyme, garlic, salt and pepper; blend in butter to make a paste-like mixture. Spread mustard over fat side of lamb. Spread with bread crumb mixture, patting down slightly. Discard any excess bread crumb mixture.

3. Place racks crumb side up on baking sheet. Roast in preheated oven for 15 to 20 minutes or until medium-rare. (Instant-read thermometer should read 130°F/55°C.) Remove from oven. Transfer to cutting board and cut into chops.

Pork Wellington

Makes 6 servings

The Duke of Wellington has a grand dish named after him that became the entertaining extravaganza of the 1960s. Here's an adaptation made with pork tenderloin that has become my family's tradition to serve on Christmas Eve.

Tips

Frozen butter puff pastry is preferred, but any brand of frozen puff pastry in a 14- to 16-oz (400 to 450 g) package will work well in this recipe.

To ensure even baking of pastry, rotate baking sheets halfway through cooking. Or, if using a small oven, bake one sheet at a time.

Pork Wellingtons can be assembled ahead early in the day and refrigerated until ready to bake.

Variation

Use veal tenderloin instead of pork.

- Preheat oven to 375°F (190°C)
- 2 baking sheets, lined with parchment paper

6	slices regular or double-smoked bacon or pancetta, chopped	6
2 cups	finely chopped shiitake mushrooms	500 mL
1/4 cup	finely chopped shallots	60 mL
2	cloves garlic, finely chopped	2
1 tbsp	chopped fresh thyme or 1 tsp (5 mL) dried thyme leaves	15 mL
2 tbsp	chopped fresh parsley	30 mL
2 tbsp	Dijon mustard	30 mL
2	pork tenderloins, trimmed (about 1 1/2 lbs/750 g total)	2
	Salt and freshly ground black pepper	
1	package (14 to 16 oz/400 to 450 g) frozen puff pastry, thawed	1
4 oz	herb and garlic cream cheese, such as Boursin	125 g

1. In a nonstick skillet, cook bacon over medium heat, stirring, for 5 minutes or until crisp. Transfer to paper towels to drain. Drain all but 1 tbsp (15 mL) fat from skillet.

2. Add mushrooms, shallots, garlic and thyme; cook, stirring, for 3 minutes or until mushrooms are tender. Stir in parsley, mustard and bacon bits. Let cool.

3. Cut pork crosswise into 24 pieces, each 3/4 inch (2 cm) in size. Season with salt and pepper.

4. Divide puff pastry in half. Roll each half into a 12- by 9-inch (30 by 23 cm) rectangle; cut each rectangle into twelve 3-inch (7.5 cm) squares. Arrange on prepared baking sheets.

5. Spread a generous teaspoon (5 mL) of the shallot-herb mixture in the center of each pastry square and top with a tenderloin piece. Season with salt and pepper.

6. Bake in preheated oven for 18 to 20 minutes or until pastry is golden. Top each pastry with 1 tsp (5 mL) of the cream cheese and return to oven for 2 to 3 minutes or until cheese softens.

Company Pork Roast
with Fruit Stuffing

I love the way the sweetness of dried fruit accents the delicate taste of pork in this recipe. And when you stuff the loin with a fruit and spice mixture, you ensure that the meat will be extra moist and flavorful.

Tips

Store-bought curry pastes vary in flavor and strength depending on the brand. Some pastes are labeled as mild but have more heat than expected. Add a smaller amount of curry paste to the recipe to test the strength and add more to get the depth of curry flavor you prefer.

To make fresh bread crumbs, process 1 slice white sandwich bread in a food processor until finely crumbled.

- Preheat oven to 350°F (180°C)
- Roasting pan, with rack

Stuffing

1 tbsp	butter	15 mL
1/3 cup	chopped green onions	75 mL
1 tsp	ground cumin	5 mL
1 tsp	mild curry paste, or to taste	5 mL
1	egg	1
1 cup	chopped mixed dried fruits, such as apricots, prunes, apples, cranberries	250 mL
1/2 cup	soft fresh bread crumbs	125 mL
1 tsp	grated orange zest	5 mL
	Salt and freshly ground black pepper	

Pork Roast

3 lb	boneless single pork loin roast	1.5 kg
2 tsp	vegetable oil	10 mL
1	large clove garlic, finely chopped	1
1 tsp	dried sage leaves	5 mL
1/2 tsp	dried thyme leaves	2 mL
	Salt and freshly ground black pepper	

Gravy

1 tbsp	all-purpose flour	15 mL
1/2 cup	white wine or chicken stock	125 mL
3/4 cup	chicken stock	175 mL
	Salt and freshly ground black pepper	

1. In a small skillet, melt butter over medium heat. Add green onions, cumin and curry paste; cook, stirring, for 2 minutes or until softened.

2. In a bowl, beat egg; add onion mixture, dried fruits, bread crumbs and orange zest; season with salt and pepper.

3. *Pork Roast:* Place roast on a cutting board, fat side up, with the shorter end facing you. With your knife parallel to board, cut pork loin in half but do not cut all the way through. Open like a book. Cover meat with plastic wrap and, using a meat mallet or rolling pin, pound to about 1 inch (2.5 cm) thickness. Season with salt and pepper. Spread stuffing down center of meat and fold meat over to enclose. Tie securely at six intervals with butcher's string.

4. Place roast on rack in roasting pan. In a small bowl, combine oil, garlic, sage and thyme; spread over pork roast and season with salt and pepper.

5. Roast in preheated oven for $1\frac{1}{2}$ to $1\frac{3}{4}$ hours or until an instant-read thermometer registers 160°F (70°C).

6. Transfer roast to cutting board; tent with foil and let stand for 10 minutes before carving.

7. *Gravy:* Drain fat from pan. Place over medium heat; sprinkle with flour. Cook, stirring, for 1 minute or until lightly colored. Add wine; cook until partially reduced. Add stock and bring to a boil, scraping any brown bits from bottom of pan. Season with salt and pepper to taste. Strain sauce through a fine sieve into a warm sauceboat. Cut pork into thick slices and serve accompanied with gravy.

Pork Chops with Honey and Thyme

Simple and tasty — this is my favorite way to cook fast-fry pork chops. Serve with rice and steamed broccoli.

Tip

To brown meat without having to add a lot of oil, pat meat dry with paper towels before cooking. Add a bit of the oil to the pan and heat until hot but not smoking. Add a small amount of the meat at a time until nicely colored; remove. Add a bit more oil to pan if necessary and reheat before adding next batch of meat.

½ cup	chicken stock	125 mL
1 tbsp	liquid honey	15 mL
1 tbsp	cider vinegar	15 mL
1 tsp	cornstarch	5 mL
1 lb	thin boneless pork chops (about 6), trimmed	500 g
1 tbsp	vegetable oil	15 mL
	Salt and freshly ground black pepper	
3	green onions, sliced	3
1½ tsp	chopped fresh thyme or ½ tsp (5 mL) dried thyme leaves	7 mL

1. In a bowl, combine stock, honey, vinegar and cornstarch. Set aside.

2. Pat pork chops dry with paper towels. In a large nonstick skillet, heat oil over medium-high heat; cook pork for 1 to 2 minutes per side or until lightly browned. Season with salt and pepper. Transfer to a plate.

3. Reduce heat to medium. Stir in green onions and thyme; cook, stirring for 30 seconds. Stir reserved chicken stock mixture and add to skillet; cook, stirring, for 1 minute or until sauce boils and thickens.

4. Return pork and any juices to skillet; cover and cook for 2 minutes or until pork is no longer pink in center. Season sauce, if necessary, with additional salt and pepper to taste.

Smothered Pork Chops with Caramelized Onions and Apple

Makes 4 servings

I serve this family favorite pork dish with baked winter squash or mashed sweet potatoes and a green vegetable, such as steamed broccoli.

Tips

You can use boneless pork loin chops; just decrease the cooking time slightly.

It is not necessary to peel the apple in this recipe.

4	bone-in pork loin chops (cut 1/2-inch/1 cm thick)	4
	Salt and freshly ground black pepper	
2 tbsp	vegetable oil, divided	30 mL
2	onions, thinly sliced	2
1	large apple, sliced	1
1 tbsp	chopped fresh sage or 1 tsp (5 mL) dried rubbed sage	15 mL
1 tbsp	honey Dijon mustard	15 mL
1/4 tsp	freshly grated nutmeg	1 mL
1/2 cup	unsweetened apple cider, unsweetened apple juice or chicken stock	125 mL
1 tbsp	all-purpose flour	15 mL

1. Season pork chops with salt and pepper. In a large nonstick skillet, heat 1 tbsp (15 mL) oil over medium-high heat. Brown pork on both sides. Transfer to a plate.

2. Add remaining oil to skillet; reduce heat to medium. Cook onion, stirring often, for about 10 minutes or until tender and light golden. Stir in apple, sage, mustard, nutmeg and 1/4 tsp (1 mL) each salt and pepper. Cook, stirring often, for 5 minutes or until apple is almost tender.

3. In a bowl, blend flour with 1/4 cup (60 mL) of the cider until smooth. Stir in remaining cider. Add to skillet and bring to a boil, stirring, until lightly thickened.

4. Return pork chops and any accumulated juices to skillet. Spoon onion mixture over pork. Cover and cook over medium heat for 5 to 7 minutes or until only a hint of pink remains in pork.

Jamaican Jerk Pork

Makes 6 servings

Double the quantities for this flavor-packed seasoning and store half in a covered jar in the refrigerator to use with chicken legs or bone-in chicken breasts.

Tips

It's advisable to wear rubber gloves when handling hot chiles to prevent burns.

You can also turn up the heat a notch or two with a generous splash of Caribbean hot sauce or cayenne pepper.

Jerk marinade will keep for up to 1 week in the refrigerator.

Variation

Substitute 2 jalapeño peppers for the Scotch bonnets, if desired.

Jerk Seasoning

3	green onions, thickly sliced	3
1	small Scotch bonnet chile pepper, seeded and quartered	1
2	cloves garlic, quartered	2
1	piece (1 inch/2.5 cm) peeled gingerroot, coarsely chopped	1
2 tbsp	red wine vinegar	30 mL
2 tbsp	soy sauce	30 mL
2 tbsp	vegetable oil	30 mL
1 tbsp	packed brown sugar	15 mL
2 tsp	chopped fresh thyme or ¾ tsp (3 mL) dried thyme leaves	10 mL
1½ tsp	ground allspice	7 mL
½ tsp	salt	2 mL
¼ tsp	ground cinnamon	1 mL
¼ tsp	freshly grated nutmeg	1 mL
¼ tsp	freshly ground black pepper	1 mL
2	pork tenderloins, trimmed (about 1½ lbs/750 g total)	2
	Mango Pepper Salsa (see recipe, page 287)	

1. *Jerk Seasoning:* In a food processor, purée green onions, chile pepper, garlic, ginger, vinegar, soy sauce, oil, brown sugar, thyme, allspice, salt, cinnamon, nutmeg and pepper until smooth.

2. Cut pork tenderloins crosswise into two pieces each. Place in a shallow bowl and spread with jerk seasoning. Marinate at room temperature, turning occasionally, for up to 15 minutes or cover and refrigerate for up to 1 day.

3. Preheat greased barbecue grill to medium. Remove pork from marinade, discarding marinade. Grill pork, turning occasionally, for 15 to 18 minutes or until pork is nicely browned with just a hint of pink inside.

4. Transfer to a cutting board and cut into thick diagonal slices. Accompany with Mango Pepper Salsa.

Orange Hoisin Pork

Tip

Use thin pork scallops, boneless pork loin chops or boneless pork tenderloin in this recipe.

2 tsp	grated orange zest	10 mL
1/3 cup	fresh orange juice	75 mL
3 tbsp	hoisin sauce	45 mL
2 tbsp	rice vinegar	30 mL
1 tbsp	soy sauce	15 mL
1 tbsp	liquid honey	15 mL
2 tsp	cornstarch	10 mL
2 tbsp	vegetable oil, divided	30 mL
1 lb	lean boneless pork (see Tip, left), cut into very thin strips	500 g
1 tbsp	minced gingerroot	15 mL
2	cloves garlic, finely chopped	2
2	small zucchini, halved lengthwise, then sliced crosswise	2
1	red bell pepper, cut into thin 2-inch (5 cm) strips	1

1. In a glass measure, stir together orange zest and juice, hoisin sauce, vinegar, soy sauce, honey and cornstarch until smooth.

2. In a large nonstick skillet or wok, heat 1 tbsp (15 mL) oil over medium-high heat. Cook pork, stirring, for 2 minutes or until lightly colored. Transfer to a plate.

3. Add remaining oil to skillet. Cook ginger and garlic, stirring, for 30 seconds or until fragrant. Add zucchini and red pepper; cook, stirring, for 2 minutes or until vegetables are tender-crisp.

4. Return pork to skillet and stir in orange juice mixture. Cook, stirring, for 1 to 2 minutes or until sauce thickens. Serve immediately.

Baked Ham with Citrus-Mustard Glaze

The orange and lemon zest add a wonderful flavor to the ham, as well as a terrific garnish.

Tips

You will need the zest from about 2 oranges and 2 lemons.

Once opened, make sure to store maple syrup in the refrigerator. It also can be frozen.

- Preheat oven to 325°F (160°C)
- Shallow roasting pan

1	bone-in smoked ham (about 8 lbs/4 kg)	1
2 tbsp	coarsely grated orange zest	30 mL
2 tbsp	coarsely grated lemon zest	30 mL
1/2 cup	citrus marmalade	125 mL
1/4 cup	maple syrup	60 mL
1/4 cup	white wine vinegar	60 mL
2 tbsp	orange juice	30 mL
2 tsp	dry mustard	10 mL
1 cup	chicken stock (approx.)	250 mL
1 tsp	cornstarch	5 mL

1. Remove skin and trim fat from ham, leaving a 1/4-inch (0.5 cm) thick layer. Score the fat to make a diamond pattern. Place ham in roasting pan and bake, uncovered, for 1 1/4 hours. Drain off any fat in pan.

2. In a small saucepan of boiling water, blanch orange and lemon zest for 1 minute to remove bitterness. Drain and reserve.

3. In a food processor, purée marmalade, maple syrup, vinegar, orange juice and mustard until smooth. Transfer to a bowl.

4. Pour glaze over ham and sprinkle with zests. Bake, basting every 15 minutes, for about 45 minutes or until nicely glazed and meat thermometer registers 140°F (60°C). (Add a small amount of stock to bottom of pan if glaze begins to brown.) Transfer ham to a warm platter, cover loosely with foil and let rest for 15 minutes before carving.

5. Place roasting pan on stovetop over medium heat. Blend stock and cornstarch until smooth; pour into pan; cook, stirring, until sauce boils and is slightly thickened.

6. Cut ham into slices and serve accompanied with sauce.

Cider Ham Steak with Apples and Cranberries

Makes 4 servings

This tasty sauce flecked with apples and dried cranberries also goes well with boneless chicken breasts or turkey scallops. Pair this dish with scalloped potatoes or rice and a green vegetable such as broccoli.

Tip

To get more juice out of a lemon, roll on countertop or microwave on High for 20 seconds before squeezing.

⅔ cup	apple cider or juice	150 mL
1 tbsp	packed brown sugar	15 mL
2 tsp	fresh lemon juice, or to taste	10 mL
1½ tsp	Dijon mustard	7 mL
1½ tsp	cornstarch	7 mL
1 lb	center-cut ham steak, trimmed and cut into 4 portions	500 g
1 tbsp	butter	15 mL
2	green onions, sliced	2
1	apple, peeled, cored and diced	1
¼ cup	dried cranberries or raisins	60 mL

1. In a glass measure, combine apple cider, brown sugar, lemon juice, mustard and cornstarch until smooth.

2. Pat ham dry with paper towels. In a large nonstick skillet, heat butter over medium-high heat; brown ham on both sides. Transfer to a plate.

3. Reduce heat to medium. Add green onions, apple and cranberries to skillet; cook, stirring, for 2 minutes or until softened. Add cider mixture; cook, stirring, until sauce is thickened.

4. Return ham to skillet; cook for 2 minutes, turning once, or until heated through. Place ham steaks on serving plates and spoon sauce over top.

Barbecued Ribs

Makes 4 servings

Grilled, succulent ribs are a frequent summer request. The only way to eat them is with your fingers, so be sure to have plenty of napkins handy.

Tip

When barbecuing ribs, watch carefully to prevent them from charring. You may need to reduce the heat to medium-low, depending on the heat output of your barbecue.

This sauce is also terrific with other grilled favorites, such as burgers or chicken wings and legs.

- Preheat oven to 375°F (190°C) or preheat barbecue grill to medium-low
- Large shallow roasting pan or heavy rimmed baking sheet, lined with foil, with a rack (if using oven)

3 to 4 lbs	pork back or side ribs, trimmed	1.5 to 2 kg
	Salt and freshly ground black pepper	
	Zesty Barbecue Sauce or Tex-Mex Barbecue Sauce (see recipes, below and opposite)	

To Oven-Roast

1. Place ribs on rack in roasting pan; season with salt and pepper. Cover with foil. Roast in preheated oven for 40 minutes or until cooked through.

2. Remove foil; brush ribs generously on both sides with sauce. Roast, uncovered, for 40 to 45 minutes, brushing generously every 15 minutes with sauce, until ribs are nicely glazed and tender. Cut into portions and serve.

To Grill

1. Season ribs with salt and pepper. Place on grill; cook, turning occasionally, for 25 to 30 minutes or until cooked through and nicely browned.

2. Brush ribs generously on both sides with sauce. Increase heat to medium and grill, turning often and brushing generously with sauce, for 20 to 25 minutes or until nicely glazed and tender. Cut into portions and serve.

Zesty Barbecue Sauce

Makes 2 cups (500 mL)

1¼ cups	chili sauce or ketchup	300 mL
½ cup	liquid honey	125 mL
1	small onion, finely chopped	1
2	large cloves garlic, finely chopped	2
2 tbsp	Worcestershire sauce	30 mL
2 tbsp	fresh lemon juice	30 mL
1 tbsp	Dijon mustard	15 mL
1 tsp	hot pepper sauce, or to taste	5 mL

Tip

This recipe makes enough for 3 to 4 lbs (1.5 to 2 kg) ribs.

Don't limit this sauce to just ribs. It's also wonderful on burgers and chicken wings and legs.

Tip

This recipe makes enough sauce for 6 to 8 lbs (3 to 4 kg) ribs. Store additional sauce in an airtight container in the refrigerator and use within 1 month.

Variation

Chipotle Tex-Mex Barbecue Sauce

If you want to turn up the heat, omit hot pepper flakes and add 1 to 2 canned chipotle peppers, seeded and chopped, and 1 tbsp (15 mL) or more canned adobo sauce, depending on how hot you want the sauce to be.

1. In a medium saucepan, combine chili sauce, honey, onion, garlic, Worcestershire sauce, lemon juice and mustard. Bring to a boil; reduce heat and simmer, partially covered, stirring occasionally, for 10 to 15 minutes or until slightly thickened. Stir in hot pepper sauce.

Tex-Mex Barbecue Sauce

Makes about 4 cups (1 L)

1	bottle (12 oz/341 mL) beer	1
2 cups	chili sauce or ketchup	500 mL
½ cup	cider vinegar	125 mL
½ cup	packed brown sugar	125 mL
¼ cup	Worcestershire sauce	60 mL
2	onions, finely chopped	2
4	large cloves garlic, finely chopped	4
2 tbsp	chili powder	30 mL
1 tbsp	dried oregano leaves	15 mL
1 tsp	hot pepper flakes, or to taste	5 mL

1. In a large saucepan, combine beer, chili sauce, cider vinegar, brown sugar, Worcestershire sauce, onions, garlic, chili powder, oregano and hot pepper flakes. Bring to a boil; reduce heat and simmer, partially covered, stirring occasionally, for 25 minutes or until thickened.

Thyme-Roasted Chicken with Garlic Gravy

Makes 4 servings

I feel like it's a special occasion when I have a roast chicken in the oven. It conjures up a homey smell and feel. In my opinion, it's one of the most satisfying dishes on earth. Here I place herbs and seasonings under the bird's skin to produce a succulent, flavorful chicken. Slow roasting with lots of garlic creates a wonderful aroma — yet, surprisingly, imparts only a subtle flavor to the gravy.

- Preheat oven to 325°F (160°C)
- Roasting pan with rack

1	chicken (about 3½ lbs/1.75 kg)	1
10	cloves garlic, peeled	10
1 tsp	dried thyme leaves	5 mL
¼ tsp	salt	1 mL
¼ tsp	freshly ground black pepper	1 mL
1⅓ cups	chicken stock (approx.), divided	325 mL
½ cup	white wine or additional chicken stock	125 mL
1 tbsp	all-purpose flour	15 mL

1. Remove giblets and neck from chicken. Rinse and pat chicken dry inside and out. Place 2 cloves garlic inside cavity. Starting at cavity opening, gently lift skin and rub thyme, salt and pepper over breasts and legs. Tie legs together with string; tuck wings under back.

2. Add remaining garlic, ⅔ cup (150 mL) chicken stock and wine to roasting pan; place chicken, breast side up, on rack in pan.

3. Roast in preheated oven, basting every 30 minutes, adding additional stock if pan juices evaporate, for 1¾ to 2 hours or until pan juices run clear when chicken is pierced and meat thermometer inserted in thigh registers 185°F (85°C).

4. Transfer to a platter; tent with foil and let stand for 10 minutes before carving. Meanwhile, strain pan juices into measure, pressing down firmly to mash garlic into juices; skim off fat. Add enough of remaining stock to make ¾ cup (175 mL).

5. In a small saucepan, stir together 2 tbsp (30 mL) of pan juices and flour; cook, stirring, over medium heat for 1 minute. Gradually whisk in remaining pan juices; cook, stirring, until boiling and thickened. Serve with chicken.

One-Hour Roast Chicken with Sage and Garlic

Makes 4 servings

Who has time to wait around for a chicken to roast when you're in a hurry? I take an hour off the roasting time by doing two things: I flatten the chicken by cutting the bird open along the backbone, placing it flat on the broiler pan, and then boosting the oven temperature. The result? A golden, succulent bird in half the time.

Tips

If you don't have a rasp grater, such as a Microplane, to grate lemon zest, use a zester to remove the zest in thin shreds, then finely chop with a knife.

When lemons are bargain-priced, stock up for the future. Grate the zest and squeeze the juice; place in separate containers and freeze.

- Preheat oven to 400°F (200°C)
- Broiler pan, greased

1	chicken (about 3½ lbs/1.75 kg)	1
1 tbsp	butter, softened	15 mL
2	cloves garlic, minced	2
1 tbsp	minced fresh sage or 1 tsp (5 mL) dried sage leaves	15 mL
1½ tsp	grated lemon zest	7 mL
½ tsp	salt	2 mL
½ tsp	freshly ground black pepper	2 mL
2 tsp	olive oil	10 mL
¼ tsp	paprika	1 mL

1. Remove giblets and neck from chicken. Rinse and pat chicken dry inside and out with paper towels. Using heavy-duty kitchen scissors, cut chicken open along backbone; press down on breast bone to flatten slightly and arrange skin side up on rack of a broiler pan.

2. In a bowl, blend butter with garlic, sage, lemon zest, salt and pepper. Gently lift breast skin; using a knife or spatula, spread butter mixture under skin to coat breasts and part of legs. Press down on outside skin to smooth and spread butter mixture.

3. In a small bowl, combine olive oil and paprika; brush over chicken.

4. Roast chicken for 1 hour or until juices run clear and a meat thermometer inserted in the thickest part of the thigh registers 185°F (85°C). Transfer chicken to a platter. Tent with foil; let rest 5 minutes before carving.

Stuffed Mediterranean Chicken for Company

Makes 4 servings

Here's what I serve when I'm entertaining and I want a dish that I can count on to impress my guests. Keep the rest of the menu simple — serve with your favorite pasta dish and a green vegetable or tossed salad.

Tip

To toast pine nuts: Place nuts in a dry skillet over medium heat, stirring, for 2 to 3 minutes or until lightly colored. Watch carefully because they burn easily.

¼ cup	chopped oil-packed sun-dried tomatoes	60 mL
¼ cup	chopped fresh parsley, divided	60 mL
2 tbsp	lightly toasted pine nuts (see Tip, left)	30 mL
2 tbsp	freshly grated Parmesan cheese	30 mL
4	large boneless skinless chicken breasts	4
	Salt and freshly ground black pepper	
¼ cup	all-purpose flour	60 mL
1 tbsp	olive oil	15 mL
½ cup	chicken stock	125 mL
⅓ cup	dry white wine	75 mL
2	cloves garlic, finely chopped	2
3	tomatoes, seeded and diced	3
¼ cup	slivered pitted kalamata olives	60 mL
1 tbsp	rinsed capers (optional)	15 mL

1. In a bowl, combine sun-dried tomatoes, 2 tbsp (30 mL) of the parsley, pine nuts and Parmesan.

2. On a cutting board, using a sharp knife, slice each breast lengthwise along one side almost in half. Open each breast like a book; season with salt and pepper. Spoon parsley mixture over half of each breast; fold top over and press gently to seal.

3. Place flour on a plate; lightly dredge breasts in flour, shaking off excess. In a large nonstick skillet, heat oil over medium-high heat; cook chicken until lightly browned on both sides. Transfer to a plate. Discard remaining flour.

4. Reduce heat to medium. Stir in stock, wine and garlic; cook for 1 minute. Stir in tomatoes, olives, capers, if using, and remaining parsley; cook for 2 to 3 minutes or until slightly reduced and thickened. Season with salt and pepper to taste.

5. Return chicken to skillet. Cover and cook over medium-low heat for 10 to 15 minutes or until chicken is no longer pink inside.

6. To serve, cut chicken into diagonal slices. Spoon sauce on plates; arrange chicken on top.

Sesame-Crusted Chicken Cutlets

This chicken cutlet with a crunchy sesame coating is delicious served with Thai peanut sauce, red chili sauce, plum sauce or any other Asian sauce.

Tips

Instead of purchasing chicken cutlets, use a sharp knife to cut 3 boneless skinless chicken breasts lengthwise into 3 thin cutlets each.

To make fresh bread crumbs, process 2 slices white sandwich bread in a food processor until finely crumbled.

1 lb	thin chicken cutlets	500 g
1	egg	1
1 tbsp	toasted sesame oil	15 mL
1 tbsp	water	15 mL
½ tsp	salt	2 mL
1 cup	soft fresh bread crumbs	250 mL
⅓ cup	sesame seeds	75 mL
2 tbsp	vegetable oil (approx.)	30 mL

1. Pound cutlets between sheets of plastic wrap to an even ¼-inch (0.5 cm) thickness.

2. In a bowl, beat egg, sesame oil, water and salt. In a shallow bowl, combine bread crumbs and sesame seeds. Dip chicken pieces in egg mixture, then coat in bread crumb mixture. Discard any excess egg and crumbs.

3. In a large nonstick skillet, heat half the oil over medium-high heat. Cook chicken, in batches, for 2 to 3 minutes per side or until golden on outside and no longer pink in center. Add more oil as needed and wipe skillet clean with paper towels between batches.

Honey Lemon Chicken

Makes 4 servings

Kids love simple dishes like this one, with its straightforward flavors. And this chicken dish is simple enough that even young cooks can make it.

Tip

This recipe also works well with a whole cut-up chicken or bone-in chicken breasts. With its tang of lemon and sweetness of honey, this dish is sure to become a family favorite.

- Preheat oven to 350°F (180°C)
- 13- by 9-inch (33 by 23 cm) baking dish

4	chicken legs, skin removed	4
2 tbsp	liquid honey	30 mL
2 tsp	grated lemon zest	10 mL
1 tsp	fresh lemon juice	5 mL
1	large clove garlic, finely chopped	1
¼ tsp	salt	1 mL
¼ tsp	freshly ground black pepper	1 mL

1. Arrange chicken in baking dish. In a bowl, combine honey, lemon zest, lemon juice, garlic, salt and pepper; spoon over chicken.

2. Bake, basting once, for 45 to 55 minutes or until juices run clear when chicken is pierced.

Chicken Cordon Bleu

Crumb-coated chicken breasts stuffed with ham and melted Gruyère cheese can be easily prepared ahead and makes for a great menu choice when entertaining.

Tip

To make 1½ cups (375 mL) fresh bread crumbs, process 3 slices white sandwich bread in a food processor until finely crumbled.

- Preheat oven to 375°F (190°C)
- Rimmed baking sheet, greased

2	eggs, lightly beaten	2
½ cup	all-purpose flour	125 mL
1½ cups	fine fresh bread crumbs	375 mL
	Salt and freshly ground black pepper	
1 tsp	dried thyme leaves	5 mL
4	large boneless skinless chicken breasts	4
4	thin slices cooked ham or prosciutto	4
4	thin slices Gruyère cheese	4
2 tbsp	butter	30 mL
2 tbsp	olive oil	30 mL

1. Place eggs, flour and bread crumbs in three separate shallow bowls. Season flour with salt and pepper. Add thyme to bread crumbs.

2. Remove the tenderloins from breasts and reserve for another use. Place breasts on cutting board. Using a sharp knife, slice each breast lengthwise along one side almost in half. Open each breast like a book.

3. Cover with a piece of plastic wrap and gently pound each breast using a meat pounder or rolling pin to an even thickness slightly less than ½ inch (1 cm) thick. Cover each opened breast with 1 slice of ham and 1 slice of cheese, tucking in any ends. Brush edge of each breast with some of the beaten egg, then fold over to enclose ham and cheese.

4. Lightly dredge each breast in flour, shaking off excess, then dip in egg and coat evenly with bread crumbs. Discard any excess flour mixture, eggs and crumbs.

5. In a large nonstick skillet, melt butter and oil over medium-high heat. Cook chicken until nicely browned, about 3 minutes per side.

6. Transfer chicken to a baking sheet and place in preheated oven for 10 to 12 minutes or until chicken is cooked through and cheese is melted.

My Favorite Chicken Dish

Makes 4 servings

Boneless chicken breasts are a staple in my weekly grocery cart. Everyone needs an all-purpose chicken dish to whip up on the spur of the moment. This is one of mine. It's a breeze to cook and always a hit with my family. Serve alongside noodles or rice. Add a salad and you've got dinner ready in 30 minutes.

Tip

Vary the flavors by using different herbs, such as tarragon or herbes de Provence.

4	boneless skinless chicken breasts	4
2 tbsp	all-purpose flour	30 mL
1/2 tsp	salt	2 mL
1/2 tsp	freshly ground black pepper	2 mL
1 tbsp	butter	15 mL
1/2 cup	chicken stock	125 mL
1/2 cup	orange juice or mixture of juice and part dry white wine	125 mL
1	large clove garlic, finely chopped	1
1/2 tsp	dried Italian herbs or basil leaves	2 mL
1/4 tsp	granulated sugar	1 mL
1 tbsp	chopped fresh parsley or chives	15 mL

1. On a cutting board, using a sharp knife, cut each breast lengthwise into two thin pieces. Place flour in a shallow bowl; season with salt and pepper. Coat chicken in flour mixture, shaking off excess.

2. Heat a large nonstick skillet over medium-high heat. Add butter; when foamy, add chicken pieces. Cook 2 minutes per side or until lightly browned. Transfer to a plate.

3. Reduce heat to medium; add stock, orange juice, garlic, Italian herbs and sugar to skillet. Bring to a boil; cook for 1 minute or until slightly reduced. Season sauce with salt and pepper to taste.

4. Return chicken to skillet; reduce heat, cover and simmer for 5 minutes or until no longer pink inside and sauce is slightly thickened. Serve sprinkled with parsley.

Cornmeal-Crumbed Chicken Drumsticks

Makes 6 servings

This popular chicken dish does double duty served warm as a family-pleasing supper or served cold, tucked into a picnic hamper or bagged lunch.

Tip

Make extras of the seasoned crumb mixture and keep in the freezer to coat boneless strips of chicken breasts or fish fillets for a quick supper.

• Rimmed baking sheet, with greased rack

½ cup	sour cream	125 mL
1 tbsp	fresh lemon juice	15 mL
1	large clove garlic, minced	1
½ tsp	salt	2 mL
¼ tsp	freshly ground black pepper	1 mL
12	chicken drumsticks, skin removed	12

Crumb Coating

⅓ cup	cornmeal	75 mL
⅓ cup	fine dry bread crumbs	75 mL
⅓ cup	freshly grated Parmesan cheese	75 mL
2 tbsp	minced fresh parsley	30 mL
1 tsp	dried basil leaves	5 mL
½ tsp	dried thyme leaves	2 mL
½ tsp	paprika	2 mL
3 tbsp	butter, melted	45 mL

1. In a bowl, combine sour cream, lemon juice, garlic, salt and pepper. Add drumsticks; stir to coat well. Cover and let marinate in the refrigerator for 2 hours or overnight.

2. *Crumb Coating:* In a large heavy plastic bag, combine cornmeal, bread crumbs, Parmesan cheese, parsley, basil, thyme and paprika. Add drumsticks, in batches, and shake to coat well in crumb mixture. Discard any excess marinade and crumbs. Place on prepared baking sheet. Brush drumsticks lightly with melted butter.

3. Preheat oven to 350°F (180°C). Bake drumsticks for 40 to 45 minutes or until golden and no longer pink when cut into at the bone. If serving cold, let cool, place in an airtight container and refrigerate.

Yummy Parmesan Chicken Fingers

Makes 4 servings

What a relief to know when you come home frazzled from a day at work, you can count on these tasty chicken fingers stashed away in your freezer. Round out the meal with rice and a steamed vegetable, such as broccoli, for a dinner that's on the table in 30 minutes.

Tips

You can also make extra batches of the crumb mixture and store in the freezer.

Instead of boneless chicken breasts, prepare skinless chicken drumsticks in the same way but bake in a 375°F (190°C) oven for 40 to 45 minutes or until tender.

* Preheat oven to 400°F (200°C)
* Rimmed baking sheet, with greased rack

½ cup	finely crushed soda cracker crumbs (about 16 crackers)	125 mL
⅓ cup	freshly grated Parmesan cheese	75 mL
½ tsp	dried basil leaves	2 mL
½ tsp	dried marjoram leaves	2 mL
½ tsp	paprika	2 mL
½ tsp	salt	2 mL
¼ tsp	freshly ground black pepper	1 mL
4	small boneless skinless chicken breasts	4
1	egg	1
2 tbsp	butter	30 mL
1	clove garlic, minced	1

1. In a food processor, combine cracker crumbs, Parmesan cheese, basil, marjoram, paprika, salt and pepper. Process to make fine crumbs. Place in a shallow bowl.

2. Cut chicken breasts into four strips each. In a bowl, beat egg; add chicken strips. Using a fork, dip chicken strips in crumb mixture until evenly coated. Discard any excess egg and crumb mixture. Arrange on greased rack set on baking sheet. In small bowl, microwave butter and garlic at High for 45 seconds or until melted. Brush chicken strips with melted butter.

3. Bake in preheated oven for 15 minutes or until no longer pink in center. (If frozen, bake for up to 25 minutes.)

Lebanese Chicken Kabobs

Makes 4 servings

Known as *shish taouk*, these kabobs are comfort food in the Middle East. I find the Mediterranean blend of lemon, olive oil and garlic used here very appealing with chicken. Use the versatile marinade for chicken breasts and legs instead of kabobs.

Variation

Turn kabobs into sandwich wraps by nestling the grilled chicken in warm pita breads along with shredded lettuce, tomato wedges and chopped onion. Top with a spoonful of store-bought hummus, or mayonnaise flavored with garlic. Roll up for a quick meal.

• Wooden skewers

¼ cup	plain yogurt	60 mL
2 tbsp	olive oil	30 mL
2 tbsp	fresh lemon juice	30 mL
2 tbsp	chopped fresh mint or 2 tsp (10 mL) dried mint leaves	30 mL
2	cloves garlic, minced	2
½ tsp	salt	2 mL
	Freshly ground black pepper	
4	boneless skinless chicken breasts, cut into 1-inch (2.5 cm) cubes	4

1. In a large bowl, combine yogurt, olive oil, lemon juice, mint, garlic, salt and pepper. Add chicken to marinade; cover and refrigerate for 1 hour or overnight.

2. Preheat greased barbecue grill to medium-high (or preheat oven broiler). Soak skewers in cold water for 15 minutes.

3. Remove chicken from marinade, discarding marinade, and thread chicken onto skewers. Place on prepared grill, turning occasionally, for about 12 minutes or until chicken is no longer pink inside. (Alternatively, arrange kabobs on broiler rack. Place under preheated broiler 4 inches/10 cm from heat, turning occasionally, for about 15 minutes or until chicken is longer pink inside.)

Rosemary Chicken Breasts with Sweet Potatoes and Onions

A breeze to prepare, this easy-to-assemble dish is elegant enough to serve to company. The herb and lemon butter tucked under the skins keeps the chicken moist, and I love the way it imparts a wonderful flavor to the vegetables layered on the bottom.

Tips

Make extra batches of rosemary butter, shape into small logs, wrap in plastic wrap and store in the freezer. Cut into slices and use to tuck under the breast skins of whole roasting chickens or Cornish hens, or to top grilled meats.

If you purchased whole breasts with backs on, cut away backbone using poultry shears.

This recipe can easily be halved to serve 2.

- Preheat oven to 375°F (190°C)
- 13- by 9-inch (33 by 23 cm) baking dish, greased

2	sweet potatoes (about 1½ lbs/750 g)	2
1	onion	1
1½ tsp	chopped fresh rosemary or ½ tsp (2 mL) dried rosemary leaves, crumbled	7 mL
	Salt and freshly ground black pepper	
4	skinless bone-in chicken breasts	4

Rosemary Butter

2 tbsp	butter	30 mL
1	large clove garlic, minced	1
1 tsp	grated lemon zest	5 mL
2 tsp	chopped fresh rosemary or ¾ tsp (3 mL) dried rosemary leaves, crumbled	10 mL
¼ tsp	salt	1 mL
¼ tsp	freshly ground black pepper	1 mL

1. Peel sweet potatoes and onion; cut into thin slices. Layer in prepared baking dish. Season with rosemary and salt and pepper to taste.

2. *Rosemary Butter:* In a small bowl, mash together butter, garlic, lemon zest, rosemary, salt and pepper. Divide into four portions

3. Place chicken breasts, skin side up, on work surface. Remove any fat deposits under skins. Press down on breast bone to flatten slightly. Carefully loosen the breast skins and tuck rosemary butter under skins, patting to distribute evenly.

4. Arrange chicken on top of vegetables in baking dish. Roast for 45 to 55 minutes or until vegetables are tender and chicken is nicely colored.

Tandoori Chicken

Ginger, cumin, coriander and cayenne pepper are signature ingredients in Indian cooking and make chicken taste wonderful. I love the way the spicy yogurt marinade in this dish keeps the chicken moist and tender. Serve with Cucumber Raita.

Tips

The marinade takes no time to make in the food processor. If you have time, let the chicken marinate in the refrigerator for several hours or overnight to intensify the flavors.

For food safety reasons, baste the chicken just once, halfway through cooking, then discard any leftover marinade.

● Rimmed baking sheet, with greased rack (if using oven)

Tandoori Marinade

½ cup	plain yogurt	125 mL
1 tbsp	tomato paste	15 mL
2	green onions, coarsely chopped	2
2	cloves garlic, quartered	2
1	piece (1½ inches/4 cm) peeled gingerroot, coarsely chopped	1
2 tsp	mild curry paste	10 mL
1 tsp	garam masala	5 mL
1 tsp	ground coriander	5 mL
½ tsp	ground cumin	2 mL
¼ tsp	salt	1 mL
¼ tsp	cayenne pepper	1 mL
4	skinless, bone-in chicken breasts	4
2 tbsp	chopped fresh cilantro or parsley	30 mL
	Cucumber Raita (see recipe, opposite)	

1. *Marinade:* In a food processor, purée yogurt, tomato paste, green onions, garlic, ginger, curry paste, garam masala, coriander, cumin, salt and cayenne until smooth.

2. Arrange chicken in a shallow dish; coat with yogurt mixture. Cover and refrigerate for at least 1 hour or for up to 1 day.

3. Preheat greased barbecue grill to medium-high. Remove chicken from marinade, discarding marinade. Place chicken bone side up on grill; cook for 15 minutes. Turn and cook for 10 to 15 minutes or until no longer pink in center. Garnish with cilantro.

Oven Method

1. Follow Steps 1 and 2, above. Preheat oven to 350°F (180°C). Place chicken on rack on baking sheet; roast for 50 to 55 minutes or until no longer pink in center. Garnish with cilantro.

Raita is a yogurt-based side dish served as a cool, refreshing accompaniment to cut the heat in Indian dishes.

Tip

Use yogurt with 2% or more milk fat; nonfat yogurt has too thin a consistency for this recipe.

Cucumber Raita

1 cup	plain yogurt	250 mL
1	small clove garlic, minced	1
1/4 tsp	salt	1 mL
1/4 tsp	ground cumin	1 mL
1/4 cup	grated seeded peeled cucumber	60 mL
2 tbsp	chopped fresh cilantro (or 1 tbsp/ 15 mL chopped fresh mint)	30 mL

1. In a bowl, combine yogurt, garlic, salt and cumin.

2. Place cucumber in sieve and squeeze out moisture. Shortly before serving, stir cucumber into yogurt mixture. Sprinkle with cilantro.

Chicken Curry with Red Peppers

Makes 4 servings

In the time it takes to cook rice or pasta, this streamlined dish is ready to serve.

Tip

Store-bought curry pastes vary in flavor and strength depending on the brand. Some pastes are labeled as mild but have more heat than expected. Add a smaller amount of curry paste to the recipe to test the strength and add more to get the depth of curry flavor you prefer.

1 cup	chicken stock	250 mL
2 tsp	cornstarch	10 mL
1/4 tsp	salt	1 mL
4 tsp	vegetable oil, divided	20 mL
1 lb	boneless skinless chicken breasts, cut into thin strips	500 g
2	cloves garlic, finely chopped	2
1 tbsp	minced gingerroot	15 mL
2 tsp	mild curry paste, or to taste	10 mL
2	large red bell peppers, cut into thin strips	2
3	green onions, sliced	3

1. In a liquid glass measure, combine stock, cornstarch and salt; set aside.

2. In a large nonstick skillet, heat 2 tsp (10 mL) oil over medium-high heat; cook chicken, stirring often, for 5 minutes or until no longer pink inside. Transfer to a plate.

3. Reduce heat to medium; add remaining oil; cook garlic, ginger and curry paste, stirring, for 1 minute. Add peppers; cook, stirring, for 2 minutes. Stir reserved stock mixture and pour into skillet; bring to a boil. Cook, stirring, until thickened. Add chicken and green onions; cook, stirring, for 2 minutes or until heated through.

Butter Chicken

Makes 4 servings

Indian cooking has become popular in North America in recent years, and it's now much easier to find ingredients, such as the complex spice blends, in large supermarkets. This is one of my favorite ways to prepare chicken. Serve with rice and naan bread to mop up the delicious sauce.

Tip

Garam masala is an aromatic blend of ground spices that often includes coriander, cumin, ginger, black pepper, black cardamom, nutmeg, cinnamon, cloves and bay leaves.

4	boneless skinless chicken breasts, halved lengthwise	4
	Tandoori Marinade (see recipe, page 274)	
4 tbsp	butter, divided	60 mL
¾ cup	canned tomato sauce	175 mL
⅓ cup	whipping (35%) cream	75 mL
¼ cup	chicken stock	60 mL
	Salt	
¼ cup	coarsely chopped fresh cilantro	60 mL

1. Arrange chicken in a shallow dish and coat both sides with tandoori marinade. Cover and refrigerate for at least 1 hour or for up to 1 day.

2. Remove chicken from marinade and place on a plate. Reserve marinade. In a large nonstick skillet over medium heat, melt 1 tbsp (15 mL) of the butter. Cook chicken, in two batches, for about 2 minutes per side or until lightly browned, melting 1 tbsp (15 mL) more butter in the skillet between batches. Remove to a plate.

3. To skillet, add tomato sauce, cream, stock and reserved marinade. Bring to a boil and cook, stirring, for 3 minutes. Whisk in remaining 2 tbsp (30 mL) butter until melted. Return chicken to skillet and coat in sauce. Reduce heat to medium-low, cover and simmer for 5 to 7 minutes or until chicken is no longer pink in center.

4. Arrange chicken on a serving platter, spoon sauce over top and sprinkle with cilantro.

Turkey Tips

- I prefer to roast a fresh turkey rather than a frozen bird, which is less moist and juicy. To streamline the preparations, I've done away with stuffing the turkey. Instead, the stuffing is packed into a casserole dish and baked in the oven for the last hour of roasting the bird.

- Not sure what size turkey to buy? Estimate 1 lb (500 g) per person.

- *Quick defrosting method:* Place frozen turkey (in original wrapping) in cold water and change water frequently. Allow 1 hour per pound (2 hours per kg). Once defrosted, cook turkey within 2 days.

- Wash hands well before and after handling turkey. Wash and disinfect work surface and utensils with hot soapy water and dry thoroughly.

- Cook turkey thoroughly. Never slow-roast at low temperatures or partially cook a bird, then continue roasting later on in day or next day.

- Roast in a 325°F (160°C) oven until a meat thermometer, inserted in the thickest portion of inner thigh, reaches an internal temperature of 170°F (80°C) for unstuffed bird; 180°F (82°C) for stuffed bird.

- Chill leftovers promptly. Do not leave cooked turkey at room temperature for more than 2 hours. Place cooked turkey meat in a casserole or wrap in foil or plastic and refrigerate immediately. Leftovers will keep in fridge for up to 4 days or freeze for 1 month.

Whole Turkey Roasting Times

Today's leaner turkeys take less time to cook than turkeys did in the past. Don't rely on outdated information from old cookbooks and recipes. Here are newly revised roasting times:

Cooking time (hours) in 325°F (160°C) oven

Weight	Stuffed	Unstuffed
6 to 8 lbs (3 to 3.5 kg)	3 to 3¼ hours	2½ to 2¾ hours
8 to 10 lbs (3.5 to 4.5 kg)	3¼ to 3½ hours	2¾ to 3 hours
10 to 12 lbs (4.5 to 5.5 kg)	3½ to 3¾ hours	3 to 3¼ hours
12 to 16 lbs (5.5 to 7 kg)	3¾ to 4 hours	3¼ to 3½ hours
16 to 22 lbs (7 to 10 kg)	4 to 4½ hours	3½ hours

Roast Turkey with Sage-Bread Stuffing

Turkey always has the place of honor when my family and friends gather for holiday meals. It's perfect when serving a crowd. It's economical, too, and everyone loves it. Best of all are the leftovers that get wrapped and placed in the fridge for hearty sandwiches the next day — or even later that night.

Tip

See Turkey Tips, page 277.

Variation

Sausage-Apple Stuffing
Cook 1 lb (500 g) bulk sausage meat in a large skillet over medium-high heat, breaking up with back of spoon, until no longer pink; drain off fat. Add 2 peeled, finely chopped apples; combine with bread stuffing mixture.

- Preheat oven to 325°F (160°C)
- 12-cup (3 L) casserole dish, greased
- Large roasting pan or broiler pan, with greased rack

Stuffing

1/3 cup	butter	75 mL
2 cups	chopped onions	500 mL
2 cups	chopped celery	500 mL
8 oz	mushrooms, chopped	250 g
4	cloves garlic, minced	4
1 tbsp	dried rubbed sage leaves	15 mL
1 tsp	dried thyme leaves	5 mL
1 tsp	dried marjoram leaves	5 mL
1 tsp	salt	5 mL
1/2 tsp	freshly ground black pepper	2 mL
12 cups	white or whole wheat bread cubes, toasted on baking sheet in 350°F (180°C) oven for 15 minutes	3 L
1/2 cup	chopped fresh parsley	125 mL
1 cup	turkey stock (approx.)	250 mL

Turkey

1	turkey (about 12 to 14 lbs/6 to 7 kg)	1
2 tbsp	melted butter	30 mL
6	cloves garlic, unpeeled	6
1	large onion, cut into 8 wedges	1
2	carrots, cut into chunks	2
1	large stalk celery, cut into chunks	1
1 tsp	dried rosemary leaves, crumbled	5 mL
1/2 tsp	dried thyme leaves	2 mL
1/2 tsp	dried marjoram leaves	2 mL
	Salt and freshly ground black pepper	

Gravy

1/4 cup	all-purpose flour	60 mL
1/2 cup	white wine or additional stock	125 mL
3 cups	turkey gravy stock	750 mL
	Salt and freshly ground black pepper	

Turkey Gravy Stock

Pat neck and giblets dry. (Do not use liver.) In a large saucepan, heat 1 tbsp (15 mL) vegetable oil over medium-high heat; cook neck and giblets, stirring, for 8 minutes or until nicely browned. Add 1 each chopped onion, carrot and celery stalk including leaves along with 1 tsp (5 mL) dried thyme; cook, stirring, for 3 minutes or until vegetables are lightly colored. Add 1 cup (250 mL) white wine, if desired. Stir in 6 cups (1.5 L) water; season lightly with salt and pepper. Bring to a boil, cover and simmer over medium-low heat for 3 hours. Strain stock through cheesecloth-lined or fine sieve; discard solids. Makes about 4 cups (1 L) stock.

1. *Stuffing*: In a large skillet, melt butter over medium heat; cook onions, celery, mushrooms, garlic, sage, thyme, marjoram, salt and pepper, stirring often, for 15 minutes or until tender.

2. In a large bowl, combine onion mixture, bread cubes and parsley. Spoon into casserole dish.

3. To bake, add enough turkey stock to moisten stuffing and toss. (If you plan to stuff the bird, omit stock.) Cover with lid or foil and place in oven for the last hour of roasting turkey, uncovering for last 30 minutes to brown and crisp the top.

4. *Turkey*: Remove neck and giblets from bird; reserve to make stock. Rinse turkey with cold water; pat dry. Secure legs by tying with string or tuck under skin around the tail; fold wings back and secure neck skin with skewer.

5. Place turkey, breast side up, on rack in roasting pan. Brush bird with melted butter. Lightly crush garlic with side of knife; scatter garlic, onion, carrots and celery in pan. Season turkey and vegetables with rosemary, thyme, marjoram, salt and pepper.

6. Insert meat thermometer into thickest part of inner turkey thigh, being careful not to touch bone. Roast turkey for $3\frac{1}{4}$ to $3\frac{1}{2}$ hours; no need to baste. (If turkey starts to brown too quickly, tent bird loosely with heavy-duty foil, shiny side down.) Turkey is done when meat thermometer registers 170°F (80°C) for unstuffed bird; 180°F (82°C) if stuffed.

7. Remove from oven; cover with foil and let stand for 15 minutes for easy carving.

8. *Gravy*: Skim fat from roasting pan; place over medium heat. Stir in flour; cook, stirring, for 1 minute. Add wine; cook, stirring, until reduced by half. Stir in stock; bring to boil, scraping up brown bits from bottom of pan, until gravy thickens. Strain through a fine sieve into a saucepan, pressing down on vegetables; discard the vegetables. Season gravy with salt and pepper to taste.

Quick Turkey Curry

Makes 4 servings

This recipe will make you want to roast a turkey just so you have some leftovers on hand. But if time does not permit, buy a roasted chicken from the deli section of the supermarket and use the diced meat in this no-fuss dish.

Tip

Mango chutney is called for in this recipe, but any type, whether store-bought or homemade, can be used; add according to taste. Serve over basmati rice and sprinkle with chopped cilantro, if desired.

2 tsp	vegetable oil	10 mL
1	small onion, chopped	1
1	large clove garlic, finely chopped	1
2 tsp	minced gingerroot	10 mL
1	apple, peeled and chopped	1
½ cup	finely diced celery	125 mL
2 tsp	mild curry paste, or to taste	10 mL
1 tbsp	all-purpose flour	15 mL
1⅓ cups	chicken stock	325 mL
3 tbsp	mango chutney	45 mL
2 cups	diced cooked turkey or chicken	500 mL
¼ cup	raisins	60 mL
	Salt and freshly ground black pepper	

1. In a large nonstick skillet, heat oil over medium heat. Add onion, garlic, ginger, apple, celery and curry paste; cook, stirring, for 5 minutes or until softened.

2. Blend in flour; add chicken stock and chutney. Cook, stirring, until sauce comes to a boil and thickens. Stir in turkey and raisins; season with salt and pepper to taste. Cook for 3 minutes or until heated through.

Crispy Almond Baked Fish

Makes 3 to 4 servings

This easy oven method is my preferred way to cook white fish fillets, such as sole, haddock or turbot. As much as I like to quickly fry a crumb-coated fillet in a skillet on the stovetop, only one or two can fit comfortably in the pan at one time. Hence the speed and practicality of cooking all the fillets at once by the oven method.

Tip

To defrost package of frozen fish fillets: Remove package wrapping; place fish on plate. Microwave at Medium (50%) for 3 minutes. Shield ends with thin strips of foil to prevent them from cooking before the rest of the fish has defrosted. Microwave at Defrost (30%) for 2 to 3 minutes more or until fish separates into fillets. Let stand for 10 minutes to complete defrosting. Pat dry with paper towels to absorb excess moisture.

- Preheat oven to 425°F (220°C)
- Rimmed baking sheet

½ cup	soft fresh bread crumbs	125 mL
⅓ cup	sliced blanched almonds	75 mL
½ tsp	dried tarragon or basil leaves	2 mL
½ tsp	grated orange or lemon zest	2 mL
1 lb	fish fillets, such as sole, haddock or turbot	500 g
2 tbsp	butter, melted	30 mL
	Salt and freshly ground black pepper	
	Lemon wedges	

1. In a food processor, combine bread crumbs, almonds, tarragon and orange zest. Process, using on-off turns, until almonds are finely chopped.

2. Wrap fish in paper towels to absorb excess moisture. Brush baking sheet with some of the melted butter. Arrange fillets on sheet in single layer. Brush tops with remaining butter; season with salt and pepper. Sprinkle crumb mixture over fish and pat lightly.

3. Bake in preheated oven for 8 to 10 minutes or until fish flakes when tested with a fork. (Time depends on thickness of fish; increase time accordingly.) Serve with lemon wedges.

Cod with Spinach and Mushrooms

Cod with Spinach

Makes 4 servings

Cod's delicate, sweet flavor and firm texture pairs well with the easy-to-prepare spinach sauce. I like to serve this dish with steamed new potatoes.

Tips

Make sure the spinach is very dry. Place in a salad spinner to remove excess moisture. If using regular spinach, remove stem ends and coarsely chop leaves.

A loin of cod is a thicker cut of fish that takes a bit longer to cook than a fillet. Cod is delicate, so only turn once or it will break up. Any thick-cut fish can be used instead, including haddock, halibut or black cod.

2 tbsp	butter, divided	30 mL
1/3 cup	finely chopped shallots	75 mL
2 cups	sliced mushrooms	500 mL
1 tsp	dried fines herbes or tarragon	5 mL
1/3 cup	vegetable or chicken stock	75 mL
8 oz	fresh baby spinach (8 cups/2 L, lightly packed)	250 g
2 tsp	cornstarch	10 mL
1/3 cup	whipping (35%) cream	75 mL
	Salt and freshly ground black pepper	
1/4 cup	cornmeal	60 mL
4	cod loins, each 5 oz (150 g)	4
1 tbsp	vegetable oil	15 mL

1. In a large saucepan, melt 1 tbsp (15 mL) butter over medium heat. Cook shallots, mushrooms and fines herbes, stirring, for 5 minutes or until softened. Increase heat to high. Add stock and spinach; cook, stirring, until spinach is just wilted.

2. Blend cornstarch with 1 tbsp (15 mL) cold water. Stir into mushroom mixture and cook until thickened. Stir in cream and heat through. Season with salt and pepper. Keep sauce warm.

3. Place cornmeal in a shallow bowl and season with salt and pepper. Roll cod loins in cornmeal mixture, shaking off excess. Discard any excess cornmeal.

4. In a large nonstick skillet, heat oil and remaining 1 tbsp (15 mL) butter over medium heat. Cook cod for about 3 minutes per side or until nicely colored and fish flakes when tested with a fork. Spoon sauce onto plates and top with cod.

Cod Provençal

What to do with fresh cod from the market and ripe tomatoes plucked from your garden? Add some briny olives and pungent capers, and make this delicious fish dish that bursts with the sunny flavors of the Mediterranean.

Tip

Don't skimp on the olive oil — it's what gives this dish its distinct character and flavor.

• Preheat oven to 425°F (220°C)
• 8-inch (20 cm) square baking dish

1¼ lbs	cod or halibut, cut into 4 pieces	625 g
	Salt and freshly ground black pepper	
2	ripe tomatoes, seeded and diced	2
2	green onions, sliced	2
1	clove garlic, finely chopped	1
¼ cup	kalamata olives, rinsed, cut into slivers	60 mL
2 tbsp	chopped fresh parsley or basil leaves	30 mL
1 tbsp	capers, rinsed	15 mL
Pinch	hot pepper flakes (optional)	Pinch
2 tbsp	olive oil (see Tip, left)	30 mL

1. Arrange cod in a single layer in baking dish. Season with salt and pepper.

2. In a bowl, combine tomatoes, green onions, garlic, olives, parsley, capers and hot pepper flakes, if using; season with salt and pepper. Spoon tomato-olive mixture over fish fillets; drizzle with oil.

3. Bake in preheated oven for 15 to 20 minutes or until fish flakes when tested with a fork. Serve in warmed wide shallow bowls and spoon pan juices over top.

Pan-Seared Halibut

Halibut is one of my favorite fish to serve. I prefer it simply pan-fried, with a refreshing sauce on the side.

Tip

The halibut steaks should be no more than ¾ inch (2 cm) thick. For thicker pieces of fish, pan-sear until browned on both sides, then transfer to a glass pie plate and bake in a 375°F (190°C) oven for 7 to 9 minutes or until cooked through.

Variation

Instead of halibut, use trout, salmon, cod, tilapia or red snapper fillets.

4	halibut steaks (each 6 oz/175 g)	4
	Salt and freshly ground black pepper	
2 tbsp	vegetable oil	30 mL
	Lemon or lime wedges	
	Cucumber Dill Sauce or Tomato Cilantro Salsa (see recipes, opposite)	

1. Pat halibut dry with paper towels. Season with salt and pepper. In a large nonstick skillet, heat oil over medium heat. Cook halibut, turning once, for 6 to 8 minutes or until golden brown on both sides and fish flakes when tested with a fork.

2. Transfer to serving plates and serve with lemon wedges and Cucumber Dill Sauce or Tomato Cilantro Salsa.

Serve this tasty sauce with my pan-seared halibut, or with other fish, such as salmon and trout.

Cucumber Dill Sauce

Makes ¾ cup (175 mL)

½ cup	regular or light sour cream	125 mL
2 tbsp	finely chopped fresh dill	30 mL
2 tbsp	finely chopped chives or green onion tops	30 mL
1 tsp	lemon juice, or to taste	5 mL
¼ tsp	salt	1 mL
¼ tsp	freshly ground black pepper	1 mL
½ cup	finely diced seedless cucumber	125 mL

1. In a bowl, combine sour cream, dill, chives, lemon juice, salt and pepper. (Can be prepared up to 2 hours ahead; cover and refrigerate.)

2. Shortly before serving, stir in cucumber.

This light, refreshing Mexican salsa is known as pico de gallo. It goes well with many dishes, from fish, seafood, chicken and egg dishes to fajitas.

Tip

Fresh cilantro, also called coriander and Chinese parsley, lasts only a few days in the fridge before it deteriorates and turns tasteless. Wash cilantro well, spin dry and wrap in paper towels; store in plastic bag in the fridge. Leave the roots on — they keep the leaves fresh.

Tomato Cilantro Salsa

Makes about 1½ cups (375 mL)

2	large tomatoes, seeded and diced	2
⅓ cup	chopped fresh cilantro	75 mL
2	green onions, sliced	2
1 to 2	jalapeño peppers, seeded and finely chopped	1 to 2
1 tbsp	lime juice, or to taste	15 mL
	Salt	

1. In a bowl, combine tomatoes, cilantro, green onions and jalapeños. (Can be prepared up to 2 hours ahead; cover and refrigerate.)

2. Just before serving, stir in lime juice and season with salt.

Cedar-Planked Salmon with Maple Ginger Glaze

Plank cooking imparts a subtle smoky flavor to fish, meat, poultry and vegetables. It's an especially popular cooking method for salmon, as the fish turns out deliciously moist and the plank prevents it from falling apart on the grill.

Tips

Use an untreated wood plank that is $\frac{1}{2}$ to 1 inch (1 to 2.5 cm) thick, 7 inches (18 cm) wide and 12 inches (30 cm) long. Red cedar is the most popular and is often sold in supermarkets or where barbecue equipment is sold. Other aromatic woods, including white cedar, maple or cherry, can also be used.

To store gingerroot: Peel gingerroot, place in glass jar and add white wine or sherry to cover. As an added bonus, you can use the ginger-infused wine or sherry to flavor other fish or chicken dishes, or stir-fries.

● Cedar plank (see Tips, left), soaked in water for at least 1 hour

Ginger Maple Glaze

$\frac{1}{4}$ cup	maple syrup	60 mL
1 tsp	grated orange zest	5 mL
$\frac{1}{4}$ cup	fresh orange juice	60 mL
2 tbsp	balsamic vinegar	30 mL
2 tsp	finely grated gingerroot	10 mL
1	clove garlic, grated	1
$1\frac{1}{2}$ lbs	skin-on salmon fillet	750 g
	Mango Pepper Salsa (see recipe, opposite)	

1. *Glaze:* In a small saucepan, combine maple syrup, orange zest and juice, vinegar, ginger and garlic. Bring to a boil over medium heat and cook for about 5 minutes or until reduced and syrupy. Let cool.

2. Baste top side of salmon liberally with glaze and let stand for 15 minutes.

3. Meanwhile, preheat barbecue grill to medium-high. Place salmon skin side down on soaked plank and brush again with glaze. Place plank on grill, close lid and grill, without turning, for about 20 minutes or until fish flakes when tested with a fork. (There should be a gentle smoke coming from the wood. Reduce heat if necessary to moderate the amount of smoke.)

4. Cut fillet into 4 pieces and arrange on serving plates. Serve with Mango Pepper Salsa.

No-Plank Method

1. Follow Steps 1 and 2, opposite. Grease barbecue grill and preheat to medium-high. Baste salmon with glaze and place skin side down on grill. Close lid and grill, turning once, for 10 minutes per inch (2.5 cm) of thickness, until fish flakes when tested with a fork.

Oven Method

1. Follow Steps 1 and 2, opposite. Preheat oven to 425°F (220°C). Line a rimmed baking sheet with parchment paper or foil. Place salmon on baking sheet and brush with glaze. Roast for 10 minutes per inch (2.5 cm) of thickness, until fish flakes when tested with a fork.

Mango Pepper Salsa

Makes about 2 cups (500 mL)

1	mango, peeled and diced	1
2	green onions, sliced	2
1	small red bell pepper, diced	1
1	jalapeño pepper, seeded and minced	1
⅓ cup	coarsely chopped fresh cilantro	75 mL
1 tsp	grated gingerroot	5 mL
1 tbsp	fresh lime juice	15 mL
1 tbsp	maple syrup or liquid honey	15 mL
	Salt	

1. In a bowl, combine mango, green onions, red pepper, jalapeño, cilantro and ginger. (Can be prepared up to 1 hour ahead; cover and refrigerate.)

2. Just before serving, stir in lime juice and maple syrup. Season with salt to taste.

Salmon with Lemon Ginger Sauce

Makes 4 servings

Fresh ginger gives such a sparkling flavor to salmon — or any fish, for that matter. Substituting dried ground ginger just doesn't come close to imparting the same crisp taste as gingerroot, which is available in most supermarkets and produce stores.

Tips

One of the best uses for the microwave in my kitchen is for quickly cooking fish such as this salmon. Arrange fish and sauce in a shallow baking dish and cover with microwave-safe plastic wrap; turn back one corner to vent. Microwave on Medium (50%) for 4 minutes. Turn fish over and re-cover; microwave on Medium (50%) for 3 to 5 minutes more or until salmon turns opaque.

This fish dish is also great to cook on the barbecue.

- Preheat oven to 425°F (220°C)
- 11- by 7-inch (28 by 18 cm) baking dish, greased

4	salmon fillets, each 5 oz (150 g)	4

Marinade

2	green onions	2
1½ tsp	minced gingerroot	7 mL
1	clove garlic, minced	1
2 tbsp	soy sauce	30 mL
1 tbsp	fresh lemon juice	15 mL
1 tsp	grated lemon zest	5 mL
1 tsp	granulated sugar	5 mL
1 tsp	sesame oil	5 mL

1. Place salmon fillets in a single layer in baking dish.

2. *Marinade:* Chop green onions; set aside chopped green tops for garnish. In a bowl, combine white part of green onions, ginger, garlic, soy sauce, lemon juice and zest, sugar and sesame oil. Pour marinade over salmon; let stand at room temperature for 15 minutes or in the refrigerator for up to 1 hour.

3. Bake, uncovered, in preheated oven for 13 to 15 minutes or until salmon turns opaque. Arrange on serving plates, spoon sauce over and sprinkle with reserved green onion tops.

Blackened Cajun Snapper

Makes 4 servings

A terrific and easy way to cook fish. Once the fillets are blackened quickly on the stovetop, the heat of the oven takes care of the rest of the cooking. The skillet needs to be hot, so turn on your oven exhaust vent and be prepared for a bit of smoke in your kitchen.

Variation

Catfish, whitefish or grouper are also good fish to try instead of the red snapper.

● Preheat oven to 400°F (200°C)

1 tbsp	sweet paprika	15 mL
1½ tsp	dried oregano leaves, crumbled	7 mL
1 tsp	dried thyme leaves	5 mL
½ tsp	salt	2 mL
½ tsp	freshly ground black pepper	2 mL
½ tsp	granulated sugar	2 mL
¼ tsp	cayenne pepper, or to taste	1 mL
4	firm-fleshed red snapper fillets (about 1½ lbs/750 g)	4
2 tbsp	butter, divided	30 mL
1 tbsp	olive oil	15 mL
1	large clove garlic, minced	1
2 tbsp	fresh lemon juice	30 mL

1. In a wide shallow bowl, combine paprika, oregano, thyme, salt, pepper, sugar and cayenne. Pat fish dry with paper towels. Dip in herb and spice mixture, coating well on both sides. Discard any excess spice mixture.

2. In a small saucepan, melt 1 tbsp (15 mL) of the butter over medium heat. Brush tops of fillets with butter.

3. Heat a large cast-iron or heavy skillet over high heat until hot. Add oil and immediately place fish buttered side down in skillet. Reduce heat to medium. Cook fish for 3 to 4 minutes or until underside is blackened.

4. Turn over and place skillet in preheated oven. Cook fish for 7 to 9 minutes or until it flakes easily.

5. Meanwhile, heat remaining butter in small saucepan over medium heat until nicely browned. Add garlic and cook, stirring, for 15 seconds or until fragrant. Add lemon juice and remove from heat.

6. Place fish on serving plates and spoon lemon-butter sauce over.

Stuffed Sole

Want to wow your guests? Put this on your menu. Tender sole fillets with vibrant red pepper stuffing marry well in a light wine and cream sauce. It makes an attractive fish dish that never fails to impress.

Tip

In the past, fish dishes were adorned with silky rich sauces loaded with cream and butter. Adding only a small amount of whipping cream still gives this sauce its luxurious and creamy appeal, but keeps the calorie count way down.

- Preheat oven to 425°F (220°C)
- 8-inch (20 cm) square baking dish

1 tbsp	butter	15 mL
¼ cup	chopped green onions	60 mL
1 cup	chopped mushrooms	250 mL
1	red bell pepper, cut into very thin 1-inch (2.5 cm) strips	1
1 tsp	dried tarragon	5 mL
	Salt and white pepper	
8	small sole fillets (about 1½ pounds/750 g)	8
⅓ cup	white wine or fish stock	75 mL
2 tsp	cornstarch	10 mL
⅓ cup	whipping (35%) cream	75 mL

1. In a nonstick skillet, heat butter over medium heat. Add green onions, mushrooms, red pepper and tarragon; cook, stirring, for 3 minutes or until softened. Let cool.

2. Lay sole fillets, skinned side down, on work surface with smaller tapered ends closest to you; season with salt and pepper. Spoon a generous tablespoonful (15 mL) of filling on bottom ends of fillets. Roll up and place fillets seam side down in baking dish. Pour wine over top. (Recipe can be prepared up to this point earlier in day, then covered and refrigerated.)

3. To bake, cover with lid or foil; place in preheated oven for 16 to 20 minutes or until fish turns opaque. Using a slotted spoon, remove fillets and arrange on serving plate; cover and keep warm.

4. Strain fish juices through a fine sieve into a medium saucepan; bring to a boil over high heat and reduce to about ½ cup (125 mL). In a bowl, blend cornstarch with 1 tbsp (15 mL) cold water; stir in cream. Pour into saucepan, whisking constantly, until sauce comes to a boil and thickens. Adjust seasoning with salt and pepper to taste. Spoon sauce over fish and serve.

Tilapia with Lemon Caper Sauce

Makes 4 servings

This garlicky lemon sauce is the perfect foil for quick-cooking fish fillets, as well as pork or chicken cutlets. Serve with roasted potato wedges and steamed green beans or broccoli.

Variation

Pork or Chicken with Lemon Caper Sauce

Replace the tilapia with 1 lb (500 g) thin pork or chicken cutlets. Brown the meat in Step 3. After the sauce is reduced in Step 4, return meat to skillet and cook in sauce for 2 to 3 minutes or until just a hint of pink remains in pork or chicken is no longer pink inside.

1/3 cup	dry white wine	75 mL
1/3 cup	chicken stock	75 mL
1 tsp	grated lemon zest	5 mL
1 tbsp	fresh lemon juice	15 mL
1 tsp	dried fines herbes or oregano leaves	5 mL
1 tbsp	small capers, rinsed	15 mL
1	clove garlic, finely chopped	1
1/4 cup	all-purpose flour	60 mL
1/2 tsp	salt	2 mL
1/4 tsp	freshly ground black pepper	1 mL
1 1/4 lbs	tilapia fillets	625 g
1 tbsp	olive oil (approx.)	15 mL
1 tbsp	butter (approx.)	15 mL

1. In a glass measure, combine wine, stock, lemon zest and juice, fines herbes, capers and garlic.

2. On a large plate, combine flour, salt and pepper. Pat fish dry with paper towels. Lightly dredge in seasoned flour, shaking off excess. Discard excess flour mixture.

3. In a large nonstick skillet, heat 1 1/2 tsp (7 mL) each oil and butter over medium-high heat until foamy. Cook fish, in two batches, for 1 to 2 minutes per side or until lightly browned and fish flakes when tested with a fork, adding more oil and butter as needed between batches. Transfer fish to a serving plate and keep warm.

4. Reduce heat to medium and add wine mixture to skillet. Cook, stirring, for about 2 minutes or until sauce is reduced and slightly thickened. Pour over fish and serve immediately.

Pan-Roasted Trout with Brown Butter Sauce and Toasted Almonds

Tip

To get more juice out of a lemon, roll on countertop or microwave on High for 20 seconds before squeezing.

¼ cup	sliced blanched almonds	60 mL
4	trout or salmon fillets with skin on, each 6 oz (175 g)	4
	Salt and freshly ground black pepper	
2 tsp	olive oil	10 mL
2 tbsp	butter	30 mL
¼ cup	dry white vermouth, white wine or stock	60 mL
1 tbsp	fresh lemon juice	15 mL
2 tbsp	chopped fresh parsley	30 mL

1. In a large nonstick skillet, toast almonds over medium heat, stirring often, for 3 to 5 minutes or until lightly colored. Transfer to a bowl.

2. Season fish with salt and pepper. Place skillet over medium-high heat and heat oil. Arrange fillets skin side down in skillet and cook for 2 minutes (do not turn). Reduce heat to medium-low, cover and cook for 4 to 5 minutes, depending on thickness, until fish is opaque. Carefully lift fillets with a spatula, remove skin and arrange fillets on serving plates; keep warm.

3. Wipe out skillet with a paper towel. Place over medium heat and add butter. Cook, swirling skillet often, until butter is a nutty golden brown. Add vermouth and lemon juice; cook, stirring, until sauce is slightly reduced. Add parsley and season with salt and pepper. Spoon sauce over fillets, sprinkle with almonds and serve immediately.

A Pound
of Ground

continued…

One-Pot Dishes

Best-Ever Meatloaf

I could make this juicy meatloaf with garlic mashed potatoes every week and never hear a complaint from my family that it's served too often.

Tips

I like to use oatmeal as a binder, since it gives a coarser texture to the meatloaf (bread crumbs produce a finer one). Use whichever binder you prefer.

I always double the recipe and wrap the extra cooked meatloaf in plastic wrap, then in foil, for the freezer. Defrost overnight in the fridge. To reheat, cut into slices and place in saucepan. Moisten with about ½ cup (125 mL) beef stock; set over medium heat until piping hot. Or place meatloaf and stock in casserole dish and microwave on Medium (50%) until heated through.

- Preheat oven to 350°F (180°C)
- 9- by 5-inch (23 by 13 cm) loaf pan, greased

1 tbsp	vegetable oil	15 mL
1	onion, chopped	1
2	cloves garlic, finely chopped	2
1 tsp	dried basil leaves	5 mL
1 tsp	dried marjoram leaves	5 mL
¾ tsp	salt	3 mL
¼ tsp	freshly ground black pepper	1 mL
1	egg	1
¼ cup	chili sauce or ketchup	60 mL
1 tbsp	Worcestershire sauce	15 mL
2 tbsp	chopped fresh parsley	30 mL
1½ lbs	lean ground beef	750 g
¾ cup	quick-cooking rolled oats or ½ cup (125 mL) dry bread crumbs	175 mL

1. In a large nonstick skillet, heat oil over medium heat. Add onion, garlic, basil, marjoram, salt and pepper; cook, stirring, for 3 minutes or until softened. (Alternatively, place in microwave-safe bowl; microwave, covered, on High for 3 minutes.) Let cool slightly.

2. In a large bowl, beat egg; stir in onion mixture, chili sauce, Worcestershire sauce and parsley. Crumble beef over mixture and sprinkle with rolled oats. Using a wooden spoon, gently mix until evenly combined.

3. Press mixture lightly into loaf pan. Bake in preheated oven for 1 hour or until meat thermometer registers 170°F (80°C). Let stand for 5 minutes. Drain pan juices; turn out onto a plate and cut into thick slices.

Southwest Meatloaf

Instead of ketchup, serve salsa with this oregano- and cumin-flavored meatloaf.

Tips

To avoid skin irritation, wear rubber gloves when handling jalapeño peppers.

To make 1 cup (250 mL) fresh bread crumbs, process 2 slices white sandwich bread in a food processor until finely crumbled.

Variation

Instead of all beef, use ¾ lb (375 g) each ground pork and ground beef, if desired.

- Preheat oven to 350°F (180°C)
- 9- by 5-inch (23 by 13 cm) loaf pan, greased

1 tbsp	olive oil	15 mL
1	small green bell pepper, finely chopped	1
2	jalapeño peppers, seeded and minced (optional)	2
1	onion, finely chopped	1
2	cloves garlic, finely chopped	2
1 tsp	dried oregano leaves	5 mL
1 tsp	ground cumin	5 mL
¾ tsp	salt	3 mL
¼ tsp	freshly ground black pepper	1 mL
1	egg	1
2 tsp	Dijon mustard	10 mL
1 cup	soft fresh bread crumbs	250 mL
1½ lbs	lean ground beef	750 g

1. In a large nonstick skillet, heat oil over medium heat; cook green pepper, jalapeño peppers, if using, onion, garlic, oregano, cumin, salt and pepper, stirring often, for 5 minutes or until softened. Let cool slightly.

2. In a bowl, beat egg and mustard. Stir in vegetable mixture, bread crumbs and beef. Using a wooden spoon, gently mix until evenly combined.

3. Press mixture lightly into loaf pan. Bake in preheated oven for 1 hour or until meat thermometer registers 170°F (77°C). Let stand for 5 minutes. Drain pan juices; turn out onto a plate and cut into thick slices.

Veal Meatloaf

Makes 6 servings

Ground meats are one of the best supermarket buys for budget-trimming meals. I serve this family favorite meatloaf accompanied with fluffy mashed potatoes and glazed carrots for a delicious, economical supper.

Variations

Mini Veal Meatloaves

Divide into 12 balls; lightly press into muffin cups. Bake at 400°F (200°C) for 20 minutes or until no longer pink in center. Drain off juice.

Ground chicken can be substituted for the ground veal.

● Preheat oven to 350°F (180°C)
● 9- by 5-inch (23 by 13 cm) loaf pan, greased

1 tbsp	olive oil	15 mL
1	onion, finely chopped	1
1	large clove garlic, finely chopped	1
½ tsp	dried thyme or marjoram leaves	2 mL
¾ tsp	salt	3 mL
¼ tsp	freshly ground black pepper	1 mL
1	egg	1
¼ cup	chicken stock	60 mL
1 tsp	grated lemon zest	5 mL
½ cup	dry seasoned bread crumbs	125 mL
2 tbsp	finely chopped fresh parsley	30 mL
1½ lbs	lean ground veal	750 g

1. In a large nonstick skillet, heat oil over medium heat; cook onion, garlic, thyme, salt and pepper, stirring often, for 3 minutes or until softened. Let cool slightly.

2. In a bowl, beat together egg, stock and lemon zest. Stir in onion mixture, bread crumbs, parsley and veal. Using a wooden spoon, gently mix until evenly combined.

3. Press mixture lightly into loaf pan. Bake in preheated oven for 1 hour or until meat thermometer registers 170°F (77°C). Let stand for 5 minutes. Drain pan juices; turn out onto a plate a cut into thick slices.

Italian Chicken Meatloaf

Makes 6 servings

This Italian-inspired meatloaf has a winning combination of sausage, mozzarella cheese and basil pesto and is sure to become a family favorite.

Tip

Hate shedding tears when chopping onions? To minimize the weeping problem, use a razor-sharp knife to prevent loss of juices and cover the cut onions with a paper towel as you chop them to prevent the vapors from rising to your eyes.

- Preheat oven to 375°F (190°C)
- 9- by 5-inch (23 by 13 cm) loaf pan, greased

1 lb	lean ground chicken, turkey or beef	500 g
8 oz	mild Italian pork, beef or chicken sausage, casings removed	250 g
1 cup	shredded mozzarella or provolone cheese	250 mL
1 cup	soft fresh Italian bread crumbs	250 mL
1	egg	1
1 cup	tomato pasta sauce, divided	250 mL
2 tbsp	basil pesto, store-bought or homemade (see recipe, page 334)	30 mL
1	small onion, finely chopped	1
1	clove garlic, finely chopped	1
1/2 tsp	salt	2 mL
1/2 tsp	freshly ground black pepper	2 mL

1. In a bowl, combine chicken, sausage meat, cheese and bread crumbs.

2. In another bowl, beat egg. Stir in 1/2 cup (125 mL) pasta sauce, pesto, onion, garlic, salt and pepper. Pour over chicken mixture and gently mix until evenly combined.

3. Press meat mixture into prepared loaf pan. Spread remaining 1/2 cup (125 mL) pasta sauce over top. Bake in preheated oven for 55 to 60 minutes or until a meat thermometer inserted into center registers 170°F (77°C). Let stand for 5 minutes. Drain pan juices; turn out onto a plate and cut into thick slices.

Turkey Mushroom Meatloaf

Makes 6 servings

Move over, meatloaves made with ground beef. This tasty meatloaf is packed with great flavor and is sure to become a favorite. Consider doubling the recipe and stash the second cooked meatloaf in the freezer to have on hand for another meal.

Tips

To wash or not wash mushrooms? You can wipe them with a damp cloth, if you wish. However, I feel it's important to wash all produce that comes into my kitchen. I quickly rinse mushrooms under cold water and immediately wrap in a clean, dry kitchen towel or paper towels to absorb excess moisture.

To make 1½ cups (375 mL) fresh bread crumbs, process 3 slices white sandwich bread in a food processor until finely crumbled.

- Preheat oven to 350°F (180°C)
- 9- by 5-inch (23 by 13 cm) loaf pan, greased

1 tbsp	olive oil	15 mL
1 cup	finely chopped mushrooms	250 mL
1 cup	diced peeled apple	250 mL
1	onion, finely chopped	1
½ cup	finely chopped celery	125 mL
2 tsp	dried sage leaves	10 mL
1 tsp	dried thyme leaves	5 mL
1 tsp	salt	5 mL
½ tsp	freshly ground black pepper	2 mL
2 tbsp	chopped fresh parsley	30 mL
2	eggs	2
1½ lbs	ground turkey or chicken	750 g
1½ cups	soft fresh bread crumbs	375 mL

1. In a nonstick skillet, heat oil over medium heat; cook mushrooms, apple, onion, celery, sage, thyme, salt and pepper, stirring often, for 10 minutes or until vegetables are tender. Add parsley and let cool slightly.

2. In a bowl, lightly beat eggs. Stir in turkey, bread crumbs and vegetable mixture. Using a wooden spoon, gently mix until thoroughly combined.

3. Press mixture lightly into loaf pan. Bake in preheated oven for 1 to 1¼ hours or until meat thermometer registers 170°F (77°C). Let stand for 5 minutes. Drain pan juices; turn out onto a plate and cut into thick slices.

Meatloaf and Mashed Potato Pie

Makes 4 to 5 servings

Everyone loves meatloaf and mashed potatoes. Here's a creative way to prepare this favorite combo.

Tip

Make a double batch of meatloaf. Press into two pie plates; bake according to recipe until no longer pink in center. Top one meatloaf with mashed potatoes; let the other one cool, wrap well and freeze for another meal.

- Preheat oven to 375°F (190°C)
- Deep 9- or 10-inch (23 or 25 cm) pie plate, greased

Mashed Potato Topping

6	russet or Yukon gold potatoes, peeled and cubed (about 2 lbs/1 kg)	6
½ cup	sour cream	125 mL
	Salt and freshly ground black pepper	

Meatloaf

1	egg	1
¼ cup	chili sauce or ketchup	60 mL
¼ cup	minced onion	60 mL
1	clove garlic, minced	1
1 tsp	Worcestershire sauce	5 mL
½ tsp	salt	2 mL
¼ tsp	freshly ground black pepper	1 mL
¼ cup	dry seasoned bread crumbs	60 mL
1 lb	lean ground beef or veal	500 g
½ cup	shredded Cheddar cheese	125 mL

1. *Mashed Potato Topping:* In a large saucepan, cook potatoes in boiling salted water until tender. Drain well and return to saucepan; place over low heat for 1 minute to dry. Mash using potato masher or electric mixer at low speed until smooth. Beat in sour cream; season with salt and pepper to taste. Keep warm over low heat.

2. *Meatloaf:* In a bowl, beat egg; stir in chili sauce, onion, garlic, Worcestershire sauce, salt and pepper. Mix in bread crumbs and beef. Press evenly into pie plate. Bake for 25 to 30 minutes or until no longer pink in center; drain juice.

3. Spread mashed potatoes over meat; sprinkle with cheese. (Can be prepared up to 1 day ahead; cover and refrigerate.) Bake for 20 to 25 minutes or until cheese is melted. (Bake 10 minutes longer, if refrigerated.)

Kids' Favorite Spaghetti Pie

Makes 4 servings

Leftover pasta in the fridge is perfect for this pizza-like supper dish that's especially appealing to the younger set.

Tip

It's easy to turn this recipe into a vegetarian dish — just omit the meat. Broccoli can be replaced by zucchini, bell peppers or whatever vegetables you have on hand.

- Preheat oven to 350°F (180°C)
- 9- or 10-inch (23 or 25 cm) glass pie plate, greased

8 oz	mild or hot Italian sausages, casings removed, or lean ground beef	250 g
2 cups	sliced mushrooms	500 mL
1	small onion, chopped	1
1	large clove garlic, finely chopped	1
1½ tsp	dried oregano leaves	7 mL
2 cups	tomato pasta sauce	500 mL
2 cups	small broccoli florets	500 mL
3 cups	cooked spaghetti or other string pasta (6 oz/175 g uncooked)	750 mL
1½ cups	shredded mozzarella cheese	375 mL

1. In a medium saucepan over medium-high heat, cook sausage meat, breaking up with a wooden spoon, for 4 minutes or until no longer pink. Drain in sieve to remove any fat. Return to saucepan. Add mushrooms, onion, garlic, and oregano; cook, stirring, for 3 minutes or until vegetables are softened. Add tomato pasta sauce; cover and simmer for 10 minutes.

2. Rinse broccoli; place in a covered casserole dish. Microwave at High for 2 to 2½ minutes or until bright green and almost tender. Rinse under cold water to chill; drain.

3. Arrange spaghetti in pie plate. Spread with meat sauce; top with broccoli and sprinkle with cheese. Bake for 25 to 30 minutes or until cheese is melted. Cut into wedges and serve.

Shepherd's Pie

Mushrooms add a depth of flavor to this dish and help cut down on the amount of meat used. When my children were young and didn't like the sight of mushrooms in their favorite supper dish, I would finely chop the mushrooms in a food processor and they never knew the difference.

Tip

To wash or not wash mushrooms? You can wipe them with a damp cloth, if you wish. However, I feel it's important to wash all produce that comes into my kitchen. I quickly rinse mushrooms under cold water and immediately wrap in a clean, dry kitchen towel or paper towels to absorb excess moisture.

- Preheat oven to 375°F (190°C)
- 10-cup (2.5 L) shallow baking dish

Mashed Potato Topping

6	potatoes, peeled and cubed (about 2 lbs/1 kg)	6
¾ cup	milk or buttermilk	175 mL
	Salt and freshly ground black pepper	

Meat Layer

1 lb	lean ground beef or veal	500 g
8 oz	mushrooms, sliced or chopped	250 g
1	onion, finely chopped	1
2	cloves garlic, finely chopped	2
½ tsp	dried thyme leaves	2 mL
½ tsp	dried marjoram leaves	2 mL
3 tbsp	all-purpose flour	45 mL
1½ cups	beef stock	375 mL
2 tbsp	tomato paste (see Tip, opposite)	30 mL
2 tsp	Worcestershire sauce	10 mL
	Salt and freshly ground black pepper	
1	can (12 oz/341 mL) corn kernels, drained	1

Bread Crumb Topping

2 tbsp	fine dry bread crumbs	30 mL
2 tbsp	freshly grated Parmesan cheese	30 mL
¼ tsp	paprika	1 mL

1. *Mashed Potato Topping:* In a large saucepan of boiling salted water, cook potatoes until tender. Drain and mash using a potato masher or hand-held electric mixer; beat in milk until smooth. Season with salt and pepper to taste.

2. *Meat Layer:* In a large nonstick skillet, cook beef over medium-high heat, breaking up with a wooden spoon, for 5 minutes or until no longer pink.

Unless you're using expensive tomato paste from a tube, you can freeze leftover tomato paste. Put tablespoons (15 mL) of leftover canned tomato paste on a waxed paper–lined plate or in ice cube trays; freeze until firm. Transfer to a small freezer bag and have handy in the freezer to add to recipes.

3. Reduce heat to medium. Add mushrooms, onion, garlic, thyme and marjoram; cook, stirring often, for 5 minutes or until softened. Sprinkle with flour; stir in stock, tomato paste and Worcestershire sauce. Bring to a boil; reduce heat and simmer, covered, for 8 minutes. Season with salt, if needed, and pepper to taste.

4. Spread meat mixture in baking dish; layer with corn. Place small spoonfuls of mashed potatoes over corn and spread evenly. (The recipe can be prepared up to this point earlier in the day or the day before, then covered and refrigerated.)

5. *Bread Crumb Topping:* In a small bowl, combine bread crumbs, Parmesan and paprika; sprinkle over top of shepherd's pie.

6. Bake in preheated oven for 25 to 30 minutes (40 minutes, if refrigerated) or until filling is bubbly.

Italian Shepherd's Pie

You won't be able to resist this old standby with new-fashioned Italian flavors. The garlic is slowly roasted in olive oil and imparts a sweet, mellow flavor to the mashed potato and bean topping.

Tips

Garlic Mashed Potatoes and Beans makes a wonderful topping for this recipe, but that's by no means its only use. Serve it as a side dish with your favourite roast, such as Tuscan Roast Veal with Rosemary and White Wine (page 246).

Like coffee, Parmesan loses its wonderful aromatic flavor and moisture if grated ahead. Choose a wedge in a cheese shop and have it grated for you. Freeze in an airtight container. Or better still, grate the cheese as you need it.

Store Parmesan wedges wrapped in plastic wrap, then in foil, in the refrigerator; it keeps well for weeks.

- Preheat oven to 350°F (180°C)
- 13- by 9-inch (33 by 23 cm) baking dish, greased

Garlic Mashed Potatoes and Beans

6	large russet potatoes, peeled and cubed (about 3 lbs/1.5 kg)	6
2 tbsp	olive oil	30 mL
8	cloves garlic, thinly sliced	8
1	can (19 oz/540 mL) white kidney beans, drained and rinsed	1
¼ cup	chopped fresh parsley	60 mL

Meat Layer

1½ lbs	lean ground beef, veal or chicken	750 g
1	large onion, finely chopped	1
3	cloves garlic, finely chopped	3
2 cups	diced carrots	500 mL
1 cup	chopped celery	250 mL
2 tsp	dried basil leaves	10 mL
1½ tsp	dried oregano leaves	7 mL
¾ tsp	salt	3 mL
¼ tsp	hot pepper flakes	1 mL
1	can (28 oz/796 mL) plum tomatoes, including juice	1
¼ cup	tomato paste	60 mL

Bread Crumb Topping

¼ cup	freshly grated Parmesan cheese	60 mL
2 tbsp	fine dry bread crumbs	30 mL

1. *Garlic Mashed Potatoes and Beans:* In a large saucepan of boiling salted water, cook potatoes for 20 minutes or until tender.

2. Meanwhile, in a small saucepan over low heat, combine oil and garlic. Cook, stirring occasionally, for 5 to 7 minutes or until garlic is tender but not browned.

Prepare this dish ahead.
Cover and refrigerate
for up to 1 day; increase
baking time by 10 minutes.

3. Drain potatoes, reserving $1/2$ cup (125 mL) cooking liquid. Using an electric mixer, mash potatoes until smooth; mash in beans and garlic mixture, adding enough of the cooking liquid to make a smooth purée. Stir in parsley.

4. In a Dutch oven or large saucepan over medium-high heat, cook beef, breaking up with a wooden spoon, for 7 minutes or until no longer pink. Reduce heat to medium; add onion, garlic, carrots, celery, basil, oregano, salt and hot pepper flakes. Cook, stirring, for 5 minutes or until vegetables are softened.

5. In a food processor, purée tomatoes with juice. Stir into beef mixture with tomato paste; bring to a boil. Reduce heat to medium-low, cover and simmer, stirring occasionally, for 20 minutes or until vegetables are tender. Spread in prepared baking dish. Spoon potato mixture evenly over meat layer.

6. *Bread Crumb Topping:* In a small bowl, combine Parmesan cheese and bread crumbs; sprinkle over top. Bake in oven for 40 to 45 minutes or until bubbly and top is golden.

Chicken Shepherd's Pie with Sweet Potato Topping

I updated the shepherd's pie with this combination of a savory chicken and mushroom filling and a sweet potato topping. This dish has become a favorite in my family.

Tips

To soften cream cheese: Place cream cheese in glass bowl and microwave on Medium (50%) for 45 to 60 seconds.

When ground chicken or turkey is browned in a skillet, it doesn't turn into a fine crumble like other ground meats. I overcome the problem by placing the cooked chicken in a food processor and chopping it using on-off turns to break up meat lumps.

- Preheat oven to 375°F (190°C)
- 10-cup (2.5 L) shallow baking dish, greased

3	sweet potatoes, peeled and cubed (about 2 lbs/1 kg)	3
2 oz	cream cheese, softened, cubed	60 g
2	green onions, sliced	2
1 lb	lean ground chicken or turkey	500 g
1 tbsp	vegetable oil	15 mL
8 oz	mushrooms, sliced	250 g
1	onion, chopped	1
1 tsp	poultry seasoning	5 mL
1½ cups	chicken stock	375 mL
1 tbsp	soy sauce	15 mL
1 tbsp	cornstarch	15 mL
	Salt and freshly ground black pepper	
2 cups	frozen corn kernels or peas	500 mL
2 tbsp	fine dry bread crumbs	30 mL

1. In a saucepan of boiling salted water, cook sweet potatoes for 10 minutes or until tender. Drain and return to pot. Add cream cheese and mash until smooth. Stir in green onions; reserve.

2. In a large nonstick skillet over medium-high heat, cook chicken, breaking up with a wooden spoon, for 5 minutes or until no longer pink. Transfer to a bowl.

3. In same skillet, heat oil over medium heat. Cook mushrooms, onion and poultry seasoning, stirring occasionally, for 5 minutes or until mushrooms are softened.

4. In a small bowl, stir together stock, soy sauce and cornstarch. Stir into skillet. Add chicken and bring to boil. Reduce heat and simmer, stirring often, for 5 minutes or until sauce is thickened and heated through. Season with salt and pepper to taste.

5. Spoon chicken mixture into prepared baking dish and top with corn. Top with reserved sweet potato mixture in an even layer. Sprinkle with bread crumbs.

6. Bake in preheated oven for 35 to 40 minutes or until top is lightly browned and filling is hot in center.

Tourtière

Makes 6 servings

There are many versions of Quebec's famous meat pie. This exceptional one is courtesy of a friend whose mother's recipe came from the late Jehane Benoit, the doyenne of French Canadian cooking. Prepare individual meat pies for easy serving, if desired.

Tip

Unbaked meat pies freeze well for up to 2 months. Let defrost in refrigerator overnight before baking.

- Preheat oven to 425°F (220°C)
- 9-inch (23 cm) pie plate, lightly greased

	Pastry for a double-crust 9-inch (23 cm) pie (see recipe, page 509)	
1 lb	lean ground pork	500 g
8 oz	lean ground veal	250 g
1	large onion, finely chopped	1
2	cloves garlic, finely chopped	2
½ tsp	dried thyme leaves	2 mL
½ tsp	dried savory leaves	2 mL
¾ tsp	salt	3 mL
¼ tsp	ground allspice	1 mL
¼ tsp	ground cloves	1 mL
¼ tsp	freshly ground black pepper	1 mL
¾ cup	beef stock or water	175 mL
⅓ cup	fine dry bread crumbs	75 mL
1	egg yolk	1

1. In a Dutch oven or large saucepan over medium-high heat, cook pork and veal, breaking up with a wooden spoon, for 5 minutes. Add onion, garlic, thyme, savory, salt, allspice, cloves and pepper; cook, stirring often, for 5 minutes.

2. Add stock; bring to a boil. Reduce heat; partially cover and simmer, stirring occasionally, for 20 minutes or until most of liquid has evaporated. Remove from heat. Stir in bread crumbs to absorb excess moisture; let cool, then refrigerate until chilled.

3. On a lightly floured surface, roll out half the pastry into a 12-inch (30 cm) round. Line prepared pie plate with pastry. Trim edges. Spoon filling into pie shell. Cover with top pastry; trim edges, crimp to seal and cut steam vents. In a small bowl, beat egg yolk with 2 tsp (10 mL) water. Brush pastry with egg wash.

4. Bake pie in preheated oven for 15 minutes; reduce heat to 375°F (190°C) and bake for 25 to 30 minutes more or until pastry is golden.

Picadillo Meat Pie

Picadillo is a ground beef
dish popular in Latin
American countries. It is
often served over rice or in
a taco. Here, meat pie takes
on a Latin flair with the
tasty filling. Serve it with
your favorite salsa.

Tips

Hate shedding tears
when chopping onions?
To minimize the weeping
problem, use a razor-sharp
knife to prevent loss of
juices and cover the cut
onions with a paper towel
as you chop them to
prevent the vapors from
rising to your eyes.

Frozen butter puff pastry
is preferred, but any brand
of frozen puff pastry in a
14- to 16-oz (400 to 450 g)
package will work well in
this recipe.

● 10-inch (25 cm) tart pan with removable bottom

1½ lbs	lean ground beef	750 g
1	large onion, finely chopped	1
2	cloves garlic, finely chopped	2
1 tsp	dried oregano leaves	5 mL
1 tsp	ground cumin	5 mL
¾ tsp	salt	3 mL
Pinch	cayenne pepper (optional)	Pinch
1 cup	tomato sauce	250 mL
½ cup	beef stock	125 mL
¼ cup	raisins	60 mL
¼ cup	green olives (about 8), pitted and finely chopped	60 mL
⅓ cup	fine dry bread crumbs	75 mL
1	package (14 to 16 oz/400 to 450 g) frozen puff pastry, thawed	1
1	egg yolk	1

1. In a Dutch oven or large saucepan, cook beef over medium-high heat, breaking up with a wooden spoon, for 7 minutes or until no longer pink.

2. Add onion, garlic, oregano, cumin, salt and cayenne, if using. Cook, stirring often, for 5 minutes or until onion is softened.

3. Add tomato sauce, stock, raisins and olives. Reduce heat, partially cover and simmer, stirring occasionally, for 15 minutes or until liquid is evaporated. Remove from heat and stir in bread crumbs. Transfer meat mixture to a bowl and let cool. Cover and refrigerate.

4. On a lightly floured surface, thinly roll out half the pastry into a 14-inch (35 cm) circle. Fit into tart pan and trim edges, leaving a ¾-inch (2 cm) overhang. Spread meat filling in pastry in an even layer. In a small bowl, combine egg yolk with 1 tsp (5 mL) water. Brush pastry edges with egg wash.

5. Roll out the remaining pastry into a 12-inch (30 cm) circle and arrange over top of pie. Pinch pastry edges to seal; trim. Brush top with egg wash; prick pastry with fork. Refrigerate for 30 minutes. (At this stage, pie can be frozen for up to 2 months; defrost overnight in fridge.)

6. Meanwhile, preheat oven to 375°F (190°C).

7. Bake pie in preheated oven for 45 to 50 minutes or until golden brown. Let cool for 10 minutes before serving.

Mama's Italian Cheeseburgers

Makes 4 burgers

If burgers are starting to become mundane, put some excitement in those patties. Instead of cheese on top of the burger, put shredded cheese right in the ground meat mixture for moist burgers with a twist. Mama would be pleased.

Tip

For an easy vegetable topping, cut bell peppers and a large red onion into rounds, brush lightly with olive oil and grill alongside burgers.

• Preheat greased barbecue grill to medium-high

1/4 cup	tomato pasta sauce	60 mL
1/4 cup	grated or minced onion	60 mL
1	clove garlic, minced	1
1/4 tsp	dried basil or oregano leaves	1 mL
1/4 tsp	salt	1 mL
1/4 tsp	freshly ground black pepper	1 mL
3/4 cup	shredded mozzarella cheese	175 mL
1/3 cup	dry seasoned bread crumbs	75 mL
1 lb	lean ground beef	500 g
4	hamburger buns, split and toasted	4

1. In a bowl, combine tomato pasta sauce, onion, garlic, basil, salt and pepper. Stir in cheese and bread crumbs; mix in beef. Shape into four 3/4-inch (2 cm) thick patties.

2. Grill, turning once, for 6 to 7 minutes on each side or until no longer pink in center. Serve in buns.

Terrific Chicken Burgers

Makes 4 burgers

Layer these patties in a toasted onion bun for an easy burger supper or accompany them with stir-fried rice and vegetables.

1	egg	1
1/2 cup	fine dry bread crumbs	125 mL
1/3 cup	finely chopped green onions	75 mL
1 tsp	ground coriander	5 mL
1 tsp	grated lemon zest	5 mL
1/2 tsp	salt	2 mL
1/4 tsp	freshly ground black pepper	1 mL
1 lb	ground chicken or turkey	500 g
1 tbsp	vegetable oil	15 mL

1. In a bowl, beat egg; stir in bread crumbs, green onions, coriander, lemon zest, salt and pepper; mix in chicken. With wet hands, shape into four 3/4-inch (2 cm) thick patties.

2. In a large nonstick skillet, heat oil over medium heat; cook patties for 5 to 6 minutes on each side or until golden brown on outside and no longer pink in center.

Middle Eastern Lamb Burgers

Makes 4 burgers

I love the combination of spices and dried fruits in Middle Eastern cooking. The Cucumber-Yogurt Sauce offers a cool counterpoint to these richly spiced burgers that can be tucked into pita bread pockets or crusty Kaiser rolls.

Tip

Instead of grilling the pitas, you can wrap them in paper towels and microwave on Medium (50%) for 1 1/2 minutes or until warm.

Variation

If ground lamb is difficult to obtain, use lean ground beef or turkey instead.

● Preheat greased barbecue grill to medium-high

Burgers

1	egg	1
1/3 cup	finely chopped green onions	75 mL
1/4 cup	raisins	60 mL
2 tbsp	fine dry bread crumbs	30 mL
1/2 tsp	ground cumin	2 mL
1/2 tsp	ground coriander	2 mL
1/2 tsp	salt	2 mL
1/2 tsp	freshly ground black pepper	2 mL
Pinch	ground cinnamon	Pinch
1 lb	lean ground lamb	500 g
4	7-inch (18 cm) pitas, halved to form pockets	4

Cucumber-Yogurt Sauce

1 cup	finely diced seedless cucumber	250 mL
1 cup	plain yogurt	250 mL
2 tbsp	chopped fresh mint, cilantro or chives	30 mL
1	small clove garlic, minced	1
	Salt	
2	tomatoes, cut into wedges	2
	Leaf lettuce	

1. *Burgers:* In a bowl, beat egg; stir in green onions, raisins, bread crumbs, cumin, coriander, salt, pepper and cinnamon; mix in ground lamb. Shape into four 3/4-inch (2 cm) thick patties.

2. Grill, turning once, for 6 to 7 minutes per side or until no longer pink in center. Wrap pitas in foil; place on grill for 10 minutes, turning once, until heated through.

3. *Cucumber-Yogurt Sauce:* Combine cucumber, yogurt, mint and garlic in a bowl; season with salt to taste.

4. Cut burgers into halves; place one half in each cut pita pocket with tomato wedges and lettuce. Top with Cucumber-Yogurt Sauce.

Salmon Burgers with Rémoulade

Dietitians recommend that we eat salmon twice a week to benefit from its heart-healthy omega-3 oils. If you're getting bored of baked salmon, try these delicious burgers, which can be made with either fresh or canned salmon.

Variation

Instead of fresh salmon, use 2 cans (each 7½ oz/ 213 g) sockeye salmon. Drain, remove skins and wrap in paper towels to absorb excess moisture. Place in a bowl and mash salmon with bones. Stir in ⅓ cup (75 mL) rémoulade, ¼ cup (60 mL) dry unseasoned bread crumbs and 1 beaten egg. Shape into four ½-inch (1 cm) thick patties and cook as directed in Steps 2 to 4.

Rémoulade is a French mayonnaise and herb sauce that is similar to tartar sauce. Serve it with grilled or baked fish and seafood.

Variation

Add 1 tbsp (15 mL) chopped capers and 1 tsp (5 mL) anchovy paste.

1 lb	skinless salmon fillet, cubed	500 g
	Rémoulade (see recipe, below), divided	
2 tbsp	dry unseasoned bread crumbs	30 mL
¼ tsp	salt	1 mL
	Freshly ground black pepper	
½ cup	panko crumbs or dry unseasoned bread crumbs	125 mL
4 tsp	vegetable oil	20 mL
4	crusty buns, split and toasted	4
8	thin slices tomato	8
	Boston or leaf lettuce	

1. In a food processor, combine salmon, ⅓ cup (75 mL) rémoulade, 2 tbsp (30 mL) bread crumbs, salt and pepper. Pulse until finely chopped. Transfer to a bowl and shape into four ½-inch (1 cm) thick patties.

2. Place panko crumbs in a shallow bowl. Lightly coat both sides of patties in crumbs.

3. In a large nonstick skillet, heat oil over medium heat. Cook burgers for 3 to 4 minutes per side or until golden and cooked through to center.

4. Spread buns with rémoulade. Place salmon burgers on buns and garnish with tomato slices and lettuce. Refrigerate any remaining rémoulade.

Rémoulade

Makes about 1 cup (250 mL)

⅔ cup	light mayonnaise	150 mL
1 tbsp	whole-seed mustard	15 mL
2	green onions, finely chopped	2
2 tbsp	finely chopped fresh parsley	30 mL
2 tbsp	finely chopped fresh dill or basil	30 mL
2 tsp	fresh lemon juice	10 mL
	Hot pepper sauce	

1. In a bowl, combine mayonnaise, mustard, green onions, parsley, dill and lemon juice. Season with hot pepper to taste. (Can be prepared up to 2 days ahead; cover and refrigerate.)

Beef Patties Parmigiana

Teaching your children how to cook? Here's a simple recipe that most kids can easily master. Serve these kid-friendly patties with pasta or tuck patties along with sauce into four split Kaiser rolls for a hearty sandwich.

Tips

Like coffee, Parmesan loses its wonderful aromatic flavor and moisture if grated ahead. Choose a wedge in a cheese shop and have it grated for you. Freeze in an airtight container. Or better still, grate the cheese as you need it.

Store Parmesan wedges wrapped in plastic wrap, then in foil, in the refrigerator; it keeps well for weeks.

- Preheat oven to 350°F (180°C)
- 8-inch (20 cm) square baking dish

1	egg	1
2 tbsp	freshly grated Parmesan cheese	30 mL
6 tbsp	fine dry bread crumbs, divided	75 mL
¼ cup	minced onion	60 mL
1 tsp	dried basil leaves	5 mL
½ tsp	salt	2 mL
	Freshly ground black pepper	
1 lb	ground beef	500 g
1 tbsp	olive oil	15 mL
1 cup	tomato pasta sauce (homemade or store-bought)	250 mL
4	slices mozzarella or provolone cheese	4

1. In a bowl, beat egg; stir in Parmesan, 2 tbsp (30 mL) of the bread crumbs, onion, basil, salt and pepper; mix in ground beef. Form into four ¾-inch (2 cm) thick patties.

2. Spread remaining bread crumbs in shallow baking dish. Dip patties in crumbs to coat on both sides. Discard any excess crumbs.

3. In a large nonstick skillet, heat oil over medium-high heat; brown patties, in batches, if necessary, about 3 minutes on each side. Arrange in baking dish.

4. Spoon tomato sauce over patties and top each with cheese slice. Bake in preheated oven for 20 minutes or until patties are no longer pink in center and sauce is bubbly and cheese is melted.

Salisbury Steak

Makes 4 servings

Here's a satisfying meatloaf-like dish with a tasty gravy that's wonderful accompanied by creamy mashed potatoes. Peel the potatoes and start them cooking on the stovetop before you begin preparing the patties so both will be ready at about the same time.

Tip

Unless you're using expensive tomato paste from a tube, you can freeze leftover tomato paste. Put tablespoons (15 mL) of leftover canned tomato paste on a waxed paper–lined plate or in ice cube trays; freeze until firm. Transfer to a small freezer bag and have handy in the freezer to add to recipes.

1	egg	1
2 tbsp	fine dry bread crumbs	30 mL
1	small onion, finely chopped	1
1 tbsp	Worcestershire sauce	15 mL
1/2 tsp	salt	2 mL
1/4 tsp	freshly ground black pepper	1 mL
1 lb	lean ground beef	500 g
2 tsp	vegetable oil	10 mL
1 1/2 cups	chopped mushrooms	375 mL
1	clove garlic, finely chopped	1
1/4 tsp	dried thyme or marjoram leaves	1 mL
1 tbsp	all-purpose flour	15 mL
1 cup	beef stock	250 mL
1 tbsp	tomato paste	15 mL

1. In a bowl, beat egg; stir in bread crumbs, half the onion, half the Worcestershire sauce, salt and pepper; mix in ground beef. Form into four ¾-inch (2 cm) thick patties.

2. In a large nonstick skillet, heat oil over medium-high heat; brown patties, about 2 minutes on each side. Transfer to a plate. Add remaining onion, mushrooms, garlic and thyme to skillet; cook, stirring, for 2 minutes or until softened.

3. Sprinkle with flour; stir in remaining Worcestershire sauce, beef stock and tomato paste. Cook, stirring, for 1 minute or until thickened. Return patties to skillet; reduce heat, cover and simmer, turning once, for 10 minutes or until patties are no longer pink in center.

Basic Meatballs

Makes 48 meatballs

Meatballs are delicious in a variety of sauces, such as Sweet-and-Sour and Spicy Black Bean (see recipes following).

Tip

For Spaghetti with Meatballs, see recipe, page 336.

- Preheat oven to 400°F (200°C)
- Rimmed baking sheets

1	egg	1
2 tbsp	water	30 mL
⅓ cup	fine dry bread crumbs	75 mL
⅓ cup	minced green onions	75 mL
1	clove garlic, finely chopped	1
¾ tsp	salt	3 mL
½ tsp	freshly ground black pepper	2 mL
1½ lbs	lean ground beef, chicken or turkey	750 g

1. In a large bowl, beat egg with water; stir in bread crumbs, green onions, garlic, salt and pepper. Mix in beef.

2. Form by tablespoonfuls (15 mL) into balls; arrange on baking sheets. Bake for 15 minutes or until browned and no longer pink inside. Drain on paper towels.

Sweet-and-Sour Meatballs

Makes 6 servings

Take advantage of supermarket specials for lean ground beef and cook batches of meatballs ahead. Freeze them for this quick dish.

1	can (14 oz/398 mL) pineapple chunks	1
¼ cup	packed brown sugar	60 mL
¼ cup	rice vinegar	60 mL
¼ cup	soy sauce	60 mL
4 tsp	cornstarch	20 mL
48	Basic Meatballs (see recipe, above)	48

1. Drain pineapple chucks and reserve. Measure pineapple juice; add enough water to make 1 cup (250 mL).

2. In a large saucepan, combine pineapple juice, brown sugar, vinegar, soy sauce and cornstarch. Place over medium heat, stirring, until sauce comes to a boil and thickens.

3. Stir in meatballs and pineapple chunks; cook for 3 to 5 minutes or until piping hot.

Meatballs in Spicy Black Bean Sauce

It takes only a few minutes to assemble the spicy-sweet sauce for these winning meatballs.

Tip

To freeze meatballs: Place meatballs in a single layer on a baking sheet until frozen, then transfer to a covered container or freezer bag. To quickly reheat, place the frozen meatballs in a casserole dish, cover and microwave on Medium (50%) until defrosted.

½ cup	orange juice	125 mL
½ cup	water	125 mL
¼ cup	packed brown sugar	60 mL
¼ cup	rice vinegar	60 mL
2 tbsp	black bean sauce	30 mL
2 tbsp	soy sauce	30 mL
1 tbsp	cornstarch	15 mL
2 tsp	minced gingerroot	10 mL
½ tsp	Asian chili sauce or hot pepper sauce	2 mL
48	Basic Meatballs (see recipe, page 315)	48
2 tbsp	chopped green onion tops	30 mL

1. In a large saucepan, combine orange juice, water, brown sugar, rice vinegar, black bean sauce, soy sauce, cornstarch, ginger and chili sauce. Cook over medium heat, stirring, for 3 minutes or until sauce boils and thickens.

2. Add meatballs and stir to coat; cook for 2 minutes or until hot. Transfer to serving bowl; sprinkle with green onion tops.

Amazing Chili

Every cook has a special version of chili. Here's mine — it's meaty and nicely spiced, with just the right amount of beans. Not everyone agrees that beans belong in a chili — witness the Texas version dubbed "bowl of red" — but I love the way the beans absorb the spices and rich tomato flavor.

Tip

The flavor of the chili hinges on the quality of chili powder used. Most powders are a blend of dried ground mild chiles, as well as cumin, oregano, garlic and salt. Read the list of ingredients to be sure you're not buying one with starch and sugar fillers. Chili powder should not be confused with powdered or ground chiles of the cayenne pepper variety.

1½ lbs	lean ground beef	750 g
2	onions, chopped	2
3	cloves garlic, finely chopped	3
2	stalks celery, chopped	2
1	large green bell pepper, chopped	1
2 tbsp	chili powder	30 mL
1½ tsp	dried oregano leaves	7 mL
1½ tsp	ground cumin	7 mL
¾ tsp	salt	3 mL
½ tsp	hot pepper flakes, or to taste	2 mL
1	can (28 oz/796 mL) tomatoes, including juice, chopped	1
1 cup	beef stock	250 mL
1	can (19 oz/540 mL) pinto or red kidney beans, drained and rinsed	1
¼ cup	chopped fresh parsley or cilantro	60 mL

1. In a Dutch oven or large saucepan, cook beef over medium-high heat, breaking up with a wooden spoon, for about 7 minutes or until no longer pink. Drain off any fat.

2. Reduce heat to medium. Add onions, garlic, celery, green pepper, chili powder, oregano, cumin, salt and hot pepper flakes; cook, stirring often, for 5 minutes or until vegetables are softened.

3. Stir in tomatoes with juice and stock. Bring to a boil; reduce heat, cover and simmer, stirring occasionally, for 1 hour.

4. Add beans and parsley; cover and simmer for 10 minutes more.

Red Hot Beanless Chili

This beanless chili has a hot kick to it, so reduce the amount of pepper flakes if you prefer it on the tamer side. Ladle into bowls and have ready shredded Cheddar cheese, sliced green onions, sour cream and chopped cilantro so everyone can choose their fixings. Terrific served with Cheddar drop biscuits.

Variation

If you wish to add beans, omit cornmeal; add 2 cans (each 19 oz/540 mL) red kidney beans, drained and rinsed, to chili instead.

3 lbs	lean ground beef	1.5 kg
2 tbsp	olive oil	30 mL
2	large onions, chopped	2
6	cloves garlic, finely chopped	6
5 to 6	jalapeño peppers, seeded and minced	5 to 6
3 tbsp	chili powder	45 mL
1 tbsp	dried oregano leaves	15 mL
1 tbsp	ground cumin	15 mL
2	bay leaves	2
1 tsp	salt	5 mL
2 tsp	hot pepper flakes, or to taste	10 mL
1	can (28 oz/596 mL) tomatoes, including juice, chopped	1
1	can (10 oz/284 mL) beef broth (undiluted)	1
1	can (5½ oz/156 mL) tomato paste	1
3	red or green bell peppers, diced	3
¼ cup	cornmeal	60 mL

1. In a large Dutch oven or stockpot, cook beef over medium-high heat in two batches, breaking up with a wooden spoon, for about 7 minutes or until no longer pink. Drain off any fat. Transfer to a bowl.

2. Reduce heat to medium; add oil to pan. Cook onions, garlic, jalapeño peppers, chili powder, oregano, cumin, bay leaves, salt and hot pepper flakes, stirring, for 5 minutes or until softened.

3. Return meat to pan; add tomatoes with juice, 2 cups (500 mL) water, broth and tomato paste. Bring to a boil; simmer, covered, for 30 minutes, stirring occasionally. Add peppers; cook for 30 minutes more.

4. In a bowl, stir together ¼ cup (60 mL) water with cornmeal; stir into meat mixture. Cook for 10 minutes or until sauce is thickened. Remove bay leaves before serving. Season with salt, if needed.

20-Minute Chili

**Makes 4 to
6 servings**

Here's a streamlined
version of chili that's
a snap. Make a double
batch and have containers
stashed away in the freezer
for quick microwave
meals. Just ladle into
bowls and, if desired, top
with shredded Monterey
Jack cheese. Set out a
basket of crusty bread —
supper is that easy.

Tip

Add just a pinch of hot
pepper flakes for a mild
chili; but if you want to turn
up the heat, use amount
specified in the recipe.

1 lb	lean ground beef, chicken or turkey	500 g
1	large onion, chopped	1
2	large cloves garlic, finely chopped	2
1	large green bell pepper, chopped	1
4 tsp	chili powder	20 mL
1 tbsp	all-purpose flour	15 mL
1 tsp	dried basil leaves	5 mL
1 tsp	dried oregano leaves	5 mL
½ tsp	hot pepper flakes, or to taste	2 mL
2 cups	tomato pasta sauce	500 mL
1⅓ cups	beef stock	325 mL
1	can (19 oz/540 mL) red kidney or pinto beans, drained and rinsed	1
	Salt and freshly ground black pepper	

1. In a Dutch oven or large saucepan over medium-high heat, cook beef, breaking up with a wooden spoon, for 5 minutes or until no longer pink. Drain off any fat.

2. Reduce heat to medium. Add onion, garlic, green pepper, chili powder, flour, basil, oregano and hot pepper flakes; cook, stirring, for 4 minutes or until vegetables are softened.

3. Stir in tomato sauce and stock. Bring to a boil; cook, stirring, until thickened. Add beans; season with salt and pepper to taste. Reduce heat and simmer, covered, for 10 minutes.

Turkey Chili with Macaroni and Vegetables

Kids love this dish and so do grownups. The spicy Mexican influence provides a nice change from the traditional Italian pasta fare.

Variations

Doctor this yummy chili according to your family's tastes by substituting their favorite vegetables, such as corn and green bell peppers, for the zucchini. Omit hot pepper flakes if you prefer a milder-tasting dish.

For an Italian version, substitute 1½ tsp (7 mL) dried basil leaves for the chili powder and cumin.

Vegetarian Variation
Chickpea Chili with Pasta and Vegetables

Omit ground turkey. Cook vegetables and seasonings in 1 tbsp (15 mL) vegetable oil. Add 1 can (19 oz/540 mL) chickpeas, drained and rinsed, along with canned tomatoes.

1 lb	lean ground turkey or chicken	500 g
1	onion, chopped	1
2	cloves garlic, finely chopped	2
2	carrots, peeled and diced	2
2	stalks celery, chopped	2
4 tsp	chili powder	20 mL
1 tsp	dried oregano leaves	5 mL
1 tsp	ground cumin	5 mL
½ tsp	salt	2 mL
¼ tsp	hot pepper flakes, or to taste	1 mL
1	can (28 oz/796 mL) plum tomatoes, including juice, chopped	1
2	small zucchini, halved lengthwise and sliced	2
2 cups	elbow macaroni or other small-shaped pasta, such as shells	500 mL
	Salt and freshly ground black pepper	

1. In a large Dutch oven or large saucepan, cook turkey over medium-high heat, breaking up with a wooden spoon, for 5 minutes or until no longer pink.

2. Reduce heat to medium. Add onion, garlic, carrots, celery, chili powder, oregano, cumin, salt and hot pepper flakes; cook, stirring often, for 5 minutes or until vegetables are softened.

3. Stir in tomatoes with juice. Bring to a boil; reduce heat, cover and simmer, stirring occasionally, for 15 minutes. Add zucchini; cover and simmer for 3 to 5 minutes or until just tender.

4. Meanwhile, in a large pot of boiling salted water, cook pasta until tender but still firm. Drain well. Stir into tomato mixture and heat through. Season with salt and pepper to taste.

Mama's Italian Cheeseburgers (page 310)

Amazing Chili (page 317)

Spaghetti
with Meatballs
(page 336)

Spanish Vegetable Paella (page 378)

Best-Ever Macaroni and Cheese (page 355)

Broccoli and Cheese–Stuffed Potatoes (page 407)

Asparagus with Parmesan and Toasted Almonds (page 414)

Chicken Paprika with Noodles

Makes 4 servings

Economical ground meats provide versatile options for the harried cook. Serve this tasty ground chicken dish with a salad or green vegetable such as broccoli. Dinner is ready in about 30 minutes.

Tip

When ground chicken or turkey is browned in a skillet, it doesn't turn into a fine crumble like other ground meats. I overcome the problem by placing the cooked chicken in a food processor and chopping it using on-off turns to break up meat lumps.

1 lb	lean ground chicken or turkey	500 g
1 tbsp	butter	15 mL
1	onion, chopped	1
8 oz	mushrooms, sliced	250 g
1 tbsp	paprika	15 mL
2 tbsp	all-purpose flour	30 mL
1⅓ cups	chicken stock	325 mL
½ cup	sour cream	125 mL
2 tbsp	chopped fresh dill or parsley	30 mL
	Salt and freshly ground black pepper	
8 oz	fettuccine or broad egg noodles	250 g

1. In a large nonstick skillet over medium-high heat, cook chicken, breaking up with a wooden spoon, for 5 minutes or until no longer pink. Transfer to a bowl.

2. Melt butter in skillet. Add onion, mushrooms and paprika; cook, stirring often, for 3 minutes or until vegetables are softened.

3. Sprinkle with flour; stir in stock and return chicken to skillet. Bring to a boil; cook, stirring, until thickened. Reduce heat, cover and simmer for 5 minutes. Remove from heat and stir in sour cream (it may curdle if added over the heat) and dill; season with salt and pepper to taste.

4. Meanwhile, cook pasta in a large pot of boiling salted water until tender but firm. Drain well. Return to pot and toss with chicken mixture. Serve immediately.

Beefy Macaroni

No need to buy pricey packaged dinner mixes when it's easy to create your own. It's just a matter of using pantry staples already in your cupboard. In about the time it takes to fix an accompanying salad, this dish is ready to set on the table.

Tip

Use your own homemade tomato sauce (see Big-Batch Tomato Sauce, page 333) or rely on one of the many pasta sauces available in supermarkets to cut down on preparation time.

1 lb	lean ground beef, chicken or turkey	500 g
1	small onion, chopped	1
2	cloves garlic, finely chopped	2
1 tsp	dried basil or oregano leaves	5 mL
1½ cups	tomato pasta sauce (see Tip, left)	375 mL
1½ cups	chicken or beef stock (approx.)	375 mL
1 cup	elbow macaroni	250 mL
2	medium zucchini, cut into ½-inch (1 cm) cubes	2

1. In a large nonstick skillet over medium-high heat, cook beef, breaking up with a wooden spoon, for 5 minutes or until no longer pink. Add onion, garlic and basil; cook, stirring, for 2 minutes.

2. Add tomato pasta sauce and stock; bring to a boil. Stir in pasta; reduce heat, cover and cook for 2 minutes.

3. Stir in zucchini; cook, covered, stirring occasionally, adding more stock if needed, for 5 to 7 minutes or until pasta and zucchini are tender.

Spanish Chicken and Rice

Makes 4 servings

Your whole family will love this easy supper dish with Southwest appeal. Serve with corn on the cob or a tossed salad.

Tip

To microwave rice: In an 8-cup (2 L) casserole dish, combine 2 cups (500 mL) stock and 1 cup (250 mL) long-grain white rice. Microwave, covered, on High for 4 to 6 minutes or until boiling. Microwave on Medium (50%) for 10 to 14 minutes or until most of the liquid is absorbed. Let stand for 10 minutes. Makes 3 cups (750 mL) rice.

2 cups	chicken stock	500 mL
1 cup	long-grain white rice	250 mL
1 lb	lean ground chicken, turkey or beef	500 g
1 tbsp	vegetable oil	15 mL
2	cloves garlic, finely chopped	2
1	small onion, finely chopped	1
1	green bell pepper, diced	1
1	large stalk celery, finely chopped	1
1-1/2 tsp	chili powder	7 mL
1 tsp	dried oregano leaves	5 mL
1 tsp	paprika	5 mL
1/2 tsp	salt	2 mL
1/4 tsp	freshly ground black pepper	1 mL
1	can (14 oz/398 mL) diced tomatoes, including juice	1

1. In a medium saucepan, bring stock to a boil. Add rice, reduce heat, cover and simmer for 20 minutes or until liquid is absorbed and rice is tender.

2. In a large saucepan over medium-high heat, cook chicken, breaking up with a wooden spoon, for 5 minutes or until no longer pink. Transfer to a bowl.

3. Add oil to pan. Cook garlic, onion, green pepper, celery, chili powder, oregano, paprika, salt and pepper, stirring often, for 4 minutes or until vegetables are softened.

4. Return chicken to pan, along with tomatoes and their juice; bring to a boil. Reduce heat to medium-low, cover and simmer for 10 minutes or until vegetables are tender.

5. Stir in cooked rice. Cover and let stand for 5 minutes to blend the flavors.

Spicy Asian Pork with Mushrooms and Rice Noodles

When you're tempted to order takeout to satisfy a craving for a spicy Asian meal, cook up this economical and easy dish of noodles with ground pork and mushrooms instead. Serve it with steamed vegetables, such as broccoli or bok choy.

Variation

Instead of noodles, add 6 cups (1.5 L) shredded Napa cabbage and cook for 1 to 2 minutes or just until wilted.

8 oz	wide rice noodles	250 g
1/4 cup	hoisin sauce	60 mL
1/4 cup	oyster sauce	60 mL
1/4 cup	water	60 mL
2 tbsp	fresh lime juice or rice vinegar	30 mL
1 to 2 tsp	Asian chili sauce, or to taste	5 to 10 mL
1 lb	lean ground pork	500 g
1 tbsp	vegetable oil	15 mL
2 tbsp	minced gingerroot	30 mL
3	cloves garlic, finely chopped	3
8 oz	white or cremini mushrooms, coarsely chopped	250 g
5	green onions, sliced	5
1	can (8 oz/ 227 mL) water chestnuts, drained, rinsed and coarsely chopped	1
1/2 cup	coarsely chopped fresh cilantro	125 mL

1. Place noodles in a large bowl and cover with boiling water. Let stand for 15 minutes or until softened; drain and reserve.

2. In a small bowl, stir together hoisin sauce, oyster sauce, water, lime juice and chili sauce; reserve.

3. In a large nonstick skillet or wok, cook pork over medium-high heat, breaking up with a wooden spoon, for 5 minutes or until no longer pink. Transfer to a bowl. Drain off any fat.

4. Add oil to skillet; cook ginger and garlic, stirring, for 30 seconds or until fragrant. Add mushrooms, green onions and water chestnuts. Cook, stirring, for 3 minutes or until mushrooms are softened. Return pork to skillet and cook, stirring, for 2 minutes.

5. Stir in hoisin mixture. Add rice noodles. Stir until combined and rice noodles are coated in the sauce and heated through. Toss with cilantro. Serve immediately.

Tex-Mex Cobbler

Makes 4 to 6 servings

Looking for an inviting dinner-in-a-dish everyone in the family will enjoy? This hearty chili-flavored beef casserole topped with a tasty cornbread crust fills the bill. I've kept the seasonings tame so it appeals to the sensitive taste buds of young diners, but boost the seasonings if desired.

Tip

Add 1 tsp (5 mL) additional chili powder along with ¼ tsp (1 mL) hot pepper flakes, or to taste, to the ground beef mixture for a more assertive chili flavor.

- Preheat oven to 400°F (200°C)
- 10-cup (2.5 L) casserole dish

1 lb	lean ground beef	500 g
1	onion, chopped	1
2	cloves garlic, finely chopped	2
1	large green bell pepper, chopped	1
2 tsp	chili powder	10 mL
1 tsp	dried oregano leaves	5 mL
½ tsp	ground cumin	2 mL
2 tbsp	all-purpose flour	30 mL
1½ cups	beef stock	375 mL
1	can (7½ oz/213 mL) tomato sauce	1
1	can (12 oz/341 mL) corn kernels, drained	1

Cheddar Cornbread Crust

⅔ cup	all-purpose flour	150 mL
½ cup	cornmeal	125 mL
1½ tsp	granulated sugar	7 mL
1½ tsp	baking powder	7 mL
¼ tsp	salt	1 mL
½ cup	shredded Cheddar cheese	125 mL
1	egg	1
⅔ cup	milk	150 mL

1. In a large nonstick skillet over medium-high heat, cook beef, breaking up with a wooden spoon, for 5 minutes or until no longer pink. Drain off any fat. Stir in onion, garlic, green pepper, chili powder, oregano and cumin; cook, stirring, for 4 minutes or until softened.

2. Blend in flour; stir in stock and tomato sauce. Bring to a boil, stirring, until thickened. Reduce heat, cover and simmer for 5 minutes. Stir in corn; cook for 2 minutes or until piping hot. Spoon into casserole dish.

3. *Cheddar Cornmeal Crust:* In a bowl, combine flour, cornmeal, sugar, baking powder and salt; mix in cheese. In another bowl, beat together egg and milk. Stir into dry ingredients to make a smooth batter.

4. Spoon crust over beef mixture in an even layer. Bake in preheated oven for 20 to 25 minutes or until top is light golden and filling is bubbly.

Beef and Potato Hash

Makes 4 servings

Looking for a fast-track dinner? Convenient frozen hash browns come to the rescue along with quick-cooking ground beef for a family-pleasing meal.

Tip

To defrost hash browns: Place hash browns on a plate lined with paper towels; microwave on High for 3 to 4 minutes, stirring once.

1 lb	lean ground beef	500 g
2 tsp	Worcestershire sauce	10 mL
1 tbsp	vegetable oil	15 mL
1	onion, chopped	1
1	green bell pepper, chopped	1
4 cups	frozen hash brown potatoes, defrosted (see Tip, left)	1 L
	Salt and freshly ground black pepper	

1. In a large nonstick skillet over medium-high heat, cook beef, breaking up with a wooden spoon, for 5 minutes or until no longer pink. Drain off any fat. Transfer to a bowl. Stir in Worcestershire sauce.

2. Add oil to skillet; cook onion, green pepper and potatoes, stirring often, for 8 to 10 minutes or until potatoes are golden. Add ground beef; season with salt and pepper to taste. Cook for 2 minutes or until heated through.

Beef and Vegetable Fried Rice

Makes 4 servings

Some days you just don't have time to think about what's for supper. Rather than getting takeout, here's an easy dish that counts on convenient frozen vegetables to get dinner on the table in 20 minutes.

Tip

Cook extra rice ahead and keep it handy in the fridge. Or use instant rice prepared according to package directions.

1 lb	lean ground beef	500 g
3	green onions, sliced	3
1	large clove garlic, finely chopped	1
2 tsp	minced gingerroot	10 mL
2 cups	cooked rice (see Tip, page 327), preferably basmati	500 mL
4 cups	frozen mixed Asian vegetables	1 L
3 tbsp	soy sauce	45 mL

1. In a large nonstick skillet over medium-high heat, cook beef, breaking up with a wooden spoon, for 5 minutes or until no longer pink. Drain off any fat.

2. Add green onions, garlic and ginger; cook, stirring, for 1 minute. Stir in rice; cook, stirring, for 2 minutes.

3. Add vegetables and soy sauce. Reduce heat to medium, cover and cook, stirring occasionally, (adding 2 tbsp/30 mL water if necessary to prevent from sticking), for 5 minutes or until vegetables are tender.

Salsa Beef and Rice Casserole

Here's a terrific make-ahead casserole dish with lots of family appeal. Either bake the dish in your oven or take a shortcut and use your microwave.

Tip

To cook rice: Bring 2 cups (500 mL) water to a boil in a medium saucepan; add 1 cup (250 mL) white long-grain rice and ½ tsp (2 mL) salt. Return to a boil; reduce heat to low, cover and simmer for 20 minutes. If using brown rice, increase water to 2½ cups (625 mL) and increase cooking time to 40 to 45 minutes. Makes 3 cups (750 mL) rice.

Variation

Replace half or all the beef with Italian sausages. Remove casings and brown sausage meat; drain well.

- Preheat oven to 375°F (190°C)
- 10-cup (2.5 L) casserole dish, greased

2 tsp	vegetable oil	10 mL
2	zucchini, halved lengthwise, then thinly sliced crosswise	2
1½ cups	fresh, frozen or canned corn kernels	375 mL
1½ cups	medium salsa	375 mL
1 lb	lean ground beef	500 g
1	onion, finely chopped	1
2	large cloves garlic, finely chopped	2
4 tsp	chili powder	20 mL
1 tsp	dried oregano leaves	5 mL
½ tsp	salt	2 mL
½ tsp	freshly ground black pepper	2 mL
3 cups	cooked white or brown rice (see Tip, left)	750 mL
1 cup	shredded Cheddar cheese	250 mL

1. In a large nonstick skillet, heat oil over medium-high heat. Add zucchini and cook, stirring, for 3 minutes or until softened. Transfer to a bowl; stir in corn and salsa.

2. Add beef to skillet; cook, breaking up with a wooden spoon, for 5 minutes or until no longer pink. Drain off any fat.

3. Add onion, garlic, chili powder, oregano, salt and pepper; cook, stirring, for 3 minutes. Stir in rice.

4. In casserole dish, layer half the beef mixture, then half the vegetable mixture. Repeat layers. Sprinkle with cheese.

5. Cover and bake in preheated oven for 40 minutes; remove cover and bake another 15 to 20 minutes or until center is piping hot and cheese is golden. Or microwave, covered, on High for 12 to 16 minutes (5 to 7 minutes longer if refrigerated) or until piping hot in center.

Rice-Stuffed Peppers

This homey dish is a great way to take advantage of the economical vegetables on display at country farm markets in the fall.

Tips

If tomatoes aren't fully ripened when you buy them, place in a paper bag on your counter for a day a two. The ethylene gas given off by the tomatoes speeds up the ripening process. Never store tomatoes in the fridge — the cold temperature numbs their sweet flavor. A sunny windowsill may seem like a good place to ripen tomatoes, but a hot sun often bakes rather than ripens them.

To seed tomatoes, cut in half crosswise and gently squeeze out seeds.

- Preheat oven to 350°F (180°C)
- 13- by 9-inch (33 by 23 cm) baking dish

4	large green or red bell peppers	4
8 oz	lean ground beef	250 g
8 oz	hot or mild Italian sausages, casings removed	250 g
2 tsp	olive oil	10 mL
4	green onions, sliced	4
2	cloves garlic, finely chopped	2
1 tsp	dried basil leaves	5 mL
2	large tomatoes, peeled, seeded and diced	2
1 cup	fresh or frozen corn kernels	250 mL
¾ tsp	salt	3 mL
½ tsp	freshly ground black pepper	2 mL
1½ cups	cooked rice	375 mL
1 cup	shredded mozzarella cheese	250 mL
⅓ cup	freshly grated Parmesan cheese	75 mL
½ cup	chicken stock	125 mL

1. Cut peppers in half lengthwise. Remove seeds and membranes. In a large pot of boiling salted water, blanch peppers for 5 minutes; drain and place cut side down on rack to cool.

2. In a large nonstick skillet, cook beef and sausage over medium-high heat, breaking up with a wooden spoon, for 5 minutes or until no longer pink. Drain in sieve to remove fat; set aside.

3. Add oil to skillet; cook green onion, garlic and basil, stirring, for 2 minutes or until softened. Stir in tomatoes, corn, salt and pepper; cook, stirring, for 3 to 5 minutes or until corn is tender. Stir in rice and ground beef; cook, stirring, for 3 minutes or until heated through.

4. In a bowl, combine mozzarella and Parmesan cheeses. Stir half of the cheese into rice mixture. Arrange peppers, cut side up, in casserole dish. Fill with rice mixture; top with remaining cheese. Pour stock into casserole dish; bake peppers for 30 to 35 minutes or until top is golden and filling is piping hot.

Beef and Potato Curry

Serve this one-pot family favorite with warm pita bread along with a cucumber and tomato salad.

Tips

Unless you're using expensive tomato paste from a tube, you can freeze leftover tomato paste. Put tablespoons (15 mL) of leftover canned tomato paste on a waxed paper–lined plate or in ice cube trays; freeze until firm. Transfer to a small freezer bag and have handy in the freezer to add to recipes.

Store-bought curry pastes vary in flavor and strength depending on the brand. Some pastes are labeled as mild but have more heat than expected. Add a smaller amount of curry paste to the recipe to test the strength and add more to get the depth of curry flavor you prefer.

1 lb	lean ground beef	500 g
1	onion, chopped	1
2	large cloves garlic, finely chopped	2
2 tbsp	tomato paste	30 mL
1 tbsp	mild curry paste, or to taste	15 mL
1 tbsp	minced gingerroot	15 mL
¼ tsp	salt	1 mL
4	potatoes, peeled and diced (about 1½ lbs/750 g)	4
2 cups	beef stock	500 mL
1½ cups	frozen peas	375 mL
¼ cup	chopped fresh cilantro or parsley (optional)	60 mL

1. In a Dutch oven or large saucepan over medium-high heat, cook beef, breaking up with a wooden spoon, for 5 minutes or until no longer pink. Drain off any fat.

2. Add onion, garlic, tomato paste, curry paste, ginger and salt; cook, stirring, for 5 minutes or until onion is softened.

3. Add potatoes and stock; bring to boil. Reduce heat, cover and simmer for 15 minutes. Stir in peas; cook, covered, for 5 minutes or until potatoes and peas are tender. Stir in cilantro, if using.

Stuffed Cabbage Rolls

Satisfying casseroles like this one are always a welcome choice when planning make-ahead meals for the freezer.

Tips

Cooked cabbage rolls can be frozen for up to 2 months.

To easily chop canned tomatoes, run a knife through the tomatoes right in the can.

If inner cabbage leaves are not softened, blanch cabbage again in boiling water to soften leaves.

- Preheat oven to 350°F (180°C)
- 12-cup (3 L) casserole dish

1	head green cabbage, cored (about 3 lbs/1.5 kg)	1
1 tbsp	vegetable oil	15 mL
1	large onion, finely chopped	1
2	large cloves garlic, finely chopped	2
1 tsp	paprika	5 mL
1½ cups	cooked rice	375 mL
1 lb	lean ground beef	500 g
	Salt and freshly ground black pepper	
1	can (28 oz/796 mL) plum tomatoes, including juice	1
2 tsp	packed brown sugar	10 mL

1. In a large pot of boiling salted water, cook cabbage for 5 to 6 minutes or until leaves are softened. Drain, rinse under cold water, carefully separating 12 leaves. Using a knife, trim coarse veins from cabbage leaves.

2. In a large saucepan, heat oil over medium heat; cook onion, garlic and paprika, stirring, for 5 minutes or until softened. In a bowl, combine half the onion mixture, rice, beef, ½ tsp (2 mL) salt and ½ tsp (2 mL) pepper; mix well.

3. In a food processor, purée tomatoes including juice. Add with brown sugar to remaining onion mixture in saucepan; bring to a boil. Cover and reduce heat; simmer for 15 minutes, stirring occasionally. Season with salt and pepper to taste.

4. Spoon ¼ cup (60 mL) rice mixture onto each cabbage leaf just above stem. Fold ends and sides over filling; roll up. Spoon 1 cup (250 mL) tomato sauce in bottom of casserole dish. Layer with half the cabbage rolls; pour 1 cup (250 mL) tomato sauce over. Top with remaining cabbage rolls and pour remaining sauce over. Cover and bake in preheated oven for 1 to 1¼ hours or until rolls are tender.

Pasta

continued...

Baked Pastas (continued)

Big-Batch Tomato Sauce

Here's an indispensable
sauce I always have handy
in the freezer to use as
a base for my family's
favorite pasta dishes. It's
a versatile sauce, and I've
included several ways
to serve it.

Tips

In summer, instead of
canned tomatoes, I make
this sauce with 5 lbs
(2.5 kg) of fresh ripe
tomatoes, preferably the
plum variety. To prepare,
remove tomato cores; cut
an X in the bottom of each
tomato. Plunge in boiling
water for 30 seconds
to loosen skins. Chill in
cold water; drain. Slip off
skins; cut tomatoes in half
crosswise and squeeze out
seeds. Chop finely.

Instead of dried basil and
oregano, replace dried
herbs with 1/3 cup (75 mL)
chopped fresh basil; add
toward end of cooking.

To save time, chop
vegetables in the food
processor.

2 tbsp	olive oil	30 mL
1	onion, finely chopped	1
2	carrots, peeled and finely chopped	2
1	stalk celery including leaves, finely chopped	1
4	cloves garlic, finely chopped	4
1 tbsp	dried basil leaves	15 mL
1½ tsp	dried oregano leaves	7 mL
1 tsp	salt	5 mL
1 tsp	granulated sugar	5 mL
½ tsp	freshly ground black pepper	2 mL
1	bay leaf	1
2	cans (28 oz/796 mL) plum tomatoes, including juice, chopped	2
1	can (5½ oz/156 mL) tomato paste	1
¼ cup	finely chopped fresh parsley	60 mL

1. In a Dutch oven or large saucepan, heat oil over
   medium-high heat. Add onion, carrots, celery, garlic,
   basil, oregano, salt, sugar, pepper and bay leaf; cook,
   stirring often, for 5 minutes or until vegetables
   are softened.

2. Stir in tomatoes with juice, tomato paste and 1 tomato-
   paste can of water. Bring to a boil; reduce heat and
   simmer, partially covered, for 35 to 40 minutes, stirring
   occasionally, until slightly thickened. Remove bay
   leaf; stir in parsley. Let cool; pack into containers and
   refrigerate or freeze.

Basil Pesto

Pesto keeps well for up to a week in the refrigerator, or pack into a small airtight container and freeze for up to 1 month.

Tip

Whenever you use a spoonful of the pesto, cover the surface of the pesto with a bit more oil to seal in flavors.

1 1/2 cups	lightly packed fresh basil leaves	375 mL
2	cloves garlic, coarsely chopped	2
3 tbsp	pine nuts or lightly toasted walnuts	45 mL
1/4 cup	olive oil (approx.)	60 mL
1/4 cup	freshly grated Parmesan cheese	60 mL
	Salt and freshly ground black pepper	

1. In a food processor, combine basil, garlic and pine nuts. While machine is running, add oil in a stream and process until smooth. Add a bit more oil if pesto appears dry.

2. Stir in Parmesan cheese; season with salt and pepper to taste. Place in a small container; cover with a thin layer of oil and refrigerate.

Sun-Dried Tomato Pesto

For a fast dinner suggestion, toss this pesto with 8 oz (250 g) pasta, cooked according to package directions, or swirl it into soup for a wonderful burst of flavor.

Tip

If fresh basil is unavailable, increase parsley to 1 cup (250 mL) and add 1 tbsp (15 mL) dried basil.

1/2 cup	sun-dried tomatoes	125 mL
1/2 cup	lightly packed fresh basil (see Tip, left)	125 mL
1/2 cup	lightly packed fresh parsley	125 mL
1	large clove garlic, quartered	1
1/3 cup	vegetable stock	75 mL
2 tbsp	olive oil	30 mL
1/3 cup	freshly grated Parmesan cheese	75 mL
1/2 tsp	freshly ground black pepper	2 mL

1. In a bowl, cover sun-dried tomatoes with boiling water; let stand for 10 minutes or until softened. Drain and pat dry; chop coarsely.

2. In a food processor, combine rehydrated tomatoes, basil, parsley and garlic. With motor running, add stock and oil in a stream. Stir in Parmesan cheese and pepper.

Pasta Tips

How to Cook Pasta

You can ruin a good pasta dish if you don't cook the pasta properly. The most common error is not using enough water to boil the pasta — with the result that it cooks unevenly and sticks together.

- *To cook 1 lb (500 g) of pasta:* Using a large pot, bring 16 cups (4 L) of water to a full rolling boil. Add 1 tbsp (15 mL) salt (this is important for flavor) and all the pasta at once. (Do not add oil.) Stir immediately to prevent pasta from sticking. Cover with a lid to return water quickly to full boil. Then uncover and stir occasionally. Taste to see if pasta is al dente, or firm to the bite. Drain immediately. Unless directed otherwise, never rinse pasta — this chills it and removes the coating of starch that helps sauce cling to pasta. Return to pot or place in large warmed serving bowl; add the sauce and toss until well coated. (Never place pasta on serving plates and ladle sauce on top.) Serve immediately.

Freezing and Refrigerating Pasta

Here are some general guidelines for making pasta dishes ahead and refrigerating or freezing:

- Make pasta sauces up to 2 days ahead and refrigerate or freeze for up to 2 months. If assembling pasta dish ahead: Cook pasta and chill under cold water; drain. Toss cold pasta with cold sauce and spoon into casserole dish. It's best to assemble casserole no more than a few hours ahead to prevent pasta from absorbing too much of the sauce.

- *To freeze:* Do not add the cheese topping (it goes rubbery when frozen). Cover with plastic wrap, then with foil. Freeze for up to 2 months. Let defrost in refrigerator overnight. Increase baking time by about 10 minutes.

Spaghetti with Meatballs

Makes 4 servings

This dish is the essence of Italian cooking — comforting, hearty and sure to please.

3 cups	Big-Batch Tomato Sauce (see recipe, page 333)	750 mL
24	Basic Meatballs (see recipe, page 315)	24
½ cup	beef stock	125 mL
12 oz	spaghetti or other string pasta	375 g
½ cup	freshly grated Parmesan cheese	125 mL

1. In a large saucepan, combine tomato sauce, meatballs and stock; bring to a boil. Reduce heat, cover and simmer for 15 minutes.

2. Cook pasta in a large pot of boiling salted water until tender but firm; drain well and toss with sauce. Place in serving bowls and sprinkle with Parmesan cheese.

Spaghetti with Meat Sauce

Makes 4 servings

Intensely flavored thanks to the addition of red wine — this easy pasta dish suits those nights when you crave something simple but satisfying.

Variation
Instead of ground beef, use half veal and half pork or a combination of all three.

12 oz	lean ground beef	375 g
½ cup	red wine or beef stock	125 mL
3 cups	Big-Batch Tomato Sauce (see recipe, page 333)	750 mL
	Salt, freshly ground pepper and hot pepper flakes	
12 oz	spaghetti	375 g
½ cup	freshly ground Parmesan cheese	125 mL

1. In a large nonstick skillet over medium-high heat, cook beef, breaking up with a wooden spoon, for 5 minutes or until no longer pink. Add wine; cook until partly reduced.

2. Stir in tomato sauce; season with salt, pepper and hot pepper flakes to taste. Reduce heat, cover and simmer for 15 minutes.

3. Cook pasta in a large pot of boiling salted water until tender but firm; drain well and toss with sauce. Place in serving bowls and sprinkle with Parmesan cheese.

Spaghetti Carbonara

Makes 4 servings

In no time at all and with a few basic ingredients on hand, you can whip up this great-tasting dish in about the same time it takes to cook the pasta.

Tips

Like coffee, Parmesan loses its wonderful aromatic flavor and moisture if grated ahead. Choose a wedge in a cheese shop and have it grated for you. Freeze in an airtight container. Or better still, grate the cheese as you need it.

Store Parmesan wedges wrapped in plastic wrap, then in foil, in the refrigerator; it keeps well for weeks.

6	slices bacon, chopped	6
2	cloves garlic, finely chopped	2
2 tbsp	chopped fresh parsley	30 mL
4	eggs	4
½ cup	freshly grated Parmesan cheese	125 mL
½ tsp	salt	2 mL
	Freshly ground black pepper	
12 oz	spaghetti or linguine	375 g

1. In a large nonstick skillet, cook bacon over medium heat, stirring, for 5 minutes or until crisp. Drain fat in skillet. Add garlic and cook, stirring, for 30 seconds or until fragrant. Add parsley and reserve.

2. In a bowl, beat eggs with Parmesan cheese, salt and pepper.

3. Meanwhile, in a large pot of boiling salted water, cook pasta until tender but firm. Drain well and return to pot.

4. Immediately pour egg and bacon mixtures over hot pasta and toss until well coated and eggs are set. Serve immediately.

Spaghetti with Chicken, Broccoli and Pesto

Vary the flavor of this dish by substituting other store-bought pestos, such as sun-dried tomato, for the basil pesto. Every brand and type of pesto varies in strength; add the smaller amount suggested in the recipe and stir in more if desired.

Tip

See page 335 for tips on cooking pasta.

1 tbsp	olive oil	15 mL
1 lb	boneless skinless chicken or turkey breasts, cut into thin strips	500 g
½ cup	chicken stock	125 mL
⅓ to ½ cup	basil pesto, store-bought or homemade (see recipe, page 334)	75 to 125 mL
12 oz	spaghettini or other string pasta	375 g
4 cups	broccoli florets and peeled chopped stems	1 L
⅓ cup	freshly grated Parmesan cheese	75 mL
	Salt and freshly ground black pepper	

1. In a large nonstick skillet, heat oil over medium-high heat. Cook chicken, stirring, for 5 minutes or until browned and no longer pink. Add stock and pesto; cook, stirring, for 1 minute or until heated through. Remove from heat.

2. Meanwhile, in a large pot of boiling salted water, cook pasta until almost tender; add broccoli. Return to a boil; cook for 2 minutes or until broccoli is tender-crisp. Drain well; return to pot. Stir in chicken mixture; toss until well coated. Sprinkle with Parmesan cheese; season with salt and pepper to taste. Serve immediately.

Mushroom Pappardelle with Prosciutto

Makes 4 to 6 servings

This rich, flavorful sauce is also excellent with polenta or as a sauce for gnocchi or cheese-stuffed ravioli.

Variation

Mushroom Ravioli Bake with Gorgonzola

Prepare mushroom sauce as directed and add 4 oz (125 g) Gorgonzola or other blue cheese, cut into pieces, stirring until melted. Replace pappardelle with 1 lb (500 g) cheese-and-spinach-stuffed ravioli and cook in a large pot of boiling salted water until almost tender (undercook slightly, as the pasta absorbs the sauce when baked). Drain ravioli well and spread in a greased 10-cup (2.5 L) shallow casserole dish. Pour mushroom sauce over top and sprinkle with Parmesan cheese. Bake in preheated 400°F (200°C) oven for 20 minutes or until bubbling and lightly browned. Serve immediately. Makes 6 servings.

1 tbsp	olive oil	15 mL
4 cups	sliced shiitake mushrooms or a combination of shiitake, cremini and white mushrooms	1 L
1 tbsp	butter	15 mL
½ cup	diced thick-cut prosciutto	125 mL
⅓ cup	finely chopped shallots	75 mL
2	large cloves garlic, finely chopped	2
1½ tsp	chopped fresh thyme or ½ tsp (2 mL) dried thyme leaves	7 mL
1 cup	whipping (35%) cream	250 mL
⅓ cup	chicken or vegetable stock	75 mL
	Salt and freshly ground black pepper	
12 oz	pappardelle, wide egg noodles or string pasta	375 g
2 tbsp	chopped fresh flat-leaf (Italian) parsley	30 mL
⅓ cup	freshly grated Parmesan cheese	75 mL

1. In a large nonstick skillet, heat oil over medium-high heat. Cook mushrooms, stirring often, for 5 minutes or until softened. Transfer to a bowl.

2. Add butter to skillet. Cook prosciutto, shallots, garlic and thyme, stirring, for 1 minute. Add cream and stock; bring to a boil and cook, stirring occasionally, for 5 minutes or until reduced and slightly thickened. Return mushrooms to skillet, reduce heat and simmer for 1 minute or until hot. Season with salt and pepper. (Can be made 1 day ahead. Cover and refrigerate. Reheat until piping hot.)

3. Meanwhile, in a large pot of boiling salted water, cook pasta until tender but firm. Drain well and return pasta to pot. Add mushroom sauce and parsley. Toss until combined. Sprinkle with Parmesan cheese and serve immediately.

Fettuccine Alfredo

Makes 6 servings

This luxurious pasta delivers so much pleasure it's worth the calorie splurge once in a while. Serve it on special occasions as a main course or as a starter dish. Delizioso!

Tips

Like coffee, Parmesan loses its wonderful aromatic flavor and moisture if grated ahead. Choose a wedge in a cheese shop and have it grated for you. Freeze in an airtight container. Or better still, grate the cheese as you need it.

Store Parmesan wedges wrapped in plastic wrap, then in foil, in the refrigerator; it keeps well for weeks.

1 cup	whipping (35%) cream	250 mL
1 cup	table (18%) cream	250 mL
¼ cup	butter, softened	60 mL
1½ cups	freshly grated Parmesan cheese	375 mL
¼ tsp	freshly ground black pepper	1 mL
	Salt and freshly grated nutmeg	
1 lb	fettuccine	500 g
¼ cup	finely chopped fresh chives, basil or parsley	60 mL

1. In a large saucepan, bring whipping cream and table cream to a boil over medium heat; boil until reduced to about 1½ cups (375 mL). Reduce heat to low; whisk in butter and cheese until sauce is smooth. Add pepper; season with salt and nutmeg to taste. Keep warm.

2. Meanwhile, in a large pot of boiling salted water, cook pasta until tender but still firm. Drain well; return to pot; pour cream sauce over pasta. Sprinkle with herbs; toss well. Serve immediately on warm plates.

> The creamy flavor of fettuccine Alfredo comes not only from the cream and butter but also from the quality of the Parmesan cheese. You're in for a rich and nutty-sweet treat when you indulge in a morsel of Parmigiano-Reggiano or its less-aged (and milder) cousin, Grana Padano. There's just no comparison between authentic Parmesan and the containers of inferior boxed grated cheese found on supermarket shelves.

Fettuccine with Shrimp and Vegetables

3 tbsp	olive oil, divided	45 mL
1½ lbs	large raw shrimp, peeled and deveined, with tails left on	375 g
2	cloves garlic, finely chopped	2
½ tsp	hot pepper flakes, or to taste	2 mL
⅓ cup	vodka (optional)	75 mL
2	small red bell peppers, cut into thin strips	2
1	fennel bulb, top trimmed and cut into thin strips	1
1 cup	fish or chicken stock	250 mL
1 cup	whipping (35%) cream	250 mL
1 tbsp	grated orange zest	15 mL
½ tsp	salt	2 mL
¼ tsp	freshly ground black pepper	1 mL
12 oz	fettuccine	375 g
⅓ cup	chopped fresh parsley	75 mL

1. In a large heavy skillet, heat half the oil over high heat until almost smoking; add shrimp, garlic and hot pepper flakes. Cook, stirring, for 1 to 2 minutes or until shrimp are pink and almost cooked through. Add vodka, if using, and ignite with a match. Cook, shaking skillet, until flames subside. Transfer shrimp and juices to a bowl.

2. Add remaining oil to pan; cook red pepper and fennel strips, stirring, for 2 minutes or until tender-crisp. Transfer to bowl with shrimp.

3. Add stock, cream, zest, salt and pepper to pan; bring to a boil. Reduce heat to medium and boil sauce until reduced by half. Return shrimp and vegetables to skillet and heat through. Season with salt and pepper to taste.

4. Meanwhile, in a large pot of boiling salted water, cook pasta until just tender but firm. Drain well. Return to pot. Toss with shrimp and vegetables; sprinkle with parsley. Serve immediately.

Frutti di Mare Linguine (Pasta with Seafood Sauce)

This recipe was given to me by a good friend who is a marvelous cook and sommelier. It may not be tradition to use red wine with seafood, but the wine adds a rich flavor to the sauce. It's also not traditional to serve cheese with seafood, but top this recipe with freshly grated Parmesan cheese — it tastes wonderful with the wine-based pasta sauce.

Tip

This is a very adaptable sauce — if fresh clams or mussels aren't available, increase the amount of shrimp and scallops or splurge on lobster tails instead. If the lobster tails are raw, remove the meat from the shell and cut into 1-inch (2.5 cm) chunks. Cook as you would the shrimp or scallops. If using cooked lobster, cut into chunks and add to sauce along with mussels, just to heat through.

1 lb	littleneck clams, scrubbed	500 g
1/2 cup	white wine, fish stock or water	125 mL
1 lb	mussels, scrubbed	500 g
2 tbsp	butter	30 mL
2 tbsp	olive oil	30 mL
4	large cloves garlic, cut into slivers	4
8 oz	large raw shrimp, peeled and deveined, with tails left on	250 g
8 oz	sea scallops, halved or quartered if large	250 g
6	vine-ripened tomatoes, peeled, seeded and chopped (2 lbs/1 kg)	6
1/2 cup	red wine	125 mL
	Salt and freshly ground black pepper	
12 oz	linguine or other string pasta	375 g
1/4 cup	chopped fresh flat-leaf (Italian) parsley	60 mL

1. In a Dutch oven or large saucepan, combine clams and white wine. Bring to a boil over high heat. Cover and steam clams for 2 minutes. Add mussels and steam, covered, for 3 minutes or until clams and mussels open. Transfer to a strainer; reserve juice and set aside. Discard any clams or mussels that do not open. When cool enough to handle, set aside 16 clams and 16 mussels in the shell. Shuck remaining clams and mussels and place in a bowl.

2. In the same Dutch oven, heat butter and oil over medium heat. Cook garlic, stirring often, for 5 minutes or until golden (do not let garlic brown or sauce will be bitter). Remove garlic from pan and discard, leaving as much butter and oil in pan as possible.

3. Increase heat to high and add shrimp and scallops to pan. Cook, stirring, for 3 minutes or until opaque. Using slotted spoon, transfer to bowl with shucked clams and mussels. Set aside.

Tip

Instead of fresh tomatoes, use 1 can (28 oz/796 mL) plum tomatoes, including juice, and 2 tbsp (30 mL) tomato paste.

4. To remaining butter and oil in Dutch oven, add tomatoes, red wine, reserved juice from steamed clams and mussels, $\frac{1}{2}$ tsp (2 mL) salt and $\frac{1}{4}$ tsp (1 mL) pepper. Increase heat to high and cook, crushing tomatoes with back of a wooden spoon, for 3 minutes or until sauce-like. Reduce heat, partially cover and simmer, stirring occasionally, for about 20 minutes or until sauce is reduced and thickened.

5. Meanwhile, in a large pot of boiling salted water, cook linguine until tender but firm. Drain well.

6. Return sauce to a boil over high heat. Add reserved shellfish and heat through. Season with salt and pepper to taste. Toss sauce with drained pasta and sprinkle with parsley. Serve immediately.

Linguine with Clam Sauce

By the time it takes to cook the pasta, a flavorful sauce using canned clams can be quickly assembled on the stovetop.

Tips

Omit the cream if you prefer a lighter sauce.

Freeze remaining clam juice to use in other fish-based soups and sauces.

2 tbsp	olive oil	30 mL
1	onion, chopped	1
3	large cloves garlic, finely chopped	3
¼ tsp	hot pepper flakes, or to taste	1 mL
2	cans (each 5 oz/142 g) baby clams, drained, juice reserved	2
½ cup	dry white wine	125 mL
2 cups	chopped seeded fresh plum tomatoes	500 mL
½ cup	whipping (35 %) cream	125 mL
¼ cup	chopped fresh parsley	60 mL
	Salt and freshly ground black pepper	
12 oz	linguine, spaghetti or fettuccine	375 g

1. In a large skillet, heat oil over medium-high heat. Cook onion, garlic and hot pepper flakes, stirring, for 2 minutes. Add clams and cook, stirring, for 2 minutes. Add wine; cook for 1 minute or until slightly reduced.

2. Stir in tomatoes and ½ cup (125 mL) of the reserved clam juice. Reduce heat to medium and cook, stirring occasionally, for 5 minutes or until sauce-like. Add cream and parsley. Season with salt and pepper to taste. Cook for 1 minute or until heated through.

3. Meanwhile, cook pasta in a large pot of boiling salted water until tender but firm. Drain well. Return to pot and add clam sauce; toss to coat pasta in the sauce. Serve immediately.

Linguine with Scallops, Lemon and Garlic

When I crave a rich and creamy pasta dish, this is it. Since this requires very little preparation, have all of the ingredients assembled before you start.

Tip

When to use curly versus flat-leaf parsley? While both are interchangeable in recipes, I like the more assertive taste of flat-leaf parsley, especially in recipes such as this one where it is a vital ingredient and balances nicely with the lemon and garlic.

1 lb	large scallops	500 g
	Salt and freshly ground black pepper	
2 tbsp	butter	30 mL
3	cloves garlic, finely chopped	3
½ cup	dry white wine	125 mL
1 tbsp	grated lemon zest	15 mL
1 tbsp	fresh lemon juice	15 mL
1 cup	whipping (35%) cream	250 mL
¼ cup	chopped fresh flat-leaf (Italian) parsley (see Tip, left)	60 mL
12 oz	linguine	375 g

1. Pat scallops dry with paper towels. Halve horizontally and season with salt and pepper.

2. Heat a large heavy skillet over high heat. Add butter; heat until foamy and butter starts to brown. Add scallops and cook for 1 minute or until lightly browned. Turn and cook second side for about 30 seconds. Do not overcook. Transfer to a plate.

3. Reduce heat to medium. Add garlic and cook, stirring, for 30 seconds or until fragrant. Stir in wine and lemon zest and juice; bring to a boil. Add cream and cook, stirring, until sauce boils and is slightly reduced.

4. Add parsley and season with salt and pepper to taste. Add scallops and cook for 1 minute or just until heated in the sauce. Do not overcook.

5. Meanwhile, in a large pot of boiling salted water, cook pasta until tender but firm. Drain and return to pot.

6. Pour sauce over pasta and toss until well coated. Spoon pasta into warm bowls and serve immediately.

Fusilli with Mushrooms and Peas

I like to use fusilli in this recipe because the sauce clings nicely to the corkscrew-shaped pasta, but feel free to use whatever pasta you have in your pantry.

Tip

You can make this 5-minute pasta sauce the day ahead and refrigerate. Reheat on stovetop or microwave before tossing with hot cooked pasta.

1 tbsp	butter	15 mL
2 cups	sliced mushrooms	500 mL
2	green onions, sliced	2
4 oz	herb and garlic cream cheese	125 g
1 cup	frozen peas	250 mL
½ cup	milk	125 mL
⅓ cup	freshly grated Parmesan cheese	75 mL
8 oz	fusilli, penne or other tube-shaped pasta	250 g
	Salt and freshly ground black pepper	

1. In a large saucepan, melt butter over medium heat. Add mushrooms and green onions; cook, stirring, for 3 minutes or until softened. Add cream cheese, peas, milk and Parmesan; cook, stirring, for 2 minutes or until piping hot.

2. Cook pasta in a large pot of boiling salted water until tender but firm. Drain well. Stir into mushroom mixture; toss to coat well. Season with salt and pepper to taste. Serve immediately.

Penne Arrabbiatta

Even when my pantry is almost empty, chances are I'll have a can of tomatoes and dried pasta on hand to whip up this easy supper dish.

Tips

If you don't have any fresh herbs, substitute 1 tsp (5 mL) each dried oregano and basil for the fresh parsley and basil and add to sauce with the tomatoes.

If wonderful ripe tomatoes are available, use 2 lbs (1 kg) tomatoes (about 5 to 6), peeled, seeded and chopped, instead of canned tomatoes.

Variation

Spicy Tomato Sauce with Cheese

Instead of the traditional accompaniment of freshly grated Parmesan cheese, toss hot pasta with 5 oz (150 g) creamy goat cheese or Gorgonzola or soft Brie, rind removed and cheese cut into small pieces.

2 tbsp	olive oil	30 mL
3	cloves garlic, thinly sliced, then coarsely chopped	3
¼ tsp	hot pepper flakes, or to taste	1 mL
1	can (28 oz/796 mL) plum tomatoes, including juice, chopped	1
Pinch	granulated sugar	Pinch
	Salt and freshly ground black pepper	
12 oz	penne pasta	375 g
2 tbsp	chopped fresh parsley	30 mL
2 tbsp	chopped fresh basil or additional parsley	30 mL
	Freshly grated Parmesan or Romano cheese (optional)	

1. In a large saucepan, heat oil over medium heat. Stir in garlic and hot pepper flakes. Reduce heat to low and cook, stirring, for 1 minute or until garlic is light golden. (Do not let garlic brown or sauce will be bitter.)

2. Add tomatoes with juice; season with sugar, salt and pepper. Bring to a boil, reduce heat and simmer, partially covered, stirring occasionally, for 15 minutes.

3. Meanwhile, in a large pot of boiling salted water, cook pasta until tender but firm. Drain well; return to pot. Add tomato sauce, parsley and basil; toss well. Adjust seasoning with salt and pepper. Serve immediately, along with Parmesan cheese, if using.

Creamy Bow Ties with Basil

Toss this luxurious basil and walnut sauce with bow ties or any other interesting pasta shapes and get ready to entertain. It takes only 5 minutes to make and can be prepared a few hours ahead and reheated over low heat just before serving.

1 tbsp	butter	15 mL
4	green onions, sliced	4
2	cloves garlic, finely chopped	2
¼ cup	finely chopped walnuts	60 mL
1 cup	table (18%) cream	250 mL
⅓ cup	freshly grated Parmesan cheese	75 mL
8 oz	bow tie pasta (farfalle)	250 g
⅓ cup	chopped fresh basil	75 mL
	Salt and freshly ground black pepper	

1. In a large saucepan, melt butter over medium heat. Add green onions, garlic and walnuts; cook, stirring, for 2 minutes or until onions are softened. Stir in cream and Parmesan. Keep warm over low heat; do not let mixture boil.

2. Cook pasta in a large pot of boiling salted water until tender but firm. Drain well; add to cream sauce along with basil and toss to coat. Season with salt and pepper to taste. Serve immediately.

Angel Hair Pasta with Spicy Ginger Beef and Vegetables

Makes 4 servings

Timing is everything when it comes to cooking pasta and preparing a stir-fry. Before you begin chopping the vegetables for this recipe, put a large pot of water on the stove to boil. The pasta takes just a few minutes to cook, so don't add it to the boiling water until just after you brown the meat. This way, both pasta and stir-fry will be ready at the same time.

Variation

Use pork, chicken or firm tofu instead of the beef.

½ cup	chicken stock	125 mL
3 tbsp	soy sauce	45 mL
1½ tsp	cornstarch	7 mL
12 oz	lean tender beef, such as sirloin, cut into very thin shreds	375 g
4 tsp	vegetable oil, divided	20 mL
2 tbsp	minced gingerroot	30 mL
2	large cloves garlic, finely chopped	2
½ tsp	hot pepper flakes, or to taste	2 mL
2 cups	snow peas, ends trimmed, halved	500 mL
1	large red bell pepper, cut into thin 2-inch (5 cm) strips	1
4	green onions, sliced	4
8 oz	angel hair pasta	250 g
⅓ cup	chopped fresh cilantro	75 mL

1. In a glass measure, combine stock, soy sauce and cornstarch. Pat meat dry with paper towels.

2. In a wok or large nonstick skillet, heat 2 tsp (10 mL) of the oil over high heat; stir-fry beef until browned. Transfer to a plate.

3. Add remaining oil to skillet; cook ginger, garlic and hot pepper flakes, stirring, for 15 seconds. Stir in snow peas, red pepper and green onions; cook, stirring, for 1 minute. Stir stock mixture and add to skillet; cook, stirring, until thickened. Return beef to skillet. Cook, stirring, for 30 seconds.

4. Meanwhile, in a large pot of boiling salted water, cook pasta until tender but firm. Drain well and return to pot. Add beef mixture and cilantro; toss well. Serve immediately.

Spicy Noodles with Vegetables and Peanut Sauce

Makes 6 servings

Vegetarians in your household will request this dish often and come to think of it as a comfort food. Its vibrant combination of Asian flavors tastes terrific and is nourishing, too. Any leftovers make a great next-day lunch.

Tips

To clean leeks: Trim dark green tops. Cut down center almost to root end and chop. Rinse in a sink full of cold water to remove sand; scoop up leeks and place in colander to drain or use a salad spinner.

Cut vegetables into uniform 2-inch (5 cm) lengths. This colorful pasta dish takes only a few minutes to cook, so have ingredients assembled before you start.

¼ cup	peanut butter	60 mL
⅓ cup	water	75 mL
2 tbsp	soy sauce	30 mL
2 tbsp	fresh lime juice	30 mL
2 tbsp	packed brown sugar	30 mL
¼ tsp	hot pepper flakes, or to taste	1 mL
1 tbsp	sesame oil	15 mL
2 tbsp	vegetable oil	30 mL
1 tbsp	minced gingerroot	15 mL
2	cloves garlic, minced	2
1	leek, white and light green parts only, cut into matchstick strips (see Tips, left)	1
2	small Italian eggplants, cut into thin strips (about 2 cups/500 mL)	2
2	bell peppers (assorted colors), cut into thin strips	2
12 oz	linguine, broken into thirds	375 g
½ cup	chopped fresh cilantro or parsley	125 mL

1. In a small saucepan, combine peanut butter, water, soy sauce, lime juice, brown sugar, hot pepper flakes and sesame oil. Stir over medium heat until mixture is warm and smooth. Set aside.

2. In wok or large nonstick skillet, heat oil over high heat. Add ginger, garlic, leek and eggplant; cook, stirring, for 2 minutes. Add peppers; cook, stirring, for 1 minute more or until vegetables are just tender-crisp. Stir in peanut sauce until heated through.

3. Meanwhile, in a large pot of boiling salted water, cook linguine until tender but firm. Drain and return to pot. Toss with vegetables and peanut sauce until well coated; sprinkle with cilantro. Serve warm or at room temperature.

Pad Thai

Makes 6 servings

Pad Thai may be the most popular dish in Thailand, but its addictive appeal has spread beyond that country's borders, based on the number of restaurants that now feature it on their menus. Here's how to make it in your home kitchen.

Tip

Fish sauce (also called *nam pla*) is an important flavoring ingredient in this dish. Look for it in the Asian foods section of most large supermarkets or in Asian markets.

8 oz	wide rice stick noodles	250 g
1/3 cup	chili sauce or ketchup	75 mL
1/4 cup	fish sauce (see Tip, left)	60 mL
3 tbsp	fresh lime juice	45 mL
1 tbsp	packed brown sugar	15 mL
1 tsp	Asian chili sauce, or to taste	5 mL
2 tbsp	vegetable oil, divided	30 mL
8 oz	medium raw shrimp, peeled and deveined	250 g
8 oz	boneless skinless chicken breasts, cut into thin strips	250 g
3	cloves garlic, minced	3
2	eggs, lightly beaten	2
2 cups	bean sprouts	500 mL
5	green onions, sliced	5
1/2 cup	coarsely chopped fresh cilantro	125 mL
1/3 cup	coarsely chopped roasted peanuts	75 mL
	Lime wedges	

1. Place noodles in a large bowl. Add hot water to cover. Let stand for 15 minutes or until softened. Drain.

2. In a bowl, combine chili sauce, fish sauce, lime juice, brown sugar and Asian chili sauce.

3. In a large wok or nonstick skillet, heat 1 tbsp (15 mL) of the oil over medium-high heat. Cook shrimp and chicken, stirring, for 3 minutes or until chicken is cooked through and shrimp are pink. Add to chili sauce mixture and toss.

4. Add remaining oil to the skillet. Cook garlic, stirring, for 15 seconds or until fragrant. Add eggs; cook, stirring constantly, for 30 seconds or until soft-scrambled. Add sprouts and green onions; cook, stirring, for 1 minute.

5. Add noodles and shrimp mixture; cook, stirring, for 2 minutes or until heated through. Transfer to a platter; sprinkle with cilantro and peanuts. Garnish with lime wedges.

Singapore Noodles

Here's a popular noodle dish you'll spot on many restaurant menus that is easy to recreate in your home kitchen.

Tips

Other pasta, such as angel hair, can be substituted. Cook noodles according to package directions before adding to recipe.

Store-bought curry pastes vary in flavor and strength depending on the brand. Some pastes are labeled as mild but have more heat than expected. Add a smaller amount of curry paste to the recipe to test the strength and add more to get the depth of curry flavor you prefer.

6 oz	rice vermicelli	175 g
3 tbsp	soy sauce	45 mL
2 tsp	mild curry paste, or to taste	10 mL
2 tbsp	vegetable oil, divided	30 mL
1	red or green bell pepper, cut into thin strips	1
5	green onions, sliced	5
2	large cloves garlic, minced	2
3 cups	bean sprouts, rinsed and dried	375 mL
12 oz	cooked peeled baby shrimp	375 g

1. Place vermicelli in a bowl and cover with boiling water. Let soak for 3 minutes to soften. Drain; chill under cold water and drain well. Cut noodles using scissors into 3-inch (7.5 cm) lengths; set aside.

2. In a small bowl, combine soy sauce and curry paste; set aside.

3. Heat a wok or large nonstick skillet over high heat until very hot; add 1 tbsp (15 mL) oil, tilting wok to coat sides. Stir-fry pepper strips, green onions and garlic for 1 minute. Add bean sprouts and shrimp; stir-fry for 1 to 2 minutes or until vegetables are tender-crisp. Transfer to a bowl.

4. Add remaining oil to wok; when very hot, add noodles and soy sauce mixture. Stir-fry for 1 minute or until heated through. Return vegetable-shrimp mixture to wok and stir-fry for 1 minute more. Serve immediately.

Spicy Noodles with Sesame Greens

This Japanese-inspired noodle dish is quick-cooking, so have all the ingredients assembled and measured before you start. As soon as the pasta goes into the water and boils, start the stir-fry. Finely chop the thicker stems of the greens and coarsely chop the leaves for even cooking. This dish goes well with grilled chicken or salmon.

Tip

To toast sesame seeds: Heat a nonstick skillet over medium heat. Add seeds and toast, stirring often, for 2 to 3 minutes or until nicely colored.

2 tbsp	soy sauce	30 mL
1 tsp	toasted sesame oil	5 mL
1 tsp	granulated sugar	5 mL
½ tsp	Asian chili oil or sauce (optional)	2 mL
1 tbsp	vegetable oil	15 mL
1 tbsp	minced gingerroot	15 mL
2	cloves garlic, finely chopped	2
4 cups	chopped Swiss chard, preferably red-stemmed	1 L
4 cups	chopped bok choy	1 L
2 tbsp	vegetable stock or water	30 mL
8 oz	soba noodles or whole wheat spaghetti	250 g
2 tbsp	toasted sesame seeds	30 mL
2	green onions, sliced	2

1. In a bowl, stir together soy sauce, sesame oil, sugar and chili oil, if using. Set aside.

2. In a wok or large nonstick skillet, heat oil over high heat. Cook ginger and garlic, stirring, for 15 seconds or until fragrant. Add Swiss chard and bok choy; cook, stirring, for 1 minute. Add stock; cover and steam for 2 minutes or until tender-crisp.

3. Meanwhile, in a large pot of boiling salted water, cook noodles until just tender but firm. Drain well; return to pot.

4. Add greens to noodles and toss; place in a large serving bowl. Sprinkle with sesame seeds and green onions. Serve warm or at room temperature.

Easy One-Pot Macaroni and Cheese

Here's a streamlined mac and cheese that's as easy to assemble as the prepackaged version.

Tips

For a speedy meal-in-one dinner, add 3 to 4 cups (750 mL to 1 L) small broccoli florets to the pot of boiling pasta for the last 3 minutes of cooking; remove from heat when broccoli is tender-crisp.

To reheat leftovers on the stovetop or in the microwave, stir in additional milk until sauce is creamy.

2 tbsp	all-purpose flour	30 mL
1½ cups	milk	375 mL
1½ cups	shredded Cheddar cheese	375 mL
¼ cup	freshly grated Parmesan cheese	60 mL
1 tsp	Dijon mustard	5 mL
	Salt and cayenne pepper	
2 cups	elbow macaroni	500 mL

1. In a large saucepan, whisk flour with ¼ cup (50 mL) milk to make a smooth paste; stir in remaining milk until smooth. Place over medium heat; cook, stirring, until mixture comes to a boil and thickens. Reduce heat to low; stir in cheeses and mustard. Cook, stirring, until melted. Season with salt and a pinch of cayenne pepper to taste; keep warm.

2. Cook pasta in a large pot of boiling salted water until tender but firm. Drain well; stir into cheese mixture. Cook for 1 minute or until sauce coats the pasta. Serve immediately.

Best-Ever Macaroni and Cheese

**Makes 4 to
6 servings**

As popular today as in the
1950s, classic macaroni
and cheese has a lot going
for it. It's not hard to make,
so why open up a box of
the prepackaged stuff when
you can create the real
thing in your kitchen?

Tip

Can't figure out the volume
of a casserole dish? Look
for the measurements
on the bottom of dish
or measure by pouring
in enough water to fill
completely.

- Preheat oven to 375°F (190°C)
- 8-cup (2 L) deep casserole dish, greased

3 tbsp	butter	45 mL
¼ cup	all-purpose flour	60 mL
1	bay leaf	1
3 cups	milk	750 mL
1 tbsp	Dijon mustard	15 mL
	Salt and cayenne pepper	
2 cups	shredded Cheddar cheese, preferably aged (about 8 oz/250 g)	500 mL
2 cups	elbow macaroni	500 mL
1 tbsp	butter, melted	15 mL
1 cup	soft fresh bread crumbs	250 mL

1. In a large saucepan, melt butter over medium heat. Blend in flour and add bay leaf; cook, stirring, for 30 seconds. Pour in 1 cup (250 mL) milk, whisking constantly, until mixture comes to a boil and is very thick. Pour in rest of milk in a slow stream, whisking constantly, until sauce comes to a full boil and is smooth. Whisk in mustard.

2. Reduce heat to low; stir in cheese until melted. Remove bay leaf; season with salt and a dash of cayenne pepper to taste. Remove from heat.

3. Meanwhile, in a large pot of boiling salted water, cook macaroni for 8 minutes or until just tender. (Do not overcook; pasta continues to cook in sauce.) Drain well. Stir into cheese sauce until well coated.

4. Spoon into prepared casserole dish. In a bowl, toss 1 tbsp (15 mL) melted butter with bread crumbs; sprinkle over top. Bake in preheated oven for 25 minutes or until bubbly and top is lightly browned.

Spinach and Ricotta Cannelloni

Makes 6 servings

To streamline this one-dish pasta, I like to use convenient bottled pasta sauces sold in supermarkets. Try one with mushrooms, roasted red peppers or basil pesto to add another flavor dimension to this dish.

Tip

To make ahead and freeze: Cover with plastic wrap, then with heavy-duty foil. Freeze for up to 2 months. Thaw in the refrigerator overnight. Add 15 minutes to baking time.

- Preheat oven to 350°F (180°C)
- 13- by 9-inch (33 by 23 cm) baking dish, greased

1 tbsp	olive oil	15 mL
1	package (10 oz/300 g) frozen chopped spinach, thawed, squeezed dry	1
4	green onions, sliced	4
2	cloves garlic, finely chopped	2
1	egg	1
2 cups	ricotta cheese	500 mL
1½ cups	shredded Asiago or provolone cheese, divided	375 mL
½ cup	freshly grated Parmesan cheese, divided	125 mL
⅓ cup	chopped fresh parsley	75 mL
¼ tsp	each salt and freshly grated black pepper	1 mL
¼ tsp	freshly grated nutmeg	1 mL
6	sheets (each 9 by 6 inches/23 by 15 cm) fresh lasagna noodles	6
3 cups	tomato pasta sauce	750 mL
½ cup	chicken stock	125 mL

1. In a large nonstick skillet, heat oil over medium-high heat; cook spinach, green onions and garlic, stirring, for 3 minutes or until softened. Remove from heat.

2. In a bowl, beat egg; stir in ricotta, ½ cup (125 mL) of the Asiago cheese, ¼ cup (60 mL) of the Parmesan cheese, parsley, salt, pepper and nutmeg. Stir in spinach mixture until combined.

3. In a large pot of boiling salted water, cook lasagna noodles until tender but firm, about 3 minutes. Drain and chill under cold water. Cut each sheet in half crosswise. Place on a damp kitchen towel.

4. In a bowl, combine pasta sauce and stock. Spread 1 cup (250 mL) of the tomato sauce in prepared baking dish.

5. Spoon ⅓ cup (75 mL) of the ricotta filling along one short edge of each lasagna sheet. Roll up and place in baking dish, making two rows. Cover with remaining tomato sauce; sprinkle with remaining Asiago and Parmesan cheeses. Bake in preheated oven for 40 to 45 minutes or until sauce is bubbly.

Easy Lasagna

Everyone loves lasagna, but who has the time to make it from scratch? Try this uncomplicated version that makes even a non-cook look like a pro in the kitchen. It's also the perfect recipe for young cooks, since there's no chopping involved. Once you assemble the ingredients, it takes a mere 15 minutes to prepare and the lasagna is ready for the oven.

Tip

Lasagna freezes well; cover with plastic wrap, then with foil and freeze for up to 2 months. Thaw in the refrigerator overnight before baking.

- Preheat oven to 350°F (180°C)
- 13- by 9-inch (33 by 23 cm) baking dish, lightly greased

2 cups	ricotta cheese	500 mL
2	eggs, beaten	2
1/3 cup	freshly grated Parmesan cheese	75 mL
1/4 tsp	freshly ground black pepper	1 mL
1/4 tsp	freshly grated nutmeg	1 mL
3 cups	spaghetti sauce (homemade or store-bought)	750 mL
12	precooked lasagna noodles	12
2 cups	shredded mozzarella cheese	500 mL

1. In a bowl, combine ricotta, eggs and Parmesan cheese; season with pepper and nutmeg.

2. Depending on thickness of the spaghetti sauce, add about 3/4 cup (175 mL) water to thin sauce. (Precooked noodles absorb extra moisture while cooking.)

3. Spoon 1/2 cup (125 mL) sauce in bottom of prepared baking dish. Layer with 3 lasagna noodles. Spread with 3/4 cup (175 mL) of the sauce and then one-third of the ricotta mixture. Repeat with two more layers of noodles, sauce and ricotta cheese. Layer with rest of noodles and top with remaining sauce. Sprinkle with mozzarella cheese.

4. Bake, uncovered, in preheated oven for 45 minutes or until cheese is melted and sauce is bubbly.

Lasagna with Roasted Butternut Squash and Sage

This hearty, white-sauced lasagna dish is a delicious alternative to tomato-sauced pasta. Serve it for dinner or as part of a buffet.

Tip

To make ahead, prepare sauce and roasted vegetables, place in separate airtight containers and refrigerate up to a day ahead. Reheat sauce, stirring until smooth, before assembling lasagna.

- Preheat oven to 400°F (200°C)
- 2 rimmed baking sheets
- 13- by 9-inch (33 by 23 cm) baking dish, well greased

1	butternut squash (about 1½ lbs/750 g), peeled, seeded and cut into thin 2-inch (5 cm) long slices	1
2	red bell peppers, cut into 2-inch (5 cm) strips	2
2 tbsp	olive oil	30 mL
	Salt and freshly ground black pepper	
12	lasagna noodles	12
2 tbsp	chopped fresh sage	30 mL
	Béchamel Sauce (see recipe, opposite)	
1½ cups	shredded Asiago cheese	375 mL
⅓ cup	freshly grated Parmesan cheese	75 mL

1. Scatter squash and red pepper on baking sheets. Drizzle with olive oil and season with salt and pepper. Roast in preheated oven for 20 to 25 minutes, stirring occasionally, until vegetables are just tender. Reduce oven temperature to 350°F (180°C).

2. Meanwhile, in a large pot of boiling salted water, cook pasta until tender but firm; drain. Rinse in cold water to chill and arrange noodles on clean, dry kitchen towels.

3. Stir sage into béchamel sauce. Spread ¾ cup (175 mL) sauce in bottom of prepared baking dish. Layer with 3 lasagna noodles. Spread one-third of the squash mixture over noodles. Spread with ¾ cup (175 mL) sauce and sprinkle with ⅓ cup (75 mL) Asiago cheese. Repeat two more layers of pasta, vegetables, sauce and Asiago. Top with last layer of lasagna noodles, remaining sauce and Asiago. Sprinkle with Parmesan cheese.

4. Cover with foil and place dish on a baking sheet. Bake for 30 minutes. Remove foil and bake for 15 to 20 minutes or until top is golden and sauce is bubbling. Let stand for 10 minutes before cutting.

Béchamel sauce, also called white sauce, is the base for most cheese sauces for pasta or vegetable dishes.

Tip

If making sauce ahead, refrigerate in an airtight container for up to 1 day. Reheat, stirring until smooth, before using.

Béchamel Sauce

Makes 4 cups (1 L)

¼ cup	butter	60 mL
1	small onion, sliced	1
1	bay leaf	1
½ tsp	salt	2 mL
¼ tsp	freshly ground black pepper	1 mL
¼ tsp	freshly grated nutmeg	1 mL
⅓ cup	all-purpose flour	75 mL
4 cups	hot milk	1 L
½ cup	freshly grated Parmesan cheese	125 mL

1. In a medium saucepan, melt butter over medium heat. Add onion, bay leaf, salt, pepper and nutmeg and cook, stirring often, for 3 minutes or until onion is softened. Sprinkle in flour and cook, whisking constantly, for 2 minutes or until bubbly.

2. Whisk in hot milk in a stream and bring sauce to a full boil, whisking constantly. Reduce heat and simmer, whisking often, for about 10 minutes or until smooth and thickened. Strain sauce through a fine sieve into a bowl; discard bay leaf. Stir in Parmesan cheese.

Roasted Vegetable Lasagna with Spicy Tomato Sauce

Today's store-bought tomato sauces and packaged shredded cheeses ease the making of traditional lasagna. This updated version serves a crowd and replaces ground meat with plenty of healthy vegetables.

Tip

Don't be intimidated by the fennel. It's simple to handle; just trim the top and cut in half lengthwise. Remove and discard the tough core.

- Preheat oven to 400°F (200°C)
- 2 rimmed baking sheets
- 13- by 9-inch (33 by 23 cm) baking dish, greased

Roasted Vegetables

2	small zucchini, diced	2
1	red onion, chopped	1
1	fennel bulb, diced	1
1	large red bell pepper, diced	1
1 tbsp	dried oregano leaves	15 mL
½ tsp	freshly ground black pepper	2 mL
2 tbsp	olive oil	30 mL

Cheese Filling

2	eggs	2
½ tsp	freshly ground black pepper	2 mL
1½ cups	ricotta cheese	375 mL
1 cup	crumbled feta cheese (about 4 oz/125 g)	250 mL
¼ cup	chopped fresh parsley	60 mL
12	lasagna noodles	12

Spicy Tomato Sauce

1	jar (26 oz/700 mL) spicy tomato sauce with roasted red peppers	1
1	can (7½ oz/213 mL) tomato sauce	1
⅓ cup	chopped kalamata olives (optional)	75 mL
1½ cups	shredded mozzarella cheese	375 mL

1. *Roasted Vegetables:* In a bowl, combine zucchini, onion, fennel, pepper, oregano and pepper; drizzle with oil and toss to coat. Spread on baking sheets. Roast in preheated oven, stirring occasionally, for 20 to 25 minutes or until tender. Remove and set aside. Reduce oven temperature to 350°F (180°C).

2. *Cheese Filling:* In a bowl, beat eggs and pepper; stir in ricotta, feta and parsley.

3. Meanwhile, in a large pot of boiling salted water, cook noodles for 8 minutes or until almost tender. Drain; chill under cold running water. Arrange in single layer on damp tea towel.

4. *Spicy Tomato Sauce:* In a large bowl, combine bottled and canned tomato sauces; spread ¾ cup (175 mL) sauce in baking dish. Stir roasted vegetables and olives, if using, into remaining tomato sauce.

5. Layer 3 noodles in baking dish. Spread with one-quarter of the vegetable sauce; top with one-third of the ricotta mixture. Repeat layers twice. Arrange remaining noodles over top; spread with remaining sauce.

6. Sprinkle top with mozzarella cheese; cover loosely with foil. Bake in 350°F (180°C) oven for 30 minutes; uncover and bake for 20 to 25 minutes more or until bubbly and top is golden. Let stand for 5 minutes before cutting.

Chicken Penne Bake

Makes 8 to 10 servings

This casual country-style dish — perfect for large potluck dinners — is an easy make-ahead casserole that's a real crowd pleaser.

Tips

Hate shedding tears when chopping onions? To minimize the weeping problem, use a razor-sharp knife to prevent loss of juices and cover the cut onions with a paper towel as you chop them to prevent the vapors from rising to your eyes.

To wash or not wash mushrooms? You can wipe them with a damp cloth, if you wish. However, I feel it's important to wash all produce that comes into my kitchen. I quickly rinse mushrooms under cold water and immediately wrap in a clean, dry kitchen towel or paper towels to absorb excess moisture.

- Preheat oven to 350°F (180°C)
- 16-cup (4 L) baking dish, greased

2 tbsp	olive oil (approx.), divided	30 mL
2 lbs	boneless skinless chicken thighs, cut into 1-inch (2.5 cm) pieces	1 kg
2	onions, chopped	2
6	cloves garlic, chopped	6
4 cups	sliced mushrooms	1 L
2 tsp	dried basil leaves	10 mL
2 tsp	dried oregano leaves	10 mL
1 tsp	hot pepper flakes	5 mL
1 tsp	salt	5 mL
1	can (28 oz/796 mL) plum tomatoes, including juice	1
1	can (5½ oz/156 mL) tomato paste	1
1½ cups	chicken stock	375 mL
1	red bell pepper, chopped	1
1	green bell pepper, chopped	1
½ cup	dry-cured black olives	125 mL
½ cup	chopped fresh parsley	125 mL
12 oz	penne or other tube-shaped pasta	375 g
2 cups	shredded mozzarella cheese	500 mL
½ cup	freshly grated Pecorino Romano or Parmesan cheese	125 mL

1. In a Dutch oven or large saucepan, heat 1 tbsp (15 mL) olive oil over medium-high heat; brown chicken in batches, adding more oil as needed. Transfer to a plate.

2. Add remaining oil; cook onions, garlic, mushrooms, basil, oregano, hot pepper flakes and salt, stirring, for 5 minutes or until softened. Return chicken to pan along with accumulated juices.

3. In a food processor, purée tomatoes with juice. Add to chicken mixture with tomato paste and stock. Bring to a boil; reduce heat, cover and cook for 25 minutes. Add red and green peppers and olives; cook, covered, for 10 minutes or until peppers are tender. Stir in parsley. (If making ahead, let cool and refrigerate.)

Variation

Substitute 1 lb (500 g) mild or hot Italian sausages for half of the chicken called for in this hearty Italian dish. Prick sausages with a fork and cook in a large skillet in 1 tbsp (15 mL) oil, turning often, until cooked through. Cut into slices and add along with browned chicken.

4. In a large pot of boiling salted water, cook pasta until tender but firm; drain. Rinse under cold water to chill; drain well. Stir pasta into sauce. Spoon half into prepared baking dish; sprinkle with half the mozzarella and Romano cheeses. Top with remaining pasta and sprinkle with remaining cheeses. (Can be prepared to this point, covered and refrigerated for up to 1 day.)

5. Cover and bake in preheated oven for 45 minutes; uncover and bake for 30 minutes more or until piping hot in center and top is golden.

Baked Penne with Italian Sausage and Sweet Peppers

Makes 6 servings

This hearty pasta dish, brimming with chunks of tasty sausage and colorful peppers, makes a delicious feast for any occasion.

Tip

To easily chop canned tomatoes, run a knife through the tomatoes right in the can.

- Preheat oven to 350°F (180°C)
- 13- by 9-inch (33 by 23 cm) baking dish, lightly greased

12 oz	hot or mild Italian sausages	375 g
2 tbsp	olive oil, divided	30 mL
3	bell peppers (assorted colors)	3
1	large onion, halved lengthwise and thinly sliced	1
2	cloves garlic, finely chopped	2
1 tsp	dried basil leaves	5 mL
1 tsp	dried oregano leaves	5 mL
½ tsp	salt	2 mL
½ tsp	hot pepper flakes, or to taste	2 mL
1	can (28 oz/796 mL) plum tomatoes, including juice, chopped	1
¼ cup	chopped oil-packed sun-dried tomatoes (optional)	60 mL
¼ cup	chopped fresh parsley	60 mL
12 oz	penne or other small tube-shaped pasta	375 g
1½ cups	grated fontina or mozzarella cheese	375 mL
⅓ cup	freshly grated Romano or Parmesan cheese	75 mL

1. Prick skins of sausages with a fork. In a Dutch oven or large saucepan, heat 1 tbsp (15 mL) oil over medium-high heat; cook sausages for 5 minutes or until browned on all sides. (Sausages will not be cooked through.) Remove from pan, cut into slices and reserve.

2. Add remaining oil to pan. Add peppers, onion, garlic, basil, oregano, salt and hot pepper flakes; cook, stirring often, for 7 minutes or until softened.

3. Return sausage slices to pan along with canned tomatoes with juice and sun-dried tomatoes, if using. Bring to a boil; reduce heat to medium-low; cover and simmer, stirring occasionally, for 20 minutes. Stir in parsley. Adjust seasoning with salt, if necessary.

Variation

Add ⅓ cup (75 mL) small black olives to the sauce along with the parsley for an added dimension of flavor. For a vegetarian version, omit the sausages.

4. Meanwhile, cook pasta in a large pot of boiling salted water until tender but firm. Drain well. Place half of the cooked pasta in prepared baking dish. Pour in half of the sauce. Layer again with remaining pasta and top with remaining sauce.

5. In a bowl, combine fontina and Romano cheeses; sprinkle over top of casserole. Bake, uncovered, in preheated oven for 30 to 35 minutes or until cheese is melted and lightly colored.

Party Pasta with Mushrooms, Spinach and Tomato

Planning a party — or going to one? This meatless dish is perfect to serve company or take along to a potluck supper. It makes a large party dish, or you can divide it into smaller portions and place into two 8-cup (2 L) baking dishes. Enjoy one now and freeze the other for another delicious meal.

Tips

Like coffee, Parmesan loses its wonderful aromatic flavor and moisture if grated ahead. Choose a wedge in a cheese shop and have it grated for you. Freeze in an airtight container. Or better still, grate the cheese as you need it.

Store Parmesan wedges wrapped in plastic wrap, then in foil, in the refrigerator; it keeps well for weeks.

- Preheat oven to 350°F (180°C)
- 16-cup (4 L) baking dish, lightly greased

2 tbsp	butter	30 mL
1	onion, finely chopped	1
4	cloves garlic, finely chopped	4
4 cups	sliced mushrooms	1 L
1 tsp	dried basil leaves	5 mL
1 tsp	dried oregano leaves	5 mL
1 tsp	dried marjoram leaves	5 mL
1 tsp	salt	5 mL
1/2 tsp	dried rosemary leaves, crumbled	2 mL
1/2 tsp	freshly ground black pepper	2 mL
1/4 cup	all-purpose flour	60 mL
1 1/2 cups	milk	375 mL
2 cups	half-and-half (10%) cream	500 mL
1	can (28 oz/796 mL) tomatoes, including juice, chopped	1
2	packages (each 10 oz/300 g) fresh or frozen spinach, cooked, squeezed dry and chopped	2
1 lb	bow tie pasta (farfalle)	500 g
2 cups	shredded fontina or provolone cheese	500 mL
1/2 cup	freshly grated Parmesan cheese	125 mL

1. In a Dutch oven or large saucepan, melt butter over medium-high heat. Add onion, garlic, mushrooms, basil, oregano, marjoram, salt, rosemary and pepper; cook, stirring often, for 5 minutes or until softened.

2. In a bowl, blend flour with just enough milk to make a smooth paste; stir in remaining milk. Gradually add milk mixture and cream to mushroom mixture, stirring constantly, until sauce comes to a full boil and thickens.

Tip

Pasta dishes often call for Italian cheeses, such as fontina, provolone or mozzarella, which are wonderfully mild melting cheeses and are interchangeable with each other. If you like, you can use another good melting cheese, such as Gouda, Gruyère, Asiago, Monterey Jack or Cheddar, to replace a portion of the milder cheese.

3. Add tomatoes with juice and spinach; cook, stirring often, for 3 to 5 minutes or until piping hot. Adjust seasoning with salt and pepper to taste. Let sauce cool to room temperature.

4. Meanwhile, cook pasta in a large pot of boiling salted water until tender but firm. Drain well. Return pasta to pot and stir in sauce until coated.

5. Place half the pasta in prepared baking dish. Sprinkle with half the fontina and half the Parmesan cheese. Layer with rest of pasta and sprinkle with remaining fontina and Parmesan cheese.

6. Bake, uncovered, in preheated oven for 40 to 45 minutes or until center is piping hot and top is lightly browned. Serve immediately.

Creamy Tuna Pasta Bake

This modern rendition of a tuna casserole includes a nutritional boost of broccoli in a creamy basil sauce. To prepare the casserole ahead, make the sauce the day before and refrigerate. Assemble the dish no more than 4 hours ahead to prevent pasta from soaking up the sauce.

Tip

If fresh basil is unavailable, substitute 2 tsp (10 mL) dried basil leaves and cook with onions.

Vegetarian Variation

For a vegetarian version, omit tuna and substitute 1 can (19 oz/540 mL) kidney beans, drained and rinsed.

- Preheat oven to 350°F (180°C)
- 13- by 9-inch (33 by 23 cm) baking dish, greased

2 tbsp	butter	30 mL
6	green onions, chopped	6
3	cloves garlic, finely chopped	3
4 cups	sliced mushrooms	1 L
½ tsp	salt	2 mL
½ tsp	freshly ground black pepper	2 mL
⅓ cup	all-purpose flour	75 mL
2 cups	light (5%) cream or milk	500 mL
1½ cups	chicken stock	375 mL
3	tomatoes, seeded and diced	3
⅔ cup	freshly grated Parmesan cheese	150 mL
½ cup	chopped fresh basil	125 mL
12 oz	penne	375 g
4 cups	broccoli florets and chopped peeled stems	1 L
2	cans (each 6 oz/170 g) solid white tuna, drained and flaked	2
1½ cups	soft fresh bread crumbs	375 mL
1 cup	shredded Asiago or mozzarella cheese	250 mL

1. In a Dutch oven or large saucepan, melt butter over medium-high heat. Cook green onions, garlic, mushrooms, salt and pepper, stirring occasionally, for 5 minutes or until softened.

2. In a bowl, whisk flour with ½ cup (125 mL) cream until smooth; add remaining cream. Add to pan along with stock. Bring to a boil, stirring, for 3 minutes or until sauce thickens. Remove from heat. Stir in tomatoes, Parmesan and basil. (Can be prepared to this point, covered and refrigerated for up to 1 day.)

3. In a large pot of boiling salted water, cook pasta for 7 minutes or until almost tender. Add broccoli; cook for 2 minutes or until broccoli is bright green and crisp, and pasta is just tender. Drain; chill under cold water. Drain well and return to pot. Stir in tuna and sauce. Spread in baking dish. (Casserole can be prepared to this point; cover and refrigerate for up to 4 hours before serving. Increase baking time by 15 minutes.)

4. In a bowl, combine bread crumbs and Asiago cheese; sprinkle over top. Bake in preheated oven for 40 to 45 minutes or until golden and center is piping hot.

Tuna Noodle Bake with Cheddar Crumb Topping

Makes 4 to 6 servings

This recipe takes an old standby to new heights. What's great, too, is that it keeps well in the fridge for up to 2 days before baking. Just pop it in the oven when you get home from work for an effortless meal. Serve with a crisp green salad.

Tip

To make ahead, cook noodles, rinse under cold water to chill; drain. Combine cold noodles and cold sauce; spoon into casserole dish, cover and refrigerate. Add crumb topping just before baking to prevent it from getting soggy.

- Preheat oven to 350°F (180°C)
- 13- by 9-inch (33 by 23 cm) casserole dish, lightly greased

1 tbsp	butter	15 mL
8 oz	mushrooms, sliced	250 g
¾ cup	chopped green onions	175 mL
2 tbsp	all-purpose flour	30 mL
1	can (10 oz/284 mL) chicken broth, undiluted	1
1 cup	milk	250 mL
4 oz	cream cheese, softened	125 g
1	can (6 oz/170 g) solid white tuna, drained and flaked	1
1 cup	frozen peas	250 mL
8 oz	broad egg noodles	250 g

Cheddar Crumb Topping

½ cup	dry bread crumbs	125 mL
2 tbsp	melted butter	30 mL
1 cup	shredded Cheddar cheese	250 mL

1. In a saucepan, melt butter over medium heat. Add mushrooms and green onions; cook, stirring, for 3 minutes or until softened.

2. Blend in flour; pour in broth and milk. Bring to a boil, stirring constantly, until slightly thickened. Stir in cream cheese until melted. Add tuna and peas; cook 2 minutes more or until heated through. Remove from heat.

3. Cook noodles in a large pot of boiling water until tender but still firm. Drain well. Stir noodles into sauce. Spoon into prepared casserole dish.

4. *Cheddar Crumb Topping:* In a bowl, toss bread crumbs with melted butter; add Cheddar cheese. Just before baking, sprinkle topping over noodles.

5. Bake in preheated oven for about 30 minutes (10 minutes longer if refrigerated) or until top is golden.

Company Chicken Tetrazzini

With leftover cooked chicken or turkey, you can make a wonderful pasta dish that's great for company. To make the dish in advance, cook the sauce, cover and refrigerate. Boil the pasta, rinse under cold water and chill. Combine the cold sauce and pasta up to 4 hours before the dish goes in the oven. (This prevents the pasta from absorbing too much of the sauce.)

Variation

This casserole also works well with ham instead of chicken.

- Preheat oven to 350°F (180°C)
- 13- by 9-inch (33 by 23 cm) baking dish, greased

2 tbsp	butter	30 mL
8 oz	mushrooms, sliced	250 g
4	green onions, finely chopped	4
1 tsp	dried basil leaves	5 mL
¼ cup	all-purpose flour	60 mL
2 cups	chicken or turkey stock	500 mL
½ cup	whipping (35%) cream or table (18%) cream	125 mL
¼ cup	medium-dry sherry	60 mL
2 cups	cubed cooked chicken or turkey	500 mL
⅔ cup	freshly grated Parmesan cheese	150 mL
	Salt and freshly ground black pepper	
8 oz	broad egg noodles	250 g

1. In a large saucepan, melt butter over medium-high heat. Add mushrooms, green onions and basil; cook for 4 minutes or until softened. In a bowl, blend flour with ⅓ cup (75 mL) stock to make a smooth paste; stir in remaining stock. Pour into saucepan; bring to a boil, stirring, until thickened. Add cream, sherry and chicken; cook over medium heat for 2 to 3 minutes or until heated through. Remove from heat. Stir in half the Parmesan cheese; season with salt and pepper to taste.

2. Cook noodles in a large pot of boiling salted water until almost tender but firm. Drain well. Return to pot; add chicken mixture and toss to coat well. Spoon into prepared baking dish. Sprinkle with remaining Parmesan cheese. Bake for 30 to 35 minutes or until heated through. (If refrigerated, cook 10 minutes more or until piping hot in center.)

Rice, Beans and Grains

Herb Rice Pilaf

This herb-infused rice makes the perfect accompaniment to a wide range of dishes. Try it with fish, chicken, beef, lamb or pork.

Tip

To save time, make ahead and reheat in the microwave before serving.

Variation

Saffron Rice Pilaf

Substitute ¼ tsp (1 mL) crushed saffron threads for the thyme.

2 tbsp	butter	30 mL
1	small onion, finely chopped	1
1	clove garlic, minced	1
½ tsp	dried thyme leaves	2 mL
	Freshly ground black pepper	
1½ cups	long-grain white rice	375 mL
3 cups	chicken or vegetable stock	750 mL
1	small red bell pepper, finely diced	1
¼ cup	chopped fresh parsley	60 mL

1. In a large saucepan, melt butter over medium heat. Add onion, garlic, thyme and pepper; cook, stirring often, for 3 minutes or until softened.

2. Add rice and stock; bring to a boil. Reduce heat to low; cover and simmer for 15 minutes or until most of stock is absorbed.

3. Stir in red pepper; cover and cook for 7 to 9 minutes more or until rice is tender. Stir in parsley; let stand, uncovered, for 5 minutes.

Wild and Brown Rice Pilaf

Makes 6 servings

You need only a small amount of expensive wild rice combined with brown rice to make this colorful side dish flecked with red pepper.

Tip

Instead of pecans, use walnuts or toasted slivered almonds.

½ cup	wild rice	125 mL
3 cups	chicken stock	750 mL
2 tbsp	butter	30 mL
1	onion, finely chopped	1
1½ tsp	chopped fresh thyme (or ½ tsp/2 mL dried)	7 mL
1 cup	long-grain brown rice	250 mL
1	red bell pepper, finely diced	1
⅓ cup	coarsely chopped pecans (optional)	75 mL
¼ cup	chopped fresh parsley	60 mL
	Salt and freshly ground black pepper	

1. Rinse wild rice under cold water. Place in small saucepan with 1 cup (250 mL) of chicken stock. Bring to a boil, reduce heat and simmer, covered, for 15 minutes or until most of stock is absorbed.

2. In a medium saucepan, heat butter over medium-high heat. Add onion and thyme and cook, stirring often, for 2 minutes or until onion is softened. Add partially cooked wild rice, brown rice and remaining stock; bring to a boil. Reduce heat to low, cover and simmer for 20 minutes or until rice is almost tender. Stir in red pepper and cook for 5 minutes more or until liquid is absorbed. Let stand, uncovered, for 5 minutes.

3. Fluff rice with a fork and stir in pecans, if using, and parsley. Season with salt and pepper to taste.

Vegetable Fried Rice

Makes 4 servings

Use this recipe as a guide to create your own versions of fried rice, depending on what type of veggies you have in the fridge. With rice cooked ahead, it takes no time to prepare this quick supper dish.

Variations
Chicken or Pork Fried Rice

Cut 8 oz (250 g) chicken breasts or lean boneless pork loin into thin strips. In a skillet, heat 1 tbsp (15 mL) oil over medium-high heat; cook meat, stirring, for 5 minutes or until no longer pink. Remove; keep warm. Continue with recipe as directed. Return meat to skillet with bean sprouts.

Instead of peas, try substituting blanched diced carrots, snow peas cut into 1-inch (2.5 cm) pieces, 1 zucchini, halved lengthwise and sliced, or small broccoli florets.

1 tbsp	vegetable oil	15 mL
3	green onions, chopped	3
1½ tsp	minced gingerroot	7 mL
1	clove garlic, minced	1
3 cups	cold cooked rice	750 mL
1 cup	frozen peas	250 mL
½	red bell pepper, cut into thin strips, 1½ inches (4 cm) long	½
1 tsp	mild curry paste (optional)	5 mL
2 cups	bean sprouts	500 mL
2 tbsp	soy sauce	30 mL

1. In a large nonstick skillet, heat oil over high heat. Add green onions, ginger and garlic; cook, stirring, for 15 seconds or until fragrant. Add rice, peas and pepper; cook, stirring often, for 5 to 7 minutes or until rice is heated through and vegetables are tender.

2. In a small bowl, combine soy sauce and curry paste, if using; stir into rice mixture along with bean sprouts. Cook, stirring, for 1 to 2 minutes or until heated through. Serve immediately.

Wild Mushroom Risotto

Risotto is hugely popular these days. And no wonder — its creamy appeal makes it a modern comfort food. It may seem intimidating to make at home, but it's easy to do provided you don't wander away from the stove. What else is key about risotto? It waits for no one, so call everyone to the table as you add the last ladle of stock to the saucepan.

Tip

A proper risotto is made with Italian short-grain rice, which has a relatively high starch content. As it cooks, it gives off the starch and the constant stirring results in a creamy, moist texture similar to porridge. Arborio rice is the most widely available short-grain variety; look for the word "superfino" on the package to ensure you are buying a superior grade. Vialone nano and carnaroli are two other types of short-grain Italian rice that make wonderful risotto. They are not quite as starchy as Arborio and require slightly less stock in cooking.

5 cups	lightly salted chicken or vegetable stock (approx.)	1.25 L
2 tbsp	butter, divided	30 mL
2 tbsp	olive oil, divided	30 mL
1 lb	assorted mushrooms, such as cremini, shiitake and oyster, coarsely chopped	500 g
2	cloves garlic, minced	2
1 tbsp	chopped fresh thyme or 1 tsp (5 mL) dried	15 mL
1/4 tsp	freshly ground black pepper	1 mL
1	small onion, finely chopped	1
1 1/2 cups	short-grain rice, such as Arborio	375 mL
1/2 cup	white wine or stock	125 mL
1/3 cup	freshly grated Parmesan cheese	75 mL
	Salt	
2 tbsp	chopped fresh parsley	30 mL

1. In a large saucepan, bring stock to a boil; reduce heat to low and keep hot.

2. In a heavy-bottomed medium saucepan, heat 1 tbsp (15 mL) each butter and oil over medium heat. Add mushrooms, garlic, thyme and pepper; cook, stirring often, for 5 to 7 minutes or until tender. Remove and set aside.

3. Add remaining butter and oil to saucepan; cook onion, stirring, for 2 minutes or until softened. Add rice; stir for 1 minute. Add wine; stir until absorbed.

4. Add 1 cup (250 mL) hot stock; adjust heat to a simmer so stock bubbles and is absorbed slowly.

5. When absorbed, continue adding 1 cup (250 mL) stock at a time, stirring almost constantly, for 15 minutes. Add mushroom mixture; cook, stirring often, adding more stock when absorbed, until rice is just tender but slightly firm in the center. Mixture should be creamy; add more stock or water, if necessary. (Total cooking time will be 20 to 25 minutes.)

6. Add Parmesan cheese; adjust seasoning with salt and pepper to taste. Spoon into warm shallow serving bowls or onto plates. Sprinkle with parsley; serve immediately.

Risotto Primavera

Feel free to change this
recipe and use the freshest
vegetables you can find
when shopping at the
market. For instance, add
mushrooms, sugar snap
peas or red bell pepper for
delectable variations.

Tip

A proper risotto is made
with Italian short-grain
rice, which has a relatively
high starch content. As
it cooks, it gives off the
starch and the constant
stirring results in a creamy,
moist texture similar to
porridge. Arborio rice is
the most widely available
short-grain variety; look
for the word "superfino"
on the package to ensure
you are buying a superior
grade. Vialone nano and
carnaroli are two other
types of short-grain Italian
rice that make wonderful
risotto. They are not quite
as starchy as Arborio and
require slightly less stock
in cooking.

5 cups	lightly salted vegetable or chicken stock	1.25 L
1 tbsp	butter	15 mL
1	small onion, chopped	1
2	small carrots, peeled and finely diced	2
1 cup	thin asparagus, cut into 1-inch (2.5 cm) diagonal pieces	250 mL
1	zucchini, finely diced	1
1	large ripe firm tomato, seeded and finely diced	1
½ cup	shelled fresh peas or thawed frozen peas	125 mL
1 tbsp	olive oil	15 mL
1½ cups	short-grain rice, such as Arborio (see Tip, left)	375 mL
⅓ cup	freshly grated Parmesan cheese	75 mL
¼ cup	chopped fresh basil	60 mL
	Salt and freshly ground black pepper	

1. In a large saucepan, bring stock to a boil; reduce heat to low and keep hot.

2. In a large heavy-bottomed saucepan, heat butter over medium heat. Cook onion and carrots, stirring occasionally, for 5 minutes. Add asparagus and zucchini; cook, stirring occasionally, for 3 minutes or until vegetables are just tender. Remove vegetables and place in a bowl along with tomato and peas.

3. Add oil to saucepan; add rice and cook over medium-high heat, stirring, until grains are coated. Add 1 cup (250 mL) of the hot stock; adjust heat to a simmer so stock bubbles and is absorbed slowly, stirring constantly. When absorbed, continue adding 1 cup (250 mL) of the stock at a time, stirring almost constantly, for 15 minutes.

4. Add vegetable mixture; cook, stirring often, adding more stock when absorbed, until rice is just tender but slightly firm in the center. Mixture should be creamy; add more stock or water, if necessary. (Total cooking time will be 20 to 25 minutes.)

5. Stir in Parmesan cheese and basil. Season with salt and pepper to taste. Spoon onto warm dinner plates and serve immediately.

Baked Risotto with Spinach

Makes 8 servings

Oven-baked risotto makes an elegant and colorful dish that's perfect for entertaining.

Tips

To clean leeks: Trim dark green tops. Cut down center almost to root end and chop. Rinse in a sink full of cold water to remove sand; scoop up leeks and place in colander to drain or use a salad spinner.

Make risotto up to 1 day ahead. Cover and refrigerate. Increase baking time by 10 minutes.

- Preheat oven to 350°F (180°C)
- 13- by 9-inch (33 by 23 cm) baking dish, greased

2	packages (each 10 oz/300 g) fresh spinach	2
2 tbsp	butter, divided	30 mL
2	leeks, white and light green parts only, cut in half lengthwise, then sliced crosswise (see Tip, left)	2
½ tsp	salt	2 mL
¼ tsp	freshly ground black pepper	1 mL
¼ tsp	freshly grated nutmeg	1 mL
2½ cups	short-grain rice, such as Arborio (see Tip, page 376)	625 mL
3	cloves garlic, finely chopped	3
7 cups	hot chicken or vegetable stock	1.75 L
4 oz	herb and garlic cream cheese or herb goat cheese	125 g
½ cup	freshly grated Parmesan cheese	125 mL

1. Rinse spinach; remove tough ends. Place in Dutch oven with just the water clinging to leaves; cook over medium-high heat, stirring, until just wilted. Drain well and squeeze dry; finely chop.

2. In a large nonstick skillet, melt 1 tbsp (15 mL) butter over medium heat; cook leeks, stirring, for 3 minutes or until softened. Add spinach, salt, pepper and nutmeg; cook, stirring, for 5 minutes or until vegetables are tender.

3. In a Dutch oven, heat remaining butter over medium heat; cook rice and garlic, stirring, for 2 minutes. Add 5 cups (1.25 L) hot stock; bring to a boil. Reduce heat to medium-low, cover and simmer for 15 minutes or until rice is almost tender and most of liquid is absorbed.

4. Stir in remaining stock and cream cheese until blended; add spinach mixture. Spread in prepared baking dish. Sprinkle with Parmesan. Bake in preheated oven for 25 to 30 minutes or until center is piping hot and top is light golden.

Spanish Vegetable Paella

Makes 4 servings as a main course or 6 as a side dish

Traditional paella is made in a wide shallow pan, but today's nonstick skillet makes a very good substitute and reduces the amount of oil needed for this dish.

Tip

Try a variety of different vegetables, including bite-size pieces of broccoli, cauliflower, asparagus, green beans, bell peppers and zucchini.

● Preheat oven to 375°F (190°C)

4 cups	assorted prepared vegetables (see Tip, left)	1 L
3½ cups	chicken or vegetable stock	875 mL
¼ tsp	saffron threads, crushed	1 mL
Pinch	hot pepper flakes	Pinch
	Salt	
2 tbsp	olive oil	30 mL
4	green onions, chopped	4
3	large cloves garlic, finely chopped	3
1½ cups	short-grain white rice, such as Arborio	375 mL

1. Cook vegetables (except peppers and zucchini) in a saucepan of boiling, lightly salted water for 1 minute. Rinse under cold water to chill; drain well.

2. In the same saucepan, bring stock to a boil. Add saffron and hot pepper flakes; season with salt to taste. Keep warm.

3. In a large nonstick skillet, heat oil over medium-high heat. Add green onions and garlic; cook, stirring, for 1 minute. Add vegetables to skillet; cook, stirring often, for 4 minutes or until lightly colored. Stir in rice and hot stock mixture. Reduce heat so rice cooks at a gentle boil: cook, uncovered, without stirring, for 10 minutes or until most of the liquid is absorbed.

4. Cover skillet with lid or foil. (If skillet handle is not ovenproof, wrap in double layer of foil.) Bake for 15 minutes or until all liquid is absorbed and rice is tender. Remove; let stand, covered, for 5 minutes before serving.

Basmati Rice with Ginger

This is my preferred way to prepare basmati rice — with ginger and aromatic spices, resulting in a wonderful flavor. Serve it to accompany a curry dish made with chicken, lamb or lentils.

Tip

Always rinse and soak the basmati rice to remove excess starch. This results in a less sticky, more fluffy rice when cooked.

Variation

Saffron Basmati Rice with Pine Nuts

Replace 1½ cups (375 mL) of the water with chicken or vegetable stock and reduce salt to ¼ tsp (1 mL). Replace gingerroot, cinnamon and bay leaf with ¼ tsp (1 mL) saffron threads, crushed. Add ¼ cup (60 mL) lightly toasted pine nuts along with cilantro.

1½ cups	basmati rice	375 mL
1 tbsp	butter or oil	15 mL
1	small onion, finely chopped	1
1 tbsp	minced gingerroot	15 mL
1	stick cinnamon, broken in half	1
1	large bay leaf, broken in half	1
1 tsp	salt	5 mL
¼ cup	chopped fresh cilantro (or 2 tbsp/ 30 mL chives or green onions)	60 mL

1. Place rice in sieve and rinse. Transfer to a bowl and add water to cover. Let soak for 15 minutes. Drain.

2. In a medium saucepan, melt butter over medium heat. Cook onion, ginger, cinnamon and bay leaf, stirring, for 2 minutes or until onion is softened.

3. Add rice, 2¼ cups (550 mL) water and salt; bring to a boil. Reduce heat to low, cover and simmer for 10 minutes or until water is absorbed. Let stand, uncovered, for 5 minutes.

4. Fluff rice with a fork and remove and discard cinnamon stick and bay leaf. Transfer to serving dish and sprinkle with cilantro.

Jamaican Rice and Peas

Rice and peas is a traditional dish served throughout the Caribbean. This Jamaican version calls for kidney beans, but you could also use canned pigeon peas or black-eyed peas.

Tip

Instead of hot pepper flakes, add a whole Scotch bonnet pepper to the rice when cooking to give it a subtle peppery flavor. Discard whole pepper before serving.

1	can (14 oz/398 mL) light or regular coconut milk	1
1 tbsp	vegetable oil	15 mL
1	large onion, chopped	1
3	cloves garlic, chopped	3
2 tsp	chopped fresh thyme or ½ tsp (2 mL) dried thyme leaves	10 mL
¼ tsp	hot pepper flakes, or to taste	1 mL
1½ cups	long-grain white rice, rinsed	375 mL
½ tsp	salt	2 mL
¼ tsp	freshly ground black pepper	1 mL
1	can (19 oz/540 mL) kidney beans, rinsed and drained	1
4	green onions, sliced	4

1. Pour coconut milk into large glass measure. Add enough water to make 3 cups (750 mL). Stir to blend.

2. In a large saucepan, heat oil over medium-high heat. Cook onion, garlic, thyme and hot pepper flakes, stirring, for 2 minutes or until softened.

3. Add rice, coconut milk mixture, salt and pepper; bring to a boil. Reduce heat to low, cover and simmer for 15 minutes or until almost all of the liquid is absorbed. Stir in kidney beans and cook for 5 minutes or until rice is tender and beans are heated through.

4. Fluff rice with a fork and stir in green onions. Let stand, uncovered, for 5 minutes before serving.

Mexican Rice and Beans

Tip

To avoid skin irritation, wear rubber gloves when handling jalapeño peppers.

1 tbsp	vegetable oil	15 mL
1	onion, chopped	1
2	cloves garlic, minced	2
1	green bell pepper, diced	1
1 to 2	jalapeño peppers, seeded and minced (optional)	1 to 2
1 tbsp	chili powder	15 mL
1 tsp	dried oregano leaves	5 mL
2	tomatoes, seeded and diced	2
2 cups	vegetable stock	500 mL
1 cup	long-grain white rice	250 mL
1	can (19 oz/540 mL) black beans or kidney beans, drained and rinsed	1
¼ cup	chopped cilantro (optional)	60 mL

1. In a large saucepan, heat oil over medium heat. Cook onion, garlic, green pepper, jalapeño peppers, if using, chili powder and oregano, stirring, for 5 minutes or until softened.

2. Add tomatoes; cook for 3 minutes or until sauce-like. Add stock and bring to a boil.

3. Stir in rice and black beans. Reduce heat to low; cover and cook for 20 minutes or until rice is tender. Stir in cilantro, if using.

Baked White Beans and Vegetables with Garlic Crumb Crust

A simple combo of beans and vegetables is a terrific side dish or main course that will delight not only the vegetarians in the crowd but everyone else as well. As a prelude to dinner, your home will be filled with the heavenly aroma of garlic from the crunchy crumb topping

Tip

To seed tomatoes, cut in half crosswise and gently squeeze out seeds.

- Preheat oven to 350°F (180°C)
- 11- by 7-inch (28 by 18 cm) baking dish, greased

1 tbsp	olive oil	15 mL
2 cups	chopped Spanish onion	500 mL
3	cloves garlic, finely chopped	3
1 tbsp	balsamic vinegar	15 mL
5	tomatoes, seeded and diced	5
1 tbsp	chopped fresh thyme or 1 tsp (5 mL) dried thyme leaves	15 mL
1	bay leaf	1
¾ tsp	salt	3 mL
¼ tsp	freshly ground black pepper	1 mL
2	small zucchini, halved lengthwise, thickly sliced	2
1	red bell pepper, diced	1
1	yellow bell pepper, diced	1
1	can (19 oz/540 mL) white kidney beans, drained and rinsed	1

Garlic Crumb Crust

1½ cups	soft fresh bread crumbs (see Tip, opposite)	375 mL
2 tbsp	chopped fresh parsley	30 mL
1	large clove garlic, minced	1
2 tbsp	olive oil	30 mL

1. In a Dutch oven or large saucepan, heat oil over medium heat. Cook onions and garlic, stirring, for 5 minutes or until softened. Add balsamic vinegar and cook until evaporated. Add tomatoes, thyme, bay leaf, salt and pepper. Bring to boil. Reduce heat, cover and simmer for 20 minutes.

2. Add zucchini and red and yellow peppers; cook for 8 to 10 minutes or until vegetables are tender-crisp. Gently stir in beans.

Tip

To make fresh bread crumbs: Place 3 slices of crusty bread in a food processor and pulse until fine.

3. Spoon mixture into prepared baking dish. (Can be prepared up to this point, covered and refrigerated for up to 1 day.)

4. *Garlic Crumb Crust:* In a bowl, combine bread crumbs, parsley and garlic. Drizzle with olive oil and toss to coat. Sprinkle crumb topping over beans; bake in preheated oven for 35 minutes (10 minutes longer if bean mixture is made ahead and refrigerated) or until bubbly and top is golden.

Easy Baked Beans

Makes 4 servings

Here's an easy, spruced-up bean dish flavored with bacon that uses a can of baked beans. No one will know that it wasn't made from scratch.

Tip

Cans of baked beans range in size depending on brand. Use 3 to 4 cups (750 mL to 1 L).

4	slices bacon, chopped	4
1	small onion, finely chopped	1
1	can (28 oz/796 mL) baked beans in tomato sauce	1
2 tbsp	packed brown sugar	30 mL
1/4 cup	barbecue sauce or ketchup	60 mL
1 tbsp	Worcestershire sauce	15 mL
1 tsp	Dijon mustard	5 mL

1. In a large saucepan over medium-high heat, cook bacon, stirring often, for 5 minutes or until crisp. Drain fat from pan.

2. Add onion and cook, stirring, for 2 minutes or until softened. Add beans, brown sugar, barbecue sauce, Worcestershire sauce and mustard; bring to a boil. Reduce heat and simmer, stirring occasionally, for 5 minutes or until flavors have blended.

Molasses Baked Beans

Here's an old-time favorite that stirs memories of the pioneer spirit. This rustic dish is a winter standby and wonderful when served with home-baked bread.

Vegetarian Variation

For a vegetarian version, omit bacon and cook onions and garlic in 2 tbsp (30 mL) vegetable oil.

- Preheat oven to 300°F (150°C)
- 12-cup (3 L) casserole dish or bean pot

1 lb	dried Great Northern or white pea beans, rinsed and picked over (about 2¼ cups/550 mL)	500 g
6	slices lean smoky bacon, chopped	6
1	large onion, chopped	1
3	cloves garlic, finely chopped	3
1	can (7½ oz/213 mL) tomato sauce	1
⅓ cup	fancy molasses	75 mL
¼ cup	packed brown sugar	60 mL
2 tbsp	balsamic vinegar	30 mL
2 tsp	dry mustard	10 mL
1 tsp	salt	5 mL
¼ tsp	freshly ground black pepper	1 mL

1. In a Dutch oven or large saucepan, combine beans with 6 cups (1.5 L) cold water. Bring to a boil over high heat; boil for 2 minutes. Remove from heat, cover and let stand for 1 hour.

2. Drain beans and cover with 8 cups (2 L) cold water. Bring to a boil; reduce heat, cover and simmer for 30 to 40 minutes or until beans are just tender but still hold their shape. Drain, reserving 2 cups (500 mL) cooking liquid. Place beans in casserole dish or bean pot.

3. Meanwhile, in a saucepan, cook bacon over medium heat, stirring often, for 5 minutes or until crisp. Drain all but 2 tbsp (30 mL) fat from pan. Add onion and garlic; cook, stirring, for 3 minutes or until softened.

4. Add 2 cups (500 mL) reserved bean-cooking liquid, tomato sauce, molasses, brown sugar, balsamic vinegar, mustard, salt and pepper. Stir into beans.

5. Cover and bake in preheated oven for 2½ to 3 hours or until most of liquid has been absorbed.

Black Bean Salsa Chili

I particularly like this meatless chili because it requires little cooking or fuss. Any kind of canned beans, such as chickpeas or kidney beans, can be used. Since canned beans and salsa tend to be salty, there's no need to season with extra salt.

Tip

Medium salsa gives a burst of heat. For a tamer chili, use mild salsa.

Variation

Add 1 cup (250 mL) diced cooked ham or sliced smoked sausage, such as kielbasa, along with beans, if desired, for a meat-based chili.

2 tsp	vegetable oil	10 mL
1	small onion, chopped	1
2	cloves garlic, minced	2
1	large green bell pepper, diced	1
2 tsp	chili powder	10 mL
1 tsp	dried oregano leaves	5 mL
½ tsp	ground cumin	2 mL
1	can (19 oz/540 mL) black beans, drained and rinsed	1
1 cup	frozen or canned corn kernels	250 mL
1½ cups	mild or medium salsa (see Tip, left)	375 mL
¾ cup	water or stock (approx.)	175 mL
1 cup	shredded Cheddar cheese	250 mL
¼ cup	chopped fresh cilantro (optional)	60 mL

1. In a large saucepan, heat oil over medium heat. Cook onion, garlic, green pepper, chili powder, oregano and cumin, stirring, for 5 minutes or until vegetables are softened.

2. Stir in black beans, corn, salsa and water to cover. Bring to a boil; reduce heat, cover and simmer for 10 minutes. Ladle into bowls and serve topped with cheese and cilantro, if using.

Southwest Tortilla Vegetable Bake

Tip

To make ahead, cover and refrigerate for up to 1 day or overwrap in heavy-duty foil and freeze for up to 1 month. Let thaw completely in refrigerator for up to 24 hours. Increase baking time by 15 minutes.

- Preheat oven to 350°F (180°C)
- 13- by 9-inch (33 by 23 cm) baking dish, greased

1 tbsp	vegetable oil	15 mL
1	large onion, chopped	1
3	cloves garlic, minced	3
2	large green bell peppers, diced	2
2 tsp	dried oregano leaves	10 mL
2 tsp	ground cumin	10 mL
1	can (12 oz/341 mL) corn kernels, drained	1
1	jar (26 oz/700 mL) medium salsa, divided	1
2	cans (each 19 oz/540 mL) black beans, drained and rinsed	2
2 tsp	chili powder	10 mL
8 oz	cream cheese, softened	250 g
¾ cup	sour cream or yogurt	175 mL
½ cup	chopped fresh cilantro or parsley	125 mL
7	9-inch (23 cm) flour tortillas	7
2 cups	shredded mozzarella cheese	500 mL

1. In a large nonstick skillet, heat oil over medium heat; cook onion, garlic, green peppers, oregano and cumin, stirring often, for 10 minutes or until vegetables are tender. Remove from heat; stir in corn and $1\frac{1}{2}$ cups (375 mL) salsa.

2. In a bowl, using a fork, mash beans with chili powder. In a separate bowl, blend cream cheese with sour cream; stir in cilantro.

3. Arrange 3 tortillas in prepared baking dish, covering bottom and sides. Spread with half the bean mixture; layer with half the vegetable and cream cheese mixtures. Top with 2 tortillas, tucking in sides. Repeat layers. Top with remaining 2 tortillas; spread with remaining salsa.

4. Sprinkle with cheese; cover loosely with foil. Bake in preheated oven for 30 minutes. Uncover and bake for 25 minutes longer or until filling is bubbly. Let stand 5 minutes before cutting.

Indian-Style Lentils

If you have a vegetarian in the family, you can count on this Indian-inspired dish with its bold seasonings as a reliable main course dish. A bowlful makes a quick and easy supper.

Variation

For a meat lover's version of this dish, add chopped leftover roast lamb, roast beef or baked ham for the last 10 minutes of cooking.

1 tbsp	vegetable oil	15 mL
1	onion, chopped	1
3	cloves garlic, finely chopped	3
1 tbsp	minced gingerroot	15 mL
2 tsp	ground cumin	10 mL
1 tsp	ground coriander	5 mL
1/2 tsp	salt	2 mL
	Freshly ground black pepper	
1 cup	green lentils, rinsed and sorted	250 mL
1	can (19 oz/540 mL) tomatoes, including juice, chopped	1
1 1/2 cups	vegetable or chicken stock	375 mL
1/3 cup	chopped fresh cilantro or parsley	75 mL

1. In a large saucepan, heat oil over medium heat. Add onion, garlic, ginger, cumin, coriander, salt and pepper; cook, stirring, for 3 minutes or until softened.

2. Add lentils, tomatoes with juice and stock. Bring to a boil; reduce heat, cover and simmer for 35 minutes or until lentils are tender. Stir in cilantro; adjust seasoning with salt and pepper to taste.

Bistro Lentils with Smoked Sausage

It's Friday night. You've worked hard all week. Don't even bother setting the table. Here's a supper dish that's easy to balance on your lap while you relax in front of the TV. As an added bonus, this dish goes great with a cold beer.

Tips

The smaller-sized green Laird lentils hold their shape in cooking and are the kind I prefer for this recipe.

Any kind of smoked sausage or ham works well.

3½ cups	chicken or vegetable stock (approx.)	875 mL
1½ cups	lentils, rinsed and sorted (see Tips, left)	375 mL
½ tsp	dried thyme leaves	2 mL
2 tbsp	olive oil	30 mL
1 cup	diced red onions	250 mL
3	cloves garlic, finely chopped	3
2	carrots, peeled and diced	2
1 cup	diced fennel or celery	250 mL
1	red bell pepper, diced	1
2 tbsp	balsamic vinegar	30 mL
8 oz	smoked sausage, such as kielbasa, cut into ½-inch (1 cm) chunks (see Tips, left)	250 g
	Freshly ground black pepper	
¼ cup	chopped fresh parsley	60 mL

1. In a large saucepan, bring stock to a boil over high heat. Add lentils and thyme; reduce heat to medium-low, cover and simmer for 25 to 30 minutes or until lentils are just tender but still hold their shape.

2. Meanwhile, heat oil in a large nonstick skillet over medium heat. Add onions, garlic, carrots and fennel; cook, stirring often, for 8 minutes. Add red pepper; cook, stirring, for 2 minutes more or until vegetables are just tender. Stir in vinegar; remove from heat.

3. Add vegetables and smoked sausage to lentils in saucepan; season with pepper to taste. Cover and cook for 5 to 8 minutes more or until sausage is heated through. (Add more stock or water, if necessary, to prevent lentils from sticking.) Stir in parsley. Serve warm or at room temperature.

Bulgur Risotto with Tomatoes and Basil

Makes 4 servings

Here is one of my favorite side dishes. It's a bulgur-based spinoff of traditional risotto, which is made with Arborio rice. Bulgur has a wonderful nutty taste and is made from wheat berries that have been cooked, dried and cracked.

Tip

Medium bulgur will take 10 minutes to cook; coarse whole-grain bulgur (sold in health food stores) will take 15 minutes. Fine bulgur is not recommended for this recipe, as it becomes mushy.

Variation

Orzo Risotto with Tomatoes and Basil

Replace bulgur with orzo, a rice-shaped pasta. Cook orzo until creamy and soft, but with a slight bite.

1 tbsp	butter	15 mL
1	small onion, finely chopped	1
1	large clove garlic, finely chopped	1
1 cup	bulgur (see Tip, left)	250 mL
1 cup	chopped seeded peeled tomatoes	250 mL
2 cups	chicken or vegetable stock (approx.)	500 mL
1/4 cup	freshly grated Parmesan cheese	60 mL
2 tbsp	chopped fresh basil	30 mL
	Freshly ground black pepper	

1. In a medium saucepan, melt butter over medium-high heat. Cook onion and garlic, stirring, for 2 minutes or until softened. Add bulgur and cook, stirring, for 1 minute or until lightly toasted.

2. Add tomatoes and $1\frac{1}{2}$ cups (375 mL) stock. Bring to a boil; reduce heat if necessary and boil gently, stirring often and adding more stock as needed, for 10 to 15 minutes or until most of liquid is absorbed and bulgur is tender but firm (mixture should still be quite moist). Stir in Parmesan and basil; season with pepper to taste. Serve immediately.

Baked Polenta
with Roasted Vegetables

Makes 8 servings

This impressive dish, which features plenty of vegetables, appeals to both vegetarians and meat eaters.

Tip

Another way to serve firm polenta is to cut it into squares and grill alongside other vegetables, such as peppers and zucchini, or with Italian sausages. Prepare half the polenta as directed and omit garlic and butter. Spread hot polenta in oiled 13- by 9-inch (33 by 23 cm) baking pan and let stand for 30 minutes or until cool and firm. Cut into squares or rectangles. Brush with a little olive oil and lightly brown on a hot, greased grill or stovetop grill or in nonstick skillet.

- Preheat oven to 425°F (220°C)
- 2 rimmed baking sheets
- 13- by 9-inch (33 by 23 cm) baking dish, greased

2	zucchini	2
1	small eggplant (about 1 lb/500 g)	1
1	red bell pepper	1
1	yellow bell pepper	1
1	large red onion	1
2 tbsp	olive oil	30 mL
1 tbsp	chopped fresh rosemary or 1 tsp (5 mL) dried rosemary leaves, crumbled	15 mL
½ tsp	salt	2 mL
½ tsp	freshly ground black pepper	2 mL
¼ cup	chopped fresh parsley	60 mL
	Garlic Polenta (see recipe, opposite)	
2 cups	tomato pasta sauce	500 mL
2 cups	shredded mozzarella cheese	500 mL
⅓ cup	freshly grated Parmesan cheese	75 mL

1. Halve zucchini lengthwise and thickly slice. Cut eggplant into ½-inch (1 cm) slices, then cut into 1½-inch (4 cm) pieces. Cut peppers into 1-inch (2.5 cm) pieces. Cut onion into thin lengthwise wedges. Arrange vegetables on baking sheets. Drizzle with oil; sprinkle with rosemary, salt and pepper. Roast in preheated oven, stirring occasionally, for 25 to 30 minutes or until tender. Transfer to a bowl; stir in parsley.

2. Cut prepared polenta in half crosswise; using two lifters, gently transfer one half to baking dish. Spread with half the tomato sauce, then half the vegetables and half the mozzarella and Parmesan cheeses. Repeat layers. (Can be prepared up to this point, covered and refrigerated for up to 2 days.) Bake in 350°F (180°C) oven for 50 to 60 minutes or until piping hot in center and cheese is melted.

Tip

Make polenta ahead.
Cover and refrigerate for
up to 1 day.

Garlic Polenta

• Rimmed baking sheet, greased

3	cloves garlic, minced	3
2 tsp	salt	10 mL
2 cups	cornmeal	500 mL
⅓ cup	freshly grated Parmesan cheese	75 mL
2 tbsp	butter	30 mL

1. In a Dutch oven or large saucepan, bring 7 cups
   (1.75 L) water, garlic and salt to a boil; gradually whisk
   in cornmeal until thickened. Reduce heat to low; cook,
   stirring often with wooden spoon, for 15 to 20 minutes
   or until polenta is thick enough to mound on spoon.
   Stir in Parmesan cheese and butter.

2. Spread onto prepared baking sheet; cover with plastic
   wrap. Refrigerate for 30 minutes or until firm.

Creamy Polenta

Makes 4 servings

Polenta is Italian comfort
food — a creamy cornmeal
porridge that is wonderful
served with any kind of
a meat or vegetable pasta
sauce or swirled with basil
pesto sauce and extra
Parmesan.

Tip

If using only water when
cooking the polenta, add
1 tsp (5 mL) salt to the
boiling water.

1½ cups	chicken stock or water	375 mL
¾ cup	yellow cornmeal	175 mL
¼ cup	freshly grated Parmesan cheese	60 mL
2 tbsp	butter	30 mL
	Salt (optional)	

1. In a large saucepan, bring stock and 1½ cups (375 mL)
   water to a boil; gradually whisk in cornmeal until
   thickened. Reduce heat to low; cook, stirring often with
   wooden spoon, for 15 to 20 minutes or until polenta is
   smooth and creamy.

2. Stir in Parmesan cheese and butter. Season with salt
   to taste.

Middle Eastern Couscous with Chickpeas

This impressive one-pot party dish features easy-to-use couscous and canned chickpeas with rich flavors of cumin, coriander and zesty orange. Refrigerate any extras and serve hot or cold for next day's lunch.

Tip

Fresh cilantro, also called coriander and Chinese parsley, lasts only a few days in the fridge before it deteriorates and turns tasteless. Wash cilantro well, spin dry and wrap in paper towels; store in plastic bag in the fridge. Leave the roots on — they keep the leaves fresh.

- 10-cup (2.5 L) casserole dish, greased

1½ cups	vegetable stock	375 mL
1½ cups	couscous	375 mL
2 cups	sliced peeled carrots (cut on the diagonal)	500 mL
1	large red bell pepper, diced	1
1	can (19 oz/540 mL) chickpeas, drained and rinsed	1
1 tbsp	olive oil	15 mL
1	large onion, chopped	1
3	cloves garlic, finely chopped	3
2 tbsp	minced gingerroot	30 mL
2 tsp	ground cumin	10 mL
1 tsp	ground coriander	5 mL
¾ tsp	salt	3 mL
¼ tsp	cayenne pepper	1 mL
1 cup	orange juice	250 mL
½ cup	raisins or dried cranberries	125 mL
1 tbsp	grated orange zest	15 mL
½ cup	chopped fresh cilantro or parsley	125 mL

1. In a saucepan, bring stock to a boil. Add couscous and remove from heat. Cover and let stand for 5 minutes. Fluff with fork. Transfer to prepared casserole dish.

2. In a small saucepan of boiling salted water, cook carrots for 3 minutes or until tender-crisp. Rinse in cold water; drain. Add carrots, red pepper and chickpeas to couscous in casserole and mix well.

3. In a large nonstick skillet, heat oil over medium-high heat. Cook onion, garlic, gingerroot, cumin, coriander, salt and cayenne, stirring, for 2 minutes. Stir in orange juice. Bring to a boil. Add raisins and orange zest. Remove from heat. Stir into couscous mixture until well combined. (Casserole can be prepared up to this point, covered and refrigerated for 1 day.)

4. Cover and microwave on High for 7 to 9 minutes (10 to 12 minutes if refrigerated), stirring once, or until mixture is steaming. Or cover and bake in preheated 350°F (180°C) oven for 45 to 50 minutes (10 minutes longer if refrigerated) or until mixture is steaming. Stir in cilantro.

Moroccan-Style Couscous

Here's a colorful side dish that's ready in 10 minutes. What could be simpler?

Tip
The dried fruits and nuts can be omitted for a basic version.

1½ cups	chicken stock	375 mL
½ tsp	ground cumin	2 mL
1 cup	couscous	250 mL
2	green onions, sliced	2
⅓ cup	raisins or slivered dried apricots	75 mL
3 tbsp	slivered almonds, shelled pistachios or chopped pecans	45 mL

1. In a small saucepan, bring chicken stock and cumin to a boil. Stir in couscous, green onions, raisins and almonds. Remove from heat; cover and let stand for 5 minutes. Fluff with fork and serve.

Mushroom Barley Pilaf

Makes 4 to 6 servings

Nutritionists recommend adding more grain to our diets. Here's a dish to serve to your family that is not only great-tasting, but wholesome besides.

Variation
Other nuts, such as skinned hazelnuts or unblanched almonds, can be substituted for the walnuts.

1 tbsp	butter	15 mL
2 cups	sliced mushrooms	500 mL
1	small onion, chopped	1
½ tsp	dried thyme or marjoram leaves	2 mL
1 cup	pearl barley, rinsed	250 mL
2½ cups	chicken or vegetable stock (approx.)	625 mL
⅓ cup	finely chopped walnuts or pecans	75 mL
¼ cup	freshly grated Parmesan cheese	60 mL
2 tbsp	chopped fresh parsley	30 mL
	Salt and freshly ground black pepper	

1. In a medium saucepan, heat butter over medium heat. Add mushrooms, onion and thyme; cook, stirring, for 5 minutes or until softened.

2. Stir in barley and stock; bring to a boil. Reduce heat, cover and simmer, stirring occasionally and adding more stock if necessary, for 30 minutes or until barley is tender.

3. Stir in walnuts, Parmesan and parsley; season with salt and pepper to taste.

Quinoa with Almonds

Thanks to a new awareness of the goodness of grains, we can find a much larger selection in supermarkets. One of my favorites is quinoa (pronounced *keen-wah*), an ancient grain that is high in protein and fiber. In this recipe, quinoa's mild, nutty flavor is paired with coriander and citrus.

Tips

When you buy quinoa, it has been rinsed and air-dried to remove the naturally occurring bitter saponins, a resin-like coating. Still, rinse it again before use to remove any powdery residue that may remain.

To toast almonds: Place nuts on a baking sheet in a 350°F (180°C) oven for 6 to 8 minutes, stirring occasionally, until lightly toasted.

1 tbsp	vegetable oil	15 mL
2	carrots, peeled and chopped	2
2	stalks celery, chopped	2
1	small onion, finely chopped	1
1½ tsp	ground coriander	7 mL
1 cup	quinoa, rinsed well	250 mL
1 cup	chicken stock	250 mL
1 tsp	grated orange or lemon zest	5 mL
1 cup	orange juice	250 mL
½ tsp	salt	2 mL
¼ tsp	freshly ground black pepper	1 mL
¼ cup	chopped fresh cilantro or parsley	60 mL
¼ cup	toasted sliced almonds	60 mL

1. In a medium saucepan, heat oil over medium heat. Cook carrots, celery, onion and coriander, stirring, for 5 minutes or until vegetables are softened. Add quinoa, stock, orange zest and juice, salt and pepper; bring to a boil. Reduce heat to medium-low, cover and simmer for 15 minutes or until quinoa is tender and liquid is absorbed.

2. Uncover and fluff quinoa with a fork. Let stand for 5 minutes. Stir in cilantro and almonds.

Vegetables

continued...

Root and Winter Vegetables

Fluffy Garlic Mashed Potatoes

Makes 6 servings

The secret to these creamy mashed potatoes is buttermilk. It adds a tangy flavor and keeps the potatoes moist so they reheat beautifully the next day.

Variation
Roasted Garlic Mashed Potatoes

Beat in a whole bulb of roasted garlic (instead of fresh garlic) in the above recipe. It may seem like a lot, but once roasted, garlic loses its harsh taste and becomes very mild and buttery.

6	large russet or Yukon gold potatoes (about 3 lbs/1.5 kg)	6
2 tbsp	butter or olive oil	30 mL
2	cloves garlic, finely chopped, or more to taste	2
½ cup	milk	125 mL
¾ cup	buttermilk or sour cream (approx.)	175 mL
	Salt and freshly ground black pepper or freshly grated nutmeg	

1. Peel potatoes and cut into 3-inch (7.5 cm) chunks. In a large saucepan, cook potatoes in boiling salted water until tender, about 20 minutes or until fork-tender. (Yukon gold potatoes take a few minutes longer.) Drain well and return to saucepan. Place over low heat and dry for 1 to 2 minutes.

2. Press potatoes through a food mill or ricer or mash with potato masher or use an electric mixer at low speed until very smooth. (Do not use a food processor or the potatoes will turn into glue.)

3. In a small saucepan, heat butter and garlic over medium-low heat for 1 to 2 minutes; do not let garlic brown. Add milk and heat until piping hot. Beat garlic mixture into potatoes along with enough buttermilk or sour cream to make a smooth purée. Adjust seasoning with salt and pepper or nutmeg to taste.

4. Place over medium heat, stirring occasionally, until potatoes are piping hot. Can be made a few hours ahead and reheated. Beat in additional milk or buttermilk to make potatoes creamy, if necessary.

Creamy Mashed Potato Casserole

Everyone's favorite do-ahead mashed potato casserole — perfect for a roast turkey or roast beef family dinner. For lump-free mashed potatoes, use a food mill or ricer instead of a potato masher.

Tips

Casserole can be prepared ahead through Step 2, covered and refrigerated for up to 2 days. Sprinkle with crumb topping before baking. Increase baking time by 10 minutes.

The type of potatoes used determines how fluffy your mashed potatoes will be. The starchy russet, or baking, variety produces fluffy mashed potatoes. Yellow-fleshed potatoes, such as Yukon gold, have a slightly buttery taste and make delicious mashed potatoes with a creamier texture. Regular white potatoes also make a creamy purée, although not as flavorful. New potatoes are not suitable for mashing as they don't have the starch content of storage potatoes.

- Preheat oven to 350°F (180°C)
- 8-cup (2 L) casserole dish, greased

6	large russet potatoes (about 3 lbs/1.5 kg) (see Tips, left)	6
4 oz	light cream cheese, softened, cubed	125 g
¾ cup	hot milk (approx.)	175 mL
	Salt and freshly grated nutmeg	
½ cup	shredded Cheddar cheese	125 mL
¼ cup	fine dry bread crumbs	60 mL
½ tsp	paprika	2 mL

1. Peel potatoes and cut into 3-inch (7.5 cm) chunks. In a large saucepan of boiling salted water, cook potatoes for 20 to 25 minutes or until fork-tender. Drain well and return to saucepan. Place over low heat and dry for 1 to 2 minutes.

2. Press potatoes through a food mill or ricer or mash with potato masher or use an electric mixer at low speed until very smooth. (Do not use a food processor or the potatoes will turn into glue.) Beat in cream cheese and milk until smooth; season with salt and nutmeg to taste. Spread evenly in prepared casserole dish.

3. In a small bowl, combine Cheddar cheese, bread crumbs and paprika. Sprinkle evenly over potatoes.

4. Bake, uncovered, in preheated oven for 40 to 50 minutes or until top is golden and a knife inserted in center is hot to the touch.

Fork-Mashed New Potatoes with Fresh Herbs

Makes 6 servings

To satisfy our cravings for mashed potatoes, here's a summer version designed for small delicious new potatoes.

2 lbs	small new potatoes	1 kg
¼ cup	sour cream	60 mL
2 tbsp	chopped fresh basil or parsley	30 mL
2 tbsp	chopped fresh chives	30 mL
2 tsp	Dijon mustard	10 mL
¼ tsp	salt	1 mL
¼ tsp	freshly ground black pepper	1 mL

1. In a large saucepan of boiling salted water, cook potatoes for 20 minutes or until tender. Drain; place in shallow bowl. Cut into quarters. (Peel if desired, but it's not necessary.)

2. Add sour cream, basil, chives, mustard, salt and pepper. Using a fork, roughly mash until potatoes are quite smooth; there should still be some lumps remaining. Serve immediately.

Roasted Garlic Potatoes

Makes 4 servings

If you're like me, you'll come to rely on this breezy side dish as the perfect complement to a Sunday roast. I also like it with Bistro Steak (see recipe, page 238) and other grilled meats.

Tip

Peel the potatoes if you like, but I find the potatoes are tastier with the skin left on.

- Preheat oven to 400°F (200°C)
- 13- by 9-inch (33 by 23 cm) baking dish, greased

4	large russet potatoes, scrubbed and cut into 1-inch (2.5 cm) chunks (about 2 lbs/1 kg)	4
2 tbsp	olive oil	30 mL
4	cloves garlic, slivered	4
	Salt and freshly ground black pepper	
1 tbsp	chopped fresh parsley	15 mL

1. Cook potato chunks in a large saucepan of boiling salted water for 5 minutes; drain well. Spread in baking dish. Drizzle with oil and garlic; season with salt and pepper to taste.

2. Roast for 40 minutes, stirring occasionally, until potatoes are tender and golden. Sprinkle with parsley.

Classic Scalloped Potatoes

I wouldn't dream of serving a baked ham without this favorite side dish. Use your food processor to quickly slice the potatoes.

Tip

To make ahead, layer potatoes in cream sauce in dish, cover and refrigerate for up to 1 day.

Variation

Scalloped Potatoes with Ham and Swiss Cheese

Add 8 oz (250 g) smoked ham, cut into 1-inch (2.5 cm) strips, along with potatoes in the sauce. Substitute Swiss Gruyère for the Cheddar cheese.

- Preheat oven to 350°F (180°C)
- 10-cup (2.5 L) shallow baking dish, greased

2 tbsp	butter	30 mL
1	large onion, halved lengthwise, thinly sliced	1
2 tbsp	all-purpose flour	30 mL
1½ cups	milk	375 mL
2 tsp	Dijon mustard	10 mL
½ tsp	salt	2 mL
Pinch	freshly grated nutmeg	Pinch
6	potatoes (about 2 lbs/1 kg)	6
1 cup	shredded aged Cheddar cheese	250 mL

1. In a saucepan, melt butter over medium heat. Cook onion, stirring often, for 3 minutes or until softened. Sprinkle with flour; stir in milk, mustard, salt and nutmeg. Bring to a boil, stirring, until sauce thickens.

2. Peel and thinly slice potatoes; rinse under cold water. Drain; wrap in a clean, dry towel to dry. Stir into sauce; bring to a boil over medium heat. Spoon into prepared baking dish; sprinkle with cheese. Bake for 45 to 50 minutes or until potatoes are tender and top is golden.

Gruyère Scalloped Potatoes

Some people think there can never be enough potato recipes in a cookbook — and I agree. Potatoes are soothing, earthy and one of the best comfort foods around. No matter how you prepare them, they always taste wonderful.

Here's an update of a French classic with half the calorie-rich cream replaced by flavorful stock. It's a perfect accompaniment to a Sunday roast or as a main course dish served with a crisp tossed salad.

Tip

Recipe can easily be doubled and baked in a 13- by 9-inch (33 by 23 cm) baking dish.

- Preheat oven to 375°F (190°C)
- 10-cup (2.5 L) shallow baking dish, greased

6	russet or Yukon gold potatoes (about 2 lbs/1 kg)	6
	Salt, freshly ground black pepper and freshly grated nutmeg	
½ cup	chicken stock	125 mL
½ cup	whipping (35%) cream	125 mL
1	clove garlic, minced	1
1 cup	shredded Gruyère or Cheddar cheese	250 mL

1. Peel and thinly slice potatoes; rinse under cold water. Drain; wrap in a clean, dry towel to dry. Arrange slices in prepared baking dish. Season with salt, pepper and nutmeg.

2. In a small saucepan, bring stock, cream and garlic to a boil. (Or place in a large glass measure; microwave on High for $2\frac{1}{2}$ minutes or until almost boiling.) Pour over potatoes. Cover with lid or foil.

3. Bake in preheated oven for 40 minutes. Sprinkle with cheese; bake, uncovered, for 20 to 25 minutes more or until cheese is bubbly and golden.

Champ

These traditional Irish mashed potatoes are made with butter and green onions and are the perfect companion to a rich dark stew.

Variation

Instead of green onions, use ⅓ cup (75 mL) snipped fresh chives or parsley.

6	russet or Yukon gold potatoes, peeled and quartered (about 2 lbs/1kg)	6
¾ cup	milk (approx.)	175 mL
¾ cup	chopped green onions	175 mL
2 tbsp	butter	30 mL
	Salt and freshly ground black pepper	
	Chopped green onion tops	

1. Peel potatoes and cut into 3-inch (7.5 cm) chunks. In a large saucepan, cook potatoes in boiling salted water until tender, about 20 minutes or until fork-tender. (Yukon gold potatoes take a few minutes longer.) Drain well and return to saucepan. Place over low heat and dry for 1 to 2 minutes.

2. Press potatoes through a food mill or ricer or mash with potato masher or use an electric mixer at low speed until very smooth. (Do not use a food processor or the potatoes will turn into glue.)

3. Meanwhile, in a small saucepan, combine milk, green onions and butter. Place over medium-low heat for 5 minutes, or until piping hot. Using an electric mixer, beat milk mixture into potatoes, adding more milk if necessary, until potatoes are creamy. Season with salt and pepper to taste.

4. Place pan over medium-low heat, if necessary, to reheat until piping hot. Spoon into serving bowl and sprinkle with green onion tops.

Potato Pudding

This classic comfort food, called *kugel*, is a staple in Jewish cooking. It's a delicious accompaniment to roasted meats and chicken.

Tip

Wrapping the grated potatoes in a clean, dry towel gets rid of excess starch. Make sure to grate potatoes just before using since they discolor quickly.

- Preheat oven to 350°F (180°C)
- 8-inch (20 cm) square baking dish, well greased

2	eggs	2
2 tbsp	all-purpose flour	30 mL
1 tbsp	chopped fresh parsley	15 mL
1	large clove garlic, minced	1
¾ tsp	salt	3 mL
¼ tsp	freshly ground black pepper	1 mL
1	onion	1
6	potatoes (about 2 lbs/1 kg)	6
1 tbsp	vegetable oil	15 mL

1. In a bowl, beat eggs; stir in flour, parsley, garlic, salt and pepper. Using a food processor, grate onion; fold into egg mixture.

2. Peel potatoes; wash and cut into quarters. Grate using a food processor. Wrap in a clean, dry kitchen towel; squeeze out excess moisture. Stir into onion mixture until combined. (Do this quickly before potatoes discolor.)

3. Spread in baking dish. Drizzle with oil and spread evenly. Bake in oven for about 1 hour or until top is nicely browned. Cut into squares and serve.

Perfect French Fries

Makes 4 servings

You won't believe how fantastic these homemade French fries taste. This two-step frying method results in wonderfully crisp potatoes that are not greasy. Fry potato strips in a large saucepan on your stovetop or use an electric deep fryer, a nifty kitchen appliance that takes the worry out of cooking with hot oil.

Tip

Place the fried potatoes on a heavy brown paper bag covered with paper towels to absorb the excess oil.

- Deep-fry thermometer

4	large or 6 medium russet potatoes (about 2 lbs/1 kg)	4
8 cups	vegetable oil (approx.)	2 L
	Salt	

1. Peel potatoes and cut into long strips $\frac{1}{2}$-inch by $\frac{1}{2}$-inch (1 cm) in diameter. Rinse in several changes cold water to remove starch. Cover with cold water until ready to cook. Drain well; wrap in a clean, dry kitchen towel to dry potatoes thoroughly.

2. Place enough oil in a large saucepan to come 3 inches (7.5 cm) up sides of pan. Insert a deep-fry thermometer into oil; place over medium-high heat. Heat oil to 325°F (160°C).

3. Add potato strips in batches; fry for 8 to 10 minutes or until potatoes start to brown. Remove with slotted spoon and drain on paper towels. (Can be prepared up to this point 1 hour before serving; remove pan from heat.)

4. Place pan over high heat and reheat oil to 375°F (190°C). Add potatoes in batches; fry briefly for 1 to 2 minutes or until crisp and golden brown. Remove with slotted spoon; drain on paper towels. Season with salt; serve immediately.

Oven French Fries

Makes 4 servings

If you love French fries (and who doesn't?), but you're concerned about calories, here's the next best thing to deep frying.

Tip

Dark rimmed baking sheets attract the oven heat and will roast the potatoes faster and give them a more intense color than shiny aluminum ones.

- Preheat oven to 450°F (230°C)
- 2 rimmed baking sheets, greased

4	large or 6 medium russet potatoes (about 2 lbs/1kg)	4
2 tbsp	olive or vegetable oil	30 mL
	Salt	

1. Peel potatoes and cut into long strips $\frac{1}{2}$-inch by $\frac{1}{2}$-inch (1 cm) in diameter. Rinse in several changes cold water to remove starch. Cover with cold water until ready to cook. Drain well; wrap in a clean, dry kitchen towel to dry potatoes thoroughly.

2. Place potatoes on prepared baking sheets; drizzle with oil and toss to coat evenly. Arrange in a single layer. Roast in preheated oven for 25 to 30 minutes, stirring occasionally, until tender and golden brown.

Sweet Potato Oven Fries

Makes 4 servings

The key to great oven fries is to cut the sweet potatoes into thin strips and roast them at a high temperature in a single layer on the baking sheet. If thickly cut, the fries don't crisp properly — they steam instead.

Variation

Instead of the spice blend, use 2 tsp (10 mL) chopped fresh rosemary or 1 tsp (5 mL) crumbled dried rosemary leaves along with salt and pepper and sprinkle over potatoes before roasting.

- Preheat oven to 425°F (220°C), with rack positioned in upper third of oven
- Large rimmed baking sheet, lined with foil

3	sweet potatoes (2 lbs/1 kg)	3
2 tbsp	olive oil	30 mL
1 tsp	brown sugar	5 mL
½ tsp	chili powder	2 mL
¼ tsp	salt	1 mL
¼ tsp	freshly ground black pepper	1 mL
¼ tsp	ground cumin	1 mL
¼ tsp	paprika	1 mL

1. Peel sweet potatoes and cut lengthwise into ½-inch (1 cm) slices. Cut slices into ½-inch (1 cm) thick strips. Place in a bowl. Pour in olive oil and toss to coat evenly.

2. In small bowl, combine brown sugar, chili powder, salt, pepper, cumin and paprika. Sprinkle evenly over sweet potatoes and toss to coat.

3. Arrange seasoned potatoes in a single layer on prepared baking sheet. Roast in upper third of preheated oven, using a spatula to turn fries over a few times during roasting, for about 30 minutes or until golden and crisp. Serve immediately.

Beef-Stuffed Spuds

Baked potatoes stuffed with a variety of fillings is a popular meal in my house. I make them ahead for those nights when everyone is on a different schedule. The potatoes need only a quick reheat in the microwave as each person walks through the door for an instant supper.

Tips

To oven-bake potatoes: Place in 400°F (200°C) oven for 1 hour or until potatoes give slightly when squeezed.

To microwave potatoes: Arrange potatoes in a circle 1 inch (2.5 cm) apart on a paper towel. Microwave at High, turning halfway through cooking, until potatoes are just tender when pierced with a skewer. *Microwave cooking times at High:* 1 potato, 4 to 5 minutes; 2 potatoes, 6 to 8 minutes; 4 potatoes, 10 to 12 minutes.

For moist potatoes, wrap cooked potatoes individually in foil. For drier potatoes, wrap in a dry towel. Let stand 5 minutes.

- Preheat oven to 400°F (200°C)
- 13- by 9-inch (33 by 23 cm) baking dish

4	large baking potatoes (each 10 oz/300 g)	4
8 oz	lean ground beef or veal	250 g
1/3 cup	finely chopped onions	75 mL
1	clove garlic, finely chopped	1
1 tsp	Worcestershire sauce	5 mL
	Salt and freshly ground black pepper	
1/2 cup	sour cream, plain yogurt or buttermilk (approx.)	125 mL
1 cup	shredded Cheddar cheese	250 mL
2 tbsp	chopped fresh parsley	30 mL

1. Scrub potatoes well and pierce skins with a fork in several places to allow steam to escape. Bake or microwave potatoes (see Tips, left).

2. In a large nonstick skillet over medium-high heat, cook beef, breaking up with a wooden spoon, for 4 minutes or until no longer pink. Drain off any fat.

3. Reduce heat to medium. Add onions, garlic and Worcestershire sauce; season with salt and pepper. Cook, stirring often, for 4 minutes or until onions are softened.

4. Cut warm potatoes in half lengthwise. Carefully scoop out each potato, leaving a 1/4-inch (0.5 cm) shell; set shells aside.

5. In a bowl, mash potatoes with potato masher or fork; beat in enough sour cream until smooth. Stir in beef mixture, half the cheese and all the parsley; season with salt and pepper to taste. Spoon into potato shells; top with remaining cheese.

6. Arrange in baking dish; bake in preheated oven for 15 minutes or until cheese is melted. (Alternatively, place on a large serving plate; microwave on Medium-High (70%) for 4 to 6 minutes or until heated through and cheese melts.)

Broccoli and Cheese–Stuffed Potatoes

Makes 4 servings

These delicious baked potatoes are great to pack along to work if you have the use of a microwave for reheating.

Tip

Cheddar and broccoli are a classic combo, but get adventurous with whatever cheese and vegetables are in the fridge. Another favorite is mozzarella cheese and lightly sautéed mushrooms and diced red peppers seasoned with basil.

- Preheat oven to 400°F (200°C)
- 13- by 9-inch (33 by 23 cm) baking dish

4	large baking potatoes (each 10 oz/300 g)	4
3 cups	small broccoli florets and chopped peeled stems	750 mL
½ cup	sour cream, plain yogurt or buttermilk (approx.)	125 mL
2	green onions, sliced	2
1⅓ cups	shredded Cheddar or Gruyère cheese, divided	325 mL
	Salt and cayenne pepper	

1. Scrub potatoes well and pierce skins with a fork in several places to allow steam to escape. Bake or microwave potatoes (see Tips, page 406).

2. In a saucepan, cook or steam broccoli until just tender-crisp. (Alternatively, place in covered casserole with 2 tbsp (30 mL) water and microwave on High for 2 to 2½ minutes.) Drain well.

3. Cut a thin slice from tops of warm potatoes. Scoop out potato, leaving a ¼-inch (0.5 cm) shell, being careful not to tear the skins.

4. In a bowl, mash potato with potato masher or fork; beat in enough sour cream until smooth. Add broccoli, green onions and 1 cup (250 mL) cheese. Season with salt and a dash of cayenne pepper to taste.

5. Spoon filling into potato shells, mounding the tops. Arrange in shallow baking dish; sprinkle with remaining cheese. Bake in preheated oven for 15 minutes or until cheese melts. (Alternatively, place on a large serving plate and microwave on Medium-High (70%) for 4 to 6 minutes or until heated through and cheese melts.)

Tuna-Stuffed Potatoes

Can't bear to see another bagged tuna sandwich for lunch? Try these tuna-stuffed potatoes instead. They're ideal to make ahead and pop into the microwave for a quick reheat.

Tips

To oven-bake potatoes: Place in 400°F (200°C) oven for 1 hour or until potatoes give slightly when squeezed.

To microwave potatoes: Arrange potatoes in a circle 1 inch (2.5 cm) apart on a paper towel. Microwave at High, turning halfway through cooking, until potatoes are just tender when pierced with a skewer. *Microwave cooking times at High:* 1 potato, 4 to 5 minutes; 2 potatoes, 6 to 8 minutes; 4 potatoes, 10 to 12 minutes.

- Preheat oven to 400°F (200°C)
- 8-inch (20 cm) baking dish

2	baking potatoes (each 10 oz/300 g)	2
1	can (6 oz/170 g) solid white or light tuna, drained and flaked	1
1	stalk celery, chopped	1
1	green onion, finely chopped	1
1/3 cup	sour cream or plain yogurt	75 mL
1/2 cup	shredded Cheddar cheese, divided	125 mL
	Salt and freshly ground black pepper	

1. Scrub potatoes well and, using a fork, pierce skins in several places to allow steam to escape. Bake or microwave potatoes (see Tips, left).

2. Cut each baked potato in half lengthwise and scoop out, leaving a 1/4-inch (0.5 cm) shell; set shells aside. Place potato in a bowl and mash with a potato masher or a fork. Stir in tuna, celery, green onion, sour cream and half the cheese. Season with salt and pepper to taste. Spoon mixture back into shells and sprinkle with remaining cheese.

3. Arrange in baking dish and bake for 15 minutes or until cheese is melted. (Alternatively, place on a large serving plate and microwave, uncovered, on Medium-High (70%) for 2 1/2 to 3 minutes or until heated through and cheese melts.)

Mashed Roasted Sweet Potatoes with Apples

Makes 6 servings

I love the combination of sweet potatoes and apples accented with maple syrup. This dish is great served with pork or chicken.

Tip

To make ahead, prepare recipe as directed, place in an airtight container and refrigerate for up to 2 days. Reheat in a saucepan over medium-low heat, stirring often, until hot. Or place in a covered casserole dish and microwave on High for 6 to 8 minutes, stirring once, until hot.

Variation

Instead of sweet potatoes, use 2 lbs (1 kg) butternut squash, peeled and seeds removed.

- Preheat oven to 375°F (190°C)
- 13- by 9-inch (33 by 23 cm) baking dish, greased

3	sweet potatoes (about 2 lbs/1 kg), peeled and cut into 1-inch (2.5 cm) chunks	3
2	apples, peeled, cored and chopped	2
1	onion, chopped	1
	Salt and freshly ground black pepper	
2 tbsp	butter, melted	30 mL
¼ cup	maple syrup	60 mL

1. Place sweet potatoes, apples and onion in prepared baking dish. Season with salt and pepper. Drizzle with melted butter and maple syrup.

2. Bake in preheated oven, stirring occasionally, for 45 to 50 minutes or until sweet potatoes are very tender.

3. In a food processor, purée vegetable mixture in batches until smooth. Transfer to a heatproof serving dish. Serve immediately or cover and place in a warm oven until serving time.

Microwave Method

1. Combine ingredients in an 8-cup (2 L) casserole dish. Microwave, covered, on High for 20 to 25 minutes, stirring once, until sweet potatoes are tender. Purée as directed in recipe.

Tomato, Zucchini and Potato Bake

Don't even bother with meat. This melt-in-the-mouth veggie dish is a scrumptious meal in itself. Hearty potatoes, sweet tomatoes and delicate zucchini are heavenly when sprinkled with a golden cheese and crumb topping.

Tip

Just add warm crusty bread to this vegetable medley for an easy supper.

- Preheat oven to 350°F (180°C)
- 13- by 9-inch (33 by 23 cm) baking dish, lightly greased

4	ripe tomatoes	4
	Salt	
2 tbsp	olive oil	30 mL
4	potatoes, peeled and thinly sliced (about 1½ lbs/750 g)	4
1	onion, thinly sliced	1
3	cloves garlic, finely chopped	3
1½ tsp	dried Italian herbs or dried oregano leaves	7 mL
	Freshly ground black pepper	
3	small zucchini, thinly sliced (about 1 lb/500 g)	3
1 cup	shredded Gruyère, provolone or mozzarella cheese	250 mL
¼ cup	freshly grated Parmesan cheese	60 mL
½ cup	soft fresh bread crumbs	125 mL
¼ cup	finely chopped fresh parsley	60 mL

1. Halve tomatoes crosswise and squeeze out seeds. Thinly slice and place on paper towels to drain. Season lightly with salt.

2. In a large nonstick skillet, heat oil over medium heat. Cook potatoes, onion, garlic and Italian herbs, stirring often, for 8 to 10 minutes or until potatoes are softened. Season with salt and pepper.

3. Layer half the sliced tomatoes, half the zucchini and half the potato mixture in prepared baking dish. Repeat layers again in same order. (The recipe can be prepared to this point up to 1 day ahead, covered and refrigerated.)

4. In a bowl, combine cheeses, bread crumbs and parsley; sprinkle over top.

5. Bake in preheated oven for 40 to 45 minutes or until top is golden and vegetables are tender.

Tomato and Zucchini Sauté

1 tbsp	olive oil	15 mL
3	small zucchini, halved lengthwise and thinly sliced	3
2 cups	cherry tomatoes, halved	500 mL
½ tsp	ground cumin (optional)	2 mL
2	green onions, sliced	2
2 tsp	balsamic vinegar	10 mL
	Salt and freshly ground black pepper	
2 tbsp	chopped fresh basil or mint	30 mL
2 tbsp	lightly toasted pine nuts (optional)	30 mL

1. In a large nonstick skillet, heat oil over medium-high heat. Add zucchini and cook, stirring, for 1 minute. Add cherry tomatoes, cumin, if using, green onions and balsamic vinegar. Cook, stirring, for 1 to 2 minutes or until zucchini is tender-crisp and tomatoes are heated through. Season with salt and pepper to taste.

2. Sprinkle with basil and pine nuts, if using, and serve immediately.

Corn with Tomatoes and Basil

2 tsp	vegetable or olive oil	10 mL
3	green onions, sliced	3
1	small green bell pepper, diced	1
3 cups	uncooked corn kernels (about 5 ears of corn)	750 mL
2	tomatoes, seeded and diced	2
2 tbsp	chopped fresh basil or 1 tsp (5 mL) dried basil leaves	30 mL
Pinch	granulated sugar	Pinch
	Salt and freshly ground black pepper	

1. In a large nonstick skillet, heat oil over medium-high heat. Cook green onions, green pepper, corn, tomatoes and basil (if using dried), stirring often, for 5 to 7 minutes (8 to 10 minutes, if using frozen corn) or until corn is tender.

2. Add sugar; season with salt and pepper to taste. Sprinkle with chopped basil (if using fresh).

Corn on the Cob with Flavored Butters and Oils

The sweetness of just-picked corn is one of summer's best pleasures. Here are different ways to cook corn on the cob (my favorite is poaching), along with flavored butters and oils to jazz it up.

Grilled Husked Corn on the Cob

Preheat greased barbecue grill to medium. Husk corn. Brush corn lightly with olive or vegetable oil and season with salt and pepper. Grill, turning often, for 10 to 15 minutes or until kernels are tender with grill marks.

Grilled Corn in the Husk

Preheat greased barbecue grill to medium-high. Remove outer layers of husk, leaving a few protective layers. (No need to soak before grilling.) Grill, turning often, for about 10 minutes or until first layer of husk is charred and corn is tender. Keep corn warm in charred husk until ready to serve. For a more intense smoky flavor, near the end of cooking pull back husk and brown kernels on the grill, turning often, for 2 to 3 minutes.

Boiled Corn on the Cob

Husk corn. Bring a large pot of water to a boil. Add corn and return to a boil. Cover and boil for 3 to 5 minutes or until tender when pierced with a fork.

Poached Corn on the Cob

Husk corn. Bring a large pot of water to a boil. Add corn and return to a boil. Cover and boil for 1 minute. Remove from heat and let stand, covered, for at least 5 minutes or up to 20 minutes.

Steamed Corn on the Cob

Husk corn. In a large pot, bring 1 inch (2.5 cm) of water to a boil. Insert steamer basket and add corn. Steam for about 10 minutes or until tender when pierced with a fork.

Microwaved Corn in the Husk

Remove outer layers of husk, leaving a few protective layers. Rinse corn under cold water. Arrange 2 inches (5 cm) apart directly on bottom of microwave. Microwave on High for the following times:

1 cob	$2\frac{1}{2}$ to 3 minutes
2 cobs	4 to 5 minutes
3 cobs	6 to 8 minutes
4 cobs	8 to 10 minutes

(Cooking times vary according to size and maturity of corn and microwave power. For even cooking, do not microwave more than 4 cobs at a time.)

Turn corn over and rearrange halfway through cooking. Let stand for 3 minutes, then pull away husk and silk.

Microwaved Husked Corn on the Cob

Place corn in a single layer in a shallow casserole dish. Add $\frac{1}{4}$ cup (60 mL) water. Cover and microwave as above, turning corn over and rearranging halfway through cooking.

Lemon Basil Butter

2 tbsp	butter, melted	30 mL
2 tbsp	finely chopped fresh basil or 1/2 tsp (2 mL) each dried basil and oregano leaves	30 mL
1/2 tsp	grated lemon zest	2 mL
1 tsp	fresh lemon juice	5 mL
	Salt and freshly ground black pepper	

In a small bowl, combine butter, basil, lemon zest and lemon juice. Season with salt and pepper. Brush over 6 hot cooked or grilled corn cobs.

Cilantro Lime Butter

2 tbsp	butter, melted	30 mL
2 tbsp	finely chopped fresh cilantro	30 mL
1/2 tsp	grated lime zest	2 mL
1 tsp	fresh lime juice	5 mL
1/4 tsp	ground cumin or coriander	1 mL
	Salt and freshly ground black pepper	

In a small bowl, combine butter, cilantro, lime zest, lime juice and cumin. Season with salt and pepper. Brush over 6 hot cooked or grilled corn cobs.

Chili Oil

2 tbsp	vegetable oil	30 mL
1/2 tsp	chili powder	2 mL
1/2 tsp	dried oregano leaves	2 mL
1/2 tsp	ground cumin	2 mL
Pinch	cayenne pepper	Pinch

In a small bowl, combine oil, chili powder, oregano, cumin and cayenne. Brush 6 husked corn cobs with flavored oil and grill following the directions for Grilled Husked Corn on the Cob.

Roasted Garlic and Herb Oil

4	cloves garlic, peeled	4
1/4 cup	olive oil	60 mL
1 1/2 tsp	chopped fresh thyme or rosemary (or a combination)	7 mL
	Salt and freshly ground black pepper	

Gently crush garlic with the side of a knife blade. In a saucepan, combine oil and garlic. Cook over medium-low heat, stirring often, for about 10 minutes or until garlic is lightly colored. Discard garlic. Add thyme and season with salt and pepper. Brush 6 husked corn cobs with flavored oil and grill following the directions for Grilled Husked Corn on the Cob.

Asparagus with Parmesan and Toasted Almonds

When locally grown asparagus appears at the market, it's one of my rites of spring. I prepare them tossed with crunchy almonds and melting Parmesan — and it's every bit as pleasing as a buttery Hollandaise.

Variation

Make this dish with green beans. Trim and cut into 1½-inch (4 cm) lengths and cook in boiling water for about 5 minutes or until tender-crisp.

1½ lbs	asparagus	750 g
¼ cup	sliced blanched almonds	60 mL
2 tbsp	butter	30 mL
2	cloves garlic, finely chopped	2
¼ cup	freshly grated Parmesan cheese	60 mL
	Salt and freshly ground black pepper	

1. Snap off asparagus ends; cut spears on the diagonal into 2-inch (5 cm) lengths. In a large nonstick skillet, bring ½ cup (125 mL) water to a boil. Blanch asparagus for 2 minutes (start timing when water returns to a boil) or until just tender-crisp. Run under cold water to chill; drain and reserve.

2. Dry the skillet and place over medium heat. Add almonds and toast, stirring often, for 2 to 3 minutes or until golden. Remove and reserve.

3. Increase heat to medium-high. Add butter to skillet; cook asparagus and garlic, stirring, for 2 to 3 minutes or until asparagus is just tender.

4. Sprinkle with Parmesan; season with salt and pepper. Transfer to serving bowl; top with almonds.

Oven-Roasted Asparagus

Roasting brings out the best in many vegetables, including asparagus. The oven-roasting method is much simpler and more flavorful than the traditional way of cooking asparagus in a steamer.

- Preheat oven to 425°F (220°C)
- Heavy rimmed baking sheet, greased

1 lb	asparagus	500 g
1 tbsp	olive oil	15 mL
	Salt and freshly ground black pepper	
1 tbsp	balsamic vinegar	15 mL

1. Snap off tough asparagus ends. If large, peel stalks. Arrange in single layer on prepared baking sheet. Drizzle with oil; season with salt and pepper.

2. Roast in oven, stirring occasionally, for 12 minutes.

3. Drizzle balsamic vinegar over asparagus and toss to coat. Roast for 3 to 5 minutes or until tender-crisp. Serve immediately.

Green Beans Stewed with Tomatoes

Makes 4 servings

This is a favorite dish to make in late summer when young beans and ripe tomatoes are at their best. But even in winter, with vine-ripened greenhouse tomatoes and imported fresh beans, this recipe is still good. If bits of tomato skin in the sauce bother you, peel the tomatoes before dicing.

Variations

For a quick supper, toss vegetable sauce with 8 oz (250 g) cooked pasta, such as penne, and sprinkle generously with Parmesan cheese.

Substitute other vegetables, such as fennel, asparagus or broccoli, for the beans.

1 lb	green beans	500 g
1 tbsp	olive oil	15 mL
1	small red onion, halved lengthwise, thinly sliced	1
2	cloves garlic, thinly sliced	2
2	ripe tomatoes, diced	2
1 tbsp	balsamic vinegar	15 mL
2 tbsp	water (approx.)	30 mL
1/4 tsp	salt	1 mL
1/4 tsp	freshly ground black pepper	1 mL
2 tbsp	chopped fresh basil	30 mL

1. Trim ends of beans; cut into $1\frac{1}{2}$-inch (4 cm) lengths. In a saucepan, cook beans in lightly salted boiling water for 3 minutes (start timing when water returns to a boil) or until still crisp. Drain well; reserve.

2. Meanwhile, in a large nonstick skillet, heat oil over medium heat. Add onion and garlic; cook, stirring, for 2 minutes or until softened.

3. Stir in tomatoes, vinegar, water, salt and pepper; cook, stirring often, for 3 minutes or until sauce-like.

4. Add beans; cover and simmer for 8 to 10 minutes, stirring occasionally, until tender. Add more water, if necessary, to keep mixture moist. Sprinkle with basil and serve warm or at room temperature.

Sugar Snap Peas in Ginger Butter

Here's a quick stir-fry with ginger and shallots that nicely complements the sweetness of emerald-green sugar snap peas.

Tip

Snow peas can be prepared in the same way, but reduce the cooking time to 1 minute or until bright green and crisp.

1½ lbs	sugar snap peas	750 g
1 tbsp	butter	15 mL
¼ cup	minced shallots	60 mL
2 tsp	minced gingerroot	10 mL
	Salt and freshly ground black pepper	

1. Remove strings from both sides of sugar snap peas. In a large nonstick skillet, melt butter over medium heat. When hot and foamy, cook shallots and ginger, stirring, for 2 minutes.

2. Add peas and cook, stirring often, for 4 minutes or until just tender. Season with salt and pepper to taste.

Teriyaki Vegetable Stir-Fry

Makes 4 servings

Use this recipe as a guideline and then get creative with whatever vegetables you have in the fridge. You'll need about 5 cups (1.25 L) in total.

Tip

Vegetables that take longer to cook, such as carrots, broccoli and cauliflower, should be added to the skillet first before adding quick-cooking ones like peppers and zucchini.

2 tbsp	teriyaki or soy sauce	30 mL
2 tbsp	water	30 mL
1 tbsp	rice vinegar	15 mL
2 tsp	packed brown sugar	10 mL
1 tsp	cornstarch	5 mL
1	large clove garlic, minced	1
1 tbsp	vegetable oil	15 mL
2 cups	small cauliflower or broccoli florets	500 mL
1	red bell pepper, cut into 2-inch (5 cm) strips	1
2	small zucchini, halved lengthwise and thinly sliced	2

1. In a glass measuring cup, combine teriyaki sauce, water, vinegar, brown sugar, cornstarch and garlic; set aside.

2. In a wok or large nonstick skillet, heat oil over medium-high heat. Add cauliflower and cook, stirring, for 1 minute. Add red pepper and zucchini; cook, stirring, for 2 minutes.

3. Reduce heat to medium. Stir teriyaki sauce and add to skillet. Cook, stirring, until sauce is slightly thickened. Cover and cook for 1 minute or until vegetables are tender-crisp.

Broccoli with Cheese Sauce

This simple vegetable side dish appears at all our family gatherings including Christmas and Thanksgiving. It's a hit with everybody. Serve the cheese sauce with other vegetables including cauliflower and Brussels sprouts.

Tip

Hot milk is the secret to lump-free sauce; microwave milk at High for 2 minutes.

● 8-cup (2 L) casserole dish

8 cups	broccoli florets and sliced peeled stems (1 large bunch)	2 L
2 tbsp	butter	30 mL
2 tbsp	all-purpose flour	30 mL
1 cup	hot milk	250 mL
1 cup	shredded aged Cheddar cheese	250 mL
	Salt and cayenne pepper	

1. Steam broccoli for 5 minutes or until just tender. Drain well. Wrap in clean, dry towel to absorb moisture. Place in casserole dish.

2. Meanwhile, in a small saucepan, melt butter over medium heat. Whisk in flour, stirring, for 15 seconds or until bubbly. Whisk in milk in a stream.

3. Bring to a boil; cook, stirring, for 1 minute or until thickened. Reduce heat to low and whisk in cheese until melted. Season with salt and pinch of cayenne pepper to taste. Pour over broccoli and serve immediately.

Orange-Glazed Broccoli

Makes 4 servings

This quick stir-fry with the lively taste of orange makes a great side dish to serve with roast chicken, beef or pork.

Variation

Any combination of vegetables can be used in this vegetable stir-fry, including bell peppers, mushrooms, snow peas, cauliflower, fennel strips and blanched green beans and carrot slices.

1/3 cup	orange juice	75 mL
1/2 tsp	cornstarch	2 mL
1 tbsp	olive oil	15 mL
1/4 cup	minced shallots	60 mL
4 cups	small broccoli florets	1 L
1	red bell pepper, cut into thin 2-inch (5 cm) strips	1
1 tsp	grated orange zest	5 mL
	Salt and freshly ground black pepper	

1. In a bowl, stir together orange juice and cornstarch until smooth; set aside.

2. In a large nonstick skillet, heat oil over medium-high heat. Cook shallots, stirring, for 20 seconds. Add broccoli and red pepper; cook, stirring, for 2 minutes. Stir in orange juice mixture. Cover and cook for 1 to 2 minutes or until vegetables are tender-crisp.

3. Sprinkle with orange zest. Season with salt and pepper to taste. Serve immediately.

Cauliflower with Hazelnut Crumb Topping

Snowy cauliflower topped with cheese and nuts makes the perfect side dish for a Sunday roast. For vegetarians, it becomes a main course dish when served along with grains or a bowl of pasta.

Tip

Sprinkle the garlic-crumb mixture over other vegetables, such as broccoli, Brussels sprouts or spinach.

Variation

Unblanched almonds, pecans or walnuts can replace the hazelnuts.

- Preheat broiler
- 10-cup (2.5 L) shallow baking dish, lightly greased

2 tbsp	butter	30 mL
¼ cup	hazelnuts or walnuts, finely chopped	60 mL
½ cup	soft fresh bread crumbs	125 mL
1	large clove garlic, minced	1
½ cup	finely shredded Gruyère or aged Cheddar cheese	125 mL
2 tbsp	chopped fresh parsley	30 mL
1	cauliflower, broken into florets	1

1. In a medium skillet, melt butter over medium heat. Add hazelnuts and cook, stirring, for 1 minute or until lightly toasted. Add bread crumbs and garlic; cook, stirring, for 1 minute more or until crumbs are lightly colored. Remove from heat; let cool.

2. In a bowl, combine crumb mixture, cheese and parsley.

3. In a large saucepan of boiling salted water, cook cauliflower for 3 to 5 minutes or until tender-crisp. Drain well. Place in prepared baking dish; sprinkle with crumb mixture. Place under preheated broiler for 1 to 2 minutes or until topping is lightly browned.

Cauliflower Fondue Bake

Makes 6 servings

This hearty vegetable dish is reminiscent of Swiss cheese fondue. It can even stand in for a light, satisfying supper when paired with crusty bread and a tossed salad.

Tip

Nutmeg is a key flavoring in this dish. Whole nutmeg is preferable to the pre-ground variety. Find it in the spice section of supermarkets and use a rasp grater (such as a Microplane), available in kitchenware shops.

- Preheat oven to 375°F (190°C)
- 8-inch (20 cm) square baking dish, greased

1	cauliflower, broken into florets	1
2 tbsp	butter	30 mL
2 tbsp	all-purpose flour	30 mL
½ cup	hot milk	125 mL
½ cup	dry white wine	125 mL
1½ cups	shredded Gruyère cheese	375 mL
	Salt and freshly grated nutmeg (see Tip, left)	

1. In a large saucepan of boiling salted water, cook cauliflower for 3 to 5 minutes or until tender-crisp. Drain well. Wrap in clean dry towel to absorb moisture.

2. In the same saucepan, melt butter over medium heat; blend in flour and cook, stirring, for 15 seconds or until bubbly. Whisk in milk in a stream; cook until smooth and very thick. Whisk in wine in a stream; cook, stirring, until thickened and bubbly. Reduce heat to low; gradually add cheese, a handful at a time, stirring, until cheese melts and sauce is smooth. Season with salt and generous pinch of nutmeg to taste. Sauce will be thick.

3. Place cauliflower in prepared baking dish. Pour sauce evenly over cauliflower. (The dish can be prepared to this point up to a day ahead; cover and refrigerate.) Bake for 20 to 25 minutes (up to 10 minutes longer, if refrigerated) or until cauliflower is just tender and top is lightly browned.

Sautéed Greens with Double-Smoked Bacon

Cooking dark greens, such as collard, kale or rapini, with smoky bacon and hot pepper flakes mellows the mild bitterness of these healthy vegetables.

Tips

To prepare greens, remove tough stem ends. Cut tender stems into 2-inch (5 cm) lengths and coarsely chop leaves. Wash well in a sinkful of cool water to remove any dirt; drain.

For a simple pasta dish, toss the cooked greens with hot cooked pasta, such as spaghetti or linguini, and sprinkle with Parmesan cheese.

8 cups	prepared greens, such as kale, collard, rapini or Swiss chard (see Tips, left)	2 L
6	slices double-smoked or regular bacon, chopped	6
1 tbsp	olive oil	15 mL
1	small onion, finely chopped	1
3	cloves garlic, finely chopped	3
¼ tsp	hot pepper flakes	1 mL
	Salt and freshly ground black pepper	

1. In a large pot of boiling salted water, blanch greens for 2 minutes. Pour into a large sieve to drain, using the back of a wooden spoon to press out as much liquid as possible.

2. In a large nonstick skillet over medium-high heat, cook bacon, stirring often, for 5 minutes or until crisp. Remove to a plate lined with paper towels. Drain any fat from skillet.

3. Reduce heat to medium and add oil to skillet. Cook onion, garlic and hot pepper flakes, stirring, for 1 minute or until onion is lightly colored.

4. Add greens and cook, stirring often, for 2 to 5 minutes or until just tender. Sprinkle with bacon bits and season with salt and pepper to taste.

Oven-Roasted Root Vegetables

I love the way oven roasting sweetens and concentrates the flavors of these sturdy root vegetables. This dish is a natural with stew and mashed potatoes.

Tip

We're used to roasting potatoes, so moving on to other vegetables isn't that much of a shift in our cooking style. Try this treatment with other vegetables, such as peppers, winter squash, beets, cauliflower and even asparagus. You'll be amazed with the results.

Variation

Use oil instead of butter and add a sprinkling of dried herbs, if you like. Reduce cooking time according to the size and type of vegetables.

- Preheat oven to 400°F (200°C)
- 13- by 9-inch (33 by 23 cm) baking dish, lightly greased

3	carrots	3
2	parsnips	2
1/2	small rutabaga (about 8 oz/250 g)	1/2
1	red onion, cut into wedges	1
2	cloves garlic, cut into slivers	2
1/4 cup	dry sherry or chicken stock	60 mL
2 tbsp	melted butter	30 mL
1/2 tsp	salt	2 mL
1/4 tsp	freshly ground black pepper	1 mL
2 tbsp	finely chopped fresh parsley	30 mL

1. Peel carrots, parsnips and rutabaga; cut into 2- by 1/2-inch (5 by 1 cm) strips. Place in prepared baking dish along with onion and garlic.

2. In a small bowl, combine sherry and butter; drizzle over vegetables. Sprinkle with salt and pepper.

3. Cover dish with foil; bake for 30 minutes. Remove foil; bake for 25 to 30 minutes more, stirring occasionally, until vegetables are tender and light golden. Sprinkle with parsley before serving.

Lemon-Glazed Baby Carrots

This is one of my favorite choices to accompany a holiday roast or turkey. Packages of ready-to-cook, peeled whole baby carrots are widely available in supermarkets. They certainly make a cook's life easier — especially when you're preparing a mammoth family dinner and plan to serve several dishes.

Tip

If doubling the recipe, glaze vegetables in a large nonstick skillet to evaporate the stock quickly.

Variation

Try this tasty treatment with a combination of blanched carrots, rutabaga and parsnip strips, too.

1 lb	peeled baby carrots	500 g
¼ cup	chicken or vegetable stock	60 mL
1 tbsp	butter	15 mL
1 tbsp	packed brown sugar	15 mL
½ tsp	grated lemon zest	2 mL
1 tbsp	fresh lemon juice	15 mL
	Salt and freshly ground black pepper	
1 tbsp	finely chopped fresh parsley or chives	15 mL

1. In a medium saucepan, cook carrots in boiling salted water for 5 to 7 minutes (start timing when water returns to a boil) or until just tender-crisp; drain and return to saucepan.

2. Add stock, butter, brown sugar, lemon zest and juice, and salt and pepper to taste. Cook, stirring often, for 3 to 5 minutes or until liquid has evaporated and carrots are nicely glazed.

3. Sprinkle with parsley or chives and serve.

Orange Honey Beets

Tender cooked beets are finished with an orange glaze that complements the natural sweetness of the beets.

Tip

To prevent beet stains, wear rubber gloves when handling beets and cover your cutting board with a sheet of waxed paper.

2 lbs	beets (about 8 small)	1 kg
1½ tsp	grated orange zest	7 mL
½ cup	fresh orange juice	125 mL
2 tbsp	liquid honey	30 mL
4 tsp	red wine vinegar or balsamic vinegar	20 mL
1 tsp	cornstarch	5 mL
1 tbsp	butter (optional)	15 mL
	Salt and freshly ground black pepper	

1. Scrub and trim beets, leaving the root and stem attached. In a saucepan of lightly salted boiling water, cook beets, partially covered, for about 40 minutes or until tender when pierced with a sharp knife. Drain and rinse under cold water. Peel and halve lengthwise; cut into wedges.

2. In same saucepan, combine orange zest, orange juice, honey, vinegar and cornstarch; stir to dissolve cornstarch. Bring to a boil over medium heat, stirring, until thickened. Stir in butter, if using. Season with salt and pepper to taste.

3. Add beets and coat in sauce. Place over medium heat, stirring, until heated through.

Roasted Pearl Onions with Cranberries

Forget the cranberry sauce the next time you serve roast turkey. Serve these tasty onions to complement a holiday bird or roast pork.

Tip

Can't figure out the volume of a baking dish? Look for the measurements on the bottom of dish or measure by pouring in enough water to fill completely.

- Preheat oven to 375°F (190°C)
- 10-cup (2.5 L) shallow baking dish

2	packages or pint baskets (each 10 oz/284 g) pearl onions	2
½ cup	fresh cranberries	125 mL
¼ cup	ruby port wine	60 mL
1 tbsp	brown sugar	15 mL
1 tsp	finely chopped fresh rosemary	5 mL
1 tbsp	butter, cut into bits	15 mL
	Salt and freshly ground black pepper	

1. In a large saucepan of boiling salted water, blanch onions for 2 minutes. Drain; run under cold water. Remove stem ends and skins. Place in a baking dish large enough to hold onions in a single layer.

2. Add cranberries, port, brown sugar and rosemary. Dot with butter and season with salt and pepper to taste.

3. Roast in preheated oven, stirring occasionally, for about 35 minutes or until onions are tender and sauce is reduced and slightly thickened. Serve warm or at room temperature.

Creamed Spinach and Mushroom Bake

Makes 6 servings

Team this creamy vegetable dish with a simple roast of pork or chicken with crispy potato wedges.

Tip

To clean leeks: Trim dark green tops. Cut down center almost to root end and chop. Rinse in a sink full of cold water to remove sand; scoop up leeks and place in colander to drain or use a salad spinner.

- Preheat oven to 375°F (190°C)
- 8-inch (20 cm) square baking dish, greased

2	packages (each 10 oz/300 g) fresh spinach	2
2 tbsp	butter	30 mL
1	leek, white and light green parts only, chopped (see Tip, left)	1
8 oz	shiitake or portobello mushrooms, sliced and chopped	250 g
1/2 cup	whipping (35%) cream	125 mL
1 tsp	grated orange zest	5 mL
	Salt, freshly ground black pepper and freshly grated nutmeg	

Crumb Topping

1/2 cup	fresh baguette bread crumbs	125 mL
1/3 cup	shredded Gruyère or Parmesan cheese	75 mL
1/4 cup	finely chopped walnuts	60 mL

1. Rinse spinach in cold water; remove large stems. Place in Dutch oven or large saucepan with just the water clinging to leaves; cook over medium-high heat, stirring, until just wilted. Drain well and squeeze dry; finely chop.

2. In a large nonstick skillet, heat butter over medium-high heat. Cook leeks and mushrooms, stirring, for 5 minutes or until tender. Stir in spinach, cream and orange zest. Cook until piping hot. Season with salt, pepper and nutmeg to taste. Transfer to prepared baking dish. (Can be prepared up to this point, covered and refrigerated for 2 days.)

3. *Crumb Topping:* In a bowl, combine bread crumbs, cheese and walnuts. Sprinkle over spinach. Bake in preheated oven for 25 to 30 minutes (5 to 10 minutes longer if refrigerated) or until top is golden and center is piping hot.

Butternut Squash Strudel

Here's an impressive side dish to replace rice or potatoes at your next dinner party. Or serve it as part of a buffet when entertaining.

Tips

Like coffee, Parmesan loses its wonderful aromatic flavor and moisture if grated ahead. Choose a wedge in a cheese shop and have it grated for you. Freeze in an airtight container. Or better still, grate the cheese as you need it.

Store Parmesan wedges wrapped in plastic wrap, then in foil, in the refrigerator; it keeps well for weeks.

- Preheat oven to 400°F (200°C)
- Rimmed baking sheet, lined with parchment paper

¼ cup	olive oil, divided	60 mL
1	large red bell pepper, cut into thin 1½-inch (4 cm) strips	1
1	onion, halved lengthwise and thinly sliced	1
3	cloves garlic, finely chopped	3
2 lbs	butternut squash, peeled, cut into large pieces and thinly sliced	1 kg
2 tbsp	chopped fresh sage	30 mL
	Salt and freshly ground black pepper	
¼ cup	freshly grated Parmesan cheese	60 mL
2 tbsp	fine dry bread crumbs	30 mL
6	sheets phyllo pastry	6
⅓ cup	melted butter	75 mL

1. In a large nonstick skillet, heat 1 tbsp (15 mL) of the oil over medium-high heat. Cook red pepper, onion and garlic, stirring, for 5 minutes or until softened. Transfer to a bowl.

2. Reduce heat to medium; add remaining oil to skillet. Cook squash, stirring, for 8 to 10 minutes or until just tender. Stir in sage and season with salt and pepper to taste. Add to bowl with red pepper mixture and combine.

3. In a bowl, combine Parmesan and bread crumbs. Place 1 sheet of phyllo on a work surface and lightly brush with some of the melted butter. (To prevent remaining sheets from drying out, keep them covered with waxed paper, then a damp kitchen towel.) Sprinkle with 1 tbsp (15 mL) of the crumb mixture.

4. Layer with 4 more sheets of phyllo, lightly brushing each layer with butter and sprinkling with 1 tbsp (15 mL) of the crumb mixture. Top with remaining sheet of phyllo and lightly brush with butter.

5. Spoon a 3-inch (7.5 cm) wide strip of squash mixture lengthwise down pastry 2 inches (5 cm) from edge. Fold 1 inch (2.5 cm) of the pastry ends over filling and carefully roll up pastry around filling. Place seam side down on prepared baking sheet. Brush with remaining butter.

6. To bake, cut 7 diagonal slits in top of pastry. Bake in preheated oven for 25 to 30 minutes or until pastry is golden. Cut into diagonal slices and serve warm or at room temperature.

Butternut Squash with Snow Peas and Red Pepper

Makes 4 servings

If the soft texture of a squash purée doesn't appeal to you, try this easy stir-fry instead.

Tip

To prepare squash: Peel squash using a vegetable peeler or paring knife. Cut into lengthwise quarters and seed. Cut into thin 1½- by ¼-inch (4 by 0.5 cm) pieces.

1 tbsp	vegetable oil	15 mL
5 cups	prepared butternut squash (see Tip, left)	1.25 L
4 oz	snow peas, ends trimmed	125 g
1	red bell pepper, cut into thin strips	1
1 tbsp	packed brown sugar	15 mL
1½ tsp	grated gingerroot	7 mL
	Salt and freshly ground black pepper	

1. In a large nonstick skillet, heat oil over medium-high heat. Cook squash, stirring, for 3 to 4 minutes or until almost tender.

2. Add snow peas, red pepper, brown sugar and ginger. Cook, stirring often, for 2 minutes or until vegetables are tender-crisp. Season with salt and pepper to taste.

Rutabaga Flan

This is a wonderful way
to dress up the humble
rutabaga. I love to serve
it as part of a traditional
holiday meal. It's always
a crowd pleaser.

Tip

To prepare ahead,
complete Steps 1 and 2.
Cover and refrigerate up to
2 days ahead. Sprinkle with
crumb topping just before
baking. Increase baking
time by 10 minutes.

- Preheat oven to 350°F (180°C)
- 8-inch (20 cm) square baking dish or 8-cup (2 L)
  casserole dish, greased

8 cups	cubed peeled rutabaga	2 L
2	eggs	2
2 tbsp	packed brown sugar	30 mL
½ tsp	salt	2 mL
¼ tsp	freshly ground black pepper	1 mL
¼ tsp	freshly grated nutmeg	1 mL
¼ cup	all-purpose flour	60 mL
1 tsp	baking powder	5 mL
¼ cup	fine dry bread crumbs	60 mL
¼ cup	freshly grated Parmesan cheese	60 mL
2 tbsp	butter, melted	30 mL

1. In a saucepan of lightly salted boiling water, cook
   rutabaga for 30 minutes or until very tender. Drain
   well and return to saucepan. Mash with a potato
   masher until smooth.

2. In a large bowl, beat eggs with brown sugar, salt,
   pepper and nutmeg. In another bowl, combine flour
   and baking powder. Stir rutabaga into egg mixture, then
   stir in flour mixture. Spread evenly in prepared baking
   dish.

3. In a bowl, combine bread crumbs, Parmesan and
   melted butter; sprinkle evenly over top.

4. Bake in preheated oven for 35 to 40 minutes or until
   top is golden and slightly puffed.

Pan-Braised Brussels Sprouts

Makes 4 to
6 servings

Brussels sprouts, with their delicate, nutty flavor, take on a pleasant sweetness in this easy-to-prepare recipe that can be doubled to serve a crowd. Like other vegetables in the cabbage family, the key is not to overcook them. Serve Brussels sprouts when they are tender-crisp and bright green in color.

1½ lbs	Brussels sprouts, trimmed and halved	750 g
2 tbsp	chicken stock	30 mL
2 tbsp	red wine vinegar	30 mL
1½ tsp	granulated sugar	7 mL
1 tbsp	butter	15 mL
2	cloves garlic, finely chopped	2
	Salt and freshly ground black pepper	

1. In a saucepan of boiling salted water, blanch Brussels sprouts for 3 minutes or until bright green and crisp; drain well. (If preparing sprouts ahead, chill in ice water. Drain well and wrap in a clean, dry kitchen towel to absorb moisture. Place in an airtight container and refrigerate for up to a day.)

2. In a glass measure, stir together stock, vinegar and sugar.

3. In a wok or large nonstick skillet, melt butter over medium-high heat and heat until foamy. Cook garlic, stirring, for 30 seconds or until fragrant. Add sprouts and cook, stirring, for 3 minutes or until lightly browned.

4. Add stock mixture. Reduce heat to medium and cook, stirring often, for about 4 minutes or until sprouts are barely tender. Season with salt and pepper to taste.

Sweet-and-Spicy Cabbage

Makes 4 servings

For a modern spin on an Oktoberfest dinner, spoon cabbage in center of serving plates and top with grilled sausages or smoked pork chops.

1	large pear or apple	1
2 tbsp	vegetable oil	30 mL
½	red onion, cut into thin wedges	½
½ tsp	hot pepper flakes, or to taste	2 mL
½	small Savoy cabbage, finely shredded	½
2 tbsp	rice vinegar	30 mL
1 tbsp	liquid honey	15 mL
	Salt	

1. Cut pear into quarters and core (not necessary to peel). Thinly slice, then cut slices in half.

2. In a large nonstick skillet, heat oil over medium-high heat. When almost smoking, add pear, onion and hot pepper flakes; stir-fry for 1 minute. Add cabbage and stir-fry for 1 minute more or until wilted.

3. Stir in rice vinegar and honey; cook, stirring, for 30 seconds. Season with salt to taste; serve immediately.

Sweet-and-Sour Red Cabbage with Apples

I consider this recipe a convenience food. I keep containers of sweet-and-sour red cabbage in my freezer, ready to microwave at a moment's notice to serve along with pork chops or roasts.

Tips

Depending on how sweet-and-sour you like your red cabbage, add more brown sugar and vinegar to taste. Most cooked red cabbage recipes, this one included, call for vinegar or wine. This adds not only flavor, but acidity, which preserves the cabbage's bright red color.

To freeze, pack cabbage into containers; it freezes well for up to 3 months.

2 tbsp	butter	30 mL
1	large onion, finely chopped	1
2	apples, peeled, cored and diced	2
1 cup	chicken or vegetable stock	250 mL
½ cup	red wine or additional stock	125 mL
⅓ cup	red wine vinegar	75 mL
⅓ cup	packed brown sugar	75 mL
1	bay leaf	1
½ tsp	salt	2 mL
¼ tsp	ground cinnamon	1 mL
¼ tsp	freshly ground black pepper	1 mL
Pinch	ground cloves	Pinch
1	red cabbage, finely shredded (about 10 cups/2.5 L)	1
1½ tsp	cornstarch	7 mL
1 tbsp	cold water	15 mL

1. In a Dutch oven or large saucepan, heat butter over medium heat. Add onion and apples; cook, stirring often, for 5 minutes or until softened.

2. Add stock, wine, vinegar, brown sugar, bay leaf, salt, cinnamon, pepper and ground cloves. Bring to a boil; stir in cabbage.

3. Cover and simmer over medium-low heat, stirring occasionally, for 45 minutes or until cabbage is tender.

4. Blend cornstarch with water; stir into cabbage. Cook for 3 minutes or until sauce is slightly thickened. Remove bay leaf before serving.

Breads and Muffins

Pizza Dough

Here is one of the easiest
and best ways to make
great pizza dough.

Tip

The ideal temperature
to let this dough rise at
is 72°F to 75°F (22°C to
25°C). However, most of
our kitchens are not this
warm. Instead, set your
oven to 200°F (100°C) (or
the lowest temperature
setting) and preheat for
3 to 5 minutes. Turn oven
off. Place covered dough
in warm oven and let rise.
Or fill a shallow roasting
pan with boiling water and
set on bottom rack of a
cold oven. Place dough
on upper rack and let rise
in closed oven.

- Heavy baking sheets, sprinkled with cornmeal, or pizza screens, greased

2¾ cups	all-purpose flour (approx.)	675 mL
1	package (2¼ tsp/11 mL) quick-rise instant yeast	1
1 tbsp	granulated sugar	15 mL
1 tsp	salt	5 mL
1 cup	warm water (120° to 130°F/50° to 55°C)	250 mL
2 tbsp	olive oil	30 mL

1. In a food processor, combine flour, yeast, sugar and salt. Process to mix ingredients. Add water and oil. Process to make soft sticky dough that forms a ball around the blade; add a small amount of flour if dough is sticky.

2. Transfer to a lightly floured board and knead, adding just enough flour to prevent dough from sticking, for 2 to 3 minutes or until smooth and elastic.

3. Place dough in a large oiled bowl, turning to coat in the oil. Cover with plastic wrap, then a dry towel; let rise in a warm place for 1 hour or until doubled in bulk.

4. Preheat oven to 450°F (230°C). Punch down dough. For medium pizzas, divide in two; or for a large pizza, do not divide.

5. Lightly flour a work surface. Flatten each ball of dough into a circle, making the outer edge thicker than the center. Lift dough from work surface, and stretch the edges and center, being careful not to tear the dough. For medium pizzas, shape into 10- to 12-inch (25 to 30 cm) circles; and for large pizza, a 15-inch (38 cm) circle. Or roll out dough using a rolling pin and pinch up the edges to form a small ridge. Place dough on prepared baking sheets. Let rest for 10 minutes before assembling pizza.

6. Spread pizzas with your favorite sauce, toppings and cheese. Bake in lower third of preheated oven. For medium pizzas, bake for 14 to 17 minutes; for large pizza, bake for 18 to 20 minutes.

Rosemary Garlic Focaccia

Makes 2 breads

Focaccia are popular Italian flatbreads used as a base for sandwiches or to serve warm with a hearty soup or stew. Warm slices are also terrific to serve as an appetizer with olive oil for dipping or to accompany with a soft cheese or spread, such as hummus.

Variation

Chopped sun-dried tomatoes or slivers of black olives can also be sprinkled on top of the focaccia, if desired, instead of sea salt.

• Two 9-inch (23 cm) cake or springform pans, greased and liberally sprinkled with cornmeal

¼ cup	olive oil	60 mL
2 tsp	dried rosemary leaves	10 mL
3	cloves garlic, finely chopped	3
3½ cups	all-purpose flour (approx.)	875 mL
1	package (2¼ tsp/11 mL) quick-rise instant yeast	1
1½ tsp	salt	7 mL
1 tsp	granulated sugar	5 mL
1½ cups	warm water (120° to 130°F/50° to 55°C)	375 mL
1½ tsp	coarse salt (optional)	7 mL

1. Place olive oil, rosemary and garlic in a small glass measure and microwave on Medium (50%) for 1 minute or until warm.

2. In a food processor, combine 3¼ cups (800 mL) of the flour, yeast, salt and sugar. Process to mix ingredients. Add water and half of the oil mixture. Process to make a soft sticky dough that forms a ball around the blade; add a small amount of remaining flour if dough is sticky.

3. Transfer to a lightly floured board and knead, adding just enough flour to prevent dough from sticking, for 2 to 3 minutes or until smooth and elastic.

4. Place dough in a large oiled bowl, turning to coat in the oil. Cover with plastic wrap, then a dry towel; let rise in a warm place for about 1 hour or until doubled in bulk.

5. Preheat oven to 375°F (190°C). Punch down dough and divide into two balls. Roll each out into a 9-inch (23 cm) circle and fit into prepared pans. Cover with towel and let rise for about 20 to 30 minutes or until doubled in size.

6. Poke your fingers in the surface of the focaccia to give it a dimpled appearance. Brush top with remaining oil mixture and sprinkle with coarse salt, if using.

7. Bake on middle rack in preheated oven for 25 to 30 minutes or until crisp and golden brown. Let cool slightly. Cut into wedges and serve warm.

Honey Oatmeal Bread

There's nothing more welcoming than the aroma of home-baked bread when you walk in the door. Who can wait to cut into a warm loaf so tasty, you don't need butter?

Tip

The ideal temperature to let this dough rise at is 72°F to 75°F (22°C to 25°C). However, most of our kitchens are not this warm. Instead, set your oven to 200°F (100°C) (or the lowest temperature setting) and preheat for 3 to 5 minutes. Turn oven off. Place covered dough in warm oven and let rise. Or fill a shallow roasting pan with boiling water and set on bottom rack of a cold oven. Place dough on upper rack and let rise in closed oven.

• Two 9- by 5-inch (23 by 13 cm) loaf pans, greased

1	package (2¼ tsp/11 mL) active dry yeast	1
1 tsp	granulated sugar	5 mL
1 cup	milk	250 mL
¼ cup	dark honey, such as buckwheat, or fancy molasses	60 mL
2 tbsp	butter	30 mL
2 tsp	salt	10 mL
1 cup	large-flake (old-fashioned) rolled oats	250 mL
2 cups	whole wheat flour	500 mL
3 cups	all-purpose flour (approx.)	750 mL
2 tsp	melted butter	10 mL
1	egg white	1
	Additional rolled oats	

1. Place ½ cup (125 mL) lukewarm water in a glass measuring cup; sprinkle with yeast and sugar. Let stand until foamy.

2. In a saucepan, combine 1 cup (250 mL) water, milk, honey, 2 tbsp (30 mL) butter and salt. Heat over medium heat, stirring, until bubbles appear around edge.

3. Place rolled oats in a large mixing bowl; pour in hot mixture. Let cool until lukewarm.

4. Stir in whole wheat flour and dissolved yeast; beat vigorously with a wooden spoon for 1 minute or until smooth. Stir in enough all-purpose flour to make a stiff dough that leaves sides of bowl.

5. Turn out onto a floured board and knead, adding just enough flour to prevent dough from sticking, for 7 to 9 minutes or until smooth and elastic.

6. Shape into a ball; place in well-buttered bowl. Turn dough to coat in butter. Cover with plastic wrap, then with clean dry towel; let rise in warm place until doubled in bulk, about 1½ to 2 hours.

Use an instant-read thermometer to measure the temperature of the water. Lukewarm water is between 105°F and 115°F (40°C and 45°C).

7. Punch down dough; knead for 1 minute to get rid of air bubbles. Divide in two. Shape into loaves and place in prepared loaf pans. Brush tops with 2 tsp (10 mL) melted butter. Cover with clean towel; let rise in a warm place for 1¼ hours or until almost doubled in bulk.

8. Preheat oven to 375°F (190°C). Lightly beat egg white with 1 tsp (5 mL) water; brush tops of loaves. Sprinkle each loaf with 1 tbsp (15 mL) rolled oats.

9. Bake in preheated oven for 45 minutes or until bottom of loaves when removed from pans sound hollow when tapped. Remove loaves from oven, turn out of pans and let cool on racks.

Hot Cross Loaf

Hot cross buns are a wonderful Easter treat, but they are so popular, you can often spot these spice- and fruit-studded buns in neighborhood bakeries year-round. Here's a streamlined method to make it in a loaf that has all of the same great taste as in a bun.

Tips

To plump currants, place in bowl and add boiling water to cover. Let stand for 1 minute. Drain and pat dry with paper towels.

If you prefer raisins, substitute them for the currants. Omit candied citron, if desired.

• 9-inch (23 cm) springform pan, greased

1 cup	milk	250 mL
1/3 cup	granulated sugar	75 mL
1/4 cup	butter, cubed	60 mL
3 1/4 cups	all-purpose flour (approx.)	800 mL
1	package (2 1/4 tsp/11 mL) quick-rise instant yeast	1
3/4 tsp	salt	3 mL
2 tsp	ground cinnamon	10 mL
1/2 tsp	freshly grated nutmeg	2 mL
1/4 tsp	ground allspice	1 mL
1/4 tsp	ground cloves	1 mL
1	egg, beaten	1
1/2 cup	dried currants, plumped (see Tips, left)	125 mL
1/4 cup	chopped candied citron or mixed peel	60 mL
1	egg white, lightly beaten	1

Icing

1/2 cup	confectioner's (icing) sugar	125 mL
2 tsp	milk	10 mL

1. In a small saucepan, combine milk, sugar and butter. Heat over medium heat, stirring, until butter melts. Let cool until warm to the touch (120°F to 130°F/50°C to 55°C on an instant-read thermometer).

2. In a large bowl, combine 2 cups (500 mL) flour, yeast, salt, cinnamon, nutmeg, allspice and cloves. Make a well in center and add warm liquid and egg. Using a wooden spoon, beat for 2 minutes to make a smooth, elastic batter. Beat in enough of the remaining flour to make a soft, slightly sticky dough.

3. Turn out onto a floured board and knead for about 5 minutes or until smooth and elastic, adding more flour as needed to prevent dough from sticking to board. Knead in currants and citron until evenly distributed. Shape dough into a ball and cover with large inverted bowl. Let rest for 20 minutes.

Tip

Here's how to use a stand mixer with a dough hook instead of making the dough by hand: In mixer bowl, combine 3 cups (750 mL) flour, yeast, salt, cinnamon, nutmeg, allspice and cloves. With machine running, beat in warm liquid and egg. Knead for 3 to 4 minutes, gradually adding reserved flour and scraping down sides of bowl using a spatula, until dough forms a soft, slightly sticky ball around dough hook. Turn out onto a floured board and knead for 1 minute or until smooth and elastic. Knead in currants and citron until evenly distributed.

4. Knead dough briefly. Shape into ball and flatten to an 8-inch (20 cm) round. Place in prepared pan. Cover with a dry towel; let rise in warm place for about 1 hour or until almost doubled in size.

5. Meanwhile, preheat oven to 375°F (190°C). Brush risen dough with egg white. With sharp knife, cut a large cross ¼ inch (0.5 cm) deep on top of loaf.

6. Bake in preheated oven for 30 to 35 minutes or until golden brown. Loosely cover loaf with a sheet of foil for last 10 minutes of baking if it is getting too brown. Remove loaf from pan and place on wire rack to cool.

7. *Icing:* In small bowl, combine confectioner's sugar with milk to make a smooth icing. Spread over cross cut in top of loaf. Let icing set. Slice and serve loaf same day it is baked.

Hot Cross Buns

Prepare dough as directed in recipe and let rest for 20 minutes. Shape into a 12-inch (30 cm) log. Cut into twelve 1-inch (2.5 cm) pieces. Shape each into ball, stretching and pinching dough underneath to make tops smooth. Flatten slightly. Place on greased baking sheet, spacing 2 inches (5 cm) apart. Cover with a dry towel and let rise in a warm place about 1 hour or until almost double in size. Brush dough with egg white. Bake rolls in preheated oven for 18 to 22 minutes or until golden. Transfer to a rack to cool. Place icing in a piping bag fitted with round tip and pipe a cross on top of each cooled bun. (Or place icing in a small plastic bag, press it into one corner and cut the tip off that corner.)

Soft Dinner Rolls

Makes 18 rolls

Hardly anyone bakes dinner rolls these days, so it's a treat when a basket of freshly baked rolls is served at dinner with a crock of butter. Just watch them disappear! If pressed for time, prepare the dough the day ahead and use the refrigerator method.

Tip

When making bread using quick-rise instant yeast, use an instant-read thermometer to ensure water is at the correct temperature of 120°F to 130°F (50°C to 55°C); otherwise, the yeast won't work properly.

● Rimmed baking sheet, greased or lined with parchment paper

3¼ cups	all-purpose flour (approx.)	800 mL
3 tbsp	granulated sugar	45 mL
1	package (2¼ tsp/11 mL) quick-rise instant yeast	1
¾ tsp	salt	3 mL
1 cup	warm water (see Tip, left)	250 mL
3 tbsp	butter, softened, divided	45 mL
1	egg, beaten	1

1. In a large bowl, combine 2½ cups (625 mL) flour, sugar, yeast and salt. Make a well in center and add water, 2 tbsp (30 mL) of the butter and egg. Using a wooden spoon, beat for 2 minutes or until batter is smooth and elastic. Beat in enough of the remaining flour to make a soft, slightly sticky dough. Turn out onto a floured board and knead for 5 minutes or until smooth and elastic, adding more flour as needed to prevent dough from sticking to board.

2. Shape dough into a ball and cover with large inverted bowl. Let rest for 20 minutes.

3. Knead dough briefly and shape into an 18-inch (45 cm) log. Cut into eighteen 1-inch (2.5 cm) pieces. Shape each into ball, stretching and pinching dough underneath to make tops smooth. Place on prepared baking sheet, spacing 1½ inches (4 cm) apart. Cover with a dry towel and let rise in a warm place about 1 hour or until almost double in size.

4. Meanwhile, preheat oven to 375°F (190°C). Bake rolls for 14 to 16 minutes or until tops are golden.

5. Melt remaining 1 tbsp (15 mL) butter and brush over tops of buns to keep crusts soft. Transfer to a rack to cool. Serve buns warm or at room temperature the same day they are baked.

Here's how to use a stand mixer with a dough hook instead of making the dough by hand: In mixer bowl, combine 3 cups (750 mL) flour, sugar, yeast and salt. Beat in water, 2 tbsp (25 mL) of the butter and egg. Knead for 3 to 4 minutes, gradually adding reserved flour and scraping down sides of bowl using a spatula, until dough forms a soft, slightly sticky ball around dough hook. Turn out onto a floured board and knead for 1 minute or until smooth and elastic.

Refrigerator Dinner Rolls

Prepare dough as directed. Once dough has rested for 20 minutes, place in a well-greased bowl, turning dough over to coat top. Cover with plastic wrap and refrigerate for 8 hours or overnight. Punch down dough and let it warm to room temperature. Or, to quickly warm the dough, place in glass bowl and microwave on Low (10%) for 12 to 15 minutes, checking every few minutes and turning dough often, until no longer cool to the touch. Shape and bake rolls as directed in recipe.

Sticky Cinnamon Buns

It's a treat to bake a batch of sticky buns and indulge in them warm from the oven. A word of warning to the calorie-conscious: it is next to impossible to eat just one of these scrumptious buns!

Tip

The ideal temperature to let this dough rise at is 72°F to 75°F (22°C to 25°C). However, most of our kitchens are not this warm. Instead, set your oven to 200°F (100°C) (or the lowest temperature setting) and preheat for 3 to 5 minutes. Turn oven off. Place covered dough in warm oven and let rise. Or fill a shallow roasting pan with boiling water and set on bottom rack of a cold oven. Place dough on upper rack and let rise in closed oven.

● 13- by 9-inch (33 by 23 cm) baking pan, well greased

1 cup	milk	250 mL
1/3 cup	granulated sugar	75 mL
1/4 cup	butter, cubed	60 mL
3 1/4 cups	all-purpose flour (approx.)	800 mL
1	package (2 1/4 tsp/11 mL) quick-rise instant yeast	1
3/4 tsp	salt	3 mL
1/2 tsp	ground cinnamon	2 mL
1	egg, beaten	1

Filling

1/2 cup	butter	125 mL
1/3 cup	maple syrup	75 mL
1 cup	packed brown sugar, divided	250 mL
1/2 cup	dark raisins	125 mL
1/2 cup	chopped pecans	125 mL
2 tsp	ground cinnamon	10 mL

1. In a small saucepan, combine milk, sugar and butter. Heat over medium heat, stirring until butter melts. Let cool until warm to the touch (120°F to 130°F/50°C to 55°C on an instant-read thermometer).

2. In a large bowl, combine 2 cups (500 mL) of the flour, yeast, salt and cinnamon. Make a well in the center and add warm liquid and egg. Using a wooden spoon, beat for 2 minutes to make a smooth, elastic batter. Beat in enough of the remaining flour to make a soft, slightly sticky dough.

3. Turn dough out onto a floured board and knead for about 5 minutes or until smooth and elastic, adding more flour as needed to prevent dough from sticking to board. Shape dough into a ball and cover with large inverted bowl. Let rest for 20 minutes.

4. *Filling:* In a small saucepan, melt butter over medium heat. Set aside 1/4 cup (60 mL) of the melted butter. Add maple syrup and 1/3 cup (75 mL) of the brown sugar to remaining butter in saucepan. Bring to a boil, stirring until smooth. Pour into prepared baking pan.

5. In a bowl, combine remaining brown sugar, raisins, pecans and cinnamon.

6. Punch down dough. On a floured surface roll out to an 18- by 10-inch (45 by 25 cm) rectangle.

7. Brush half of the remaining melted butter over dough. Sprinkle with raisin mixture, leaving a $\frac{1}{2}$-inch (1 cm) border along the long sides. Starting at one long side, roll up into a cylinder, pinching edges to seal. Cut into 12 even slices and place cut side down in pan. Brush with remaining melted butter. Cover with a dry towel; let rise in a warm place for about 1 hour or until almost doubled in size.

8. Meanwhile, preheat oven to 375°F (190°C).

9. Bake in preheated oven for 25 to 30 minutes or until buns are golden. Let cool on wire rack for 5 minutes. Invert onto a baking sheet and pull buns apart. Serve warm or at room temperature.

Yorkshire Pudding

Makes 8 servings

The quintessential English side dish to accompany roast beef is also just as delicious with roast pork and lamb, or serve with a hearty soup.

- Preheat oven to 450°F (230°C)
- 12-cup muffin pan

2	eggs	2
1 cup	milk	250 mL
1 cup	all-purpose flour	250 mL
$\frac{1}{4}$ tsp	salt	1 mL
2 tbsp	butter, melted	30 mL

1. In a bowl, whisk eggs with milk until frothy; whisk in flour and salt until batter is quite smooth.

2. Place muffin pan in preheated oven for 10 minutes, until hot.

3. Pour 1 scant teaspoon (5 mL) of melted butter into 8 muffin cups and, using a pastry brush, generously brush cups with melted butter. Fill muffin cups three-quarters full with batter.

4. Bake on middle rack in preheated oven for 18 to 20 minutes or until puffed and golden. With skewer, puncture each popover; bake for 4 to 5 minutes longer or until golden brown, crisp and puffed. Serve warm.

Banana Nut Bread

Everyone has a recipe for banana bread in their files. I've included my best. It's a simple bread that just relies on the flavor of banana and walnuts. Honey gives extra moistness that keeps it fresh for days — if it lasts that long.

Tips

Lining the bottom of baking pan with waxed or parchment paper ensures that you'll never have trouble removing the bread from the pan.

Left with ripe bananas on your counter but have no time to bake a bread? Simply freeze whole bananas with the peel, then leave at room temperature to defrost. Or peel and mash bananas; pack into containers and freeze for up to 2 months. Defrost at room temperature. Frozen banana purée may darken slightly but will not affect the delicious baked results.

- Preheat oven to 325°F (160°C)
- 9- by 5-inch (23 by 13 cm) loaf pan, greased

1¾ cups	all-purpose flour	425 mL
1 tsp	baking soda	5 mL
¼ tsp	salt	1 mL
2	eggs	2
1 cup	mashed ripe bananas (about 3)	250 mL
⅓ cup	vegetable oil	75 mL
½ cup	liquid honey	125 mL
⅓ cup	packed brown sugar	75 mL
½ cup	chopped walnuts	125 mL

1. In a bowl, stir together flour, baking soda and salt.

2. In another bowl, beat eggs. Stir in bananas, oil, honey and brown sugar.

3. Stir dry ingredients into banana mixture until combined. Fold in walnuts.

4. Pour batter into prepared loaf pan. Bake on middle rack in preheated oven for 1¼ hours or until cake tester inserted in center comes out clean. Let pan cool on rack for 15 minutes. Run knife around edge; turn out loaf and let cool on rack.

Orange Pumpkin Loaf

This bread is so much easier to bake than pumpkin pie, but still loaded with all the spice-scented flavors we love.

Tips

Baking powder and baking soda have a shelf life of only 6 months once opened, so make sure to replenish both regularly. As a reminder, write the date when they need to be replaced on the container.

The brown sugar you use in recipes is totally your preference. Brown sugar comes in both light and dark brown. Dark brown sugar is noticeably darker in color and has a stronger molasses taste.

- Preheat oven to 350°F (180°C)
- 9- by 5-inch (23 by 13 cm) loaf pan, greased

1 cup	all-purpose flour	250 mL
¾ cup	whole wheat or all-purpose flour	175 mL
2 tsp	baking powder	10 mL
½ tsp	baking soda	2 mL
½ tsp	salt	2 mL
1½ tsp	ground cinnamon	7 mL
½ tsp	freshly grated nutmeg	2 mL
¼ tsp	ground cloves or allspice	1 mL
1¼ cups	packed brown sugar	300 mL
2	eggs	2
1 cup	canned pumpkin purée (not pie filling)	250 mL
⅓ cup	vegetable oil	75 mL
2 tsp	grated orange zest	10 mL
¼ cup	fresh orange juice	60 mL

1. In a bowl, combine flours, baking powder, baking soda and salt; stir well.

2. In a small bowl, combine cinnamon, nutmeg and cloves. Transfer 1 tsp (5 mL) of the spice mixture to another bowl; add 2 tbsp (30 mL) brown sugar. Set aside for topping.

3. Place remaining spices and brown sugar in a bowl; add eggs and beat well. Stir in pumpkin, oil, orange zest and juice. Stir dry ingredients into pumpkin mixture until combined.

4. Spoon batter into prepared loaf pan. Sprinkle top with reserved spiced-sugar mixture. Bake on middle rack in preheated oven for 50 to 55 minutes or until toothpick inserted in center comes out clean. Let pan cool on rack for 15 minutes; turn loaf out and let cool completely.

Lemon Yogurt Loaf

Makes 1 loaf

Here's a lemony-flavored loaf that stays moist for days — if it lasts that long.

Tip

I like to double this recipe so that I have an extra loaf handy in the freezer. Wrap in plastic wrap, then in foil and freeze for up to 1 month.

Variation

Lemon Poppy Seed Loaf

Stir 2 tbsp (30 mL) poppy seeds into flour mixture before combining with yogurt mixture.

- Preheat oven to 350°F (180°C)
- 9- by 5-inch (23 by 13 cm) loaf pan, greased

1¾ cups	all-purpose flour	425 mL
1 tsp	baking powder	5 mL
½ tsp	baking soda	2 mL
¼ tsp	salt	1 mL
2	eggs	2
¾ cup	granulated sugar	175 mL
¾ cup	plain yogurt	175 mL
⅓ cup	vegetable oil	75 mL
1 tbsp	grated lemon zest	15 mL

Topping

⅓ cup	fresh lemon juice	75 mL
⅓ cup	granulated sugar	75 mL

1. In a bowl, combine flour, baking powder, baking soda and salt. In another large bowl, beat eggs. Stir in sugar, yogurt, oil and lemon zest. Fold in flour mixture to make a smooth batter.

2. Spoon into prepared pan; bake on middle rack in preheated oven for 50 to 60 minutes or until cake tester inserted in center comes out clean. Place pan on rack.

3. *Topping:* In a small saucepan, heat lemon juice and sugar; bring to a boil. Cook, stirring, until sugar is dissolved. (Alternatively, place in a glass bowl and microwave on High for 1 minute, stirring once.) Pour over hot loaf in pan; let cool completely before turning out of pan.

Tea Time Scones

Makes about 12 scones

Bring out the clotted cream or the sweet butter. Set out the thick jam or fruit preserves. Brew a steaming pot of tea, invite some good friends over, then spoil them with these tender, light scones.

Variation

Apricot and Candied Ginger Scones

Substitute slivered dried apricots for the currants and add 2 tbsp (30 mL) finely chopped candied ginger to flour mixture.

- Preheat oven to 400°F (200°C)
- Large baking sheet, greased or lined with parchment paper

2 cups	all-purpose flour	500 mL
¼ cup	granulated sugar	60 mL
1 tbsp	baking powder	15 mL
½ tsp	baking soda	2 mL
¼ tsp	salt	1 mL
½ cup	cold butter, cut into pieces	125 mL
½ cup	dried currants or raisins	125 mL
1	egg	1
½ cup	buttermilk	125 mL

Topping

1 tbsp	buttermilk	15 mL
2 tsp	granulated sugar	10 mL

1. In a large bowl, stir together flour, sugar, baking powder, baking soda and salt. Cut in butter using a pastry blender or fork to make coarse crumbs. Stir in currants.

2. In another bowl, beat egg with buttermilk; stir into dry ingredients with a few light strokes to make a soft dough.

3. Turn out onto floured board and knead dough gently three to four times; pat or roll out using a floured rolling pin into a circular shape about ¾ inch (2 cm) thick. Cut out rounds using a 2½-inch (6 cm) floured cutter; arrange on prepared baking sheet.

4. Brush with buttermilk and sprinkle with sugar. Bake in preheated oven for 16 to 20 minutes or until golden. Transfer to rack.

Oatmeal Scones with Cranberries

These scones are my favorite treat for a weekend breakfast at the cottage. I like to serve them warm from the oven with cold unsalted butter and a pot of thick strawberry jam or marmalade.

Tip

Any type or combination of dried fruits, such as golden raisins, chopped apricots, mangos and figs, can be used instead of cranberries.

- Preheat oven to 400°F (200°C)
- Large baking sheet, greased or lined with parchment paper

2 cups	whole wheat flour (approx.)	500 mL
1/3 cup	packed brown sugar	75 mL
1 tbsp	baking powder	15 mL
1/4 tsp	salt	1 mL
1/2 cup	cold butter, cut into pieces	125 mL
1/2 cup	large-flake (old-fashioned) rolled oats	125 mL
1/2 cup	dried cranberries	125 mL
1 1/2 tsp	finely grated orange zest	7 mL
1	egg	1
1/2 cup	half-and-half (10%) cream or milk	125 mL
	Additional cream and rolled oats	

1. In a large bowl, combine flour, brown sugar, baking powder and salt. Cut in butter using a pastry blender or fork to make coarse crumbs. Stir in rolled oats, dried cranberries and orange zest.

2. In bowl, beat egg with cream; stir into dry ingredients to make a soft, slightly sticky dough. Turn out onto a well-floured board and, with floured hands, knead gently two to three times, working in a bit more flour to prevent dough from sticking.

3. Pat into a 12- by 9-inch (30 by 23 cm) rectangle. Cut into twelve 3-inch (7.5 cm) squares; arrange on prepared baking sheet. Brush tops with cream and sprinkle lightly with rolled oats.

4. Bake in preheated oven for 18 to 22 minutes or until golden. Transfer to rack to cool.

Whole-Grain Irish Soda Bread

Makes 1 loaf

Old-fashioned soda bread is a wonderful accompaniment to a hearty soup or stew. Any leftovers are delicious toasted and spread with butter and homemade preserves.

- Preheat oven to 375°F (190°C)
- Baking sheet, greased or lined with parchment paper

2 cups	whole wheat flour	500 mL
1⅔ cups	all-purpose flour	400 mL
⅔ cup	large-flake (old-fashioned) rolled oats	150 mL
1 tbsp	granulated sugar	15 mL
1½ tsp	baking soda	7 mL
½ tsp	salt	2 mL
2 cups	buttermilk	500 mL

Topping

1 tbsp	buttermilk	15 mL
1 tbsp	large-flake (old-fashioned) rolled oats	15 mL

1. In a large bowl, combine flours, rolled oats, sugar, baking soda and salt. Stir well. Make a well in center; add buttermilk. Stir until a soft dough forms.

2. Turn out onto lightly floured board; knead five or six times until smooth. Shape dough into a ball; pat into an 8-inch (20 cm) round. Place on prepared baking sheet. With a sharp knife dipped in flour, cut a large ½-inch (1 cm) deep cross on top of loaf.

3. *Topping:* Brush loaf with buttermilk and sprinkle with oats. Bake in preheated oven for 50 to 60 minutes until well risen and golden; loaf sounds hollow when tapped on base. Immediately wrap in clean, dry tea towel; set aside to cool. This prevents crust from becoming too hard.

Cheddar Drop Biscuits

Makes 12 biscuits

Serve these wonderful biscuits straight from the oven. Consider baking a double batch if expecting a hungry crowd.

Tip

To assemble recipe ahead, place dry ingredients in a bowl. Cut in butter, add cheese, cover and refrigerate. While oven is preheating, stir in the milk and continue with recipe.

- Preheat oven to 400°F (200°C)
- Baking sheet, greased or lined with parchment paper

2 cups	all-purpose flour	500 mL
1 tbsp	baking powder	15 mL
¼ tsp	salt	1 mL
⅓ cup	butter, at room temperature, cut into pieces	75 mL
1 cup	coarsely shredded aged Cheddar cheese	250 mL
2 tbsp	chopped fresh chives	30 mL
1 cup	milk	250 mL
	Additional chopped chives	

1. In a large bowl, combine flour, baking powder and salt. Cut in butter using a pastry blender or fork to make coarse crumbs. Add Cheddar cheese and chives.

2. Stir in milk to make a soft, sticky dough. Drop 12 heaping tablespoonfuls (15 mL) onto prepared baking sheet. Sprinkle tops with chopped chives.

3. Bake on middle rack in preheated oven for 18 to 20 minutes or until edges are golden. Transfer biscuits to a rack to cool.

Green Beans Stewed with Tomatoes (page 415)

Carrot Raisin Muffins (page 451)

Classic Chocolate Chip Cookies (page 458)

Farmhouse Apple Pie (page 513)

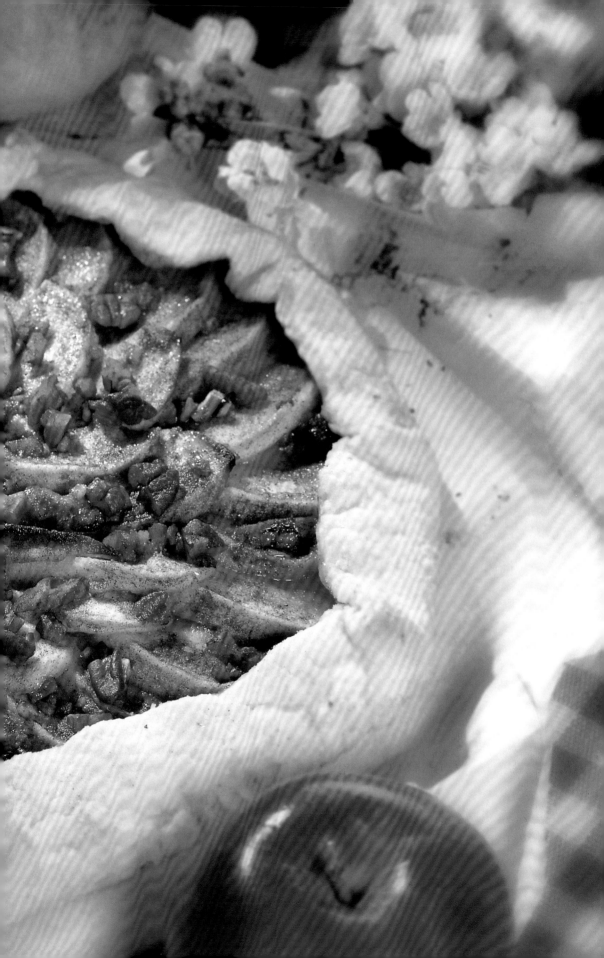

Strawberry Cream Cake (page 496)

Bread Pudding with
Caramelized Pears (page 528)

Lemon Fool with Fresh Berries (page 544)

Cheese Cornbread

Cut this savory cornbread into small squares and serve with a salad. Or cut into 6 large squares and slice in half lengthwise to use as sandwich bases. Spread with herb cream cheese or goat cheese, or layer with your favorite cold cuts, such as smoked ham or turkey, topped with tomato slices and lettuce.

Variation
Jalapeño Cornbread
Add 1 diced small red bell pepper and 2 tbsp (30 mL) minced seeded jalapeño peppers to flour mixture along with cheese.

- Preheat oven to 375°F (190°C)
- 13- by 9-inch (33 by 23 cm) baking pan, greased

1¼ cups	all-purpose flour	300 mL
1 cup	cornmeal	250 mL
2 tbsp	granulated sugar	30 mL
1 tbsp	baking powder	15 mL
¼ tsp	salt	1 mL
¾ cup	shredded Cheddar cheese	175 mL
2	eggs	2
1¼ cups	milk	300 mL
¼ cup	vegetable oil	60 mL

1. In a bowl, combine flour, cornmeal, sugar, baking powder and salt. Stir in cheese.

2. In another bowl, beat eggs with milk and oil. Pour over flour mixture and stir until combined.

3. Pour batter into prepared baking pan. Bake in preheated oven for 25 to 30 minutes or until top springs back when lightly touched in center. Let cool on rack. Cut into squares.

Maple Walnut Apple Muffins

I discovered that these wholesome muffins have great appeal. When I was a food columnist for *The Gazette* newspaper in Montreal, this recipe was featured in one of my weekly columns. The maple syrup amount was omitted due to a technical problem when going to press and the paper received more than 500 telephone calls from readers requesting how much maple syrup to add to the recipe. Here it is — with the right amount of maple syrup!

- Preheat oven to 400°F (200°C)
- 12-cup muffin pan, well greased or with paper liners

1¼ cups	all-purpose flour	300 mL
2½ tsp	baking powder	12 mL
½ tsp	baking soda	2 mL
¼ tsp	salt	1 mL
⅓ cup	finely chopped walnuts	75 mL
1	egg	1
1 cup	large-flake (old-fashioned) rolled oats	250 mL
1 cup	coarsely grated apple	250 mL
⅔ cup	maple syrup	150 mL
½ cup	plain yogurt	125 mL
¼ cup	vegetable oil	60 mL

1. In a bowl, combine flour, baking powder, baking soda, salt and walnuts.

2. In another bowl, beat egg. Stir in oats, grated apple, maple syrup, yogurt and oil. Stir into flour mixture just until combined; do not overmix.

3. Spoon batter into prepared muffin cups, filling three-quarters full.

4. Bake in preheated oven for 20 minutes or until tops spring back when lightly touched. Let cool in pan for 5 minutes, then transfer muffins to a wire rack to cool.

Carrot Raisin Muffins

Packed with nuts, fruits and carrots, these scrumptious muffins are perfect for breakfast. But they are just as tasty for afternoon snacks or stowed away in a lunch box.

Tip

Have only one muffin pan? Place muffin paper liners in 6-oz (175 mL) glass custard cups or small ramekins and fill with extra batter. Bake alongside muffin pan.

- Preheat oven to 375°F (190°C)
- Two 12-cup muffin pans, well greased or with paper liners

2 cups	all-purpose flour	500 mL
¾ cup	granulated sugar	175 mL
1½ tsp	ground cinnamon	7 mL
1 tsp	baking powder	5 mL
1 tsp	baking soda	5 mL
½ tsp	freshly grated nutmeg	2 mL
¼ tsp	salt	1 mL
1½ cups	grated carrots (about 3 medium)	375 mL
1 cup	grated peeled apples	250 mL
½ cup	raisins	125 mL
½ cup	sweetened shredded coconut	125 mL
½ cup	chopped walnuts (optional)	125 mL
2	eggs	2
⅔ cup	plain yogurt	150 mL
⅓ cup	vegetable oil	75 mL

1. In a large bowl, stir together flour, sugar, cinnamon, baking powder, baking soda, nutmeg and salt. Stir in carrots, apples, raisins, coconut and walnuts, if using.

2. In another bowl, beat eggs; add yogurt and oil. Stir into flour mixture just until combined. (Batter will be very thick.)

3. Spoon batter into prepared muffin cups, filling almost to the top.

4. Bake in preheated oven for 25 to 30 minutes or until tops spring back when lightly touched. Let cool in pans for 5 minutes, then transfer muffins to a wire rack to cool.

Lemon Blueberry Muffins

Blueberries contain powerful antioxidants, and what better way to enjoy them than in muffins that are easy to make year-round with frozen blueberries? The smaller-sized wild blueberries are ideal for making these yummy muffins.

Tips

When using frozen blueberries, the batter often gets tinted with juice from the berries. To reduce this effect, add a spoonful of batter to each muffin cup. Layer with some of the frozen blueberries and top with more batter. Scatter more berries over top.

Instead of serving cupcakes at a children's party, serve blueberry mini muffins — they are perfect for little ones to enjoy. Frost with Lemon Buttercream Frosting (variation, page 501), if desired.

To prepare 24 mini muffins, use a mini muffin pan, well greased or with paper liners. Fill prepared muffin cups three-quarters full and bake for 12 to 15 minutes or until lightly browned and tops spring back when lightly touched.

- Preheat oven to 375°F (190°C)
- 12-cup muffin pan, well greased or with paper liners

1¾ cups	all-purpose flour	425 mL
⅔ cup	granulated sugar	150 mL
2½ tsp	baking powder	12 mL
¼ tsp	salt	1 mL
2	eggs	2
¾ cup	milk	175 mL
⅓ cup	butter, melted	75 mL
2 tsp	grated lemon zest	10 mL
1 cup	fresh or frozen blueberries	250 mL

1. In a large bowl, combine flour, sugar, baking powder and salt.

2. In another bowl, beat eggs. Stir in milk, melted butter and lemon zest. Stir into flour mixture until just combined. Gently fold in blueberries.

3. Spoon batter into prepared muffin cups, filling three-quarters full.

4. Bake in preheated oven for 22 to 25 minutes or until lightly browned and tops spring back when lightly touched. Let cool in pan for 5 minutes, then transfer muffins to a wire rack to cool.

Bran Muffins

Bran muffins are never out of style. Nicely moistened with molasses, these muffins will become a morning favorite.

Tip

Always measure the oil before measuring sticky sweeteners such as molasses or honey. For recipes that don't call for oil, spray measure with nonstick vegetable spray or lightly coat with oil. You'll find every last drop of sweetener will easily pour out.

- Preheat oven to 400°F (200°C)
- 12-cup muffin pan, well greased or with paper liners

1¼ cups	whole wheat flour	300 mL
1 cup	natural bran	250 mL
1 tsp	baking soda	5 mL
½ tsp	baking powder	2 mL
¼ tsp	salt	1 mL
2	eggs	2
1 cup	buttermilk	250 mL
⅓ cup	packed brown sugar	75 mL
¼ cup	vegetable oil	60 mL
¼ cup	fancy molasses	60 mL
½ cup	raisins or chopped dried apricots	125 mL

1. In a bowl, combine flour, bran, baking soda, baking powder and salt.

2. In another bowl, beat eggs. Add buttermilk, brown sugar, oil and molasses. Stir into flour mixture to make a smooth batter; fold in raisins.

3. Spoon batter into prepared muffin cups, filling three-quarters full.

4. Bake in preheated oven for 20 to 24 minutes or until tops spring back when lightly touched. Let cool in pan for 10 minutes, then transfer muffins to a wire rack to cool.

Muesli Applesauce Muffins

Wholesome and nutritious, these tasty muffins are great to serve for breakfast or as a snack when kids come home from school. I often prepare a double batch and freeze them in an airtight container or heavy plastic storage bag. To quickly defrost, wrap each muffin in a paper towel and microwave on High for about 20 seconds or until warmed through.

Tip

Use a traditional muesli mix containing a variety of rolled grains such as oats and rye and lots of assorted fruits and nuts. A blended muesli cereal containing large cereal flakes does not work as well in this recipe.

- Preheat oven to 375°F (190°C)
- 12-cup muffin pan, well greased or with paper liners

1½ cups	whole wheat flour	375 mL
1 cup	muesli with dried fruits and nuts	250 mL
2 tsp	baking powder	10 mL
1½ tsp	ground cinnamon	7 mL
½ tsp	baking soda	2 mL
½ tsp	freshly grated nutmeg	2 mL
1	egg	1
1 cup	unsweetened applesauce	250 mL
⅔ cup	packed brown sugar	150 mL
½ cup	vanilla or plain yogurt	125 mL
¼ cup	vegetable oil	60 mL
	Additional muesli for topping	

1. In a large bowl, combine flour, muesli, baking powder, cinnamon, baking soda and nutmeg.

2. In another bowl, beat egg. Stir in applesauce, brown sugar, yogurt and oil. Stir into flour mixture until just combined.

3. Spoon batter into prepared muffin cups, filling three-quarters full. Sprinkle tops with additional muesli.

4. Bake in preheated oven for 20 to 25 minutes or until tops spring back when lightly touched. Let cool in pan for 5 minutes, then transfer muffins to a wire rack to cool.

Banana Spice Muffins

Whip up this batch of muffins and they'll be gone in no time. They are especially child-friendly, but they'll also be enjoyed by the adults in the house.

Tip

Don't overmix the batter. Use quick, gentle strokes to combine the dry and liquid ingredients together. It's normal to have a few lumps remaining in the batter.

- Preheat oven to 400°F (200°C)
- 12-cup muffin pan, well greased or with paper liners

2 cups	all-purpose flour	500 mL
1½ tsp	baking powder	7 mL
1½ tsp	ground cinnamon	7 mL
½ tsp	baking soda	2 mL
½ tsp	freshly grated nutmeg	2 mL
¼ tsp	ground cloves	1 mL
¼ tsp	salt	1 mL
1	egg	1
1 cup	mashed ripe bananas (about 3)	250 mL
¾ cup	packed brown sugar	175 mL
½ cup	plain yogurt	125 mL
¼ cup	vegetable oil	60 mL
½ cup	raisins	125 mL

1. In a bowl, combine flour, baking powder, cinnamon, baking soda, nutmeg, cloves and salt.

2. In another bowl, beat egg. Stir in bananas, brown sugar, yogurt and oil until smooth. Stir into flour mixture until just combined. Fold in raisins.

3. Spoon batter into prepared muffin cups until level with top of pan.

4. Bake in preheated oven for 20 to 25 minutes or until tops spring back when lightly touched. Let cool in pan for 5 minutes, then transfer muffins to a wire rack to cool.

Baking Tips

Accurate Measuring

- To measure flour correctly for all baking, give flour a quick stir, spoon into dry measure and use a knife to level the top. Do not pack the dry measure down by tapping on the countertop; this increases the amount.

Bread Baking Know-How

- For yeast to work properly, liquids must be at the correct temperature to activate the yeast. Liquids that are too hot will kill the action of yeast and dough will not rise. Cold temperatures will shock the yeast and it will not have its full leavening strength. Use an instant-read thermometer for accuracy.

- Do not work in too much flour when mixing and kneading, or dough will be heavy. Depending on the humidity of the flour used, you may need less or more than the amount called for.

Perfectly Baked Cookies

- Place baking sheet on middle rack of oven. Bake only one sheet at a time.

- Wipe sheets with paper towels or a damp cloth to remove grease.

- Let sheets cool completely before using again to prevent dough from melting and spreading out too much during baking.

- Double the recipe, bake half and freeze dough to bake later.

- To grease pans and baking sheets, lard, vegetable shortening or unsalted or lightly salted butter is recommended.

Cutting Bars or Squares

- Line sides and bottom of baking pan with foil or parchment paper.

- Bake as directed and let bars cool completely in pan.

- Place in freezer for up to 30 minutes or until partially frozen.

- Lift out entire batch. Cut into bars or squares with a sharp knife.

- Arrange in cookie tin with waxed paper or parchment paper separating the layers and freeze. Most bars, like cookies, freeze well.

About Nuts

- *Toasting nuts:* Place on a baking sheet in a 350°F (180°C) oven for 6 to 8 minutes or until lightly fragrant. You'll find the nuts easier to chop when warm, too.

- Nothing ruins baked goods more than rancid nuts, in particular walnuts. Taste before purchasing, if possible, to make sure nuts are fresh. Store them in an airtight container in the fridge or freezer.

Cookies, Bars and Squares

Classic Chocolate Chip Cookies

I'm never short of taste testers when the first warm batch of these cookies come out of the oven. My family loves them flecked with chocolate chips and walnuts. Served with a cold glass of milk, they're pure heaven.

Variation

Double Chocolate Chunk Cookies

Decrease all-purpose flour to 1½ cups (375 mL). Sift flour with ½ cup (125 mL) cocoa powder and baking soda. Replace chocolate chips with white chocolate chunks instead.

* Preheat oven to 350°F (180°C)
* Baking sheets, lightly greased or lined with parchment paper

¾ cup	butter, softened	175 mL
½ cup	granulated sugar	125 mL
½ cup	packed brown sugar	125 mL
2	eggs	2
2 tsp	vanilla	10 mL
1¾ cups	all-purpose flour	425 mL
½ tsp	baking soda	2 mL
¼ tsp	salt	1 mL
1½ cups	semisweet or milk chocolate chips	375 mL
1 cup	chopped walnuts or pecans (optional)	250 mL

1. In a large bowl, using an electric mixer, cream butter with granulated and brown sugars until fluffy; beat in eggs and vanilla until incorporated.

2. In another bowl, stir together flour, baking soda and salt. Beat into creamed mixture until combined; stir in chocolate chips and walnuts, if using.

3. Drop by tablespoonfuls (15 mL) about 2 inches (5 cm) apart onto prepared baking sheets.

4. Bake one sheet at time on middle rack in preheated oven for 10 to 12 minutes or until edges are firm. (Bake for the shorter time if you prefer cookies with a soft, chewy center.) Let cool for 2 minutes on baking sheet; remove to a wire rack and let cool completely.

Scrumptious Oatmeal Cookies

Makes 36 cookies

Kids love home-baked cookies especially moist and chewy ones like these made with wholesome oatmeal.

Tip

Use whatever combination of dried fruits and nuts appeals to your family or whatever you happen to have on hand. Just add 1½ cups (375 mL) in total to the batter.

- Preheat oven to 350°F (180°C)
- Baking sheets, greased or lined with parchment paper

¾ cup	butter, softened	175 mL
1¼ cups	packed brown sugar	300 mL
2	eggs	2
1 tsp	vanilla	5 mL
1¼ cups	all-purpose flour	300 mL
½ tsp	baking soda	2 mL
¼ tsp	salt	1 mL
1½ cups	large-flake (old-fashioned) rolled oats	375 mL
¾ cup	sliced almonds or chopped pecans	175 mL
¾ cup	dried cherries, dried cranberries, raisins or chocolate chips	175 mL

1. In a large bowl, using an electric mixer, cream butter and brown sugar until fluffy; beat in egg and vanilla until incorporated.

2. In another bowl, stir together flour, baking soda and salt. Stir into butter mixture, mixing well. Stir in rolled oats, almonds and dried cherries.

3. Drop by heaping tablespoonfuls (15 mL) about 2 inches (5 cm) apart onto prepared baking sheets and flatten with a fork.

4. Bake one sheet at a time on middle rack in preheated oven for 12 to 14 minutes or until edges are golden. Let cool for 5 minutes on baking sheet; remove to a wire rack and let cool completely.

Lemon Sugar Cookies

When my children were
young, this was their
favorite cookie dough
to roll out and cut into
various cookie shapes.
Sampling the unbaked
cookie dough and then
the warm-from-the-oven
cookies were the delicious
rewards for their efforts.
It's a tradition that they
still carry on today.

Tips

Instead of granulated
sugar, sprinkle tops of
the cookies with colored
sprinkles.

The cookie dough can
be made ahead. Place
in heavy-duty plastic
bags and freeze for
up to 1 month. Thaw
in refrigerator.

● Baking sheets, well greased

1 cup	butter, softened	250 mL
1¼ cups	granulated sugar	300 mL
1	egg	1
1	egg yolk	1
1 tbsp	grated lemon zest	15 mL
3 cups	all-purpose flour	750 mL
½ tsp	baking powder	2 mL
½ tsp	salt	2 mL
1	egg white, lightly beaten	1
	Granulated sugar	

1. In a large bowl, using an electric mixer, cream butter with sugar until light and fluffy; beat in egg, egg yolk and lemon zest until incorporated.

2. In another bowl, stir together flour, baking powder and salt; stir into butter mixture until combined.

3. Divide dough into thirds and shape each into a flattened disc. Wrap well in plastic wrap and refrigerate for 1 hour or until chilled.

4. Preheat oven to 350°F (180°C). On a lightly floured board, roll each disc to ¼-inch (0.5 cm) thickness. Using assorted cutters and rerolling scraps, cut out shapes; place on prepared baking sheets. Brush lightly with egg white and sprinkle lightly with granulated sugar.

5. Bake one sheet at a time on middle rack in preheated oven for 12 to 14 minutes or until edges are light golden. Let cool for 5 minutes on baking sheet; remove to a wire rack and let cool completely.

Peanut Butter Cookies

Makes 40 cookies

These crisp cookies are sure to satisfy a craving for something sweet and indulgent.

Tip

The brown sugar you use in recipes is totally your preference. Brown sugar comes in both light and dark brown. Dark brown sugar is noticeably darker in color and has a stronger molasses taste.

● Preheat oven to 375°F (190°C)
● Baking sheets, lightly greased

½ cup	butter, softened	125 mL
⅔ cup	smooth peanut butter	150 mL
1 cup	packed brown sugar	250 mL
1	egg	1
1 tsp	vanilla	5 mL
1¾ cups	all-purpose flour	425 mL
½ tsp	baking soda	2 mL
¼ tsp	salt	1 mL

1. In a large bowl, using an electric mixer, cream butter, peanut butter and brown sugar until fluffy. Beat in egg and vanilla until incorporated.

2. In another bowl, stir together flour, baking soda and salt. Stir into creamed mixture until combined.

3. Form into 1-inch (2.5 cm) balls and place 2 inches (5 cm) apart on prepared baking sheets. Using the tines of a fork, flatten by making criss-cross patterns on tops.

4. Bake one sheet at a time on middle rack in preheated oven for 11 to 13 minutes or until light golden. Transfer to a wire rack to cool.

Gingersnaps

I have been making these old-fashioned spice cookies as long as I can remember and especially love the delicious aroma that fills my kitchen when I bake a batch.

Tip

Be sure to use fresh baking soda as it makes these cookies crisp and light. Like baking powder, an open box of baking soda has a shelf life of only 6 months, so make sure to replenish both regularly. As a reminder, write the date when they need to be replaced on the container.

● Baking sheets, well greased or lined with parchment paper

¾ cup	butter, softened	175 mL
1 cup	packed brown sugar	250 mL
¼ cup	fancy molasses	60 mL
1	egg	1
2¼ cups	all-purpose flour	550 mL
1 tsp	baking soda	5 mL
2 tsp	ground ginger	10 mL
1½ tsp	ground cinnamon	7 mL
½ tsp	ground cloves	2 mL
¼ tsp	salt	1 mL
⅓ cup	granulated sugar	75 mL

1. In a large bowl, using an electric mixer, cream butter with brown sugar until light and fluffy; beat in molasses and egg until creamy.

2. In another bowl, stir together flour, baking soda, ginger, cinnamon, ground cloves and salt. Stir into creamed mixture to make a soft dough. Refrigerate for 1 hour or until firm.

3. Preheat oven to 350°F (180°C). Shape dough into 1-inch (2.5 cm) balls; roll in bowl of granulated sugar. Arrange 2 inches (5 cm) apart on prepared baking sheets. Flatten to ¼-inch (0.5 cm) thickness using bottom of large glass dipped in sugar.

4. Bake one sheet at a time on middle rack in preheated oven for 12 minutes or until golden. Let cool for 2 minutes on baking sheet; remove to a wire rack and let cool completely.

Coconut Macaroons

**Makes
36 macaroons**

Moist and chewy, these
macaroons are sure to
disappear quickly!

Tip

Separate eggs while they
are cold, but let egg whites
warm to room temperature
before beating. To speed
up the process, place the
bowl of egg whites in a
larger bowl of hot water
and let stand for 5 minutes.

- Preheat oven to 300°F (150°C)
- Baking sheets, lined with parchment paper

3 cups	sweetened flaked coconut	750 mL
2/3 cup	granulated sugar, divided	150 mL
1/4 cup	all-purpose flour	60 mL
4	egg whites	4
1/2 tsp	almond extract or vanilla	2 mL
Pinch	salt	Pinch

1. In a bowl, combine coconut, 1/3 cup (75 mL) of the sugar and the flour.

2. In another bowl, using an electric mixer, beat egg whites, almond extract and salt until soft peaks form. Beat in remaining sugar, 1 tbsp (15 mL) at a time, to make a stiff meringue. Fold in coconut mixture until evenly combined.

3. Drop by heaping teaspoonfuls (5 mL) onto prepared baking sheets, about 2 inches (5 cm) apart.

4. Bake one sheet a time on middle rack in preheated oven for 20 to 25 minutes or until firm to the touch and lightly colored. Let cool for 5 minutes on baking sheet; remove to a wire rack and let cool completely.

Scottish Shortbread

The secret to this tender, easy-to-make shortbread is to have a light touch and not to overhandle the dough.

Tip

To make your own superfine sugar: Place granulated sugar in a food processor; process until very fine.

- Preheat oven to 300°F (150°C)
- Baking sheets

1 cup	unsalted butter, softened	250 mL
½ cup	superfine sugar	125 mL
2 cups	all-purpose flour	500 mL
¼ tsp	salt	1 mL

1. In a bowl, cream butter with wooden spoon until fluffy. Beat in sugar, a spoonful at time, until well blended. Stir in flour and salt; gather into a ball.

2. On a lightly floured work surface, gently knead dough four or five times until smooth. Roll out a portion of the dough on a lightly floured surface to ⅓-inch (0.8 cm) thickness. Cut out shapes using cooking cutters and place on baking sheets.

3. Bake one sheet at a time on middle rack in preheated oven for 25 to 30 minutes or until edges are light golden. Transfer cookies to a wire rack to cool.

Crunchy Almond Biscotti

Makes 60 cookies

Biscotti are much easier to bake than delicate cookies like shortbread and they're also less rich. A double whammy — perfect for these twice-baked Italian specialties.

Tip

Store cookies in an airtight container, separating layers with waxed or parchment paper, for 1 week, or freeze for up to 1 month.

- Preheat oven to 325°F (160°C)
- Baking sheets, lined with parchment paper

½ cup	butter, softened	125 mL
1¼ cups	granulated sugar	300 mL
3	eggs	3
1 tbsp	finely grated lemon zest	15 mL
1 tsp	almond extract	5 mL
3 cups	all-purpose flour	750 mL
2½ tsp	baking powder	12 mL
¼ tsp	salt	1 mL
1 cup	whole unblanched almonds, coarsely chopped	250 mL

1. In a bowl, using an electric mixer, cream butter with sugar until light and fluffy; beat in eggs, lemon zest and almond extract until incorporated.

2. In another bowl, stir together flour, baking powder and salt; stir into butter mixture until combined. Stir in almonds.

3. Turn dough out onto lightly floured surface. With floured hands, shape into a ball and divide in two. Pat into 2 logs, each about 2½ inches (6 cm) wide and 14 inches (35 cm) long. Place on prepared baking sheet, about 2 inches (5 cm) apart.

4. Bake on middle rack in preheated oven for 25 to 30 minutes or until firm to the touch. Let cool for 10 minutes. Using a long spatula, transfer to a cutting board. With a serrated knife, cut diagonally into ½-inch (1 cm) slices.

5. Place cookies upright on sheet ½ inch (1 cm) apart, using 2 sheets, if necessary. Return to oven and bake for 20 to 25 minutes or until dry and lightly browned. Transfer cookies to a wire rack to cool.

Hazelnut and Dried Cranberry Biscotti

Makes 48 cookies

These crunchy morsels make wonderful gifts for friends and family. Pack biscotti in fancy containers or tins, or wrap in clear cellophane and add a bright ribbon.

Tip

To toast and skin hazelnuts: Place nuts on a rimmed baking sheet in preheated 350°F (180°C) oven for 8 to 10 minutes or until lightly browned. Place in a clean, dry towel and rub off most of the skins.

Variation

Dried cranberries add a sweet-tart flavor; substitute golden raisins or chopped dried apricots, if desired.

- Preheat oven to 325°F (160°C)
- Baking sheets, lined with parchment paper

½ cup	butter, softened	125 mL
1 cup	packed brown sugar	250 mL
2	eggs	2
2⅓ cups	all-purpose flour	575 mL
1½ tsp	baking powder	7 mL
1½ tsp	ground cinnamon	7 mL
¼ tsp	ground cloves	1 mL
¼ tsp	ground allspice	1 mL
¼ tsp	salt	1 mL
½ cup	dried cranberries	125 mL
¾ cup	hazelnuts, toasted, skinned and coarsely chopped (see Tip, left)	175 mL

1. In a bowl, using an electric mixer, cream butter with brown sugar until light and fluffy; beat in eggs until incorporated.

2. In another bowl, combine flour, baking powder, cinnamon, cloves, allspice and salt; stir into butter mixture until combined. Fold in dried cranberries and hazelnuts.

3. Turn dough out onto lightly floured surface. With floured hands, shape into a ball and divide in two. Pat into 2 logs, each about 2½ inches (6 cm) wide and 12 inches (30 cm) long. Place on prepared baking sheet, about 2 inches (5 cm) apart.

4. Bake on middle rack in preheated oven for 25 to 30 minutes or until firm to the touch. Let cool for 10 minutes. Using a long spatula, transfer to a cutting board. With a serrated knife, cut diagonally into ½-inch (1 cm) slices.

5. Place cookies upright on sheet ½ inch (1 cm) apart, using 2 sheets, if necessary. Return to oven and bake for 15 to 20 minutes or dry and lightly browned. Transfer cookies to a wire rack to cool.

Fudgy Chocolate Brownies

Makes 32 brownies

So moist and chewy, these brownies will disappear in no time. Luckily, this recipe makes a big batch, so you can stash half in the freezer — which is certainly recommended, if you want them to last more than a day!

Tip

Baking powder has a shelf life of only 6 months once opened, so make sure to replenish it regularly.

- Preheat oven to 350°F (180°C)
- 13- by 9-inch (33 by 23 cm) baking pan, greased

1 cup	butter, softened	250 mL
1½ cups	granulated sugar	375 mL
4	eggs	4
2 tsp	vanilla	10 mL
1 cup	all-purpose flour	250 mL
1 cup	unsweetened cocoa powder	250 mL
¾ tsp	baking powder	3 mL
¼ tsp	salt	1 mL
1 cup	walnuts, chopped	250 mL

Frosting

1 cup	confectioner's (icing) sugar	250 mL
⅓ cup	unsweetened cocoa powder	75 mL
2 tbsp	butter, softened	30 mL
2 tbsp	milk	30 mL

1. In a bowl, using an electric mixer, cream butter with sugar until light and fluffy. Beat in eggs, one at a time, until incorporated; add vanilla.

2. In a separate bowl, sift together flour, 1 cup (250 mL) cocoa powder, baking powder and salt. Beat into butter mixture to make a smooth batter. Fold in walnuts.

3. Spread in prepared baking pan. Bake on middle rack in preheated oven for 25 to 30 minutes or until cake tester inserted in center comes out clean. Place pan on a wire rack to cool completely.

4. *Frosting:* In a bowl, using an electric mixer, cream confectioner's sugar, ⅓ cup (75 mL) cocoa powder, butter and milk until smooth. Spread over slightly warm brownies. When set, cut into bars.

Skor Fudge Brownies

These brownies are the perfect chocolate indulgence — rich, dense and chocolatey with a crunchy layer of toffee. Baking is a breeze with this streamlined recipe that requires only a saucepan and a baking pan lined with foil for easy cleanup.

Tip

Look for Skor toffee bits in the baking section of supermarkets. If unavailable, use 5 finely chopped Skor bars instead. Reduce chocolate chips to ¾ cup (175 mL).

- Preheat oven to 350°F (180°C)
- 13- by 9-inch (33 by 23 cm) baking pan, bottom and sides lined with heavy foil with edges overhanging the sides

1 cup	butter, cut into pieces	250 mL
6 oz	unsweetened chocolate, coarsely chopped	175 g
2 cups	granulated sugar	500 mL
4	eggs	4
2 tsp	vanilla	10 mL
1¼ cups	all-purpose flour	300 mL
¼ tsp	salt	1 mL
1	package (8 oz/227 g) Skor toffee bits	1
1 cup	semisweet chocolate chips	250 mL

1. In a medium saucepan, melt butter and chocolate over medium heat, stirring often, until melted and smooth.

2. Remove from heat; stir in sugar. Beat in eggs and vanilla. Stir in flour and salt to make a smooth batter.

3. Spread evenly in prepared baking pan. Bake on middle rack in preheated oven for 18 minutes or until top is almost set. Sprinkle Skor toffee bits over top and return pan to oven.

4. Bake for 8 to 10 minutes more or until a toothpick inserted in center comes out with a few moist crumbs clinging to it.

5. Place pan on a wire rack; sprinkle with chocolate chips. Let stand for 5 minutes or until chocolate is melted. Spread evenly. Let cool until chocolate is set.

6. Lift brownies out of pan; carefully remove foil and cut into bars using a sharp knife.

Nanaimo Bars

Makes 36 squares

These buttery coconut concoctions were said to be invented in Nanaimo, British Columbia — hence the name — and became popular in the 1950s. No matter where they were invented, they're delicious anywhere.

Tip

Traditionally, 2 tbsp (30 mL) custard powder is used in the icing of Nanaimo Bars. If available in your supermarket, add custard powder to confectioner's sugar and omit vanilla.

• 9-inch (23 cm) square baking pan, lined with parchment paper or foil (see Tip, page 471)

Base

1	egg	1
¼ cup	granulated sugar	60 mL
½ cup	butter	125 mL
⅓ cup	unsweetened cocoa powder	75 mL
2 cups	graham wafer crumbs	500 mL
1 cup	sweetened shredded coconut	250 mL
½ cup	chopped walnuts	125 mL

Icing

¼ cup	butter, softened	60 mL
2 cups	confectioner's (icing) sugar	500 mL
2 tbsp	milk	30 mL
1½ tsp	vanilla	7 mL

Topping

¾ cup	semisweet chocolate chips	175 mL
2 tbsp	butter	30 mL

1. *Base:* In a bowl, beat egg with sugar. In a medium saucepan, melt butter over medium heat. Whisk in cocoa powder and egg mixture until combined. Cook, stirring, for about 3 minutes or until sauce is slightly thickened. Remove from heat and stir in graham wafer crumbs, coconut and walnuts. Press mixture firmly into prepared baking pan.

2. *Icing:* In a bowl, using an electric mixer, cream butter, confectioner's sugar, milk and vanilla until smooth. Spread evenly over base and refrigerate for 30 minutes or until firm.

3. *Topping:* In a glass bowl, microwave chocolate chips on Medium (50%) for 2 to 2½ minutes or until chocolate is melted; stir until smooth. Stir in butter until melted. Spread chocolate mixture over icing layer. Refrigerate for 1 hour or until chilled and firm before cutting into squares.

Chocolate Peanut Butter Toffee Bars

Makes 24 bars

Rich and oh so delicious, what could be more tempting than these yummy bars made with chocolate, toffee and peanut butter!

Tip

The brown sugar you use in recipes is totally your preference. Brown sugar comes in both light and dark brown. Dark brown sugar is noticeably darker in color and has a stronger molasses taste.

- Preheat oven to 350°F (180°C)
- 8-inch (20 cm) square baking pan, lined with parchment paper or greased foil (see Tip, right)

Crust

1 cup	all-purpose flour	250 mL
¼ cup	packed brown sugar	60 mL
½ cup	cold butter, cut into pieces	125 mL

Peanut Butter Filling

½ cup	smooth or crunchy peanut butter, at room temperature	125 mL
¾ cup	confectioner's (icing) sugar	175 mL
2 tbsp	butter, softened	30 mL
½ cup	Skor toffee bits	125 mL

Chocolate Topping

½ cup	semisweet or milk chocolate chips	125 mL
2 tbsp	half-and-half (10%) cream	30 mL
⅓ cup	finely chopped unsalted peanuts or pecans	75 mL

1. *Crust:* In a food processor, process flour and brown sugar until evenly mixed. Add butter and pulse until mixture starts to get crumbly. Press dough firmly into prepared pan. Bake in preheated oven for 18 to 20 minutes or until light golden.

2. *Filling:* In a bowl, using an electric mixer, beat peanut butter, confectioner's sugar and butter until smooth. Drop spoonfuls of filling over warm crust. Let stand for 2 minutes or until soft. Using a knife or metal spatula, spread filling evenly over crust. Sprinkle with toffee pieces and press gently into filling. Refrigerate until chilled.

3. *Topping:* In a small saucepan, combine chocolate chips and cream. Heat on medium-low, stirring, until chocolate melts. (Or combine in a glass bowl and microwave on Medium (50%) for 1 to 1½ minutes. Stir until chocolate is melted and smooth.)

4. With a metal spatula, spread topping over chilled peanut butter filling to cover evenly. Refrigerate for 1 hour or until chocolate is set. Run a knife around the edge and carefully lift from the pan using the parchment ends. Transfer to a cutting board and cut into bars.

Peanutty Cereal Snacking Bars

Makes 24 bars

Peanut butter fans will love these no-bake bars. They're a breeze to make and taste so much better than the expensive packaged snack bars sold in supermarkets.

Tip

Wrap bars individually in plastic wrap and freeze.

- 13- by 9-inch (33 by 23 cm) baking pan, greased

1 cup	smooth or crunchy peanut butter	250 mL
2/3 cup	liquid honey or golden corn syrup	150 mL
4 cups	toasted rice cereal	1 L
2 cups	muesli-type cereal with fruit and nuts	500 mL

1. In a large saucepan, combine peanut butter and honey; cook over medium heat, stirring constantly, until smooth. (Or place in large glass bowl and microwave on High for 2 minutes or until smooth, stirring once.)

2. Fold in cereals until evenly coated. Press firmly into prepared baking pan. Let cool; cut into bars.

Fabulous Date Squares

Here's a heritage recipe that never grows old. My version of date squares has a burst of lemon in the filling, which only enhances its traditional appeal.

Tip

Rather than using a knife to cut sticky dried fruits like dates and apricots, you'll find that kitchen scissors do a better job.

- Preheat oven to 350°F (180°C)
- 8-inch (20 cm) square baking pan, lined with parchment paper or greased foil (see Tip, page 471)

Filling

3 cups	chopped pitted dates (about 12 oz/375 g)	750 mL
1 cup	water	250 mL
1/4 cup	packed brown sugar	60 mL
1 tsp	grated lemon zest	5 mL

Crumb Layer

1 1/2 cups	quick-cooking rolled oats	375 mL
1 cup	all-purpose flour	250 mL
3/4 cup	packed brown sugar	175 mL
1/2 tsp	baking powder	2 mL
1/4 tsp	salt	1 mL
3/4 cup	cold butter, cut into pieces	175 mL

1. *Filling:* In a saucepan, combine dates, water, brown sugar and lemon zest. Place over medium heat; cook, stirring, for 8 to 10 minutes or until dates form a smooth paste. Let cool.

2. *Crumb Layer:* In a bowl, combine rolled oats, flour, brown sugar, baking powder and salt. Cut in butter with a pastry cutter or fork to make coarse crumbs.

3. Press two-thirds of crumb mixture in bottom of baking pan. Spread evenly with date filling. Sprinkle with remaining crumb mixture, pressing down lightly.

4. Bake in preheated oven for 25 to 30 minutes or until golden. Let cool on a wire rack; cut into squares.

Cranberry Ginger Streusel Bars

- Preheat oven to 350°F (180°C)
- 13- by 9-inch (33 by 23 cm) baking pan, lined with parchment paper or greased foil (see Tip, page 476)

Filling

3 cups	fresh or frozen cranberries	750 mL
½ cup	chopped dried apricots	125 mL
½ cup	raisins	125 mL
1 cup	packed brown sugar	250 mL
1 cup	apple juice	250 mL
¼ cup	minced candied ginger	60 mL

Crumb Mixture

2 cups	all-purpose flour	500 mL
½ cup	packed brown sugar	125 mL
1 tsp	ground ginger	5 mL
¼ tsp	salt	1 mL
1 cup	cold butter, cubed	250 mL
1 cup	quick-cooking rolled oats	250 mL

1. *Filling:* In a large saucepan, combine cranberries, apricots, raisins, brown sugar, apple juice and candied ginger. Bring to a gentle boil over medium heat, stirring often. Boil gently, stirring often, for 5 minutes or until mixture thickens. Remove from heat; let cool.

2. *Crumb Mixture:* In large bowl, combine flour, brown sugar, ground ginger and salt. Cut in butter with a pastry blender or fork until mixture resembles coarse crumbs. Stir in oats. Reserve 1½ cups (375 mL) of the crumb mixture for topping.

3. Press remaining crumb mixture into prepared pan. Bake in preheated oven for 15 to 18 minutes or until light golden. Spread with cranberry mixture. Sprinkle with reserved crumb mixture and press down lightly.

4. Bake in preheated oven for 25 to 30 minutes or until golden. Place on a wire rack; let cool completely. Carefully lift from the pan using the parchment ends. Transfer to a cutting board and cut into small bars.

Luscious Lemon Squares

These classy lemon treats with a shortbread crust are always appreciated when friends are invited for a fresh-brewed cup of tea or coffee.

Tips

If you don't have a rasp grater, such as a Microplane, to grate lemon zest, use a zester to remove the zest in thin shreds, then finely chop with a knife.

When lemons are bargain-priced, stock up for the future. Grate the zest and squeeze the juice; place in separate containers and freeze.

To get more juice out of a lemon, roll on countertop or microwave on High for 20 seconds before squeezing.

- Preheat oven to 350°F (180°C)
- 8-inch (20 cm) square baking pan, lined with parchment paper or greased foil (see Tip, page 471)

1 cup	all-purpose flour	250 mL
¼ cup	granulated sugar	60 mL
½ cup	butter, cut into pieces	125 mL

Filling

2	eggs	2
1 cup	granulated sugar	250 mL
2 tbsp	all-purpose flour	30 mL
½ tsp	baking powder	2 mL
Pinch	salt	Pinch
1 tbsp	grated lemon zest	15 mL
¼ cup	fresh lemon juice	60 mL
	Confectioner's (icing) sugar	

1. In a bowl, combine flour and sugar; cut in butter with a pastry blender to make coarse crumbs. Press into bottom of baking pan. Bake in preheated oven for 15 minutes or until light golden. Let cool on rack.

2. *Filling:* In a bowl, beat eggs with sugar; stir in flour, baking powder, salt, lemon zest and juice. Pour over base.

3. Bake for 25 to 30 minutes or until filling is set and light golden. Place pan on a wire rack to cool. Dust with confectioner's sugar; cut into small squares.

Apricot Pecan Bars

- Preheat oven to 350°F (180°C)
- 8-inch (20 cm) square baking pan, lined with parchment paper or greased foil (see Tip, page 471)

1 cup	all-purpose flour	250 mL
½ cup	cold butter, cut into pieces	125 mL
¼ cup	packed brown sugar	60 mL

Topping

1 cup	dried apricots	250 mL
2	eggs	2
1 tsp	vanilla	5 mL
¾ cup	packed light brown sugar	175 mL
2 tbsp	all-purpose flour	30 mL
½ tsp	baking powder	2 mL
½ cup	chopped pecans	125 mL

1. In a food processor, combine flour, butter and brown sugar; pulse to make fine crumbs. Press mixture evenly in bottom of prepared baking pan. Bake for 15 minutes or until light golden. Let cool; leave oven on.

2. *Topping:* Using scissors, cut apricots into thin slivers. In a bowl, beat eggs with vanilla; stir in brown sugar, flour and baking powder. Add apricots. Spread mixture evenly over baked crust; sprinkle with pecans.

3. Bake in preheated oven for 22 to 25 minutes or until top is golden brown. Place on a wire rack; let cool. Carefully lift from the pan using the parchment ends. Cut into bars.

Lunch Box Oatmeal Raisin Bars

Makes 24 bars

Ideal for school lunches, these chewy bars travel well. I like to package bars individually in plastic wrap, place in an airtight container and freeze. It's so easy to pop a bar from the freezer into lunch bags or take them along for snacks.

Tip

To remove bars easily, line baking pan with parchment paper or heavy-duty foil. Cut sheet of parchment paper or foil 9 inches (23 cm) wide or same width as baking pan, with length to overhang. Fit into baking pan with ends overhanging edge.

- Preheat oven to 350°F (180°C)
- 13- by 9-inch (33 by 23 cm) baking pan, lined with parchment paper or greased foil (see Tip, left)

2/3 cup	packed brown sugar	150 mL
1/3 cup	butter	75 mL
1/3 cup	golden corn syrup	75 mL
2 1/2 cups	quick-cooking rolled oats	625 mL
1/4 cup	all-purpose flour	60 mL
1/2 cup	raisins or chopped dried apricots	125 mL
1	egg	1
1 tsp	vanilla	5 mL

1. In a large glass bowl, combine brown sugar, butter and corn syrup. Microwave at High for 2 minutes; stir until smooth. Microwave 1 minute more or until sugar dissolves and mixture comes to a full boil.

2. Stir in rolled oats, flour and raisins. In a small bowl, beat egg with vanilla. Stir into rolled-oats mixture.

3. Spread evenly in prepared pan. Bake in preheated oven for 20 to 25 minutes or until golden around edges. Let cool for 10 minutes in pan. Carefully lift from the pan using the parchment ends. Cut into 3- by 1 1/2-inch (7.5 by 4 cm) bars. Transfer to a wire rack to cool completely.

Pecan Toffee Crunch

Makes 1 lb (500 g) candy

Don't expect to keep these easy-to-make candies for a long time. They vanish as fast as you can make them!

Variation

Use walnuts instead of pecans.

* Candy thermometer
* Rimmed baking sheet, generously buttered

½ cup	butter	125 mL
1 cup	granulated sugar	250 mL
¼ cup	water	60 mL
¼ tsp	salt	1 mL
¾ cup	finely chopped pecans, divided	175 mL
⅔ cup	semisweet chocolate chips	150 mL
1 tsp	butter	5 mL

1. In a medium saucepan, melt ½ cup (125 mL) butter over medium heat. Stir in sugar, water and salt. Bring to a boil, stirring, until sugar is dissolved.

2. Using a candy thermometer, boil mixture, stirring occasionally, for about 10 minutes or until mixture turns a rich golden caramel color and temperature reaches 300°F (150°C).

3. Remove from heat and stir in half of the chopped nuts. Immediately pour onto prepared baking sheet. Working quickly, use a metal spatula to spread mixture in a thin even layer. Let cool until candy is firm.

4. Meanwhile, place chocolate chips and 1 tsp (5 mL) butter in a bowl and microwave on Medium (50%) for 1½ to 2 minutes or until melted. Spread evenly over hardened candy while still warm.

5. Sprinkle with remaining nuts. Let cool until chocolate is firm. Using a sharp knife, cut into candy and break into pieces.

Chocolate Marshmallow Fudge

The combination of chocolate and marshmallow is an old-time favorite. It's sure to satisfy any craving for something sweet and chocolatey.

- 8-inch (20 cm) square baking pan, lined with parchment paper or foil

⅔ cup	chopped walnuts or pecans, divided	150 mL
1	small can (5½ oz/160 mL) evaporated milk, undiluted	1
1⅔ cups	granulated sugar	400 mL
1½ cups	semisweet chocolate chips	375 mL
1½ cups	miniature marshmallows	375 mL
1 tsp	vanilla	5 mL

1. Finely chop 2 tbsp (30 mL) of the walnuts for the topping and set aside.

2. In a large saucepan, combine evaporated milk and sugar. Bring to a full boil over medium-high heat, stirring constantly. Continue to boil mixture (it should be a steady rolling boil — decrease heat, if necessary) for 5 minutes without stirring.

3. Remove from heat. Stir in chocolate chips, marshmallows and vanilla until melted and mixture is smooth. Fold in remaining chopped nuts.

4. Spread in prepared baking pan. Sprinkle top with reserved 2 tbsp (30 mL) finely chopped nuts. Let cool completely before cutting into small squares.

Cakes and Pies

Baking Tips

- Incorrect measurement is a major cause of baking failures. Use a liquid cup measure for fluids and a dry measure for dry ingredients such as flour. When measuring flour, stir first, then spoon into dry measure and level off using a knife. Do not pack the dry measure down by tapping on the countertop; this increases the amount.

- In baking, always use large eggs, not medium or extra large, either of which can affect the baking result.

- Ingredients, such as eggs and butter, should be used at room temperature. Leave eggs on the counter for 30 minutes or place in a bowl of warm (not hot) water for 10 minutes.

- To soften butter, microwave on Defrost and check at 15-second intervals.

- Replace your supplies of baking powder and baking soda every 6 months; once opened, they oxidize and lose their leavening power.

- Replenish your spices regularly; buy the freshest dried fruits and nuts.

- For walnuts, the light-colored Californian walnuts are preferred.

- Always store nuts in a container in the refrigerator or freezer to keep them fresh.

- For perfect cakes, loaves, bars and squares, it's essential to use the correct size of baking pan specified in each recipe.

- When a recipe calls for a baking pan, it refers to a metal pan, while a baking dish refers to glass.

- Light baking sheets, particularly the nonstick variety, are generally better than dark sheets, which attract heat and cause cookies to bake faster and/or cause the undersides to darken too quickly.

- To grease pans or baking sheets, lard, vegetable shortening or unsalted or lightly salted butter is recommended.

Mennonite Streusel Blueberry Cake

Makes 10 to 12 servings

More commonly known as fruit *platz*, this delectable recipe was given to me by a Mennonite family in Niagara whose ancestors settled the region over two centuries ago. It makes use of seasonal fruits from sweet-and-sour pitted cherries, raspberries, sliced peaches, nectarines, apricots to blue plums.

Tip

For a smaller-size cake, halve the ingredients and bake in a greased 8-inch (20 cm) square pan for 35 to 40 minutes.

- Preheat oven to 350°F (180°C)
- 13- by 9-inch (33 by 23 cm) baking pan, generously greased

2 cups	all-purpose flour	500 mL
½ cup	granulated sugar	125 mL
1 tbsp	baking powder	15 mL
¼ tsp	salt	1 mL
⅓ cup	butter, softened	75 mL
1	egg	1
1 cup	half-and-half (10%) cream	250 mL
1½ tsp	vanilla or grated lemon zest	7 mL
4 cups	fresh or frozen blueberries or other seasonal sliced fruits	1 L

Crumb Topping

1 cup	all-purpose flour	250 mL
¾ cup	packed brown sugar	175 mL
½ cup	butter, softened	125 mL

1. In a large bowl, stir together flour, sugar, baking powder and salt. Cut in butter using a pastry blender or fork to make coarse crumbs.

2. In another bowl, beat egg with cream and vanilla. Stir into flour mixture to make a thick batter.

3. Drop tablespoonfuls of batter into prepared baking dish and spread evenly. Top with blueberries in a single layer.

4. *Crumb Topping:* In a bowl, combine flour and brown sugar. Cut in butter using a pastry blender or fork to make coarse crumbs. Sprinkle evenly over fruit. Bake on middle rack in preheated oven for 45 to 50 minutes or until crumb topping is golden. Place on a wire rack and let cool. Cut into squares and serve.

Harvest Apple Cake

An old Quebec recipe from the Eastern Townships.

Tip

Choose an apple variety that softens and loses its shape when cooked, such as Cortland.

- Preheat oven to 350°(180°C)
- 13- by 9-inch (33 by 23 cm) baking pan, greased

2 cups	all-purpose flour	500 mL
1½ tsp	baking powder	7 mL
1 tsp	ground cinnamon	5 mL
½ tsp	baking soda	2 mL
¼ tsp	freshly grated nutmeg	1 mL
¼ tsp	salt	1 mL
½ cup	butter, softened	125 mL
¾ cup	granulated sugar	175 mL
½ cup	packed brown sugar	125 mL
2	eggs	2
1 cup	apple cider or juice	250 mL
1½ cups	finely chopped peeled apple	375 mL
¾ cup	finely chopped walnuts	175 mL
½ cup	sultana raisins	125 mL
	Apple Frosting (see recipe, below)	

1. In a bowl, stir together flour, baking powder, cinnamon, soda, nutmeg and salt.

2. In another bowl, using an electric mixer, cream butter with granulated and brown sugars until fluffy. Beat in eggs. Beat in flour mixture alternately with apple cider until smooth. Fold in apples, walnuts and raisins.

3. Spread batter in prepared baking pan. Bake on middle rack in preheated oven for 30 to 35 minutes or until cake tester inserted in center comes out clean. Let cake cool on a wire rack. Spread with Apple Frosting.

Apple Frosting

Makes ½ cup (125 mL) frosting

2 tbsp	butter, softened	30 mL
1 cup	confectioner's (icing) sugar	250 mL
½ tsp	vanilla	2 mL
2 tbsp	apple cider or juice (approx.)	30 mL

1. In a bowl, using a wooden spoon, cream butter with confectioner's sugar and vanilla. Add apple cider to make a smooth frosting that spreads easily.

Gingerbread Cake

Makes 9 servings

A yummy cake to serve alone, or topped simply with a spoonful of applesauce or with custard sauce poured over top.

Tip

For an extra ginger hit, add 2 to 4 tbsp (30 to 60 mL) finely chopped crystallized ginger.

- Preheat oven to 350°F (180°C)
- 8-inch (20 cm) square baking pan, greased

1½ cups	all-purpose flour	375 g
1 tsp	baking soda	5 mL
1½ tsp	ground ginger	7 mL
¾ tsp	ground cinnamon	3 mL
¼ tsp	ground cloves	1 mL
¼ tsp	salt	1 mL
⅓ cup	butter, softened	75 mL
⅔ cup	packed brown sugar	150 mL
½ cup	fancy molasses	125 mL
1	egg	1
⅔ cup	hot water	150 mL

1. In a bowl, stir together flour, baking soda, ginger, cinnamon, cloves and salt.

2. In another bowl, using an electric mixer, beat butter with brown sugar until fluffy. Beat in molasses and egg. Add flour mixture; beat until well blended. Beat in hot water.

3. Spread batter in prepared baking pan. Bake on middle rack in preheated oven for 35 to 40 minutes or until cake tester inserted in center comes out clean. Place on a wire rack to cool. Cut into squares.

Peach Almond Cake

Makes 8 servings

This coffee cake is welcome at brunch, afternoon tea or dessert time. Make it year-round with other seasonal fruits such as pears, apples, pitted cherries or plums.

Tip

To peel peaches: Plunge peaches in boiling water for 15 to 30 seconds to loosen skins.

- Preheat oven to 350°F (180°C)
- 9-inch (23 cm) springform pan or cake pan, greased

1½ cups	all-purpose flour	375 mL
¾ cup	granulated sugar	175 mL
1½ tsp	baking powder	7 mL
½ tsp	baking soda	2 mL
¼ tsp	salt	1 mL
2	eggs	2
¾ cup	vanilla or plain yogurt	175 mL
¼ cup	butter, melted	60 mL
½ tsp	almond extract	2 mL
3	peaches, peeled and sliced	3
3 tbsp	sliced blanched almonds	45 mL
2 tbsp	granulated sugar	30 mL
½ tsp	ground cinnamon	2 mL

1. In a mixing bowl, stir together flour, ¾ cup (175 mL) sugar, baking powder, baking soda and salt.

2. In another bowl, beat eggs, yogurt, melted butter and almond extract until smooth. Stir into dry ingredients to make a smooth thick batter. Spread in prepared pan. Arrange peaches on top in a circular fashion.

3. In a small bowl, combine almonds, 2 tbsp (30 mL) sugar and cinnamon. Sprinkle over peaches. Bake on middle rack in preheated oven for 45 to 50 minutes or until cake tester inserted in center comes out clean.

Double Chocolate Zucchini Cake

Zucchini gives this cake a rich, moist texture. There's no visible trace of it when the cake is baked, so it's perfect to serve to reluctant zucchini eaters. I don't bother to peel the zucchini, but you can if you prefer. Shredding the zucchini in a food processor saves time.

Tips

If you don't have a flour sifter, sift the dry ingredients through a fine-meshed sieve to remove any lumps.

The chocolate glaze is optional; instead, you can sift confectioner's sugar over cake just before serving.

- Preheat oven to 350°F (180°C)
- 13- by 9-inch (33 by 23 cm) baking pan, greased

2¼ cups	all-purpose flour	550 mL
1½ cups	granulated sugar	350 mL
⅔ cup	unsweetened cocoa powder	150 mL
1 tsp	baking powder	5 mL
1 tsp	baking soda	5 mL
¼ tsp	salt	1 mL
2	eggs	2
1 cup	sour cream or plain yogurt	250 mL
½ cup	vegetable oil	125 mL
2 tsp	vanilla	10 mL
2 cups	finely shredded zucchini	500 mL
1 cup	semisweet chocolate chips	250 mL
1 cup	chopped walnuts	250 mL

Chocolate Glaze (optional)

1 cup	confectioner's (icing) sugar	250 mL
2 tbsp	unsweetened cocoa powder	30 mL
2 tbsp	milk	30 mL

1. In a large bowl, sift together flour, sugar, cocoa powder, baking powder, baking soda and salt.

2. In another bowl, beat eggs, sour cream, oil and vanilla. Stir in shredded zucchini. Stir into flour mixture until just combined. Fold in chocolate chips and walnuts.

3. Spread batter evenly in prepared pan. Bake for 45 to 50 minutes or until a cake tester inserted in center comes out clean. Let stand on a wire rack for 15 minutes to cool.

4. *Chocolate Glaze:* In a bowl, combine confectioner's sugar, cocoa powder and milk; stir to make a smooth, spreadable glaze. Spread glaze, if using, over warm cake; let cool completely.

Orange Rhubarb Cake with Walnut Crumbs

The refreshing tartness of rhubarb in this snacking cake is nicely complemented by the orange zest and walnut crumbs, which make for a simple, sweet, nutty topping.

- Preheat oven to 350°F (180°C)
- 13- by 9-inch (33 by 23 cm) baking pan, greased

Cake

2 cups	all-purpose flour	500 mL
2 tsp	baking powder	10 mL
1/4 tsp	salt	1 mL
1/2 cup	butter, softened	125 mL
1 cup	packed brown sugar	250 mL
2	eggs	2
1 1/2 tsp	grated orange zest	7 mL
1/2 cup	milk	125 mL
2 cups	finely chopped fresh or frozen rhubarb	500 mL

Walnut Crumbs

1/2 cup	finely chopped walnuts	125 mL
1/3 cup	packed brown sugar	75 mL

1. *Cake:* In a bowl, stir together flour, baking powder and salt.

2. In another bowl, using an electric mixer, cream butter and brown sugar until light and fluffy. Beat in eggs and orange zest until incorporated. Beat in dry ingredients alternately with milk to make a smooth batter. Fold in rhubarb. Spoon batter into prepared baking pan and spread evenly.

3. *Walnut Crumbs:* In a bowl, combine walnuts and brown sugar until evenly mixed. Sprinkle over top of batter.

4. Bake on middle rack in preheated oven for 35 to 40 minutes or until cake tester inserted in center comes out clean. Place on a wire rack to cool and cut into squares.

Sour Cream Raspberry Coffee Cake

I keep individual quick-frozen berries stocked in my freezer to make this delectable cake year-round.

Tip

If using individual quick-frozen berries, do not thaw before adding to batter.

- Preheat oven to 350°F (180°C)
- 9-inch (23 cm) springform pan, greased

1½ cups	all-purpose flour	375 mL
¾ cup	granulated sugar	175 mL
½ cup	sweetened shredded coconut	125 mL
2 tsp	baking powder	10 mL
½ tsp	baking soda	2 mL
¼ tsp	salt	1 mL
2	eggs	2
1 cup	full-fat sour cream	250 mL
1 tsp	vanilla	5 mL
1 cup	fresh or frozen raspberries or blueberries	250 mL

Crumb Topping

⅓ cup	packed brown sugar	75 mL
¼ cup	quick-cooking rolled oats	60 mL
¼ cup	all-purpose flour	60 mL
¼ cup	sweetened shredded coconut	60 mL
½ tsp	ground cinnamon	2 mL
¼ cup	butter, cut into pieces	60 mL

1. In a bowl, stir together flour, sugar, coconut, baking powder, baking soda and salt. In another bowl, beat eggs with sour cream and vanilla. Stir in flour mixture; mix well. Gently fold in raspberries; spread batter in prepared pan.

2. *Crumb Topping:* In a bowl, combine brown sugar, oats, flour, coconut and cinnamon. Cut in butter using a pastry blender or fork to make coarse crumbs. Sprinkle evenly over top.

3. Bake on middle rack in preheated oven for 40 to 45 minutes or until tester inserted in center comes out clean. Set cake on a wire rack to cool. Serve warm or at room temperature.

Cinnamon Streusel Coffee Cake

Makes 10 to 12 servings

This old-fashioned coffee cake, layered with cinnamon-walnut crumbs, is a favorite to serve for coffee or brunch.

Tip

Baking powder and baking soda have a shelf life of only 6 months once opened, so make sure to replenish both regularly. As a reminder, write the date when they need to be replaced on the container.

- Preheat oven to 350°F (180°C)
- 10-inch (25 cm) Bundt or tube pan, well greased and lightly floured

Streusel

½ cup	packed brown sugar	125 mL
⅓ cup	all-purpose flour	75 mL
¼ cup	cold butter, cut into pieces	60 mL
1 tbsp	ground cinnamon	15 mL
¾ cup	finely chopped walnuts or pecans	175 mL

Batter

2½ cups	all-purpose flour	625 mL
1 cup	granulated sugar	250 mL
1½ tsp	baking powder	7 mL
1 tsp	baking soda	5 mL
¼ tsp	salt	1 mL
3	eggs	3
1 cup	sour cream	250 mL
⅔ cup	vegetable oil	150 mL
2 tsp	grated orange zest	10 mL
⅓ cup	fresh orange juice	75 mL

1. *Streusel:* In a food processor, combine brown sugar, flour, butter and cinnamon. Pulse to make fine crumbs. Transfer to a bowl and stir in walnuts. Sprinkle ½ cup (125 mL) streusel in bottom of prepared pan.

2. *Batter:* In a bowl, stir together flour, sugar, baking powder, baking soda, and salt.

3. In another bowl, beat eggs with sour cream, oil, zest and juice. Stir liquid ingredients into flour mixture until combined; do not overmix.

4. Spread half the batter over streusel mixture in pan. Sprinkle with 1 cup (250 mL) streusel mixture. Top with remaining batter and streusel. Tap pan several times on counter to expel air bubbles.

5. Bake on middle rack in preheated oven for 50 to 60 minutes or until a cake tester inserted in center comes out clean. Let cool on rack for 10 minutes. Carefully run a knife around sides and inner tube and invert coffee cake onto a wire rack to cool completely.

Golden Citrus Fruitcake

Makes 1 loaf

Microplane zester/graters are a handy kitchen gadget for shredding citrus peel. They come in a variety of grate sizes from fine to coarse and also work magic when grating fresh ginger, garlic and hard cheeses such as Parmesan.

- Preheat oven to 300°F (150°C)
- 9- by 5-inch (23 by 13 cm) loaf pan, greased, bottom and sides lined with parchment paper and greased
- Shallow pan of hot water placed on bottom rack in oven

1½ cups	chopped dried apricots	375 mL
1 cup	chopped dried figs	250 mL
1 cup	golden raisins	250 mL
1 cup	dark raisins or pecans	250 mL
½ cup	orange-flavored liqueur or orange juice	125 mL
¾ cup	butter, softened	175 mL
¾ cup	granulated sugar	175 mL
3	eggs	3
1 tbsp	finely grated orange zest	15 mL
1 tbsp	finely grated lemon zest	15 mL
1¾ cups	all-purpose flour	425 mL
1½ tsp	baking powder	7 mL
¼ tsp	salt	1 mL
	Additional orange-flavored liqueur (optional)	

1. In a large glass bowl, combine apricots, figs, golden and dark raisins and liqueur. Microwave on High for 2 minutes, stirring once. Let cool, stirring occasionally.

2. In a large bowl, using an electric mixer, cream butter and sugar until fluffy. Beat in eggs, one at a time, until incorporated. Stir in orange and lemon zests.

3. In another bowl, stir together flour, baking powder and salt. Using electric mixer, beat into creamed mixture until combined. Using a spatula, fold in fruit mixture including any remaining liqueur that hasn't been absorbed by the fruit.

4. Spoon batter into prepared pan. Bake in preheated oven for 2 hours or until cake tester inserted in center comes out clean. Transfer to a wire rack. Let stand for 15 minutes. Lift cake out of pan and place on rack until cool.

5. Remove parchment paper. If desired, wrap cake in cheesecloth and drizzle with about 2 tbsp (25 mL) orange-flavored liqueur. Wrap in heavy-duty foil or plastic storage bag. Store in cool, dry place or refrigerate. Age fruitcake for at least 1 week before serving.

Pineapple Upside-Down Cake

The upside-down cake — so popular in the '50s and '60s — has been making a comeback. This is the traditional version, but other fruits, such as sliced peaches and plums, can also be used.

Tip

The brown sugar you use in recipes is totally your preference. Brown sugar comes in both light and dark brown. Dark brown sugar is noticeably darker in color and has a stronger molasses taste.

- Preheat oven to 350°F (180°C)
- 9-inch (23 cm) round or square baking dish or springform pan, greased, bottom lined with parchment paper

2 tbsp	butter, melted	30 mL
1/3 cup	packed brown sugar	75 mL
1	can (14 oz/398 mL) pineapple rings	1
1/4 cup	dried cranberries	60 mL

Batter

1 1/3 cups	all-purpose flour	325 mL
1 1/2 tsp	baking powder	7 mL
1/4 tsp	salt	1 mL
6 tbsp	butter, softened	90 mL
2/3 cup	granulated sugar	150 mL
1	egg	1
1 1/2 tsp	grated orange zest	7 mL
1/2 cup	milk	125 mL

1. Drizzle melted butter in bottom of prepared dish; sprinkle evenly with brown sugar.

2. Drain pineapple and reserve juice for another use. Arrange pineapple rings to fit snugly in bottom of pan (there may be one pineapple ring leftover.) Place dried cranberries in center of each ring.

3. *Batter:* In a bowl, stir together flour, baking powder and salt. In another bowl, using an electric mixer, cream butter with sugar until smooth. Beat in egg and orange zest until incorporated. Beat in flour mixture alternately with milk to make a smooth batter. Spoon over pineapple, spreading evenly.

4. Bake on middle rack in preheated oven for 30 to 35 minutes or until cake tester inserted in center comes out clean. Let cool in pan for 5 minutes. Invert onto serving plate. Serve warm or at room temperature.

Carrot Cake with Orange Cream Cheese Frosting

Here's a cake that is so moist with just a hint of spice. Topped with a luscious orange frosting, it's sure to please the most discerning carrot cake fan.

Tip

To soften cream cheese: Place cream cheese in glass bowl and microwave on Medium (50%) for 45 to 60 seconds.

● Preheat oven to 350°F (180°C)
● 13- by 9-inch (33 by 23 cm) baking pan, greased

2 cups	all-purpose flour	500 mL
2 tsp	baking powder	10 mL
1½ tsp	ground cinnamon	7 mL
½ tsp	salt	2 mL
3	eggs	3
1⅓ cups	granulated sugar	325 mL
¾ cup	vegetable oil	175 mL
⅓ cup	fresh orange juice	75 mL
2 cups	finely shredded carrots	500 mL
1 cup	chopped walnuts or pecans	250 mL

Orange Cream Cheese Frosting

4 oz	cream cheese, softened	125 g
2 cups	confectioner's (icing) sugar	500 mL
1 tsp	finely grated orange zest	5 mL

1. In a bowl, stir together flour, baking powder, cinnamon and salt. In another bowl, beat eggs with sugar, oil and orange juice; stir in carrots and walnuts. Stir in flour mixture until combined; spread batter in prepared baking pan.

2. Bake on middle rack in preheated oven for 35 to 40 minutes or until cake tester inserted in center comes out clean. Place on a wire rack to cool.

3. *Orange Cream Cheese Frosting:* In a bowl, using an electric mixer, beat cream cheese, confectioner's sugar and orange zest until smooth. Spread evenly over cooled cake.

Sour Cream Fudge Layer Cake with Chocolate Frosting

Moist, rich and chocolatey — everything that you would expect in an old-fashioned layer cake. Serve as is or top with a scoop of vanilla ice cream for added indulgence.

Tip

Like baking powder, an open box of baking soda has a shelf life of only 6 months, so make sure to replenish both regularly. As a reminder, write the date when they need to be replaced on the container.

- Preheat oven to 350°F (180°C)
- Two 9-inch (23 cm) round baking pans, bottoms lined with parchment paper

1 cup	strong coffee	250 mL
4 oz	unsweetened chocolate, chopped	125 g
1 cup	sour cream	250 mL
1½ tsp	baking soda	7 mL
¼ tsp	salt	1 mL
¾ cup	butter, softened	175 mL
1¾ cups	granulated sugar	425 mL
2	eggs	2
2 tsp	vanilla	10 mL
2¼ cups	all-purpose flour	550 mL

Chocolate Frosting

2½ cups	confectioner's (icing) sugar	625 mL
½ cup	unsweetened cocoa powder	125 mL
½ cup	butter, softened	125 mL
3 tbsp	dark rum, coffee-flavored liqueur or milk	45 mL
3 tbsp	sour cream or milk (approx.)	45 mL

1. Brush parchment and sides of baking pan with melted butter and dust with cocoa powder, shaking out excess.

2. In a large glass bowl, microwave coffee and chocolate at High for 1 to 2 minutes, stirring once, until piping hot and chocolate is melted. Let cool to room temperature.

3. In a bowl, whisk together sour cream, baking soda and salt.

4. In large bowl, using an electric mixer, cream butter and sugar until fluffy. Beat in eggs, one at a time, until incorporated. Beat in chocolate-coffee mixture and vanilla. Beat in half of the flour with half of the sour cream mixture; beat in remaining flour and sour cream mixture to make a smooth batter. Spread evenly in prepared pans.

5. Bake on middle rack in preheated oven for 35 to
   40 minutes or until cake feels firm in the center and
   edges begin to pull away from sides. Let cool in pans
   on wire racks for 5 minutes; turn out onto racks to
   cool completely.

6. *Chocolate Frosting:* In a bowl, sift confectioner's sugar
   with cocoa powder. Using an electric mixer on low
   speed, beat in butter and rum until smooth. Beat in
   enough sour cream to make a spreadable frosting.

7. Arrange one cake layer on a large plate. Spread with
   some of the frosting. Top with second layer and spread
   frosting over tops and sides of cake.

Brown Sugar Pound Cake with Caramel Frosting

This is a wonderful, crowd-pleasing cake that can satisfy a large gathering.

Tip

Instead of baking the cake in a tube pan, bake in two 9- by 5-inch (23 by 13 cm) greased loaf pans, with bottoms lined with parchment paper. Bake for 50 minutes or until toothpick inserted in center comes out clean. Let cool in pans for 5 minutes. Turn loaves out of pans and let cool on a wire rack for 10 minutes. Spread tops of warm loaves with frosting.

- Preheat oven to 350°F (180°C)
- 10-inch (25 cm) tube pan, greased and floured, bottom lined with parchment paper

3 cups	all-purpose flour	750 mL
1 tsp	baking soda	5 mL
¼ tsp	salt	1 mL
1½ cups	butter, softened	375 mL
2¼ cups	packed dark brown sugar	550 mL
6	eggs	6
2 tsp	vanilla	10 mL
1 cup	sour cream	250 mL
1 cup	finely chopped pecans	250 mL

Caramel Frosting

¼ cup	butter	60 mL
½ cup	lightly packed dark brown sugar	125 mL
3 tbsp	half-and-half (10%) cream	45 mL
1½ cups	sifted confectioner's (icing) sugar	375 mL

Additional chopped pecans

1. In a bowl, stir together flour, baking soda and salt.

2. In a stand mixer bowl, beat butter and brown sugar on high speed for 3 minutes or until pale and fluffy. Add eggs, one at a time, scraping down sides of bowl and beating well after each addition. Beat in vanilla. On low speed, beat in dry ingredients alternately with sour cream, making three additions of dry and two of sour cream, until just incorporated; do not overmix. Fold in pecans.

3. Spoon batter into prepared pan and smooth top with a spatula. Tap pan on counter to expel any air bubbles. Bake in preheated oven for 60 to 75 minutes or until a toothpick inserted in the center comes out clean. Let cool on a wire rack for 10 minutes.

The brown sugar you use in recipes is totally your preference. Brown sugar comes in both light and dark brown. Dark brown sugar is noticeably darker in color and has a stronger molasses taste. Some recipes, such as this pound cake, specify dark brown sugar because it gives the cake a richer molasses flavor. It is fine to use light brown sugar if that is what you have.

4. Carefully run a knife around sides and center tube. Invert cake out of pan and remove center tube. Peel off parchment paper. Place cake on a rack.

5. *Caramel Frosting:* In a small saucepan, melt butter over medium heat. Add brown sugar and cream. Heat, stirring, until almost boiling and sugar is dissolved. Remove from heat and let cool for 3 minutes. Stir in confectioner's sugar until smooth. Spread warm frosting over top of warm cake, allowing frosting to drip down sides. Sprinkle top with pecans. Leave cake on rack until completely cool and frosting is set.

Strawberry Cream Cake

Nothing is more seductive than crimson strawberries, cold whipped cream and buttery lemon cake. For me, this perfect summer dessert beats out shortcake hands down as the ultimate strawberry creation.

Tips

Strawberries can be replaced with 2 cups (500 mL) other small fruits such as raspberries, blueberries or blackberries. Or use a combination of several berries.

To make your own superfine sugar: Place granulated sugar in a food processor; process until very fine.

For fluffy whipped cream, make sure whipping cream is very cold before beating. As well, place the beaters and bowl in the freezer for 10 minutes before you start.

Dessert can be assembled up to 4 hours ahead of serving time.

- Preheat oven to 350°F (180°C)
- 9-inch (23 cm) springform pan, greased and lightly dusted with flour (tap out excess)

Sponge Cake

3	eggs	3
1 cup	granulated sugar	250 mL
1½ cups	all-purpose flour	375 mL
2 tsp	baking powder	10 mL
¼ tsp	salt	1 mL
¾ cup	milk	175 mL
⅓ cup	butter, melted	75 mL
1 tsp	grated lemon zest	5 mL

Filling

1½ cups	whipping (35%) cream	375 mL
1 tsp	vanilla	5 mL
¼ cup	superfine sugar (see Tips, left)	60 mL
3 cups	sliced strawberries	750 mL
1 cup	whole small strawberries	250 mL
	Mint sprigs	

1. *Sponge Cake:* In a bowl, using an electric mixer at high speed, beat eggs and sugar for 3 minutes or until thick and creamy.

2. In a separate bowl, stir together flour, baking powder and salt. In a glass measuring cup, combine milk, melted butter and lemon zest.

3. Beat dry ingredients into egg mixture alternately with milk mixture until batter is just smooth.

4. Pour into prepared pan. Bake on middle rack in preheated oven for 30 to 35 minutes or until cake tester inserted in center comes out clean.

5. Let cake cool for 5 minutes; run knife around edge and remove sides. Place on a wire rack to cool completely. Using a long serrated knife, slice cake horizontally to make three layers, each about ½ inch (1 cm) thick.

6. *Filling:* In a bowl, using an electric mixer, whip cream until soft peaks form. Beat in vanilla and sugar, a spoonful at a time, until stiff peaks form.

7. Arrange one cake layer, cut side up, on a large serving plate. Spread with one-third of the whipped cream; top with half the sliced berries, including some juice. Arrange second cake layer on top. Spread with one-third of the whipped cream and remaining sliced berries with juice. Arrange third layer on top; spread top with remaining whipped cream. Garnish with small whole berries and mint sprigs.

Strawberry Shortcake

Although strawberries are available year-round, it's a true occasion when sweet local strawberries appear in markets and roadside stands. Sweeter and more juicy, they are a scrumptious treat when served with tender biscuits and cold whipped cream.

Tips

If you don't have a rasp grater, such as a Microplane, to grate lemon zest, use a zester to remove the zest in thin shreds, then finely chop with a knife.

When lemons are bargain-priced, stock up for the future. Grate the zest and squeeze the juice; place in separate containers and freeze.

- Preheat oven to 400°F (200°C)
- 2½-inch (6 cm) cookie cutter, floured
- Baking sheet, lined with parchment paper

Shortcake

2 cups	all-purpose flour	500 mL
5 tbsp	granulated sugar, divided	75 mL
1 tbsp	baking powder	15 mL
¼ tsp	salt	1 mL
6 tbsp	butter, cut into pieces	90 mL
1	egg	1
¾ cup	milk (approx.)	175 mL
1 tsp	grated lemon zest	5 mL
2 tbsp	sliced almonds (optional)	30 mL

Filling

4 cups	strawberries, sliced	1 L
6 tbsp	granulated sugar, divided	90 mL
1½ cups	whipping (35%) cream	375 mL
1 tsp	vanilla	5 mL

1. *Shortcake:* In a large bowl, stir together flour, 4 tbsp (60 mL) of the sugar, baking powder and salt. With a pastry blender or fork, cut in butter until crumbly.

2. In another bowl, beat egg with milk and lemon zest. Make a well in center of dry ingredients and stir in milk mixture until dough just comes together. Turn out onto lightly floured surface. Gently knead four to five times to form a smooth dough.

3. Pat into a circle about 1 inch (2.5 cm) thick. Using prepared cookie cutter, cut out 8 biscuits, rerolling scraps.

4. Place on prepared baking sheet, 2 inches (5 cm) apart. Brush tops with milk; sprinkle with almonds, if using, and remaining 1 tbsp (15 mL) of the sugar.

5. Bake on middle rack in preheated oven for 14 to 16 minutes or until golden and puffed. Transfer to a wire rack and let cool.

6. *Filling:* Meanwhile, place 1 cup (250 mL) of the strawberries in a bowl and mash with 4 tbsp (60 mL) of the sugar. Gently stir in remaining sliced berries. Let stand at room temperature for up to 2 hours.

7. In a bowl, whip cream with 2 tbsp (30 mL) of the sugar and vanilla until stiff peaks form.

8. *To serve:* For each shortcake, split biscuit in half horizontally; place bottom half on dessert plate. Spoon about $\frac{1}{3}$ cup (75 mL) of the sliced berries and juices over biscuit. Top with whipped cream, then biscuit top. Serve immediately.

Vanilla Cupcakes with Buttercream Frosting

Makes 18 cupcakes

Most of us have fond memories of cupcakes — peeling back the paper liner and taking a delicious bite into the soft cake and sweet, creamy frosting. Lucky for us cupcakes are in vogue again, showing up at parties and celebrations so we can enjoy this yummy treat all the time.

Variations

Lemon Cupcakes

Substitute 1 tbsp (15 mL) grated lemon zest for vanilla in cake batter.

See Lemon Buttercream Frosting variation, page 501.

- Preheat the oven to 350°F (180°C)
- Two 12-cup muffin pans, with paper liners sprayed with nonstick cooking spray

2 cups	all-purpose flour	500 mL
2 tsp	baking powder	10 mL
¼ tsp	salt	1 mL
¾ cup	milk	175 mL
2 tsp	vanilla	10 mL
¾ cup	butter, softened	175 mL
1¼ cups	granulated sugar	300 mL
2	eggs	2
	Buttercream Frosting (see recipe, opposite)	

1. In a bowl, stir together flour, baking powder and salt. In a glass measure, combine milk and vanilla.

2. In a large bowl, using an electric mixer, cream butter with sugar until light and fluffy. Add eggs, one at a time, beating well after each addition.

3. Reduce speed to low, then add flour and milk mixtures alternately in batches, beginning and ending with flour and mixing until just combined.

4. Spoon batter into prepared muffin cups, filling them two-thirds full. Bake on middle rack in preheated oven for 20 to 22 minutes or until tops are pale golden and a cake tester inserted in centers comes out clean. Remove from oven and let cool for 10 minutes. Turn cupcakes out of the pan and place on a wire rack to cool completely. Frost with Buttercream Frosting.

Variations

Lemon Buttercream Frosting

Use lemon juice instead of milk and 2 tsp (10 mL) lemon zest for vanilla.

Chocolate Buttercream Frosting

Beat in ⅓ cup (75 mL) unsweetened cocoa powder along with confectioner's sugar and increase milk to 3 to 4 tbsp (45 to 60 mL) to make a creamy frosting.

Buttercream Frosting

Makes 1½ cups (375 mL) frosting

½ cup	butter, softened	125 mL
2½ cups	confectioner's (icing) sugar	625 mL
2 tbsp	milk	30 mL
1 tsp	vanilla	5 mL

1. In a bowl, using an electric mixer, cream butter with confectioner's sugar. Beat in milk and vanilla to make a smooth, fluffy frosting.

Easy Chocolate Cupcakes

Makes 18 large cupcakes

Here is a simple and economical old-fashioned recipe for chocolate cupcakes that is easy enough for kids to help make.

Tips

To sour milk, add 1 tbsp (15 mL) lemon juice to a glass measuring cup and add milk to make 1 cup (250 mL).

If you don't have two muffin pans, bake cupcakes in two batches.

Variation

To make a layer cake instead of cupcakes, pour batter into two greased and floured 9-inch (23 cm) round cake pans and bake for 30 to 35 minutes or until tester inserted in center comes out clean.

- Preheat oven to 350°F (180°C)
- Two 12-cup muffin pans, with paper liners sprayed with nonstick cooking spray

2 cups	all-purpose flour	500 mL
1½ cups	granulated sugar	375 mL
⅔ cup	unsweetened cocoa powder	150 mL
1 tsp	baking soda	5 mL
¼ tsp	salt	1 mL
2	eggs	2
1 cup	sour milk (see Tip, left) or buttermilk	250 mL
½ cup	vegetable oil	125 mL
2 tsp	vanilla	10 mL
½ cup	hot water	125 mL
	Buttercream Frosting or Chocolate Buttercream Frosting (see recipes, page 501)	

1. In a large bowl, sift together flour, sugar, cocoa powder, baking soda and salt.

2. In another bowl, beat eggs. Stir in milk, oil and vanilla; whisk in hot water. Stir in flour mixture until combined. (Batter is quite thin.)

3. Pour batter into prepared muffin cups, filling two-thirds full. Bake on middle rack in preheated oven for 18 to 20 minutes or until tops of cupcakes spring back when lightly touched. Let cool on wire racks. Spread with Buttercream Frosting.

Individual Warm Chocolate Cakes

Makes 6 servings

This decadent, rich chocolate dessert is popular on restaurant menus, but it's easy to make at home. I find raspberries the perfect fruit to pair with chocolate; strawberries are my second choice to serve with this impressive dessert.

Tips

"Bittersweet" (not to be confused with unsweetened bitter chocolate) refers to dark chocolate with at least 70% cacao content. It's recommended in this recipe for its superior flavor and can be found in supermarkets and fine bakeries. If unavailable, semisweet baking chocolate can be substituted.

The cakes are baked just before serving, but the batter can be made earlier in the day and refrigerated. Remove batter from fridge 1 hour before baking to bring it to room temperature.

- Preheat oven to 375°F (190°C)
- 6 ramekins (each 6 oz/175 mL), well greased and lightly dusted with cocoa powder, tapping out excess
- Rimmed baking sheet

½ cup	butter, cut into pieces	125 mL
8 oz	bittersweet chocolate (see Tip, left), chopped	250 g
2 tsp	vanilla	10 mL
2	eggs	2
2	egg yolks	2
⅓ cup	granulated sugar	75 mL
Pinch	salt	Pinch
2 tbsp	all-purpose flour	30 mL
	Vanilla Custard Sauce (page 533) or Raspberry Sauce (page 547)	
1 cup	fresh raspberries	250 mL
	Whipped cream (optional)	

1. In a metal bowl set over a saucepan of simmering water, melt butter and chocolate, stirring occasionally. (Or place butter and chocolate in 4-cup (1 L) glass bowl and microwave on Medium (50%) for 3 to 4 minutes or until chocolate is melted.) Stir in vanilla. Let chocolate cool until lukewarm.

2. In another bowl, using an electric mixer, beat eggs, egg yolks, sugar and salt on high speed for 2 minutes or until thick and pale. On low speed, beat in flour. Fold in chocolate mixture until combined. Spoon batter into prepared ramekins and arrange on baking sheet.

3. Bake in preheated oven for 15 to 17 minutes or until sides of the cakes are firm and centers are soft. Transfer to a wire rack and let cool for 1 minute. Run a knife around the edge to loosen each cake. Invert a plate over each ramekin and carefully turn each one over to unmold. Spoon Vanilla Custard Sauce or Raspberry Sauce around cakes and garnish with raspberries (and whipped cream, if serving with the raspberry sauce). Serve immediately.

Classic Deli Cheesecake with Glazed Strawberries

If you're tempted to use all low-fat dairy products in this classic cheesecake, you might be disappointed, because the cake just won't have the same creamy taste and texture as the authentic cheesecakes served in a Jewish deli.

Tip

For a super-creamy cheesecake, purée pressed cottage cheese in a food processor before beating with cream cheese.

- Preheat oven to 300°F (150°C)
- 9-inch (23 cm) springform pan

1 tbsp	butter, melted	15 mL
2 tbsp	fine dry bread crumbs	30 mL
1 lb	pressed cottage cheese	500 g
2	packages (each 8 oz/250 g) cream cheese, cubed, softened	2
4	eggs	4
1¼ cups	granulated sugar	300 mL
⅓ cup	all-purpose flour	75 mL
1 cup	full-fat sour cream	250 mL
2 tsp	vanilla	10 mL
2 tsp	grated lemon zest	10 mL

Topping

4 cups	small whole strawberries (approx.)	1 L
⅓ cup	strawberry or red currant jelly	75 mL

1. Brush bottom and sides of springform pan with melted butter; coat with bread crumbs and shake out excess.

2. In a bowl, using a stand mixer or hand-held electric mixer, combine cottage cheese, cream cheese, sugar and flour. Beat on high speed for 3 minutes, occasionally scraping down sides, until smooth and creamy. On low speed, beat in eggs, one at a time, until incorporated. Beat in sour cream, vanilla and lemon zest until combined.

3. Pour batter into prepared pan. Bake in preheated oven for 70 minutes or until cake rises to top of pan, edges are firm and center is still moist. Turn off oven. Leave cheesecake in closed oven for 1 hour.

4. Remove from oven and place on a wire rack. Carefully run a knife around edge of pan and let cool. Cover and refrigerate for at least 1 day before serving.

Tip

Instead of topping the cheesecake with glazed strawberries, serve it with Lemon Blueberry Sauce (see recipe, below).

This fruity sauce makes a delicious topping for blintzes or cheesecake.

5. *Topping:* Wash strawberries and let dry completely on a clean, dry kitchen towel. Remove stem ends. Arrange whole berries, stem side down, in an even layer on top of cake.

6. Place jelly in a glass bowl with 1 tsp (5 mL) water; microwave on High for 1 minute or until melted and boiling. Brush berries with hot jam mixture. Refrigerate for 4 hours or overnight.

7. Remove cake from fridge 30 minutes before serving. To serve, cut into slices using a warm knife dipped in hot water and dried with a towel.

Lemon Blueberry Sauce

Makes about 2 cups (500 mL)

⅓ cup	granulated sugar	75 mL
¼ cup	unsweetened apple juice or water	60 mL
1½ tsp	grated lemon zest	7 mL
1 tbsp	fresh lemon juice	15 mL
1 tbsp	cornstarch	15 mL
3 cups	frozen blueberries	750 mL

1. In a medium saucepan, stir together sugar, apple juice, lemon juice and cornstarch until smooth. Stir in blueberries. Bring to a full boil over medium-high heat, stirring often. Boil, stirring, for 2 minutes or until thickened.

2. Remove from heat and stir in lemon zest. Let cool. Transfer to an airtight container and refrigerate for up to 3 days.

Chocolate Swirl Cheesecake

The combination of chocolate swirling through thick cream cheese on top of a chocolate nut crust makes this a decadent splurge. It's hard to resist having seconds.

Tips

To prevent the top of the cheesecake from cracking, don't overbake it; it should still appear slightly underbaked in the center.

To melt chocolate: Place chopped chocolate in bowl and microwave on Medium (50%) for 2½ to 3 minutes.

- Preheat oven to 325°F (160°C)
- 9-inch (23 cm) springform pan, lightly greased

Crust

1 cup	chocolate baking crumbs	250 mL
⅓ cup	chopped walnuts or pecans	75 mL
2 tbsp	butter, melted	30 mL
2 tbsp	granulated sugar	30 mL

Filling

1 lb	cream cheese, softened (two 8 oz/250 g packages)	500 g
⅔ cup	granulated sugar	150 mL
3	eggs	3
½ cup	sour cream	125 mL
1½ tsp	vanilla	7 mL
3 oz	semisweet chocolate, melted	90 g

1. *Crust:* In a food processor, combine crumbs, walnuts, butter and sugar. Process using on-off turns until nuts are finely chopped. Press in bottom and 1 inch (2.5 cm) up sides of springform pan. Bake in preheated oven for 10 minutes or until just set. Let cool.

2. *Filling:* In a large bowl, using electric mixer, beat cream cheese and sugar until smooth. Beat in eggs, one at a time, until incorporated. Beat in sour cream and vanilla.

3. Transfer 1 cup (250 mL) of the batter to a bowl; stir in melted chocolate until smooth.

4. Spoon white batter into prepared pan. Top with six distinct spoonfuls of chocolate batter. Using a knife, cut through batter in a zigzag pattern, being careful not to cut through to crust.

5. Bake on middle rack in preheated oven for 30 minutes or until firm around outside and slightly moist in center. Turn off oven, leave door ajar and let cake cool in oven for 1 hour. Remove and carefully run a knife around outside edge; refrigerate.

Luscious Tropical Cheesecake

Making a cheesecake may seem like a half-day production, but not with this no-bake method that is guaranteed to win raves for the cook.

Tips

Can be made the day ahead; cover and refrigerate.

To toast coconut: Place coconut on baking sheet in a 350°F (180°C) oven, stirring once, for 5 to 7 minutes.

● Preheat oven to 350°F (180°C)
● 9-inch (23 cm) springform pan, lightly greased

Crust

1 cup	digestive cookie or graham wafer crumbs	250 mL
2 tbsp	granulated sugar	30 mL
2 tbsp	butter, melted	30 mL

Filling

1	can (14 oz/398 mL) crushed pineapple	1
1	package (¼ oz/7 g) unflavored gelatin	1
8 oz	cream cheese, softened and cubed	250 g
1 cup	ricotta cheese	250 mL
½ cup	granulated sugar	125 mL
2 tsp	grated orange zest	10 mL
1 cup	whipping (35%) cream	250 mL
½ cup	sweetened shredded coconut, toasted (see Tips, left)	125 mL

1. *Crust:* In a bowl, combine cookie crumbs, sugar and butter. Press in bottom of springform pan. Bake for 8 minutes or until set. Chill until firm. Fit a 3-inch (7.5 cm) wide strip of waxed or parchment paper around inside of pan.

2. *Filling:* Drain pineapple in sieve set over bowl; press with rubber spatula to extract juice. Pour ½ cup (125 mL) of the juice into a small saucepan; sprinkle gelatin over. Let stand for 2 minutes to soften. Cook over low heat, stirring, until gelatin is dissolved. (Or put juice and gelatin in a measuring cup; let stand 2 minutes to soften, then microwave on Medium (50%) for 1 minute.) Let cool slightly.

3. In a food processor, combine cream cheese, ricotta, sugar and warm gelatin mixture; process until smooth. Transfer to a large bowl; stir in drained pineapple and orange zest.

4. In a bowl, using an electric mixer, whip cream until stiff peaks form. Fold into pineapple mixture until smooth. Pour into prepared pan; smooth top and sprinkle with toasted coconut. Chill until set, about 4 hours. Remove side of pan and waxed or parchment paper; arrange on a serving plate.

Single-Crust Pie Pastry

Makes enough pastry for a 9- or 10-inch (23 or 25 cm) single-crust pie shell

¼ cup	cold butter	60 mL
¼ cup	lard or shortening	60 mL
1¼ cups	all-purpose flour	300 mL
Pinch	salt	Pinch
2 tbsp	ice water (approx.)	30 mL

Tips

Traditional pie pastry is made with shortening, but I prefer to make mine using a combination of butter and lard or shortening. The reason? Not only does the buttery taste come through, but butter produces a golden crust. Another plus: the pastry is easy to handle and roll.

If you prefer, you can omit the lard and use ½ cup (125 mL) cold butter.

1. Place butter and lard in a bowl; freeze for 20 minutes or until firm. Cut into small pieces.

2. In a food processor, combine flour, salt, butter and lard. Pulse to make fine crumbs. Transfer mixture to a bowl.

3. Using a fork, stir in enough water to hold dough together. Gather dough into a ball. Gently knead two to three times on a lightly floured pastry board.

4. With floured hands, flatten dough into a 5-inch (13 cm) round. Wrap in plastic wrap; refrigerate for 1 hour.

Mixing the Dough by Hand

Have butter and lard at room temperature. Place flour and salt in a bowl. Using a pastry blender, cut in butter and lard. Continue with Step 3.

Double-Crust Pie Pastry

Tips

To get more juice out of a lemon, roll on countertop or microwave on High for 20 seconds before squeezing.

If you prefer, you can omit the lard and use 1 cup (250 mL) cold butter.

½ cup	cold butter	125 mL
½ cup	lard or shortening	125 mL
2½ cups	all-purpose flour	625 mL
¼ tsp	salt	1 mL
1	egg yolk	1
1 tsp	lemon juice	5 mL
3 to 4 tbsp	cold water (approx.)	45 to 60 mL

1. Place butter and lard on a plate; place in freezer for 20 minutes or until firm. Cut into small pieces.

2. In a food processor, combine flour, salt, butter and lard. Pulse to make fine crumbs. Transfer mixture to a bowl.

3. In a small bowl, beat egg yolk with lemon juice and 2 tbsp (30 mL) water. Drizzle over flour mixture and toss using a fork. Sprinkle with additional water just to hold pastry together and gather into a ball. Gently knead two to three times on a lightly floured pastry board.

4. Divide dough in two. With floured hands, flatten dough into 5-inch (13 cm) rounds. Wrap each in plastic wrap; refrigerate for 1 hour.

Mixing the Dough by Hand

Have butter and lard at room temperature. Place flour and salt in a bowl. Using a pastry blender, cut in butter and lard. Continue with Step 3.

Lemon Meringue Pie

Tart, sweet and lemony —
who can resist indulging in
a slice of this tempting pie?

Tips

If you don't have a
rasp grater, such as a
Microplane, to grate
lemon zest, use a zester
to remove the zest in
thin shreds, then finely
chop with a knife.

When lemons are
bargain-priced, stock up
for the future. Grate the
zest and squeeze the
juice; place in separate
containers and freeze.

To get more juice out of a
lemon, roll on countertop
or microwave on High
for 20 seconds before
squeezing.

Make sure to seal edges
of crust with meringue to
prevent the meringue from
shrinking when baked.

- Preheat oven to 425°F (220°C)
- 9-inch (23 cm) pie plate, lightly greased

Pastry for a single-crust 9-inch
(23 cm) pie (see recipe, page 508)

Filling

1 cup	granulated sugar	250 mL
¼ cup	cornstarch	60 mL
Pinch	salt	Pinch
4	egg yolks	4
½ cup	fresh lemon juice	125 mL
2 tbsp	butter, cut into pieces	30 mL
1 tbsp	finely grated lemon zest	15 mL

Meringue

4	egg whites	4
¼ tsp	cream of tartar	1 mL
½ cup	granulated sugar	125 mL

1. On a lightly floured surface, roll out pastry into a
   12-inch (30 cm) round. Roll pastry loosely around
   rolling pin; unroll into prepared pie plate. Trim edge,
   leaving a ½-inch (1 cm) overhang; turn pastry edge
   under and flute edge. Prick with a fork and line with a
   sheet of parchment paper or foil; fill with dried beans
   or pie weights.

2. Bake in preheated oven for 10 minutes or until
   edges are set. Remove pie weights and bake for 5 to
   6 minutes more or until pastry is light golden. Place
   on rack to cool.

3. *Filling:* In a medium saucepan, combine sugar,
   cornstarch and salt; whisk in 1½ cups (375 mL) cold
   water until smooth. Add egg yolks and lemon juice.
   Cook over medium heat, whisking constantly, until
   mixture comes to a boil. Boil, stirring constantly,
   for 1 minute; remove from heat. Whisk in butter
   and lemon zest until butter is completely melted.
   Let mixture cool for 10 minutes; pour into pie shell.
   Let cool completely until filling is set, about 2 to
   3 hours.

4. *Meringue:* In a large bowl, using an electric mixer, beat
   egg whites and cream of tartar until soft peaks form.

Gradually add sugar, a spoonful at a time, until stiff glossy peaks form. Spread over lemon filling, making sure to seal edges of the crust. Make decorative swirls with the back of a spoon.

5. Bake in preheated 350°F (180°C) oven for 10 to 12 minutes or until light golden. Place on a wire rack to cool; refrigerate. To serve, cut with sharp knife dipped in hot water.

Ginger Peach Pie

Makes 8 servings

When I lived in Niagara, in the heart of peach country, I couldn't wait for the first baskets of rosy-blushed peaches to appear at neighboring roadside stands in late July to make my all-time favorite pie. Serve warm, with ice cream if desired.

Tip

To peel peaches: Plunge peaches in boiling water for 15 to 30 seconds to loosen skins.

- Preheat oven to 425°F (220°C)
- 9-inch (23 cm) pie plate, lightly greased

	Pastry for a double-crust 9-inch (23 cm) pie (see recipe, page 509)	
6 cups	sliced peeled peaches (about 8)	1.5 L
1½ tsp	grated lemon zest	7 mL
2 tbsp	fresh lemon juice	30 mL
¾ cup	packed brown sugar	175 mL
¼ cup	cornstarch	60 mL
¼ cup	finely chopped candied ginger	60 mL

1. On a lightly floured surface, roll out half of the pastry into a 12-inch (30 cm) round. Roll pastry loosely around rolling pin; unroll into prepared pie plate and trim edges.

2. In a large bowl, toss peaches with lemon zest and juice; stir in brown sugar, cornstarch and candied ginger. Spoon into prepared pie shell.

3. Roll out remaining pastry and fit over filling. Trim, leaving a ½-inch (1 cm) overhang. Tuck top edge of pastry under bottom edge. Press edges together with a fork or flute edges with fingers to seal. Cut steam vent in center and make small slashes using a knife.

4. Bake in preheated oven for 15 minutes; reduce temperature to 375°F (190°C). Bake for 35 to 40 minutes or until pastry is golden and filling is bubbly. Place on a wire rack to cool.

Cinnamon Apple Crumble Pie

When you arrive home with your bounty of rosy apples in the fall, whip up this family treat. You won't regret it. A thick slice of warm-from-the-oven pie topped with a scoop of vanilla ice cream is pure comfort food no one can resist.

Variation

Apple Walnut Crisp

Omit pastry shell. Arrange apple filling in 9-inch (2.5 L) round or square baking dish. Prepare crumble topping. Toss with ½ cup (125 mL) chopped walnuts or pecans. Sprinkle evenly over fruit. Bake in preheated 375°F (190°C) oven for 35 to 40 minutes or until apples are tender and topping is golden.

- Preheat oven to 425°F (220°C)
- 9-inch (23 cm) pie plate, lightly greased

Pastry for a single-crust 9-inch (23 cm) pie shell (see recipe, page 508)

Filling

8 cups	sliced peeled tart apples, such as McIntosh	2 L
½ cup	granulated sugar	125 mL
2 tbsp	all-purpose flour	30 mL
1½ tsp	ground cinnamon	7 mL
¼ tsp	freshly grated nutmeg	1 mL

Crumble Topping

¾ cup	large-flake (old-fashioned) rolled oats	175 mL
½ cup	all-purpose flour	125 mL
⅔ cup	packed brown sugar	150 mL
½ cup	cold butter, cut into pieces	125 mL

1. On a lightly floured surface, roll out pastry to a 12-inch (30 cm) round. Roll pastry loosely around rolling pin; unroll into prepared pie plate. Trim edges, leaving a ½-inch (1 cm) overhang. Turn pastry edge under and flute the edge. Refrigerate.

2. *Filling:* In a large bowl, toss apples with sugar, flour, cinnamon and nutmeg. Spoon into prepared pie shell, packing lightly.

3. *Crumble Topping:* In a bowl, combine rolled oats, flour and brown sugar; cut in butter using a pastry blender or fork until mixture resembles coarse crumbs. Sprinkle over apples, packing lightly.

4. Bake in lower third of preheated oven for 15 minutes; reduce temperature to 350°F (180°C) and bake for 40 to 45 minutes more or until apples are tender.

5. Place on a wire rack to cool. Serve warm or at room temperature with ice cream, if desired.

Farmhouse Apple Pie

Intimidated by the thought of making two-crust pies? Try this simple free-form pie — it only needs a single pie crust and looks like it came from a pastry shop.

Tip

Store-bought pastry for a single-crust pie can be used instead of the suggested homemade pastry.

• Baking sheet, lightly greased

Pastry

1¼ cups	all-purpose flour	300 mL
1 tbsp	granulated sugar	15 mL
	Salt	
½ cup	butter, cut into pieces	125 mL
2 tbsp	cold water (approx.)	30 mL

Filling

4	apples, such as Golden Delicious, Spy or Granny Smith, peeled, cored and sliced	4
⅓ cup	granulated sugar	75 mL
¼ cup	finely chopped pecans	60 mL
½ tsp	ground cinnamon	2 mL

1. *Pastry:* In a bowl, combine flour, sugar and generous pinch of salt. Cut in butter with a pastry blender or fork to make coarse crumbs. Sprinkle with enough water to hold dough together; gather into a ball. Gently knead two to three times on a floured board. Flatten to a 5-inch (13 cm) circle; wrap in plastic wrap and refrigerate for 1 hour.

2. Preheat oven to 375°F (190°C).

3. On a lightly floured surface, roll pastry to a 13-inch (32 cm) round; transfer to prepared baking sheet. Using a sharp knife, trim pastry edge to form an even circle.

4. *Filling:* Starting 2 inches (5 cm) from edge, overlap apple slices in a circle; arrange another overlapping circle of apples in center. In a bowl, combine sugar, pecans and cinnamon; sprinkle over apples. Fold pastry rim over apples to form a 2-inch (5 cm) edge.

5. Bake on middle rack in preheated oven for 35 to 40 minutes or until pastry is golden and apples are tender. Place baking sheet on a wire rack to cool. With a spatula, carefully slide pie onto serving platter.

Pecan Pie

• 9-inch (23 cm) pie plate or tart pan with removable bottom, lightly greased

	Pastry for a single-crust 9-inch (23 cm) pie crust (see recipe, page 508)	
2	eggs	2
¾ cup	packed brown sugar	175 mL
¾ cup	golden corn syrup	175 mL
2 tbsp	butter, melted	30 mL
1 tsp	vanilla	5 mL
1¼ cups	pecan halves	300 mL

1. On a lightly floured surface, roll pastry out to a 12-inch (30 cm) round. Roll pastry loosely around rolling pin; unroll into prepared pie plate. Trim edge, leaving a ½-inch (1 cm) overhang. Turn pastry edge under and flute the edge. Refrigerate for 30 minutes to chill.

2. Preheat oven to 375°F (190°C).

3. In a bowl, beat eggs. Stir in brown sugar, corn syrup, melted butter and vanilla until smooth.

4. Coarsely chop 1 cup (250 mL) pecans (chop nuts into three pieces each). Stir into filling.

5. Pour into prepared crust; sprinkle top with remaining ¼ cup (60 mL) whole pecans. Bake on middle rack in preheated oven for 35 to 40 minutes or until filling is set around edges but is slightly moist in the center. Place on a wire rack to cool. Serve at room temperature.

Pumpkin Pie

Makes 8 servings

This classic pie is the highlight of Thanksgiving dinner for my family. The whipped cream topping is a must to complete the holiday indulgence!

Tip

To make pumpkin (or squash) purée: Cut pumpkin into halves, quarters or chunks (depending on size) and remove seeds. Place in a 12- to 16-cup (3 to 4 L) casserole dish. Add ½ cup (125 mL) water. Microwave, covered, on High for 15 to 30 minutes or until tender when tested in several places with a knife. (Cooking time will vary according to the amount and type of pumpkin or squash.) Let stand for 10 minutes or until cool enough to handle. Scoop out pulp and mash or purée in a blender or food processor.

Pumpkin tends to be very watery, so place purée in a fine-mesh strainer for several hours to drain excess moisture. Freeze in airtight containers for up to 3 months.

• 9-inch (23 cm) pie plate, lightly greased

	Pastry for a single-crust 9-inch (23 cm) pie (see recipe, page 508)	
2	eggs	2
1 cup	packed brown sugar	250 mL
2 cups	pumpkin purée (not pie filling)	500 mL
1 cup	half-and-half (10%) cream	250 mL
1½ tsp	ground cinnamon	7 mL
½ tsp	ground allspice	2 mL
½ tsp	freshly grated nutmeg	2 mL
¼ tsp	ground cloves	1 mL
¼ tsp	salt	1 mL

1. On a lightly floured surface, roll out pastry into a 12-inch (30 cm) round. Roll pastry loosely around rolling pin; unroll into pie plate. Trim edge, leaving a ½-inch (1 cm) overhang; turn pastry edge under and flute edge. Refrigerate for 30 minutes to chill.

2. Preheat oven to 425°F (220°C).

3. In a bowl, beat eggs with brown sugar. Stir in pumpkin purée, cream, cinnamon, allspice, nutmeg, cloves and salt until spices are well combined.

4. Pour filling into pie shell; bake on middle rack in preheated oven for 15 minutes, then reduce temperature to 350°F (180°C). Bake for 35 to 40 minutes or until tip of knife inserted in center comes out clean. Place on a wire rack to cool; refrigerate.

French Plum Almond Tart

While North American fruit pies are typically made with a double crust and thickened fruit filling, European tarts are made with a single crust topped with a layer of fresh fruits and sweetened egg custard or a nut-based filling. With puff pastry handy in the freezer, it's easy to turn out this impressive-looking French fruit tart in short order.

Tips

Puff pastry comes in 14- to 16-oz (400 to 450 g) packages, depending on the brand. You'll be using half a package for this recipe. Frozen butter puff pastry is preferred, but any brand of frozen puff pastry will work.

Instead of plums, use quartered apricots or sliced peeled peaches, apples or pears.

- Preheat oven to 400°F (200°C)
- 9-inch (23 cm) tart pan with removable bottom

8 oz	frozen puff pastry, thawed	250 g
6 tbsp	granulated sugar, divided	90 mL
1/4 tsp	ground cinnamon	1 mL
Pinch	freshly ground nutmeg	Pinch
2 tbsp	butter, softened	30 mL
1	egg	1
1/2 cup	ground blanched almonds (2 oz/60 g)	125 mL
1/2 tsp	almond extract	2 mL
2 cups	thickly sliced damson or prune plums	500 mL
	Ice cream	

1. On lightly floured surface, roll out pastry to fit tart pan and trim edges. Prick bottom of pastry with a fork. Freeze for 15 minutes or until pastry is firm. Bake in preheated oven for 10 to 12 minutes or until crust is light golden and slightly puffed. Let cool slightly.

2. In a small bowl, combine 2 tbsp (30 mL) sugar, cinnamon and nutmeg; reserve.

3. In a bowl, using a wooden spoon, cream butter and remaining sugar. Beat in egg until smooth. Beat in almonds. Spread mixture evenly in partially baked tart shell. Arrange plums in a circular pattern over top. Sprinkle with reserved spice mixture.

4. Bake on middle rack in preheated oven for 30 to 35 minutes or until pastry is browned and filling is golden. Transfer to a wire rack to cool. To serve, cut into wedges and accompany with ice cream.

Linzertorte

Makes 8 to 10 servings

This Austrian specialty that takes its name from the city of Linz is especially famous throughout Europe. It is a tradition in my family to bake this delectable dessert at Christmas and for special family gatherings.

Tip

To get 1½ cups (375 mL) ground almonds, you'll need to purchase about 6 oz (175 g).

- Preheat oven to 350°F (180°C)
- 9-inch (23 cm) tart pan with removable bottom, greased

¾ cup	butter, softened	175 mL
⅔ cup	granulated sugar	150 mL
2	egg yolks	2
1 tsp	grated lemon zest	5 mL
1 tbsp	lemon juice	15 mL
1¼ cups	all-purpose flour	300 mL
½ tsp	baking powder	2 mL
¾ tsp	ground cinnamon	3 mL
¼ tsp	salt	1 mL
1½ cups	ground unblanched almonds	375 mL
1 oz	semisweet chocolate, grated	30 g
1 cup	raspberry jam (approx.)	250 mL
1	egg white, lightly beaten, for glaze	1
	Confectioner's (icing) sugar	

1. In a bowl, using an electric mixer, cream butter and sugar until light and fluffy. Beat in yolks and lemon zest and juice.

2. In another bowl, stir together flour, baking powder, cinnamon and salt. Add to creamed mixture until combined. Stir in ground almonds and chocolate.

3. Break off one-third of the dough, shape into a ball and flatten. Roll out dough between sheets of waxed or parchment paper into a 9-inch (23 cm) circle. Place on baking sheet and freeze for 15 minutes or until firm.

4. Meanwhile, using floured hands, press remaining dough evenly into bottom and sides of prepared tart pan. Spread with raspberry jam.

5. Remove dough from freezer and cut into twelve ¾-inch (2 cm) strips. Arrange 6 strips in the same direction on jam layer, spacing about 1 inch (2.5 cm) apart; layer remaining 6 over top in the opposite direction. Trim ends of pastry strips and press into rim of torte. Brush pastry edge and strips with egg white.

6. Bake tart on middle rack in preheated oven for 30 to 35 minutes or until golden. Let cool completely on a wire rack; remove sides of pan. Dust top with confectioner's sugar. Cut into small wedges and serve.

Butter Tarts

Scrumptious is the best way to describe these old-time favorite tarts with a moist, not too sweet, filling.

Tip

The brown sugar you use in recipes is totally your preference. Brown sugar comes in both light and dark brown. Dark brown sugar is noticeably darker in color and has a stronger molasses taste.

- Preheat oven to 425°F (220°C)
- Two 12-cup muffin pans, lightly greased

	Pastry for a double-crust 9-inch (23 cm) pie (see recipe, page 509)	
½ cup	raisins, dried currants, chopped walnuts or pecans	125 mL

Filling

2	eggs	2
¾ cup	corn syrup	175 mL
¾ cup	packed brown sugar	175 mL
¼ cup	butter, melted	60 mL
2 tsp	vanilla	10 mL
2 tsp	fresh lemon juice	10 mL
¼ tsp	salt	1 mL

1. On a lightly floured surface, roll out pastry to ⅛-inch (3 mm) thickness. Cut out 4-inch (10 cm) rounds and fit into muffin cups. Sprinkle raisins in bottom.

2. *Filling:* In a bowl, beat eggs. Stir in corn syrup, brown sugar, butter, vanilla, lemon juice and salt. Spoon 2 tbsp (30 mL) filling into each tart shell.

3. Bake on rack in lower third of preheated oven for 14 to 16 minutes or until pastry is golden and filling is bubbly. Remove from oven; let stand for 1 minute. Run a knife around pastry edge to loosen tarts; using a pastry spatula, carefully remove to a wire rack to cool.

Desserts

continued...

Warm Maple Apple Pudding

Saucy fruit topped with a light cake batter makes one of the most soothing desserts ever created. This version hails from Quebec, where sweet and snappy McIntosh apples are paired with amber maple syrup.

Tip

Once opened, make sure to store maple syrup in the refrigerator. It also can be frozen.

- Preheat oven to 350°F (180°C)
- 8-inch (20 cm) square baking dish, greased

4 cups	peeled sliced apples, such as McIntosh or Golden Delicious	1 L
⅔ cup	maple syrup	150 mL
⅓ cup	raisins	75 mL
1 cup	all-purpose flour	250 mL
¼ cup	granulated sugar	60 mL
1½ tsp	baking powder	7 mL
½ tsp	baking soda	2 mL
¼ tsp	salt	1 mL
¼ cup	butter, cut into pieces	60 mL
1	egg	1
½ cup	buttermilk	125 mL
1 tsp	vanilla	5 mL

1. In a saucepan, bring apples and maple syrup to a boil; simmer 3 minutes or until softened. Add raisins. Pour into prepared baking dish.

2. In a bowl, combine flour, sugar, baking powder, baking soda and salt. Cut in butter using pastry blender or two knives to make fine crumbs. In a bowl, beat egg, buttermilk and vanilla. Pour over flour mixture; stir just until combined.

3. Drop by large spoonfuls onto warm apple slices. Bake in preheated oven for 30 minutes or until top is golden and cake tester inserted in center comes out clean. Serve warm with ice cream, if desired.

Sticky Toffee Pudding

Sticky toffee pudding is a scrumptious British dessert that consists of a moist date or prune cake topped with a sticky-sweet toffee sauce. This retro dessert has gained in popularity in recent years, and it's always a hit when I serve it to friends and family.

Tip

Sticky Toffee Pudding can be prepared through step 5 up to 1 day ahead. Cover pudding with plastic wrap and store at room temperature. Transfer sauce to an airtight container, cover and refrigerate. Reheat pudding in a 300°F (150°C) oven for about 15 minutes or until warm. Reheat sauce briefly in the microwave or on the stovetop. Continue with step 6.

- Preheat oven to 350°F (180°C)
- 13- by 9-inch (33 by 23 cm) baking dish, greased

1½ cups	chopped pitted dates	375 mL
1 tsp	baking soda	5 mL
1½ cups	boiling water	375 mL
2 cups	all-purpose flour	500 mL
2 tsp	baking powder	10 mL
¼ tsp	salt	1 mL
⅓ cup	butter, softened	75 mL
1 cup	packed brown sugar	250 mL
3	eggs	3

Toffee Sauce

1 cup	whipping (35%) cream	250 mL
1 cup	lightly packed dark brown sugar	250 mL
¼ cup	butter	60 mL
1 tsp	vanilla	5 mL
	Pouring Vanilla Custard (page 533), whipped cream or ice cream	

1. In a heatproof bowl, combine dates and baking soda. Pour boiling water over and let stand until mixture cools to room temperature, about 20 minutes.

2. In a bowl, stir together flour, baking powder and salt.

3. In another bowl, using an electric mixer, beat butter and brown sugar until light and fluffy. Beat in eggs, one at a time, until incorporated. With the mixer on low speed, beat in flour mixture until just combined. Stir in date mixture.

4. Spoon batter into prepared baking dish. Bake in preheated oven for 35 to 40 minutes or until toothpick inserted in center comes out clean. Place on a wire rack to partially cool for 15 minutes.

5. *Toffee Sauce:* In a medium saucepan, combine cream, brown sugar and butter. Bring to a boil over medium-high heat, stirring, to dissolve brown sugar. Reduce heat and boil gently, stirring often for about 3 minutes or until sauce is reduced and slightly thickened. Remove from heat and stir in vanilla.

6. Using a skewer, pierce surface of cake at 1-inch (2.5 cm) intervals and slowly pour half of the warm sauce over warm pudding, spreading evenly. Let stand for 15 minutes or until most of the sauce is absorbed.

7. To serve, cut into squares and top with some of the remaining toffee sauce. Serve warm or at room temperature, with Pouring Vanilla Custard.

Easy Vanilla Pudding

2 cups	milk	500 mL
2	egg yolks	2
1/3 cup	granulated sugar	75 mL
3 tbsp	cornstarch	45 mL
2 tsp	vanilla	10 mL

1. In a small saucepan, whisk together milk and egg yolks. Stir in sugar and cornstarch until smooth. Place over medium heat and cook, stirring, for 5 minutes or until pudding comes to a full boil and thickens.

2. Remove from heat. Stir in vanilla. Pour pudding into individual serving dishes. Serve warm or cold. If serving cold, let cool slightly, and place plastic wrap directly on the surface to prevent the formation of a skin.

Microwave Method

1. Using an 8-cup (2 L) glass bowl or casserole dish, whisk together milk and egg yolks. Stir in sugar and cornstarch until smooth. Microwave, uncovered, on High for 2 minutes. Whisk well. Continue to microwave on High for 2 to 4 minutes, whisking every minute, until pudding comes to a full boil and thickens. Stir in vanilla.

Lemon Sponge Pudding

Makes 6 servings

Nice and lemony, this old-fashioned dessert is often called a self-saucing pudding. It has a separate sponge cake layer on top and luscious, tart-sweet lemon sauce underneath.

Tips

If you don't have a rasp grater, such as a Microplane, to grate lemon zest, use a zester to remove the zest in thin shreds, then finely chop with a knife.

When lemons are bargain-priced, stock up for the future. Grate the zest and squeeze the juice; place in separate containers and freeze.

To get more juice out of a lemon, roll on countertop or microwave on High for 20 seconds before squeezing.

• Preheat oven to 350°F (180°C)
• 6 ramekins or custard cups (each 6 oz/175 mL), well greased
• 13- by 9-inch (33 by 23 cm) baking pan

3	eggs, separated	3
¼ tsp	salt	1 mL
¾ cup	granulated sugar, divided	175 mL
3 tbsp	butter, softened	45 mL
¼ cup	all-purpose flour	60 mL
1¼ cups	milk	300 mL
1 tbsp	grated lemon zest	15 mL
⅓ cup	fresh lemon juice	75 mL

1. In a bowl, using an electric mixer, beat egg whites with salt until soft peaks form. Beat in ¼ cup (60 mL) of the sugar, 1 tbsp (15 mL) at a time, until stiff and glossy.

2. In another bowl, using the same beaters, beat butter and remaining sugar until fluffy. Beat in egg yolks until incorporated. On low speed, beat in flour, milk, lemon zest and juice. Using a rubber spatula, fold in one-quarter of the egg whites; fold in remaining egg whites until completely combined.

3. Pour batter into prepared ramekins (batter will almost come to top of each dish). Place ramekins in baking pan and pour enough boiling water into pan to reach halfway up the sides of ramekins.

4. Bake on middle rack in preheated oven for 40 to 45 minutes or until lightly browned on top. Remove ramekins from pan and let stand for 30 minutes to set. Serve either warm or cool.

Kids' Favorite Chocolate Pudding

Makes 4 servings

Why rely on expensive store-bought puddings, when you can make nourishing homemade ones that take little time to make on the stovetop or in the microwave? Milk puddings are also a great way to boost calcium.

Tips

Whole milk gives a creamier consistency than lower-fat 1% or skim milk in this easy-to-make dessert.

If cooking pudding in the microwave, be sure to use a large bowl to prevent boil-overs.

Variation

Butterscotch Pudding

Cook pudding as directed. Substitute ½ cup (125 mL) butterscotch chips for the chocolate chips; reduce sugar to ¼ cup (60 mL).

⅓ cup	granulated sugar	75 mL
¼ cup	cornstarch	60 mL
2¼ cups	milk	550 mL
⅓ cup	semisweet chocolate chips	75 mL
1 tsp	vanilla	5 mL

1. In a medium saucepan, whisk together sugar and cornstarch; add milk, whisking until smooth. Place over medium heat; cook, stirring, for 5 minutes or until mixture comes to a full boil; cook for 15 seconds.

2. Remove from heat. Stir in chocolate chips and vanilla; blend until smooth. Pour pudding into individual serving dishes. Let cool slightly; cover surface with plastic wrap to prevent skins from forming on surface. Refrigerate.

Microwave Method

1. In an 8-cup (2 L) glass bowl or casserole dish, whisk together sugar and cornstarch; add milk, whisking until smooth. Microwave, uncovered, on High for 2 minutes. Whisk well; microwave on High for 2 to 4 minutes more, whisking every minute, until pudding comes to a full boil and thickens. Stir in chocolate chips and vanilla.

Creamy Rice Pudding

Makes 6 servings

When it comes to comfort food, I put rice pudding at the top of my list. It's creamy, luscious and oh so satisfying.

Tips

If short-grain rice is unavailable, use long-grain rice (not converted) instead. Long-grain rice is not as starchy, so reduce the amount of milk to 4 cups (1 L) in total. Combine long-grain rice with 3½ cups (875 mL) of the milk and continue with recipe as directed.

Be careful of spillovers: Add a walnut-size piece of butter to rice mixture to reduce milk from foaming.

Variation

Instead of using vanilla for flavoring, add two 2-inch (5 cm) strips of lemon peel to the milk-rice mixture when cooking. Remove before serving.

½ cup	short-grain rice, such as Arborio	125 mL
5 cups	whole milk, divided	1.25 L
⅓ cup	granulated sugar	75 mL
¼ tsp	salt	1 mL
1	egg yolk	1
¼ cup	sultana raisins	60 mL
1 tsp	vanilla	5 mL
	Ground cinnamon (optional)	

1. In a large saucepan, combine rice, 4½ cups (1.125 L) milk, sugar and salt. Bring to a boil; reduce heat to medium-low and simmer, partially covered, stirring occasionally, for 45 to 50 minutes or until rice is tender and mixture has thickened.

2. Beat together remaining ½ cup (125 mL) milk and egg yolk; stir into rice mixture, stirring, for 1 minute or until creamy. Remove from heat. Stir in raisins and vanilla.

3. Serve either warm or at room temperature. (Pudding thickens slightly as it cools.) Sprinkle with cinnamon, if desired.

Cinnamon Raisin Bread Pudding

On a comfort scale, bread puddings, with their old-fashioned appeal, rate as one of the most-loved desserts. This simple bread pudding, which features cinnamon bread in a custard base, takes no time to put together.

- Preheat oven to 375°F (190°C)
- Rimmed baking sheets
- 10-cup (2.5 L) shallow baking dish, generously buttered
- Large shallow roasting pan or deep broiler pan

12	slices cinnamon raisin swirl bread (1 lb/500 g loaf)	12
6	eggs	6
2 cups	whole milk	500 mL
1 cup	half-and-half (10%) cream	250 mL
¾ cup	granulated sugar	175 mL
2 tsp	vanilla	10 mL

Topping

2 tbsp	granulated sugar	30 mL
½ tsp	ground cinnamon	2 mL

1. Place bread slices in a single layer on baking sheets and lightly toast in preheated oven for 10 to 12 minutes. Let cool. Leave oven on. Cut bread into cubes and place in prepared baking dish.

2. In a bowl, whisk together eggs, milk, cream, ¾ cup (175 mL) sugar and vanilla. Pour over bread. Let soak for 10 minutes, pressing down gently with a spatula.

3. *Topping:* In a small bowl, combine 2 tbsp (30 mL) sugar and cinnamon. Sprinkle over top.

4. Place baking dish in roasting or broiler pan; add enough boiling water to come halfway up sides of dish. Bake in preheated oven for 45 to 50 minutes or until top is puffed and custard is set in center. Remove from water bath; place on a wire rack to cool. Serve warm or at room temperature.

Bread Pudding
with Caramelized Pears

In the old days, bread puddings were an economy dish, simply made with stale bread and custard. But there's nothing humble about this recipe. The golden pear topping flecked with raisins transforms it into a special dessert fit for company.

Tip

Use whole milk to give this pudding an extra creamy texture.

- Preheat oven to 350°F (180°C)
- 8-inch (20 cm) square baking dish, greased
- 13- by 9-inch (33 by 23 cm) baking pan

6	slices egg bread (challah) or white sandwich bread	6
2 tbsp	butter, softened	30 mL
4	eggs	4
1/3 cup	granulated sugar	75 mL
2 tsp	vanilla	10 mL
2 cups	hot milk	500 mL

Pear Topping

1/3 cup	granulated sugar	75 mL
4	pears, such as Bartlett, peeled, cored and sliced	4
1/2 tsp	freshly grated nutmeg	2 mL
1/3 cup	raisins or dried cranberries	75 mL
1/4 cup	sliced blanched almonds	60 mL

1. Trim crusts from bread; butter one side of each bread slice. Cut into 4 triangles each; layer in prepared baking dish, overlapping the triangles.

2. In a large bowl, whisk together eggs, sugar and vanilla. Whisk in hot milk in a stream, stirring constantly. Pour over bread.

3. *Pear Topping:* In a large nonstick skillet over medium heat, cook sugar and 2 tbsp (30 mL) water, stirring occasionally, until mixture turns a deep caramel color. Immediately add pears and nutmeg (be careful of spatters). Cook, stirring often, for 5 minutes or until pears are tender and sauce is smooth. Stir in raisins; spoon evenly over bread slices. Sprinkle almonds over top.

4. Place baking dish in baking pan; add enough boiling water to come halfway up sides of dish. Bake in preheated oven for 40 to 45 minutes or until custard is set in center. Remove from water bath; place on a wire rack to cool. Serve warm or at room temperature.

Bananas Foster Bread Pudding

It might come as a surprise that one of my most requested desserts is a homey bread pudding fancied up with a classic topping of Bananas Foster and served drizzled with Pouring Vanilla Custard. A perfect "Yum" dessert!

Tip

The brown sugar you use in recipes is totally your preference. Brown sugar comes in both light and dark brown. Dark brown sugar is noticeably darker in color and has a stronger molasses taste.

- Preheat oven to 350°F (180°C)
- 11- by 7-inch (28 by 18 cm) baking dish, greased
- 13- by 9-inch (33 by 23 cm) baking pan

6	thick slices egg bread (challah) or home-style firm white bread	6
2 tbsp	butter, softened	30 mL
4	eggs	4
1/3 cup	packed brown sugar	75 mL
2 tbsp	amber rum	30 mL
2 tsp	vanilla	10 mL
2 cups	hot half-and-half (10%) cream	500 mL
	Bananas Foster (page 549)	
	Pouring Vanilla Custard (page 533)	

1. Trim crusts from bread; butter one side of each slice. Cut into 1-inch (2.5 cm) cubes; spread in prepared baking dish.

2. In a large bowl, whisk together eggs, brown sugar, rum and vanilla. Whisk in hot cream in a stream, stirring constantly. Pour over bread. Let soak for 10 minutes, pressing down gently with a spatula.

3. Meanwhile, prepare Bananas Foster as directed. Spoon banana mixture and sauce evenly over bread mixture.

4. Place baking dish in baking pan and add enough boiling water to come halfway up sides of dish. Bake in preheated oven for 40 to 45 minutes or until custard is set in center. Remove from water bath; place on a wire rack to cool. Serve warm or at room temperature, accompanied with Pouring Vanilla Custard.

Panna Cotta

Panna cotta is Italian for "cooked cream" and refers to a cream-based gelatin pudding typically flavored with vanilla and served with berries. This impressive dessert is easy to make and can be made a day or two before you plan to serve it.

Tips

If making ahead, cover ramekins before refrigerating at the end of Step 2. Store for up to 2 days.

Nonfat vanilla yogurts are already thickened with gelatin, so select a yogurt with at least 2% fat content (but no more than 5%) for a more richly textured dessert.

• 6 ramekins or custard cups (each 6 oz/175 mL), lightly oiled

1	package (¼ oz/7 g) unflavored gelatin	1
1 cup	whipping (35%) cream	250 mL
¼ cup	granulated sugar	60 mL
1½ cups	vanilla yogurt (see Tip, left)	375 mL
1 tsp	vanilla	5 mL
	Raspberry Sauce (page 547)	
	Fresh raspberries or blueberries	
	Mint sprigs	

1. Place 2 tbsp (30 mL) cold water in a small bowl and sprinkle gelatin over. Let stand to soften.

2. In a small saucepan, combine whipping cream and sugar. Heat over medium-high heat, stirring, until sugar is dissolved and cream is steaming. Remove from heat and stir in gelatin mixture until dissolved. Whisk in yogurt and vanilla. Pour into ramekins and refrigerate for 4 hours or until set.

3. To serve, run a paring knife around sides of each ramekin. Place hot tap water in a shallow bowl. Dip bottom of ramekins, one at a time, into hot water for about 15 seconds to loosen. Wipe ramekin bottoms dry and, using the tip of the knife to nudge each panna cotta out, carefully invert on serving plates. Spoon Raspberry Sauce around each panna cotta and garnish with fresh berries and mint.

Crème Caramel

This self-saucing French custard was the rage in the '70s. French cuisine is back in vogue, and so too is this appealing dessert that is surprisingly easy to make and serve.

Tip

Can be made up to 2 days ahead of serving.

- Preheat oven to 325°F (160°C)
- 6 ramekins or custard cups (each 6 oz/175 mL), lightly greased
- 13- by 9-inch (33 by 23 cm) baking pan

Caramel

½ cup	granulated sugar	125 mL
¼ cup	water	60 mL

Custard

2	eggs	2
2	egg yolks	2
½ cup	granulated sugar	125 mL
1 tsp	vanilla	5 mL
2 cups	whole milk	500 mL
½ cup	whipping (35%) cream	125 mL

1. *Caramel:* In a heavy-bottomed medium saucepan, combine sugar and water. Place over medium heat until sugar melts; increase heat to medium-high and cook until sugar mixture boils (do not stir). When syrup has turned a rich caramel color, remove from heat; pour into ramekins. Quickly rotate dish to spread caramel evenly over bottom.

2. *Custard:* In a bowl, whisk together eggs, egg yolks, sugar and vanilla. In another saucepan, heat milk and cream over medium heat until almost boiling. Pour hot milk mixture in a thin stream into egg mixture, whisking constantly. Strain through a sieve into prepared ramekins.

3. Arrange in baking pan; carefully pour in boiling water to come 1 inch (2.5 cm) up sides of dish. Place pan in oven; bake for 25 minutes or until tester inserted in center comes out clean. Let cool to room temperature; refrigerate. To serve, run a knife around edges to loosen custards. Invert onto serving plates.

Crème Brûlée with Fresh Berries

Makes 6 servings

Crème brûlée is such a popular restaurant dessert, but you can easily make it in your home kitchen. Use a combination of fresh berries flavored with a fruit liqueur to top the custards and get ready to impress your guests.

Tip

Instead of vanilla extract, use a 2-inch (5 cm) piece of vanilla bean. Split the bean, scrape seeds from the inside; add seeds and bean halves to cream when heating in Step 1. Strain out the pods and discard.

Variation

Instead of liqueur, place 2 tbsp (30 mL) raspberry or black currant jelly in a bowl and microwave on High for 30 seconds or until melted. Stir in 1 to 2 tsp (5 to 10 mL) water. Let cool, then pour over fruit.

- Preheat oven to 325°F (160°C)
- 6 ramekins or custard cups (each 6 oz/175 mL), arranged in a 13- by 9-inch (33 by 23 cm) baking pan
- Rimmed baking sheet

2 cups	whipping (35%) cream	500 mL
6	egg yolks	6
1/3 cup	granulated sugar	75 mL
1½ tsp	vanilla	7 mL
6 tbsp	packed brown sugar (approx.)	90 mL
2 cups	fresh berries, including blueberries, raspberries and blackberries	500 mL
2 tbsp	Chambord (raspberry liqueur) or crème de cassis (black currant liqueur)	30 mL

1. In a saucepan, heat cream over medium heat until piping hot; do not boil.

2. In a bowl, whisk egg yolks and sugar until thick and smooth, about 2 minutes. Gradually whisk in hot cream in a stream. Whisk in vanilla.

3. Strain custard through a fine sieve into a 4-cup (1 L) glass measure and skim off foam. Pour into ramekins. Pour enough hot water into baking pan to come halfway up sides of ramekins.

4. Bake in preheated oven for 40 to 45 minutes or until just set in center. Remove ramekins from water bath. Let cool, then refrigerate, uncovered, for 3 hours, until firm, or for up to 1 day.

5. Place oven rack 4 inches (10 cm) from broiler and preheat broiler. Place custards on baking sheet. Press brown sugar through a fine sieve and coat tops of custard in a thin even layer. Broil for 2 minutes or until sugar bubbles; watch carefully to prevent burning. Rotate ramekins and remove as each top is caramelized.

6. Place ramekins in freezer for 15 minutes to firm the caramel topping or refrigerate, uncovered, for up to 3 hours.

7. In a bowl, combine berries and liqueur. Let stand at room temperature for at least 15 minutes or for up to 1 hour. Spoon berry mixture atop custards and serve.

Vanilla Custard Sauce

Makes about 2 cups (500 mL)

This all-purpose sauce dresses any dessert from a bowl of fruit salad to fruit crisps to angel or pound cake topped with fresh berries.

Variation

Instead of vanilla, add 2 tbsp (30 mL) orange-flavored liqueur or brandy.

⅓ cup	granulated sugar	75 mL
1 tbsp	cornstarch	15 mL
1 cup	milk	250 mL
1	egg yolk	1
2 tsp	vanilla	10 mL
½ cup	whipping (35%) cream	125 mL

1. In a small saucepan, stir together sugar and cornstarch. Blend in milk and egg yolk until smooth. Place over medium heat, whisking constantly, until sauce comes to a boil and thickens.

2. Remove from heat and stir in vanilla. Transfer to a bowl. Let cool slightly. Cover surface with plastic wrap and let cool slightly, then refrigerate.

3. In a bowl, using an electric mixer, whip cream until soft peaks form. Fold cream into chilled custard until sauce is smooth. Refrigerate until ready to serve. Can be made up to 1 day ahead.

Pouring Vanilla Custard

Makes 2 cups (500 mL)

This delicious sauce can top any number of desserts, from warm chocolate cake to sticky toffee pudding.

Tip

This sauce can be made ahead, placed in an airtight container and refrigerated for up to 2 days.

1 cup	milk	250 mL
⅔ cup	half-and-half (10%) cream	150 mL
¼ cup	granulated sugar	60 mL
4	egg yolks	4
1 tsp	vanilla	5 mL

1. In a small saucepan, combine milk, cream and sugar. Heat over medium-high heat, whisking until milk mixture is steaming and sugar has dissolved.

2. In a bowl, whisk egg yolks. Pour in hot milk mixture in a thin stream, whisking constantly. Return mixture to saucepan and cook over low heat, whisking, for 4 to 5 minutes or until thick enough to coat the back of a wooden spoon. Do not let boil or sauce will curdle.

3. Remove from heat and strain through a fine sieve. Stir in vanilla. Let cool slightly. Serve sauce warm or place plastic wrap directly on the surface and refrigerate until chilled.

Mixed Berry Granola Crisp

Makes 6 to 8 servings

Summer is never far away now that today's supermarkets feature a great selection of frozen berries. They're ideal to use in this pleasing dessert.

Tips

Use a combination of fresh or frozen fruits, such as blueberries, strawberries, raspberries and blackberries.

Use granola with nuts, such as almonds; do not use granola with added raisins or dried fruit.

- Preheat oven to 350°F (180°C)
- 8-cup (2 L) baking or casserole dish, greased

5 cups	assorted fresh or frozen berries (see Tips, left)	1.25 L
½ cup	granulated sugar	125 mL
2 tbsp	cornstarch	30 mL
1½ tsp	grated orange zest	7 mL

Granola Topping

1 cup	granola with nuts (see Tips, left)	250 mL
¾ cup	all-purpose flour	175 mL
½ cup	packed brown sugar	125 mL
1 tsp	ground cinnamon	5 mL
¼ tsp	freshly grated nutmeg	1 mL
⅓ cup	butter, melted	75 mL

1. Place berries in prepared baking dish. In a bowl, combine sugar, cornstarch and orange zest. Sprinkle over fruit and toss to combine.

2. *Granola Topping:* In a bowl, combine granola, flour, brown sugar, cinnamon and nutmeg. Pour in melted butter and toss to combine. Spread topping over fruit.

3. Bake in preheated oven for 40 to 45 minutes (10 minutes longer, if using frozen fruit) or until fruit mixture is bubbly and top is golden.

Peach Almond Crumble

When you pair fresh ripe peaches with a crumbly nut topping, it's a juicy sweet treat. Served warm with ice cream, it's the ultimate comfort food dessert.

Tip

Fresh peaches work best, but in a pinch you can substitute 1 can (28 oz/796 mL) peaches, drained and sliced. Omit the cornstarch.

- Preheat oven to 375°F (190°C)
- 8-inch (20 cm) baking dish, greased

Fruit

4 cups	peeled sliced peaches or nectarines	1 L
2 tsp	cornstarch	10 mL
1/3 cup	peach or apricot preserves	75 mL

Topping

1/2 cup	large-flake (old-fashioned) rolled oats	125 mL
1/2 cup	all-purpose flour	125 mL
1/3 cup	packed brown sugar	75 mL
1/3 cup	sliced blanched almonds	75 mL
1/4 tsp	ground ginger	1 mL
1/3 cup	butter, melted	75 mL

1. *Fruit:* In a bowl, toss peaches with cornstarch; stir in preserves. Spread in prepared baking dish.

2. *Topping:* In a bowl, combine rolled oats, flour, brown sugar, almonds and ginger. Drizzle with butter; stir to make coarse crumbs. Sprinkle over fruit.

3. Bake in preheated oven for 30 to 35 minutes or until topping is golden and filling is bubbly. Serve warm or at room temperature with ice cream, if desired.

Strawberry-Rhubarb Cobbler

I look forward to indulging in this old-fashioned dessert when local berries and rhubarb are in season. But it's also good in winter, when I turn to my freezer for my stash of summer fruits. Serve the cobbler warm and top with good-quality vanilla ice cream.

Tips

If using frozen fruit, there's no need to defrost before using.

If you prefer to bake the cobbler earlier in the day, reheat in 350°F (180°C) oven for about 15 minutes.

Variation
Blueberry-Peach Cobbler

Use 2 cups (500 mL) fresh or frozen blueberries and 4 cups (1 L) sliced peaches. Reduce sugar to ⅔ cup (150 mL).

- Preheat oven to 400°F (200°C)
- 9-inch (23 cm) round or square baking dish

4 cups	chopped fresh rhubarb	1 L
2 cups	sliced strawberries	500 mL
¾ cup	granulated sugar	175 mL
2 tbsp	cornstarch	30 mL
1 tsp	grated orange zest	5 mL

Biscuit Topping

1 cup	all-purpose flour	250 mL
¼ cup	granulated sugar	60 mL
1½ tsp	baking powder	7 mL
¼ tsp	salt	1 mL
¼ cup	cold butter, cut into pieces	60 mL
½ cup	milk	125 mL
1 tsp	vanilla	5 mL
	Additional granulated sugar	

1. Place rhubarb and strawberries in baking dish. In a small bowl, combine sugar, cornstarch and orange zest; sprinkle over fruit and gently toss.

2. Bake in preheated oven for 20 to 25 minutes (increase to 30 minutes if using frozen fruit) or until hot and fruit bubbles around edges.

3. *Biscuit Topping:* In a bowl, combine flour, sugar, baking powder and salt. Cut in butter using a pastry blender or fork to make coarse crumbs. In a glass measure, combine milk and vanilla; stir into dry ingredients to make a soft, sticky dough.

4. Using a large spoon, drop 8 separate spoonfuls of dough onto hot fruit; sprinkle with 2 tsp (10 mL) sugar.

5. Return to oven and bake for 25 to 30 minutes or until top is golden and fruit is bubbly. Serve warm or at room temperature.

Plum-Peach Gingerbread Cobbler

This biscuit topping, with all the old-fashioned flavor of gingerbread, marries well with summery ripe peaches and plums. Serve warm with a custard sauce or topped with ice cream.

Tip

Baking powder and baking soda have a shelf life of only 6 months once opened, so make sure to replenish both regularly. As a reminder, write the date when they need to be replaced on the container.

- Preheat oven to 400°F (200°C)
- 8-cup (2 L) baking or casserole dish

2 cups	sliced purple plums	500 mL
2 cups	sliced peaches	500 mL
½ cup	packed brown sugar	125 mL
1½ tsp	grated orange zest	7 mL
1 tbsp	cornstarch	15 mL
2 tbsp	orange juice	30 mL

Biscuit Topping

1 cup	all-purpose flour	250 mL
1 tsp	baking powder	5 mL
½ tsp	baking soda	2 mL
¾ tsp	ground ginger	3 mL
½ tsp	ground cinnamon	2 mL
¼ tsp	ground allspice	1 mL
¼ tsp	salt	1 mL
¼ cup	butter, melted	60 mL
⅓ cup	liquid honey	75 mL
½ cup	plain or vanilla-flavored yogurt	125 mL
1	egg	1
¼ cup	sliced almonds	60 mL

1. In a baking dish, combine plums, peaches, brown sugar and orange zest. In a small bowl, blend cornstarch with orange juice; stir into fruit mixture. Bake in preheated oven for 20 to 25 minutes or until hot and fruit bubbles around edges.

2. *Biscuit Topping:* In a bowl, stir together flour, baking powder, soda, ginger, cinnamon, allspice and salt.

3. In another bowl, whisk together butter, honey, yogurt and egg until smooth. Stir into flour mixture to make a smooth batter. Drop spoonfuls of dough evenly over hot fruit; smooth batter with back of spoon. Sprinkle with almonds.

4. Return to oven and bake for 25 to 30 minutes or until top is golden and fruit is bubbly. Serve warm or at room temperature.

Apple Brown Betty

A betty is a yummy pudding-like baked dessert that dates back to colonial times. It's layered with buttered bread crumbs and spiced sweetened fruit, typically apples because they were the most abundant.

Tips

Golden Delicious, McIntosh or Cortland apples work well in this dessert, but use whatever firm, slightly tart apples you have on hand.

Use stale bread to make your crumbs. Leftover egg bread or French loaf is preferred, but any day-old, firm white bread will also work. Leave the sliced bread out on the counter to dry for several hours or place slices on a baking sheet in a 350°F (180°C) oven for 5 to 10 minutes. Let cool before making crumbs.

- Preheat oven to 375°F (190°C)
- 8-inch (20 cm) square baking dish, greased

6	slices stale egg bread (challah) or firm white bread (approx.)	6
¼ cup	butter, melted	60 mL
6 cups	sliced peeled apples, such as Golden Delicious, McIntosh or Cortland (about 6)	1.5 L
½ cup	packed brown sugar	125 mL
1 tsp	ground cinnamon	5 mL
¼ tsp	freshly grated nutmeg	1 mL
2 tbsp	apple juice or water	30 mL
1 tsp	grated lemon zest	5 mL
1 tbsp	fresh lemon juice	15 mL
	Ice cream	

1. Trim crusts from bread; tear bread into pieces. Place in a food processor and pulse to make enough coarse crumbs to measure 2 cups (500 mL), lightly packed. Transfer to a bowl, pour melted butter over and toss.

2. In a bowl, combine apples, brown sugar, cinnamon, nutmeg, apple juice, lemon zest and lemon juice. Spoon half into baking dish. Sprinkle with half of the buttered bread crumbs.

3. Top with remaining apples and bread crumbs. Bake in preheated oven for 40 to 45 minutes or until crumbs are nicely toasted on top and apples are tender. Serve warm or at room temperature, topped with ice cream.

Warm Brown Sugar Pears with Pecan Oat Crunch

Makes 6 servings

Serve these delectable pears warm over ice cream and topped with a sweet, nutty crumble. It makes a terrific do-ahead dessert when you've got company for dinner.

Tips

Make the Pecan Oat Crunch up to 1 week ahead and store in an airtight container in the refrigerator, or freeze for up to 1 month.

Cook the pears as directed and store in an airtight container in the refrigerator for up to 2 days. To serve, place pears with sauce in a saucepan and reheat on the stovetop, or microwave on High, stirring once, until heated through.

- Preheat oven to 350°F (180°C)
- Rimmed baking sheet

Pecan Oat Crunch

¾ cup	large-flake (old-fashioned) rolled oats	175 mL
½ cup	all-purpose flour	125 mL
⅔ cup	packed brown sugar	150 mL
¾ cup	pecans, coarsely chopped	175 mL
½ cup	butter, melted	125 mL

Brown Sugar Pears

2 tbsp	butter	30 mL
4	firm but ripe Bartlett or Anjou pears, peeled, cored and sliced	4
⅓ cup	packed brown sugar	75 mL
¼ cup	pear or apple juice	60 mL
¼ tsp	freshly grated nutmeg	1 mL
	Premium vanilla or praline ice cream	

1. *Pecan Oat Crunch:* In a bowl, stir together rolled oats, flour, brown sugar and pecans. Pour melted butter over and toss well to distribute. Spread mixture evenly on baking sheet. Bake in preheated oven, stirring often, for 18 to 22 minutes or until mixture turns golden and crisp. Let cool.

2. *Brown Sugar Pears:* In a large nonstick skillet, melt butter over medium-high heat. Add pears and cook, stirring often, for 3 minutes or until pears are lightly colored. Stir in brown sugar, juice and nutmeg; cook, stirring, for 4 to 5 minutes or until sauce is slightly reduced and pears are tender-crisp.

3. Place a generous scoop of ice cream in each serving bowl. Top with warm pear slices and sauce and sprinkle with Pecan Oat Crunch. Serve immediately.

Pear-Raisin Strudel

For a simple, elegant presentation, dust the top of the strudel with confectioner's sugar, slice and arrange on dessert plates spread with Vanilla Custard Sauce (see recipe, page 533).

Tip

The taste of freshly grated nutmeg is so much better than the pre-ground variety. Whole nutmeg can be found in the spice section of your supermarket or bulk food store. Use a rasp grater (such as a Microplane) to grate nutmeg.

- Preheat oven to 375°F (190°C)
- Rimmed baking sheet, lined with parchment paper

4	large firm but ripe Bartlett, Bosc or Anjou pears, peeled, cored and thinly sliced	4
1/3 cup	sultana raisins	75 mL
1/3 cup	packed brown sugar	75 mL
2 tbsp	all-purpose flour	30 mL
1 tsp	grated lemon zest	5 mL
1/4 tsp	freshly grated nutmeg or ground ginger	1 mL
1/3 cup	gingersnap, amaretti or graham wafer cookie crumbs	75 mL
2 tbsp	granulated sugar	30 mL
7	sheets phyllo pastry	7
1/2 cup	butter, melted	125 mL

1. In a bowl, combine pears, raisins, brown sugar, flour, lemon zest and nutmeg.

2. In a small bowl, combine crumbs and granulated sugar.

3. Place 1 sheet of phyllo on work surface. (To prevent remaining sheets from drying out, keep them covered with waxed paper, then a damp towel.) Lightly brush phyllo with melted butter and sprinkle with 1 tbsp (15 mL) crumb mixture.

4. Layer 5 sheets of phyllo, lightly brushing each layer with melted butter and sprinkling with 1 tbsp (15 mL) crumb mixture. Top with remaining sheet of phyllo and lightly brush with melted butter.

5. Spoon a 3-inch (7.5 cm) wide strip of fruit mixture lengthwise down pastry 2 inches (5 cm) from edge. Fold 1 inch (2.5 cm) of the pastry ends over filling and carefully roll up pastry around filling. Place seam side down on prepared baking sheet. Brush with remaining butter. (Can be assembled up to 4 hours ahead of baking and refrigerated.)

6. Cut seven diagonal slits in top of pastry. Bake in preheated oven for 30 to 35 minutes or until pastry is golden. Cut into diagonal slices and serve warm or at room temperature.

Mocha Toffee Mousse

Makes 6 servings

This delicious mocha dessert relies on the coffee flavor from a liqueur or very strong coffee to nicely balance the dark chocolate. Espresso is preferred, or double-strength coffee brewed using dark-roasted beans.

Tip

If you can't find toffee bits, break up toffee candy bars, such as Skor.

1 cup	milk	250 mL
1/3 cup	granulated sugar	75 mL
3	egg yolks	3
5 oz	bittersweet chocolate (see Tip, page 542), chopped	150 g
1/4 cup	coffee liqueur or strong coffee	60 mL
1 cup	whipping (35%) cream	250 mL
1/2 cup	Skor toffee bits	125 mL
	Unsweetened cocoa powder	

1. In a small saucepan, combine milk and sugar. Heat over medium-high heat, stirring occasionally, until milk is steaming and sugar is dissolved.

2. In a bowl, whisk yolks. Pour in hot milk in a thin stream, whisking constantly. Return mixture to saucepan and cook over medium-low heat, whisking, for 3 to 4 minutes or until mixture coats the back of a wooden spoon.

3. Add chocolate and stir until melted. Remove from heat. Stir in coffee liqueur. Transfer to a bowl and let cool to room temperature. Refrigerate for 1 to 1½ hours, stirring occasionally, until mixture starts to thicken.

4. In a bowl, using electric mixer, beat cream until stiff peaks form. Whisk one-third of the whipped cream into chocolate mixture. Fold in remaining whipped cream and toffee bits. Spoon into dessert dishes or large wine glasses. Cover with plastic wrap and refrigerate for 4 hours or overnight. To serve, sift cocoa powder over top.

Ultimate Chocolate Mousse

There is no more sinful and satisfying combination than rich dark chocolate and whipped cream. Serve small portions of this silky classic. It's rich. And wonderful.

Tips

Mousse can be made up to 3 days ahead. It also can be frozen; let defrost in the refrigerator for several hours or overnight.

"Bittersweet" (not to be confused with unsweetened bitter chocolate) refers to dark chocolate with at least 70% cacao content. It's recommended in this recipe for its superior flavor and can be found in supermarkets and fine bakeries. If unavailable, semisweet baking chocolate can be substituted.

2	eggs	2
½ cup	milk	125 mL
⅓ cup	granulated sugar	75 mL
6 oz	bittersweet chocolate (see Tip, left), finely chopped	175 g
1 tsp	vanilla	5 mL
1½ cups	whipping (35%) cream	375 mL
2 oz	bittersweet chocolate, at room temperature	60 g

1. In a metal bowl, whisk together eggs, milk and sugar until smooth. Place over a saucepan of simmering water; cook, whisking constantly, for 4 minutes or until foamy and hot to the touch. Remove bowl from heat; whisk in chopped chocolate until melted. Stir in vanilla.

2. Refrigerate for about 15 minutes, whisking every 5 minutes, until mixture cools and is slightly thickened. (Do not chill chocolate until completely set.)

3. In another bowl, using an electric mixer, beat cream until stiff peaks form. Whisk one-third of the whipped cream into the chocolate mixture; gently fold in remaining whipped cream until well combined.

4. Spoon mousse into six stemmed wine glasses or serving dishes. Cover with plastic wrap and refrigerate 4 hours or overnight.

5. With a vegetable peeler, shave curls of chocolate onto a sheet of waxed paper; garnish mousse with chocolate curls just before serving.

Tiramisu

Makes 10 to 12 servings

Who doesn't love tiramisu, which transforms rich mascarpone, chocolate and sweet biscuits soaked in coffee into one of the most delectable desserts imaginable? Here is a streamlined version made without raw eggs.

Variation

Instead of Amaretto, use 2 tbsp (30 mL) each orange-flavored liqueur and rum or brandy.

● 10-cup (2.5 L) baking or serving dish

1	container (16 oz/450 g) mascarpone cheese	1
1/3 cup	Amaretto	75 mL
1/4 cup	granulated sugar	60 mL
1 cup	whipping (35%) cream, whipped	250 mL
1 1/2 cups	cold espresso or strong brewed coffee	375 mL
24	savoiardi biscuits or dry ladyfingers (one 7 oz/200 g package), divided	24
5 oz	bittersweet chocolate (see Tip, page 542), grated	150 g
	Unsweetened cocoa powder	

1. In a large bowl, whisk together mascarpone, Amaretto and sugar. Fold in whipped cream.

2. Place coffee in a shallow bowl. Dip 12 of the savoiardi biscuits, one at a time, in coffee until moistened and place in a single layer in baking dish. Spread with half of the mascarpone mixture. Sprinkle with half of the grated chocolate. Sift a thin layer of cocoa powder over filling.

3. Dip remaining savoiardi biscuits in coffee in the same way and arrange in a single layer in baking dish. Spread with remaining mascarpone mixture and grated chocolate; sift cocoa powder evenly over top.

4. Chill before serving. Cover with plastic wrap and refrigerate for 2 hours or overnight.

Lemon Fool with Fresh Berries

Makes 6 servings

Here's an updated version of the traditional "fool" — an old-fashioned dessert with fruit or berries folded into whipped cream or custard. This dessert is ideal for entertaining since it can be assembled earlier in the day.

Tip

Instead of individual serving dishes, layer berries and lemon fool in a deep 6-cup (1.5 L) glass serving bowl.

1 cup	whipping (35%) cream	250 mL
1 cup	Lemon Curd (see recipe, below)	250 mL
3 cups	fresh berries, such as sliced strawberries, raspberries or blueberries	750 mL
	Additional berries, mint sprigs and grated lemon zest	

1. In a chilled bowl, using an electric mixer, whip cream until stiff peaks form.

2. In another large bowl, whisk Lemon Curd until smooth. Whisk in one-quarter of the whipped cream; using a spatula, fold in remaining whipped cream.

3. Arrange half the berries in six parfait glasses or large wineglasses. Top with half the lemon fool. Layer with remaining berries and lemon fool. (Recipe can be prepared to this point and refrigerated for up to 4 hours.)

4. To serve, garnish with berries, mint and lemon zest.

Lemon Curd

Makes about 1½ cups (375 mL)

Here's a zesty sauce to fill baked tart shells and layer cakes. You can also whisk lemon curd into yogurt or whipped cream and use to top fresh fruit, gingerbread or pound cake. Or serve it with warm scones.

1	egg	1
2	egg yolks	2
1 tbsp	grated lemon zest	15 mL
⅓ cup	fresh lemon juice	75 mL
¾ cup	granulated sugar	175 mL
¼ cup	butter, softened	60 mL

1. In a medium saucepan, lightly whisk the egg and egg yolks. Whisk in lemon zest and juice. Add sugar and butter.

2. Cook over medium heat, whisking constantly, until mixture thickens, about 5 minutes. Transfer to a bowl. Serve hot or cover surface with plastic wrap and refrigerate until chilled. Or spoon into a preserving jar and refrigerate.

Strawberry Mascarpone Trifle with Chocolate

No cooking is involved in this sensational dessert! It's only a matter of assembling layers of pound cake, luscious strawberries, creamy mascarpone and dark chocolate. Sinful — and oh so simple.

Tip

Instead of the mascarpone cheese, you can use 1 package (8 oz/250 g) light cream cheese, softened.

1 cup	mascarpone cheese	250 mL
2/3 cup	granulated sugar	150 mL
2 tbsp	orange juice	30 mL
1 tbsp	grated orange zest	15 mL
1½ cups	whipping (35%) cream	375 mL
5 cups	fresh strawberries	1.25 L
1/3 cup	orange-flavored liqueur or orange juice	75 mL
1	frozen pound cake (10 oz/298 g)	1
4 oz	bittersweet chocolate (see Tip, page 542), grated	125 g
	Mint sprigs	

1. In a bowl, beat mascarpone cheese with sugar, orange juice and zest until creamy. In another bowl, using an electric mixer, beat cream until stiff peaks form; fold into mascarpone mixture until smooth.

2. Set aside 1 cup (250 mL) small whole strawberries. Slice remaining berries and place in a bowl; stir in orange-flavored liqueur.

3. Cut cake into 1- by ½-inch (2.5 by 1 cm) pieces. Arrange half the cake cubes in bottom of an 8-cup (2 L) glass serving bowl. Top with half the sliced strawberries, including some juice. Spread with half the mascarpone mixture; sprinkle with half the grated chocolate. Repeat layers with remaining ingredients.

4. Cover and refrigerate at least 4 hours and up to 12 hours before serving. Garnish with reserved whole strawberries and mint sprigs.

Fresh Fruit Trifle

A fresh twist on classic trifle, this sensational recipe stars seasonal fruits drizzled with a special orange custard cream. Traditional jam also gets replaced by tart-sweet raspberry sauce. I can count on this surprisingly light dessert to fit in well at a summer barbecue or a winter holiday meal.

Tips

Try any combination of fruits — raspberries, blueberries, sliced strawberries, halved green and red grapes, peeled kiwi slices, orange sections, apple, pear and pineapple pieces, cut into $\frac{1}{2}$- to $\frac{3}{4}$-inch (1 to 2 cm) cubes.

Toss fruits that discolor in 1 tbsp (15 mL) lemon juice; drain before using.

To toast almonds: Place nuts on a baking sheet in a 350°F (180°C) oven for 6 to 8 minutes, stirring occasionally, until lightly toasted.

$\frac{1}{2}$ cup	granulated sugar	125 mL
1 tbsp	cornstarch	15 mL
$\frac{1}{2}$ cup	orange juice	125 mL
2	egg yolks	2
4 oz	cream cheese, cubed and softened	125 g
2 tsp	grated orange zest	10 mL
$\frac{1}{4}$ cup	orange-flavored liqueur or orange juice	60 mL
1 cup	whipping (35%) cream	250 mL
1	frozen pound cake (10 oz/298 g), cut into $\frac{3}{4}$-inch (2 cm) cubes	1
	Raspberry Sauce (see recipe, opposite)	
6 cups	prepared fresh fruits	1.5 L
$\frac{1}{4}$ cup	toasted sliced almonds	60 mL
	Fresh or frozen raspberries	
	Mint sprigs	

1. In a small saucepan, whisk together sugar, cornstarch and orange juice until smooth; beat in egg yolks. Cook over medium heat, whisking constantly, for 3 minutes, until mixture comes to a full boil and thickens. Remove from heat. Beat in cream cheese, orange zest and orange-flavored liqueur until smooth.

2. Transfer custard to a bowl and cool. (Can be made 1 day ahead, covered and refrigerated.) In a bowl, using an electric mixer, whip cream until stiff peaks form. Fold into orange custard just before using.

3. Arrange half the cake cubes in bottom of a 10-cup (2.5 L) trifle or straight-sided glass serving bowl. Drizzle with half the raspberry sauce. Add half the fruit, pressing an occasional piece of fruit flat against sides of the bowl. Spoon half the orange custard cream over fruit.

4. Layer with remaining cake cubes, patting down lightly. Spoon remaining raspberry sauce over and top with fruit mixture. Spread with rest of orange custard cream.

5. Cover and chill for at least 4 hours or up to 1 day ahead. Just before serving, sprinkle with toasted almonds and garnish with raspberries and mint.

For a decorative top,
spoon 2 tbsp (30 mL) of
the raspberry sauce into a
small plastic storage bag.
Press mixture into one
corner of the bag. Poke
a small hole in tip of bag
using a skewer and pipe
mixture in a thin stream
over top in a zigzag or
lattice pattern.

Raspberry Sauce

1	package (10 oz/300 g) frozen unsweetened raspberries, defrosted	1
¼ cup	granulated sugar	60 mL
1½ tsp	cornstarch	7 mL
2 tsp	fresh lemon juice	10 mL

1. Place raspberries in a fine sieve set over a bowl. Using a rubber spatula, press berries to extract juice and remove seeds. There should be 1 cup (250 mL).

2. Place in a saucepan; stir in sugar and cornstarch until smooth. Bring to a boil over medium heat, stirring constantly, until thickened. Remove from heat. Let cool; add lemon juice. Cover and refrigerate. The sauce can be made up to two days ahead.

Ginger Fresh Fruit Compote

Candied ginger dresses up a simple homemade or store-bought fruit salad. To further enhance this dessert, add 2 tbsp (30 mL) orange-flavored liqueur with the zest. Serve with crisp cookies, such as biscotti.

Tip

Any combination of fruits cut into bite-size pieces can be used, including pears, peaches, plums, apples, pineapple and strawberries. Prepare fruit mixture no more than 4 hours ahead of serving to prevent discoloration.

1⅓ cups	orange juice	325 mL
¼ cup	liquid honey	60 mL
2 tbsp	finely chopped candied ginger	30 mL
2 tsp	grated orange zest	10 mL
6 cups	prepared fresh fruit	1.5 L
2 tbsp	chopped fresh mint (optional)	30 mL

1. In a small saucepan, combine orange juice, honey and candied ginger. Bring to a boil; boil for 2 minutes. Remove from heat; stir in orange zest. Let cool to room temperature.

2. Place fruit in a serving bowl and stir in ginger mixture. Cover and refrigerate for up to 4 hours. Sprinkle with mint, if using, before serving.

Strawberry-Rhubarb Compote

Makes 6 servings

Serve this warm, homey dessert with a dollop of vanilla yogurt or ice cream.

2 cups	chopped fresh or frozen rhubarb	500 mL
½ cup	packed brown sugar	125 mL
¼ cup	orange juice	50 mL
2 cups	quartered fresh strawberries	500 mL
1 tsp	grated orange zest	5 mL

1. In a small saucepan, combine rhubarb, brown sugar and orange juice; bring to a boil. Reduce heat and simmer for 3 minutes or until rhubarb is tender but still holds its shape; do not stir, or rhubarb will break up.

2. Remove from heat and stir in strawberries and orange zest. Serve warm or transfer to a bowl, let cool, then refrigerate and serve chilled.

Bananas Foster

Bananas Foster is a classic New Orleans dessert that dates back to the 1950s and was made famous by Brennan's Restaurant.

Tips

Nutmeg gives the bananas a Caribbean flare to go along with the amber rum and raisins. If desired, use 1 tsp (5 mL) cinnamon instead.

The classic recipe for Bananas Foster calls for both banana liqueur and rum. Add 2 tbsp (30 mL) banana liqueur, if desired, when adding brown sugar and raisins to the skillet.

Variation

Instead of bananas, use 6 slices of fresh pineapple, cut ½-inch (1 cm) thick, and omit raisins.

2 tbsp	butter	30 mL
⅓ cup	packed brown sugar	75 mL
¼ cup	dark raisins	60 mL
½ tsp	freshly grated nutmeg	2 mL
6	firm but ripe bananas (small size)	6
⅓ cup	amber rum	75 mL
	Ice cream	

1. In a large nonstick skillet, melt butter over medium heat. Add sugar, raisins and nutmeg, and cook, stirring, until sugar is dissolved.

2. Peel bananas and cut in half lengthwise. Add to skillet, cut side down, and simmer, carefully turning over once, for 4 to 5 minutes or until just tender.

3. Pour rum over bananas in skillet. Standing back, ignite with long wooden match and, once flames subside, baste bananas with sauce.

4. Serve warm bananas with sauce over ice cream.

Baked Apples with Buttered Rum Sauce

Serve 6

What could be more quintessentially comfort food that homespun baked apples? Here they take on an entertaining flair with a splash of rum. Terrific served warm.

Tip

If baking apples ahead, reheat in the microwave on Medium-High (70%) for 3 to 4 minutes or until warm.

Variation

Instead of rum, replace with additional water and 1 tsp (5 mL) vanilla.

- Preheat oven to 350°F (180°C)
- Shallow baking dish just large enough to hold apples

6	apples, such as Spartan or Cortland	6
1/2	lemon	1/2
1/3 cup	chopped pecans	75 mL
1/3 cup	sultana raisins or dried cranberries	75 mL
2 tbsp	butter, cut into pieces	30 mL
3/4 cup	packed brown sugar	175 mL
1/4 tsp	freshly grated nutmeg	1 mL
1/4 cup	dark rum or brandy	60 mL

1. Core apples; peel skins starting at top, leaving 1-inch (2.5 cm) band at bottom. Rub apples with lemon half to prevent browning. Arrange in baking dish.

2. In a bowl, combine pecans and raisins; stuff into apple cavities and top with butter.

3. In a small saucepan, combine brown sugar, 1/3 cup (75 mL) water and nutmeg; place over medium heat and bring to a boil, stirring, until sugar is dissolved. Stir in rum. Pour over apples. Bake in oven, basting occasionally with sauce, for 45 to 50 minutes or until apples are just tender when pierced with a knife.

4. Place in individual serving dishes and drizzle with sauce. Serve warm.

Wine-Poached Pears

Makes 4 servings

When I want elegance and style, I turn to this classic preparation for pears. It's an impressive way to end a special meal.

Tips

Poach the pears the day ahead. They are best served well chilled.

Select pears that are not overly ripe so they will hold their shape when sliced.

2 cups	red wine or cranberry juice cocktail	500 mL
½ cup	granulated sugar	125 mL
1	stick cinnamon	1
3	whole cloves	3
2	strips orange peel (each 3 inches/7.5 cm long)	2
4	Bartlett pears, peeled, halved lengthwise and cored	4
	Whipped cream or extra-thick yogurt	
	Freshly grated nutmeg	
	Mint sprigs	

1. In a saucepan, combine wine, sugar, cinnamon stick, cloves and orange peel. Bring to a boil; stir to dissolve sugar. Add pear halves; reduce heat, cover and simmer for 15 minutes or until just tender when pierced with a knife. Remove with a slotted spoon to a dish; let cool.

2. Bring poaching liquid in saucepan to a boil over high heat; boil until reduced to ¾ cup (175 mL). Strain through a sieve to remove spices; let cool and refrigerate.

3. Place pears cut side down on work surface. Beginning near the stem end, cut each pear half into ¼-inch (0.5 cm) lengthwise slices. (Do not cut through the stem itself; slices will still be attached at stem end.) Arrange 2 pear halves on each dessert plate, pressing down gently to fan out slices. Spoon syrup over top. Garnish with a dollop of whipped cream or extra-thick yogurt and sprinkle with grated nutmeg. Garnish with mint sprigs.

Chocolate Fondue

Everyone loves chocolate fondue, and it's so easy to serve when you don't want to fuss over dessert. Serve a colorful plate of bite-size pieces of fresh fruit and, if desired, include cubes of pound or sponge cake and assorted cookies, such as biscotti, alongside the fondue for dipping. Provide everyone with plates and wooden skewers or fondue forks for dipping.

Tips

Omit sugar when making the fondue with milk chocolate.

Make the chocolate sauce ahead, let cool, cover and refrigerate for up to 1 day. Reheat in a saucepan over low heat or in the microwave.

If you don't have a chocolate fondue pot, place the warm sauce in a warm serving bowl and reheat sauce as needed if it cools after serving.

For best flavor, use good-quality chocolate when making fondue.

¾ cup	whipping (35%) or table (18%) cream	175 mL
2 tbsp	granulated sugar	30 mL
6 oz	bittersweet chocolate (see Tip, page 554), chopped	175 g
½ tsp	vanilla	2 mL
	Assorted fresh fruits, dried fruits, cake pieces and cookies	

1. In a small heavy-bottomed saucepan, combine cream and sugar and heat over medium-high heat, stirring, until cream is steaming and sugar is dissolved. Reduce heat to low and add chocolate. Heat, stirring, until chocolate is melted and mixture is smooth. (Do not allow the mixture to boil.) Or place cream, granulated sugar and chocolate in a 4-cup (1 L) glass bowl or casserole. Microwave at Medium (50%) for 3 to 4 minutes or until chocolate is melted and sauce is smooth, stirring twice.

2. Stir in vanilla and transfer to a chocolate fondue pot set over a candle or a serving bowl. Serve warm with fruit and baked items for dipping.

Fondue Dippers

Try these dippers with chocolate fondue:

- Strawberries, pears, apples, bananas, kiwi, pineapple, honeydew melon and cantaloupe
- Dried fruits, including figs, apricots, mangos and peaches
- Cubes of pound or sponge cake, cookies such as biscotti, ladyfingers and rolled wafers

Lemon Mascarpone Semifreddo

Makes 12 servings

Italian for "half cold," *semifreddo* refers to a partially frozen dessert. A favorite do-ahead dessert when serving a crowd, this semifreddo is refreshing and attractive when topped with juicy, fresh berries. Best of all, it holds well for up to an hour when set out on a dessert table. (If left longer, it will become too soft to slice.)

Tips

To completely line a springform pan with parchment, cut a circle of parchment paper to fit the bottom. Cut a 30- by 3-inch (75 by 7.5 cm) strip to fit the inside edge of pan.

Dessert can be frozen in an airtight container for up to 2 weeks.

Variation

Lemon Mascarpone Mousse

Omit crust. Halve the ingredients for the filling and prepare as directed. Place in a bowl, cover and refrigerate for at least 4 hours or up to 1 day. To serve, scoop Lemon Mascarpone Mousse into large wine glasses. Garnish with berries and lemon zest. Serves 6.

- 9-inch (23 cm) springform pan, bottom and sides lined with parchment paper

Crust

1 cup	lemon cookie crumbs	250 mL
2 tbsp	granulated sugar	30 mL
2 tbsp	butter, melted	30 mL

Filling

1½ cups	granulated sugar	375 mL
2 tbsp	cornstarch	30 mL
1 cup	fresh lemon juice	250 mL
4	eggs, beaten	4
3 tbsp	grated lemon zest	45 mL
1	container (1 lb/450 g) mascarpone cheese	1
2 cups	whipping (35%) cream	500 mL
	Fresh raspberries or strawberries and grated lemon zest as garnish	

1. *Crust:* In a bowl, combine crumbs, sugar and butter. Press evenly into bottom of pan and refrigerate until firm, about 30 minutes.

2. *Filling:* In a medium stainless steel saucepan, combine sugar and cornstarch. Whisk in lemon juice, then beaten eggs until smooth. Cook over medium heat, whisking constantly, for about 5 minutes or until sauce thickens to a pudding-like consistency. Remove from heat and stir in lemon zest. Transfer to a large bowl and let cool to room temperature. Whisk in mascarpone until smooth.

3. In a bowl, using an electric mixer, beat whipping cream until stiff peaks form. Whisk in one-third of the whipped cream into mascarpone mixture, then fold in remaining whipped cream until incorporated. Spoon cream mixture into prepared pan and use a spatula to smooth top. Rap pan on counter several times to settle filling. Cover with plastic wrap, then foil. Freeze for 8 hours or overnight.

4. To serve, remove sides of pan. Remove base and carefully remove parchment paper. Transfer to a serving plate and remove parchment paper from around sides. Cover loosely with plastic wrap and refrigerate for 4 hours to soften slightly. Garnish with fresh berries and lemon zest. To serve, cut into wedges.

Frozen Skor Bar Mousse

This fabulous crowd-pleasing dessert can be made ahead and tucked away in the freezer to serve at a moment's notice.

Tips

Separate eggs while they are cold, but let egg whites warm to room temperature before beating. To speed up the process, place the bowl of egg whites in a larger bowl of hot water and let stand for 5 minutes.

"Bittersweet" (not to be confused with unsweetened bitter chocolate) refers to dark chocolate with at least 70% cacao content. It's recommended in this recipe for its superior flavor and can be found in supermarkets and fine bakeries. If unavailable, semisweet baking chocolate can be substituted.

- Preheat oven to 275°F (140°C)
- 2 baking sheets, lined with parchment paper
- 13- by 9-inch (33 by 23 cm) baking dish

Meringue

¾ cup	confectioner's (icing) sugar	175 mL
¼ cup	unsweetened cocoa powder	60 mL
4	egg whites, at room temperature	4
¼ tsp	cream of tartar	1 mL
¾ cup	superfine sugar	175 mL

Mousse

1½ cups	milk	375 mL
4	egg yolks	4
⅓ cup	granulated sugar	75 mL
5 oz	bittersweet chocolate (see Tip, left), chopped	150 g
⅓ cup	coffee liqueur or strong coffee	75 mL
2 cups	whipping (35%) cream	500 mL
6	Skor candy bars (each 1¼ oz/39 g), finely chopped	6
1 tbsp	unsweetened cocoa powder	15 mL

1. *Meringue:* Trace two 12- by 8-inch (30 cm by 20 cm) rectangles on parchment paper; turn paper over and place on baking sheets.

2. In a bowl, sift confectioner's sugar with cocoa powder. In a large bowl, using an electric mixer, beat egg whites with cream of tartar until soft peaks form. Beat in sugar, a spoonful at a time, until stiff glossy peaks form. Using a rubber spatula, fold in cocoa mixture in two additions.

3. Spoon meringue onto parchment rectangles evenly to edges. Bake in oven for 1½ hours or until crisp and dry, rotating baking sheets halfway through to bake evenly. Place on rack; let cool. Peel off paper. (Meringues can be wrapped in foil and stored in cool, dry place for up to 3 days.)

4. *Mousse:* In a heatproof bowl, whisk together milk, egg yolks and sugar. Place over saucepan of simmering water; cook, whisking often, for 8 minutes, or until thick enough to coat a spoon. Remove from heat. Add chocolate and stir until melted; stir in coffee liqueur. Let cool to room temperature. Cover and refrigerate, stirring occasionally, for 4 hours or until thickened.

5. In a bowl, whip cream; whisk one-third into chocolate mixture. Fold in remaining whipped cream. Set aside ⅓ cup (75 mL) chopped Skor bars; fold remaining candy into chocolate mixture.

6. Place one meringue in baking dish, trimming to fit, if necessary. Spread with half the mousse. Top with remaining meringue; spread with remaining mousse. Sprinkle with reserved candy. Wrap in heavy-duty foil. Freeze for 8 hours. Sift cocoa powder over top. Transfer to refrigerator for 30 minutes before cutting into squares.

Strawberry Ice Cream Cake

Surprisingly easy to prepare, this impressive frozen dessert is sublime when fresh berries are in season.

Tip

Instead of orange-flavored liqueur, substitute the same quantity of undiluted frozen orange juice concentrate.

● 9- by 5-inch (23 by 13 cm) loaf pan, lined with plastic wrap with ends hanging generously over sides of pan

1	frozen pound cake (10 oz/298 g)	1
6 cups	fresh strawberries, hulled	1.5 L
6 tbsp	orange-flavored liqueur	75 mL
4 tbsp	fresh lime juice	60 mL
1/3 cup	granulated sugar	75 mL
4 cups	strawberry ice cream, softened slightly	1 L
	Whipped cream (optional)	

1. Slightly defrost pound cake. Trim dark crusts from top and sides of cake and discard. Cut cake into 24 slices, each 1/4 inch (0.5 cm) thick.

2. Quarter and slice 2 cups (500 mL) berries. Place in bowl with 3 tbsp (45 mL) orange-flavored liqueur and 2 tbsp (30 mL) lime juice. Set aside.

3. In a food processor, purée remaining berries, orange-flavored liqueur, lime juice and sugar; pour into a bowl.

4. Spread scant 1/4 cup (60 mL) strawberry purée in pan. Layer with 8 slices of cake, arranging them lengthwise with slightly overlapping edges. Spread cake with scant 1/4 cup (60 mL) strawberry purée, then top with 2 cups (500 mL) ice cream and another scant 1/4 cup (60 mL) strawberry purée.

5. Repeat layers of cake, strawberry purée, ice cream and strawberry purée. Arrange remaining cake slices on top and spread with 1/4 cup (60 mL) strawberry purée. Fold plastic wrap over top, pressing gently down on cake. Freeze for 8 hours.

6. Stir reserved purée into sliced strawberry mixture. Cover and refrigerate.

7. To serve, place cake in refrigerator for 30 minutes to soften slightly. Lift out of pan and remove plastic wrap. Cut into slices and arrange on serving plates. Top with a generous spoonful of strawberry mixture and a dollop of whipped cream, if desired.

Lemon Raspberry Ice Cream Torte

Makes 8 to 10 servings

This delectable ice cream cake is a simple assembly of store-bought ice cream layered with tart lemon curd and raspberries.

Tip

To get more juice out of a lemon, roll on countertop or microwave on High for 20 seconds before squeezing.

- 9-inch (23 cm) springform pan, bottom lined with parchment paper

1¼ cups	chocolate baking crumbs	300 mL
3 tbsp	butter, melted	45 mL
¾ cup	Lemon Curd (see recipe, page 544)	175 mL
2 tsp	fresh lemon juice	10 mL
1½ cups	fresh raspberries	375 mL
6 cups	vanilla ice cream, softened slightly	1.5 L

1. In a bowl, combine chocolate crumbs and butter. Press into bottom of pan. Freeze for 15 minutes or until firm.

2. In a bowl, whisk Lemon Curd with lemon juice. Spread 2 cups (500 mL) ice cream in pan. Spread with half of the lemon curd mixture, leaving 1-inch (2.5 cm) border around edge. Freeze for 1 hour or until firm. Spread with 2 cups (500 mL) ice cream.

3. Meanwhile, in a food processor, purée ¾ cup (175 mL) raspberries; spread over ice cream, leaving 1-inch (2.5 cm) border around edge. Freeze for 1 hour or until firm.

4. Spread with remaining ice cream and top with remaining lemon curd. Lightly press remaining whole raspberries into lemon curd. Wrap well and freeze overnight or for up to 2 weeks.

5. To serve, place in refrigerator for 20 minutes to soften slightly. Remove sides of pan, place on serving plate and cut into wedges.

Crunchy Ice Cream Sandwiches with Chocolate Sauce

Makes 6 servings

Here's a kid-friendly treat that is as much fun for them to make as it is to eat.

Tips

Chocolate sauce thickens slightly if made in advance; microwave briefly on Defrost until warmed slightly and easy to spread.

If Skor bits are not available, use 2 chopped Skor bars (each 1 oz/39 g) instead.

● 8-inch (20 cm) square baking pan, lined with plastic wrap with ends hanging generously over sides of pan

1 cup	finely chopped crunchy granola bars	250 mL
½ cup	finely chopped pecans	125 mL
½ cup	Skor bits	125 mL
4 cups	mocha almond fudge or butterscotch ripple ice cream, softened slightly	1 L

Chocolate Sauce

¾ cup	whipping (35%) cream	175 mL
½ cup	semisweet or milk chocolate chips	125 mL
½ tsp	vanilla	2 mL
	Strawberries or raspberries	

1. In a bowl, combine granola bar crumbs, pecans and Skor bits. Sprinkle half of the crumb mixture into prepared pan; spread with ice cream. Sprinkle remaining crumbs over top; using back of a spoon, pat gently. Cover with plastic wrap, then foil, and freeze for 8 hours or until firm.

2. *Chocolate Sauce:* In a saucepan, heat whipping cream over medium heat until piping hot; remove from heat. Whisk in chocolate chips until melted and smooth; stir in vanilla. Let cool slightly; transfer to an airtight container and refrigerate.

3. To serve, lift dessert out of pan and cut into six pieces. Spread chocolate sauce on serving plates and top with ice cream sandwiches. Garnish with berries.

Quick Butterscotch Sauce

Here's another great sauce for pouring over ice cream. You can also drizzle it over cake, apple pie or fresh fruit.

Tip

Let sauce come to room temperature before using. Sauce can be stored in an airtight container in fridge for up to 1 month.

¾ cup	packed brown sugar	175 mL
¾ cup	whipping (35%) cream	175 mL
¼ cup	golden corn syrup	60 mL
½ tsp	vanilla	2 mL

1. In a large glass bowl or casserole dish, combine brown sugar, cream and corn syrup. Microwave at High, stirring twice, for 5 to 6 minutes. Add vanilla; let cool to room temperature. Sauce thickens as it cools.

Amazing Marshmallow Fudge Sauce

It's great poured over ice cream; it's even better when you add sliced bananas or strawberries and a dollop of whipped cream. To create a scrumptious brownie sundae, place a large brownie on a dessert plate, top with a scoop of ice cream and pour sauce over.

Tip

Keep the sauce in an airtight container in the fridge for up to 1 month. The sauce thickens when refrigerated, so let it come to room temperature before using.

1 cup	canned evaporated milk	250 mL
¾ cup	semisweet chocolate chips	175 mL
1 cup	miniature marshmallows	250 mL
1 tsp	vanilla	5 mL

1. Pour evaporated milk in a large glass bowl or casserole dish; microwave on High for 2 to 2½ minutes or until almost boiling. Add chocolate chips; let stand for 2 minutes to melt. Stir well. Add marshmallows; microwave on Medium (50%) for 1½ to 2 minutes or until marshmallows are melted. Add vanilla; stir until smooth. Let cool to room temperature before using. Sauce thickens as it cools.

Library and Archives Canada Cataloguing in Publication

Burkhard, Johanna
   500 best comfort food recipes / Johanna Burkhard.

Previous title: 400 best comfort food recipes.
ISBN 978-0-7788-0248-8

   1. Cookery. 2. Comfort food. I. Burkhard, Johanna. 400 best comfort food recipes.
II. Title. III. Title: Five hundred best comfort food recipes.

TX714.B876 2010   641.5   C2010-903256-X

Index